Brief Contents

PART ONE — Joining a Conversation 1

1. Understanding Yourself as a Writer 1
2. Finding and Listening In on Conversations 32
3. Reading to Write 49
4. Assessing and Evaluating Sources 84
5. Working Together 98

PART TWO — Contributing to a Conversation 119

6. Choosing Your Writing Role 119
7. Writing to Reflect 131
8. Writing to Inform 181
9. Writing to Analyze 233
10. Writing to Evaluate 297
11. Writing to Solve Problems 348
12. Writing to Convince or Persuade 404

PART THREE — Conducting Research 467

13. Focusing Your Search 467
14. Locating Sources 480
15. Conducting Field Research 499
16. Managing Your Sources 515
17. Avoiding Plagiarism 525

PART FOUR — Crafting and Polishing Your Contribution 539

18. Developing Your Thesis Statement 539
19. Organizing Your Ideas 547
20. Drafting Your Document 560
21. Using Sources Effectively 582
22. Designing Your Document 606
23. Working with Genres 618
24. Revising and Editing 653

PART FIVE — Documenting Sources 667

25. Using MLA Style 667
26. Using APA Style 691

PART SIX — Handbook 713

27. Style: Writing Confidently 713
28. Grammar: Writing Skillfully 742
29. Punctuation and Mechanics: Giving Your Readers Direction 771

Joining the Conversation
A Guide and Handbook for Writers

FIFTH EDITION

Mike Palmquist
Colorado State University

Barbara Wallraff

Boston | New York

For Bedford/St. Martin's

Vice President: Leasa Burton
Program Manager: Laura Arcari
Director of Content Development: Jane Knetzger
Development Manager: Maura Shea, Susan McLaughlin, Caroline Thompson
Senior Development Editor: Sherry Mooney
Assistant Editor: Paola García-Muñiz
Director of Media Editorial: Adam Whitehurst
Media Editor: Dan Johnson
Marketing Manager: Vivian Garcia
Senior Director, Content Management Enhancement: Tracey Kuehn
Senior Managing Editor: Michael Granger
Senior Content Project Manager: Kendra LeFleur
Senior Project Manager, Workflows: Lisa McDowell
Production Supervisor: Robin Besofsky
Director of Design, Content Management: Diana Blume
Interior Design: Claire Seng-Niemoeller
Cover Design: William Boardman
Text Permissions Editor: Allison Ziebka-Viering
Text Permissions Researcher: Elaine Kosta, Lumina Datamatics, Inc.
Director Rights and Permissions: Hilary Newman
Photo Researcher: Cheryl DuBois, Lumina Datamatics, Inc.
Director of Digital Production: Keri deManigold
Advanced Media Project Manager: Rand Thomas
Copyeditor: Rosemary Winfield
Composition: Lumina Datamatics, Inc.
Printer and Binding: King Printing Co., Inc.

Copyright © 2023, 2020, 2017, 2014 by Bedford/St. Martin's. All rights reserved. No part of this book may be reproduced, stored in a retrieval system, or transmitted in any form or by any means, electronic, mechanical, photocopying, recording, or otherwise, except as may be permitted by law or expressly permitted in writing by the Publisher.

Library of Congress Control Number: 2021952507

ISBN: 978-1-319-33494-9 (paperback)
ISBN: 978-1-319-41226-5 (Loose-leaf Edition)

Printed in the United States of America

2 3 4 5 6   27 26 25 24

Acknowledgments

Text acknowledgments and copyrights appear at the back of the book on pages 793–794, which constitute an extension of the copyright page. Art acknowledgments and copyrights appear on the same page as the art selections they cover.

At the time of publication all Internet URLs published in this text were found to accurately link to their intended website. If you do find a broken link, please forward the information to english@macmillan.com so that it can be corrected for the next printing.

For information, write: Bedford/St. Martin's, 75 Arlington Street, Boston, MA 02116

Preface for Instructors

When my son was young (perhaps five years old), he would often say, "I'm a lucky guy." That's how I feel about my work on this book. I am fortunate indeed to be able to work on a project that has touched the lives of so many writers and writing teachers—and that enacts a pedagogy in which I believe so strongly. In the preface to the previous edition of *Joining the Conversation*, I wrote that my work on this book has been one of those rare projects that has drawn on almost every aspect of my teaching and scholarly life. I noted that it had woven together and deepened my interest in Kenneth Burke's notion of academic discourse as a form of conversation, my commitment to bringing the scholarship of writing into my classes, my fascination with the intersections between writing and information technology, and my deep belief that writing is at once a rhetorical act and a means of creating and sharing new knowledge.

In this edition, I continue my efforts to weave those threads together and, in particular, to continue to explore what it means to write and to be a writer in the twenty-first century. But now I do so in the midst of a worldwide pandemic and in the face of serious questions about whether our democracy will survive the next few elections. These challenges underscore the importance of examining how writers can better understand and contribute to the professional, disciplinary, and civic conversations that shape our society. They call our attention to the complexity of writers' efforts to navigate the often conflicting motivations, expectations, and biases of their readers. And they make abundantly clear the central importance of being able to read critically, recognize misinformation and disinformation, and assess and evaluate the discourse shaping the conversations in which we are engaged.

With that in mind, my work on this new edition has focused even more on the complex relationships between writers and readers and between writers and the sources they draw on. You'll find greater attention to the roles writers adopt in relation to their readers. You'll find a much more nuanced and extensive discussion of how to work with sources and, in particular, how to assess the credibility and relevance of the information writers encounter as they join written conversations. And you'll find three new student essays that take on issues that speak to the environmental and social concerns that engage and motivate our students.

Joining the Conversation continues to emphasize rhetorical situation, disciplinary context, composing processes, research strategies, and the strong relationship between writing and critical thinking. It continues to rely on material drawn from the rich history and practices of writing studies. And it continues to draw on Kenneth Burke's notion of the parlor (although admittedly one that is both less confrontational and more collaborative than Burke's early vision) to help students grow as writers. It also maintains its commitment to recognizing how the composing process is necessarily shaped by technology, examining how computers, tablets, and phones allow us to access information, ideas, and arguments and the ways in which what we access informs our interactions with readers and peers. Finally, it continues to focus strongly on genre and document design as key strategies for achieving a writer's goals.

New to the Fifth Edition

This edition of *Joining the Conversation* includes the following new features.

- **GREATER EMPHASIS ON WRITING ROLES**

Part Two, "Contributing to a Conversation," opens with a new chapter that provides a thorough exploration of the roles writers take on in their documents. This chapter considers what it means to adopt a role as a writer, what factors can shape a writer's choice of role, and how a writer might rely on more than one role in a document. These roles give students crucial lenses for understanding their rhetorical situations and empower them to make informed decisions about every aspect of their writing process. Writers will benefit from a greater understand of why and how they might adopt roles and how they might find themselves shifting among them as they develop their contributions to the conversations they've decided to join.

- **EXPANDED TREATMENT OF SOURCE CREDIBILITY AND BIAS**

In an era of fake news and information bubbles, it's hard to understate the importance of assessing sources and understanding the biases of their authors and publishers. Chapter 4, "Assessing and Evaluating Sources," is significantly expanded from the previous edition, offering new strategies for recognizing and responding to misinformation and disinformation, addressing the lure of new but unproven information, and escaping information bubbles. Most important, it provides a detailed discussion of a new process for assessing and evaluating sources. This process incorporates lateral reading — a technique used by fact checkers — and rhetorical listening to help writers select the best sources for their writing projects.

- **NEW READINGS TO CHALLENGE AND ENGAGE STUDENTS**

The updated readings in this edition — and the **"Start a Conversation"** activities that accompany them — offer engaging readings by a wide range of authors whose work appears in mainstream media and scholarly publications. Professional documents such as infographics, videos, and progress reports offer a variety of genres, purposes, and tones.

Seven engaging new readings include

- a literacy narrative by Sandra Cisneros that explores the influence of her father on her development as a writer (Writing to Reflect)
- an informative article about gymnast Simone Biles's decision to withdraw from the team competition in the Tokyo Olympics (Writing to Inform)
- a YouTube video that explores how Temple Grandin, who is autistic, sees the world (Writing to Analyze)

● **THREE NEW THOUGHT-PROVOKING STUDENT ESSAYS**

Three of the six featured student writers in the fifth edition are new, and they write on three of the key tasks writers take on: informing, solving problems, and convincing or persuading. Like the other featured student writers in *Joining the Conversation*, these writers put a face on purpose-based writing, while **"In Process" boxes** trace their progress with glimpses of their notes, outlines, and other process documents.

Key Features of *Joining the Conversation*

● **THE CONVERSATION METAPHOR THAT MAKES SENSE TO STUDENTS**

Lucid and easy to understand, the conversation metaphor that underpins the book inspires students to become the best writers they can be. It guides students in considering purpose, readers, sources, context, and genre in everything they read and write. Understanding writers' roles, such as interpreter or problem solver, helps students keep the rhetorical situation at the forefront of their writing activities.

● **A VARIETY OF READINGS ACROSS GENRES AND MEDIA**

Chapters 7 through 12 include a diverse selection of professional readings by authors such as Margo Jefferson, James Parker, Rivka Galchen, Brooke Gladstone, Anu Partanen, and Sandra Cisneros. Readings not only serve as examples of admirable writing but also demonstrate successful design choices, whether they are print essays, magazine articles, blog posts, infographics, or videos. The layout of the readings has been carefully designed to give students a realistic sense of the original source. Each selection is accompanied by questions for critical reading that ask students to consider both the piece's writing situation and its genre.

Each assignment chapter also includes a **"Genre Talk" feature**, which focuses on the distinctive design features of particular genres and highlights how purpose, audience, sources, and context shape a document and its design.

● AN EMPHASIS ON HELPING STUDENTS UNDERSTAND THEMSELVES AS WRITERS

Chapter 1, "Understanding Yourself as a Writer," establishes a strong foundation for successful writing, including an emphasis on writing as a form of conversation, on writing as a rhetorical act, and on writing as a complex and recursive, yet ultimately highly individualized, process. The book as a whole emphasizes reflection and transfer as key skills, concepts that are developed in particular in Chapter 7, "Writing to Reflect." Scenarios featuring student writers illustrate the centrality of inquiry and reflection skills, while model readings from composition studies give students further practice in summary, paraphrase, and note taking. Chapter 5, "Working Together," along with twenty **"Working Together" activities** throughout the book, help students understand both why and how to work with other writers in activities including collaborative idea generation, role-play, and peer review, allowing them to shape their own writing processes with input and inspiration from their peers.

● COMPREHENSIVE TREATMENT OF RESEARCH PROCESSES

From its first edition, *Joining the Conversation* has provided one of the most comprehensive treatments of research methods. This edition continues to do so, offering up-to-date discussions of searching for sources, working with libraries, and conducting field research. Students will find advice on the full range of research issues, from developing plans to search for, locate, and manage sources to understanding how to work with librarians and how to conduct and analyze the results of observations, interviews, and surveys.

● AMPLE STUDENT SUPPORT

The true measure of a textbook should be how well it works for student writers. *Joining the Conversation* supports students as they work through their own writing processes. **"Your Turn" boxes** offer specific, accessible strategies for finding a conversation to join, gathering information from sources, and preparing a draft, while **"Working Together" boxes** provide opportunities for collaboration. Throughout Chapters 7 through 12, **"In Process" boxes** highlight the featured student writers' processes, showing their brainstorming notes, outlines, survey questions, and peer-review materials.

- **PROJECT IDEAS FOR INNOVATIVE ASSIGNMENTS**

The suggested projects at the end of each chapter offer models for both essays and public genres. Each set includes extended treatments of rhetorical situations, sources, and writing and design conventions.

- **INTEGRATED HANDBOOK**

Joining the Conversation offers three chapters of lively examples and friendly advice on matters of style, grammar, punctuation, and mechanics. Written by professional editor and writer Barbara Wallraff, formerly a senior editor at *The Atlantic* magazine, the brief handbook acts as both a quick reference tool and a foundation for in-depth revision and editing.

- **ALIGNMENT WITH THE COUNCIL OF WRITING PROGRAM ADMINISTRATORS' OUTCOMES STATEMENT**

As an inquiry-based rhetoric focusing on purpose and genre, *Joining the Conversation* helps instructors and students accomplish the teaching and learning goals published by the Council of Writing Program Administrators. See the catalog page for *Joining the Conversation* for detailed information on how the text supports each outcome.

Acknowledgments

This project represents another long stretch of weekends and evenings that might otherwise have been spent with my family. I offer my deepest thanks to them for their patience and support as I've worked on this new edition. I offer my thanks as well to the colleagues who have inspired me as I worked on this book. David Kaufer and Chris Neuwirth helped me understand the power of the conversation metaphor and provided valuable advice as I entered the discipline. Richard Young not only inspired me but also provided me with the tools to think carefully and productively about the role of textbooks within the discipline. Dick Hayes, Tom Huckin, Rich Enos, and Mike Rose provided me with the guidance that helped me become a contributing member of the writing studies community. And the colleagues with whom I have discussed the teaching of writing over the years — Tim Amidon, Chuck Bazerman, Nick Carbone, Sue Doe, Caleb Gonzales, Lynda Haas, Will Hochman, Asao Inoue, Lisa Langstraat, Sue McLeod, Aimee McLure, Joan Mullin, Michael Pemberton, Janice Walker, Aleashia Walton, and Terry Myers Zawacki, among many others — have provided me with knowledge and ideas that have shaped this book. *Joining the Conversation* would be far less useful without their insights.

PREFACE FOR INSTRUCTORS

A project like this necessarily involves the contributions of a wide range of colleagues who worked on key resources for the book. I am grateful to Barbara Wallraff for her work on the handbook, to Heather Landers for her contributions to the materials on oral and multimedia presentations, and to Sue Doe for her work on the original instructor's guide for the book.

I am also indebted to the following reviewers who offered careful critiques of drafts of this book:

Kodwo Adam-Moses, Auburn University; Gina Atkins, North Carolina State University at Raleigh; Eric D. Brown, Arizona State University; Sylvia Hayes, Midlands Technical College; Michael Horton, Midlands Tech College — Beltline; Mark Lamoureux, Housatonic Community College; Hyuong Min Lee, Texas A&M University — College Station; Angie Mckinnon Carter, Utah Valley University; Nicholas G. Palombo, Auburn University; Michael A. Reyes, California Lutheran University; and Yingying Tang, Auburn University. Their feedback and thoughtful suggestions helped me understand how I could improve on the previous edition of *Joining the Conversation*, and I thank them for the time and care they took in their reviews.

Once again, I have been extraordinarily fortunate to find, in my colleagues at Bedford/St. Martin's, a group of editors who care deeply about producing the best possible textbooks. For their support, encouragement, and generous approach to editing, I thank my developmental editors, Kate George and Sherry Mooney, and associate editor Paola García-Muñiz. They have been constant sources of support and good ideas throughout the work on this new edition and I feel extraordinarily fortunate to have been able to work with them. I am indebted, as well, to Anna Palchik and Claire Seng-Niemoeller for the outstanding design of this book; to my content project manager, Kendra LeFleur, for her attention to detail in directing its complex production, and to Rosemary Winfield for her careful copyediting. I also offer my thanks to vice president Leasa Burton for her leadership throughout the editions of this book, and to senior program manager Laura Arcari and Marketing Manager Vivian Garcia for their work in helping instructors understand how *Joining the Conversation* might make a contribution in their classrooms.

Finally, I offer my thanks to the six student writers whose work is featured in this book: Jeremy Alcazar, Caitlin Guariglia, Gabriella Guerrero, Sophie Kimble, Brooke Shannon, and Kelsey Smith. I deeply appreciate their willingness to share their work and their insights about their writing processes with other student writers. I hope that their superb examples inspire the students who use this book to join and contribute to their own written conversations.

Mike Palmquist
Colorado State University

Bedford/St. Martin's puts you first

From day one, our goal has been simple: to provide inspiring resources that are grounded in best practices for teaching, reading, and writing. For more than forty years, Bedford/St. Martin's has partnered with the field, listening to teachers, scholars, and students about the support writers need. No matter the moment or teaching context, we are committed to helping every writing instructor make the most of our resources — resources designed to engage every student.

How can we help *you*?

- Our editors can align our resources to your outcomes through correlation and transition guides for your syllabus. Just ask us.
- Our sales representatives specialize in helping you find the right materials to support your course goals.
- Our learning solutions and product specialists help you make the most of the digital resources you choose for your course.
- Our *Bits* blog on the Bedford/St. Martin's English Community (**community .macmillan.com**) publishes fresh teaching ideas regularly. You'll also find easily downloadable professional resources and links to author webinars on our community site.

Contact your Bedford/St. Martin's sales representative or visit **macmillanlearning.com** to learn more.

● DIGITAL AND PRINT OPTIONS FOR *JOINING THE CONVERSATION*

Choose the format that works best for your course, and ask about our packaging options that offer savings for students.

Digital

- *Achieve with Joining the Conversation.* Achieve offers a dedicated composition space for writing instructors and students of all comfort levels with course technology. It provides trusted content with a robust e-book, as well as diagnostics with personalized study plans. Achieve's dedicated writing tools break down the writing process for students, make revision choices more visible to instructors, and guide students through drafts, peer review, avoiding plagiarism, reflection, and revision. Fully editable prebuilt assignments support the book's approach. To order *Achieve with Joining the Conversation*, use ISBN 978-1-319-41230-2. For details, visit **macmillanlearning.com/college /us/achieve/english.**
- *Popular E-Book Formats.* For details about our ebook partners, visit **macmillanlearning.com/ebooks**.

- **Inclusive Access.** Enable every student to receive their course materials through your LMS on the first day of class. Macmillan Learning's Inclusive Access program is the easiest, most affordable way to ensure all students have access to quality educational resources. Find out more at **macmillanlearning.com/inclusiveaccess.**

Print

- **Paperback.** To order the paperback edition, use ISBN 978-1-319-33494-9. To order the paperback packaged with Achieve, use ISBN 978-1-319-50360-4.
- **Looseleaf Edition.** This format does not have a traditional binding; its pages are loose and hole punched to provide flexibility and a lower price to students. It can be packaged with Achieve for additional savings. To order the loose-leaf packaged with Achieve, use ISBN 978-1-319-50362-8.
- **Student's Companion.** To order the supplemental workbook *A Student's Companion for Joining the Conversation* packaged with the paperback edition, use ISBN 978-1-319-50368-0.

YOUR COURSE, YOUR WAY

No two writing programs or classrooms are exactly alike. Our Curriculum Solutions team works with you to design custom options that provide the resources your students need. (Options below require enrollment minimums.)

- **ForeWords for English.** Customize any print resource to fit the focus of your course or program by choosing from a range of prepared topics, such as Sentence Guides for Academic Writers.
- **Macmillan Author Program (MAP).** Add excerpts or package acclaimed works from Macmillan's trade imprints to connect students with prominent authors and public conversations. A list of popular examples or academic themes is available upon request.
- **Mix and Match.** With our simplest solution, you can add up to 50 pages of curated content to your Bedford/St. Martin's text. Contact your sales representative for additional details.

INSTRUCTOR RESOURCES

You have a lot to do in your course. We want to make it easy for you to find the support you need — and to get it quickly.

Teaching with Joining the Conversation is available as a PDF that can be downloaded from **macmillanlearning.com** and is also available in Achieve. Visit the instructor resources tab for *Joining the Conversation*. In addition to chapter overviews and teaching tips, the instructor's manual includes sample syllabi, context and suggested responses for questions within the book, and suggestions for expanding activities and writing projects.

Contents

PREFACE FOR INSTRUCTORS v

PART ONE Joining a Conversation 1

 UNDERSTANDING YOURSELF AS A WRITER 1

Why think of writing as conversation? 2
You already know how conversations work — online and off 3
Conversations help you share information, ideas, and arguments 5
Conversations allow you to adopt roles 7

What should I know about writing situations? 9
Writing situations are rhetorical situations 9
Writing has a purpose 9
Readers have purposes, needs, interests, knowledge, and backgrounds 11
Writing builds on the work of others 12
Writing takes place in context 13
Writing situations are an important area of scholarly inquiry 15

What should I know about genre and design? 16
Genres are general categories of documents 16
Design is a writing tool 17
Genre and design are related 17
Genres and design help writers achieve their goals 21

What should I know about writing processes? 22
Writing is like other complex activities 22
It takes time and effort to become a good writer 23
Writing processes vary from project to project 24
Writing processes are recursive 25
Writing processes involve critical thinking 25
  Writing relies on critical thinking 25
  Writing supports critical thinking 26
  Writing assignments call for different types of critical thinking 26
Writing processes are studied intensely 27

How can I prepare for a successful writing project? 29
Take ownership 29
Create a writer's notebook 31
Manage your time 31
● **In Summary: Understanding Yourself as a Writer** 31

 FINDING AND LISTENING IN ON CONVERSATIONS 32

How can I analyze an assignment? 32
Assess your writing situation 33
  Determine your purpose and role 33
  Determine who your readers are and what motivates them 33
  Consider the role of sources 33
  Identify the context and genre 35
  Note requirements, limitations, and opportunities 35

How can I find interesting conversations? 36
Generate ideas 37

xiii

Brainstorm   37
Freewrite   37
Loop   38
Cluster   39
Map   40
Use sentence starters   40
Ask questions   44

How can I "listen in" on written conversations?   45
Discuss the topic with others   46
Observe the topic firsthand   46
Read what others have written   46
Review your sources   47
- **In Summary: Finding and Listening In on Conversations   48**

3 READING TO WRITE   49

How can I read critically?   49
Read with an attitude   50
Consider writing situations   50
Draw on critical thinking skills   50

How can I read actively?   51
Skim for an overview   51
  Peter Johnston, *Guiding the Budding Writer*   54
Mark and annotate   58
Pay attention   59
  Recognize the genre   60
  Consider illustrations   60
  Record new information and challenging ideas   61
  Identify similarities and differences   61
  Evaluate and reflect on what you've learned   61
Understand the writer's argument   62
  Identify the main point   62
  Find reasons and evidence that support the main point   62

How can I take notes?   63
Quote directly   64
Paraphrase   65
Summarize   66
Use notes to improve your understanding of an issue   67
  Record your reactions and impressions   67
  Compare sources   67
  Classify sources   68
  Plan your document   70

How can I engage with my sources?   70
Read to understand   70
  Nancy Sommers, *Living Composition*   71
  Main-point summaries   76
  Key-point summaries   76
  Outline summaries   76
Read to respond   77
  Agree/disagree responses   78
  Reflective responses   78
  Analytic responses   78
Read to make connections   79
  Literature reviews   80
- **In Summary: Reading to Write   83**

4 ASSESSING AND EVALUATING SOURCES   84

What should I consider as I begin to assess sources?   85
Consider the function and biases of your sources   85
Consider the lure of new and exciting information   86
Avoid information bubbles   86

What strategies should I use to evaluate a source?   87
Explore connections to your conversation   87
Read laterally to assess a source's credibility   87
Read closely to evaluate the source   89
  Evaluate relevance   89

CONTENTS xv

Evaluate evidence 90
Evaluate the author 90
Evaluate the publisher 91
Evaluate timeliness 91
Evaluate comprehensiveness 91
Evaluate genre 92
Ask what you can learn from the source 93

Should I evaluate all types of sources in the same way? 93
Evaluate the relevance and credibility of digital sources 93
Evaluate the relevance and accuracy of field sources 96
- **In Summary: Assessing and Evaluating Sources** 97

5 WORKING TOGETHER 98

How can collaborative activities improve my writing? 99
Work together to generate ideas 99
  Group brainstorming 99
  Role-playing 100
Work together to collect and work with information 102
Work together to refine your argument 102

How can I work with other writers on a group project? 104
Understand the purposes of working in a group 105
Understand potential problems and develop solutions 106
Establish ground rules 107
Create a plan 108

How can I use peer review to improve my writing? 108
Use peer review to enhance your writing process 109
Use peer review to improve your document 109

How can I conduct an effective peer review? 110
Consider context 110
Consider technology 110
Consider your needs as a writer 111
  When you ask for feedback on a draft 111
  When you receive feedback on a draft 111
Consider your role as a reviewer 112
  To prepare for a peer-review session 112
  Before you make comments 113
  As you make comments 114

What resources can I draw on as I review and collaborate? 116
Use technological tools 116
Consult instructors, classmates, friends, and family 118
- **In Summary: Working Together** 118

PART TWO   Contributing to a Conversation 119

6 CHOOSING YOUR WRITING ROLE 119

What is a writing role? 120

What roles can I adopt? 120
Observer 121
Reporter 121
Interpreter 121
Evaluator 122
Problem solver 122
Advocate 123
Other roles 123

How can I choose my role? 125

Your purpose 125
Your readers 125
   Observer 125
   Reporter 125
   Interpreter 126
   Evaluator 126
   Problem Solver 126
   Advocate 127

Your context 127

How will my role affect my work on my document? 128

Your role will shape your choice of sources 128
Your role will influence your critical thinking 128

Can I adopt more than one role? 130

- **In Summary: Choosing Your Writing Role** 130

7 WRITING TO REFLECT 131

What is writing to reflect? 131

THE WRITER'S ROLE: Observer 132

What kinds of documents are used to share reflections? 132

Meditations 133
   James Parker, *An Ode to Not Being a Morning Person* 133
Photo essays 135
   James Mollison, *Where Children Sleep* 135
Literacy narratives 148
   Sandra Cisneros, *Only Daughter* 148
Memoirs 152
   Margo Jefferson, *Are We Rich?* 152

Genre Talk: Reflective Writing 157

How can I write a reflective essay? 158

- **IN PROCESS: A Reflective Essay about a Family Vacation** 158

Find a conversation and listen in 158
   Explore your experiences 158
   Ask questions about promising subjects 159
   Conduct an observation 159
Reflect on your subject 160
- **IN PROCESS: Conducting an Observation** 161
   Examine your subject 162

Collect details 163
Find significance 164
- **IN PROCESS: Making Comparisons** 164
Prepare a draft 165
   Convey your main idea 165
   Tell a story 166
   Go into detail 167
   Choose your point of view 167
   Consider genre and design 168
   Frame your reflections 168
Review and improve your draft 169
   Ensure that your main idea is clear 169
   Examine the presentation of your observations 169
   Review dialogue 169
   Show, don't tell 170
- **IN PROCESS: Adding Dialogue** 170
   Respond to feedback from your instructor 171
- **IN PROCESS: Responding to Instructor Feedback** 171
   PEER REVIEW: Improve Your Reflective Essay 172

✱ **Student Essay** 173
   Caitlin Guariglia, *Mi Famiglia* 173

✱ **Project Ideas** 177

- **In Summary: Writing a Reflective Essay** 180

8 WRITING TO INFORM 181

What is writing to inform? 181

THE WRITER'S ROLE: Reporter 182

What kinds of documents are used to inform? 183

Informative essays and articles 183

Alice Park and Sean Gregory, *Time 2021 Athlete of the Year: Simone Biles*   183
Infographics   190
International Networks Archive, Princeton University, *The Magic Bean Shop* and *The Fries That Bind Us*   190
Profiles   192
Rivka Galchen, *An Unlikely Ballerina: The Rise of Misty Copeland*   192
Newsletter articles   200
Illyanna Maisonet, *Why Aren't There More Puerto Rican Restaurants . . . In California?*   200

Genre Talk: Informative Writing   204

How can I write an informative essay?   205

- **IN PROCESS:** An Informative Essay about Fast Fashion   205

Find a conversation and listen in   205
Reflect on your interests   205
- **IN PROCESS:** Using the Library Catalog   207
Ask questions about promising subjects   208

Gather information   208
Create a search plan   208
Collect sources   210
Assess and evaluate your sources   210
Take notes   210
Consider field research   211

Prepare a draft   211
- **IN PROCESS:** Assessing and Evaluating Sources   212
Present your main point   214
Develop supporting points and evidence   214
- **IN PROCESS:** Developing Support   215
Consider genre and design   217
Frame your information   218

Review and improve your draft   219
Focus your discussion   220
Ensure clarity   220
Review your use of sources   220
Assess your introduction and conclusion   220
Respond to feedback from your instructor   221
- **IN PROCESS:** Responding to Instructor Feedback   221

PEER REVIEW: Improve Your Informative Essay   222

✶ **Student Essay**   222
Gabriella Guerrero, *Fast Fashion? Not So Fast!*   222

✶ **Project Ideas**   229
- **In Summary:** Writing an Informative Essay   232

9 WRITING TO ANALYZE   233

What is writing to analyze?   233

THE WRITER'S ROLE: Interpreter   234

What kinds of documents are used to present an analysis?   235

Articles   235
Carly Lewis, *The Writing on the Virtual Bathroom Wall*   235
Issue analyses   240
Peter C. Baker, *Reform of the Nerds, Starring Arthur Chu*   240
Rhetorical analyses   248
Brooke Gladstone, *The Goldilocks Number*   248
Videos   252
Blank on Blank, *Temple Grandin on Her Search Engine*   252

Genre Talk: Analytical Writing   255

How can I write an analytical essay?   256

- **IN PROCESS:** An Analysis of a Cultural Trend   256

Find a conversation and listen in   256
Reflect on your surroundings   256
Ask interpretive questions   257
Search for sources   259
- **IN PROCESS:** Searching Databases   260

Conduct your analysis   261
Refine your question   261
Seek a fuller understanding of your subject   262
Apply an interpretive framework   264
- **IN PROCESS:** Applying Interpretive Frameworks   273

Prepare a draft 274
   Make an interpretive claim 274
   Explain your interpretation 274
- **IN PROCESS:** Supporting Reasons with Evidence 277
   Consider genre and design 277
   Frame your analysis 278
Review and improve your draft 279
   Ensure that your claim is debatable 279
   Challenge your conclusions 279
   Examine the application of your interpretive framework 279

Assess your organization 280
- **PEER REVIEW:** Improve Your Analytical Essay 280
Respond to feedback from your instructor 281
- **IN PROCESS:** Responding to Instructor Feedback 281

✱ **Student Essay** 282
   Kelsey Smith, *Art Theft on the Rise with Social Media* 282

✱ **Project Ideas** 292
- In Summary: Writing an Analytical Essay 296

10 WRITING TO EVALUATE 297

What is writing to evaluate? 297

 THE WRITER'S ROLE: Evaluator 298

What kinds of documents are used to share evaluations? 299

Scholarly articles 299
   Thomas Polk, *A Review of the* MLA Handbook, *Eighth Edition* 299
Web-based articles 304
   Marie-Helen Maras, *4 Ways 'Internet of Things' Toys Endanger Children* 304
Media reviews 307
   Justin Kanoya, *Thoughts on* Crazy Rich Asians: *How Representation Impacts Self-Worth* 307
Progress reports 311
   National Cancer Institute, *Excerpts from* Cancer Trends Progress Report 311

Genre Talk: Evaluative Writing 321

How can I write an evaluative essay? 322

- **IN PROCESS:** An Evaluative Essay about the Effectiveness of a Media Production 322

Find a conversation and listen in 322
   Explore your needs, interests, and concerns 323
   Locate sources 324
- **IN PROCESS:** Searching the Web 325
   Narrow your focus by asking questions 326
- **IN PROCESS:** Focusing on a Subject 326

Conduct your evaluation 327
   Define your criteria 327
   Identify evidence 328
   Make your judgments 329
- **IN PROCESS:** Making Judgments 330
Prepare a draft 331
   State your overall judgment 331
   Present your evaluation 332
- **IN PROCESS:** Using Evidence to Support Judgments 333
   Consider genre and design 334
   Frame your evaluation 335
Review and improve your draft 336
   Review your criteria 336
   Reconsider your evidence 336
   Ensure that your judgments are fair and reasonable 337
   Respond to feedback from your instructor 337
- **IN PROCESS:** Responding to Instructor Feedback 337
- **PEER REVIEW:** Improve Your Evaluative Essay 338

✱ **Student Essay** 339
   Brooke Shannon, *Is Wicked* All That Wicked? 339

✱ **Project Ideas** 344
- In Summary: Writing an Evaluative Essay 347

CONTENTS | **xix**

11 WRITING TO SOLVE PROBLEMS 348

What is writing to solve problems? 348

THE WRITER'S ROLE: Problem Solver 349

What kinds of documents are used to solve problems? 350

Problem-solving articles and essays 350
- Anneke Jong, *Leveling the Playing Field: How to Get More Women in Tech* 350

Proposals 354
- Dave Krepcho, *Grant Proposal for Second Harvest Food Bank of Central Florida* 354

Opinion pieces 363
- Sapna Maheshwari, *Why Elite Female Athletes Are Turning Away from Major Sponsors* 363

Advice 369
- Savannah Peterson, *Advice for Generation Z from a Savvy Millennial* 369

Genre Talk: Problem-Solving Writing 375

How can I write a problem-solving essay? 376

- **IN PROCESS:** A Problem-Solving Essay about Shark Finning 376

Find a conversation and listen in 376
- Explore difficulties 377
- Ask questions about promising subjects 378
- Locate relevant sources and conduct field research 378

Develop a solution 379
- Define the problem 380
- Consider potential solutions 381
- **IN PROCESS:** Developing a Survey 382
- **IN PROCESS:** Defining a Problem 383
- Assess the practicality of your solution 384
- **IN PROCESS:** Developing a Solution 385

Prepare a draft 386
- Explain the problem 386
- Propose your solution 387
- Explain your solution 388
- Consider genre and design 389
- **IN PROCESS:** Providing Support for Key Points 390
- Frame your essay 391

Review and improve your draft 391
- Reassess your problem definition 392
- Review the presentation of your solution 392
- Check the feasibility of your solution 392
- Consider objections and alternative solutions 393
- Respond to feedback from your instructor 393
- **IN PROCESS:** Responding to Instructor Feedback 393
- **PEER REVIEW:** Improve Your Problem-Solving Essay 394

✱ **Student Essay 394**
- Sophie Kimble, *Sharks for Profit* 394

✱ **Project Ideas 401**
- In Summary: Writing a Problem-Solving Essay 403

12 WRITING TO CONVINCE OR PERSUADE 404

What is writing to convince or persuade? 404

THE WRITER'S ROLE: Advocate 405

What kinds of documents are used to convince or persuade? 406

Argumentative essays 406
- Anu Partanen, *What Americans Keep Ignoring about Finland's School Success* 406

Advertisements 413
- Men Can Stop Rape, *Where Do You Stand?* 413

Point/counterpoint editorials 418
- Katharina Nieswandt, Point: *Basic Income after Automation? That's Not How Capitalism Works!* 418
- Ben Bloch, Counterpoint: *Tax Robots and Universal Basic Income* 423

Open letters   426
   Angela Nickerson, *An Open Letter to Lands' End*   426

Genre Talk: Argumentative Writing   430

How can I write an argumentative essay?   431

- **IN PROCESS:** An Argumentative Essay about Police Reform   431

Find a conversation and listen in   431
   Explore disagreements   432
- **IN PROCESS:** Generating Ideas about Conversations   432
   Track online conversations   434
   Ask questions about promising issues   434

Build your argument   435
- **IN PROCESS:** Locating Sources   436
   Define your overall claim   437
   Develop reasons to accept your overall claim   437
   Choose evidence to support your reasons   439
- **IN PROCESS:** Choosing Evidence   441
   Identify and consider opposing claims   442
   Ensure the integrity of your argument   443

Prepare a draft   445
   Make an argumentative claim   445
   Appeal to your readers   446
   Address counterarguments   449
   Consider genre and design   451
   Frame your argument   451

Review and improve your draft   452
   Consider your overall claim   452
   Review your reasons, evidence, and appeals   452
   Examine your treatment of counterarguments   452
   Ensure the integrity of your argument   453
   Respond to feedback from your instructor   453
- **IN PROCESS:** Responding to Instructor Feedback   453
   PEER REVIEW: Improve Your Argumentative Essay   454

✱ Student Essay   455
Jeremy Alcazar, *Reforming, Not Defunding, the Police*   455

✱ Project Ideas   463
- In Summary: Writing an Argumentative Essay   465

PART THREE   Conducting Research   467

13   FOCUSING YOUR SEARCH   467

What should I consider as I develop my research question?   467
   Consider your issue and disciplinary context   468
   Reflect on your purpose and role   470
   Look for gaps in the conversation   472

How can I draft my research question?   473
Generate questions about your issue   473
Select and refine your question   474
   Refer to shared assumptions and existing conditions   474
   Narrow your scope   475
   ✏ Tech Tip: Conduct preliminary searches   476

Be open to change   476

How can I develop my search plan?   477
Identify relevant types of sources   477
   Consider the scope of your conversation   477
   Consider the timeliness of your subject   477
   Consider what you need to learn   477
   Consider the evidence you'll need   478
Identify appropriate search tools and research methods   478
Review and refine your plan   479
- In Summary: Focusing Your Search   479

14 LOCATING SOURCES   480

How can I locate sources using digital resources?   480

Generate search terms   481
Choose search strategies   482
- Plan basic searches   482
- 🖅 Tech Tip: Plan advanced searches   483

Search library catalogs   485
- 🖅 Tech Tip: Search with multiple strategies   487

Search databases   487
- Identify relevant databases   487
- Search within database fields   488

Search the web   489
- Use web search engines   489
- Use news search sites   491
- Use reference sites   491
- Use government search sites and directories   491
- Search social media sites   492

Search media sites   492
- Use image search sites and directories   492
- Use audio search sites   492
- Use video search sites   493

How can I locate sources using print resources?   493

Discuss your search plan with a librarian   494
Visit the library stacks   494
- 🖅 Tech Tip: Use interlibrary loan   494

Browse periodicals   495
Check reference works   495
- Consult bibliographies   496
- Review indexes   497
- Check biographies   497
- Browse specialized encyclopedias   498
- Consult handbooks   498
- Review almanacs   498
- Scan atlases   498

- **In Summary: Locating Sources**   498

15 CONDUCTING FIELD RESEARCH   499

When should I use field research methods?   499

How can I conduct an interview?   500

Plan your interview   501
- Identify interview candidates   501
- Develop interview questions   501
- Decide how to conduct your interview   502
- Decide whether to share questions in advance   502
- Decide how to record and take notes   503

Conduct your interview   504
Analyze your results   505

How can I conduct an observation?   505

Plan your observation   505
- Determine what, how, and how often to observe   505
- Determine whether to ask permission to observe   506

Conduct your observation   507
Analyze your results   508

How can I conduct a survey?   509

Plan your survey   509
- Identify potential survey respondents   509
- Decide what to ask and how to ask it with integrity   509
- Determine whether you are asking your questions clearly   511

Distribute your survey   511
Analyze your results   512

How can I engage in other forms of field research?   513

Engage in correspondence   513
Attend public events   513
Collaborate with others   514

- **In Summary: Conducting Field Research**   514

16. MANAGING YOUR SOURCES 515

How can I keep track of print materials? 515

How can I keep track of digital materials? 516
Download sources 517
Copy and paste 518
Use email 518
Take photos, make recordings, and save notes 519
Save bookmarks and favorites in your browser 519
Use web tools 520
Back up your files 520

How can I create a bibliography? 520
List sources in a working bibliography 521
Summarize sources in an annotated bibliography 522
- In Summary: Managing Your Sources 524

17. AVOIDING PLAGIARISM 525

What is plagiarism? 526
Unintentional plagiarism 526
Intentional plagiarism 527
Plagiarism in group projects 527
Self-plagiarism 528
Tech Tip: Translation tools 528

What are research ethics? 528

What is common knowledge? 530
What is fair use and when should I ask permission to use a source? 530
Tech Tip: Seeking permission 530

How can I avoid plagiarism? 532
Conduct a knowledge inventory 532
Take notes carefully 533
Attribute ideas appropriately 534
Identify sources in your document 534
Understand why writers plagiarize 535

What should I do if I'm accused of plagiarism? 535
- In Summary: Avoiding Plagiarism 537

PART FOUR: Crafting and Polishing Your Contribution 539

18. DEVELOPING YOUR THESIS STATEMENT 539

How can I develop my position on an issue? 539
Review your notes 540
Consider your writing situation 540

How can I draft my thesis statement? 541
Consider your genre 541
Identify important information, ideas, and arguments related to your position 542
Draft alternatives 543
Focus your thesis statement 543

How can I support my thesis statement? 544
Choose reasons to accept your thesis statement 544
Select evidence to support your reasons 545
- In Summary: Developing Your Thesis Statement 546

19 ORGANIZING YOUR IDEAS 547

How can I choose an organizing pattern? 547
Understand the types of organizing patterns 548
Reflect on your writing situation 549

How can I arrange my ideas? 550
Labeling 550
Grouping 551
Clustering 551
Mapping 551

How can I create an outline? 554
Create an informal outline 554
Create a formal outline 556

What if I'm not ready to organize my ideas? 558
Create a zero draft 558
Create an outline or a map from a zero draft 559
- **In Summary: Organizing Your Ideas** 559

20 DRAFTING YOUR DOCUMENT 560

How can I use my outline or map to write a first draft? 561

How can I draft an effective document? 562
Create paragraphs that focus on a central idea 562
Create paragraphs that use appropriate organizing patterns 563
Integrate information from sources effectively 563
Write clearly and concisely 564
Engage your readers 566
Use details to capture your readers' attention 566
Create transitions within and between paragraphs 567

How can I help readers follow my ideas? 569
Let readers know where your document is taking them 569
    Give readers a map 570
    Build on readers' experiences 570
Keep related ideas together 570
Keep the flow of your document moving forward 570
Say things just once 571

How can I draft my introduction? 571
Frame your introduction 572
Select an introductory strategy 573
    State the topic 573
    Establish the context 574
    State your thesis 574
    Define a problem 575
    Make a surprising statement 575
    Ask a question 575
    Tell a story 575
    Provide a historical account 576
    Lead with a quotation 576
    Draw a contrast 576
    Provide a map 577

How can I draft my conclusion? 577
Reinforce your points 577
Select a concluding strategy 578
    Offer additional analysis 578
    Speculate about the future 578
    Close with a quotation 579
    Close with a story 579
    Close with a question 580
    Call your readers to action 580
    Link to your introduction 580
Reinforce your efforts to frame your subject or issue 581
- **In Summary: Drafting Your Document** 581

21 USING SOURCES EFFECTIVELY 582

How can I use sources to accomplish my purposes as a writer? 583
Introduce a point 583
Contrast ideas 584
Provide evidence 585
Align yourself with an authority 585
Define a concept, illustrate a process, or clarify a statement 586
Set a mood 587
Provide an example 587
Amplify or qualify a point 587

How can I integrate sources into my draft? 588
Identify your sources 588
　Use attributions and in-text citations 588
　Provide a context 589
Quote strategically 590
　Use partial, complete, or block quotations 590
　Modify quotations appropriately 591
　Punctuate quotations correctly 593
Paraphrase information, ideas, and arguments 595
　Ensure the accuracy and fairness of each paraphrase 595
　Integrate each paraphrase into your document 595
Summarize sources 596
　Summarize an entire source 596
　Summarize specific information and ideas from a source 596
　Summarize a group of sources 597
Present numerical information 598
Use images, audio, and video 598

How can I ensure I've avoided plagiarism? 601
Quote, paraphrase, and summarize accurately and appropriately 601
Distinguish between your ideas and ideas in your sources 601
Check for unattributed sources in your document 603

How should I document my sources? 603
Choose a documentation system 603
Provide in-text references and publication information 604

● **In Summary: Using Sources Effectively** 605

22 DESIGNING YOUR DOCUMENT 606

How can I design my document? 606
Understand design principles 607
　⚐ Tech Tip: Check accessibility 609
Design for a purpose 609
Design for your readers 610
Design to address genre conventions 611

What design elements can I use? 612
Use fonts, line spacing, and alignment 612
Use page layout elements 612
Use color, shading, borders, and rules 615
Use illustrations 615
　Photographs and other images 615
　Charts and graphs 615
　Tables 615
　Other digital illustrations 615
Use navigation tools 617

● **In Summary: Designing Your Document** 617

23 WORKING WITH GENRES 618

How can I choose the right genre? 619
Analyze your assignment 619
Reflect on your purpose, role, readers, and context 620
Consider your writing resources 620

What should I consider as I design an academic essay? 621
Consider how design can help you achieve your goals 621
Consider reader expectations 622
Consider your context 622
View an essay 623

How can I write and design an article? 625
Analyze your target publication 625
Develop and organize your argument 627
Collect and work with sources 627
Draft, design, and review your article 628
View an article 628

How can I create a multimodal essay? 630
Build on your experiences writing academic essays 630
Develop and organize your argument 630
Collect and work with sources 631
    Choose your sources 631
    Place and stage your sources 631
    Import or link to media sources 632
Choose composing tools 633
Develop a consistent design 634
View a multimodal essay 635

How can I create a website? 637
Plan your site 637
    Create content 637
    Choose navigation tools 638
Design your site 638
Create your site 639
Publish your site 639
View web pages 639

How can I make a presentation? 641
Consider your speaking situation 642
Plan your presentation 642
    Create a bare-bones outline 642
    Consider your words 643
    Prepare speaker's notes 643
Create a multimedia presentation 645
    Choose media sources 645
    Choose composing tools 646
    Develop a consistent design 647
    Prepare for challenges 648
Engage with your audience 648
If necessary, present virtually 649
View a presentation 649
- **In Summary: Working with Genres** 652

REVISING AND EDITING 653

What should I focus on when I revise? 653
Consider your writing situation 654
Consider your argument and ideas 654
Consider your use, integration, and documentation of sources 655
Consider the structure and organization of your document 656
Consider genre and design 656

What strategies can I use to revise? 657
Save multiple drafts 657
Highlight your main point, reasons, and evidence 657
Challenge your assumptions 659
    Put yourself in the place of your readers 659
    Play devil's advocate 659
    Play the "So what?" game 659
Scan, outline, and map your document 659
Ask for feedback 661

What should I focus on when I edit? 662
Focus on accuracy 662
Focus on economy 662
Focus on consistency 663
Focus on style 663
Focus on spelling, grammar, and punctuation 663

What strategies can I use to edit? 664
Read carefully 664
Mark and search your document 664

Use spelling, grammar, and style tools with caution 665
Ask for feedback 666
- In Summary: Revising and Editing 666

PART FIVE — Documenting Sources 667

25 USING MLA STYLE 667

How do I cite sources within the text of my document? 669

How do I prepare the list of works cited? 672
Books 673

Sources in journals, magazines, and newspapers 678
Reference works 683
Field sources 684
Media sources 684
Other digital sources 687

26 USING APA STYLE 691

How do I cite sources within the text of my document? 693

How do I prepare the reference list? 696
Books 697
Sources in journals, magazines, and newspapers 702

Reference works 705
Field sources 705
Media sources 706
Other digital sources 707
Other sources 711

PART SIX — Handbook 713

27 STYLE: WRITING CONFIDENTLY 713

Write clear, logical sentences 714
Choose the right sentence structures 714
    Put your main ideas in main clauses 714
    To give multiple ideas equal weight, use a compound sentence 714
    To emphasize one idea over another, use a complex sentence 715
    Combine coordination and subordination in a compound-complex sentence 717

Write in complete sentences 717
    Watch out for subordinate clauses posing as sentences 718
    Watch out for verbals posing as verbs 719
    Watch out for fragments that begin with prepositions 719
    Watch out for fragments consisting of examples 720

Avoid run-ons and comma splices   720
   Use a comma and a coordinating conjunction   720
   Use a semicolon   721
   Break the sentence in two   721
   Subordinate one of the clauses   721

Use parallel structures to help readers understand your ideas   722
   When you write a series, make all the elements in it parallel   722
   Compare like with like   722
   Connect elements in a series to the rest of the sentence   723

Let readers know where your sentence is going   724
   Use conjunctions and transition words as signposts   724
   Keep related ideas together   725
   Keep the flow of the sentence moving forward   727

Avoid dangling words and phrases   728
   Avoid dangling modifiers   728
   Avoid dangling prepositions   729

Choose language that will earn you respect   730
Match your style to your writing situation   730
   Choose the right level of formality   730
   Avoid unnecessarily technical language   731

Use language that is free of bias and stereotyping   732
Avoid exaggeration   733
Use only words you know   734

Choose lively, concise phrasing   735
To be vivid, be specific   735
Give every word a job to do   735
Favor the active voice   736
Look for alternatives to forms of the verb *to be*   737
If you want to use figures of speech, invent your own   738
Pay attention to relationships among words   738
Avoid using too many *-tion*, *-ing*, and *-ly* endings   740
Make a habit of stating things in an affirmative way   741

- **In Summary: Style: Writing Confidently**   741

28 GRAMMAR: WRITING SKILLFULLY   742

Make verbs work for you   743
Match the number of a verb to the number of its subject   743
   Watch out for words that come between the subject and verb   744
   Treat most compound subjects as plural   744
   Match the number of the verb to the nearer or nearest of alternative subjects   745
   Make the subject and verb agree, even when the verb comes first   745
   Do not confuse the subject with a noun complement   746
   Use singular verbs with singular indefinite pronouns   746
   Use the right verb forms with collective nouns   747
   Watch out for nouns that look plural but are not   748

Use verb tense and mood to convey timing and possibility   748
   Don't get tripped up by irregular verbs   751
   Use verbs in special moods in special cases   755

Use pronouns to help readers   757
Match subject pronouns with subjects and object pronouns with objects   757
   Watch out when using subject or object pronouns together or with a name   758
   Use *who* for subjects and *whom* for objects   759
   Use reflexive pronouns to refer to the subject of the sentence or clause   759
   Choose the right pronouns in comparisons   760
   Use a subject pronoun for a subject complement   760

Make pronouns agree with their antecedents 761
   Watch out for indefinite pronouns 761
   Watch out for collective nouns 762
Avoid vague or ambiguous pronoun references 762
   Watch out for pronouns whose antecedents are whole clauses or sentences 763
   Avoid using the same pronoun when referring to different things 763
   Avoid using a pronoun when it might refer to more than one thing 764
   Use the pronoun *you* only when you mean your readers 764
   Use *they* only to refer to particular people or things 765

Use the placeholder pronoun *it* sparingly 765

Use adjectives and adverbs to clarify your ideas 766
Use adjectives to modify nouns and pronouns 766
Use adverbs to modify verbs, adjectives, and adverbs 767
Know when to use *good*, *well*, *bad*, and *badly* 768
Use *-est*, *most*, or *least* only when comparing three or more items 769
Watch out for adverbs with absolute concepts 769
- **In Summary: Grammar: Writing Skillfully** 770

29 PUNCTUATION AND MECHANICS: GIVING YOUR READERS DIRECTION 771

Use commas to keep your sentences organized and readable 772
Use a comma and a coordinating conjunction to separate two main clauses 772
Use commas to set off introductory elements 773
Use commas to set off detours 773
Use commas in series 775
Use commas to set off most quotations 776
Use commas in other places where readers expect them 776

Use periods, question marks, and exclamation points correctly 777
End most sentences with periods 777
Reserve question marks for actual questions 777
Use exclamation points sparingly 778

Use quotation marks when you borrow words 778
Put quotation marks around direct quotations 778
Put quotation marks around new terms and words used as words 779
Put quotation marks around the titles of short works 779
Place quotation marks correctly with other punctuation 780

Use apostrophes in contractions and possessives 780
Use apostrophes in contractions 780
Use apostrophes to show possession 781
Distinguish among possessives, adjectives, and attributive nouns 781
Give possessive pronouns special treatment 782

Use colons to point to what comes next 782

Use semicolons between equivalent elements 783

Use other punctuation marks in specific situations 783
Use hyphens mainly to help readers understand relationships between adjacent words 783
   Check a dictionary 784
   Use hyphens to make compound adjectives 784
   Do not add hyphens to internet addresses 785
   Hyphenate between syllables at the end of a line 785
Use dashes for breaks in thought that are larger than commas suggest 785
Use parentheses for explanatory and other minor asides 786
Use brackets inside parentheses and quotations 787

Use ellipsis marks to indicate omissions   787

Use a slash when quoting poetry or song lyrics and sparingly for alternatives   788

Use sentence mechanics to help readers follow your ideas   788

Use capitalization to mark beginnings   788

   Capitalize proper names   788

   Capitalize titles that immediately precede a person's name   788

   Capitalize adjectives derived from proper names   789

   Capitalize most words in the titles of works   789

   Follow the specialized capitalization style of organizations and brands   789

Use italics for titles of substantial works, for foreign words, and sparingly for emphasis   790

   Italicize the titles or names of substantial works   790

   Italicize foreign words   790

   Use italics for emphasis   790

Use abbreviations and acronyms to help, not frustrate, readers   791

   Use standard abbreviations   791

   Use acronyms to simplify and clarify   792

- **In Summary: Punctuation and Mechanics: Giving Your Readers Direction**   792

INDEX   795

PART ONE
Joining a Conversation

01 Understanding Yourself as a Writer

Why think of writing as conversation? 2
You already know how conversations work — online and off 3
Conversations help you share information, ideas, and arguments 5
Conversations allow you to adopt roles 7

What should I know about writing situations? 9
Writing situations are rhetorical situations 9
Writing has a purpose 9
Readers have purposes, needs, interests, knowledge, and backgrounds 11
Writing builds on the work of others 12
Writing takes place in context 13
Writing situations are an important area of scholarly inquiry 15

What should I know about genre and design? 16
Genres are general categories of documents 16
Design is a writing tool 17
Genre and design are related 17
Genres and design help writers achieve their goals 21

What should I know about writing processes? 22
Writing is like other complex activities 22
It takes time and effort to become a good writer 23
Writing processes vary from project to project 24
Writing processes are recursive 25
Writing processes involve critical thinking 25
Writing processes are studied intensely 27

How can I prepare for a successful writing project? 29
Take ownership 29
Create a writer's notebook 31
Manage your time 31

What do you think when you hear someone say, "I'm a writer"? Do you think *Novelist*? *Poet*? *Journalist*? *Blogger*?

Or do you simply wonder what they mean?

Our understanding of what is involved in being a writer is complicated by characterizations of writers in the news media, movies, books, and television. It's not unusual, for example, to hear someone say, "But I'm not a *real writer*."

But of course they are. Almost everyone is. Writing is something most of us do on a daily basis. Whether we're tweeting, texting, posting on Facebook, adding a caption to a photo on Instagram, or responding to a discussion forum in a class, we're writing.

The idea that we're all writers becomes clearer when you think of writing as a form of conversation. When we join this kind of conversation, we read what others have written. We think about the information, ideas, and arguments they've shared. We decide whether we want to respond. And we shape our contributions to the conversation, if we make them, to fit the writing situation in which we find ourselves.

That said, it's the details that matter. This chapter explores those details by examining how writing is similar to engaging in conversation, considering key aspects of the situations in which writers find themselves, discussing genre and design, considering the composing processes we can use to engage in written conversations, and exploring strategies we can use to succeed as writers.

Why Think of Writing as Conversation?

Writing is often referred to as a mysterious process. Some people even consider the ability to write well a rare and special gift. Well ... perhaps. But only if you're talking about the ability to write a prize-winning novel or a poem that will be celebrated for generations. If, on the other hand, you're talking about conveying information, ideas, and arguments clearly and convincingly, the writing process is anything but mysterious.

In fact, once you realize that writing shares a surprising number of similarities with participating in a conversation, you'll find that writing is an activity you can approach with confidence. In this book, writing is treated as an activity similar to conversation. The documents you'll write are contributions that move a conversation forward. The designs you'll choose reflect your purposes and those of your readers. And the roles you'll adopt as a writer are much like those you've adopted as you've discussed issues with your friends and family. By thinking of writing as conversation, you'll be able to use your already extensive understanding of how conversations work to become a confident, effective writer.

You Already Know How Conversations Work — Online and Off

Imagine yourself at a party. When you arrive, you say hello to friends and get something to eat or drink. Then you walk around, listening briefly to several conversations. Eventually, you join a group that is talking about something you find interesting.

If you're like most people, you won't jump right into the conversation. Instead, you'll listen for a few minutes and think about what is being said. Perhaps you learn something new. Eventually, you add your voice to the conversation, other members of the group pick up on what you've said, and the conversation moves along.

The same thing happens when you join a new group online. Whether you join a discussion board or a Facebook group, more than likely you listen in (or read what's been posted) to learn about the group's interests before you make any posts.

You can use your understanding of how conversations work to become a better writer. You'll realize fairly quickly that good writing involves more than simply stating what you know. You'll see writing, instead, as a process of joining, reflecting on, and contributing to a conversation about something that interests you.

Because written conversations take place over much longer periods of time than spoken conversations, you can use your conversational skills to greater advantage. You can thoroughly consider your purposes and analyze your readers' needs, interests, and backgrounds. And you can explore the contexts — physical, social, cultural, and disciplinary — that will shape how your document is written and read.

Today, many of us are as likely to engage in conversations through writing as through speaking. Most people, however, don't think of creating text messages, email messages, status updates, comments, notes, forum posts, or blog posts as writing. Yet it is. And the writing you've done in these settings can help prepare you for the writing you'll be asked to do in class or at a job.

Certainly, there are differences between the writing you do on social media and the writing you do in an academic essay. Using abbreviations such as *omg* or *lol* in an essay might go over just about as well as writing "In summary, the available evidence suggests" in a text message. Despite these differences, you can build on your experiences as a writer in a wide range of settings. Just as you adapt your tone or level of formality in a spoken conversation to the people involved in the conversation — for example, treating new acquaintances differently than you treat old friends — you can adapt your writing to the situation in which you find yourself. Just as you tailor your comments to friends when you write on their Facebook pages, you can consider the interests and experiences of the people who will read your next academic essay. And just as you've learned to be critical — even suspicious — of what you find on social media, you can apply the same caution to your reading of the sources you encounter as you work on a writing project for a class or your job.

Your Turn: Inventory Your Writing Life

We all have writing lives. In fact, you probably do much more writing than you think. Conduct an inventory of your writing activities and reflect on how your experiences might enhance the writing you do for class assignments. To get started, use the following prompts:

1. **Create a list of everything you do that involves typing.** Be sure to include typing on phones, tablets, and computers.

2. **List everything you do that involves handwriting.** Include everything from grocery lists to notes taken in class to personal letters.

3. **Identify the purposes and audiences of each activity you've listed.** For each item, indicate why you do it or what you hope to accomplish by doing it (purpose). Then indicate who reads it (audience). In some cases, such as shopping lists or class notes, your audience will most likely be yourself.

4. **Identify activities that involve locating information.** For each activity on your list, indicate whether you read sources (such as newspaper or magazine articles, websites, blogs, or books), search the web, collect information through observation, or talk to others in the course of carrying out the activity.

5. **Review your list to identify writing activities that might prepare you for academic writing.** Look for activities that involve accomplishing a purpose; thinking about the needs, interests, and experiences of your readers; or collecting information. Consider how carrying out these activities might help you succeed at academic writing assignments.

Conversations Help You Share Information, Ideas, and Arguments

Much like a spoken conversation, a written conversation involves an exchange of information, ideas, and arguments among readers and writers. Instead of using spoken words, however, participants in a written conversation can communicate through text, images, audio, and video. And just as most people listen to what's being said before contributing to a spoken conversation, most writers begin the process of writing about a topic by reading and then reflecting on what they've learned.

To advance the conversation, writers search for something new to offer readers, and then they write their own document. In turn, that document is read by other members of the conversation. If some of them are interested, concerned, or even offended by the writer's contribution, they might respond. In this sense, a conversation among writers and readers becomes a circular process in which the information, ideas, and arguments shared through documents lead to the creation of new documents.

Consider the experiences of Gina Colville, a college student taking a first-year writing course at Front Range Community College north of Denver. Gina's instructor was teaching a writing-about-writing course, in which the content of the course focuses not on a particular theme or topic but on research and theory about writing. Gina's instructor had asked her to reflect on her experiences as a writer and to locate a few recent articles and blog posts that might speak to those experiences. To learn about writing research and theory, Gina started to "listen in" on written conversations about writing instruction, academic writing, professional writing, and writing on social media. She looked for information in her library's databases (see *Search Library Catalogs* in Chapter 14), searched the web (see *Search the Web* in Chapter 14), and read articles and social media posts. Some of the sources she read were written by writing instructors, some by journalists and professional writers, and still others by students. Gina found herself drawn to discussions of different approaches to preparing future high school teachers to teach writing. She compared what she read with her own experiences as a student and reflected on how she was taught to write during high school. Eventually, she wrote an evaluative essay that compared and made judgments about various instructional approaches.

As she learned more about how high school teachers are trained to teach writing, Gina decided to share her ideas about these approaches with friends and family, as well as with others who were interested in the topic. To get started, she shared her ideas on Twitter, Instagram, and Facebook and read the comments she received.

Writers learn about a topic through reading.

Eventually, a student reporter for her college newspaper responded to her ideas in an article about Colorado guidelines for teaching writing to high school students.

You can see conversational exchanges among readers and writers in numerous contexts. Articles in scholarly and professional journals almost always refer to previously published work. Similarly, letters to the editors of newspapers and magazines often make references to earlier letters or articles. You can even see this process in writing classes. As writers share their work with classmates and instructors, they receive feedback that often leads to important changes in their final drafts. In turn, as writers read the work of their classmates, they often refine their thinking about their own writing projects.

As you work on your own writing projects, keep in mind the circular nature of written conversations. Remember: just as when you join a group of friends who are chatting at a party, you'll be entering a situation in which others have already contributed their observations and ideas. Your contribution should build on what has been written by others. In turn, other members of the conversation will read what you've written and build on the ideas, information, and arguments you've shared with them.

After reading about a topic, writers share information with readers, who may respond in writing themselves.

Conversations Allow You to Adopt Roles

In spoken conversations, we often take on roles. A speaker might explain something to someone else, in a sense becoming a guide through the conversation. Another speaker might advance an argument, taking on the role of an advocate for a particular position. These roles shift and change as the conversation moves along. Depending on the flow of the conversation, a person who explained something at one point in the conversation might make an argument later on.

A similar form of role-playing takes place in written conversation. The roles writers take on reflect their purpose, their understanding of their readers, and the types of documents they plan to write. To help them achieve their purposes, writers typically adopt one or more of the roles you'll learn about in later chapters of this book.

Those roles include the following:

- *Observers*, who reflect on an event, individual or group, object, idea, or issue (Chapter 7)
- *Reporters*, who provide detailed but neutral information about a topic or an issue (Chapter 8)
- *Interpreters*, who analyze and explain the significance of ideas, individuals, groups, or events (Chapter 9)
- *Evaluators*, who assess how well something meets a given set of criteria (Chapter 10)
- *Problem Solvers*, who identify, define, and propose solutions to problems (Chapter 11)
- *Advocates*, who engage in arguments about issues and ideas (Chapter 12)

Learn more about roles in Part 2 of this book.

Your Turn: Find a Written Conversation

We're surrounded by written conversations. Some focus on politics, others on sports, and still others on issues in an academic discipline. You'll find contributions to conversations on the front page of newspapers, on websites such as CNN.com and Foxnews.com, in academic and professional journals, and on social media. Spend some time locating a conversation about a topic that interests you. Use the following prompts to find the conversation:

1. **List a topic that interests you.** Because you'll be searching for sources, jot down a list of search terms, or keywords (see *Generate Search Terms* in Chapter 14), that you can use to locate sources on the topic.
2. **Choose a newspaper or magazine or search for sources.** Browse a newspaper or magazine or search for sources on a web search, in a library database, or in a library catalog using the keywords you jotted down about your topic (see Chapter 14).
3. **Identify sources that seem to address the topic.** Skim each source to get a sense of how it addresses your topic (see *What Strategies Can I Use to Read Actively?* in Chapter 3).
4. **Decide whether the sources are engaged in the same conversation.** Ask whether the sources are addressing the same topic. If they are, list the ways in which they are "talking" to one another about the topic. Identify any agreements, disagreements, or differences in their approach to the topic.
5. **Reflect on the conversation.** Ask whether the sources you've identified tell you enough to understand the conversation. Consider whether you might need to locate more sources to give you a fuller picture of the conversation.

What Should I Know about Writing Situations?

When people participate in a spoken conversation, they pay attention to a wide range of factors: why they've joined the conversation, who's involved in the conversation, and what's already been said. They also notice the mood of the people they're speaking with, their facial expressions and body language, and physical factors such as background noise. In short, they consider the situation as they listen and speak. Similarly, when writers engage in written conversation, they become part of a **writing situation** — the setting in which writers and readers communicate with one another. Writing situations are shaped by these and other important factors, including the sources you use and the type of document you decide to write.

Writing Situations Are Rhetorical Situations

A writing situation is another name for a **rhetorical situation**, a concept that has been studied for thousands of years. The ancient Greeks, particularly Plato, Socrates, and Aristotle, contributed in important ways to our understanding of rhetorical situations. So did rhetoricians such as Gongsun Long and Gui Guzi in China, the early Buddhist writers in India, Wénjìng Mìfû in Japan, Cicero and Quintilian in Rome, Al-Kindi and Al-Farabi in the Arab world, and those whose names have been lost to antiquity in the early empires of Nubia, Axum, and Mali in Africa, among those from many other cultures. Viewing writing as a rhetorical act helps us understand how writers or speakers pursue their purposes; consider the needs and interests of their audiences; adapt to the conditions in which they address their audiences; and organize, design, or present their documents or speeches.

This book is based strongly on a *rhetorical approach* to writing. Throughout the book, you'll find yourself considering why writers pursue particular purposes and adopt specific roles; how readers' reactions are affected by their needs, interests, knowledge, and backgrounds; and how the contexts in which documents are written and read shape the experience of reading them. You'll also consider not only the opportunities you can take advantage of as you create your contribution to the conversation but also the limitations you'll face as you craft your document.

Writing Has a Purpose

As is the case with spoken conversations, writers join written conversations for particular **purposes**, which in turn affect the roles they adopt (see *Conversations Allow You to Adopt Roles* earlier in this chapter). Writers hoping to persuade or convince their readers, for example, take on the role of advocate, while those hoping to inform readers take on the role of reporter. You can read more about the roles writers adopt in Chapters 6 to 12.

Writers often have more than one purpose for writing a document.

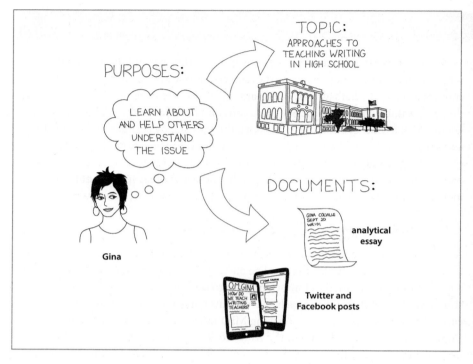

Writers often have more than one purpose for writing a document. Writers of academic essays, for instance, might complete their essays not only to earn a grade and pass a course but also to learn about a particular topic or improve their composing skills. Writers of newspaper and magazine articles may have been assigned their topics, but they often find themselves interested in their subjects and end up writing as much for themselves as for their readers.

Writers' purposes for joining a conversation are shaped by their **needs**, **interests**, and **backgrounds**. For example, a person who lives along a river in the western United States might wonder how a proposed new reservoir would affect the flow of the river. Urban planners charged with ensuring adequate water supplies might want to understand how the proposed reservoir would affect communities along the river. Still others, such as those employed by white water rafting companies, might want to learn how reduced stream flows will affect their jobs.

Your purposes will affect what you choose to write about and how you compose a document. Gina Colville, the student who posted on social media about preparing future high school teachers to teach writing, wanted not only to learn about the issue but also to call attention to the training and support high school teachers need to do a good job in the classroom. As she wrote in her posts, her purposes affected her choice of what to write about, which information to use as supporting evidence for her points, and how to address the information, ideas, and arguments she encountered in her reading.

Readers Have Purposes, Needs, Interests, Knowledge, and Backgrounds

Just as writers have purposes, so do readers. Among other purposes, readers often want to learn about a subject, assess or evaluate ideas and arguments, or understand opposing perspectives. And like writers' purposes, readers' purposes are strongly influenced by both their own needs, interests, and knowledge of a subject and by their backgrounds — their values, beliefs, and experiences. Gina's interest in how high school teachers learn how to teach writing, for example, was driven by the experiences she and her friends and family had had in high school. Her readers were probably drawn to her post by similar personal experiences — their memories of writing assignments, their knowledge of the challenges faced by high school teachers, or the perspective they had gained through reading a magazine article or hearing a news report about the issue.

Writers consider the needs, interests, and backgrounds of their readers.

As writers craft their contributions to a written conversation, they ask who their readers are likely to be. They reflect on their readers' values and beliefs, determine what their readers might already know about a subject, and take into account their readers' likely experiences — if any — with the subject. They consider what readers need to learn about a subject and what readers may be interested in knowing. They ask why potential readers would want to read their document — and what might cause them to stop reading. In short, writers try to understand and connect with their readers.

Writing Builds on the Work of Others

In spoken conversations — at least in those that are productive — people take turns sharing their ideas. To move the conversation forward, speakers build on what has been said, often referring to specific ideas or arguments and identifying the speakers who raised them. Comments such as "As Ellen said …" and "Reid made a good point earlier when he pointed out that …" are frequently made in spoken conversations or class discussions. They show respect for the contributions made by others and help speakers align themselves with or distance themselves from other members of the conversation.

Written conversations also build on earlier contributions. Writers refer to the work of other authors to support their arguments, to provide a context for their own contributions, or to differentiate their ideas from those advanced by other authors. For example, an opinion columnist might contrast her ideas with those offered by other members of the conversation by quoting another columnist. Later in the same column, she might include a statement made by yet another author to support her argument.

As she listened in on the conversation about how high school teachers are trained to teach writing, Gina read a blog post by a graduate student in teacher education. The blogger was concerned about standardized testing in schools and how these high-stakes tests were affecting both students and teachers. The blogger posted national survey data showing the number of classroom hours devoted to preparing students for these kinds of tests. Other students and teachers around the country commented on the blog post, sharing anecdotal evidence about how standardized tests were affecting their classroom experiences. When writers use sources in this way, they provide citations to indicate where the information comes from and to help readers locate the sources in case they wish to review them.

Even when writers do not refer directly to other sources, the work of other writers may influence their thinking about a subject. As you write, be aware that what you've read, heard, seen, and experienced will shape your thinking about the subject — and what you choose to include in your document.

Writing Takes Place in Context

Just as in spoken conversations, written conversations are affected by the contexts — or settings — in which they take place.

- **Physical context** affects how you write and read (on paper or on a screen) and how well you or your readers can concentrate. For example, consider the differences between trying to read or write in a noisy, crowded, jolting bus and trying to do so in a quiet, well-lit room.
- **Social context** affects how easily writers and readers can understand one another. Readers familiar with topics such as violence in American high schools, for example, do not need to be educated about them — they already know the key points. This reduces the amount of time and effort writers need to devote to providing background information.
- **Cultural context** refers to a larger set of similarities and differences among readers. For instance, readers from the American Midwest might find it easier to understand the allusions and metaphors used in a document written by someone from Kansas than those in a document written by someone who grew up in another country. Similarly, today's teenagers might find it easier to follow what's being said in a document written one month ago by a high school senior in Milwaukee than a document written in 1897 by a retired railroad engineer from Saskatchewan.
- **Disciplinary context** refers to the shared writing practices, general agreements about appropriate types of documents, and shared assumptions about what is worth writing about that are common to a particular profession or academic discipline, such as history, accounting, construction management, or chemistry.

For students, one of the most important social and cultural contexts shaping their written work is academic life itself, that complex mix of instructors, fellow students, classes, tests, labs, and writing assignments that they negotiate on a daily basis. Academic culture — U.S. and Canadian academic culture in particular — is the product of hundreds of years of arguments, decisions, revisions, and reinventions of a way of thinking and behaving. Academic culture affects far more than how you behave in class or interact with others online,

Physical, social, cultural, and disciplinary contexts affect the writing and reading of documents.

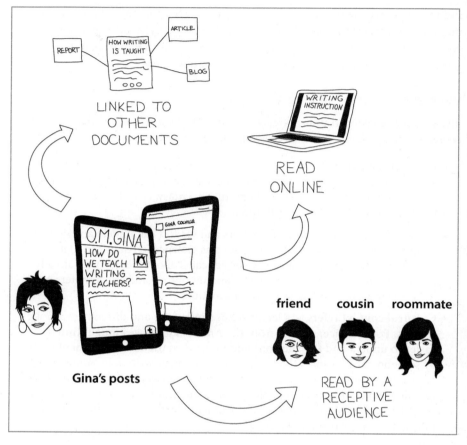

although that's certainly an important element of it. It also shapes the writing you'll do during and after your time in college.

In nearly every instance, what you say and how you say it will reflect a combination of contexts. For example, the fact that Gina's posts were both written and read online allowed her to link directly to other digital documents, such as news articles, scholarly articles, Facebook posts, and tweets. At the same time, because her work would most likely be read on a phone, she was cautious about readers having to scroll through multiple screens. As a result, her posts tended to be brief. Because she was writing to an audience who knew her well (friends and family), she didn't need to provide a great deal of information about her background. And because so many of her friends and family had had similar experiences in high school, she did not feel that she had to explain her perspective as clearly as she might have had she been writing to people with different backgrounds.

Writing Situations Are an Important Area of Scholarly Inquiry

It's also useful to understand that writing is the subject of intense scholarship. For more than a century, researchers and theorists have approached the study of writing from a wide range of perspectives: historical, cultural, psychological, social, anthropological, educational, and rhetorical, to name only a few. From teachers who focus on the creative side of writing to theorists who explore the political implications of writing in the world (and in the classroom) to cognitive scientists who try to understand the thinking processes involved in writing, scholars have published research findings, theoretical insights, and innovative approaches to writing instruction since the early 1900s.

Despite those early studies, writing research was for most of the twentieth century an underemphasized part of academic scholarship in the United States.

Working Together: Analyze a Writing Situation

Work together with your classmates to analyze a writing situation. Generate a list of documents that members of the group have written recently. Then choose one, and analyze its writing situation. To conduct your analysis, respond to the following prompts:

1. **What was written?** Describe the document in enough detail to allow other members of the class to understand its main point.

2. **What were the writer's purposes?** List the purpose or purposes that drove the writer's work on the document. Why did the writer decide to create the document? What did the writer hope to gain by writing it? How was the writer's purpose shaped by their needs, interests, values, beliefs, knowledge, and experience?

3. **Who were the intended readers?** Describe the people who might have been expected to read the document, and list their purpose or purposes for reading it. How would their reading of the document have been shaped by their needs, interests, values, beliefs, knowledge, and experience?

4. **What sources were used in the document?** Identify the sources of information, ideas, and arguments used in the document. Indicate how the sources were used (for example, to support a point or to differentiate the writer's ideas from those of another author).

5. **What contexts shaped the writing and reading of the document?** Identify the physical, social, cultural, and disciplinary contexts that shaped the writer's work on the document and the readers' understanding of it.

That began to change in the 1960s and 1970s as increasing numbers of students sought college degrees, including many who might not have attended college in earlier decades — and faculty members began studying how best to teach them. By the early 1980s, English departments had begun offering doctorates in the study of writing and rhetoric. And, by the late 1990s, doctoral programs were being offered by independent writing programs that had broken away from English departments.

The strong growth in scholarly work on writing and writing instruction over the past six decades has fueled significant changes in how writing is taught. More recently, transformative changes in information technology — in particular, the web and social media — and in the tools we use to create and distribute texts and media, have influenced writing instruction. Throughout this book, you'll find discussions of relevant research on writing and writing instruction, the role of technology in writing, and the implications of writing in society.

What Should I Know about Genre and Design?

As you craft your contribution to a written conversation, you can draw on two powerful, closely related tools to create an effective document: **genre** and **design**.

Genres Are General Categories of Documents

Given the influx of technology and the ease of sharing ideas on the web and in social media, writers have tremendous choice in the types of documents they create. General categories of documents are called *genres*. When you use the word *novel*, for example, you're referring to a general category of long fiction. If you say that you like to read novels, you aren't talking about reading a particular book; instead, you're expressing a preference for a type of writing that is distinct from poetry or biography, for instance.

Opinion columns, academic essays, scholarly articles, and Instagram posts are all genres. So are personal journals, thank-you letters, and entries on personal blogs. In fact, there are a wide variety of genres, and the number seems to grow larger every few years. Until the 1990s, for example, personal and company web pages didn't exist. Nor did blogs. Nor, for that matter, did text messages, tweets, or Facebook posts. Yet they have all become important genres.

Although the term *genre* typically refers to general categories of documents, such as novels or websites, it can also be used to refer to more specific categories. For example, you might refer not simply to novels but also to romance novels, mystery novels, and historical novels. Or you might refer to different types of academic essays, such as reflective essays, argumentative essays, or analytical essays. The word *genre*, in this sense, can be used flexibly. Sometimes it's used in the largest possible sense, and sometimes it refers to highly specific categories of documents.

Design Is a Writing Tool

Document design is the use of visual elements — such as fonts, colors, columns, and illustrations — to enhance the effectiveness of written documents. A well-designed chart, for example, can be far more effective at conveying complex information than even the most clearly written paragraph. Similarly, the emotional impact of a well-chosen illustration, such as a photograph of a starving child or a video clip of aid workers rushing to help victims of a natural disaster, can do far more than words alone to persuade a reader to take action. By understanding and applying the principles of document design, you can increase the likelihood that you'll achieve your purposes as a writer and address the needs and interests of your readers. Throughout this book, you'll find design treated as a central writing strategy, and you'll find numerous examples of the design characteristics of the genres discussed in each chapter. You'll also find an in-depth discussion of design in Chapters 22 and 23.

Genre and Design Are Related

Think about a website you visited recently. Now picture the opening pages of a novel. The differences that come to mind reflect how genre and design are intertwined. You can tell genres apart by focusing on why they are written, how they are written, and what they look like. On the basis of appearance alone, it's usually fairly easy to tell the difference between an academic essay and an article in a popular magazine. Similarly, the style in which a document is written, the organizational pattern it follows, and the ways in which it uses sources work together to help you understand that a document is, for example, a scholarly journal article, a social media post, or a brochure. As you read a document (and often without really thinking about it), you may notice characteristic features of a genre, such as the use of boldface headlines or detailed footnotes. And once you've identified the genre, you can read the document more effectively, locate information within it more easily, and know when to approach it with a bit of skepticism.

18 CHAPTER 01 | Understanding Yourself as a Writer

Brochures provide information by using large, descriptive titles to draw attention to important information.

Including an eye-catching image makes this brochure even more persuasive than text alone might have.

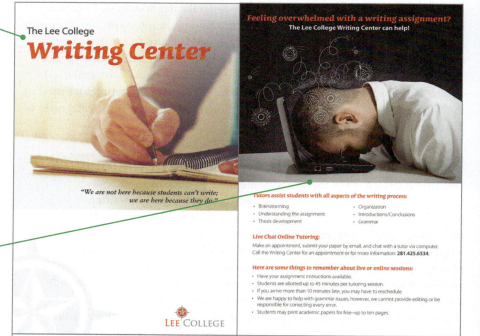

If you recognize a document as an advertisement, for example, you're less likely to be swayed by questionable reasoning.

The following documents illustrate a wide range of genres that might be used to write about a topic. Each document addresses the topic of preparing future high school teachers to teach writing effectively. The documents range from a brochure and a PowerPoint presentation to a website and a journal article. As you look at each document, think about the purpose for which it was written, the readers it addresses, the genre conventions it follows, and the design it uses.

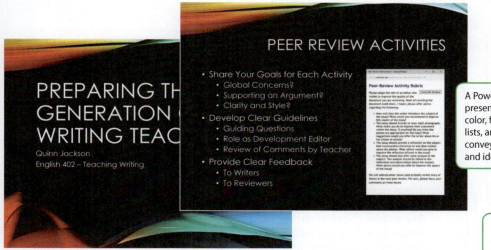

A PowerPoint presentation uses color, fonts, bulleted lists, and images to convey information and ideas.

Websites provide information, links to other documents, and contact information.

AMERICAN SECONDARY EDUCATION 41(1) FALL 2012

TEACHING WRITING IN THE SHADOW OF STANDARDIZED WRITING ASSESSMENT: AN EXPLORATORY STUDY

Authors

HUNTER BRIMI, ED.D., is an English teacher at Farragut High School in Knoxville, Tennessee.

Abstract

This exploratory study results from interviews with five high school English teachers regarding their writing instruction. The researcher sought to answer these questions: (1) How had the Tennessee Comprehensive Assessment Program's (TCAP) Writing Assessment affected their teaching as gauged by the teachers' statements regarding the assessment, emphasis on the writing process, and use of multiple writing genres? and (2) How did these teachers learn to teach writing, and did their training mitigate the influence of standardized testing? The teachers indicated that the TCAP Writing Assessment palpably affected their instruction. Additionally, the teachers revealed that they struggled to teach the writing process and showed reluctance to teach or assign multi-genre writing. This may result from their dearth of training to teach writing before entering the field.

"Most of us are English majors and not writing teachers. I think teachers need much more instruction on how to teach writing," said Layla Canton, a 20-year veteran English teacher. Ms. Canton's words illustrate the frustration that many English teachers feel concerning teaching composition. Teachers often enter the field inadequately prepared to teach this cardinal component of their subject matter due to preparation programs that do not always give abundant instruction on how to teach writing (Smith, 2003).

In a summary of "professional trends and issues," the commissioners of

Genres and Design Help Writers Achieve Their Goals

Genres develop to help writers accomplish a general purpose. Academic essays help writers demonstrate their knowledge to an instructor, while informative articles in newspapers, magazines, and newsletters help writers share information and ideas with their readers. Opinion columns and letters to the editor, in contrast, are often used by writers to advance arguments.

Documents in a particular genre usually share a general purpose and tend to use similar writing conventions, such as level of formality or the type of evidence used to support a point. For example, newspaper obituaries are usually formal and serious, while email messages are often informal and relaxed. Scholarly articles almost always refer to the sources of evidence offered to support their points, while letters to the editor sometimes offer no evidence at all. In addition, documents in a particular genre often use similar design elements. Academic essays, for example, are usually formatted with wide margins and double-spaced lines, while magazine articles often use columns and make extensive use of color and illustrations.

In most cases, genres are shaped by the social, cultural, and disciplinary contexts from which they emerge. When writers and readers form a community — such as an academic discipline, a professional association, or a group that shares an interest in a particular topic or activity — they develop characteristic ways of communicating with one another. Over time, members of a community will come to an agreement about the type of evidence that is generally accepted to support arguments, the style

Your Turn: Analyze a Genre

For this exercise, analyze the Lee College Writing Center brochure and respond to the following prompts:

1. **Writing style.** Is the brochure written in a formal or an informal style? Somewhere in between? How would you describe the relationship that the authors of the brochure attempt to establish with readers?

2. **Evidence.** What types of evidence are used in the brochure? Why do you think the authors chose these types of evidence?

3. **Organization.** How is the brochure organized? Do you find it easy to follow? Difficult? Somewhere in between? Why?

4. **Citation style.** Are sources cited in the brochure? If so, how are the sources cited — in a works cited list, in footnotes, or in the text itself? Why do you think the author cites (or doesn't cite) sources in this way?

5. **Design.** Briefly identify the design elements used in the document, such as columns, photographs, and text formatting. (For more information on design elements, see Chapter 22.) How does the design of the document set up expectations about its content? To what extent does the design help or hinder your ability to read and understand the document?

in which sources should be cited, and the manner in which documents should be designed and organized. As the needs of a community evolve, the genre changes as well. Articles in magazines for automobile or motorcycle enthusiasts, for example, differ in important ways from articles in magazines about contemporary music. In the same way, scholarly articles written by sociologists, civil engineers, and chemists use evidence or organization in distinct ways.

Changes in our ability to design documents also have important effects on genres. Academic essays, for example, have begun to make greater use of color and illustrations. In other cases, what was once a single genre has become several distinct genres. For example, as the number of readers on the web has exploded over the past few decades, websites have become far more specialized. In the mid-1990s, most websites looked alike. Today, characteristic differences can be seen among personal blogs, commercial websites, government websites, and entertainment websites.

Consider the role that genre and design might play in your writing process (see *What Should I Know about Writing Processes?* later in this chapter). Your choice of genre should reflect your writing situation, in particular your goals, your readers, and the context in which your document will be read. The design of your document should also align with your writing situation. You can think of these choices as part of your effort to share your ideas with your readers. The rhetorical concept of *delivery* — one of the five canons of classical rhetoric — has most often been associated with techniques for delivering a speech, but as writers have gained greater control over how they can design and share their documents, delivery has become an increasingly important consideration.

What Should I Know about Writing Processes?

If you ask most writing instructors what's involved in writing, they'll likely say something about the composing process. If they say more than a sentence or two, you'll almost certainly hear that the process varies from writer to writer and situation to situation. Writing, they'll tell you, is a series of decisions and activities shaped by the distinctive demands writers face as they work on particular writing projects.

Writing Is Like Other Complex Activities

Writing is a lot like snowboarding. It's also a lot like teaching, coaching, playing a musical instrument, and selling trucks.

It might seem absurd to compare writing to snowboarding or selling trucks, but there are surprising similarities among these and other complex activities. As a boarder, your goals might vary each time you get off a lift at the top of a mountain. You might want to make it down the slope safely. You might want to win a race. Or perhaps you might want to work on a new skill, such as carving turns or landing jumps. To accomplish your goals, you can draw on your knowledge of snow conditions, weather, the training techniques used by professional boarders, and so on. You can use specific strategies, such as slowing down where trails merge or timing your run to avoid that group of skiers who seem to be enjoying life a bit too much. And you can draw on a set of processes, such as steering with both feet and shifting your stance as you initiate turns, to accomplish your goals — and stay upright.

The key factors in complex activities such as snowboarding — goals, knowledge, strategies, and processes — are similar to those involved in writing. In fact, what you've learned in other areas can often help you gain new knowledge and skills as a writer.

It Takes Time and Effort to Become a Good Writer

As a writer, you will benefit from understanding your writing situation and the kinds of composing processes and strategies you might use to accomplish your goals. You'll also benefit from practice. The more you write, and the more often you receive useful feedback on your writing, the better you'll become. Just as musicians benefit from lessons, feedback, and practice, writers benefit from time spent writing and the guidance and feedback they receive from instructors and other writers.

Since the middle of the nineteenth century, a surprisingly large number of teachers have told their students, "Writers are born, not made." That notion emerged from a mixture of romantic theory (which swept Europe and the United States in the eighteenth and nineteenth centuries and continues to have a strong influence today) and faculty psychology (a psychological theory with eighteenth-century roots that held that people are born with or without innate "faculties" — or abilities). Some writing teachers went as far as to discourage any students they felt lacked the "gift" to write well from even attempting to improve their skills.

It is true that some people are born with a combination of cognitive abilities and emotional sensibilities that allows them to be truly exceptional writers, much as basketball players like Stephen Curry and LeBron James are born with a mix of exceptional physical abilities, spatial reasoning aptitudes, and emotional sensibilities that allows them to succeed as athletes. But the idea that the lack of these abilities will doom you to failure in a particular area — to the point that you might as well not even try to develop those abilities — is nonsense. You don't need to be a LeBron James to enjoy — and enjoy success at — basketball. You don't need to be a Mozart or a Beethoven to be a fine musician. You don't need to be a "gifted" writer to be a successful writer.

That said, success in writing requires time and effort. And all writers can benefit from good advice. Seeking guidance from more experienced writers — including writing teachers, writing center consultants, and colleagues or supervisors who understand what makes a successful document — will help you improve more quickly.

Writing Processes Vary from Project to Project

Most of the writing projects you'll work on over your lifetime will share some basic characteristics. For each, you will have a purpose, a set of readers, and a context within which your writing will take place. You also might have a deadline or expectations about length or the kinds of sources you might use to support your argument.

These similarities in writing projects contribute to similarities in the processes writers use as they work on a project.

As you start a project, remember two things. First, because general types of writing projects share similarities, you can build on what you've learned from past projects. Second, despite these similarities, it's rare to use every one of the typical writing processes in a particular writing project. You might already know a great deal about a topic, for instance, or design choices might be limited or nonexistent. Whatever the cause, you'll almost always find that some aspect of a writing project will distinguish it from the projects you've worked on in the past.

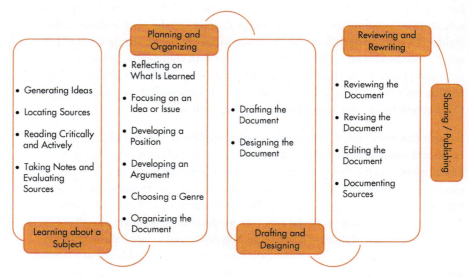

Writers can draw on a wide range of composing processes.

Writing Processes Are Recursive

Writing is anything but a step-by-step process. You'll repeat processes, rethink earlier decisions, and delete sentences that no longer work. If you don't like your first or second or third draft, you can learn more about your subject to improve it, revise it, or reorganize it. At its heart, writing is a process of making judgments about whether you've done enough to accomplish your goals and deciding what to do if you haven't.

Cognitive scientists call this pattern of returning to and repeating processes *recursion*. Some writers call it frustrating, since it is seldom as orderly as the sequence shown in the figure on the facing page suggests. The process of writing this book, for example, involved repeated and often unexpected movement from one composing process to another.

Understanding that writing is recursive can help you avoid such frustration. Knowing that learning more about an issue may lead you to rethink your position will prepare you to return again and again to the work of developing and refining your ideas or argument. Rather than viewing this work as unnecessary and repetitive, you'll understand it as a reasonable and effective process.

Writing Processes Involve Critical Thinking

Critical thinking is a widely used and broadly defined set of ideas about how people approach complex situations and challenges. In a way, it's like the general notion of *creativity*: almost everyone thinks it's a good idea — and almost everyone defines it in their own way. In higher education, critical thinking has been defined as a set of attitudes, as a group of thinking activities, and as a way of defining and solving problems. In this book, critical thinking is viewed as both an attitude and a set of activities. That view is shaped in part by Benjamin Bloom's taxonomy of cognitive objectives, which includes activities such as understanding, applying, analyzing, and evaluating. It is also shaped by developmental frameworks such as Karen Kitchener and Patricia King's reflective judgment model. Together, the work of these scholars and their colleagues provides a strong basis on which to understand what it means to think critically.

● WRITING RELIES ON CRITICAL THINKING

Every kind of writing — from taking notes to crafting an argument to writing a sonnet — requires the writer to engage in one or more forms of critical thinking. Whether you are trying to remember and understand key concepts related to an issue or are trying to craft a complex argument, you will find yourself reflecting, analyzing, making judgments, and creating new work. You'll adopt a critical attitude as you read and evaluate sources. You'll rely on activities such as analysis and evaluation as you plan and develop your contribution to a conversation. And you'll engage in creation as you design, draft, revise, and edit your document.

We call your attention to critical thinking activities and attitudes throughout this book and especially in our discussions of composing particular genres and working with sources. You'll find that the roles you adopt as you make your contribution to a conversation will rely more heavily on some critical thinking activities than others.

● WRITING SUPPORTS CRITICAL THINKING

You've almost certainly been asked to write a report, a term paper, or an essay that addressed a complex topic or issue. The written work you turned in for a grade presented your conclusions about your subject. In this sense, it served as a record of the critical thinking you engaged in as you planned, researched, composed, and designed the document.

But the act of composing a document involves much more than simply translating thoughts into sentences and paragraphs. Few writers ever figure things out completely and then sit down to record their fully formed thoughts. Instead, the process of composing a document involves assessing and reassessing ideas. It can lead you to change your mind as you learn more about your subject. And it can result in significant changes in how you share your conclusions with your readers.

In this way, writing allows you to do more than share the results of your thinking as you work on your document. It also leads you to engage in various types of critical thinking as you carry out that work.

● WRITING ASSIGNMENTS CALL FOR DIFFERENT TYPES OF CRITICAL THINKING

Understanding the kinds of critical thinking a writing assignment requires can help you anticipate the kinds of research and composing processes you'll engage in as you work on your project. It's typical, for example, to engage in efforts to remember and understand information and ideas. And you might be asked to apply that understanding to specific situations, problems, or subjects. Depending on the type of assignment, you might also be asked to analyze or evaluate information. And, of course, you'll be creating a document.

As you start working on a writing project, assess the kinds of critical thinking you'll need to carry out. You can find clues in the words used to describe the activities involved in completing the assignment.

Critical Thinking Activity	Goal	Associated Words
Remembering	Committing information to memory so that it can be recalled later	Define, duplicate, learn, list, memorize, recall, repeat, reproduce, retain
Understanding	Working with information so that you can explain the who, what, when, where, how, and why associated with information and ideas	Classify, describe, discuss, explain, identify, locate, recognize, report, select, translate, paraphrase, summarize, comprehend
Reflecting	Considering the meaning and implications of information, ideas, and events	Contemplate, consider, explore, indicate, muse, ponder, reveal, think about, wonder
Applying	Using your understanding of information and ideas to explore a situation, problem, subject, or issue	Apply, choose, demonstrate, dramatize, employ, illustrate, interpret, operate, solve, use, write
Analyzing	Assessing the parts of a subject and how those parts function as a whole and/or in relationship to other subjects	Analyze, appraise, compare, contrast, criticize, differentiate, discriminate, distinguish, examine, experiment, question, test
Evaluating	Making criterion-based judgments about a subject	Appraise, argue, assess, calculate, defend, evaluate, gauge, judge, select, support, value
Creating	Making something new	Assemble, build, craft, conceive, construct, create, design, develop, fashion, formulate, generate, invent, write

Writing Processes Are Studied Intensely

The idea that writing is a process is far from new. In the late nineteenth century, rhetorician John Quackenbos, citing Benjamin Franklin, characterized writing as a four-part process that modern writing teachers would immediately recognize as generating ideas, planning, drafting, and revising. This conception of writing as a process was widely shared by other nineteenth-century rhetoricians, and these ideas influenced writing instruction well into the twentieth century. Yet, as scholars such as James Berlin, Sharon Crowley, David R. Russell, and Richard E. Young have argued, prior to the early 1980s most writing instruction in higher education involved a highly reductive notion of what aspects of writing could and could not be taught.

That began to change only after three groups of scholars came into conflict — and eventually into a semblance of cooperative coexistence. In the 1960s, drawing on strong roots going back to the early twentieth century, writing scholars such as Peter Elbow, Ken Macrorie, and Donald Murray took an *expressivist* perspective on writing, arguing that good writing resulted from a search for an authentic voice that expressed a genuine self. Writing, these scholars believed, could be learned — through experience and with feedback from teachers and other writers — but it couldn't be taught directly. To become a writer, you needed to write.

In the 1970s and 1980s, writing scholars such as Janet Emig, John R. Hayes, Linda Flower, Sondra Perl, Marlene Scardamalia, and Carl Bereiter began studying the cognitive processes writers used as they wrote. Scholars taking this approach focused on composing processes such as planning (setting goals, generating ideas, and organizing ideas), drafting, and reviewing and revising — all of which interact with the writer's memory, the tools used during composing, and the writing situation. Eventually, recognizing the important role played by social context in cognition, these scholars came to be referred to as *socio-cognitive rhetoricians*.

In the early to late 1980s, *social-epistemic rhetoricians* argued that we needed to look at the various contexts in which writers worked. Scholars such as David Bartholomae, James Berlin, Patricia Bizzell, Joseph Harris, and James Porter argued from various historical and theoretical perspectives that the thinking of the individual — cognition — is linked deeply and inseparably to social interaction. Essentially, they argued, no one is an island. We are all connected to each other through language, and those connections shape how we think and what we do.

Since these critical debates in the 1970s, 1980s, and 1990s, writing scholars have looked broadly at issues that extend fairly naturally from the ideas that writing is a form of expression that requires complex thinking processes and that these processes are shaped in important ways by social, political, cultural, historical, disciplinary, and technological contexts. Applying theoretical lenses ranging from feminism to cultural materialism to critical pedagogy, writing scholars such as Vershawn Ashanti Young, Kathleen Blake Yancey, Asao Inoue, Jacqueline Jones Royster, Cynthia Selfe, and Victor Vitanza, among many others, have sought to understand writing processes by exploring the cultural, historical, and political aspects of writing; by looking at the interactions between writing and technology; and by considering the place of writing in a complex, multiracial, multiethnic, gender-inclusive world. Some recent scholars have argued for a "post-process" perspective on writing, contending that it is useful to look beyond the questions that preoccupied writing scholarship as it established itself as a distinct discipline and to begin to grapple with newer and potentially larger questions about what it means to write and to be a writer.

As you work on your writing projects, consider your own composing processes. Note how they change from one project to another, especially when those projects rely on sources in different ways, when they are addressed to different groups of readers, and when they involve different genres than those you've used in the past. Understanding your own composing processes — and how they vary from project to project — can help you better understand what you already do well and how you might improve your writing knowledge and skills. And that, in turn, will help you become a stronger, more confident writer.

How Can I Prepare for a Successful Writing Project?

You can improve your chances of successfully completing a writing project by taking ownership of your writing project, creating a writer's notebook, and learning to manage your sources and your time.

Take Ownership

Successful writers have a strong personal investment in what they write. Sometimes this investment comes naturally. You might be interested in a topic, committed to achieving your purposes as a writer, intrigued by the demands of writing for a particular audience, or excited about the challenges of composing and designing a new type of document. At times, however, you need to create a sense of personal investment by looking for connections between your interests and your writing project. This can be a challenge, particularly when you've been assigned a project that normally wouldn't interest you.

The key to investing yourself in a project you don't initially care about is to make it your own. Look for ways in which your project can help you pursue your personal, professional, and academic interests. Consider how it might help you meet new people or develop new skills. Or look for opportunities associated with the project, such as learning how to build arguments or design documents. Your goal is to find something that appeals to your interests and helps you grow as a writer.

To take ownership of a writing project, carry out the following activities:

- **Explore academic connections.** Is the writing project relevant to work you are doing in other classes or, more generally, in your major or minor? Look for ways that working on this project might help you develop useful academic skills or expose you to information, ideas, or arguments that allow you to make progress as a student.
- **Consider personal connections.** Sometimes your personal interests — such as hobbies and other activities — can spark an interest in the writing project. Do any of your experiences relate to the project in some way? Will working on this project allow you to develop skills and abilities that might help you in your personal life?
- **Look for professional connections.** Does the writing project have any relevance to the job you currently have or one day hope to have? Will working on this project help you develop skills or expose you to information, ideas, or arguments that might be relevant to your professional goals?

Your Turn: Create a Project Timeline

In your writer's notebook, create a project timeline like the one shown here. The steps in your process might be slightly different, but most writing projects involve these general stages. As you create your timeline, keep in mind any specific deadlines given in your assignment, such as the dates when you must hand in first drafts and revised drafts.

Project Timeline

Activity	Start date	Completion date
Analyze your assignment		
Generate ideas		
Collect and read potential sources		
Choose a focus		
Develop your ideas		
Write a first draft		
Review and revise your first draft		
Write and revise additional drafts		
Polish your final draft		
Edit for accuracy and correctness		
Finalize in-text citations and works cited list		

Create a Writer's Notebook

A writer's notebook — where you can keep the sources you collect along the way and record your thoughts, observations, and progress — can help you keep track of what you find and think about as you work on your project. A writer's notebook can take many forms:

- a paper notebook
- a word-processing file or a folder on your computer
- a folder or binder
- a set of note cards
- notes or voice recordings on a phone or tablet

Although it might seem like extra work now, creating a writer's notebook at the beginning of your project will save you time in the long run.

Manage Your Time

Time management should be a high priority as you begin your writing project. Without it, you might, for example, spend far too much time collecting information and far too little time working with it. As you begin to think about your writing project, consider creating a project timeline. A project timeline can help you identify important milestones in your project and determine when you need to meet them.

In Summary: Understanding Yourself as a Writer

- ★ Think of writing as a form of conversation (p. 2).
- ★ Understand the rhetorical nature of writing situations (p. 9).
- ★ Learn about genre and design (p. 16).
- ★ Understand composing processes (p. 22).
- ★ Lay the foundation for a successful writing project by taking ownership of your project, creating a writer's notebook, and managing your time (p. 29).

02 Finding and Listening In on Conversations

How can I analyze an assignment? 32
Assess your writing situation 33
Note requirements, limitations, and opportunities 35

How can I find interesting conversations? 36
Generate ideas 37
Ask questions 44

How can I "listen in" on written conversations? 45
Discuss the topic with others 46
Observe the topic firsthand 46
Read what others have written 46
Review your sources 47

In the most general sense, getting started on a writing project involves "listening in" on conversations and choosing one that interests you. To begin this process, analyze your assignment and generate ideas about potential topics. Then spend time learning about the conversations that interest you most.

How Can I Analyze an Assignment?

Writers in academic and professional settings usually work in response to an assignment. You might be given general guidelines, you might be asked to choose a topic within a general subject area, or you might be given complete freedom. No matter how much freedom you have, however, your assignment will provide important clues about what your instructor and your other readers will expect.

A close reading of an assignment can reveal not only its goals and basic requirements but also useful information about your purpose, readers, role, sources, and context. Most important, a close reading can help you complete the assignment successfully.

Assess Your Writing Situation

What you write about depends on your writing situation — your purpose, readers, role, sources, and context. In many cases, your assignment will identify or suggest these elements for you. If it doesn't, take some time to think about the situation that will shape your work.

● DETERMINE YOUR PURPOSE AND ROLE

Every writer has a purpose, or reason, for writing. In fact, most writers have multiple purposes (see *Writing Has a Purpose* in Chapter 1). In Chapters 6 to 12, you'll explore a range of goals that you might be asked to pursue: to reflect, to inform, to analyze, to evaluate, to solve problems, and to convince or persuade. In turn, your purpose will shape the role you adopt in relation to your readers (see Chapter 6). You will also bring your personal goals to a writing project, such as learning something new, improving your writing skills, convincing others to adopt your point of view, gaining respect from others, getting a good grade, or earning a promotion.

● DETERMINE WHO YOUR READERS ARE AND WHAT MOTIVATES THEM

Your assignment might identify your readers, or audience, for you. If you are working on a project for a class, one of your most important readers will be your instructor. Other readers might include your classmates, people who have a professional or personal interest in your topic, or, if your project will be published, the readers of a particular newspaper, magazine, or website. If you are writing in a business or professional setting, your readers might include supervisors, customers, or other people associated with the organization. You can read more about readers in *Readers Have Purposes, Needs, Interests, Knowledge, and Backgrounds* in Chapter 1.

● CONSIDER THE ROLE OF SOURCES

Most documents are influenced by the work of other writers (see *Writing Builds on the Work of Others* in Chapter 1). As you analyze an assignment, determine whether you'll need to draw on information from sources, such as magazine or journal articles, websites, or scholarly books. Ask whether you'll need to cite a minimum or a maximum number of sources and whether you're required to use a specific documentation system, such as those created by the Modern Language Association (MLA) or the American Psychological Association (APA) (see Chapters 25 and 26).

Whether or not an assignment provides guidelines for sources, ask what you'll need to learn to complete your project, and then identify potential information resources. You can read more about finding and using sources in Part Three of this book.

Essay Assignment

For this assignment, you'll identify and describe a problem that affects veterans as they return from active duty. Your purpose will be to inform members of your community about how the problem affects them, the consequences of not addressing the problem, and the costs of addressing it effectively.

Due Date: October 1, at the beginning of class

Your Readers: Your audience will be the members of your community. I will also be a reader, but my primary role will be to consider how well you've addressed the members of your community.

Essay Requirements: Your essay should be between 750 and 1,000 words in length. Your essay should

- introduce the problem you are addressing
- describe the potential effects of the problem
- propose a solution to the problem
- estimate the costs of putting the solution into effect
- support your points with evidence (personal experience, information from sources)
- clearly document your sources following MLA style

Conclude your essay by doing more than simply summarizing what you've said so far. In general, try to leave your readers with something to think about after they've read your essay. Finally, revise to clarify and strengthen your argument, and edit to remove errors in spelling, grammar, and mechanics so that your writing is clear and readable.

Format: Please submit your essay in a folder clearly labeled with your name and email address. Your folder should contain the following:

- the final draft of your essay, formatted with one-inch margins, double-spaced lines, and a readable (in particular, not italic or script) 12-point font
- rough drafts of your essay
- a list of additional sources you consulted as you created your essay
- the homework you completed as you worked on your essay
- the workshop comments you received from your classmates on drafts of your essay
- your workshop comments on your classmates' essays

▲ Essay assignment

Annotations:
- The choice of topic is left to the writer, although some general guidelines are provided. The purpose is discussed here and in the requirements section.
- The assignment specifies the readers and defines the role the instructor will play as a reader.
- The genre is identified as a standard academic essay.
- The repeated use of the words *problem* and *solution* indicates that the writer's purpose is to write a problem-solving essay.
- Aside from the due date, requirements are listed in a separate section. Key requirements include length, content, and documentation system.
- The assignment requires students to turn in not only the final essay but also rough drafts, homework, and comments on classmates' drafts.

IDENTIFY THE CONTEXT AND GENRE

Context refers to the physical, social, disciplinary, and cultural settings that shape the writing and reading of a document (see *Writing Takes Place in Context* in Chapter 1). To identify the context for your writing project, ask whether your document will be read in print or online. Ask whether it will need to take the form of a particular genre (or type of document), such as a report, an opinion column, a blog post, or a multimedia presentation. Consider how social and cultural contexts — such as recent events and shared history — will shape the attitudes and understanding of your readers. Consider as well how the genre and context will influence your decisions as a writer.

Note Requirements, Limitations, and Opportunities

Your analysis should identify your assignment's requirements. You should also consider potential limitations and look for opportunities. Being aware of these

Working Together: Analyze an Assignment

Work together with your classmates to analyze your assignment. Use the following prompts to guide your analysis:

1. **Consider your topic.** If a topic has been assigned, look for indications of how you should address it. If you are allowed to choose your own topic, look for indications of what the instructor considers an appropriate topic.

2. **Examine the assignment for discussions of purpose and roles.** Consider the purposes and roles you might pursue through the assignment. Identify your own purposes — personal, professional, academic — and those of your classmates for working on this assignment. Consider the roles you might adopt.

3. **Identify and describe potential readers.** Describe their likely needs, interests, backgrounds, and knowledge of the topic. Ask why readers would want to read your document.

4. **Explore the use of sources in your document.** Identify potential sources of information that will help you learn about your topic. Then determine whether you need to cite a minimum number of sources or use a specific documentation system, such as MLA or APA.

5. **Identify the contexts in which the document will be written and read.** Ask, for example, whether your document will be read in print or online. Ask how historic or recent events might shape your readers' understanding of and attitudes toward your topic.

6. **Identify the genre, if any, defined by the assignment.** If the assignment leaves the choice of genre open, identify genres that are well suited to the assignment.

7. **Understand requirements and limitations.** Look for requirements and limitations, such as document length and due date, that will affect your ability to address a particular topic. Identify other requirements, such as number of sources, documentation system, and intermediate assignments or rough drafts.

8. **List potential opportunities.** Identify opportunities that might save time or enhance the quality of the document.

factors will help you weigh the potential drawbacks of choosing a particular topic. In the face of a looming due date or a limited word count, for example, you might find that you need to narrow the scope of a topic significantly.

Requirements can include

- word count or page length
- due date
- number and type of sources you must use (digital, print, and field)
- suggested or required resources
- document organization (title page, introduction, body, conclusion, works cited list, and so on)
- documentation format (such as MLA or APA)
- intermediate reports or activities due before you turn in the final document (such as thesis statements, notes, outlines, and rough drafts)

Limitations might include lack of access to sources, insufficient time to work on a project, or limited access to hardware or software (such as printers or video editing apps) that would help you produce a quality document.

Sometimes writers get so wrapped up in the requirements and limitations of an assignment that they overlook their opportunities. As you think about possible topics, ask whether you can take advantage of opportunities such as

- access to a specialized or particularly good library
- personal experience with and knowledge about a topic
- access to experts on a topic

How Can I Find Interesting Conversations?

Writers aren't mindless robots who create documents without emotion or conviction — or at least they shouldn't be. One of the most important things you can do as a writer is to look for a conversation that will hold your interest as you work on your writing project.

Even if you are assigned a specific topic, you can almost always find an approach that will engage you and still accomplish the goals of the assignment. In fact, most successful writers have learned to deal with "boring" topics by creating personal or professional connections to them. Essentially, they try to persuade themselves to care about a topic — and in many cases, they end up developing a genuine interest. You can do this by generating ideas and asking questions about potential topics, taking care not to rule out any topics until you've given them a chance.

Generate Ideas

You can generate ideas about possible topics of conversation by using prewriting activities such as brainstorming, freewriting, looping, clustering, mapping, and using sentence starters. These activities are useful not only for deciding which topics interest you most but also for identifying a focus that is well suited to your writing situation.

● BRAINSTORM

Brainstorming involves making a list of ideas as they occur to you. This list should not consist of complete sentences — in fact, brainstorming is most successful when you avoid censoring yourself. Don't worry about weeding out ideas. You'll have time for that later.

Brainstorming sessions usually respond to a specific question, such as "What interests me personally about this project?" or "Why would anyone care about _____?" For example, Henry Garcia, a student in the same writing course as Gina Colville (see *Conversations Help You Share Information, Ideas, and Arguments* in Chapter 1), was planning to pursue a career in marketing. That semester, he had joined the staff of the college newspaper to gain some practical experience as a writer. He drew on his experiences as he brainstormed the following list in response to the question "What do I want to learn from a writing course?"

How to write a good argument	How to connect with my readers
How to use sources	How to prep for my career
How to have a good style	Which courses to take next
How to use good grammar	Whether I like this career idea

This brainstorming list helped Henry recognize that he might take a reflective approach to the assignment, contemplating his own plans for a career in light of what he might learn from articles and other sources that address his topic.

● FREEWRITE

Freewriting involves writing full sentences quickly, without stopping and — most important — without editing what you write. You might want to start with an idea you generated during brainstorming, or you could begin your freewriting session with a prompt, such as "I am interested in _____ because. . . ." Some writers set a timer and freewrite for five, ten, or fifteen minutes; others set a goal of a certain number of words or pages and keep writing until they meet that goal.

After brainstorming about what he wanted to learn from a writing course, Henry freewrote about how to connect with his readers' purposes and interests.

> I'll have to find a way to explain it and make a career in marketing interesting. I don't have a lot of experiences to draw on, just some work with my high school newspaper and now at Front Range. But maybe those experiences writing for an audience can come in handy as I learn to develop a marketing campaign. In all those situations, I think you need to get in people's heads, figure out their interests and what drives them, get a sense of what they want and need.

To freewrite, write as much as you can, don't pause to consider whether your sentences are "good" or "bad," and don't pay attention to details such as spelling and grammar. If all this work results in a single good idea, your freewriting session will be a success.

TECH TIP: If you find it difficult to freewrite without editing, try freewriting on a computer with the monitor turned off. Or consider dictating. Many apps allow you to speak your thoughts aloud and convert them immediately to text. These forms of freewriting can take your focus away from generating text, largely because you can carry them out without looking at the screen. You can also record your ideas using an app and listen to them later to identify promising ideas.

● LOOP

Looping is a specialized form of freewriting. During a looping session, you write (or dictate) for a set amount of time (five minutes works well) and then read what you've written. As you read, identify one key idea in what you've written, and then repeat the process with this new idea as your starting point. If you're using a word-processing program, you can copy the sentence and paste it below your freewriting; if you are writing by hand, highlight or draw a circle around the sentence. Repeat the looping process as needed to refine your ideas.

Henry's looping session built on the last sentence of his freewriting exercise.

> I could think about how you need to get in people's heads, figure out their interests and what drives them, get a sense of what they want and need. I like that aspect of marketing, and of writing, too. It's a challenge for marketing professionals to make consumers pay attention to the product or service you are offering, just like it's a challenge for reporters to grab the attention of their readers. People are

Writers consider what connects them to the topic.

bombarded by so much media and advertising these days that good marketing and good writing need to stand out to get noticed. That's what I really want to practice in this course.

● CLUSTER

Clustering involves putting your ideas about a topic into graphic form. As you map out the relationships among your ideas, clustering can help you gain a different perspective on a topic. It can also help you generate new ideas.

To cluster ideas about a topic, place your main idea, or a general topic that interests you, at the center of a page. Jot down key ideas — such as subcategories, causes and effects, or reasons supporting an argument — around the main idea. Then create clusters of ideas that branch out from the key ideas. In these clusters, list groups of related ideas, evidence, effects, causes, consequences — in short, ideas that are related to your key ideas.

Henry created a cluster to explore the topic of connecting his writing class to a career in marketing.

• MAP

Mapping is similar to clustering in that it places related ideas about a topic in graphic form. Unlike clustering, however, mapping helps you define the relationships among your ideas. The practice is especially helpful if you are exploring a topic in terms of causes and effects, sequences of events, costs and benefits, or advantages and disadvantages. For example, you might create a map to predict what would happen if tobacco taxes were doubled. Or you might create a map to identify factors that led to an oil spill along the Oregon coast.

To map a topic, place your main idea at the top of a page. If you are looking at more than one aspect of a topic, such as costs and benefits, list as many relationships as you can think of. If you are looking at causes and effects, start with a single effect. Then explore the topic by identifying related causes and effects, costs and benefits, advantages and disadvantages, and so on. For example, if you are mapping a topic using causes and effects, treat each effect as a new cause by asking yourself, "If this happened, what would happen next?" Then use arrows to show the consequences. If you are mapping a topic using costs and benefits, show groups of costs and identify the relationships among them.

Henry used his word-processing program to create a map that explored the kinds of courses he might take to prepare for a career in marketing.

• USE SENTENCE STARTERS

Sentence starters like the following help you generate ideas by "filling in the blanks" in each sentence.

> **Sentence Starter:** Although we know that _____, we also know that _____.
>
> ==Although we know that== the growing opposition to standardized testing in high schools should encourage more teachers to use writing assignments instead, ==we also know that== most high school teachers typically teach so many students that it can be difficult to respond effectively to all of those assignments.

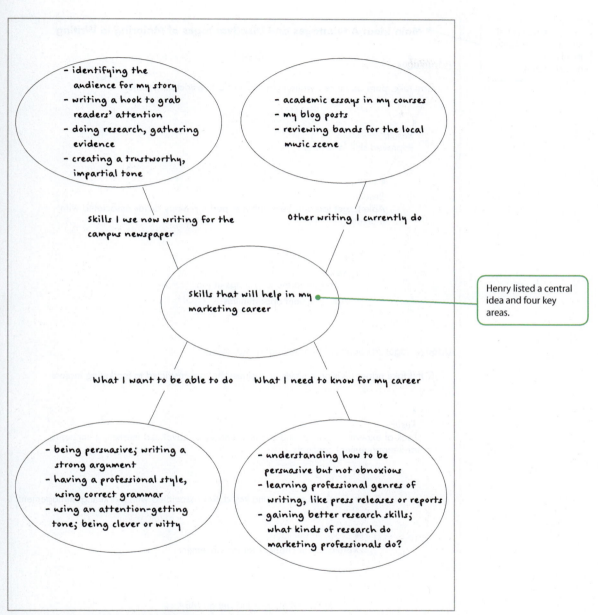

▲ A cluster of ideas about preparing for a career in marketing

> Henry listed a central idea and then mapped its advantages and disadvantages.

Main Idea: Advantages and Disadvantages of Majoring in Writing

Advantages

Can take more advanced writing classes that are restricted to majors

  Result:
  Improved skill in writing

    Result:
    Able to get job and better able to perform many duties associated with marketing position

      Result:
      Good performance ratings in job
      Advancement opportunities

Disadvantages (as opposed to majoring in marketing)

Can't take upper division courses in business that are restricted to marketing majors

  Result:
  Lack of expertise in advanced business concepts, advanced marketing concepts, and management concepts

    Result: Can't do some of the key duties associated with marketing management

      Result: Lower chances for advancement

        Result: Might need to get an MBA

▲ A map exploring the advantages and disadvantages of majoring in writing versus majoring in marketing

There are nearly as many sentence starters as there are ideas about how to structure a sentence. You can make up your own or you can try some of the following.

Exploring Interests

I would like to understand [how / why / whether] _____ happened.

I want to know more about _____, especially the aspects of _____.

I am interested in _____ because _____.

Explaining

There are three reasons this is [true / not true / relevant / important / essential]. First, _____. Second, _____. Third, _____.

We can [change / improve / fix] this by _____.

To accomplish _____, we must _____.

People do this because _____.

We were trying to _____, but we ended up _____.

Interpreting and Analyzing

This means that _____.

If we were starting over, we would _____.

It has always been the case that _____.

Comparing and Contrasting

Like _____, _____.

Unlike _____, _____.

I know _____, but I don't know _____.

Predicting

When this happens, _____.

We would prefer that _____ is true, but we must recognize that _____.

Too often, we _____. This leads to _____.

If we _____, then _____.

Stating Beliefs

I believe _____.

We have to _____.

I want to _____.

Exploring Possibilities

If this is [true / happening / important], then _____.

Sometimes, _____.

We could _____.

How can we _____?

Evaluating

The most important aspect of _____ is _____.

This is better because _____.

Understanding Causes and Effects

When I was _____, I decided _____. That decision has _____.

When I was _____, I believed _____. But now I believe _____.

The root cause of this problem is _____.

This happened because _____.

Ask Questions

When you have completed your brainstorming, freewriting, looping, clustering, mapping, or sentence starter activities, review what you've written. Ideally, these idea-generating techniques have provided you with some useful ideas for a topic. You can select the strongest candidate and generate additional ideas by asking questions. Writers often ask questions to

- define a topic
- evaluate a topic
- consider goals
- explore potential outcomes
- consider appropriate courses of action
- compare and contrast topics
- understand causes and effects
- solve problems

Chapters 7 through 12 each provide a series of questions that will help you narrow your focus and explore ideas for a particular kind of writing project. You can create your own exploratory questions by pairing question words — *what, why, when, where, who, how, would, could, should* — with words and phrases that focus on

Your Turn: Find a Topic That Interests You

Generate ideas for possible writing topics by conducting at least three of the prewriting activities described earlier in this chapter: brainstorming, freewriting, looping, clustering, mapping, using sentence starters, and asking questions. Then use your responses to the following prompts to decide which topic interests you most.

1. What are the three most important topics I have identified so far?
2. Of these topics, which one will best sustain my interest in this project?
3. Which one will best help me achieve my purposes as a writer?
4. Which one will best address my readers' needs, interests, and backgrounds?
5. Which one best fits the requirements of my assignment?
6. Which one is most appropriate for the type of document I plan to write?
7. Which one has the fewest limitations?
8. Which one allows me to best take advantage of opportunities?
9. Based on these answers, the topic I want to choose is _____.

different aspects of a topic. Asking questions can help you think critically about your topic and explore options you might not otherwise consider.

Gina, for example, generated the following questions to explore and focus her topic on how to prepare high school teachers to teach writing:

> *What are the biggest challenges facing high school writing teachers?*
>
> *What kinds of support do teachers who use writing in their courses need?*
>
> *Which kind of feedback did I get on my writing assignments in high school? How useful was it?*
>
> *Should the state mandate particular types of writing assignments?*

As you ask questions, be aware of the role you are adopting as a writer (see Chapter 6). If you are writing an informative essay, for example, the words *what*, *when*, and *where* are appropriate. If you are conducting an analysis, you might use the words *why* and *how*. If you are interested in goals and outcomes, try the words *would* and *could*. If you want to determine an appropriate course of action, ask questions using the word *should*.

The questions you ask will probably change as you learn more about a topic, so it's best to think of them as flexible and open ended. By continuing to ask questions that reflect your growing understanding of a topic, you can build a solid foundation for your own contribution to the conversation.

How Can I "Listen In" on Written Conversations?

If you've chosen a topic that appeals to more than a few individuals, you can be sure it's the subject of several ongoing conversations. Listening in on these conversations can familiarize you with various aspects of the topic. Written conversations about the broad topic of federal regulation of new drugs, for example, might focus on issues such as childhood vaccination, prevention of birth defects, and the treatment of illnesses such as AIDS, SARS-CoV-2, and Alzheimer's disease. Each of these issues, in turn, might be addressed by different groups of people, often for quite different purposes. Childhood vaccination, for instance, might draw the attention of parents worried about potential side effects, health officials concerned about epidemics and pandemics, and researchers interested in the growth of drug-resistant diseases.

Listening in on these conversations allows you to determine which group you want to join. To make that decision, you don't have to engage in a full-blown research project. At this early stage in your writing project, you simply have to invest enough time to determine whether you want to learn more. To get started, discuss your ideas with others, observe a situation firsthand, and review published sources.

Discuss the Topic with Others

Discussing your writing project can provide insights you might not find on your own. Identify resources by talking with an instructor, a supervisor, or a librarian. Learn what other people think about a topic by conducting interviews (see Chapter 15). Gather information and insights by corresponding with experts or with people who have been affected by a topic (see Chapter 15). Get a sense of how readers might respond to your ideas by posting on social media and seeing the responses to your ideas.

Observe the Topic Firsthand

Observing something for yourself allows you to learn about a topic without filtering it through the interpretation of other writers. If you are considering a topic that focuses on a particular place, event, or activity, you might want to conduct one or more observations. If you're interested in a local issue, attend a community meeting and listen to what people have to say. If you're interested in the impact of parental involvement in youth sports, spend time at a youth soccer game. If you're interested in the importance of strength training to reduce pain, you might spend some time in a gym speaking with personal trainers. For more on planning and conducting observations, see *How Can I Conduct an Observation?* in Chapter 15.

Read What Others Have Written

Even if you are familiar with a topic, you need to learn as much about it as you can before you begin to write. Reading what others have written about a topic will help you gather new information and ideas; it is also an important step in identifying conversations and determining which ones interest you.

- **Search online library catalogs** for sources using title, author, and subject words. Before you begin your search, generate a list of words and phrases that are related to the topic you want to explore.
- **Browse library shelves** to find sources related to those you've already located. Review the works cited lists, footnotes, endnotes, or in-text citations or particularly useful sources. Then find and review these cited sources.
- **Visit the periodicals room** to find the latest magazines, newspapers, and scholarly journals.

- **Search databases** just as you would search an online library catalog. To identify relevant databases, ask a reference librarian for assistance.
- **Search the web** using the search terms you used for your catalog and database searches. Remember, though, that many web-based sources will not have undergone the same scholarly review process applied to sources in library catalogs and databases.
- **Browse the web** by following useful links from one site to another.
- **Use social media** since tweets, Facebook updates, or blog posts on your topic can lead to other relevant sources.
- **Visit online discussion groups**, such as email lists, newsgroups, and web discussion forums, to find everything from expert opinions to the musings of people who know little or nothing about a topic. If you read with a bit of skepticism, however, you can begin to learn about the issues surrounding a topic.

To learn more about locating digital and print sources, see Chapters 13 and 14.

Review Your Sources

As you learn about a topic, you'll begin the process of focusing your attention on a specific *issue* — a point of disagreement, uncertainty, concern, or curiosity that is being discussed by a community of readers and writers. Look for patterns in the information, ideas, and arguments you encounter.

- **Notice central concepts.** When several sources refer to the same idea, you can assume that this information is central to the topic.

Your Turn: Choose a Conversation

Working with the topic you selected at the end of the previous Your Turn activity, listen in on a few of the conversations taking place about it. You might discuss this topic with other people, conduct an observation, or read a few sources that address your topic. Identify the three most promising conversations you've found. To choose among the conversations, ask the following questions about each one:

1. Will joining this conversation help me accomplish my purpose?
2. Do my readers need to be exposed to this conversation?
3. Do my readers want to be exposed to this conversation?
4. How will my readers' backgrounds affect their reactions to this conversation?

- **Find broad themes.** Sources that discuss the same general theme are most likely involved in the same conversation. By recognizing these broad themes, you can identify some of the key issues addressed in the conversations about your topic.
- **Look for disagreements.** Some sources will explicitly indicate that they disagree with the arguments, ideas, or information in other sources. If you look for explicit statements of disagreement, you can identify a group of sources that are engaged in conversation with one another.
- **Recognize recurring voices.** You might find that some authors write frequently about your topic or that some are cited frequently. These authors might have significant experience or expertise related to the topic, or they might represent particular perspectives on the topic.

You can learn more about searching for patterns for sources and other critical reading strategies in Chapter 3.

As you review the conversations you've identified, ask what interests you most about each one. At a minimum, you'll want to choose a focus that interests you and is appropriate for your assignment. Ideally, this focus will also match up well with the purposes, needs, interests, and backgrounds of your readers.

In Summary: Finding and Listening In on Conversations

★ Get started by analyzing your assignment and assessing your writing situation (p. 32).

★ Generate ideas for finding conversations about interesting topics (p. 37).

★ Ask questions about the conversations you've found (p. 44).

★ Listen in on promising conversations by discussing your topic with others, observing the topic firsthand, and reading what others have written (p. 46).

★ Review what you've learned to determine which conversation to join (p. 47).

03 Reading to Write

How can I read critically? 49
Read with an attitude 50
Consider writing situations 50
Draw on critical thinking skills 50

How can I read actively? 51
Skim for an overview 51
Mark and annotate 58
Pay attention 59
Understand the writer's argument 62

How can I take notes? 63
Quote directly 64
Paraphrase 65
Summarize 66
Use notes to improve your understanding of an issue 67

How can I engage with my sources? 70
Read to understand 70
Read to respond 77
Read to make connections 79

As you join a written conversation, you'll "listen in" to find out what other writers have already contributed to the discussion and begin developing your own thoughts about the subject. In this chapter, you'll learn how to read these contributions critically and actively, how to record your reactions and ideas as you read them, and how to take notes on sources that merit a second read. You'll also learn how to engage in writing with the information, ideas, and arguments you encounter as you read.

How Can I Read Critically?

Reading critically means reading with an attitude. It also means reading with your writing situation in mind. As you read critically, you'll recognize the questions — points of disagreement, uncertainty, concern, or curiosity — that are under discussion in a written conversation. You'll also begin to think about how you might respond to these questions. This kind of reading draws on a range of critical thinking skills, including analysis, evaluation, and reflection. Reading critically, in this sense, helps you strengthen your critical thinking skills.

Read with an Attitude

As you learn about and prepare to contribute to a written conversation, both your point of view and your attitude are likely to change. Initially, you might be curious, noting new information and marking key passages. Later, as you determine whether sources fit into the conversation or are reliable, you might adopt a more questioning attitude. Eventually, after you begin to draw conclusions about the conversation, you might become skeptical and more willing to challenge the arguments you read.

Regardless of where you are in your writing process, you should always adopt a critical attitude. Accept nothing at face value, ask questions, look for both similarities and differences among the sources you read, examine the implications of what you read for your writing project, be on the alert for unusual information, and note relevant sources and information. Most important, be open to ideas and arguments, even if you don't agree with them. Give them a chance to affect how you think about the conversation you've decided to join.

Consider Writing Situations

Reading critically involves approaching each source with an awareness not only of your own writing situation but also of the writing situation that shaped the source. Remember that each document you read was written to accomplish a particular purpose and was intended for a particular group of readers. Realize that the physical, technological, social, disciplinary, and cultural contexts in which the document was produced affected how the writer presented information, ideas, and arguments. And be aware that the writing situation that helped produce the source might differ significantly from your own.

As you read, remember what you are trying to accomplish. Your purpose and role will affect your assessment of the information, ideas, and arguments you encounter. Moreover, your understanding of your readers' purposes, needs, interests, and backgrounds will affect how you use what you've learned.

Draw on Critical Thinking Skills

As you read, you'll draw on your critical thinking skills. You'll work to understand important information, ideas, and arguments. You'll compare the document you're reading now to those you've read earlier. You'll try to understand the motivations behind a document. You'll reflect on what you've learned. And you'll make judgments about the quality of the ideas and arguments you encounter. In short, you'll find that critical reading relies on critical thinking.

The decisions you make as you read, review, and assess potential sources will have a profound effect on what you write in your project document. Remember that you are working on your writing project to make a contribution, to shape your readers' thinking about your subject. Avoid being overly deferential to the authors who have written before you. You should respect their work, but you shouldn't assume that their conclusions about the subject are the final word. Be prepared to challenge their ideas and arguments. In short, be critical. If you aren't, there's little point in working on your project, since you'll simply repeat the ideas of others instead of advancing your own.

How Can I Read Actively?

Once you've thought about your writing situation and the writing situations that shaped your sources, you're ready to start reading actively. Reading actively means interacting with sources and considering them in light of the conversation you've decided to join. When you read actively, you might do one or more of the following:

- Skim the source to get a general sense of what it's about.
- Write questions in the margins.
- Jot down your reactions.
- Identify key information, ideas, and arguments.
- Note how you might use information, ideas, and arguments in your document.
- Visually link one part of the source to another.
- Identify important passages for later rereading.

To read actively, focus on three strategies: skimming, marking and annotating, and examining sources closely.

Skim for an Overview

Before investing too much time in a source, skim it. *Skimming* — reading just enough to get the general idea of what a source is about — can tell you a great deal in a short amount of time. It's an important first step in reading a source critically. To skim sources, glance at surface elements without delving too deeply into the content.

How to skim a print document

Identify the type of document to remind yourself of typical purposes, forms of evidence, and genre conventions. This page is part of an article from the professional journal *Educational Leadership*.

Check the title (and table of contents, if one is provided) for cues about content.

Check headings and subheadings to learn about content and organization.

Look for pull quotes (quotations or passages called out into the margins or set in larger type) for a sense of the writer's main idea.

Read the first and last sentences of paragraphs to find key information.

Skim captions of photos and figures, which often highlight important arguments, ideas, and information.

Look for publication information, such as journal title and publication date.

Skim opening paragraphs to learn about the purpose and scope of the document.

Peter Johnston, "Guiding the Budding Writer," *Educational Leadership* 70.1 (September 2012), pp. 64–67. Copyright © 2012 by ASCD. Republished with permission of the ASCD; permission conveyed through Copyright Clearance Center, Inc. (top left) Photo: © Stefanie Felix; (top right and bottom right) Photos © Susie Fitzhugh.

How Can I Read Actively? | CHAPTER 03   53

Check the page title in the title bar of the browser for information about the purpose and content of the page.

Check the URL to learn about the purpose of a web page — for instance, whether the page is part of a larger site. Extensions such as .com (for business), .edu (for education), .org (for nonprofit organizations), and .gov (for government) can provide clues about the site's purpose.

Check the navigation headers and menus to learn about the site's content and organization.

Check for information about the author to learn about the author's background, interests, and purposes for writing the document.

Check the title.

Check for links to other sites to learn more about the issue.

Skim captions of photos and figures, which often highlight important arguments, ideas, and information.

Read the first and last sentences of paragraphs to find key information.

Scan for boldface, colored, or italic text, which might be used to emphasize important information.

View media such as video files and scan for links to social-media sites.

▲ **How to skim a web page**

Retrieved from www.ascd.org/publications/educational-leadership/mar16/vol73/num06/toc.aspx on March 14, 2016. Copyright 2016 by ASCD. Reprinted with permission. All rights reserved.

Quinn Jackson, a student working on an assignment in the same writing-about-writing course as Gina Colville (see *Conversations Help You Share Information, Ideas, and Arguments* in Chapter 1) and Henry Garcia (see *Generate Ideas* in Chapter 2), used skimming to gain a quick overview of an article published in the scholarly journal *Educational Leadership*. The article explored the impact of teacher comments on student writing. She also skimmed the journal's website to locate additional articles on the topic.

Guiding the Budding Writer

How we comment on students' work can give students a larger vision for their own potential.

Peter Johnston

Thomas Newkirk, a seasoned and successful writer, once took a draft of his writing to the Pulitzer Prize–winning author Donald Murray for feedback. After scanning the draft, Murray simply asked, "What's this about?" His question caused Newkirk to reflect on this piece of writing and better focus it by cutting the first three pages (Newkirk, 2012, p. 116).

Four-year-old Abby had a similar experience when she made a book in preschool and showed it to educator Matt Glover. Matt asked her what the book was about. Seeing that she didn't understand his question, he said, "Remember how *Owl Babies* was all about the owls and their mommy, and Tessa's book was all about a butterfly and a lady? What's your book about?" (Ray & Glover, 2008, p. 144).

In both these cases, feedback helped develop the authors' vision for themselves and their work. Both anecdotes shed light on the relationship between feedback and the development of authors of all ages. Let's consider the significance of the feedback for Abby. With two sentences, Matt helped her understand that books are *about* something, that a book is an important social contract. He accomplished this by drawing Abby's attention to a helpful resource for reflection — other authors' work. He made it clear that Abby is an author, just like Martin Waddell, who wrote *Owl Babies*, and Tessa, who wrote about the lady and the butterfly.

Matt's feedback positioned Abby to begin to think, as authors do, about other authors' work and what she might learn from them. In response to this feedback and the related classroom conversations, Abby began to have conversations with her peers about their writing. Thus Matt began the process of making Abby independent of her teachers' feedback. This is one thing effective feedback accomplishes; beyond improving one particular

> If teachers commit to involving students in personally meaningful projects, productive feedback will follow.

book, essay, or assignment, it has a larger vision. Matt's feedback looked to the future, inviting Abby to become the kind of person who makes books about something and who observes work by people similar to herself to learn new possibilities.

Four Truths about Feedback
These examples illustrate four important points about feedback that we often miss. First, giving feedback doesn't necessarily mean telling students what's good or bad. Actually, it doesn't necessarily mean *telling* them anything; notice how Donald Murray and Matt Glover began with questions.

Second, feedback should be inseparable from the larger classroom conversations. Matt's feedback to Abby didn't stand alone. Abby's preschool teacher had already fostered conversations that drew attention to the choices authors make and the logic of those choices. We might call this *public feedback*. In a 1st grade class, public feedback might include observations like,

> I notice Jamal made this word big and bold and in uppercase letters with an exclamation point. That means he wants me to read it very loudly. Remember how in *Roller Coaster*, Marla Frazee wrote the word WHOOSH in big uppercase letters, too?

Such public feedback is part of the same conversation that identifies students as authors. It draws the classroom community's attention to processes that inform authors' decisions. Adding, "That means he wants me to read it very loudly" reminds students that the teacher, now in the role of reader, is partly under the control of the writer, thus focusing young authors on strategic thinking in relation to readers.

Similarly, when reading *What Happened to Cass McBride?* to 8th graders, the teacher might say, "I wonder why Gail Giles chose to use so many flashbacks in the story." Such conversations about authors' mental processes have an additional benefit. They require imagining what's going on in another person's mind. The more students practice imagining authors' thinking, the more they are inclined to do so independently and to become better writers and readers. At the same time, as students imagine fellow authors' thoughts and feelings, their social imagination expands—which leads to better social behavior (Johnston, 2012).

Third, feedback is not merely cognitive in reach, nor merely corrective in function. Like the rest of classroom talk, feedback affects the ways students understand themselves and one another—how they perceive themselves as writers. When a teacher draws a student's attention to the compositional choices he or she made to construct a convincing argument, the teacher invites that student to construct a self-narrative that says, I did *x* (added a detail to my illustration of a key point), the consequence of which was *y* (I got my meaning across better). This kind of feedback positions students as people who can accomplish things by acting strategically.

Fourth, optimal feedback is responsive, meaning it's adjusted to what the individual writer is likely to need. To give Abby feedback, Matt had to know something about what young authors need to understand—and he had to recognize the signs of her understanding.

> Feedback sets in motion conversations that affect how students make sense of themselves.

Teachers who want to provide feedback that strengthens each learner's writing skills, motivation, and independence should keep five principles in mind. Although I've used writing as the focus of my examples, the same principles hold for other areas of academic learning.

Five Key Principles
1. Context matters
Context affects feedback. When students are fully engaged, we can provide ample differentiated feedback to individuals because we don't have to worry about managing the behavior of other students. Students who are working on something personally and socially meaningful know when they need feedback and come looking for it (Ivey & Johnston, 2012), and they are more receptive to critical feedback. By contrast, a student reading an unengaging text or doing a math problem that's too difficult will likely disengage. Teachers' feedback will then be about behavior rather than academic learning, and any academic feedback will likely be given too quickly, leaving little thinking time and undermining the student's control. If teachers commit to involving students in personally meaningful projects, productive feedback will follow.

There are, of course, contexts in which feedback is unlikely to be heard. When we give a grade as part of our feedback, students routinely read only as far as the grade. In general, students value feedback less after the work is completed than when it's still in progress. If we give a writer more control over the feedback — such as by asking what aspect of the work he or she would like feedback on — the writer is more likely to tune in.

2. Teachers aren't the sole source
Feedback comes from other students as much as from teachers — which is a good thing if we capitalize on it. When we teach students to teach as well as to learn about good writing, feedback becomes more immediately available and plentiful. This means that part of our students' language arts development should involve learning how to give feedback to others — how to respond to other learners. Fostering peer feedback expands the reach of our teaching.

With peer feedback, classroom talk becomes a reflective surface in which students can see their own work. They hear students talking with peers or with the teacher about writing and use those conversations to reflect on their own writing. Ideally, community conversations will respond to all students' efforts. Students will then have a forum in which they can request feedback from peers and teach others.

3. A focus on process empowers students
Responsive feedback communities use three key practices. The first is listening. Until we understand where a person is coming from, it's hard to provide responsive feedback. The second is publicly noticing the significant decisions authors make and encouraging students to do the same. The third practice I call *causal process feedback*. This is feedback on how a student's choices affected the finished product. For example, "Look how you revised that — you added examples of the colonists' complaints against tyranny to your essay. Now I see what you mean" (Ray & Glover, 2008, p. 164). This feedback turns the student's attention to the writing process and makes the student's experience into a tool for future composing. Causal process feedback is at the heart of building a sense of agency: It helps demystify the skill of writing.

We can turn students' attention to the process by asking something like, "How did you solve that problem with your lead paragraph?" The question invites students to articulate a causal connection between a set of behaviors and an outcome.

Feedback that emphasizes processes helps learners not only persist in the face of difficulty but also find more solutions to problems. Feedback that focuses on effort ("You really tried hard") has the same benefits (Kamins & Dweck, 1999). In my view, however, it's less useful for two reasons. First, you can't say it unless you know the student *did* try hard. Second, a comment focused only on effort misses the chance that other students will overhear — and benefit from — a teacher's comment about how a strategy one student used improved a piece of writing.

4. "Positive" doesn't mean praising

Positive feedback motivates students and gives them the tools to improve. Teachers often confuse being positive with providing praise. They are not the same. The trouble with praise is that it has side effects (Dweck, 2007). If we praise a student who's fully engaged, we simply distract her and suggest that her real goal should be to please us. In Matt's feedback to Abby, he did not say, "I like the way you …" because that would place him in the authority role and suggest that the goal of Abby's efforts is to please him. Feedback like, "Good girl," is even less helpful because it carries no useful information — it merely lets the student know that she is being judged. Public praise is even more problematic: If we say "good" to one student and "excellent" to another, suddenly "good" damns with faint praise.

Praise is not so good for creating independently driven writers, and sometimes it's downright destructive. Phrases that invite a symmetrical power relationship and a message of student contribution ("Thank you for helping us figure that out" or even "Thank you") are more useful.

Ordinarily, teachers don't need praise to make a student feel good about the book he has just made or the math problem she has solved. We can just point out what was accomplished and ask, "How did you do that?" Or, respond to each as one writer (or researcher or filmmaker) to another ("Your piece made me really want to do something about homelessness"). Or, we might ask, "How does it feel to have completed your first poem?"

The challenge in being positive comes when students attempt something that stretches them beyond what they can do and results in errors. These errors may nonetheless reflect useful strategic thinking. Being positive here requires not being distracted by the many things that did *not* go well, and instead focusing students' attention on what was partially successful. For example, "I see you figured out the first part of that word by using a word you already know. I wonder whether that would also work for the second part of the word." Drawing attention to the successful part not only consolidates a useful strategy, but also builds a foundation for further productive writing.

5. Feedback shifts how students see themselves

Feedback sets in motion conversations that affect how students make sense of themselves. Thus, it's particularly important that feedback not contain judgmental comments or comments that cast students in terms of permanent traits. This includes comments like, "You're a good writer," "That's what good readers do,"

> Teachers often confuse being positive with providing praise. They are not the same.

and even, "I'm proud of you." If we make these statements when students are successful, when they fail, they will fill in the other end of the conversation ("You're not good at this," "I'm disappointed in you") (Kamins & Dweck, 1999). Judgment-tinged feedback nudges students toward a world made up of people who are good artists or not good artists, smart or not.

By contrast, students who hear "You did a good job," which mildly turns attention to the process rather than the person, are more likely to try again the activity at which they were previously unsuccessful. Even better is something akin to "You found a way to solve the problem. Are there any other ways you can think of to solve it?"

What's the Point?
The primary goal of feedback is to improve the future possibilities for each individual learner and for the learning community. This means expanding, for every learner, the vision of what's possible, the strategic options for getting there, the necessary knowledge, and the learner's persistence. Teachers aren't merely teaching skills and correcting errors. We're teaching *people* who wish to competently participate in valued social practices—the practices that writers, mathematicians, artists, and others do every day.

References
Dweck, C. S. (2007). The perils and promises of praise. *Educational Leadership, 65*(2), 34–39.
Ivey, G., & Johnston, P. H. (2012). *Engagement with young adult literature: Processes and consequences*. Manuscript submitted for publication.
Johnston, P. H. (2012). *Opening minds: Using language to change lives*. Portland, ME: Stenhouse.
Kamins, M. L., & Dweck, C. S. (1999). Person versus process praise and criticism: Implications for contingent self-worth and coping. *Developmental Psychology, 35*(3), 835–847.
Newkirk, T. (2012). *The art of slow reading: Six time-honored practices for engagement*. Portsmouth, NH: Heinemann.
Ray, K. W., & Glover, M. (2008). *Already ready: Nurturing writers in preschool and kindergarten*. Portsmouth, NH: Heinemann.

Mark and Annotate

Marking and annotating are simple yet powerful active-reading strategies. Mark a source to identify key information, ideas, and arguments. Annotate a source to note agreements and disagreements, to identify support for your argument, or to remind yourself about alternative perspectives on your issue. Common techniques include the following:

- using a highlighter, a pen, or a pencil to identify key passages in a print source
- attaching sticky notes or flags to printed pages
- identifying important passages in digital texts using a highlighting tool
- writing reactions and notes in the margins of print sources
- creating comments in digital texts

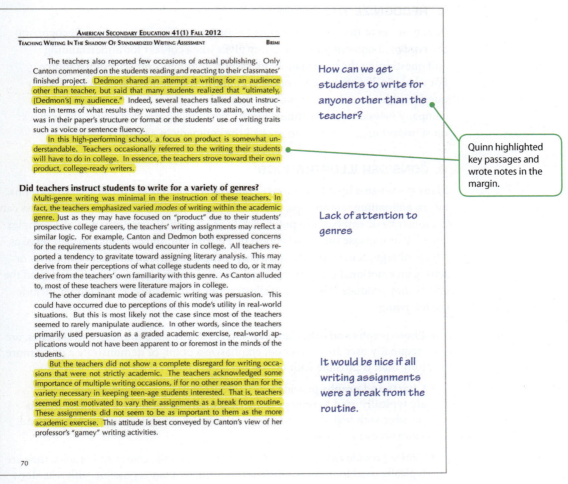

▲ Marking and annotating a source

You can also create notes, which provide a compact, easy-to-review record of the most important information, ideas, and arguments you've found in your sources. You can read more about taking notes later in this chapter.

Pay Attention

Examine at least some sources closely for key information, ideas, and arguments. Noting various aspects of a source during your active reading will help you better understand its argument, its role in the conversation you've decided to join, and its potential role in your own contribution to the conversation.

RECOGNIZE THE GENRE

Pay attention to the type of document — or genre — you are reading. Recognizing the type of document you are reading gives you a context for understanding and questioning the information, ideas, and arguments presented in a source. For example, if a source is an opinion column, you're more likely to watch for a questionable use of logic or analysis. Similarly, if you're reading an article in a company newsletter or an annual report, you'll recognize that one of the writer's most important concerns is to present the company in a positive light.

CONSIDER ILLUSTRATIONS

Many documents use illustrations — photographs and other images, charts, graphs, tables, animations, audio clips, and video clips — in addition to text. Illustrations can demonstrate or emphasize a point, clarify or simplify the presentation of a complex concept, or increase the visual appeal of a document. Illustrations can also serve as a form of argument by presenting a surprising or even shocking set of statistics or setting an emotional tone. As you read, be aware of the types of illustrations and the effects they produce. The types of illustrations you are likely to encounter include the following:

- **Photographs and other images,** such as drawings, paintings, and sketches, are frequently used to set a mood, emphasize a point, or demonstrate a point more fully than is possible with text alone.

- **Charts and graphs** provide a visual representation of information. They are typically used to present numerical information more succinctly than is possible with text alone or to present complex information in a compact and more accessible form.

- **Tables** provide categorical lists of information. Like charts and graphs, they are typically used to make a point more succinctly than is possible with text alone or to present complex information in a compact form. Tables are frequently used to illustrate contrasts among groups, relationships among variables (such as income, educational attainment, and voting preferences), or change over time (such as growth in population during the past century).

- **Digital illustrations,** such as PowerPoint presentations, web pages, and word-processing documents intended for reading on computers, tablets, or phones, can include a wider range of illustrations than print documents can. Illustrations such as audio, video, and animations differ from photographs, images, charts, graphs, and tables in that they don't just appear on the page — they do things.

Read more about the uses of illustration in Chapter 22.

- **RECORD NEW INFORMATION AND CHALLENGING IDEAS**

As you read, mark and annotate passages that contain information that is new to you. In your writer's notebook, record new information in the form of a list or as a series of brief descriptions of what you've learned and where you learned it.

You might be tempted to ignore material that's hard to understand. If you do, however, you could miss critical information. When you encounter something difficult, mark it and make a brief annotation reminding yourself to check it out later. Sometimes you'll learn enough from your continued reading that the passage won't seem as challenging when you come back to it. Sometimes, though, you won't be able to figure out a passage on your own. In that case, turn to someone else for help — your instructor, a librarian, members of an online forum — or try searching a database, library catalog, or the web using keywords or phrases from the passage.

- **IDENTIFY SIMILARITIES AND DIFFERENCES**

You can learn a lot by looking for similarities and differences among the sources you read. For example, you might identify which authors take a similar *approach* (see *Read to Make Connections* later in this chapter) to an issue, such as favoring increased government support for solar energy. You could then contrast this group with other groups of authors, such as those who believe that market forces should be the primary factor encouraging solar power and those who believe we should focus on other forms of energy. Similarly, you might create marginal annotations or digital comments when information in one source agrees or disagrees with information in another. Doing so can help you build your own argument or identify information that will allow you (and potentially your readers) to better understand the issue.

Learn more about comparing sources in *How Can I Take Notes?* later in this chapter.

- **EVALUATE AND REFLECT ON WHAT YOU'VE LEARNED**

Critical reading relies heavily on skills typically referred to as critical thinking, in particular understanding, analyzing, evaluating, and reflecting. As you discover similarities and differences among the documents you've read, you'll begin to decide which sources align best with your evolving understanding of your issue. You'll begin to determine which sources might help you illustrate the full range of ideas that are being considered in the conversation — including those with which you disagree. And you'll likely find yourself reflecting on the information, ideas, and arguments you've encountered. In the next section, "Understand the Writer's Argument," you can read about understanding an author's position on an issue. In Chapter 4, you'll find a detailed discussion of assessing and evaluating sources.

Understand the Writer's Argument

Written conversations typically include a range of positions on an issue. Determining where authors agree and disagree can help you understand the conversation as a whole. Similarly, identifying the reasons and evidence authors offer to support their positions — an author's main point or argument about an issue — can help you gain insights into the conversation and think critically about the issue.

● IDENTIFY THE MAIN POINT

Sources typically have a main point. An editorial in a local newspaper, for example, might urge voters to approve financing for a new school. An article might report a new advance in automobile emissions testing, or a website might emphasize the benefits of a new technique for treating a sports injury. The main point will often be expressed in the form of a thesis statement (see Chapter 18). As you read critically, make sure you understand what the writer wants you to accept, believe, or do.

● FIND REASONS AND EVIDENCE THAT SUPPORT THE MAIN POINT

Once you've identified the main point, look for the reasons given to accept it. If an author is arguing, for instance, that tuition at public colleges and universities should be funded by the federal government, that author might support their argument with the following reasons:

> Everyone, regardless of socioeconomic background, should have the opportunity to pursue a higher education.
>
> The number of college graduates is falling short of the number of employees needed to fill jobs in the private and public sectors.
>
> All members of society will benefit from a highly educated workforce.

Reasons can take a wide range of forms and are often presented in ways that appeal to emotions, logic, principles, values, or beliefs (see *Appeal to Your Readers* in

---

Working Together: Understand the Argument in a Source

Working with a group of classmates, identify the main point, reasons, and evidence in the article "Guiding the Budding Writer" earlier in this chapter.

1. **List the main point at the top of your page.** Determine what the author is asking you to know, believe, or do.
2. **Briefly list each reason to accept the main point in the order in which it appears in the source.** You might want to brainstorm lists individually based on your reading of the article and then share your ideas to create the group's list.
3. **Determine the most important evidence offered as proof for each reason.** Once you've agreed on the reasons, work together to identify the evidence used to support each reason.

Chapter 12). As persuasive as these reasons might seem, they are only as good as the evidence offered to support them. In some cases, evidence is offered in the form of statements from experts on a subject or from people in positions of authority. In other cases, evidence might include personal experience. In still other cases, evidence might include firsthand observations, excerpts from an interview, or statistical data.

When you find empirical evidence used in a source, consider where the evidence comes from and how it is being used. If the information appears to be presented fairly, ask whether you might be able to use it to support your own ideas, and try to verify its accuracy by consulting additional sources.

Learn more about arguments in *How Can I Write an Argumentative Essay?* in Chapter 12.

How Can I Take Notes?

Notes — in the form of direct quotations, paraphrases, and summaries — provide you with a collection of important information, ideas, and arguments from your sources, as well as a record of your reactions to your sources. Taking brief notes when you are first looking at a source allows you to keep track of your evolving understanding of your topic or issue. Later, when you've decided that a source is worth a closer read, you might take more extensive notes that will help you as you plan, draft, and design your document.

The methods you use to take notes — such as using note cards, a paper notebook, a word-processing program, web-based tools, or an app on a phone or tablet, for example — should reflect how you like to work with information. If you're uncertain about which method might suit you, talk to other writers, your instructor, or a librarian, and then try a few of the most promising methods. Each method has its own advantages and disadvantages, and no single method is always right for every situation.

Learn more about planning, drafting, and designing your document in Part Four.

You should take notes when a source

- features an idea that surprises or interests you or that you think you might want to argue for or against
- provides a statement that enhances your understanding of the issue
- offers insights into how an authority or expert understands the issue
- conveys an understanding of someone else's firsthand experience with an issue or event

As you take notes, remember that they should help you accomplish your purposes as a writer and address your readers effectively. Make sure that you quote your sources accurately, paraphrase passages fairly and appropriately, and summarize clearly and fairly. In every case, provide enough source information so you can locate the original source when you need to check for accuracy or want to find additional information.

As you use your notes, do so thoughtfully. Be sure that the information you are including in your document has been verified. Consider whether alternative perspectives might help you craft a better document — and then seek out sources that provide those perspectives. Your notes should be a source of support for your argument, but they should not limit your efforts to learn more about your issue even in the later stages of your composing process.

Quote Directly

A direct quotation is an exact copy of words found in a source. Taking notes that contain quotations can help you accurately keep track of the information, ideas, and arguments you encounter as you learn about a conversation.

When you use quotations in your notes, be sure to place quotation marks around any quoted passage. If you don't, you might think that the passage is a paraphrase or a summary when you review your notes later and then unintentionally plagiarize it when you draft your document (see Chapter 20). The solution to this problem is simple: ensure that you take notes carefully and accurately. Be sure to do the following:

- Enclose quoted passages in quotation marks.
- Identify the author and title of the source for every quotation.
- List the page number (or paragraph number, if you are using a source that does not have page numbers) where the quotation can be found.
- Proofread what you have written to make sure it matches the original source exactly — including wording, punctuation, and spelling.

Learn more about plagiarism in Chapter 17.

Quinn Jackson decided to quote from an article about teaching writing that appeared in the academic journal *Teaching English in the Two-Year College*. The article, written by Nancy Sommers, describes her growth as a teacher over the past three decades.

> Source: Nancy Sommers, "Living Composition," p. 34
>
> "If, after three decades, I'm more surefooted about teaching writing and more passionate about it, I imagine it is because I teach not from a set of secret codes or passwords, but from my own work as a writer, waiting to be surprised by the alphabet's infinite possibilities; and from encouraging students to write as if they have an audience, a gathering, waiting to receive their words."

See Chapter 21 to learn more about using direct quotations.

▲ A direct quotation

Nancy Sommers, "Living Composition," *Teaching English in the Two-Year College* 43.1 (September 2015). Copyright 2015 by the National Council of Teachers of English. Reprinted with permission.

Paraphrase

When you restate a passage from a source in your own words, you are paraphrasing. Using paraphrases in your notes serves three purposes. First, restating a passage in your own words can help you remember it better than if you simply copy and paste a quotation. Second, because paraphrases are written in your own words, they're usually easier to understand later, when you're drafting. Third, paraphrasing as you take notes will help you save time during drafting, since good writers seldom rely exclusively on direct quotations.

Paraphrasing is a useful skill that takes practice. One of the most common problems writers have as they paraphrase is mirroring the source material too closely — that is, making such minor changes to the wording and sentence structure of a source that the paraphrase remains nearly identical to the original passage. Another common problem is distorting the meaning of the source.

Consider the differences among the original passage (shown on the facing page) and the appropriate and inappropriate paraphrases shown next.

Appropriate Paraphrase

Sommers' growth as a teacher has little to do with some sort of privileged, insider knowledge and everything to do with her own work as a writer who loves language and her desire to help students understand that they write best when they write for an interested and receptive group of readers.

> Preserves the meaning of the original passage without replicating the sentence structure and wording.

Inappropriate Paraphrase

Sommers notes that, after roughly thirty years, she is more confident about teaching writing and more excited about it. It is not because she draws on a sort of secret sauce for teaching, but because of her experiences working as a writer. She is always ready to be surprised by the possibilities of language and wants to help students write as if they are addressing readers who care about the words they have to share.

> Does not differ sufficiently from the original; uses similar sentence structures and changes only some key words.

Inappropriate Paraphrase

Sommers writes that she continues to be passionate about teaching writing because she remains open to the infinite possibilities of language and its power to reach an audience.

> Distorts the meaning of the original passage.

When paraphrasing, focus on understanding the key ideas in the passage, and then restate them in your own words. You might find it useful to begin a paraphrase with the phrase "In other words." This strategy reminds you that it's important to do more than simply change a few words in the passage. You might want to set the original source aside while you paraphrase so that you won't be tempted to copy sentences directly from it.

See Chapter 21 to learn more about using paraphrases.

In your note, identify the author and title of the source, and list the page number (or paragraph number, if you are using a source that does not have page numbers) where the passage that you paraphrased can be found. After you've completed your paraphrase, check it for accuracy and ensure that the wording and sentence structure differ from the original passage.

Summarize

A summary is a concise statement of the information, ideas, and arguments in a source. You can write summaries to capture the overall argument and information in a source or to record a writer's main idea so that you can respond to it later. The following notes contain appropriate and inappropriate summaries of the journal article "Teaching Writing in the Shadow of Standardized Writing Assessment: An Exploratory Study."

Appropriate Summary

In the article "Teaching Writing in the Shadow of Standardized Writing Assessment: An Exploratory Study," Hunter Brimi reports on a study in which five high school teachers considered the impact of a state-mandated standardized writing assessment on their efforts to teach writing. Brimi based his conclusions about the impact of the writing assessment on the teachers' comments about the assessment itself, the importance of teaching composing processes, and their willingness to assign multiple genres. Analysis of the interviews indicated that the standardized writing assessment affected their teaching and their willingness to assign genres that were not addressed in the state-mandated writing assessment. The interviews also suggested that the teachers' lack of preparation to teach writing might have affected their behaviors regarding the standardized writing assessment.

> The summary gives a broad overview of the article's argument and avoids close paraphrases of key points.

Problems can arise when a writer fails to summarize ideas and instead either creates a close paraphrase or writes a patchwork summary that is little more than a series of passages copied from the source.

Inappropriate Summary

An exploratory study involving interviews with five high school English teachers regarding their writing instruction showed that the Tennessee Comprehensive Assessment Program's (TCAP) Writing Assessment affected their teaching, particularly in terms of its impact on teaching the writing process and their use of multiple writing genres. The teachers indicated that the TCAP Writing Assessment measurably affected their teaching. Additionally, the teachers revealed that they struggled to teach the writing process and showed reluctance to teach or assign multi-genre writing. It is possible that this might be the result of their lack of training to teach writing before becoming teachers.

> The summary consists of a series of unattributed quotations and close paraphrases of the article's abstract.

In your note, identify the author, the title, and, if you are summarizing only part of a source, the pages, paragraphs, or section where the information can be found. To avoid mirroring the language and sentence structure of the source, begin your summary with "The author argues that" or "The author found that." As with paraphrases, you might want to put aside the original source so that you won't be tempted to copy sentences directly from it. After you've completed your summary, check it for accuracy and unintentional plagiarism.

Use Notes to Improve Your Understanding of an Issue

Because taking notes requires thought and effort, the process of choosing quotations, creating paraphrases, and summarizing sources can help you gain a deeper understanding of an issue. Yet taking notes can do far more than simply help you remember and understand your sources. It can help you keep track of ideas that occur to you as you work with sources and gain insights into how they are related to each other. Taking notes, in a real sense, plays an important role in planning your contribution to the conversation you've decided to join.

You can learn more about annotating sources during critical reading earlier in this chapter.

● RECORD YOUR REACTIONS AND IMPRESSIONS

You can use your notes to keep track of your reactions and impressions. You might have created annotations in the margins or added comments using a word-processing program. As you take more formal notes, you can use them as the basis for a more substantial reflection on the source. For example, you might have written, "This makes sense" in the margin. If so, take some time to create a note that explains why it makes sense and what the source adds to your understanding of the issue. You can learn more about annotating sources during critical reading earlier in this chapter.

● COMPARE SOURCES

Reviewing your notes can help you identify relationships among information, ideas, and arguments. Paying attention to your sources as a group — not just to individual sources — helps you gain a more complete understanding of your issue. It also can be useful when you begin planning and organizing your document, since those connections can help you frame your argument. To compare sources, use the following techniques.

- **Look for similarities.** As you take notes, identify similarities among your sources. Later, this can help you define groups of authors that you can use to support your argument, point to as misguided for the same general reason, or use to illustrate a particular point.
- **Look for disagreements.** Taking note of disagreements among your sources can help you determine the sticking points in the conversation you've decided to join. In turn, understanding where your sources disagree can help you decide where to make your contribution to the conversation.

Notes on "Guiding the Budding Writer" by Peter Johnston

Quotes	Notes and Reactions
"Public feedback is part of the same conversation that identifies students as authors. It draws the classroom community's attention to processes that inform authors' decisions" (p. 64).	An interesting observation, since so many people (including a lot of teachers, I think) consider feedback on writing a quiet, private event. I can use this to push back against the idea that classroom writing is just between student and teacher.
"Feedback is not merely cognitive in reach, nor merely corrective in function. Like the rest of classroom talk, feedback affects the ways students understand themselves and one another — how they perceive themselves as writers" (p. 64).	A key observation here. I'd like to see if I can find another source to back this up.
"Teachers aren't merely teaching skills and correcting errors. We're teaching *people* who wish to competently participate in valued social practices — the practices that writers, mathematicians, artists, and others do every day" (p. 66).	This ties into the idea of why writing instruction is so important. It's not just about communication — and it's not just about correctness. It's about getting people ready to contribute to society.

Annotations:
- The title of the source is listed at the top of the note.
- The quotation is surrounded by quotation marks.
- The writer jots down reactions to the quotations.
- Page numbers follow quotations.

Peter Johnston, "Guiding the Budding Writer," *Educational Leadership* 70.1 (September 2012), pp. 64–67. Copyright © 2012 by the Association for Supervision and Curriculum Development. Republished with permission of the Association for Supervision and Curriculum Development; permission conveyed through Copyright Clearance Center, Inc.

- **Look for common citations.** Any source that is being referenced frequently is likely to contain important information, ideas, or arguments. Take note of frequently cited sources and consult them later.

CLASSIFY SOURCES

As you take notes, use them to classify your sources. Among other purposes, you can keep track of sources that include important information or ideas, that represent various approaches to your issue, and that might be used to support particular points in the document you plan to write. Strategies for classifying sources include tagging, labeling, grouping, listing, and visualizing.

- **TECH TIP: Tagging and Labeling.** Tags are words or phrases that can be associated with digital notes. Labels can be applied to print notes. You can use tags and labels to remind yourself about the purpose or content of a note or to help you remember something about the source. You might tag a note with one of the reasons you're planning to use in your document, for example, or you might label a note as useful for your introduction. Later, as you're working on your introduction or fleshing out that reason, you can quickly call up your tagged notes. Similarly, you might label a note to remind yourself about the approach taken in the source to which it refers and later, as you draft, look for notes with that label. Apply as many tags or labels as are relevant to each note.

- **Grouping.** Use groups to organize notes by the part of the document in which you plan to refer to the source, the approach advanced in the source, or the kind of evidence contained in the source. If you are working with print notes, put them in piles, envelopes, or folders. If you are working with digital notes, drag each note into a group (within, for example, a word-processing file) or into a folder (if you are saving each note as a distinct file).

- **Listing.** Listing is similar to grouping, but it does not require you to move your notes into a particular location. Instead, create notes that list your sources. You might, for example, create a list of all the sources that contain information used to support your position and then make another list of sources that contain information that contradicts your position.

- **Visualizing.** As you take notes, you can use the same mapping and clustering techniques that you can use as you generate ideas and organize your document (see *Generate Ideas* in Chapter 2 and *How Can I Arrange My Argument?* in Chapter 19). For example, you can create notes that contain a sketch of the relationships among the sources you've read so far. Or you could draw clusters of sources that support or illustrate a particular approach to your issue, and then write brief notes about what they have in common, how the clusters of sources differ from each other, and so on. Similarly, you can draw maps showing the relationships among important ideas in your sources and identify which sources are associated with each idea.

Your Turn: Respond to Sources

As you take notes, you'll gain a deeper understanding of your sources, both individually and as a group. Use your knowledge of your sources to create a response that will help you plan and draft your project document. Use one or more of the following prompts as the basis for your response.

1. **What do you agree with in one or more of your sources?** Briefly summarize the idea or argument with which you agree, and then explain why you agree.

2. **What do you disagree with in one or more of your sources?** Briefly summarize the idea or argument with which you disagree, and then explain why you disagree.

3. **What do you see as the most important idea emerging from your research so far?** Briefly summarize the idea, and then explain its importance.

4. **Why do you think one or more of the authors you've taken notes on so far approaches the issue as they have?** Briefly describe their approach, and then explain why they are taking it.

5. **What approach do you think should be taken on this issue?** Briefly describe the approach, and then explain its importance.

- **PLAN YOUR DOCUMENT**

    Planning notes include directions to yourself about how you might use a source in your project document, thoughts about how you might organize the document, or ideas you will want to remember later. You can use planning notes to keep track of how you want to use the information, ideas, and arguments you encounter. Consider jotting down notes — such as *How will this tie in? Use in introduction? Is this verified?* or *Are there alternative explanations or perspectives on this information?* — as you work with your sources.

How Can I Engage with My Sources?

When you read like a writer, you prepare yourself to become an active member of the conversation you've decided to join. You learn where the conversation has been — and where it is now. In short, reading like a writer helps you think critically about what you've read and prepares you to write your own document.

To engage more fully with the information, ideas, and arguments you encounter in your reading, go beyond simply knowing what others have written. By reading to understand, reading to respond, and reading to make connections, you can begin to find your voice.

Read to Understand

Reading to understand involves gaining an overview of the most important information, ideas, and arguments in a source. When writers read to understand, they often create summaries — brief descriptions of the main idea, reasons, and supporting evidence in a source. Depending on the complexity of the source, summaries can range from a brief statement about the argument found in a source to a detailed description of the key points and evidence it provides.

Many writers believe that a summary should be objective. It would be more precise to say that a summary should be accurate and fair. That is, you should not misrepresent the information, ideas, or arguments in a source. Achieving accuracy and fairness, however, does not necessarily mean that your summary will be an objective presentation of the source. Instead, your summary will reflect your purpose and role and — if you're writing for an audience — the purpose, needs, and interests of your readers. As a result, your summary is likely to differ from one written by another writer. Both summaries might be accurate and fair, but each one will reflect its writer's writing situation.

As you read to understand, highlight key points in the source, and note passages that include useful quotations or information you might use to add detail to your summary. If you are writing a summary for a class, it will typically take one of three forms: a main-point summary, a key-point summary, or an outline summary.

In doing research for her essay, Quinn Jackson found this article during her search for information about preparing teachers to teach writing. Published by *Teaching English in the Two-Year College*, an academic journal, the article focused on keeping the teaching of writing "fresh and new."

Living Composition

Nancy Sommers | A veteran writing teacher asks the question — What keeps teaching fresh and new? — and discovers, in the process of writing a teaching narrative, how her teaching voice and writing voice intertwine, both in the classroom and on the page.

It is 1965, career day at Woodrow Wilson Junior High. Girls assemble in the home economics room to learn about becoming nurses, homemakers, or teachers; boys assemble down the hallway in the woodworking room to learn about careers as doctors, lawyers, or engineers. My friends and I aren't surprised to be sitting in a room of stoves and sewing machines, where we've learned to bake biscuits and wind bobbins, cook Welsh rarebit and sew aprons. What surprises me now is that we never thought of storming the wood shop to demand a seat at the workbench. But feminism hadn't found its voice in our corner of Indiana; we were content then with the choices given.

At the end of career day, we are asked to choose one profession. Rather randomly, and without any particular passion for teachers or teaching, I announce that I will become a teacher, an idea that sticks in my head throughout college and graduate school, more as default than commitment. But teaching, especially teaching writing, wasn't an inevitable choice. In my family, reading was fine, in moderation, but too much reading could be dangerous. Various aunts who wore thick glasses or needed cataract surgery, for instance, were held up as object lessons from the *Merck Manual* of maladies, proof of the dangers of excessive reading under bed covers with a flashlight. And writing — even more fraught, warned my parents, nervous immigrants: if you write down what you believe, people will know your thoughts.

Despite all these warnings, I loved to read and write, studied American literature in college, and imagined teaching to be nothing more than bringing my love of Walt Whitman to my first classroom, eighth graders in Chicago. I imagined my students would love Whitman, too, if they could read poetry outdoors, luxuriating in the leaves of grass, marveling at the conjugation of the color green. I'm not sure whether my students learned to become better readers and writers that year, but I do know that I couldn't control them, either inside or outside the classroom. They laughed and hooted when I announced, meekly, at the start of class: "Let's be quiet now." They had no desire to be quiet or to celebrate leaves of grass, though they had plenty to say, their bodies electric, brimming with the rhythms of Chicago's South Side.

Looking back on the naïveté and youthful arrogance of that first year of teaching, I see that it's clear how much that year was a song of myself, more soliloquy than exchange of voices, more my performance than the students'. It would take a decade or more for me to understand that teaching requires both humility and leaps of faith, and most importantly, a willingness to listen to, and learn from, students.

Narratives often unfold in surprising ways and as improbable as it seems from that first unsuccessful performance, I became a teacher and have stayed a teacher for thirty-five years. After all these years, I have started to wonder what sustains a life of teaching writing over a long career. Semester after semester, how do I find those corners in myself that rhyme with my students — and subject matter — to keep it fresh and new? When mentoring new teachers, their passions palpable, enthusiasm unbridled, I ask them to reflect on what brought them to education and find myself asking, after all these years of teaching, what has kept me here?

It is easy to answer such questions with a simple — well, of course, the students! Teaching, as Theodore Roethke remarked, "is one of the few professions that permits love." And I love my students in all their particularity — the infinite variety of subjects they choose to write about, their compelling cultural backstories, present on every page, and their specific questions that unhinge long-held assumptions about writing. I can't imagine more intimate and more important work than helping students develop as thinkers and writers. After class, I walk around, absorbed, as if in a trance, their questions and stories lodged in my brain.

Teaching writing is like that, absorbing and exhausting, in equal measures, and occupationally strange; we spend more time with students' papers than with the students themselves — devoting nights and weekends to their words, careful not to leave traces of mustard or spill coffee on their pages, and puzzling, in their absence, about how to respond to their ambitious, sweeping introductions — "Since the dawn of humankind."

I do not believe that I would return to the classroom, year after year, with the same passion for students or for teaching writing if I hadn't joined my students on the page, not simply as the critic in the margins of their drafts, but as a fellow writer. When I began college teaching, I wouldn't have dared to consider myself a writer, let alone someone who would pen anything other than required graduate seminar papers and a dissertation. It was my students, though, who in their struggles to become college writers gave me a subject to write about: it started with revision, and a passionate curiosity to understand why students' revised drafts were often weaker than their initial attempts. What was going on, I wondered — why do some students prosper as college writers, while others lag, and what does revising have to do with these differences? In my students' struggle to revise and in my difficulties responding to their drafts, I found subjects I loved writing about.

If my students gave me permission to write about them, and teaching gave me a subject, then CCCC* gave me an audience. Most of my published essays were first delivered as talks in convention centers, or in Hyatt and Hilton hotels, where writing teachers mingle each year with other professional associations — Kiwanis and Elk, African violet growers and Bovine practitioners — also gathered for their national conventions. In my gathering, I found a generous audience of fellow teachers, a willing group of listeners who might, if I could make the research interesting, listen to my observations about students and their writing. What I learned from my fellow teachers is the power of an audience to shape ideas and be shaped by them.

My students often ask me, "How do you write?" as if I might, magically, pull back a swirling curtain and offer passage through writing's secret door. They want writing to become easier, more predictable, and seek a pass code to manage their unruly writing process. In answering, I like to defer to Saul Bellow, who when asked that question responded: "I wake up in the morning and check the alphabet to see if all the letters are still there. Then it is simply a matter of arrangement." And sometimes writing seems that simple, moving the letters around to see where they land, being surprised, like a child playing with primary-colored block letters, to find these twenty-six letters arranging into recognizable words. At other times it feels as though I'm working in the wrong mother tongue, with consonants that don't shape into words, an alphabet splayed on a page without form or meaning.

I don't know how I write, really, only that when I write, the world has a certain tilt — everything is more interesting and vivid; everything becomes relevant in a different way, as if I'm searching for clues on a great scavenger hunt, filtering life through an idea I'm trying to locate. Like teaching, writing has its own consuming trance. If, after three decades, I'm more surefooted about teaching writing and more passionate about it, I imagine it is because I teach not from a set of secret codes or passwords, but from my own work as a writer, waiting to be surprised by the alphabet's infinite possibilities; and from encouraging students to write as if they have an audience, a gathering, waiting to receive their words.

Perhaps my teaching narrative, when told retrospectively, seems inevitable, as narratives often do. But my narrative, more oscillating than sequential, has its threads of discontinuities and detours — of not being hired, six-months pregnant, because a department chair thought it unfair to students if I gave birth in the classroom; or of finding myself, in rural New Jersey, balancing motherhood with part-time teaching, a double life of diapering by day / teaching by night.

*CCCC: Conference on College Composition and Communications.

As my children grew up and I started writing, I led another kind of double life—teaching by day / writing by night or vice versa. The teacher in the classroom, dressed in a pin-stripe suit, exhorting her students not to split infinitives or dangle modifiers, sounded very different from the writer at home who composed sentences as she curried chicken, wiping cumin, cardamom, and cayenne off her fingers; or as she crafted essays to include all the living, breathing sources around her—found objects from home and work. The writer by night wanted to connect the dots, to figure out what she could make of these sources and her double life, teaching and writing, and to write as if everything were relevant.

It all sounds simple in retrospect, but writing is neither simple nor straightforward. I tell my students—writing is so uncomfortable and difficult at times, so always wear socks. And as I write, I wear my winter woolen socks, even in summer, to protect against the inevitable—an idea that seemed so interesting in its conception, but insubstantial in its execution; or a reviewer's big red question marks to say, "You were really seeking the wrong clues on that scavenger hunt of yours; try again." It takes many leaps of faith to write into, and not away from, the jumble of confused ideas in an early draft, and even more leaps to know how to do something different, better, in the next draft, hoping that on the other side, possibly, perhaps, a clearer vision will emerge.

Over the years as my teaching and writing narratives intertwined, I pulled up my socks and worked across drafts, seeking a voice that could push against the either/or categories of being personal *or* being academic. Voice is that elusive category we talk about with students—"find your voice," we urge, as if they left it somewhere, in a dresser drawer, perhaps, as if they could purchase it on Amazon. But there is no lost and found drawer for voice, no way to shop for it, or stumble upon it. It is something you have to write your way into, something that takes practice and play, attempt after attempt, as you arrange the alphabet into comfortable shapes and sounds, listening for your own idiosyncratic take on the world. I tell my students they can't park their voice at the college gates; they can't write as if they're wearing someone else's socks. I, too, had to learn that I couldn't write in the meek voice of a girl who winds bobbins, nor in the strident voice of a feminist who storms the woodworking shop. Part and parcel of who I am in the world is a teacher, and I want to write as I have come to teach: setting out on a quest, with leaps of faith and good humor, attempting, as essayists do, to figure something out, and always, always imagining an audience on the other end.

What sustains a career in teaching writing, year after year, to keep it fresh and new? Looking back, I see that what brought me to teaching—a desire to convert students into people who love to read poetry and conjugate the color green—is quite different from what has kept me in the classroom. What has kept me here is the passionate belief that teaching writing is, as it has always been "since the dawn of humankind," both a literary and civic calling: helping students write clear declarative sentences repairs the world. To write "Be Specific" in the margins of students' papers is to encourage a habit of mind—an attentiveness to details and particulars, to words and their meanings—a way of being thoughtful, both on the page and in life. And to comment on their drafts "Develop this" or "Analyze more" is to encourage students to add to the world through writing, to make new ideas possible, by contributing their idiosyncratic voices to the ongoing conversation of humankind.

What keeps me in the classroom, exhilarated each September to return after summer's interlude, is that teaching, by now, *is* practiced and comfortable, familiar and recognizable, and not at all fresh and new. Perhaps these terms "fresh and new" are more suited to a double life, where something new, something fresh is always needed. Yes, each semester brings the excitement of new students, but after decades of teaching, you come to welcome being practiced and surefooted, with an anecdote always at hand, building on what you've done before, with a keener sense of *how* to help students write with clarity and precision. And you welcome the comfortable feeling that you and your students, collectively, have a hunch that the writing class matters—that if you do your part, and they theirs, they'll become stronger writers. You believe it because you've seen it happen, abundantly so. You've sat with students, bewildered when their ideas wouldn't arrange, and gently asked: "Tell me what are you trying to say?" You've found ways to coax the saying, ways to turn students into writers, a class into an audience for each other's work. And you know if you didn't quite get it right one semester, you'll tweak and adjust, revise it the next; teaching, like writing, is always a work-in-progress. You welcome the chance for your teaching voice and your writing voice to merge, giving you a sense of belonging, both in the classroom and on the page.

Sometimes I like to imagine a gathering of all my former students, a reunion of sorts, nothing gauzy or sentimental, no need for streamers or balloons, toasts or fancy speeches. I just want to ask: What did you make of our time together? Where have you taken your writing as you moved through college and into the wider world?

Writing is too small a word to describe what happened in our class. And if *writing* is too small a word, *teaching writing* is too small a phrase for something I hope extends beyond the classroom walls. I hope that they've taken the lessons of our class—about argument and audience, voice and style—to enter public debates as thoughtful educated citizens. And I hope that they've found their own writing trances, their worlds tilting, absorbed and consumed by the pleasures of writing. Yet perhaps that's not what they took from our time together. What I know, though, is that our narratives are inevitably woven together—that during our time together, we've helped each other find something to say, and a reason to say it.

● MAIN-POINT SUMMARIES

A main-point summary reports the most important information, idea, or argument presented in a source. You can use main-point summaries to keep track of the overall claim made in a source, to introduce your readers to a source, and to place the main point of that source into the context of an argument or a discussion of a subject. Quinn might have written the following main-point summary of Nancy Sommers' article:

> In her article "Living Composition," Nancy Sommers reflects on how her work as a writer and as a teacher of writing have combined to keep classroom teaching "fresh and new" (33).

Main-point summaries are brief. They identify the source and its main point.

● KEY-POINT SUMMARIES

Like a main-point summary, a key-point summary reports the most important information, idea, or argument presented in a source. However, it also includes the reasons (key points) and evidence the author uses to support their main point. Key-point summaries are useful when you want to keep track of a complex argument or understand an elaborate process.

> In her article "Living Composition," Nancy Sommers reflects on how her work as a writer and as a teacher of writing have combined to keep classroom teaching "fresh and new." Recounting how her varied experiences as a teacher, mother, and writer have shaped her understanding of writing, she notes the shift in her perspective over the many years since she was a novice teacher. "I see that it's clear how much that year was a song of myself, more soliloquy than exchange of voices, more my performance than the students'," she writes. "It would take a decade or more for me to understand that teaching requires both humility and leaps of faith, and most importantly, a willingness to listen to, and learn from, students" (33). Looking back on her students, she notes her hope that they've left her classrooms to become active writers, participating in public and professional discourse as well as in the kind of personal writing that she has enjoyed. No matter what her students have done, however, she points out that "our narratives are inevitably woven together — that during our time together, we've helped each other find something to say, and a reason to say it" (36).

The author, source, and main point are identified.

Quotations from the article are provided.

Key lessons learned over a lifetime of teaching are identified.

● OUTLINE SUMMARIES

Sometimes called a plot summary, an outline summary reports the information, ideas, and arguments in a source in the same order used in the source. In a sense, an outline summary presents the overall "plot" of the source by reporting what was written in the order in which it was written. Outline summaries are useful when you need to keep track of the sequence of information, ideas, and arguments in a source.

> In her article "Living Composition," Nancy Sommers reflects on how her work as a writer and as a teacher of writing have combined to keep classroom teaching "fresh and new." Recalling her early life as a writer and reader, she points out that despite growing up in a family where reading was considered "fine, in moderation, but too much reading could be dangerous" (32), she would go on to study literature in college and eventually find herself teaching writing to eighth graders in Chicago. Noting her "naïveté and youthful arrogance" (33), she points out that in retrospect her first year of teaching "was a song of myself, more soliloquy than exchange of voices, more my performance than the students'" (33).
>
> Over the years, Sommers would grow as a teacher and writer, balancing writing, the teaching of writing, and family life. Along the way, she encountered the — at the time — normal challenges facing women pursuing a career, including not being hired for a teaching position because she was pregnant and dividing time between caring for her family, teaching her students, and pursuing her work as a writer and writing scholar. Yet Sommers also notes that it was through writing and the teaching of writing that she found a professional community, the Conference on College Composition and Communication, where she could share her ideas and benefit from a larger audience of writing scholars.
>
> Sommers shares the hopes she has for her students — that they have all become active writers, participating in public and professional discourse as well as in the kind of personal writing that she has enjoyed. She concludes, however, that no matter what her students have done as writers, "our narratives are inevitably woven together — that during our time together, we've helped each other find something to say, and a reason to say it" (36).

Annotations:
- The author, source, and main point are identified.
- The summary identifies each of the major points made in the article in the order in which they were made.
- The author's name is mentioned whenever information from the source is used.
- Phrases such as "shares" and "She concludes" provide a sense of movement through the source.

Read to Respond

Reading to respond allows you to begin forming your own contribution to a conversation. Your response will help you focus your reactions to the information, ideas, and arguments you've encountered in a source. To prepare to write a response to a source, note passages with which you agree or disagree, reflect on interesting information and ideas, and record your thoughts about the effectiveness of the argument advanced in the source.

- **AGREE/DISAGREE RESPONSES**

    If you want to explore an idea or argument in a source, try freewriting about why you agree or disagree with it. In your response, clearly define the idea or argument to which you are responding. Then explain whether you agree or disagree with the idea or argument — or whether you find yourself in partial agreement with it — and why.

- **REFLECTIVE RESPONSES**

    A reflective response allows you to consider the meaning or implications of what you read. You might focus on a key passage or idea from a source, explaining or elaborating on it. Or you might reflect on your own experiences, attitudes, or observations in relation to a piece of information, an idea, or an argument. You can also use a reflective response to consider how an idea or argument might be interpreted by other readers, how it might be applied in a new context, or how it might be misunderstood.

- **ANALYTIC RESPONSES**

    An analytic response focuses on the important elements of a source, such as its purpose, ideas, argument, organization, focus, evidence, and style. For example, you might ask whether the main point is stated clearly, or whether appropriate types of evidence are used to support an argument. You might also analyze the logic of an argument or map its organization. Or you might offer suggestions about how an author could have made the source more effective.

Even when writers choose a particular type of response, they often draw on the other types to flesh out their ideas. For example, you might consider why you

Your Turn: Summarize a Source

Using the following guidelines, write an outline summary of the article "Guiding the Budding Writer" earlier in this chapter:

1. **Identify the author and title of the source.**
2. **Convey the main point and key points made by the writer.** Present the main point and key points in the order in which they appear in the source. For each point, briefly describe the evidence provided to back it up.
3. **Clearly credit the author for any information, ideas, and arguments you include in your summary.** Use quotation marks for direct quotations, and identify the page or paragraph from which you've drawn a paraphrase or quotation. (See Chapter 21 for guidelines on integrating information from sources into your draft.)

disagree with an argument by analyzing how effectively the source presents the argument. Or you might shift from agreeing with an idea to reflecting on its implications.

Read to Make Connections

You can learn a lot by looking for similarities and differences among the sources you read. Do sources make use of the same information or evidence? Is the information or evidence across the sources consistent or is it contradictory? Do groups of authors view the subject or issue in distinctly different ways? Are the similarities among the positions (see *Understand the Writer's Argument* earlier in this chapter) taken by authors in a group distinctive enough to constitute a general approach — a shared perspective — on the subject or issue? Making connections like these can help you build your own argument or identify information that will allow you (and your readers) to better understand a conversation.

As you read more and more about a subject, you'll gain a better understanding of the status of the conversation. For example, knowing that people involved in your conversation agree on the overall definition of a problem might lead you to focus your efforts on either challenging that definition or suggesting a possible solution. If you find yourself agreeing with one group of authors, you might start to think of yourself as a member of that group — as someone who shares their approach to the

Your Turn: Respond to a Source

Putting your response into words can help you sort out your reactions to the ideas, information, and arguments in a source. Use the following guidelines to write an informal response to Peter Johnston's article "Guiding the Budding Writer" or Nancy Sommers' article "Living Composition" both of which can be found earlier in this chapter.

1. **Identify a focus for your response.** You might select important information, an intriguing idea, or the author's overall argument.
2. **Decide what type of response you are going to write.** Will you use agree/disagree, reflective, analytical, or some combination of the three types?
3. **Write an introduction that identifies the information, idea, argument, or source** to which you are responding, lays out your overall response (your main point), and identifies the source's author and title.
4. **Provide reasons to support your main point and evidence to support your reasons.**
5. **Clearly credit the sources of any information, ideas, or arguments you use to support your response.** Use quotation marks for direct quotations, and identify the page or paragraph from which you've drawn a paraphrase or quotation. (See Chapter 21 for guidelines on documenting sources.)

subject or issue. If you don't agree with any of the groups you've identified, perhaps you are ready to develop a new approach to the subject or issue.

To explore potential connections among authors, jot down notes in the margins of your sources or in your writer's notebook. Each time you read a new source, think about what you've already read, and make note of similarities and differences among your sources. Ask whether the source you've just read aligns with an approach you've already identified or whether it might represent a new approach.

Beyond a collection of notes and annotations, reading to make connections might also result in longer pieces of freewriting (see *Freewrite* in Chapter 2). In some cases, you might create a literature review — a brief essay that defines and considers existing approaches to an issue.

● LITERATURE REVIEWS

A review of literature presents an overview of the key information, ideas, and arguments that are being discussed by other writers who are addressing your issue or topic. An effective review of literature goes beyond the simple list of sources that are typically found in a working bibliography (see *How Can I Create a Bibliography?*

Working Together: Make Connections among Sources

Work together with a group of classmates to identify general approaches to the subject of how writing is taught. To prepare for the group activity, each member should read, mark, and annotate the articles and website in this chapter. During class, you should carry out the following activities:

1. Members of the group should take turns reporting what they've learned about one of the sources.

2. As each report is made, the other members of the group should take notes on the key ideas highlighted by the reporter.

3. When the reports have been completed, the group should create an overall list of the key ideas discussed in the individual reports.

4. Identify sources that seem to share similar approaches to the issue. Give each group of sources a name, and provide a brief description of the ideas its authors have in common.

5. Describe each group of sources in detail. Explain what makes the authors part of the same group (their similarities) and how each group differs from the others you've defined.

Once you've completed the activity, consider how you would respond to each group of authors. Ask whether you agree or disagree with their approaches, and describe the extent to which you agree or disagree. Consider whether you would want to join a group, whether you would want to refine a particular approach to better fit your understanding of the subject, or whether you would rather develop a new approach.

in Chapter 16) by offering a discussion of important approaches to your issue. That is, a review of literature focuses not so much on individual documents as on groups of documents and the ideas shared by their authors. For example, you might find that the work you've read about the use of social media in writing instruction addresses three general approaches: (1) supporting interaction among members of a given writing class, (2) allowing instructors to share course materials with students, and (3) helping instructors and students share feedback on writing projects. You can see an example of how approaches are defined in the discussion of different approaches to writing instruction in the section *Writing Situations Are an Important Area of Scholarly Inquiry* in Chapter 1.

Focusing on approaches to an issue, as opposed to the positions adopted by individual authors (see *Understand the Writer's Argument* earlier in this chapter), can help you understand the major ideas that are being considered in the conversation you are planning to join. By understanding existing approaches to an issue, you can determine whether you agree with any of those approaches or whether you want to introduce a completely new approach. In turn, this will help you develop your own position on the issue.

Reviews of literature, such as the example that follows, can be written not only as an intermediate genre intended primarily for your own use but also for other readers. Some academic journals publish reviews of literature on a regular basis, providing their readers with overviews of and commentary on new work in a given area, such as teaching with technology or new work in teaching English as a second language.

> Ask any high school language-arts teacher what they find most challenging and you're more likely than not to hear something about writing. They'll tell you they wish they had learned more about how to teach and respond to student writers during college. They'll point to the difficulty of responding thoughtfully and substantively to writing assignments from as many as 150 students at a time. They'll explain that they spend more time on writing than on any other part of their teaching lives. — The writer frames the issue as a problem for teachers.
>
> What is the thoughtful faculty member in a school of education or an English education program to do? That's not clear. While there is no lack of agreement that preparation in writing instruction is critical for any language-arts teacher, there's little consensus on how best to prepare future teachers to handle the challenges of assigning and responding to student writing. Suggested directions include methods courses that focus exclusively on writing instruction, attention to writing

— The writer suggests that it's not clear how best to solve the problem.

— The writer lists four possible approaches to solving the problem.

> instruction in courses across the education curriculum, ensuring that future writing teachers are themselves strong writers, and in-service (on-the-job) training that focuses on the rhetorical and writing process issues teachers face as they work with their students.
>
> The argument that future language-arts teachers should be required to take methods courses in writing instruction is far from new. Christine Tulley, in her extensive review of the issue, notes that Emma J. Breck called for the establishment of a methods course in writing in 1923 and observes that calls for this kind of course have been made regularly since the 1960s (see for example Grommon, Larson, Martin and Dismuke, Myers et al., Neville and Papillion, and Rider and Rusk). Yet far less progress has been made in this area than scholars such as Tulley desire. "Historically, composition was seldom considered a worthy area of study in its own right as literature often remained the focus in writing courses," writes Tulley, who notes that this "contributes to a cycle where literary study was more valued among English students and faculty" (26). . . .

Annotations:
- The first approach is defined and addressed from a historical perspective.
- The writer identifies a scholar who has written extensively about the approach.
- The author lists several other scholars. Following MLA style, she lists author names in parentheses.
- Quotations are used to illustrate key aspects of the approach.
- Following MLA style, a page number is provided to help readers locate the quotation.

Your Turn: Write a Review of Literature

Complete a literature review for your project. To prepare for the review, read your sources carefully and identify two to four approaches to your issue. Provide an overview of each approach, and then discuss some of the most important or representative sources. Use quotations, paraphrases, and summaries (see *How Can I Take Notes?* earlier in this chapter) to share information from the sources with your readers. Use in-text citation and a works cited or references list (see Chapter 25 and Chapter 26) to identify your sources.

As you develop your review of literature, do the following:

1. **Introduce the issue.** Explain its importance and indicate where disagreement exists among the authors who are discussing the issue.
2. **Identify and define approaches to the issue.** Use descriptive names, such as the three types of rhetoricians discussed in *Writing Processes Are Studied Intensely* in Chapter 1. Describe what authors who take the approach agree on. Drawing on evidence from your sources, describe how each approach differs from the other approaches you've defined.
3. **Identify authors whom you think are representative of positions taken** within each approach or are noteworthy for the clarity or novelty of their ideas. If appropriate, briefly discuss disagreements among authors who take the same approach. Draw on evidence from your sources.
4. **Offer an overall assessment of the state of the conversation about your issue.** Indicate which approach you align yourself with. If you don't agree with one of the approaches you've identified, explain why and offer a new approach that reflects your take on the issue.

In contrast to the dedicated writing methods course, a number of scholars have argued for broad integration of attention to writing instruction across the courses future teachers take during college, with a particular focus on linking methods of writing instruction to methods of reading instruction. David Griffith and Amber Northern argue in a recent report from the Thomas B. Fordham Institute that "teachers would do well to think of reading and writing as complementary activities, rather than as separate subjects" (9). Similarly, but with an emphasis on linking literacy instruction with instruction in other content areas, such as the sciences, Roni Jo Draper and her colleagues argue that we should modify teacher preparation curricula to prepare them to support the learning of both content and discipline-specific literacies. Other scholars, including . . . .

The second approach is introduced using a transitional phrase.

A brief summary of the approach is provided.

A quotation helps define the approach.

A position within the approach is illustrated.

While there is debate about how best to develop methods courses, there is wide consensus that language-arts teachers should themselves be writers. Writing in 1985 for the National Writing Project's journal, *The Quarterly*, Tim Gillespie observes, "Writing makes us experts on teaching writing" (par. 13). Gillespie is far from alone, and he's far from the first to make this argument.

A third approach is introduced.

In Summary: Reading to Write

★ Read with a purpose (p. 49).

★ Read actively (p. 51).

★ Summarize useful ideas, information, and arguments (p. 66).

★ Respond to what you read (p. 77).

★ Explore connections among sources (p. 79).

04 Assessing and Evaluating Sources

What should I consider as I begin to assess sources? 85

Consider the function and biases of your sources 85
Consider the lure of new and exciting information 86
Avoid information bubbles 86

What strategies should I use to evaluate a source? 87

Explore connections to your conversation 87

Read laterally to assess a source's credibility 87
Read closely to evaluate the source 89
Ask what you can learn from the source 93

Should I evaluate all types of sources in the same way? 93

Evaluate the relevance and credibility of digital sources 93
Evaluate the relevance and accuracy of field sources 96

We live in a time when news reports and opinion pieces that criticize or refute someone's understanding of an issue can be dismissed as "fake news." We regularly see news that truly is fake distributed widely via social media — often by people who are unaware that it's not based in fact and sometimes by people who make up information or promote conspiracy theories simply to upset and build walls between people. We often find it difficult to tell hoaxes from hard news. And we know that many people get their news only from sources that reflect their political and cultural views.

As a writer, one of the biggest challenges you'll face is finding your way through the maze of real news, fake news, and deliberate deception.

What Should I Consider as I Begin to Assess Sources?

It can be difficult at times to determine whether the news and opinion pieces we encounter online and in print are based on accurate information, inaccurate information (misinformation), or inaccurate information that is shared deliberately to influence opinions and beliefs (disinformation). For instance, it can sometimes be difficult to tell whether a scholarly journal is well respected or considered to be "predatory" — that is, a journal that exists solely to make a profit from those who are willing to pay to have their articles published.

As you begin assessing sources, consider their function and the likely biases of their authors and publishers. Be wary of the excitement that often accompanies the discovery of new and intriguing information. And ask yourself whether you are considering a wide enough array of sources to gain a comprehensive understanding of the issue.

Consider the Function and Biases of Your Sources

Depending on your purpose and role, you might find yourself working with sources that serve quite different purposes. If you are exploring the impact of new government rules on safeguarding endangered species, for example, you might find yourself reading news reports, opinion columns, scholarly journal articles, and reports found on informative websites, to name only a few. As you read or view a source, consider its function. Are you reading an article that purports to be objective? Are you viewing a video in which pundits share their opinions on the issue?

Consider as well the biases of the authors and publishers associated with a source. *Bias* refers to our tendency to view something from a particular perspective. The biases of authors are shaped in large part by their interests, experiences, values, and beliefs, while the biases of publishers have more complex sources, including the mission of the publication, the biases of its owners and employees, and the perspectives of the authors it publishes. If you are working with sources from a news organization — such as CNN, Fox News, MSNBC, or National Public Radio — reflect on what you know about the organization and its staff. If you are unfamiliar with it, search for reviews or commentary about it. While many news organizations claim to be fact-based, fair, and balanced — or some variant of that theme — their coverage of major events and issues can vary significantly. Understanding tendencies among the news organization you use — and by extension, the newspapers, magazines, journals, websites, and social media that provide access to your sources — can help you avoid uncritical acceptance of how issues are framed, how facts are presented (or not), and how differing perspectives are considered (or not).

Comparatively, it might seem much less complicated to understand the bias of a major media organization, a newspaper, or a magazine than it is to determine the bias of a website, podcast, blog, tweet, or social media post. In the past few years, social media platforms such as Facebook and Twitter have been criticized repeatedly for their responses to sources of demonstrably inaccurate and misleading news. It has proven extremely challenging to balance the diverse needs, interests, values, and beliefs of hundreds of millions of social media users (billions, in the case of Facebook) with the need to reduce the spread of misinformation and disinformation, particularly in light of arguments about free speech and freedom of expression.

Consider the Lure of New and Exciting Information

It's normal to be enthusiastic about new and intriguing ideas and information, but you would be wise to exercise caution. Some of the most widely circulated fake news over the past few years has been spread by people who were intrigued by something that seemed extraordinary. In 2018, Soroush Vosoughi, Deb Roy, and Sinan Aral reported in an article in the journal *Science* that, of 126,000 rumors circulated on Twitter over more than a decade, false information spread far more widely and quickly than factual information — especially if the fake news aroused a strong emotional response in the reader. Between a thousand and a hundred thousand people saw tweets and retweets about rumors — up to a hundred times more people than those who saw tweets about fact-based stories. Simply put, people are attracted to interesting and intriguing ideas, especially when those ideas are consistent with their expectations and experiences or when they resonate emotionally.

Avoid Information Bubbles

Getting trapped in an information bubble — sometimes referred to as a *filter bubble* or an *echo chamber* — is a common problem. We enter information bubbles when we turn only to information sources that are consistent with our values, beliefs, and experiences. For example, Americans who are politically conservative appear to be more likely to view Fox News than MSNBC, a news source that is widely viewed as politically progressive (the reverse is also true). Similarly, people appear to be more likely to associate themselves with social media users and groups who share their perspectives and beliefs. As a result, the news they obtain from social media tends to be consistent with their worldviews.

It's pretty natural, then, to find yourself living in an information bubble. Fortunately, there is hope. You can pop an information bubble by using the following strategies:

- **Develop a healthy skepticism about all news, especially news distributed via social media.** Given the tendency for rumors and fake news to influence the feeds on social media, put your skepticism into high gear every time you view a tweet or social media post, every time you view a politically oriented video on the web, and every time you see yet another interesting item on a news show or in your email inbox.

- **Seek alternative perspectives.** It's reasonable to double- and triple-check your facts. It might seem less vital to double-check an opinion. Yet the commentary you hear on a regular basis might lead you to understand an issue in a particular way. That is, repeated appeals to the same set of values and beliefs can frame your understanding in ways that might seem so reasonable that alternative viewpoints will seem uninformed. Avoid getting into a rut with your viewing and reading habits. While it might be reassuring to find that you agree with much of what you hear on your preferred news sources, it can also decrease your willingness to consider other perspectives. As you work to develop a document that will appeal to readers who might not share your values and beliefs, consider the benefits of taking a broader view of the issue.
- **Consume news differently.** Change your viewing and reading habits. In the same way that you might strive to eat a balanced diet, balance your intake of information and ideas. It might be uncomfortable to spend time viewing news from sources that espouse values different from your own, but it's likely to help you write more effective documents.

What Strategies Should I Use to Evaluate a Source?

Writers quickly learn that evaluating a source involves more than looking at the source itself. Experienced writers also consider how the source fits into the wider conversation about their issue, how it is viewed by the writers of other sources, and how effectively it conveys information, ideas, and arguments. Experienced writers also consider how what they learn from their sources might affect their own position on an issue.

Explore Connections to Your Conversation

The first strategy you should use as you evaluate a source is to ask whether the source is related to your conversation. If it isn't, set it aside. If it is, ask whether it will help you to learn anything new about the issue, whether it provides a good example of a particular approach to the issue, or whether it is frequently referred to by the authors of other sources. If it doesn't do one or more of these three things, move on to other sources.

Read Laterally to Assess a Source's Credibility

You might be familiar with the term *lateral thinking*, a process in which you consider a subject from a variety of perspectives. *Lateral reading*, a concept developed by researchers Sam Wineburg and Sarah McGrew to describe the behavior of experienced fact checkers, asks you to approach reading in a similar way. Rather than focusing solely on what the source says, how it says it, and who produced it, you look at how the information, ideas, and arguments in the source fit within the many sources addressing an issue.

The *lateral* part of the phrase *reading laterally* also reflects how you might physically work within a web browser to determine how a source fits into a conversation. If you are viewing your source in a browser tab, you might open information about the site you are viewing in a new browser tab. You might follow links from the source to other sources, opening each source in a new tab. You might conduct a web search for related sources, again opening each source in a new tab. If the source offers information that surprises you or is inconsistent with what you've already learned about the issue, turn to fact-checking websites such as Snopes.com, FactCheck.org, and PolitiFact.

The following figure shows how Quinn Jackson used lateral reading to assess a source about teacher comments on student drafts. She opened links about the publisher

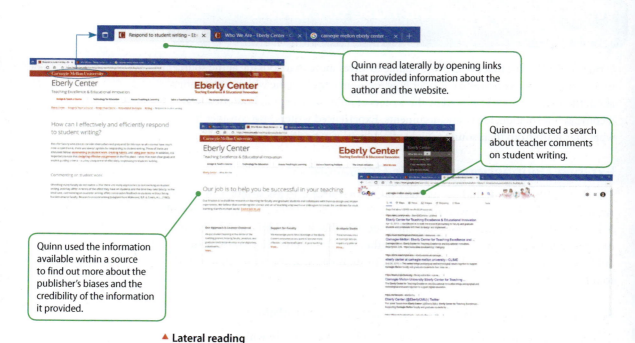

▲ Lateral reading

of the site she was viewing (in this case, the Eberly Center at Carnegie Mellon University). She also searched for information about the center. Based on her reading, Quinn concluded that the source was worth considering further.

In most cases, reading laterally should take only a few minutes. You should spend only enough time on each link you open and each search you conduct to gain a general sense of the source. If you decide that the source is worth considering further, return to the source, and carry out a closer examination of its information, ideas, and arguments.

> **Checklist for Reading Laterally**
>
> ✔ **Look for information about the author.** If a link is not provided, conduct a web search (see Chapter 14).
>
> ✔ **Look for information about the publisher.** Most websites provide links in their headers, footers, or menus. Periodicals typically provide information in a masthead near the beginning of an issue.
>
> ✔ **Search for reactions to the source.** If you cannot find any, search for reactions to other sources by the author.
>
> ✔ **Search for information about the subject.** Assess the accuracy of the conclusions provided in the source. Consider using fact-checking websites such as Snopes.com, FactCheck.org, and PolitiFact.

Read Closely to Evaluate the Source

If a source seems promising, read it more closely. Close reading involves examining the information, ideas, and arguments in a source carefully. It involves thinking critically about the content of the source and how it might connect with the other sources you've read. And it involves reflecting on how the source might contribute to your project document.

As you read a source closely, consider its relevance, evidence, author, publisher, timeliness, comprehensiveness, and genre.

● **EVALUATE RELEVANCE**

Relevance is the extent to which a source provides information you can use in your research writing project. Remember your purpose when you evaluate potential sources. Even if a source provides a great deal of information, it might not meet your needs. For example, a review of the latest iPhone might contain a great deal of accurate and up-to-date information — but it won't be of much use if you're writing about the use of tablets in college classrooms.

● EVALUATE EVIDENCE

Evidence is information offered to support a point. Statistics, facts, expert opinions, and firsthand accounts are among the many types of evidence you'll find. As a writer, you can evaluate not only the kinds of evidence in a source but also the quality, amount, and appropriateness of that evidence. Ask yourself the following questions about each source.

- **Is enough evidence offered?** A lack of evidence might indicate fundamental flaws in the author's argument.
- **Is the right kind of evidence offered?** More evidence isn't always better evidence. Ask whether the evidence is appropriate for the reasons offered and whether more than one type of evidence is used.
- **Is the evidence used fairly?** Look for reasonable alternative interpretations, questionable or inappropriate use of evidence, and evidence that seems to contradict points made elsewhere in a source. If the source uses statistics, are they interpreted fairly and presented clearly? If a quotation is offered to support a point, is the quotation used appropriately or out of context?
- **Are sources identified?** Knowing the origins of evidence can make a significant difference in your evaluation of a source. For example, if a writer quotes a political poll but doesn't say which organization conducted the poll, you might reasonably question the reliability of the source.

Your lateral reading of the source will provide you with some sense of the overall accuracy of the evidence provided in the source. Use your close reading to think more deeply about how the author presents and uses evidence in the source.

● EVALUATE THE AUTHOR

The significance of *authorship* is affected by context. Take, for example, two editorials that make similar arguments and offer similar evidence. Both are published in your local newspaper. One is written by a fourteen-year-old middle school student, and the other by a U.S. senator. You would certainly favor the senator's editorial if the subject was U.S. foreign policy. If the subject was student perceptions about drug abuse prevention in schools, however, you might value the middle school student's opinion more highly.

You can use the results of your lateral reading to gain insights into the author's expertise about an issue, their experience with the issue, and their biases.

● **EVALUATE THE PUBLISHER**

Publishers are the groups that produce and provide access to sources, including books, newspapers, journals, websites, sound and video files, and databases. Like authors, publishers have biases. Unlike authors, they often advertise them. You might already be familiar with some publishers. If not, your lateral reading will have provided you with some insights into the publisher's purpose and bias. Use your close reading to determine whether the publisher's biases seem to play too great a role in the information, ideas, and arguments presented in the source.

● **EVALUATE TIMELINESS**

The importance of *timeliness* — a source's publication date — varies according to your writing situation. If your research project would benefit from sources that have recently been published, then evaluate recent sources more favorably than dated ones. If you're writing an article on the use of superconducting materials in new mass transportation projects, you probably won't want to spend a lot of time with articles published in 1968. On the other hand, if you're writing about the 1968 presidential contest between Hubert Humphrey and Richard Nixon, sources published during that time period will take on greater importance.

Print sources usually list a publication date. It can be more difficult, however, to tell when web sources were created. When in doubt, back up undated information found on the web with a dated source.

● **EVALUATE COMPREHENSIVENESS**

Comprehensiveness is the extent to which a source provides a complete and balanced view of a topic. Like timeliness, the importance of comprehensiveness varies according to the demands of your writing situation. If you are working on a narrowly focused project, such as the role played by shifts in Pacific Ocean currents on snowfall patterns in Colorado in the winter of 2022, you might not find this evaluation criterion as useful as the others. However, if you are considering a broader issue (such as the potential effects of global climate change on agricultural production in North America) or if you are still learning as much as you can about your issue, give preference to sources that provide more complete treatment.

● **EVALUATE GENRE**

Understanding the typical characteristics of a *genre* can help you identify the roles authors take on as they develop their contributions to a written

General Genre Characteristics

	Scholarly Publications	Trade and Professional Publications	Popular Publications
Purposes	Report original research, review original research, or analyze trends in recent research	Focus on new developments within a field but are not usually as technically challenging as scholarly publications	Report or comment on events, individuals, groups, or activities
Writers	Have significant expertise in a given field	Usually have expertise on an issue but can be freelancers hired by a company or professional organization	Know a great deal about a subject but more accurately are characterized as generalists
Readers	Possess specialized knowledge about the subject	Are members of a profession interested in developments in the field	General audience; most articles are written at a reading level appropriate for an eighth- to tenth-grade education
Sources	Extensive in-text citations and works cited lists or bibliographies	Sources cited less thoroughly than in scholarly publications	Seldom include citations, although newspapers, magazines, and blogs often identify sources in general terms or by using hyperlinks
Reviews	Almost always reviewed by other experts in the same field	Sometimes peer-reviewed but usually reviewed only by the editorial staff	Not peer-reviewed and not always carefully reviewed by the editorial staff
Genres	Journal articles, books, conference papers	Journal articles, newsletter articles, blogs, websites	Newspaper and magazine articles, blogs, websites, wikis, videos

conversation. This is true not only for individual genres (such as articles and blogs) but also for more general categories (such as scholarly publications, trade and professional publications, and popular publications). Sources in these general categories are typically written for distinctly different purposes, are directed toward readers who have strikingly diverse levels of expertise on a subject, and undergo widely varying levels of review by experts on a subject. As you evaluate your sources, consider the characteristics of these three types of publications.

Ask What You Can Learn from the Source

If the work you've done so far to assess and evaluate a source gives you confidence that it can play a role in your project document, ask one additional question: does what you've learned from the source suggest that you might want to change your position on the issue? Keep an open mind. Writers often find themselves rethinking their understanding of an issue as they encounter new insights and perspectives in the sources they read.

This kind of approach to sources is similar to the notion of *rhetorical listening* that was put forward by twentieth-century rhetorician Wayne Booth and that scholars such as Sonja Foss, Cheryl Glenn, and Krista Ratcliffe have explored more recently. Being open to new ideas should be a central part of your approach to assessing and evaluating sources. It can make a critical difference in your success as a research writer.

Should I Evaluate All Types of Sources in the Same Way?

Most types of sources can be assessed and evaluated using the strategies discussed in the previous section. Some digital and field sources, however, pose additional challenges or may benefit from additional attention.

Evaluate the Relevance and Credibility of Digital Sources

TECH TIP: Because anyone can create a polished website, contribute to a wiki, start a blog, post a message to social media, or upload a podcast or a video that looks like it was produced by a professional, approach these sources with more caution than you would reserve for print sources such as books and journal articles, which typically are published only after a lengthy editorial review process.

Websites and blogs. To assess the relevance and credibility of a website or a blog, examine its domain (.edu, .com, and so on), and look for information about the site (often available through an About page).

Social media, email lists, discussion forums, podcasts, and videos. To assess the relevance and credibility of a message or upload on one of these online venues, try to learn something about the author:

- On social media sites and apps, you can usually link back to an author's personal pages.
- In email lists and discussion forums, check for a "signature" at the end of the message, and try to locate a Frequently Asked Questions (FAQ) list.
- In comments lists following articles and blogs, look for signed comments that reveal more information about the author's expertise or bias.
- For podcasts and videos, search for information about the author or sponsor of the media items. Look at lists of related media that might be provided to gain insights into biases about the issue.

Wikis. Wikis are websites that can be added to or edited by visitors to the site. Wikis such as Wikipedia (en.wikipedia.org) have grown in importance on the web, and many Wikipedia pages are highly ranked by web search sites. Wikis can be good resources as you start a writing project because they help you gain an initial understanding of an issue. In some cases, people who are experts on an issue contribute to wikis and provide information and analyses. Wikis also may link to other resources that can help you learn about the issue. Unfortunately, it can be difficult to evaluate the credibility of wiki pages because their creators and editors are often not known and because changes to wiki pages can occur quickly. Some entries are edited so frequently that they become the subject of "edit wars," in which edits to a page are undone almost instantly by those who disagree with the edits. In some cases, the entry you found yesterday might bear little or no resemblance to the entry available today.

With this in mind, it is best to use wikis when you are beginning to learn about an issue. Avoid citing them as the "last word" on a topic because those words might change before you submit your final draft.

Should I Evaluate All Types of Sources in the Same Way? | CHAPTER 04

Check its domain (.com, .edu, .gov, and so on) to learn about its purpose and publisher:

.biz, .com, .coop	business	.name	personal
.edu	higher education	.net	network organization
.gov	government	.org	nonprofit organization
.mil	military	.pro	professional

Check the title bar, page header, and page titles to learn about the site's purpose, publisher, and relevance.

Search for information — on the site or through a separate web search — about the author or publisher, if identified.

Read the body text, and review illustrations to evaluate relevance, evidence, and comprehensiveness.

Check timeliness by looking for a publication or "last modified" date.

Check page footers for information about the publisher and author. Look for About This Site or Contact links (not shown).

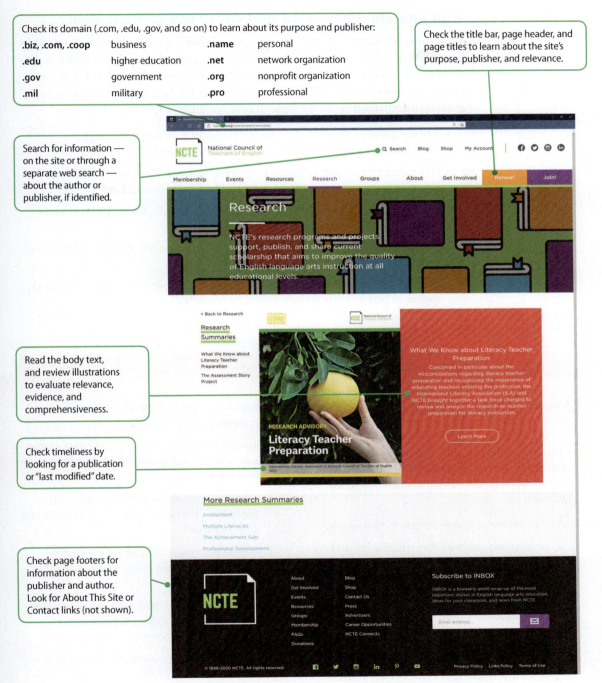

▲ Evaluating a website

Evaluate the Relevance and Accuracy of Field Sources

With some adjustment, most of the evaluation criteria discussed in this chapter can be applied to field sources such as interviews, correspondence, observations, and surveys (see Chapter 15). The relevance and the accuracy of the information you collect, however, deserve additional attention. Ask the following questions as you evaluate information collected through field research:

- Are the questions you asked in an interview, in a survey, or through correspondence still relevant to your research project?
- Is the information you collected in an observation still relevant? Are your observation notes as complete as you had hoped they would be?
- Are the individuals you interviewed or corresponded with as qualified and knowledgeable as you expected?
- Were questions in interviews, surveys, and correspondence answered fully and honestly?
- Did survey respondents have adequate time to complete the survey? Did they appear to believe their privacy would be respected?

Your Turn: Conduct a Source Evaluation

A source evaluation applies the evaluation criteria you've read about in this chapter to a single source. You should consider each criterion in light of your writing situation and then determine the suitability of the source for your research writing project. To carry out a source evaluation, respond to the following prompts:

1. Provide the complete citation for the source.
2. In what ways are the information, ideas, and arguments in the source relevant to your research writing project?
3. Is the line of argument in the source sound and well supported? In what ways can you use it in your project?
4. What have you learned about the author and publisher that would lead you to accept, question, or reject the line of argument presented in the source?
5. In what ways does the publication date of the source affect your judgment of its usefulness for your project?
6. In what ways does the comprehensiveness of the source affect your judgment of its usefulness for your project?
7. In what ways does the genre of the source affect your judgment of its usefulness for your project?
8. In what ways could this source help you achieve your purpose and address the needs and interests of your readers?
9. How are you likely to use this source in your project?

As you assess and evaluate sources, keep in mind the strategies discussed in this section. Cultivate a sense of skepticism about everything you read, no matter how much you agree with its sentiments and perspective. Apply evaluative criteria with a critical attitude. Verify, and then trust. Verify more than once. And as you plan, draft, and revise your document, keep alternative perspectives in mind. You should be skeptical even of your own attitudes and beliefs.

In Summary: Assessing and Evaluating Sources

★ **Decide whether sources are appropriate and credible (p. 85).**
- Consider the function and biases of your sources.
- Consider the lure of new and exciting information.
- Avoid information bubbles.

★ **Evaluate sources (p. 87).**
- Explore connections to your conversation.
- Read laterally to assess a source's credibility.
- Read closely to evaluate each source.
- Ask what you can learn from the source.

★ **Consider the genre and medium of the source (p. 93).**
- Evaluate the relevance and credibility of digital sources.
- Evaluate the relevance and accuracy of field sources.

05 Working Together

How can collaborative activities improve my writing? 99

Work together to generate ideas 99

Work together to collect and work with information 102

Work together to refine your argument 102

How can I work with other writers on a group project? 104

Understand the purposes of working in a group 105

Understand potential problems and develop solutions 106

Establish ground rules 107

Create a plan 108

How can I use peer review to improve my writing? 108

Use peer review to enhance your writing process 109

Use peer review to improve your document 109

How can I conduct an effective peer review? 110

Consider context 110

Consider technology 110

Consider your needs as a writer 111

Consider your role as a reviewer 112

What resources can I draw on as I review and collaborate? 116

Use technological tools 116

Consult instructors, classmates, friends, and family 118

With rare exceptions, writing is a social act. We write to inform, to entertain, to bring about change. We write to share ideas. We write to make a difference. In every case, we write *to someone* and *for a purpose*. To create more effective documents, writers frequently turn to other writers for feedback and advice. The skills required to give useful feedback and advice — and to put that feedback and advice to good use — are among the most important a writer can have. In fact, they're strongly related to the skills you use in conversation — listening carefully, treating others with respect, and deciding how to make a useful contribution. In this chapter, you'll learn how to benefit from working with other writers and how to do so effectively and efficiently.

How Can Collaborative Activities Improve My Writing?

Writers frequently ask for help from other writers as they work on their projects. In some cases, they seek this support independently by asking for advice about their choice of a topic or by requesting feedback on a draft. In other cases, a writing instructor might direct students to work together to generate ideas, collect sources on a common topic, engage in peer review, or develop and refine arguments.

Work Together to Generate Ideas

Writers often collaborate to generate ideas, typically by engaging in group brainstorming and role-playing activities.

GROUP BRAINSTORMING

Group brainstorming draws on the differing backgrounds and experiences of the members of a group to generate ideas for a writing project. For example, you might work with a group to create a list of ideas for an essay about new advances in communication technologies or social media, or you might collaborate to generate possible solutions to a problem with funding for a local school district.

To engage in group brainstorming, follow these guidelines:

- **Take notes.** Ask someone to record ideas.
- **Encourage everyone in the group to participate.** Consider taking turns. Establish a ground rule that no one should cut off other group members as they're speaking.
- **Be polite. Avoid criticisms.** Treat every idea, no matter how odd or useless it might seem, as worthy of consideration.
- **Build on one another's ideas.** Try to expand on ideas that have already been generated, and then see where they take you.
- **Generate as many ideas as possible.** If you get stuck, try asking questions about ideas that have already been suggested.
- **Review the results.** Once you've stopped brainstorming, look over the list of ideas, and then identify the most promising ones.

● **ROLE-PLAYING**

Role-playing activities are frequently used to generate and refine ideas. By asking the members of a group to take on roles, you can apply a variety of perspectives to a subject. For example, you might ask one person to play the role of a "doubting Thomas," someone who demands evidence from a writer for every assertion. Or you might ask someone to play the role of a "devil's advocate," someone who responds to a writer's arguments with counterarguments. (The term is drawn from the process by which the Roman Catholic Church confers sainthood, in which an advocate of the devil argues that the candidate is not worthy of sainthood.) Role-playing activities that are useful for generating and refining ideas include staging debates, conducting inquiries, and offering first-person explanations.

Staging a debate In a debate, speakers who represent different perspectives argue politely with one another about an issue. You might try one or more of the following role-playing activities:

- **Adopt the role of the authors of readings used in a class.** Each member of the group can adopt the perspective of one of the authors.

- **Adopt the role of a political commentator or celebrity who has taken a strong stand on an issue.** One member of a group might adopt the role of Rachel Maddow, for example, while another might adopt the role of Tucker Carlson, and still others might adopt the roles of Anderson Cooper or Laura Ingraham. Each "commentator" or "celebrity" presents a perspective on the issue that is consistent with their past statements. To prepare for the debate, learn about the positions these commentators have taken in the past by watching or listening to commentaries on a site such as YouTube.

- **Adopt the role of an authority on an issue,** such as a scientific adviser to a local zoning commission, the manager of a small business, or the director of a nonprofit organization. To prepare for the debate, conduct research in your library's databases or on the web about the person whose role you are adopting.

- **Adopt the role of someone affected by an issue or event.** For example, if you were generating ideas about a natural disaster, such as the effects of a flood in the Missouri River valley, you might take on the roles of people who lost their homes and were forced to move, health-care workers and police officers who stayed on duty, students who lost their schools, or small-business owners who lost their livelihoods, all of whom could discuss the impact of this natural disaster on their lives. To prepare for the debate, you could conduct research on how the community was affected by the event.

Conducting an inquiry An inquiry is an attempt to understand a situation or an event. For example, a military tribunal might review soldiers' actions during a military operation, while a medical inquiry might focus on the causes of a problem that occurred during a medical procedure. To conduct an inquiry, try the following role-playing activities:

- **Defend a contemporary or historical figure.** The writer presents a case, and then the other group members ask questions about the person's actions or ideas.
- **Review a proposal.** The writer presents a proposal to address an issue or a problem. The other members of the group can then raise questions about the merits of the proposal and suggest alternatives.

Giving testimony First-person explanations offer insights into the causes of, effects of, or solutions to a particular issue or problem. Role-playing activities that involve giving testimony include the following:

- **Adopt the role of devil's advocate.** The writer offers an explanation, and then respondents offer reasonable objections. Each devil's advocate asks for clarification of the points made by the writer and suggests alternative explanations.
- **Adopt the role of a person affected by an issue.** The writer takes on the role of someone who has been affected by the issue. After the writer explains the effects, the other members of the group ask questions about the writer's experiences.

Working Together: Role-Play

Work together with your classmates to generate and refine ideas for your writing project. Choose one of the categories of role-playing activities — staging a debate, conducting an inquiry, or giving testimony — and assign roles to the members of your group. Then do the following:

1. Appoint a member of your group — someone who is not contributing to the role-playing activity — to record the ideas.
2. Create a framework for the role-play. Decide who will speak first, how long each person will speak, and what sort of responses are appropriate.
3. As you conduct the role-play, be polite (within bounds, of course — some political commentators are far from polite to their opponents).
4. If you are responding to a writer's ideas, ask that person for evidence that supports their arguments or explanations.
5. If you are adopting a role that requires you to disagree, don't overdo it. Be willing to accept a reasonable explanation or argument.

Once you've completed the activity, review your recorder's notes and assess what you've learned.

Work Together to Collect and Work with Information

You might be asked — by an instructor or by another writer — to work together to collect, critically read, evaluate, and take notes on information from sources. Common collaborative activities for collecting and working with information include the following:

- **Develop a search strategy for published sources.** Depending on the scope of a writing project, creating a plan for finding sources can be quite challenging. Working with other writers can improve the odds of developing an effective and appropriate plan. You can learn more about developing a search plan in *How Can I Develop a Search Plan?* in Chapter 13.

Need a refresher on assessing and evaluating sources? See Chapter 4.

- **Assign responsibility for locating sources.** When a group is working on a shared topic, dividing up research responsibilities can be an efficient way to create a collection of sources. For example, one person might search for sources through a library catalog, another through full-text databases, and still another through searches on the web. Each person can locate promising sources and make copies for other members of the group. See Chapters 13 and 14 for more information about locating sources.

- **Assign responsibility for field research.** In writing projects that involve surveys, interviews, observation, or correspondence (see Chapter 15), individual members of the group can carry out their assigned research tasks and share the results with the group.

- **Create shared annotated bibliographies.** Members of a group working on a shared topic can create citations and annotations (brief summaries) for each source they collect. You can learn more about creating annotated bibliographies in Chapter 16.

- **Share evaluations of sources.** Writers working on a shared topic can discuss the merits of the sources they've collected and read. For more information on evaluating sources, see *Read Closely to Evaluate the Source* in Chapter 4.

- **Share notes on sources.** Writers working on a shared topic can compile their notes on the sources they've read. You can learn more about taking notes in Chapter 3.

Work Together to Refine Your Argument

Writers usually express their main point through a thesis statement (see Chapter 18). A good thesis statement invites readers to learn something new, change their attitudes or beliefs, or take action of some kind. In effect, your thesis statement serves as a brief summary of the overall argument you want to make to your readers.

To determine whether your thesis statement conveys your main point clearly and effectively, ask for feedback from other writers. You might ask friends or family members to read your thesis statement and tell you what they think it means, as Quinn Jackson did with an early draft of a thesis statement she developed for an argumentative essay about preparing teachers to teach writing. You might ask them to offer counterarguments or alternative perspectives on your issue or to engage in a role-playing activity in which they pretend to disagree with your perspective. Or you might ask for feedback during a peer-review session in class.

Regardless of where it comes from, listen carefully to the feedback you receive. Your thesis statement plays a central role in shaping the decisions you'll make about the reasons and evidence you'll offer to support your main point, and it can also affect the organization and design of your document.

> I'm not sure how you'd define "future writing teachers." Do you mean only English language arts students or do you mean anyone — even a biology major — who will be using writing assignments when they teach?

Future writing teachers should receive much stronger preparation than they currently receive in the theory and practice of writing instruction.

> Do you have any ideas about what "much stronger preparation" would involve? Are you thinking about hands-on training? Theory? Actual writing that they do themselves?

▲ **Feedback on a draft of Quinn Jackson's thesis statement**

As you develop a set of reasons to accept your main point, ask for feedback on them as well. You might create an outline of your argument (see *How Can I Create an Outline?* in Chapter 19) or write a rough draft (see Chapter 20). Friends, family, and classmates should be able to provide their reactions to the reasons you are offering. They can give you feedback on the appropriateness and effectiveness of the evidence you've selected to support your reasons and the order in which you present your reasons and evidence. And they can help you generate ideas for new and potentially more effective reasons and sources of evidence. Just as you can with a thesis statement, you can ask people to offer counterarguments or to adopt roles. And, of course, you can solicit feedback on your reasons and evidence from classmates during peer-review or idea-generation sessions.

> Teacher education programs should provide strong theoretical grounding in writing instruction for all future teachers, help future teachers understand how to assign and respond to student writing, and require future teachers to take advanced writing courses.
>
> Reason 1. Because writing is used in all courses — not just language arts — all future teachers should receive instruction in writing theory and practice.
>
> Reason 2. It's important to understand how to teach writing — and even more important to understand why some instructional choices are better than others.
>
> Reason 3. Teachers who assign writing should be good writers themselves.
>
> Evidence: Brimi, Johnston, Sommers

Comments:
- Do you really think you can make all teachers good writers?
- How will faculty in the sciences react to the writing requirement? Won't they worry about adding more credits to the major?
- Good choice of articles. But are three enough to support your argument?

▲ Feedback on an informal outline

Your argument — your main point, reasons, and evidence — is the heart of your contribution to the conversation you've decided to join. By working with other writers, you can gain valuable feedback on your argument, feedback that can help you refine and improve it.

How Can I Work with other Writers on a Group Project?

Group projects have become common not only in writing and writing-intensive classes but also in business, nonprofit, and government settings. The extent of collaboration can vary widely: each member of the group might be assigned to work on a different section of a document or presentation, or the whole group might work together — online, on the phone, or in person — to plan, design, draft, polish, revise, and edit the project. To prepare to work collaboratively on a group project, become familiar with the purposes, processes, and potential pitfalls of working with a team. Learning how to work together while you are a student can help you succeed on projects long after you've completed your degree.

Understand the Purposes of Working in a Group

Asking a group to work together reflects belief in the value of collaboration. In corporate settings, for example, working together might be a means not only of ensuring that a project succeeds but also of building a sense of togetherness and commitment among team members. In an academic setting, a group project allows students to carry out a project that a single student would find difficult to produce alone, helps them learn more about a subject, and familiarizes them with the collaborative processes they might encounter

Working Together: Learn from Past Experiences with Group Work

Most writers can look back at a group project and find something they didn't like about the experience. They might have been in a group dominated by an ineffective leader. They might have had to do far more than their fair share on a project. At the last minute, they might have been left in the lurch by someone who failed to deliver a critical part of the project. Whatever the reason, some writers prefer to work alone. Yet group work can be productive and satisfying, and most experienced writers can point to a wide range of situations in which working with other writers significantly improved their work on a writing project.

To get ready to work with other writers, reflect on your experiences with group work. Then, working with the members of your group, develop a set of guidelines that would improve the quality of group work. To carry out this activity, follow these steps.

1. Individually, spend five minutes brainstorming or freewriting (see *Generating Ideas* in Chapter 2) about your experiences with collaborative work. List both positive and negative experiences.

2. As a group, discuss your experiences. Each person should note the advantages and disadvantages of collaborative work.

3. As a group, identify the most significant challenges to working together effectively.

4. As a group, create a list of guidelines that would address these challenges.

Once you've completed the activity, share your guidelines with other groups in the class. As a class, create a list of guidelines for collaborative work in your course.

in their professional lives. In this sense, collaborating on a project might be as important as — or even more important than — producing a document or making a presentation.

Understand Potential Problems and Develop Solutions

Recognizing potential pitfalls can increase the likelihood that a collaborative project will succeed. Common problems encountered during group work range from individual concerns about participating in a group to behaviors that undermine the group's effectiveness. If you want to collaborate successfully, be aware of these problems and learn how to avoid them.

- **Some people prefer to work alone,** and they make those feelings all too clear, often to the point of insulting their classmates. Remind such people of the reasons the group is working together and the danger their attitude poses to the long-term success of the project.

- **Some people worry about losing a sense of individual worth.** Assure them that their contributions not only are important but also will be recognized as such — if not formally, then by other members of the group.

- **Some individuals will try to dominate a group,** perhaps believing that the project will fail unless they take control. Make sure at the outset of the project that everyone's ideas are heard and respected, and explain that developing a plan for the project is not a process of arguing for the superiority of a particular set of ideas so much as it is the synthesis of useful ideas.

- **Some members will find it difficult to schedule or attend group meetings.** Ensure that meeting times and venues accommodate everyone's needs. If you can't do so, have the group discuss the problem with the instructor.

- **Some members of a group will use meeting time unproductively** — at least in the eyes of other members of the group. This can cause problems, particularly when it is difficult to find time to meet or if meeting time is limited. To address this issue, be sure the group establishes and sticks to an agenda for each meeting.

- **Some group members will want to work only on what they feel capable of doing well.** In nonacademic settings, where a strong emphasis is often placed on the effectiveness of the final document, this is usually not a problem. In academic settings, however, where the goals of most collaborative projects include learning new skills and acquiring new knowledge, it is important that all members of a group take on new challenges.

- **Some members of a group won't contribute as much as others — and some won't contribute at all.** In collaborative projects for a class, you'll find that some members refuse to participate. Perhaps they assume that they can't make much of a contribution, or perhaps they're trying to save time by not participating. Regardless of their intentions, their lack of participation causes hurt feelings and might affect the overall quality of the project. Discuss as a group how you will address unequal participation.
- **Some members of a group will resent the extra time required to coordinate work on a project.** Remind these people of the reasons for working together and the benefits of doing so.
- **As the group works on a project, disagreements will arise.** As you develop ground rules for working together, consider how you'll address disagreements. Strategies include voting, discussing until consensus emerges, and seeking guidance from an instructor or a supervisor.

Establish Ground Rules

Use your discussion of potential difficulties to establish ground rules for working together. These can include guidelines for selecting meeting times and locations,

Working Together: Establish Ground Rules for a Group Project

In your writer's notebook, develop a set of ground rules for your group by responding to the following prompts. Share your responses with the members of your group and then agree on a formal set of rules.

1. Meetings will be held [at location or on Zoom, Teams, Google Hangouts, etc.] on [dates and times].
2. Discussions will be [moderated by the same person at each meeting, moderated by a different person at each meeting, unmoderated], and notes will be taken by [the same person at each meeting, a different person at each meeting].
3. When disagreements arise, they will be resolved by _____.
4. The following members of the group will take the lead on the following activities: [list names and activities].
5. To ensure equitable contributions by each group member, we will _____.
6. Group members who do not contribute equitably will face the following consequences: [list consequences].
7. Group members who drop out of the project will face the following consequences: [list consequences].

conducting discussions, resolving disputes, determining individual contributions to the project, ensuring equitable contributions from group members, and defining the consequences for inadequate participation. Ground rules can take various forms, ranging from an informal agreement among group members to a detailed statement signed by each member.

Create a Plan

An effective plan will define the overall goals of the project, identify key steps and deadlines for the completion of each step, establish who is responsible for specific activities, and suggest strategies for carrying out those activities.

How Can I Use Peer Review to Improve My Writing?

When designed carefully and treated seriously, peer review can provide valuable information to writers about the effectiveness, clarity, and organization of their drafts. Few experienced writers, in fact, produce major documents without asking for feedback on their drafts. They've learned that it can help them enhance their composing processes and improve their documents.

Working Together: Create a Plan for a Group Project

In your writer's notebook, develop a plan to complete your project. Then share your plan with the members of your group, and develop a group plan.

1. The overall goal of this project is _____.

2. This project will require completing the following steps: [Fill out this information for each step.]

Step:
_____

Deadline:
_____

Ideas for completing the step:
_____

Responsible group member:
_____

Use Peer Review to Enhance Your Writing Process

Peer review benefits the reviewer as well as the writer. By helping another writer generate ideas, you can practice effective brainstorming strategies. By participating in a planning session, you can learn something new about planning your own documents. By reading and responding to documents written by other writers, you might pick up some new strategies for organizing an essay, crafting an introduction, incorporating illustrations, or using evidence effectively. Perhaps most important, learning how to analyze other people's work can help you assess your own writing more productively.

Use Peer Review to Improve Your Document

Peer review gives you the benefit of multiple perspectives. The feedback you receive from other writers can help you learn whether you have conveyed your main point clearly, offered sufficient evidence, and organized your document effectively. It can help you gain insights into how your readers are likely to react to the information, ideas, and arguments you have presented in your draft. And it can help you identify passages in a draft that might benefit from additional revision, polishing, or editing.

To increase your chances of creating an effective document, you might ask for feedback on your overall argument, your reasoning about an issue, and your use of evidence. You might ask a friend or classmate, "What do you know about …?" or "Do you think it would be effective if …?" or "Does this seem convincing to you?" You might ask a reviewer to pretend to be part of the intended audience for your document, or you might ask for feedback on specific aspects of your document, such as its organization, style, or design.

Your Turn: Using Feedback from Peer Review

When you receive feedback on a draft, ask yourself the following questions.

1. What was I most interested in learning from the reviewer?
2. Did the reviewer provide the kind of feedback I had hoped to receive? If so, how can I use it to improve my document? If not, how can the feedback help me in other ways?
3. What does the feedback suggest to me about my writing processes? Can I use the feedback to improve my composing and research processes, my knowledge of writing situations, or my knowledge of genre and design?
4. What can I learn from this experience to improve my request for feedback in future writing projects?

How Can I Conduct an Effective Peer Review?

As you engage in peer review, either as a writer or as a reviewer, consider the stage the project is in. Early in a writing project, a writer is likely to be most interested in feedback about the overall direction of the project. Big-picture concerns — such as the purpose of the document, the general soundness of an argument, and the likely reactions of readers to that argument — will probably be more important than issues such as style and tone. Later, questions about the integration of evidence from sources, style and tone, and design will grow in importance, particularly in terms of how they help advance the writer's purpose and goals. Consider, too, the contexts in which a peer review takes place and the technologies that might be used to carry out the review.

Consider Context

As you begin a peer review, consider the context in which it is taking place. If you are conducting a peer review in a classroom, you might have limited time to read and reflect on a document. Try to focus specifically on a few primary concerns — either those defined by your instructor, perhaps through a rubric or a set of key questions, or those defined by the writer, who might ask for help in particular areas. If you are conducting a peer review outside of class, you might have more time to consider a fuller range of issues related to the document. If so, think carefully about the kind of feedback that would help the writer, and then read the document — ideally more than once — with those concerns in mind.

Consider Technology

Peer review often calls to mind images of students hunched over desks in a classroom, marking paper drafts with pens or pencils before they offer feedback to one another. Increasingly, however, peer review takes place on computers, tablets, or phones, both inside and outside the classroom. Most programs allow you to save comments and revise them before you return a draft to a writer. You'll find tools for highlighting text and suggesting text edits. You'll be able to link to related documents, websites, and databases. And you will be able to share your comments not only with the writer but also with other members of the class, including your instructor. Some instructors, in fact, ask to see the feedback writers give to one another as a means of ensuring greater attention to the peer-review process and also to get a sense of the kinds of writing issues members of the class are struggling to address.

Consider Your Needs as a Writer

Whenever you ask for feedback from other writers, keep the following guidelines in mind.

- **WHEN YOU ASK FOR FEEDBACK ON A DRAFT:**
  - **Be clear.** Tell your reviewers where you'd like them to focus. For example, let them know that you are struggling with the transition from one point to another or that you would appreciate feedback on your conclusion.
  - **Be reasonable.** Your reviewers have more to do in life than review your draft. Don't expect — or ask — them to spend more time reviewing a draft than you spent writing it. For that matter, don't expect them to put more than half an hour into a review — if that.
  - **Be prepared.** Provide a draft that is easy to review. If you are asking the reviewer to comment on a printed draft, format it with double-spaced lines and wide margins. If you are providing a digital draft, make sure the reviewer can access, read, and comment on your file easily.

- **WHEN YOU RECEIVE FEEDBACK ON A DRAFT:**
  - **Be open to criticism.** Don't dismiss constructive criticism as a problem with the reviewer's comprehension. A reviewer might make poor suggestions for revision, but it's more likely that those suggestions are a reaction to a problem in the draft. Even when the suggested revision is inappropriate, it might point to an area that needs attention.
  - **Be willing to ask questions.** If you aren't sure what a reviewer's comments mean, ask for clarification.
  - **Be willing to change.** If a reviewer offers a critique of your argument or ideas, consider addressing it in your document. You will make a stronger argument if you tell readers about alternative ways of looking at an issue — particularly when you can counter the alternatives effectively.
  - **Be fair to yourself.** It's your draft. Don't feel obligated to incorporate every suggested change into your draft.
  - **Create a plan for revision.** After you review the feedback on your draft, decide how you'll revise your draft. Your plan might take the form of a brief list of tasks; it might involve your reflections on directions you might take in your next draft; or it might be something else entirely.

> **Thesis statement:** Teacher education programs should require all preservice teachers to take advanced writing courses and methods classes in writing instruction.
>
> **To do:** My three reasons should remain unchanged. I should respond to how faculty will react to the addition of new required courses. They can either drop some existing requirements or increase the number of required credits. The latter will be a problem since our teacher licensure program already has room for only two electives. Adding more will be a problem and students will suffer from it. I'll need to read more sources on this. Perhaps there are examples of programs that have done this well.
>
> I need to read more sources in general. I only have three so far that are worth using. Probably take a look at the sources they use and work backward through the web of Science citation database. I need to identify more evidence to support my reasons.

- Quinn Jackson's original thesis statement is clarified in response to peer feedback. *(annotation to thesis statement)*
- Quinn lists potential opposing arguments and summarizes likely responses to them. *(annotation to second paragraph)*
- Quinn notes the need for further reading. *(annotation to "need to read more sources on this")*
- Quinn adds a research technique — using a citation database to see who has cited a useful article — to her to-do list. *(annotation to third paragraph)*

▲ **Quinn Jackson's revision plan**

Consider Your Role as a Reviewer

When you provide feedback to another writer, consider the following guidelines.

- ● **TO PREPARE FOR A PEER-REVIEW SESSION:**
    - **Understand the assignment.** Read the assignment sheet, if there is one, and ask the writer to describe the draft's purpose and audience.
    - **Understand the writer's needs.** Ask the writer what type of response you should provide. If you are reviewing an early draft that will be revised before it's submitted for a grade, focus on larger writing concerns such as the overall argument, evidence, and organization (see *What Should I Focus on When I Revise?* in Chapter 24). If the writer wants help with proofreading and editing, focus on accuracy, economy, consistency, biased language, style, spelling, grammar, and punctuation (see *What Should I Focus on When I Edit?* in Chapter 24).
    - **Understand any peer-review guidelines.** If you are using a feedback form or a set of questions provided by your instructor, make sure you understand these guidelines. If you don't, ask the instructor or the writer for clarification.

- **Set aside sufficient time to review the draft.** Take your job seriously, and give the draft the time it deserves. You'll want the same courtesy when your draft is reviewed.

---

1. The introduction should clearly identify and describe the issue, explaining its importance, explaining why readers should take the issue seriously, and arguing that it is complex (that is, that it is more than a pro/con debate between two opposing approaches). How would you improve the description of the issue?

   The guidelines are intended for a draft that explores a complex issue.

   The peer reviewer is asked to provide advice about how to improve the draft.

2. The writer should clearly identify and describe the main approaches taken by writers arguing about the issue. Please indicate how the writer could improve the explanation of the approaches to this issue.

   The guidelines ask for advice on how to improve the review of literature in the draft.

3. The report should provide evidence to support the writer's points. Evidence can include quotations, paraphrases, summaries, and personal experience. Please indicate how the writer could improve the use of evidence in the draft.

   Types of evidence are defined (see Select Evidence to Support Your Reasons in Chapter 18). The writer is asked to provide suggestions for improvement in the use of evidence.

4. Writers should use author tags to distinguish between their work and the work of other authors. Please identify any concerns you have in this area and suggest strategies for improving the draft.

5. The report should be organized in a manner that readers will find easy to follow. Please indicate how the organization of this draft could be improved.

   The reviewer is asked to assess and offer advice on organizational patterns (see Chapter 19).

▲ **Sample peer-review guidelines**

● **BEFORE YOU MAKE COMMENTS:**

- **Be prepared.** Read the draft all the way through at least once before making any comments. This will help you understand its overall structure and argument.
- **Be organized.** Take a few minutes to identify the areas most in need of work. On a first draft, for instance, you might identify three main areas that need the writer's attention, such as thesis statement, organization, and effective use of sources.

Ineffective and effective feedback on Quinn Jackson's first draft

> Nice introduction!

> Are you being serious?

> Awkward sentence! You might want to buy a better handbook.

> Great job so far.

> Maybe include some evidence that teachers don't always provide substantive feedback. Did you find any studies about feedback?

> Do you have any information on how many hours a week teachers typically work or on the number of students they usually teach?

> I think you might want to introduce these ideas in a different order and then make changes to reflect that order later in the document.

How would you feel if the only feedback you received on a 2,500-word writing assignment was "nice job" or "needs work" or "good argument"? How would you feel if the only feedback you received was on grammar and style?

Too many high school students receive little or no feedback on their work — even on assignments that require literally hours of work. Most shrug it off and say, "What can you expect? The teacher is incredibly busy" or "It makes sense. It was just an assignment for a science class." But a growing number are asking for more. They want to improve as writers. They want to be prepared for college or a job. They want to see some return on their investment of time and effort.

These students need to be heard. High school principals need to reward teachers who design good assignments and provide strong feedback. College and university teacher education programs need to pay serious attention to writing theory, instruction, and practice. And teachers themselves need to recognize that it's never enough to read and grade an assignment. They need to see that feedback on writing is a critical part of the teaching process.

● **AS YOU MAKE COMMENTS**:

- **Be positive.** Identify the strengths of the draft. Be specific in your praise: "This quotation really drives home your point about teachers' frustrations with changing standards" is more helpful, for instance, than "Nice quotation" because the first comment allows the writer to see why a certain strategy is effective.

- **Be judicious.** Focus on the areas of the draft most in need of improvement. Avoid commenting on everything that might be improved. In most cases, a limited set of suggested changes — particularly those that focus on bigger-picture concerns such as purpose, audience, argument, and organization — will ripple through a document in ways that make many of the other changes you might have suggested irrelevant.

- **Be clear.** If you are addressing an overall issue such as structure or integration of evidence from sources, discuss it thoroughly enough that the writer will understand your concerns. If you are addressing a specific passage, indicate where it can be found.

- **Be specific.** Avoid general comments, such as "The writing isn't clear enough." This kind of statement doesn't give the writer direction for improving the draft. Instead, offer specific comments, such as "I found it difficult to understand your explanation of the issue in the second paragraph." Similarly, focus your questions. Instead of asking, "What are you trying to do here?" ask a question such as "It seems as though you are trying to build on what you stated in the previous paragraph. Can you show the connection more clearly?"
- **Be constructive.** Offer concrete suggestions about how the draft might be improved, rather than just criticizing what you didn't like. Being constructive can also mean encouraging the writer to continue doing what you see as effective.
- **Be reasonable.** Keep the writing assignment in mind as you make suggestions for improvement. Don't hold the draft to a higher standard than the instructor will.
- **Be kind.** Be polite. Don't put down the writer simply because you find a draft inadequate, confusing, or annoying.
- **Be responsible.** Review your comments before you give them to the writer.

How would you feel if the only feedback you received on a 2,500-word writing assignment was "nice job" or "needs work" or "good argument"? How would you feel if the only feedback you received was on grammar and style? According to writing researchers Elaine Wang, Lindsay Clare Matsumura, and Richard Correnti this is all too common. "[T]eachers' written feedback tends to be superficial, focused on grammar and mechanics rather than the substance of students' ideas," they write. "Meanwhile, written feedback about content instead of surface features is associated with higher quality revisions" (p. 101).

Wang and her colleagues are far from alone in concluding that the best way to improve student writing is to make comments on students' ideas and arguments rather than on surface features such as grammar and mechanics. They cite research by scholars such as Matsumura, Patthey-Chavez, Valdés, Garnier, whose work focuses on teacher feedback and writing quality, as well as Graham, Harris, and Hebert, who report on the value of formative assessment on student writing.

The research tells us that students benefit from comments that focus on their ideas and arguments, rather than on grammar errors. Yet the research also tells us all too clearly that this is the least common kind of feedback students receive. Why is there such a clear disconnect?

> The evidence you provide here seems solid. I did a quick check, however, and I see that Wang, Matsumura, and Correnti are reporting on research with elementary and middle school teachers. Can you find research that is more directly related to your argument about feedback to high school students?

> Again, I like the use of evidence from sources here. You might want to point out, however, that the Matsumura cited here is one of the persons you cited in the first paragraph. Perhaps find another source? Otherwise, it sounds like they are citing themselves.

> You are setting up this introduction well. As a reader, I want to know the answer to your question about the disconnect. If you do a bit more work on your sources, you'll have a very strong setup for your essay.

▲ **Sample peer-review feedback**

Understanding how to conduct and use feedback from peer review not only will help you improve a particular document but also will enable you to become a better writer. As you consider the type of document you'll write to contribute to a written conversation, keep these principles in mind. Also keep in mind the distinctive characteristics of writing for particular purposes, such as writing to inform or writing to solve problems. Chapters 7 to 12 provide carefully designed peer-review activities that will help you get feedback on drafts for the kinds of writing projects featured in those chapters. These activities can be found immediately before the essays written by each of the featured student writers.

What Resources Can I Draw On as I Review and Collaborate?

Resources that support peer review and other forms of collaborative work include technological tools as well as your instructor, classmates, friends, and family.

Use Technological Tools

For many writers, the phrase "working together" implies face-to-face meetings, often during class. In fact, many collaborative activities can be carried out without the need to meet in person.

- If you are working with other writers to generate and refine ideas, use chat, text messaging, or video tools to meet online.
- If you are collaborating with other writers to collect and work with sources for a shared topic, use discussion forums, wikis, email, or cloud-based file sharing (such as Dropbox, Google Drive, iCloud, and OneDrive) to distribute sources, source citations, source evaluations, and source notes.
- If your class is supported by a learning management system such as Blackboard or Canvas, ask your instructor to create discussion forums, wikis, and file-sharing folders to support your group work. Take advantage of email to share ideas, schedule meetings, and exchange files. You might also have access to electronic whiteboard programs that allow you to meet online and work on drafts of your document.
- If you are using Macmillan Learning's Achieve platform or another tool that supports peer review, review the guidance provided by your instructor about

how to focus your review, and then follow links to related material that might be suggested by your classmates and instructor.

- If you are conducting a peer review, you can share your drafts by sending them as email attachments, uploading them to the cloud, or posting them to a learning management system. Reviewers can open the attachments in a word-processing program, comment on them using Comment and Track Changes tools, save the file with a new name, and return them to you.

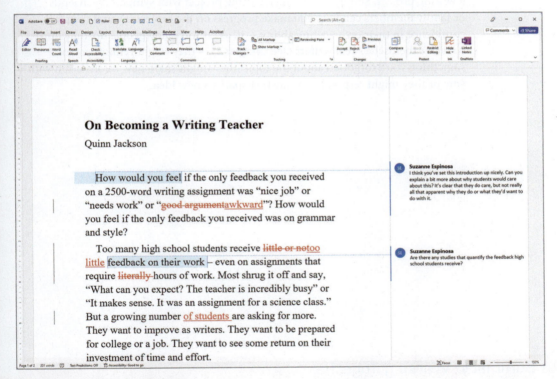

▲ Using comments and track changes

Consult Instructors, Classmates, Friends, and Family

The most important resources for peer review and collaboration are your instructor, your classmates, and your friends and family. Classmates and instructors can help you fine-tune a draft by serving as a sounding board for your ideas and by responding to it. Instructors can show you how to work with peer-review forms, provide feedback on the quality of the comments you offer your classmates, and help you better understand the goals of the assignment.

Your family and friends can not only provide honest feedback on the quality of your drafts, but they can also be resources for generating ideas about and planning a writing project. Simply discussing a writing project with sympathetic friends or family members can help you make progress on the project. Even if they lack confidence in their own writing ability — if, as far too many people do, they don't consider themselves real writers (see Chapter 1) — they might remind you of something you'd forgotten about the topic; they might share new information with you; or they might respond in a way that sparks a new idea.

In Summary: Working Together

★ Understand how collaborative activities can improve your writing (p. 99).

★ Use peer review to enhance your writing process, improve your document, and succeed on writing projects (p. 108).

★ Take advantage of resources that help writers work together (p. 116).

PART TWO
Contributing to a Conversation

06 Choosing Your Writing Role

What is a writing role? 120

What roles can I adopt? 120
Observer 121
Reporter 121
Interpreter 121
Evaluator 122
Problem solver 122
Advocate 123
Other roles 123

How can I choose my role? 125
Your purpose 125
Your readers 125
Your context 127

How will my role affect my work on my document? 128
Your role will shape your choice of sources 128
Your role will influence your critical thinking 128

Can I adopt more than one role? 130

Even if the idea of a writing role is new to you, you've certainly seen it in action. In spoken conversations, speakers might share new information, reflect on ideas shared by others, or offer their take on an issue, to name only a few of the moves speakers make as they add their voice to a discussion. Over the course of the conversation, they might shift their roles, offering new information as the conversation is getting underway, for example, and arguing later on for a particular approach to the issue.

As a writer, you'll also adopt a role, and you might find yourself shifting among more than one as you develop your contributions to the conversation you've decided to join. This chapter considers what it means to adopt a role as a writer, which factors can shape your choice of role, and how you might rely on more than one role in the document you create. The chapters in Part Two explore six of the most common roles writers adopt.

What Is a Writing Role?

You can think of a role as a way of relating to your readers. You might want to share information with them. Or perhaps you want to convince them to change their beliefs or persuade them to take action. Making decisions about the kind of relationship you want to have with your readers allows you to focus on improving your understanding of your writing situation and exploring how best to contribute to the conversation you've decided to join.

Thinking of the relationship you hope to have with your readers as a role can help you write a more focused document. It can help you make decisions about how to develop your main point, craft your thesis statement, choose your supporting points and evidence, and appeal to your readers. It can also help you choose an appropriate genre and design your document. In each of the following chapters in this part of *Joining the Conversation*, you'll find examples of how published authors have taken on various roles and how featured student writers have written essays that reflect their choice of role.

What Roles Can I Adopt?

Your choice of role reflects in large part what you want to share with your readers. In particular, it reflects what you want to share that's new. Newness can range from modest contributions of new information, ideas, or arguments to a conversation to potentially prize-winning contributions that change the direction of a conversation. The former is far more common than the latter (see *Look for Gaps in the Conversation* in Chapter 13). The nature of what you will add to the conversation — new information, a new way of looking at the issue, or a new argument — will have an impact on the role you adopt.

The primary roles discussed in this book are observer, reporter, interpreter, evaluator, problem solver, and advocate.

Observer

If you are sharing your reflections on something related to your conversation — perhaps about an event, an experience, a person, or a work of art or literature — you are adopting the role of *observer* (see Chapter 7). Writers who adopt this role spend time learning about and considering a subject. Sometimes they explore the implications of putting a particular idea into practice. Sometimes they trace relationships among ideas and information. Sometimes they ask whether or how an author's words might help them better understand their own lives. Sometimes they ask whether their understanding of one situation can help them better understand another.

Reporter

When you add information to a conversation — perhaps by bringing in information from sources that haven't been part of the conversation or perhaps by sharing information you've collected yourself — you are adopting the role of *reporter* (see Chapter 8). The information you share might advance the conversation in minor ways, perhaps by bringing in some new but hardly earth-shattering facts or data. Or you might be sharing information that fundamentally reshapes a conversation. In either case — and at points along a spectrum from "Oh, that's interesting" to "That changes everything" — you'll be advancing the conversation by reporting new information.

Writers who adopt this role vary widely in their purposes. Typically, though, they seek to make others aware of facts that are central to a written conversation. If you adopt this role, you might provide background information for people just starting to learn about a subject, or you might present new information to readers with a long-standing interest in it. You might, for example, describe the events leading to elections in a new democracy. Or you might explain the United Nations' role in monitoring those elections.

Interpreter

If you share your analysis of a subject, you are adopting the role of *interpreter* (see Chapter 9). Writers who adopt this role help readers understand the origins, qualities, significance, or potential impact of a subject. One interpreter might address the causes of a recent economic downturn, for example, while another might explore the cultural implications of a new album by Kanye West. Another writer might present a historical analysis of U.S. involvement in foreign wars, while yet another might try to help college students understand the impact of proposed legislation on the cost of attending college.

In some cases, writers who take on the role of interpreter already know a great deal about their subjects. More often, however, they spend time learning about a subject to ensure that they can offer a well-grounded interpretation. Whether they draw on the subject itself, interview experts, collect information from published sources, or use statistical evidence, effective interpreters provide even knowledgeable readers with enough information about a subject to explain the focus of their analyses and to ensure that their interpretations will make sense in the context in which they're read.

Evaluator

When you share an informed, well-reasoned conclusion about a subject's worth or effectiveness, you are adopting the role of *evaluator* (see Chapter 10). Adopting this role involves clearly conveying your judgments to your readers. Writers who take on this role typically evaluate a subject with one of three general goals: to determine whether something has succeeded or failed, to help readers understand how something might be improved or refined, or to help readers choose among alternatives. They form their conclusions by learning about their subject and considering how well it meets a given set of criteria — the standards or principles on which judgments are based. Their writing is usually balanced, and they generally offer clear reasoning and ample evidence to support their judgments.

Problem Solver

When you try to understand or address a problematic situation, you are adopting the role of *problem solver* (see Chapter 11). Sometimes, your contribution might be a new definition of the problem. At other times, it might be a new solution. At still other times, it might consist of a strong argument in favor of a solution that other writers have already proposed. If you adopt this role, you'll need a clear understanding of the problem, an awareness of solutions (if any) that have already been proposed, and a clear sense of what is needed to address the problem. Writers who take on the role of problem solver will often acknowledge the contributions made by other writers who have addressed the problem. But they will also explain why those contributions have not *fully* addressed the problem. If you choose to redefine the problem — a key step in moving toward a new solution — you will focus primarily on the origins and effects of the situation. If you choose to offer a new solution or argue for one that has already been advanced, you'll likely point out the flaws in solutions that have already been proposed, explain why the solution you favor is better, and provide a plan for implementing that solution.

Advocate

When you make an argument, you adopt the role of *advocate* (see Chapter 12). You might try to convince your readers to accept your argument, persuade them to take action, or serve as a mediator to find common ground among opposing positions on an issue. If you wish to convince or persuade your readers, you will present your overall argument, offer reasons to support it, provide evidence to support your reasons, develop appeals to increase the likelihood that your readers will accept your reasons and evidence, and consider opposing arguments. You can read more about convincing and persuading in Chapter 12.

Other Roles

In addition to the roles discussed in this part of *Joining the Conversation*, you can adopt many others. In the sense that roles reflect the relationship you want to establish with your readers, you can imagine numerous other possibilities. You might be trying to *entertain* your readers, either as a primary purpose (as writers such as Dave Barry and numerous comedians do) or as part of a larger purpose. Getting readers to smile as they read your document might lead them to look favorably on your ideas or arguments. You might be trying to share the results of *original research*. This would be similar to the role of reporter, but this role — *inquirer* — might focus not only on the results of your investigation or study but also on the methods used to carry it out (think of the methods sections in a scientific article). Still other roles might involve writing in ways that lead your readers to feel *strong emotions*, such as the feelings they might experience after hearing a powerful political speech, a religious sermon, or a eulogy for someone who died tragically or too young. These roles will often be used in conjunction with others, such as advocate, interpreter, or observer.

OBSERVERS (Chapter 6) focus on learning about and exploring the implications of a person, an event, an object, an idea, or an issue. They typically reflect on their subject and often trace their thinking about it.

> I wonder what my life would be like if I majored in advertising.

REPORTERS (Chapter 7) present themselves as experts and give detailed but neutral information. A reporter might also provide an overview of competing ideas about a topic, such as a guide to the positions of candidates for public office.

> I'm focusing on the advertising dollars generated by sites like Facebook and Amazon.

INTERPRETERS (Chapter 8) analyze and explain the significance of ideas or events.

> I have to wonder about the truthfulness of the ads aired during this year's Super Bowl. I think I'll check a few of them out.

EVALUATORS (Chapter 9) consider how well something meets a given set of criteria. Their judgments are usually balanced, and they offer evidence and reasoning to support their evaluation.

> Who cares about the truth? I wonder which ads were most effective. Did sales actually go up as a result of the ads? Did people view the products more favorably?

PROBLEM SOLVERS (Chapter 10) identify and define a problem, discuss its impact, and offer solutions based on evidence and reasoning.

> The problem I'm wrestling with is how smaller companies can benefit from events like the Super Bowl. How can they get their message out when the ads are so expensive?

ADVOCATES (Chapter 11) present evidence in favor of their side of an argument and, in many cases, offer evidence that undermines opposing views.

> If anybody cares about the truth, it's me. And I'm sure I'm not alone. We need to do something about deceptive advertising. And I know just what that is.

How Can I Choose My Role?

The role you adopt will strongly affect both your overall argument and the manner in which you present your information, ideas, or argument to your readers. Your decision about which role (or roles) to adopt will be influenced by your purpose, your readers' expectations, and the context in which your document will be written and read.

Your Purpose

Your purpose will shape your choice of role and how you carry it out. The idea of roles, in fact, emerges primarily from differences in purpose among activities such as writing to inform, to evaluate, to make an argument, and so on. Having a clear understanding of your overall goal as a writer will help you define your role. In turn, your role will shape how you work to accomplish your purpose in your document. Your purpose might also lead you to adopt other roles at various points in your document. For instance, in a document in which you work as an advocate to convince someone to think differently about the use of personal gender pronouns, you might shift at one point in your document to a secondary role, such as informing your readers about the historical use of pronouns and more recent efforts to use pronouns to recognize the choices people make about their genders.

Your Readers

Your understanding of your readers' expectations about the type of document you've decided to write will affect both your choice of role and how you carry it out. Those expectations include the typical reasons for reading a particular type of document; the manner in which information, ideas, and arguments are presented; and the goals for writing a particular type of document. As you plan, draft, and revise your document, consider how your readers' expectations will influence how you carry out your role.

- **OBSERVER**

Readers of reflective documents usually share a writer's interest in a subject. Your readers will want to learn what you think about the subject, and they'll often use what they've read as the basis for their own reflections. In general, your readers will expect you to provide a personal treatment of a subject, and they will be willing to accept — and will likely welcome — an unusual perspective.

- **REPORTER**

Readers of informative documents might be interested in a subject for personal or intellectual reasons, but they are usually looking for an answer to a question — whether it's a simple quest for a fact or a more general desire to understand an issue. They will expect a focused treatment of a subject, and they will welcome the use of visual elements — such as photos, images, charts, graphs, and tables — to help them understand key points. Your readers will expect you to be fair and reasonable, they will appreciate clarity, and they will expect you to document your sources.

● INTERPRETER

Readers of analytical documents will usually share the writer's interest in the subject and want to understand it in greater depth, either because it affects them in some way or because they are curious about it. Your readers will expect a clear introduction to your subject, a focused interpretation, thorough explanations of how you arrived at your conclusions, and reasonable support for those conclusions. Your readers are also likely to expect you to use an interpretive framework that is appropriate to the subject and similar to those typically used by other writers in your discipline or profession. For example, readers with a literary background would be surprised if an analysis of a major novel was based on the book's sales history rather than on some form of textual interpretation. Similarly, readers with a background in political science might find an article that focused on the aesthetic qualities of a speech by a presidential candidate less interesting than one that analyzed the political implications of the candidate's arguments.

● EVALUATOR

Readers of evaluative documents will typically share a writer's interest in a subject and hope to learn more about it. Your readers, as a result, will probably share your assumptions about which criteria are appropriate to use in an evaluation. Few readers, for example, expect movie reviewers to justify their choice of criteria, since they are so widely used and understood. Your readers will expect you to provide evidence and reasoning to support your judgments, and they will usually want you to acknowledge and address alternative opinions about the subject. In fact, your readers are likely to know that alternative opinions exist (usually through reading other evaluations), and they might even hold those opinions themselves. As a result, your readers are likely to dismiss an evaluation that seems unfair or unaware of different points of view.

● PROBLEM SOLVER

Readers of problem-solving documents expect a clear definition of the problem and a thorough discussion of options for addressing it. Although your readers might not be surprised by the use of emotionally charged language, they will usually prefer that a problem-solving document discusses the issue in a straightforward, balanced manner. Most readers will also expect you not only to explain and discuss the benefits of your proposed solution but also to address its advantages over other solutions. They will expect a fair and reasonable presentation of a subject, clear explanations of important ideas and concepts, and thorough documentation of sources. Readers are also likely to react favorably to the use of visual elements — such as photos, images, charts, graphs, and tables — that help them understand the problem and its solution.

ADVOCATE

Readers of argumentative documents will usually share the writer's assumption that an issue is important. While they are typically willing to consider new ideas, they will bring their own values, beliefs, and experiences to their reading of your document. To change your readers' minds or persuade them to act, you must give careful thought to who your readers are and where they come from, what they value, how resistant or receptive they might be to an argument, and what kinds of argumentative strategies — such as appeals to logic, emotion, or authority — are most likely to sway them. Your decisions about the characteristics of your readers will shape how you carry out your role. It will influence, for example, how forcefully you make your argument, how considerately you treat counterarguments, and how you present your ideas and evidence to your readers.

Your Context

The context in which your document is written and read will also have a strong influence on your choice of role and how you carry it out. Writers often connect their observations to the social, cultural, and historical contexts they share with their readers. For example, they might refer to events or people who have recently been featured in the news media, and they might mention important sources that address the subject. At the same time, they will take into consideration what their readers might already know, leaving out details and explanations that are unnecessary for their purposes and focusing instead on what they want readers to understand about their subject.

The role you adopt might also focus your attention on more specific aspects of your context. Writers who adopt the role of evaluator, for instance, will need to make decisions about the criteria on which they base their judgments. If they are addressing a general audience, they might need to define their criteria carefully. In contrast, if they are writing to professionals in a particular field, they might reasonably expect their readers to be familiar with the criteria they've selected. The same is true for writers who are offering solutions to problems or advancing an argument. If they are addressing specialists in a field, they can expect them to understand fairly technical issues. This will not be the case if they are writing to a general audience.

How Will My Role Affect My Work on My Document?

Just as your purpose, readers, and context will shape how you carry out your role, your role will influence the type of sources you use in your document and the type of critical thinking activities in which you engage as you work on your writing project.

Your Role Will Shape Your Choice of Sources

Given the differences in the documents produced by writers who adopt roles as different from each other as observer, evaluator, and advocator, it won't be surprising to learn that writers who adopt each role choose different types of sources. While a writer can draw on virtually every type of source, the role you adopt will tend to direct your attention to particular types of sources.

Role	News media	Historical works	Scholarly books, journal articles, and professional articles	Popular works (blogs, websites, videos, podcasts)	Field research (interviews, surveys, observation)
Observer	✓	✓		✓	✓
Reporter	✓	✓	✓	✓	✓
Interpreter	✓		✓	✓	
Evaluator			✓	✓	✓
Problem solver	✓		✓	✓	✓
Advocate	✓	✓	✓	✓	✓

Your Role Will Influence Your Critical Thinking

Carrying out a role, such as observer or interpreter, leads to particular types of critical thinking (see *Writing Processes Involve Critical Thinking* in Chapter 1). Bloom's taxonomy (with the addition of reflection as a form of critical thinking) provides a lens through which we can see differences in the critical thinking process that are typically involved in carrying out each of the roles addressed in this part of *Joining the Conversation*.

Role	Remembering	Understanding	Reflecting	Applying	Analyzing	Evaluating	Creating
Observer	•	•	↑	↓	↓	↓	↑
Reporter	•	↑	↓	↓	↓	↓	↑
Interpreter	•	•	•	•	↑	↓	↑
Evaluator	•	↑	•	↓	•	↑	↑
Problem solver	•	↑	•	•	↑	↑	↑
Advocate	•	↑	↑	↑	↑	↑	↑

Legend: ↓ Less frequently used, • Commonly used, ↑ Frequently used

Working Together: Explore Roles

Explore the roles you and your classmates take on during a conversation. In a group of five, ask three people to talk about a topic that has recently been in the news or that has been the focus of attention on campus. As the conversation unfolds, the other two members of the group should listen and write down the different roles that are adopted during the conversation, noting when and why the roles were adopted. After five minutes of conversation, respond to the following prompts:

1. **What roles were adopted?** The two observers should share their lists of roles. Ask whether each observer noticed the same roles. If there are differences, discuss them.

2. **When were different roles adopted?** Ask when each role was adopted. Which roles were adopted at the beginning of the conversation? Did the members of the conversation shift roles during the conversation? If so, when?

3. **Why were different roles adopted?** Explore the reasons for adopting each role. For example, ask whether people who knew more about the topic adopted different roles than those who knew less. If you saw shifts in roles, ask why those shifts occurred.

4. **Connect the activity to your work as a writer.** Consider how the idea of roles might play out in your own writing. As a group, discuss roles you've adopted in the past and consider how you might use the idea of roles in your future writing.

Can I Adopt More Than One Role?

As in spoken conversation, the roles writers play are not mutually exclusive. In an introduction to an argumentative essay, you might find yourself adopting the role of reporter, helping your readers understand an issue so that they are better positioned to understand the argument you'll advance later. Similarly, you might find yourself adopting the role of advocate in a problem-solving essay as you shift from explaining a potential solution to arguing that it should be put into effect. To understand how this fluid shifting of roles can take place — and make sense — reflect on your experiences in spoken conversations. Thinking of writing as a conversation makes it easier to understand how and when to shift roles.

In Summary: Choosing Your Writing Role

* ★ Understand the nature of writing roles (p. 120).
* ★ Understand the types of roles you can adopt (p. 120).
* ★ Consider how your writing situation helps you choose your role (p. 124).
* ★ Explore how your role shapes your use of sources and critical thinking skills (p. 128).
* ★ Understand the use of multiple roles (p. 130).

07 Writing to Reflect

What is writing to reflect? 131

What kinds of documents are used to share reflections? 132

Meditations 133
    James Parker, *An Ode to Not Being a Morning Person* 133

Photo essays 135
    James Mollison, *Where Children Sleep* 135

Literacy narratives 148
    Sandra Cisneros, *Only Daughter* 148

Memoirs 152
    Margo Jefferson, *Are We Rich?* 152

Genre Talk: Reflective Writing 157

How can I write a reflective essay? 158
Find a conversation and listen in 158
Reflect on your subject 160
Prepare a draft 165
Review and improve your draft 169

✳ **Student Essay** 173
    Caitlin Guariglia, *Mi Famiglia* 173

✳ **Project Ideas** 177

What Is Writing to Reflect?

Writing to reflect is carried out by writers who adopt the role of *observer* (see Chapter 6). It is one of the most common activities writers undertake. At the beginning of almost every writing project, writers spend time exploring and deepening their understanding of their subject. In this sense, writing to reflect provides a foundation for documents that inform, analyze, evaluate, solve problems, and convey arguments.

Reflection can also be the primary purpose for writing a document. In journals and diaries, writers reflect on a subject for personal reasons, often with the expectation that no one else will read their words. In more public documents — such as memoirs, letters, opinion columns, and blogs — writers also use reflection to share their thoughts in ways that benefit others.

Whether writing for themselves or others, writers use reflective writing to connect ideas and information, often in new and intriguing ways. Through reflection, writers can create new ways of understanding the world in which we live.

CHAPTER 07 | Writing to Reflect

THE WRITER'S ROLE:
Observer

"I write as an **observer** when I reflect on a topic."

PURPOSE
- To share a writer's insights about a subject
- To connect with readers

READERS
- Want to learn about other people's ideas and experiences
- Expect a personal treatment of the subject
- Welcome an unusual perspective

SOURCES
- Personal experiences and observations are often the major sources for reflective writing.
- Published sources might provide additional information to support a reflection.
- Cultural productions, such as music, art, movies, plays, and literature, can inspire reflection.

CONTEXT
- Reflections often draw on readers' knowledge of social events and their awareness of cultural context.
- Design choices anticipate the physical context in which the document is likely to be read.

CRITICAL THINKING

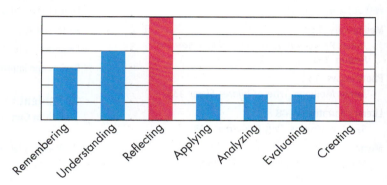

What Kinds of Documents Are Used to Share Reflections?

As a writer, you can use the reflections of other writers in many ways. Among other purposes, they can help you gain firsthand impressions from people who have been affected by an event. They can allow you to learn more about a particular historical period. They can help you understand the motivations and experiences of key figures in a political, cultural, or social movement. And they can help you develop a fuller understanding of your own experiences as you prepare your own reflective document.

You can begin to understand the contributions made by reflective documents by learning about the purposes, readers, sources, and contexts that have influenced other writers. In the following sections, you'll find discussions and examples of memoirs, meditations, photo essays, and literacy essays.

Meditations

James Parker
An Ode to Not Being a Morning Person

Meditations convey a writer's observations and thoughts on a subject to the members of a written conversation. Like memoirs and literacy narratives, meditations draw on personal experience and are often written from a first-person (*I*, *me*, *my*) point of view. However, writers of reflective essays generally move beyond themselves as the primary focus of their essays, typically by using personal experience as a foundation for exploring more abstract ideas. In doing so, they show the significance of their experiences in a broader context.

In "An Ode to Not Being a Morning Person," James Parker shares his reflections on the differences between morning people and those who struggle to face the day. His brief essay ultimately highlights his own ways of dealing with the unpleasantness of waking up far too early, all shared with the wit and good humor that characterizes much of his writing for the *Atlantic*.

An Ode to Not Being a Morning Person

James Parker

> Parker is a staff writer for the *Atlantic* and the author of the book *Turned On: A Biography of Henry Rollins*.

Me, I can fake it.

Stale as I may be from the night before, one foot — one leg — stuck in the underworld, I can still crank up the sociability. I can manufacture perkiness at an early hour. Good morning! Good morning! Am I even faking it? Perhaps not. It *is* good to wake up. I *do* rejoice in the restoration of consciousness, the grand democracy of daylight. Yes! Good morning!

You, on the other hand . . . No faking for you. You're condemned to a splendid and groaning authenticity. Waking is suffering, humans are intolerable, and you cannot, you will not, hide it. You wince, you flinch, you shuffle around. Should you happen, by some mischance, to encounter another person before you've gotten yourself together, you rear back like a scalded troll. The hours of sleep, it appears, have not refreshed you — they have *flayed* you.

> In nonacademic essays, writers frequently assume the role of observers and interpreters. In this brief essay, humor is used to share the author's reflections.

And that's what I like about you, non-morning person: your fastidiousness. Your great delicacy of being. You don't bounce giddily from oblivion to wakefulness, taking it all for granted, confident of finding things more or less as you left them at bedtime. No, no, it's a change; it's arduous; it's *real*. Deflector shields: gone. Resilience: none. The world is upon you as a pressure, an aesthetic offense, a ghastly payload of noise and glare and babbling, galumphing people. You'll be okay, you'll get there, but you need time. Complex operations of personal reassembly are required. There's an essential, existential honesty to what you're doing: Every morning, out of old socks and empty bottles of ibuprofen, you build yourself anew.

Morning person versus non–morning person. It's a classic duality, isn't it? It's Hardy versus Laurel. It's McCartney versus Lennon: *Woke up, fell out of bed, / Dragged a comb across my head* versus *Please don't wake me, no, don't shake me, / Leave me where I am*. And, this being America, we're heavily weighted in favor of productivity and go-get-'em-ness. What politician will confess to having trouble waking up? You're a bit countercultural, non–morning person, sunk in your vibes, crowned with your bedhead. You're a subversive.

And here's a truth: Morning people fizzle. They front-load the day, they burn all their energy before 10 o'clock, and the remaining hours are just a kind of higher zombiedom. By mid-afternoon, a morning person is wan and sugar-starved. But you non–morning people get stronger: Like Antaeus, whose power increased every time Hercules took him down, you are nourished by contact with the Earth. You run on heavy fuel. You draw your strength from the slumbering core of the planet, where morning never breaks.

> Parker concludes on an optimistic note, praising the strength and resilience of non-morning people.

In your writer's notebook, analyze how Parker's writing strategies contribute to his humorous reflection by responding to the following questions:

Starting a Conversation: Thinking Critically about "An Ode to Not Being a Morning Person"

1. What roles does Parker take on in this piece? At what points in the reading would you describe him as an observer, an interpreter, or an advocate?

2. How does Parker share his observations about the differences between morning people and non-morning people? In what ways does he draw on his personal experiences to move his meditation forward?

3. "An Ode to Not Being a Morning Person" originally appeared in the *Atlantic*, which generally has an educated and relatively affluent audience. What aspects of this meditation reflect that readership and the assumptions Parker makes about them?

4. As a staff writer for the *Atlantic*, Parker publishes a range of longer and shorter pieces. In addition to meditation, what other genres might you use to classify this reading? What elements of this piece make the "meditation" label suitable?

5. **Reflection:** Toward the end of the essay, Parker muses, "You're a bit countercultural, non-morning person, sunk in your vibes, crowned with your bedhead. You're a subversive." How does his witty, humorous tone throughout the essay affect your view of him and his reflections?

Photo Essays

James Mollison
Where Children Sleep

A photo essay combines text and photographs to create a dominant impression of a subject, often suggesting the author's main idea rather than stating it outright. As a visual document, a photo essay offers a powerful and refreshing opportunity to convey thoughts and emotions that might not easily be put into words and to present complex concepts in a way that readers can grasp almost intuitively.

The photos reprinted on the following pages are from *Where Children Sleep*, a collection of photographer James Mollison's portraits of children from around the world and the rooms in which they sleep. When he embarked on the project, Mollison says, "I soon realized that my own experience of having a 'bedroom' simply doesn't apply to so many kids." Born in Kenya, Mollison grew up in England and currently lives with his family in Venice. His work has been featured in many international publications.

Many reflective photo essays visually explore subjects that have spurred debate, seem misunderstood, or are relatively unknown to readers. Others are deeply personal, highlighting images and experiences intimately connected to the writer's life. In this photo essay, Mollison tries to do both, showing unfamiliar places where children around the world do a very familiar thing: sleep.

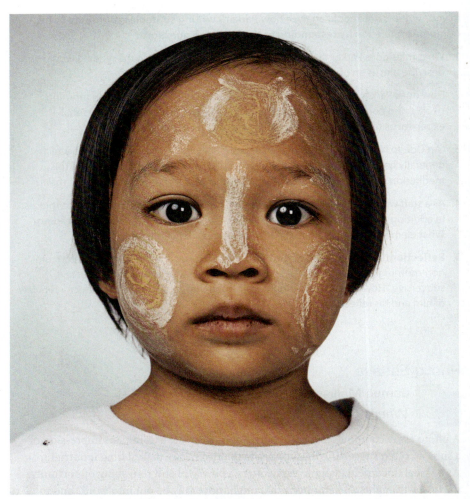

▲ Lay Lay is four years old. The cream she has on her face is made from the bark of the thanaka tree, used to condition and protect the skin. Lay Lay lives in Mae Sot, Thailand, close to the border with Burma. When her mother died, no other members of her family came to claim her, so she was placed in an orphanage. She shares this home with twenty-one other nursery-aged children. The orphanage consists of two rooms. During the day, one room is the classroom and the other is a dining room. At night, these rooms become bedrooms. The tables are pushed to one side and mats are rolled out for the children to sleep on. Each child has one drawer in which to keep their belongings. Lay Lay does not have many belongings — just a few clothes. All that is known of her background is that she is from an ethnic group of people called the Karen, one of the persecuted minority ethnic groups which make up about forty percent of the Burmese population. Lay Lay and her mother fled from the brutal Burmese military dictatorship and arrived in Thailand as refugees.

Where Children Sleep by © James Mollison, published in 2010

What Kinds of Documents Are Used to Share Reflections? | CHAPTER 07

Where Children Sleep by © James Mollison, published in 2010

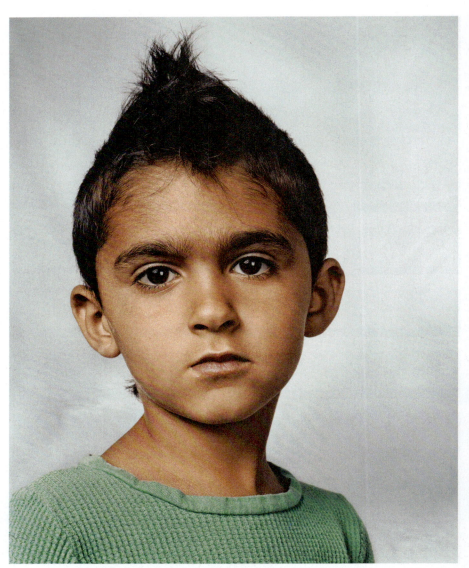

> Along with each set of photographs, Mollison includes biographical details about each child to provide context for the portraits.

▲ Jivan is four years old. He lives with his parents in a skyscraper in Brooklyn, New York. From his bedroom window, he can see across the East River to New York's Manhattan Island and the Williamsburg Suspension Bridge, which connects it to Brooklyn. Jivan has his own bedroom with an en-suite bathroom and a toy cupboard. The room was designed by Jivan's mother, who is an interior designer. His father is a DJ and music producer. Jivan's school is only a ten minute walk away. To gain a place at his school, Jivan had to take a test to prove that he can mix socially with other children. He found this quite stressful as he is a very shy boy. His parents were also interviewed before he was accepted by the school. Jivan's favorite foods are steak and chocolate. He would like to be a fireman when he grows up.

Where Children Sleep by © James Mollison, published in 2010

Where Children Sleep by © James Mollison, published in 2010

> Writers might rely on published images from historical and contemporary sources or present original photographs. In this essay, Mollison traveled around the world to collect the photographs for his essay.

▲ Kaya is four years old. She lives with her parents in a small apartment in Tokyo, Japan. Most apartments in Japan are small because land is very expensive to buy and there is such a large population to accommodate. Kaya's bedroom is every little girl's dream. It is lined from floor to ceiling with clothes and dolls. Kaya's mother makes all Kaya's dresses — up to three a month, usually. Now Kaya has thirty dresses and coats, thirty pairs of shoes, sandals, and boots, and numerous wigs. (The pigtails in this picture are made from hairpieces.) Her friends love to come around to try on her clothes. When she goes to school, however, she has to wear a school uniform. Her favorite foods are meat, potatoes, strawberries, and peaches. She wants to be a cartoonist when she grows up, drawing Japanese anime cartoons.

Where Children Sleep by © James Mollison, published in 2010

What Kinds of Documents Are Used to Share Reflections? | CHAPTER 07

Where Children Sleep by © James Mollison, published in 2010

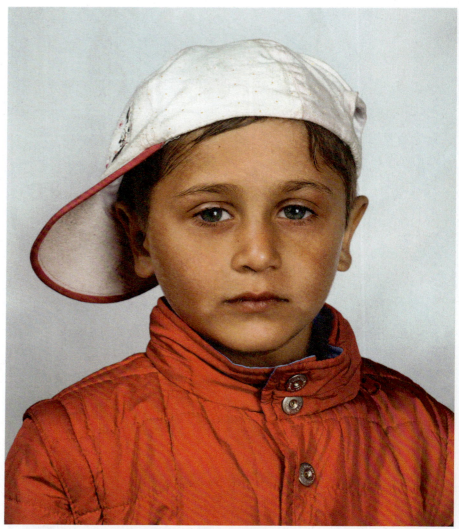

▲ Home for this four-year-old boy and his family is a mattress in a field on the outskirts of Rome, Italy. The family came from Romania by bus, after begging on the streets for enough money to pay for their tickets (€100 per adult and €80 per child). When they first arrived in Rome, they camped in a tent, but the police threw them off the site because they were trespassing on private land and did not have the correct documents. Now the family sleeps together on the mattress in the open. When it rains, they hastily erect a tent and use umbrellas for shelter, hoping they will not be spotted by the police. They left Romania without identity documents or work papers and so are unable to obtain legal employment. This boy sits by the curbside while his parents clean car windshields at traffic lights, to earn thirty to fifty cents a time. No one from the boy's family has ever been to school. His parents cannot read or write.

Where Children Sleep by © James Mollison, published in 2010

What Kinds of Documents Are Used to Share Reflections? | CHAPTER 07

Where Children Sleep by © James Mollison, published in 2010

> Photos serve a central role in the author's reflection because they contribute to the meaning of the document. Text and image play off each other to reinforce ideas and to clarify what the writer has to say.

▲ Indira lives with her parents, brother and sister near Kathmandu in Nepal. Her house has only one room, with one bed and one mattress. At bedtime, the children share the mattress on the floor. Indira is seven years old and has worked at the local granite quarry since she was three. The family is very poor so everyone has to work. There are 150 other children working at the quarry, some of whom will lose their sight because they do not have goggles to protect their eyes from stone splinters. Indira works five or six hours a day and then helps her mother with household chores such as cleaning and cooking. Her favorite food is noodles. She also attends school, which is a thirty minute walk away. She does not mind working at the quarry but would prefer to be playing. She would like to be a Nepalese dancer when she grows up.

Where Children Sleep by © James Mollison, published in 2010

What Kinds of Documents Are Used to Share Reflections? | CHAPTER 07

Where Children Sleep by © James Mollison, published in 2010

Readers are invited to draw their own conclusions from what they see, although authors of photo essays typically use the surrounding text to nudge readers in a particular direction. In this essay, Mollison presents the facts and photos of each child's situation, trusting them to be powerful enough that readers will not need his explicit commentary to draw the conclusions he is intending.

▲ Li is ten years old and lives in an apartment block in Beijing, China, with her parents. She is an only child — as a result of the Chinese government's "one child per family" policy, introduced to control population growth. China has since ended the policy. Li goes to a school nearby, where she enjoys learning math, singing, and music. She is a perfectionist and will spend up to three hours each night completing her homework to the highest standard. She also attends ballet classes twice a week after school. Three times during her school life, she will have to attend a compulsory army summer camp organized by the People's Liberation Army. In preparation for this she has to attend army training. Li does not want to be in the army when she grows up. She wants to be a policewoman so that she can protect people.

Where Children Sleep by © James Mollison, published in 2010

What Kinds of Documents Are Used to Share Reflections? | CHAPTER 07

Where Children Sleep by © James Mollison, published in 2010

Starting a Conversation: Thinking Critically about "Where Children Sleep"

In your writer's notebook, reflect on the ideas presented in Mollison's photo essay by responding to the following questions:

1. A reflective photo essay such as this one might not have a strictly defined thesis statement. But how would you describe the main idea of Mollison's work? What is the dominant impression created by his mix of words and pictures?

2. While he acknowledges the issues of poverty and wealth that inform his photos, Mollison says, "There is no agenda to the book other than my own journey and curiosity, and wanting to share in pictures and words the stories that I found interesting, or that moved me." In what ways does this statement fit with the purpose of a reflective document? What changes do you think Mollison would have made to his approach if he had, in fact, been creating an analytical or argumentative photo essay?

3. As you look at the photographs and their accompanying text, consider this statement from Mollison: "The book is written and presented for an audience of 9–13 year olds . . . intended to interest and engage children in the details of the lives of other children around the world, and the social issues affecting them, while also being a serious photographic essay for an adult audience." How successfully do you think Mollison's work reaches each of those audiences? What do you see in Mollison's writing style and in the composition of his photographs that would appeal to adults and to older children? What do you think members of each audience — nine-to-thirteen-year-olds, older teens, and adults — would take away from his work?

4. Why do you suppose that Mollison chose to use color images? Would black-and-white photographs have had as much impact, more impact, or less impact? Why do you think so?

5. **Reflection:** Consider how Mollison's photographs might have been different if he had chosen to focus on one country or region of the world. How do you think his audience and their expectations of his work would have changed, and how would they have remained the same?

Literacy Narratives

Sandra Cisneros
Only Daughter

Literacy narratives allow writers to reflect on the people, ideas, and events that have shaped them as writers and readers. What distinguishes literacy narratives from other reflective documents is not their design — they are often indistinguishable in appearance from essays or brief memoirs — but their purpose. They exist solely to help writers share their reflections about their relationship with reading and writing. Sandra Cisneros' literacy narrative "Only Daughter" focuses on the influence of her father on her development as a writer.

Only Daughter

Sandra Cisneros

Once, several years ago, when I was just starting out my writing career, I was asked to write my own contributor's note for an anthology I was part of. I wrote: "I am the only daughter in a family of six sons. *That* explains everything."

Well, I've thought about that ever since, and yes, it explains a lot to me, but for the reader's sake I should have written: "I am the only daughter in a *Mexican* family of six sons." Or even: "I am the only daughter of a Mexican father and a Mexican-American mother." Or: "I am the only daughter of a working-class family of nine." All of these had everything to do with who I am today.

I was/am the only daughter and *only* a daughter. Being an only daughter in a family of six sons forced me by circumstance to spend a lot of time by myself because my brothers felt it beneath them to play with a *girl* in public. But that aloneness, that loneliness, was good for a would-be writer—it allowed me time to think and think, to imagine, to read and prepare myself.

Being only a daughter for my father meant my destiny would lead me to become someone's wife. That's what he believed. But when I was in the fifth grade and shared my plans for college with him, I was sure he understood. I remember my father saying, "*Que bueno, mi'ha*, that's good." That meant a lot to me, especially since my brothers thought the idea hilarious. What I didn't realize was that my father thought college was good for girls — good for finding a husband. After four years in college and two more in graduate school, and still no husband, my father shakes his head even now and says I wasted all that education. In retrospect, I'm lucky my father believed daughters were meant for husbands. It meant it didn't matter if I majored in something silly like English. After all, I'd find a nice professional eventually, right? This allowed me the liberty to putter about embroidering my little poems and stories without my father interrupting with so much as a "What's that you're writing?"

But the truth is, I wanted him to interrupt. I wanted my father to understand what it was I was scribbling, to introduce me as "My only daughter, the writer." Not as "This is only my daughter. She teaches." *Es maestra* — teacher. Not even *profesora*.

Sandra Cisneros is a poet, short story writer, novelist, essayist, performer, and artist whose work explores the lives of the working class. Her numerous awards include fellowships in both poetry and fiction from the National Endowment for the Arts, the Texas Medal of the Arts, a MacArthur fellowship, several honorary doctorates, and national and international book awards, including the National Medal of the Arts award presented to her by President Barack Obama in 2016.

"Only Daughter" appeared in *Latina: Women's Voices from the Borderlands*, published by Touchstone/Simon & Schuster in 1995.

Literacy narratives are often assigned in college classes because they give students an opportunity to examine their past experiences with written expression and, in doing so, to overcome any assumptions or fears they might have.

Some literacy narratives, such as this one, focus on a critical event or series of events that influenced a person's identity as a writer. Others offer a comprehensive overview of the experiences that shaped the writer's relationship with words.

Because of their focus on the writer's life, most literacy narratives use details drawn from personal experience to support points. In this case, Cisneros offers a series of concrete, evocative details drawn from her early years as a member of her family.

> Sometimes writers of literacy narratives draw on information from published sources to provide a context for their narrative. In this case, Cisneros draws on examples from popular culture.

In a sense, everything I have ever written has been for him, to win his approval even though I know my father can't read English words, even though my father's only reading includes the brown-ink *Esto* sports magazines from Mexico City and the bloody *¡Alarma!* magazines that feature yet another sighting of *La Virgen de Guadalupe* on a tortilla or a wife's revenge on her philandering husband by bashing his skull in with a *molcajete* (a kitchen mortar made of volcanic rock). Or the *fotonovelas*, the little picture paperbacks with tragedy and trauma erupting from the characters' mouths in bubbles.

My father represents, then, the public majority. A public who is disinterested in reading, and yet one whom I am writing about and for, and privately trying to woo.

When we were growing up in Chicago, we moved a lot because of my father. He suffered bouts of nostalgia. Then we'd have to let go of our flat, store the furniture with mother's relatives, load the station wagon with baggage and bologna sandwiches and head south. To Mexico City.

We came back, of course. To yet another Chicago flat, another Chicago neighborhood, another Catholic school. Each time, my father would seek out the parish priest in order to get a tuition break, and complain or boast: "I have seven sons."

He meant siete *hijos*, seven children, but he translated it as "sons." "I have seven sons." To anyone who would listen. The Sears Roebuck employee who sold us the washing machine. The short-order cook where my father ate his ham-and-eggs breakfasts. "I have seven sons." As if he deserved a medal from the state.

My papa. He didn't mean anything by that mistranslation, I'm sure. But somehow I could feel myself being erased. I'd tug my father's sleeve and whisper: "Not seven sons. Six! and *one daughter*."

When my oldest brother graduated from medical school, he fulfilled my father's dream that we study hard and use this — our heads, instead of this — our hands. Even now my father's hands are thick and yellow, stubbed by a history of hammer and nails and twine and coils and springs. "Use this," my father said, tapping his head, "and not this," showing us those hands. He always looked tired when he said it.

Wasn't college an investment? And hadn't I spent all those years in college? And if I didn't marry, what was it all for? Why would anyone go to college and then choose to be poor? Especially someone who had always been poor.

Last year, after ten years of writing professionally, the financial rewards started to trickle in. My second National Endowment for the Arts Fellowship. A guest professorship at the University of California, Berkeley. My book, which sold to a major New York publishing house.

At Christmas, I flew home to Chicago. The house was throbbing, same as always: hot tamales and sweet tamales hissing in my mother's pressure cooker, and everybody — my mother, six brothers, wives, babies, aunts, cousins — talking too loud and at the same time. Like in a Fellini film, because that's just how we are.

I went upstairs to my father's room. One of my stories had just been translated into Spanish and published in an anthology of Chicano writing and I wanted to show it to him. Ever since he recovered from a stroke two years ago, my father likes to spend his leisure hours horizontally. And that's how I found him, watching a Pedro Infante movie on Galavisión and eating rice pudding.

There was a glass filled with milk on the bedside table. There were several vials of pills and balled Kleenex. And on the floor, one black sock and a plastic urinal that I didn't want to look at but looked at anyway. Pedro Infante was about to burst into song, and my father was laughing.

I'm not sure if it was because my story was translated into Spanish, or because it was published in Mexico, or perhaps because the story dealt with Tepeyac, the *colonia* my father was raised in and the house he grew up in, but at any rate, my father punched the mute button on his remote control and read my story.

I sat on the bed next to my father and waited. He read it very slowly. As if he were reading each line over and over. He laughed at all the right places and read lines he liked out loud. He pointed and asked questions: "Is this So-and-so?" "Yes," I said. He kept reading.

When he was finally finished, after what seemed like hours, my father looked up and asked: "Where can we get more copies of this for the relatives?"

Of all the wonderful things that happened to me last year, that was the most wonderful.

> Experienced writers frequently write literacy narratives, sometimes to share their joy of reading or their reasons for writing but just as often to connect with their readers by exploring the challenges and rewards of learning to read and write.

Starting a Conversation: Thinking Critically about "Only Daughter"

In your writer's notebook, consider Cisneros's reflections on her writing life by responding to the following questions:

1. How does Cisneros re-create the experience of her younger self throughout this piece? Do phrases such as this one — "What I didn't realize was that my father thought college was good for girls — good for finding a husband" (para. 4) — seem realistic to you? Why or why not?

2. Cisneros, reflecting on her relationship with writing and her father, writes, "In a sense, everything I have ever written has been for him, to win his approval even though I know my father can't read English words. . . ." As you think about the success she eventually enjoyed, what do these words reveal about her motivations as a writer? Do you think her success is related only to her father? What else might have motivated her?

3. In the middle of the essay, Cisneros includes a brief paragraph: "My father represents, then, the public majority. A public who is disinterested in reading, and yet one whom I am writing about and for, and privately trying to woo." What do you think Cisneros would regard as success in wooing a disinterested public — or, more specifically, her father?

4. Literacy narratives focus on moments or events that shape a person's relationship with words. How would you describe the change in Cisneros's attitude toward writing and reading?

5. **Reflection:** In what ways does Cisneros's essay lead you to reflect on your own development as a writer? If you had the opportunity to sit down with Cisneros, what stories might you share with her? What would those stories say about you as a writer?

Memoirs

Margo Jefferson
Are We Rich?

A memoir is a narrative that presents and reflects on personal experience, usually from a writer's past. "Are We Rich?" is an excerpt from Margo Jefferson's memoir *Negroland*. A personal reflection, but also a meditation on the larger discussion of race in America, the memoir recounts Jefferson's experience as a young Black girl in an affluent Chicago family. Jefferson is a Pulitzer Prize winner and a professor of writing at the Columbia University School of the Arts. She has also taught at Eugene Lang College and New York University. Formerly a cultural critic for the *New York Times* and a staff writer for *Newsweek*, Jefferson has also been published in *Vogue*, *Harper's*, and other magazines. Her first book was *On Michael Jackson*.

ARE WE RICH?

I

Are we rich? Mother raises those plucked, deep-toned eyebrows that did such good, expressive work for women in the 1950s. Lift the penciled arch by three to four millimeters and you had bemused doubt, blatant disdain, or disapproval just playful enough to lure the speaker into more error. Mother's lips form a small, cool smile that mirrors her eyebrow arch. She places a small, emphatic space between each word—"Are We Rich?"—then adds, "Why do you ask?"

I ask because I have been told that day: "Your family must be rich." A schoolmate told me and I faltered, then stalled—flattered and ashamed to be. We are supposed to eschew petty snobberies at the University of Chicago Laboratory School: intellectual superiority is our task. Other fathers are doctors. Other mothers dress well and drive stylish cars. Wondering what stirred that question has left me anxious and a little queasy.

Mother says: "We are not rich. And it's impolite to ask anyone that question. Remember that. If you're asked again, you should just say 'we're comfortable.'" I take her words in and push on, because my classmate has asked a second question.

Are we upper class?

Mother's eyebrows settle now. She sits back in the den chair and pauses for effect. I am about to receive general instruction in the liturgies of race and class.

"We're considered upper-class Negroes and upper-middle-class Americans," Mother says. "But most people would like to consider us Just More Negroes."

II

"D. and J. asked me if we know their janitor, Mr. Johnson. They think he lives near us." (They had spoken of him so affectionately that I wished I could say I knew our janitor that well and that he liked me as much as Mr. Johnson seemed to like them. They had rights of intimacy with their janitor that I lacked.)

I have to stop here, though. My policy in these pages is to use initials when I recall the mishaps or misdeeds of my peers. Their words and acts belong to me; their names belong to them. I know initials look silly in dialogue that aims for realism. But I didn't want to use their names. They were my dear friends—one from sixth grade on, the other from our twenties on—and we grew into talking honestly about these matters. They were twins and now they're dead, killed by cancer. I didn't want them to be so starkly flawed here. But for now, they must be. And so:

> Memoirs can vary greatly in length, from a few hundred words to multiple-volume books. In this case, Jefferson paints a brief but compelling portrait of her childhood explorations about race and wealth.

> Writers of memoirs usually employ the first-person point of view (*I*, *me*, *we*), emphasize text over visuals, and look for ways to make their personal stories relevant for readers.

> Jefferson's experience in *Negroland*, her term for "the colored elite" or privileged, educated African Americans of the 1950s, reveals fraught comparisons between "us" and "them"—comparisons not only between Blacks and Whites but also between well-to-do Blacks and working-class Blacks.

> In retelling a story from her childhood, Jefferson explores class through the complication of race, juxtaposing her childhood questions with her now adult knowledge.

"Debi and Judi asked me if we know their janitor, Mr. Johnson. They think he lives near us."

"It's a big neighborhood," Mother says. "Why would we know their janitor? White people think Negroes all know each other, and they always want you to know their janitor. Do they want to know our laundryman?"

That would be Wally, a smiling, big-shouldered white man who delivers crisply wrapped shirts and cheerful greetings to our back door every week.

"Good morning, Mrs. Jefferson," he says. "Good morning, Doctor. Hello, girls."

"Hello, Wally," we chime back from the breakfast table. Then, one weekend afternoon, I was in the kitchen with Mother doing something minor and domestic, like helping unpack groceries, when she said slowly, not looking at me: "I saw Wally at Sears today. I was looking at vacuum cleaners. And I looked up and saw him—" (Here she paused for the distancing Rodgers and Hammerstein irony, "*across a crowded room.*") "He was turning his head away, hoping he wouldn't have to speak. Wally the laundryman was trying to cut me." If this had been drama, she would have paused and done something with a telling prop—one of the better brands of an everyday food, or a nice-looking piece of flatware. Then she said, "And I don't even shop at Sears except for appliances."

Humor is laughing at what you haven't got when you ought to have it—the right, in this case, to snub or choose to speak kindly to your laundryman in a store where he must shop for clothes and you shop only for appliances.

Still, Wally went on delivering laundry with cheerful deference, and we responded with cooler—but not intrusively cool—civility.

Was there no Negro laundry to do Daddy's shirts as well or better? Our milkman was a Negro. So were our janitor, our plumber, our carpenter, our upholsterer, our caterer, and our dressmaker. Though I don't remember all their names, I know their affect was restful. Comfortable. If a Negro employee did his work in a sloppy or sullen way (and it did happen), Mother and Daddy had two responses. One was your standard folk wisecrack, something like "Well, some of us *are* lazy, quiet as it's kept." *Humor is laughing at what you haven't got when you ought to have it:* in this case, a spotless race reputation.

The second response was disquieting. "Some Negroes prefer to work for white people. They don't resent their status in the same way."

All right then, let's say you are a Negro cleaning woman, on your knees at this moment, scrubbing the bathtub with its extremely visible ring of body dirt, because whoever bathed last night thought, *How nice. I don't have to clean the tub because Cleo / Melba / Mrs. Jenkins comes tomorrow!* Tub done, you check behind the toilet (a washcloth has definitely fallen back there); the towels are scrunched, not hung on the racks, and you've just come from the children's bedroom, where sheets have to be untangled and almost throttled into shape before they can be sorted for the wash.

Would you rather look at the people you do this for and think: I will never be in their place if the future is like the past. Or would you rather look at your employers and think: Well, if I'd been able to get an education like Dr. and Mrs. Jefferson, if I hadn't had to start doing housework at fifteen to help my family out when we moved up here from Mississippi, then maybe I could be where they are.

Whose privilege would you find easier to bear?

Who are "you"? How does your sociological vita — race or ethnicity, class, gender, family history — affect your answer?

Whoever you are, reader, please understand that neither my parents, my sister, nor I ever left a dirty bathtub for Mrs. Blake to clean. (My sister and I called her Mrs. Blake. Mother called her Blake.) She was broad, not fat. She had very short, very straightened hair that she patted flat and put behind her ears. When it got humid in the basement, where the washer and dryer were, or in the room where she ironed clothes, short pieces of hair would defy hot comb and oil to stick up and out. We never made direct fun of her hair — we would have been punished. But we regularly mocked Negro hair that blatantly defied rehabilitation. Mrs. B.'s voice was Southern South Side: leisurely and nasal. Now that I've given my adult attention to the classic blues singers, I can say she had the weighted country diction of Ma Rainey and the short nasal tones of Sippie Wallace. Vowels rubbed down, end-word consonants dropped or muffled.

Mother made it clear that we were never to leave our beds unmade when Mrs. Blake was coming. She was not there to pick up after us. When we were old enough, we stripped our own beds each week and folded the linen before putting it in the hamper for her to remove and wash.

Mother's paternal grandmother, great-aunt, and aunt had been in service, so she was sensitive to inappropriate childish presumption.

Mrs. Blake ate her lunch (a hot lunch that Mother had made from dinner leftovers) in the kitchen. When her day was done, Mr. Blake and their daughters drove to our house. He sent his daughters to the front door to pick her up. They had the same initials we did. Mildred and Diane. Margo and Denise. Mother brought us to the front door to exchange hellos with them. Sometimes Mrs. Blake left carrying one or two bags of neatly folded clothes. Did Mildred and Diane enjoy unfolding, surveying, and fitting themselves into our used ensembles and separates?

> Writers of longer (book-length) memoirs usually address a more general audience of readers who share their interest in a certain aspect of their lives. Writers of shorter memoirs often focus on a specific moment and address readers of a particular publication, such as a newspaper, magazine, journal, or website. In this memoir, Jefferson assumes a relatively educated audience with some familiarity with issues of race and class.

Starting a Conversation: Thinking Critically about "Are We Rich?"

In your writer's notebook, reflect on the ideas presented in Jefferson's memoir by responding to the following questions:

1. The primary question, "Are we rich?," suggests that Jefferson is reflecting on social class. Yet she does more than this. What are the other underlying themes that she calls into question? How do these other themes change the implication of the question "Are we rich?" Does Jefferson answer the question? If so, in what ways is the question answered? If not, how does she leave the question unanswered?

2. The essay is divided into two sections. What is the effect of this structure? How do the sections complement or contrast with one another?

3. The essay begins and ends with a question, and there are a number of questions throughout the narrative. Do you find this pattern effective? Why or why not? Why do you think Jefferson thought it would be a good way to engage her readers?

4. Note a few of the moments in which the narrator switches from the past to the present. How does the narrator's voice change? Why do you think Jefferson alternates between reporting and reflecting? In what ways does this engage the reader?

5. **Reflection:** Think back on whether you were aware of your family's social or economic standing as a child. How has your understanding changed since then?

GENRE TALK

Reflective Writing | Informative Writing | Analytical Writing | Evaluative Writing | Problem-Solving Writing | Argumentative Writing

In the post-9/11 era, stories of returning home from war are gaining attention as more and more veterans decide to speak out about the lasting effects — both physical and psychological — of war. While some veterans opt for persuasive or problem-solving writing in the form of editorials or opinion columns, many prefer reflective documents, such as short stories, documentaries, and feature films. Run by the American Folklife Center at the Library of Congress, the Veterans History Project is a multimedia effort to collect and preserve the reflections of those who have fought in the U.S. armed services. The project contains letters, diaries, scrapbooks, drawings, photographs, videotaped interviews, and audio interviews with veterans from World War I up through the Iraq and Afghan wars. An audio interview is featured here.

A quotation by Gunnery Sgt. Noël and a photograph of her in uniform emphasize the difference between her civilian identity ("Rosie") and her identity as a marine ("Gunny Noël").

The record contains biographical information, details of Gunnery Sgt. Noël's deployments, and a brief description of her war experience.

Both the full audio interview and clips of highlights are available on the web as part of the Library of Congress Veterans History Project.

Links to additional documents, including photos and correspondence.

How Can I Write a Reflective Essay?

For some writers, the greatest challenge in writing a reflective essay is getting past the idea that no one would be interested in reading their reflections on a subject. In fact, readers show a great deal of interest in reflective writing. They buy memoirs and autobiographies, visit blogs, and read opinion columns. They read articles and essays in which writers share their thoughts about their experiences and ideas. Some readers even try to pick the locks on their siblings' diaries or journals.

Writing a reflective essay involves choosing and reflecting on a subject, preparing a draft, and reviewing and improving what you've written. As you work on your draft, you'll draw primarily on critical thinking skills that involve remembering, understanding, reflecting, and creating. As you work on your essay, you'll follow the work of Caitlin Guariglia, an Italian American student who wrote a reflective essay about a family trip to Italy.

In Process

A Reflective Essay about a Family Vacation

Caitlin Guariglia wrote a reflective essay for her introductory composition course. Caitlin based her reflection on a family trip to Italy, using her observations of the people she met in Rome to consider how cultural influences affect her Italian American family's behavior. Follow her efforts to write the essay as you read the In Process boxes throughout this chapter.

Courtesy of Caitlin Guariglia

Find a Conversation and Listen In

Reflective essays allow you to share your thoughts about a subject with readers who might have a common interest in it. You might reflect on a personal experience, an idea you've encountered in a book or a blog, a photograph or other physical object that holds special meaning for you, a person you've met or read about, a troubling conversation with a friend, or a recent event. In fact, you can reflect on almost anything. To get started on your reflective essay, spend some time thinking about your purpose, your readers, and the context in which your writing will be read (see *What Should I Know about Writing Situations?* in Chapter 1). Then generate some ideas about possible subjects for your reflection, choose one that seems promising, and learn more about it by observing it closely or discussing it with others.

- **EXPLORE YOUR EXPERIENCES**

Brainstorming (see *Generate Ideas* in Chapter 2) provides a good way to generate ideas for the subject of a reflective essay. Start by asking questions about your past or recent experiences, such as the following:

- Why is my favorite childhood memory so special to me?
- Did I learn anything about myself this weekend?

- What surprised me in my history class this week?
- What story that is currently in the news annoys me the most?
- What is the last thing that made me laugh?

Use your imagination to come up with questions about your personal, academic, and professional experiences. Quickly jot down answers to your questions. Then review your answers to identify a subject that will meet your purpose, interest your readers, and be suitable for the context, requirements, and limitations of your writing assignment. If you're still not sure you've found the right inspiration for a topic, check the writing project ideas at the end of this chapter.

● ASK QUESTIONS ABOUT PROMISING SUBJECTS

You can begin to focus on a subject by asking questions about it (see *Generate Ideas* in Chapter 2). If you were considering writing a reflective essay about online communities such as Facebook or Twitter, for example, you might use the following strategies to identify interesting aspects of the subject.

- **Ask *why, why not, when, where,* and *who.*** You might ask why some people react negatively to social-media sites such as Facebook, or you might ask who is likely to cause difficulties for members of online communities.

- **Ask how your subject functions as a whole.** You might ask how social media is changing how people communicate, whether they represent a distinctly different kind of community, or why they're so popular with a particular age group.

- **Ask about parts of a whole.** You might ask which aspects of online communities are more attractive than others or whether one subgroup in an online community is likely to behave differently than another subgroup.

- **Ask questions about degree and extent.** You can ask about the degree to which something affects something else or about the extent of a problem. For instance, you might ask whether friendships formed at a school are similar to the formation of online communities.

● CONDUCT AN OBSERVATION

If you've chosen a subject that lends itself to observation, you might find it useful to conduct one. Observing a subject firsthand can provide you with valuable insights that simply aren't possible when you're learning about the subject secondhand — for example, through discussion or through reading a book, magazine, or web page. In addition, conducting an observation can increase your credibility as a writer.

A reflective essay usually carries more weight if the writer has taken the time to observe the subject personally.

Although some observations can involve a significant amount of time and effort, an observation need not be complicated to be useful.

Reflect on Your Subject

Perhaps you've had the opportunity to listen to musicians jamming during a concert, or perhaps you're a musician yourself. If so, you know about the ebb and flow of the music, how one line of melody plays off another, how the music circles and builds. Reflection is similar to this process. As you reflect on a subject, your thinking moves from one aspect to another, flowing smoothly forward at some times and circling back at others. Reflection can involve seeking understanding, making connections, and exploring contrasts. In the same way that a jam session offers surprises not only to listeners but also to the musicians, reflection can lead you in unexpected directions. The key to reflecting productively is a willingness to be open to those new directions.

Reflection is most effective when you record your thoughts. Writing them down as notes in a writer's notebook or as entries in a journal allows you to keep track of your thinking. As you make decisions about your writing project, you can turn to your notes to review your reflections.

Working Together: Try It Out Loud

Before you start writing a reflective essay, try having a conversation with your classmates about a common experience. Form small groups and list the subjects each of you is considering writing about. Choose one that most people in the group can relate to (such as an embarrassing moment, a fight with a friend, or the first day of class). Take turns sharing your memories about the experience while the other members of the group listen, respond, and ask questions. Your purpose is to connect with the other members of your group, so try to present an honest, personal view of the event.

When you are finished, take a few minutes to reflect on the exercise. What did you learn about your audience? Did you have to adapt what you said based on their interest level or on those parts of your story they didn't understand? What did you discover about what you have in common and what you do not?

Reflection begins with viewing your subject from a particular perspective. It also involves collecting details and finding significance. To prepare to reflect, place yourself in a relaxing situation that will allow you to think. Take a walk, ride a bike, go for a run, enjoy a good meal, listen to music, lie down — do whatever you think will free you from distractions.

In Process

Conducting an Observation

Caitlin Guariglia's reflective essay was based on a series of informal observations of strangers in Rome and family members at home. She recorded her observations in a journal.

> 5-24
>
> Saw the funniest thing today — Dad and I were waiting for Mom to come out of a shop by Piazza di Spagna, so we got to stand on a side street for a while and watch people go by. There was water in the street by this one restaurant, and the guy who owned the place was pacing around the sidewalk. Practically everyone walking by felt like they had to stop and put in their two cents about the problem! And they would all wind up gesturing and pointing. Dad and I just kept trying not to laugh. Dad said it was the same way where he grew up — if something went wrong, everyone tried to help, even though half the time they just ended up getting in the way.

▲ Caitlin reviewed her notes as she planned and then began to draft her essay

Courtesy of Caitlin Guariglia

● EXAMINE YOUR SUBJECT

Begin to reflect on your subject by viewing it through a particular lens, such as how it compares to something else, what caused it or what effects it might have, or what challenges and difficulties you associate with it. Drawing on your ability to analyze (see Chapter 9), you can begin to look at your subject from more than one angle.

Explore processes Thinking of something as a process can help you understand how it works as well as how it contributes to the context in which it takes place. For example, instead of reflecting on text messaging as a social phenomenon, reflect on the processes involved in text messaging. Ask how it works, what steps are involved in composing and sending a message, and how people understand and respond to messages.

Consider implications Considering the implications of a subject can help you understand its impact and importance. You can ask questions such as what is likely to happen, what if such-and-such happens, what will happen when, and so on. As you reflect on implications, stay grounded: don't get so carried away by speculation that you lose track of your reason for reflecting.

Examine similarities and differences Use comparison and contrast to find points of connection for your subject. You might examine, for example, the similarities and differences between new communication technologies, such as email and text messaging, and older means of staying in touch, such as letter writing and hanging out together.

Trace causes and effects Thinking about causes and effects can help you better understand a subject (see *Apply an Interpretive Framework* in Chapter 9). For example, you might reflect on the origins of complaints — some dating back to the ancient Greeks — that the latest generation of young people is not only impolite and uncultured but also likely to undo the accomplishments of previous generations. You might also reflect on the effects that this attitude has on relationships between the old and the young.

Consider value Reflection often involves considering factors such as strengths and weaknesses, costs and benefits, and limitations and opportunities. For example, you might reflect on the relative strengths and weaknesses of a candidate for political office. Or you might weigh the costs and benefits of a proposed law to make the internet safer for children.

Identify challenges and difficulties Getting to the heart of an issue or idea often involves determining how it challenges your assumptions or values or identifying the nature of the difficulties it poses for you. For example, ask yourself why an idea bothers you, or ask why it might bother someone else.

Reflect on your experiences As you reflect on your subject, search for connections to your own life. Ask whether your personal experiences would lead you to act in a particular way. Ask how they are likely to influence your reactions and attitudes. Ask whether you've found yourself in situations that are relevant to your subject.

● COLLECT DETAILS

People are fond of saying, "It's all in the details." Although this is true for nearly all types of writing, it's especially true for reflective essays. Without details, even the best essay can fall flat. You might get a laugh out of the following story, for example, but few people will find it truly satisfying:

> Once upon a time, they all lived happily ever after.

To collect details for a reflective essay, use the following strategies.

Describe your subject If you can, use observation to collect details about your subject (see *Ask Questions about Promising Subjects* earlier in this chapter). If you have firsthand experience with the subject, freewrite or brainstorm about it to refresh your memory: write down what you saw and heard, what you felt, even what you smelled. Provide as much detail as possible.

Compare your subject with something else Many subjects are best understood in relation to others. Darkness, for example, is difficult to understand without comparing it to light. Success is best understood in the context of its alternatives. And for those who live in colder climates, spring is all the more welcome because it follows winter. To find useful points of comparison, create a two-column log: place your subject at the top of one column and a contrasting subject at the top of the other, and then record your reflections on the similarities and differences between the two subjects in each column.

Discuss your ideas If you talk about your subject with other people, you might be able to use their comments to add detail to your essay. You might want to set up a formal interview with someone who is an expert on the subject or with someone who has been affected by it (see Chapter 15), but you can also simply bring up your subject in casual conversations to learn what others think. If they tell a story about their experiences with your subject, ask whether you might add their anecdote to your reflection. Similarly, if you hear an interesting turn of phrase or a startling statement related to your subject, consider quoting it. (See Chapter 21 to learn more about integrating quotations into an essay.)

Learn more about your subject As you gain a better idea of how you'll focus your essay, look for opportunities to add to your understanding of the subject. Browse newspapers and magazines in your library's periodical room to pick up bits of information that will add depth to your essay, or see what's been written recently about your subject on news sites and in blogs (see Chapter 14). Take note of interesting details that might grab your readers' attention.

● **FIND SIGNIFICANCE**

Every good story has a point. Every good joke has a punch line. Every good reflective essay leaves its readers with something to think about. As you reflect on your subject, consider why it's important to you, and think about how you can make it important for your readers.

Freewrite or brainstorm about your subject for ten or fifteen minutes. Ask yourself what your readers will need or want to know about it. Ask what will spark their imaginations. Ask what will stir their emotions. Then ask whether the ideas you've come up with will help you accomplish your goals as a writer.

The main idea of your reflective essay should hold some significance for your readers. Ideally, after reading your essay, they'll continue to think about what you've written.

In Process

Making Comparisons

Caitlin Guariglia used comparison to reflect on her experiences with strangers in Rome and with her family. She used a two-column table to make direct comparisons. Her work involved several critical thinking skills: remembering, understanding, and reflecting.

Strangers in Rome	Family in America
get involved in other people's business if they feel like they know how to do it better and can help	get involved in your business, whether you like it or not!
cool, confident, witty, LOUD	not always so cool, but definitely loud, full of themselves, and usually really funny
passionate about their city, its history, and its food	love NY, but not all are passionate about it, definitely opinionated about Italian food
beautiful Italian accents	only speak a little Italian, NY accents
really big on family, and like to make you feel like part of theirs	exactly the same

Caitlin used her notes to shape a point in her final essay:

> Our ancestors may have brought the food, the expressions, and the attitudes with them to the United States a few generations ago, but it is safe to say that over the years we have lost some of the style and the musical language that Italians seem to possess from birth.

Courtesy of Caitlin Guariglia

Prepare a Draft

As you prepare to draft your reflective essay, you'll think about how to convey your main idea, how to shape your reflection, which details to include, and what point of view to take. You'll also make decisions about how to design and craft your essay. You can read about other strategies related to drafting academic essays, such as writing strong paragraphs and integrating information from sources, in Part Four.

● CONVEY YOUR MAIN IDEA

Reflective essays, like other kinds of academic essays, should have a point. Before you begin writing, try to express your main idea in the form of a tentative thesis statement, a single sentence that articulates the most significant aspect of your reflections on your subject. By framing your main idea in a particular way, you can focus your efforts and help your readers see why your reflection should matter to them.

Consider the differences among the following tentative thesis statements about pursuing a career as a writer:

> Without commitment and discipline, pursuing a career as a writer would be a waste of time.

> Without a genuine love of words and a desire to share your ideas with others, pursuing a career as a writer would be a waste of time.

> The paths that lead to a career in writing are as varied as the writers who follow them.

Each of these statements would lead to significantly different reflective essays. The first frames becoming a writer as a test of character. It implies that writers can't succeed unless they are prepared to dedicate themselves to the hard work of writing. The second thesis statement shifts the focus from discipline and commitment to the writer's relationship with words and readers. It paints a warmer, less intimidating picture of what it takes to become a writer. The third thesis statement shifts the focus completely away from the qualities shared by successful writers, suggesting instead that each writer has different reasons for pursuing a career in writing. You can read more about developing a thesis statement in Chapter 18.

Even though having a main idea is necessary, the final draft of a reflective essay doesn't always include a formal thesis statement. Depending on the nature of the reflection, writers sometimes choose to use their observations to create a dominant impression of a subject. That is, they tell a story or build up details to show — rather than state outright — why the subject is significant.

Need help with main ideas? See Chapter 18.

● **TELL A STORY**

Almost every type of writing — at least, writing that's interesting — tells a story. An autobiography tells readers about events in the writer's life. An opinion column uses an anecdote — a brief description of an event or experience — to personalize an abstract issue. An article on ESPN.com describes what happened in a game — and speculates about what it means for the playoffs. In fact, some people have said that everything we do can be understood as a story.

If the subject of your reflection is an event in your past, shaping your essay as a story (that is, a chronological narrative with a beginning, a middle, and an end) is a natural way to proceed. But other kinds of subjects also lend themselves to storytelling. For example, because writers of reflective essays often share their thinking about a subject by explaining how they arrived at their conclusions, they essentially tell a story about their reflections.

As you draft, think about what kind of story you want to share. Will it be a tale of triumph against all odds? Will it lead to a surprising discovery? Will it have a happy ending? Will it be a tragedy? A comedy? A farce?

To create a story, consider the following elements:

- **Setting.** Where does your story take place? What are the characteristics of the setting? How does the setting affect the story?
- **Character.** Who is involved in your story? What motivates them? What do they want to accomplish? What are their hopes and dreams?
- **Plot.** What happens in your story? In what order do the events take place?
- **Conflict.** Do the characters in your story disagree about something? What do they disagree about? Why do they disagree?
- **Climax.** What is the defining event in the story? What does the story lead the reader toward?
- **Resolution.** How is the conflict resolved in your story?
- **Point of view.** Who is telling this story? How is it told?

Even if you don't present your reflection as a traditional story, the elements of storytelling can help you shape your observations in a more concrete manner. For example, by asking who is involved in your subject and how they have dealt with conflicts, you can decide whether you should focus on a character's actions or on the reasons leading to a conflict. By asking about the climax of your story, you can decide whether to focus your reflection on a single event or on the results of that event.

GO INTO DETAIL

Experienced writers are familiar with the advice "Show. Don't tell." This advice, more often applied to creative writing than to academic writing, is founded on the belief that characters' words and actions should be used to convey a story. Simply learning what happened is far less satisfying for readers than viewing it through a series of unfolding events.

In the sense that a reflective essay conveys the story of your thinking about a subject, showing how you came to your main idea can be preferable to telling readers what it is. As you reflect, consider sharing what you've seen and heard about your subject that places others — the characters in your story — at the center of your essay. Use details to convey their actions. Use dialogue to convey their words.

Each point you present in your essay, each event you describe, and each observation you make should be illustrated with details. As you reflected on your subject, you collected details that helped you understand the subject. Now, return to those details, and choose the ones that will best help your readers understand your subject and grasp its significance.

CHOOSE YOUR POINT OF VIEW

In academic writing, point of view refers to the perspective the writer takes. Sometimes a writer will choose to reflect on a subject as a *detached observer*. Rather than participating in the action, the writer stands outside it, making observations or showing what happened without becoming a part of the story. This detached point of view is characterized by the use of third-person pronouns (*he, she, they*) and a seemingly objective relationship with the subject. James Mollison, for example, adopts a detached point of view for his photo essay "Where Children Sleep" earlier in this chapter. By distancing himself from the lives of the children he has photographed, Mollison enables readers to consider his observations in a broader context.

At other times, a writer will reflect on a subject as a *participant observer*, someone who is centrally involved in the story being told. In this case, the writer shares experiences and observations from a personal perspective. This participatory point of view is characterized by the use of first-person pronouns (*I, me, we*) and a more personally involved relationship with the subject. By adopting this perspective, writers become key players in their own stories and can connect with their readers on a more intimate level. Consider, for example, "Are We Rich?" earlier in this chapter, in which Margo Jefferson uses the first-person point of view to convey her childhood questions about her family's class status among Chicago's Black elite in the 1950s.

Your decision about point of view will depend on the subject of your reflection, your relationship to the subject, and the amount of information you want to reveal about yourself. If you are reflecting on a subject with which you have little or no personal experience or if you want to downplay your involvement, it's usually more effective to adopt the role of a detached observer. If, on the other hand, you want to directly convey your experiences with and perceptions of an event or if you want to make an abstract subject more personal for readers, writing as a participant observer is often the better choice.

● CONSIDER GENRE AND DESIGN

Reflective essays, like other academic essays, use design elements to make it easier for instructors and classmates to read and comment on drafts. As you draft your essay, consider how decisions about fonts, line spacing, margins, and illustrations will help your readers respond to your ideas. You can learn more about these and other elements of document design in Chapters 22 and 23.

● FRAME YOUR REFLECTIONS

Once you've made decisions about the content and design of your essay, consider how you'll frame it, or direct your readers' attention to particular aspects of your reflections rather than to others. Framing your reflections allows you to influence your readers' understanding of, and attitudes toward, what's most important to you.

Organization The organization of a reflective essay is typically determined by the nature of the subject. Most stories, for instance, are arranged chronologically so that readers can easily follow the sequence of events. Reflections on a place or an object, on the other hand, might be arranged spatially, tracing the way a reader's eyes would take in the subject in person: top to bottom, left to right, near to far, and so on. If your reflections consider similarities and differences between your subject and something else, ordering your ideas by points of comparison and contrast might be most effective. (For more on these and other organizing patterns, see Chapter 19.)

Introduction and conclusion Your introduction and conclusion are important parts of the framework within which your readers will understand and interpret your reflections, so spend some time experimenting with them until they feel right. (Because these elements of an essay often prove the most challenging to draft, you might want to put them off until you finish the rest of the essay.) Several strategies are available for writing introductions and conclusions, but a few are particularly useful for reflective essays. For instance, you might open with a surprising statement or an anecdote — a brief, pointed story — that sets the stage for your main idea. As you close your essay, consider circling back to a detail from the beginning or reiterating the significance of your reflections. (For advice on drafting introductions and conclusions, see Chapter 20.)

Review and Improve Your Draft

Completing your first draft is a major milestone. However, additional consideration of your subject and a careful review of your draft will no doubt provide numerous opportunities to improve your essay. As you review your draft, pay particular attention to how you've presented and framed your main idea, the order in which you've presented your reflections, any use of dialogue, and your inclusion of details that show rather than tell.

● ENSURE THAT YOUR MAIN IDEA IS CLEAR

Readers should be able to identify the point of your essay, even if you haven't provided a thesis statement. As you review your essay, ask whether your reflections support the position statement you drafted before writing (see *How Can I Develop a Position on My Issue?* in Chapter 18), and ask if everything you wrote helps your readers understand your subject in the way you intended. You might find that you need to revise your thesis statement to reflect your draft, or that you need to adapt your draft to better support your main idea.

● EXAMINE THE PRESENTATION OF YOUR OBSERVATIONS

Reflective essays frequently rely on narrative, or storytelling. Review your draft to find out whether the order in which you've told your story makes sense and whether the details you have included will lead readers to be sympathetic to your observations. Upon review, you might decide that you should change the order, add important ideas or observations, or remove details that seem unnecessary or irrelevant.

● REVIEW DIALOGUE

Many reflective essays use dialogue — spoken exchanges between key figures in a story — to help readers better understand a subject. Dialogue can underscore the significance of your subject and help readers gain insight into how people are affected by or react to the subject. Dialogue can also add interest to a story or allow others to make a point that you might not want to state outright. If you've included dialogue, ask whether you've used it effectively. For example, have you relied too heavily on other people's words? Are the right people engaged in dialogue? Does what they say make sense in the context of your story? If you haven't used dialogue, ask yourself where you might include it to liven up your essay or engage readers with your subject.

● SHOW, DON'T TELL

As you review your draft, think about how you can bring your observations to life by placing the people and events involved with your subject at the center of your essay. Have you done more than simply summarize your points? Will adding details help your readers better understand and connect to your subject? Can you make your points more effectively by quoting dialogue among the characters in your story? Can you illustrate key ideas by showing characters in action?

In Process

Adding Dialogue

As she reviewed her first draft, Caitlin worried that a particularly important passage felt less interesting than it should:

> Anytime our group slowed down or started to get tired, Marco would yell to us to keep going, and suddenly we were revived. He knew everything about Rome, and everywhere we went, he knew someone. He loved his city and loved sharing it with all of us.

By adding dialogue, she created a better sense of Marco's personality and helped readers imagine themselves on a tour with him:

> Anytime our group slowed down or started to get tired, Marco would yell, "Andiamo! (Let's go!)," and suddenly we were revived. He knew everything about Rome, and everywhere we went, he knew someone. All day he was calling out to friends, "Ciao bella!" or "Come stai?" He loved his city and loved sharing it with all of us.

Courtesy of Caitlin Guariglia

● RESPOND TO FEEDBACK FROM YOUR INSTRUCTOR

Instructors will sometimes offer feedback on drafts of a writing assignment, particularly if the assignment is a major project for a course. Typically, this kind of feedback focuses on larger issues, such as support for your points, the ways in which you've addressed your readers, or the way you've organized your document. If your instructor has offered feedback on more than one draft, later drafts might address concerns at the sentence or word levels.

After reviewing feedback on your essay, ask yourself first how you might address larger issues and then how you might polish and edit your draft so that your readers will find it easy to read (see Chapter 24).

If you've drawn on ideas, information, or examples from written works, such as essays or stories, or cultural productions, such as movies or concerts, make sure that you've documented those sources in the body of your essay and in a works cited or reference list. For guidelines on the MLA and APA documentation systems, see Chapters 25 and 26.

Do you know why you should document sources? See Chapter 17.

In Process

Responding to Instructor Feedback

Caitlin received comments from her instructor on her first draft. While her instructor praised the way in which she had brought to life the scenes in her essay, the instructor suggested that she might add even more detail. Her instructor noted that, while she described key encounters and had added some important dialogue, she was still missing some key descriptions of people and places that would help readers envision Caitlin's family and experiences as clearly as she herself did.

When responding to feedback from your instructor, consider whether the comment applies to only a single passage in your essay or whether it might be best applied to your entire document. In addition, consider whether the feedback might be applied to your writing assignments in the future or in other classes.

Courtesy of Caitlin Guariglia

Peer Review: Improve Your Reflective Essay

One of the biggest challenges writers face is reading a draft of their own work as a reader rather than as the writer. Because you know what you're trying to say, you find it easy to understand your draft. To determine how you should revise your draft, ask a friend or classmate to read your essay and to consider how well you've adopted the role of observer.

Purpose	1. Did you understand the significance of my observations? Do I need to state my main idea more directly or say anything more to clarify what's important about my subject?
	2. Does my subject seem relevant to you personally? Why or why not? Is there anything I can do to forge a better connection with readers?
	3. How did you respond to my reflections and observations? Do you accept what I had to say? Have I left you with something to think about?
Readers	4. Did the story of my experiences and insights make sense to you? Do you want to know anything else about them?
	5. Does my personality come through in my writing? Should I put more (or less) of myself into the essay?
	6. Have I offered you a fresh or an unusual perspective on my subject?
Sources	7. Is it clear which experiences and observations are my own and which I brought in from other sources?
	8. If I have referred to any published works or recent events, have I cited my source(s) appropriately?
	9. How well does my use of details show, rather than tell, the significance of my subject? Should I add or remove any details?
	10. Have I used dialogue effectively? Is there too little or too much?
Context	11. Did you understand any references I made to cultural, political, or social contexts? Do I need to explain anything more directly?
	12. Is the physical appearance of my essay appropriate? Did you find the font easy to read? Did I use illustrations effectively?

For each of the points listed above, ask your reviewers to offer concrete suggestions for improving your essay. You might want to ask them to adopt the role of an editor — someone who is working with you to improve your draft. You can read more about peer review in Chapter 5.

Student Essay

Caitlin Guariglia, "Mi Famiglia"
The following reflective essay was written by featured writer Caitlin Guariglia. *Courtesy of Caitlin Guariglia*

Information about the writer, class, and submission date is formatted according to MLA guidelines.

Guariglia 1

Caitlin Guariglia
Professor Edwards
ENG 1011.04
September 28, 2016

The opening paragraph grabs the reader's attention.

Following MLA guidelines, the title is centered.

Mi Famiglia

Crash! The sound of metal hitting a concrete wall is my first vivid memory of Rome. Our tour bus could not get any farther down the tiny road because cars were parked along both sides. This, our bus driver told us, was illegal. He did not tell us, exactly; he grumbled it as he stepped out of the bus. He stood there with his hands on his hips, pondering the situation. Soon, people in the cars behind us started wandering up to stand next to the bus driver and ponder along with him. That, or they honked a great deal.

The writer begins to reflect on the experience. See the beginning of Chapter 7 for more on reflecting as a critical thinking activity.

This is when I found out that Italians are resourceful people. They do not stand around waiting for someone else to fix a problem for them. They take initiative; they do what needs to be done to get things moving. Our bus driver and three other men started rocking the small cars parked crookedly along the sides of the narrow road, with every push moving them toward the concrete wall that lined the road. CRASH! The sound of the car hitting the wall was their signal that they were done pushing that car. And then they'd move to the next one in their way.

The writer returns to the image in the opening paragraph.

Angry people on Vespas sped by, making various hand gestures; some I knew and understood, but others I did not. The bus driver boarded the bus, his sleeves rolled up, sweat pouring down his face, and told us that these kind people on their Vespas were wishing us good luck. He moved the bus up about ten feet before he encountered another car he could not pass. The process repeated itself. CRASH! Another car moved. Soon a police officer walked up, talked to the bus driver, looked around, shrugged, and helped them shove the

Details help the reader visualize the writer's experience.

Guariglia 2

cars into the wall. People who had parked there began to come back and move their cars before it was done for them. When we finally made it the hundred feet down the rest of the road, everyone on our tour bus cheered. Our bus driver smiled sheepishly, as if to say, "Eh, it was nothing."

This was the sort of thing I hoped to see in Italy. I wanted to see how Italians live. My dad's side of the family is Italian, so I wanted to understand more about our heritage and our family traits, like why my family is so loud and concerned with everyone else's business. Was it a cultural thing? Or was it a family thing? Was it just something about the region of Italy where my family is from? I smiled when I read Elizabeth Gilbert's memoir *Eat, Pray, Love*. Gilbert writes, "The Neapolitan women in particular are such a gang of tough-voiced, loud-mouthed, generous, nosy dames, all bossy and annoyed and right up in your face just trying to friggin' help you for chrissake, you dope — *why they gotta do everything around here?*" (78). This sounds exactly like almost all of my great-aunts, and I was curious to find out if the women in Rome would have the same attitude.

And the obsession with eating! My grandmother feeds us constantly. My dad and I always laugh at that scene in *Goodfellas* where the mobsters show up at two in the morning after killing someone, and one mobster's mother whips up a full pasta meal for them. We know that my grandmother would do the same thing: "Are you hungry? Here, sit, eat!" Grandma holds interventions over pasta. If she is unhappy with something someone in the family is doing, she invites everyone over for pasta, and we hash it out together. Was this something all Italians do? Or was my idea of a typical Italian person all wrong? Our time in Rome clarified some of these questions for me.

When we finally got to our hotel, we met our tour guide Maresa. This small, stout, sweet Italian woman said we could call her Mama. Mama looked up our reservation, glanced at it, and said our last name. Normally, that would be nothing to celebrate. But she said our last name perfectly. Actually, not just perfectly, she said it *beautifully*. After listening to Americans butcher my difficult Italian last name my entire life, hearing this Italian woman say it was music to my ears. My grandfather would have given her a standing ovation.

The next morning we met our tour guide Marco. A large, sturdy man who looked like my grandmother cooked for him, he was confident and full of life. He took us to the main historical sites that day: the Vatican, the Colosseum, the Pantheon, the Roman Forum. While all of that was spectacular, I enjoyed listening to Marco more than anything we saw. He was a true Roman, big, proud, and loud. The Italian accent made it seem like he was singing everything he said, making it all seem that much more beautiful. Anytime our group slowed down or started to get tired, Marco would yell, "Andiamo! (Let's go!)," and suddenly we were revived. He knew everything about Rome, and everywhere we went, he knew someone. All day he was calling out to friends, "Ciao bella!" or "Come stai?" He loved his city and loved sharing it with all of us. He had such a passion for Rome, and it made me passionate about it, too. He was also an entertainer; he enjoyed making us laugh. When our group reached a crosswalk near the Vatican, he knew all of us would not make it across in one light, so he told us to try to hurry up across the street. He told us if we did not make it before the light changed, it's okay, the cars won't hit us. "And if they beep at you," he added, "it's because they like-a the music."

> The writer uses dialogue to make the scene more vivid.

    Marco fit into what my family came to know as the image of the quintessential Roman man. All of the men have two-day stubble, enough to look chic and sophisticated, but not so much as to look scruffy or messy. They also have half-smoked cigarettes hanging from their mouths. It is never a freshly lit cigarette, or a little butt, but right at that perfect halfway mark. There is a confidence, but not arrogance, in their walk. In essence, Roman men are eternally cool. In *Eat, Pray, Love*, Elizabeth Gilbert remembers watching a group of Roman men outside a bakery on their way home from a soccer game. They are "leaning up against their motorcycles, talking about the game, looking macho as anything, and eating *cream puffs*" (Gilbert 70). She is surprised at how cool they can look while eating something like cream puffs, but I have definitely seen what she means. Somehow they are manly without even having to try.

> The writer returns to her reflections about the connections between her family and her Italian heritage.

> The writer draws on a source to illustrate a point.

    Romans, like many Italian Americans I've known, also have an opinion on everything and want you to know what that opinion is. Walking by the Spanish Steps on our second day in Rome, we saw a restaurant with a water leak that had spilled out into the street. It was a narrow street with mostly pedestrian traffic. As the water trickled between the cobblestones, the restaurant owner stood over the mess, looking a lot like our bus driver with his hands on his hips. Every Italian walking by had to stop and talk to this man, and then give him advice on how to go about fixing it. The two would wave their hands at each other, sometimes nodding in agreement, sometimes yelling and waving their hands harder. This reminded me of many of my own family. When any problem arises, all the men in the house stand around looking at it saying, "No! What you gotta do is . . ." None of them are listening to each other, but each of them wants their point to be heard. It felt like déjà vu watching the same thing happen on this street in Rome. It was funny that they were all being stubborn and acting like know-it-alls, but I saw underneath it that the people stopping by really thought they were helping. They were not being rude or bossy in their minds; they were just looking out for their fellow Roman.

The last morning, Mama herded our tour group onto a bus to take us to the train station. When she got to my family, she gave us all a kiss on the cheek and a hug. She told us, "You must come back again and visit!" Then she looked at my sister and me, winked, and said, "And bring some husbands!" She must have channeled my grandmother at that moment, telling us to settle down with a nice Italian boy. We laughed and thanked Mama for her kindness during our visit.

- As we pulled away from the station, I thought of all the wonderful people we met in Rome. I imagined them coming to our family reunion barbecue that takes place every summer. I think they'd fit right in. Mama would sit with Grandma and my father's aunts and talk about how beautiful their family is. Marco would sit with my dad and his cousins, drinking scotch and smoking cigars and cigarettes. Everyone would have a place.

- But then I thought of my cousin with two-day stubble, sitting on a Vespa, and I giggled. The image was ridiculous. Our ancestors may have brought the food, the expressions, and the attitudes with them to the United States a few generations ago, but it is safe to say that, over the years, we have lost some of the style and the musical language that Italians seem to possess from birth. Then why did so much of what I saw and heard in Italy feel strangely familiar? It seems that for Italians and Italian Americans, the traits we share are not just a cultural thing or just a family thing; they are both. It is impossible to separate the two. My time in Rome showed me that to Italians, a shared culture is a kind of family, one that extends even across the ocean.

The writer begins her conclusion by sharing her thoughts as her trip comes to a close.

The conclusion offers reflections on differences between Italians and Italian Americans.

Works Cited

Gilbert, Elizabeth. *Eat, Pray, Love: One Woman's Search for Everything across Italy, India and Indonesia*. Viking, 2006.

Goodfellas. Directed by Martin Scorsese, performances by Robert De Niro, Ray Liotta, Joe Pesci, and Lorraine Bracco, Warner Bros., 1990.

Project Ideas

The following suggestions provide ways to focus your work on a reflective essay or another type of reflective document.

Suggestions for Essays

1. REFLECT ON A PERSONAL EXPERIENCE

Write a reflective essay about something you've done or something that happened to you within the last month or so. (Choosing a recent experience enables you to focus on the interaction itself, rather than on its aftermath.) Provide sufficient details about the experience so readers will be able to picture it. Consider whether you need to supply background information as well. Support your reflections with personal observation and reasoning. You might also consider discussing the experience with friends or family members to gain their perspectives on it. If the experience was of a public nature or was related to a public event, consult news reports for background information and alternate perspectives.

2. REFLECT ON A PUBLIC EVENT

Reflect on a recent event covered in your local newspaper, a local television or radio news program, or a local news website. You might choose a cultural event, such as a local music festival; a civic event, such as a Labor Day celebration; or a school event, such as a lecture or campus protest. In your essay, describe the event and offer your reflections on its significance for you and your readers. Use details, and perhaps even dialogue, to convey the flavor of the event. Depending on the context, consider who your primary audience might be. Does the event have more significance for particular groups of readers? If so, how do you think it affects them? Support your reflection with examples from personal experience, information published in news media, or an interview with someone associated with the event (see Chapter 15). If you attended the event or participated in it yourself, be sure to include your observations of what happened.

3. REFLECT ON A POEM, SHORT STORY, NOVEL, PLAY, OR MOVIE

Respond to a work of literature that you've read recently, or attend a play or movie and reflect on it. Support your reflection by describing your reactions to the work, drawing on any relevant personal experiences or knowledge, or your own reasoning. You might also read published reviews, analyses, or comments posted to online forums to get an idea of other readers' reactions, or discuss the work with a friend, a family member, a classmate, or an instructor who has read it or seen it. In your essay, briefly describe the work to which you're responding, summarizing the plot and any key themes. Then offer your reflections on it: share with your readers why it affected you the way it did and consider how it relates to your own experiences or beliefs. Offer your reflections on the meaning of the work, its larger significance, or its emotional impact.

4. REFLECT ON AN ISSUE OF INTEREST

Reflect on an issue in a discipline, profession, or current news topic that interests you. For example, a writer interested in nuclear technology might reflect on the political or environmental implications of plans to store nuclear waste in Nevada. Or a student curious about allegations of voter suppression (denying or discouraging citizens from exercising their right to vote) might visit a local polling place on Election Day and reflect on what was observed. Ask who your audience might be. Are they already interested in the issue, as you are, or are they affected by it? Are they unfamiliar with the issue? Are they unfamiliar but likely to want to understand it more deeply? Support your reflection by drawing on your personal knowledge, experiences, and concerns, referring to information or arguments from published sources as necessary to inform your readers about the issue at hand. (Observers often need to adopt the role of reporter, at least initially, to ensure that their readers have a thorough understanding of the subject.) If appropriate, you might also interview an expert on the issue or conduct an observation to get a firsthand look at your subject. In your essay, introduce the issue and offer your reflections on it. Be careful to avoid composing an argument. Instead, focus on how the issue affects you and how it might affect your readers.

5. WRITE A LITERACY NARRATIVE

Write a focused literacy narrative that identifies and reflects on a personal experience (or a series of closely related experiences) that strongly influenced you as a writer or reader. You might focus on an experience in early childhood, or one from college or later. Shape your reflection as a story, building to a moment of insight to which your readers will relate. Conclude with a brief assessment of your current relationship with literacy. Discuss whether your feelings about reading and writing have changed since that experience and explore how this has taken place.

Alternatively, rather than focusing on a specific experience that relates to literacy, you might write a literacy narrative that reflects on your overall attitudes about reading and writing. Do you enjoy reading and writing, avoid them, struggle with them, find strength from engaging with them? Have your attitudes toward reading and writing changed over time? Are your feelings about reading similar to your feelings about writing, or do you have a stronger relationship with one or the other? Perhaps you have been surprised by the development of your literacy throughout the course of your life. Support your reflections on your experiences with reading and writing by drawing on your memories of events that have shaped your attitudes. Offer an assessment of your current relationship with writing and reading. Consider including a few telling comments by family members or teachers about your experiences with literacy to support your reflections.

Suggestions for Other Genres

6. WRITE A MEMOIR

Write a brief memoir that reflects on a key event in your life. Carefully describe the event and offer your insights into its meaning and significance, keeping in mind the need to help readers understand, connect to, and benefit from your reflections. Be sure to choose a discrete event or a limited time period — a move to a new town, for example, or a particularly memorable trip. A strong memoir has a narrow focus; if you try to address too much — for example, your complicated relationship with a relative — your writing might become abstract and lose both emotional power and narrative detail. Choose narrowly for the best result. Although the event will undoubtedly be significant in your life, consider why your readers would care about it. Does the event have larger significance? Is it something shared by others? Is it a universal experience or personal and particular?

Your memoir should be based primarily on your memories. You can use description to evoke the time and place of the event, and you might even choose to re-create dialogue. If you like, discuss the event with friends or family members and include some of their recollections and insights, or draw on published sources to give readers background information and context. Even if you make use of other sources, remember that your own memories should serve as the foundation for your memoir.

7. CREATE A PHOTO ESSAY

Take or gather several photographs that illustrate an important aspect of your life or a public issue that intrigues you. The pictures might be from your personal collection of photographs or from published sources such as history books, magazines, or websites. Select five to seven images that create a dominant impression of your subject. Think about what connects the images you have chosen. How do they work together to tell a story, convey a mood, or offer a commentary on a subject? The images need not be chronological, but they should invite readers to make connections among them.

Introduce the photos with a few paragraphs that reflect on what they show, or else write an introduction along with a sentence-length caption for each image. As you write the introduction, consider whether your readers will be familiar with the subject.

Is there something you want them to know or understand before they view the photographs? The introduction allows you to provide a framework or lens through which they will view the photo essay. The final mix of images and words should lead your readers to think about the subject from a perspective they wouldn't have developed on their own. You can learn about photo essays earlier in this chapter.

8. SHARE A BLOG POST

Like an essay, a blog post can share your reflections on a personal or public event or on a work of art. Unlike an essay, which is often shared only with an instructor or classmates, a blog post is available to a wide audience and invites immediate responses from readers. As a result, choose your topic carefully, with an awareness that your reflections might be read by people who will know little about you or the contexts that shaped your experiences.

As you draft a blog post reflecting on an experience, consider the opportunities afforded to you by the context, genre, and design of a blog. Consider as well the wide range of sources you can use to share your reflections and illustrate your ideas. Blog posts can include not only your insights and ideas from personal experiences but also images and photographs, video and audio, and links to other web-based documents. Finally, consider the capabilities offered by the platform on which you choose to share your reflections. Blog tools such as WordPress and Tumblr allow you to choose a wide range of designs. Think carefully about how the design choices you might make will shape the impressions of your readers.

In Summary: Writing a Reflective Essay

★ **Find a conversation and listen in (p. 158).**
- Explore your experiences (p. 158).
- Ask questions about promising subjects (p. 159).
- Conduct an observation (p. 159).

★ **Reflect on your subject (p. 160).**
- Examine your subject (p. 162).
- Collect details (p. 163).
- Find significance (p. 164).

★ **Prepare a draft (p. 165).**
- Convey your main idea (p. 165).
- Tell a story (p. 166).
- Go into detail (p. 167).
- Choose your point of view (p. 167).
- Consider genre and design (p. 168).
- Frame your reflections (p. 168).

★ **Review and improve your draft (p. 169).**
- Ensure that your main idea is clear (p. 169).
- Examine the presentation of your observations (p. 169).
- Review dialogue (p. 169).
- Show, don't tell (p. 170).
- Respond to feedback from your instructor (p. 171).

08 Writing to Inform

What is writing to inform? 181

What kinds of documents are used to inform? 183

Informative essays and articles 183
    Alice Park and Sean Gregory, *Time 2021 Athlete of the Year: Simone Biles* 183

Infographics 190
    International Networks Archive, Princeton University, *The Magic Bean Shop* and *The Fries That Bind Us* 190

Profiles 192
    Rivka Galchen, *An Unlikely Ballerina: The Rise of Misty Copeland* 192

Newsletter articles 200
    Illyanna Maisonet, *Why Aren't There More Puerto Rican Restaurants... In California?* 200

Genre Talk: Informative Writing 204

How can I write an informative essay? 205
Find a conversation and listen in 205
Gather information 208
Prepare a draft 211
Review and improve your draft 219

✷ **Student Essay** 222
    Gabriella Guerrero, *Fast Fashion? Not So Fast!* 222

✷ **Project Ideas** 229

What Is Writing to Inform?

Many of the documents you encounter on a regular basis are informative: newspaper and magazine articles, manuals, brochures, and books (including this textbook) are among the genres — or types of documents — that allow writers to add information to conversations about a wide range of subjects. In writing and writing-intensive courses, typical informative-writing assignments include essays, reports, and websites. You might also be asked to create pamphlets, multimedia presentations, memos, or posters.

Writing to inform involves adopting the role of *reporter* (see Chapter 6). Writers who adopt this role seek to make others aware of facts that are central to a written conversation. Reporters typically refrain from interpreting or analyzing the information they provide, and they seldom ask their readers to respond in a particular way. Instead, reporters allow readers to draw their own conclusions and to decide whether — and how — to act on what they've learned.

Writers of informative documents are concerned primarily with helping readers and other writers advance their understanding of a subject. They do this in a variety of ways. They might report original research or provide a broad summary of existing knowledge or offer a detailed discussion of a narrow area of interest. Regardless of their focus on the subject or the originality of their research, their contributions to a written conversation are essential to moving the conversation forward.

THE WRITER'S ROLE:
Reporter

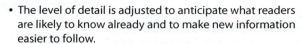

"When I take on the role of a **reporter**, I focus on informing my readers about a topic."

PURPOSE
- To share information
- To answer questions

READERS
- Want to be informed
- Expect a fair and reasonable presentation of information, ideas, and arguments
- Need clear explanations of important ideas and concepts

SOURCES
- Information can be drawn from published studies and reports, news media, and personal experience.
- Information can be obtained firsthand, through interviews, observation, surveys, correspondence, and attendance at public events.
- Reporters check that their sources are credible and accurate.

CONTEXT
- The level of detail is adjusted to anticipate what readers are likely to know already and to make new information easier to follow.
- Informative documents often use illustrations — such as charts, tables, graphs, and images — to help readers understand concepts and ideas.

CRITICAL THINKING

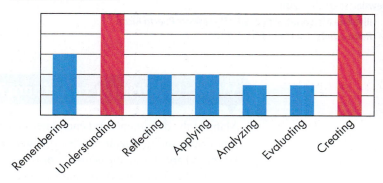

What Kinds of Documents Are Used to Inform?

Whether you are writing for a course, for publication, or in the workplace, you'll find yourself turning to — and creating — informative documents on a regular basis. If you are new to a conversation, informative documents can help you learn about a subject. As you prepare to contribute to the conversation, they can help you understand what is generally agreed upon about the subject and what remains unknown or open to debate. And as you draft your contribution, you can use information and ideas from informative documents to introduce your subject, to support your points, or to illustrate alternative perspectives.

Good writers select a genre that allows them to best address their purpose, their readers, and the context of the conversation they want to join. In the following sections, you'll find examples and discussions of some of the most common types of documents used to inform readers: informative essays and articles, infographics, profiles, and news reports.

Informative Essays and Articles

Alice Park and Sean Gregory
Time 2021 Athlete of the Year: Simone Biles

Informative essays and articles share information about a subject in a well-organized, well-supported, readable form. Essays and articles are frequently written for academic settings, such as classes, but they are also often shared in anthologies, magazines, and news sites. Writers like Alice Park and Sean Gregory, who wrote this article, often write with a primary goal of informing readers about new products, political or social events, or even the thoughts and feelings of others. Park and Gregory have written for a variety of magazines and news organizations, including *Time*, *Sports Illustrated*, and CNN.

Time 2021 Athlete of the Year: Simone Biles

Alice Park and Sean Gregory

> Alice Park and Sean Gregory are reporters for *Time* magazine. Park's reporting often focuses on health and medicine, while Gregory frequently reports on sports.

> When essays are written for academic purposes, student writers often view instructors as their primary readers. Yet teachers commonly ask their students to address a different audience, such as other students, parents, politicians, or members of a particular profession. The audience for this informative article, which appeared in both the print edition of *Time* and its website, is interested in current information on a variety of topics.

Around 9 p.m. on July 27, as Simone Biles soared high above the vault at the Tokyo Olympics, she lost herself. You could see the confusion in her eyes, which darted sideways instead of locking onto the ground as she made her way back to earth. She would later reveal that she was suffering from a frightening mental hiccup, known as "the twisties," that left her unsure of her whereabouts in midair.

As the Greatest of All Time (GOAT) in a sport that captivates the globe every four years, Biles is all about control. Her life is dedicated to micromanaging every possible element—her diet, her training, her sleep—that goes into performing, so when the lights are brightest, and the stakes highest, little is left to chance. But for Biles, control isn't just about winning; it can be the difference between life and death. She now has four skills named after her, each a breathtaking combination of daring flips and twists. Avoiding disaster requires a constant, firm grip on mental acuity.

On that night, however, the careful tapestry of control that Biles, 24, had stitched began to unravel. Or at least started to, until she responded in a way that stunned millions of viewers around the world. In the middle of the Olympics for which she had trained for five years, and which was supposed to be the triumphant capstone on a historic career, Biles slipped on her warm-up suit, packed her competition bag and told her teammates she wouldn't be competing with them, but rather cheering them on in the team event. Her mind and body weren't in sync, she said, which put her at serious risk. She also withdrew from her next four events, returning only to participate in the final one. At an Olympics in which five gold medals for Biles seemed preordained, she won a team silver and a balance-beam bronze.

For her teammates, her withdrawal from events was a decision they didn't have time to process as they scrambled to fill her position in the lineups. "We all knew we had

Alice Park and Sean Gregory, "*Time* 2021 Athlete of the Year: Simone Biles," *Time*, December 9, 2021. Copyright © 2021 by Time, Inc. All rights reserved. Used under license. https://time.com

to continue not without her, but for her," says Sunisa Lee, who stepped up to win the all-around gold in Tokyo. "What Simone did changed the way we view our well-being, 100%. It showed us that we are more than the sport, that we are human beings who also can have days that are hard. It really humanized us."

An athlete's clout is increasingly measured in much more than wins and losses. If 2020 showcased the power of athletes as activists after the murder of George Floyd, this year demonstrated how athletes are uniquely positioned to propel mental health to the forefront of a broader cultural conversation. While a few sports stars have opened up about mental health—Michael Phelps, for instance, has been candid about his post-Olympic depression—in 2021, the discussion became more wide-reaching and sustained. After withdrawing from the French Open in May to prioritize her well-being, citing anxiety, Naomi Osaka wrote in a *Time* cover essay, "It's O.K. not to be O.K." Biles, by dint of her status at one of the world's most watched events, raised the volume. "I do believe everything happens for a reason, and there was a purpose," she tells *Time* in an interview nearly four months later. "Not only did I get to use my voice, but it was validated as well."

Alice Park and Sean Gregory, "*Time* 2021 Athlete of the Year: Simone Biles," *Time*, December 9, 2021. Copyright © 2021 by Time, Inc. All rights reserved. Used under license. https://time.com.

While supporters lauded Biles, critics lambasted her for "quitting." But what Biles did transcended the chatter: she fought the stigma that has long silenced athletes, and shrugged off the naysayers who belittled her decision. "If I were going to quit, I had other opportunities to quit," she says. "There is so much I've gone through in this sport, and I should have quit over all that—not at the Olympics. It makes no sense."

A month after the Games, Biles put her vulnerability on display once again. Along with three other of the hundreds of other athletes who had been sexually abused by former team doctor Larry Nassar,

> Writers of articles often draw on quotations from interviews to present or expand on important points.

Pool/Getty Images

Biles gave emotional testimony before the Senate about the failures of institutions like the FBI, USA Gymnastics (USAG) and the U.S. Olympic and Paralympic Committee (USOPC) to stop him.

Colin Kaepernick, no stranger to criticism for taking a stand, praises Biles' "grace, eloquence and courage." "Simone Biles has used her remarkable position as the world's greatest gymnast ever to inspire a long overdue global conversation on mental health," he tells *Time*. "Her influence extends far beyond the realm of sports and shows us that another world—a better world—is possible when we speak our truths with integrity and authenticity."

At a time when anxiety and depression rates are skyrocketing—the CDC reports a 50% rise in suicide attempts by teenage girls during the pandemic—and many people are struggling with what they owe themselves vs. what others demand of them, Biles made clear the importance of prioritizing oneself and refusing to succumb to external expectations. With the eyes of the world upon her, she took the extraordinary step of saying, *That's enough. I'm enough.*

Biles thought she was, as she puts it, "good to go" before the Games. In retrospect, she acknowledges that she was shouldering a heavy load as she trained. She was the face of Team USA, and fans around the globe were anticipating watching her gravity-defying skills. Gradually, she began to feel the Olympics were less about her fulfillment and more about theirs.

In the past, when she left the gym, she didn't allow issues with

> A partial quotation is integrated into the sentence.

certain skills to spill over into the rest of her day. But as Tokyo loomed, "my mind was racing and I wasn't going to sleep as easily," she says. The pandemic, which had delayed the Games from 2020, played a huge role in that, she thinks, since safety protocols meant she was limited to going to the gym and staying home. For the gregarious Biles, that meant more time alone with her thoughts. Things only got worse in Japan. "We couldn't hang out because of COVID-19 protocols," she says, "so things you normally don't think about because you don't have time, now you have hours on end to think about—those doubts, those worries and those problems."

Biles is the only survivor of the Nassar sexual abuse scandal still competing, and pushing for USAG and USOPC to be held responsible is part of what's driven her over the past few years. "I definitely do think it had an effect," she says of that burden. "It's a lot to put on one person. I feel like the guilt should be on them and should not be held over us. They should be feeling this [pain], not me."

It took Biles about a year after the first Nassar survivors came forward to reveal publicly that she is one of them; her mother Nellie remembers Biles calling her in tears in 2017, saying she needed to talk to her. Training every day only served as a reminder of what she had been through and the lack of accountability by USAG. Biles didn't feel she could even drive herself to and from her therapy sessions, so Nellie did, waiting outside in the car in case her daughter needed her.

That work, Biles felt, mentally prepared her for her second Olympics, which she attended without family because of COVID-19 restrictions. She had stopped going to therapy for about six months before the Games, Nellie says, insisting, "I'm fine, Mom." But after her scare on the vault, she called Nellie crying. "The only thing Simone kept saying was, 'Mom, I can't do it. I can't do it,'" says Nellie. In the days that followed, Biles says she got support from Team USA's mental-health experts, who were on-site for the first time at an Olympics. That helped her make another courageous choice: competing in the balance-beam final. "At that point, it was no longer about medaling, but about getting back out there," she says. "I wanted to compete at the Olympics again and have that experience that I came for. I didn't really care about the outcome. On that beam, it was for me."

Biles' assuredness in speaking her truth and taking ownership of her fate offered permission for athletes and non-athletes alike to talk more openly about challenges they'd once kept to themselves. "Sacrifice gives back way more than it costs," says Kevin Love, a five-time NBA All-Star whose 2018 discussion of his in-game panic attacks helped start to destigmatize mental struggles in his sport. "I do believe that it often takes one person to change the trajectory of a whole system."

Olympian Allyson Felix, who gave birth to her daughter Camryn in 2018, knows how athletes are expected to make winning their everything. She says Biles will have more influence for stepping back and taking stock of what really mattered than she would have by snapping up more medals. "To see her choose herself, we're going to see the effects of that for the next generation," says Felix, who became the most decorated female track-and-field athlete of all time in Tokyo. "When thinking about role models for Cammy, wow, here is someone showing you can choose your mental health over what the world says is the most important thing."

The message is already being put into practice. As head coach for women's gymnastics at the University of Arkansas, Olympian Jordyn Wieber, another Nassar survivor, sees Biles' decision as an opportunity for her team to "take those lessons she's displaying on a worldwide level and apply them to their daily lives as student athletes." During the Olympics, Ty-La Morris, 14, an aspiring gymnast from the Bronx, stayed up past her bedtime to watch coverage of the gymnastics events. When she heard people questioning Biles' fortitude, she defended her. "Everybody kept coming after her, and nobody was in her shoes," she says. Witnessing a Black woman thrive in a traditionally white sport gives Morris the confidence that she too can make the Olympics, but in addition, she's now more likely to tell her coach if she's having difficulty, which she wouldn't have been comfortable doing before.

Experts agree that especially for young Black women, Biles' actions were a signal that it's acceptable to claim agency over both their minds and their bodies. Since the days of slavery, says LaNail Plummer, a therapist who specializes in providing mental-health services to Black and LGBTQ communities in the D.C. area, the bodies of Black women have been subject to fetishization: for purposes of labor, reproduction or athletic entertainment. Throughout their careers, for example, tennis stars Venus and Serena Williams have been the targets of racist and sexist comments because of their appearances. "Our bodies have always been under scrutiny," says Plummer. "Oftentimes, Black women are not given the freedom to be able to just be authentic. Oftentimes, they have to be what somebody asked them or designed for them to be."

So when a Black female athlete like Biles takes visible steps to safeguard her own mental and

> Authors of articles often include evidence, usually in the form of a quotation or paraphrase, from experts in a field.

physical health, to indicate that it's worth protecting, that action carries a special power. Plummer has noticed that since Tokyo, more personal and professional contacts have initiated conversations about their mental health. This is significant, as research has found that many Black women feel they must project an image of invulnerability and the stigma around mental health deters them from seeking help. And although Black adults are more likely than white ones to report symptoms of emotional distress, only 1 in 3 Black adults who needs mental-health care receives it. "It is a privilege of people who have money to see a therapist," says Reuben Buford May, a professor of sociology at the University of Illinois Urbana-Champaign who studies race and culture. "Intertwined with that is that African Americans have disproportionately been among the poor and have not been able to have health care to pay for mental-health services."

Biles alone won't change mental-health inequities or force a society that has long paid lip service to the importance of mental health to do more. But she made it that much harder to look away. And, according to school psychologist Shawna Kelly, a member of the National Association of School Psychologists' board of directors, Biles' actions will help accelerate a trend that was already under way. Recently, Kelly has seen more kids asking for help, as well as expressing concern for their friends. "Often that's before a real crisis, which is where I feel there is more opportunity to work with kids preventively and proactively."

In June, before she had any idea of the experiences to come, Biles had Maya Angelou's *And still I rise* tattooed on her collarbone. "It's a reminder and a tribute to everything I had been through, and that I always come out on top," she says. The Olympics did not go the way she or anyone else expected, but she's not wallowing in what-ifs. She's back in therapy, just finished headlining a U.S. tour and is feeling confident about the decision she made in Tokyo. "I was torn because things weren't going the way I wanted," she says. "But looking back, I wouldn't change it for anything." — *With reporting by Nik Popli and Simmone Shah*

> In general, writers of informative articles tend to cite their sources in a more journalistic manner and typically do not provide a works cited or references list to identify their sources. In academic writing, sources should always be cited using a documentation system, such as MLA or APA.

Starting a Conversation: Thinking Critically about "*Time* 2021 Athlete of the Year: Simone Biles"

In your writer's notebook, consider how Park and Gregory respond to their writing situation by answering the following questions:

1. Informative essays and articles often begin with a question that readers might have about a subject. What question(s) does "*Time* 2021 Athlete of the Year: Simone Biles" attempt to answer?

2. Who is the intended audience for this article? What clues lead you to that conclusion? What assumptions do Park and Gregory make about their readers?

3. What types of evidence do Park and Gregory use in the article? Which type is most effective? Why?

4. On the *Time* website, this article included a video compilation of interviews with Biles, photos, and social-media clips. The video can be viewed at https://youtu.be/VOZ3VEgg2Us. In what ways does the use of multimedia add to — or distract from — Park and Gregory's argument about athletes' mental health challenges?

5. **Reflection:** Park and Gregory note that even as athletes like Simon Biles and Naomi Osaka call attention to the importance of mental health, they feel the pressure of larger societal expectations. Do you think that star athletes will ever feel comfortable resisting those expectations? What would have to happen to make that possible?

Infographics

International Networks Archive, Princeton University
The Magic Bean Shop and *The Fries That Bind Us*

An infographic is a visual representation of a set of facts or data. Because of their versatility and ability to present complex data in a format that is easy for readers to parse, infographics are useful in magazines and newspapers, on websites and blogs, in journal articles, and in a variety of other contexts. An infographic's design contributes in large part to its effectiveness, and a clear, cohesive design is key to its success. These infographics were created by Jonathan Harris of Flaming Toast Productions for the International Networks Archive (INA) at Princeton University.

What Kinds of Documents Are Used to Inform? | CHAPTER 08

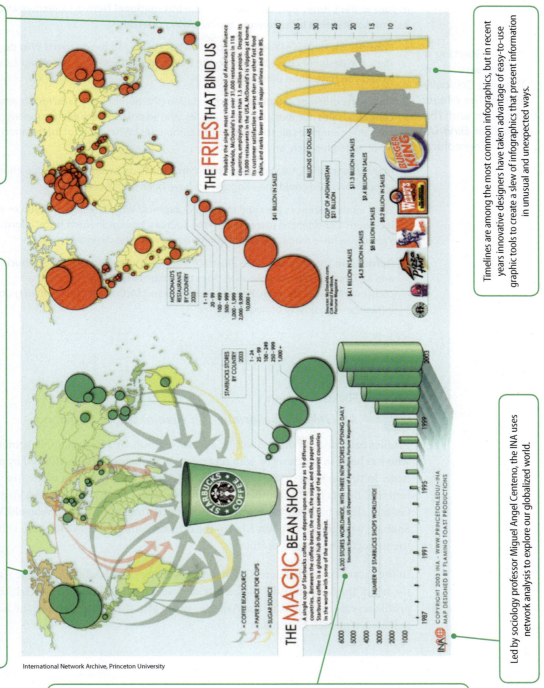

International Network Archive, Princeton University

The Magic Bean Shop and The Fries That Bind Us use text, images, corporate logos, graphs, maps, and statistics to visualize the global reach of both Starbucks and McDonald's.

The infographics illustrate the large multinational presence of these companies and the ways in which they connect the wealthiest and the poorest nations.

Timelines are among the most common infographics, but in recent years innovative designers have taken advantage of easy-to-use graphic tools to create a slew of infographics that present information in unusual and unexpected ways.

Led by sociology professor Miguel Angel Centeno, the INA uses network analysis to explore our globalized world.

As informative documents, infographics typically present information in a seemingly unbiased way, and they sometimes include a list of sources for the facts and data presented.

Starting a Conversation: Thinking Critically about *The Magic Bean Shop* and *The Fries That Bind Us* Infographics

In your writer's notebook, consider how the International Networks Archive addresses its writing situation by answering the following questions:

1. Consider the design of the infographics. What stands out to you most? Why do you think the designer chose to incorporate that feature? If you were the designer, what would you have done differently?

2. Notice the different categories of information (the number of stores/restaurants by company, sales numbers, product sources, and so on) listed for each company. Are the same categories illustrated for both companies? What types of information are emphasized for each, and why?

3. In the infographics, two companies are compared side by side. What is the effect of this layout? How else could the infographics have been structured?

4. What kinds of sources are cited in the infographics? Why do you think sources are included? Consider the placement of the sources. How prominent is the information? Would you have made a different choice if you were the designer?

5. **Reflection:** These infographics illustrate the expansive reach of both Starbucks and McDonald's. What implication does this information have for you as a consumer? In your opinion, how do Starbucks and McDonald's utilize their global influence — positively or negatively?

Profiles

Rivka Galchen
An Unlikely Ballerina: The Rise of Misty Copeland

Profiles use information to describe a place, a group, or a person, often someone who has been in the news or who represents a number of people affected by an issue. In the summer of 2021, for example, following the launches of the first "space tourism" flights by the commercial companies Blue Origin, SpaceX, and Virgin Galactic, their billionaire owners and passengers (including ninety-year-old William Shatner, who played Captain Kirk in the original *Star Trek* television series) became the subject of numerous profiles.

In the excerpt provided here, Galchen traces Misty Copeland's improbable rise to the top of the ballet world. Using a mix of observation and interviews, Galchen's profile reveals not only Copeland's tenacity but also the challenges that she has had to address to reach her dream.

An Unlikely Ballerina

The Rise of Misty Copeland

Rivka Galchen

> Rivka Galchen is the author of *Atmospheric Disturbances* (2008), *Little Labors* (2016), and *Everyone Knows Your Mother Is a Witch* (2021). Galchen's writing has been featured in such publications as *Harper's* and the *New York Times Magazine*. She is also a regular contributor to the *New Yorker*, where this article was first published in 2014.

On a recent August afternoon, near Nineteenth Street, two young girls with blond hair pulled back in ponytails ran past me, one of them calling out, "Daddy, Daddy, I just saw Misty Copeland!" The tone of voice might as well have been used to announce a sighting of Katy Perry, or Snow White. A few steps later, I entered the tiny lobby of a building on Broadway, where an old electric fan was not quite keeping the doorman cool. A caged elevator took me up to the third floor, where I passed through a low-ceilinged hallway crowded with unlabeled posters of ballet greats, until I reached an expansive fluorescent-lit room with two walls of slightly warped mirrors and air-conditioning units sealed into the windows with black electrical tape. The American Ballet Theatre soloists Misty Copeland and Alexandre Hammoudi were rehearsing the pas de deux from Act II of *Swan Lake*, the scene in which we first meet Odette; an evil sorcerer's spell has left her a swan by day and a human by night. Prince Siegfried is poised to kill the swan, but then witnesses its transformation into a beautiful young woman. "It's not that you turn her," Kevin McKenzie, A.B.T.'s artistic director since 1992 and a former principal dancer, told Hammoudi. "It's that she's startled, so she turns to you." In the movement they were practicing, Odette is downstage left and Prince Siegfried walks up behind her. Odette is naïve, uncannily beautiful, and destined to die, but she is also, in each production, a very particular dancer. McKenzie continued, "And then you're near this creature, and you're both surprised by your proximity."

Although ballet fans never lack for darlings, rarely does a dancer become an old-fashioned star, one recognized outside the realm of people with nuanced opinions about the alternative endings to *Swan Lake*. But Misty Copeland, who is thirty-two, has not only performed some of the most coveted and challenging roles in classical ballet; she has also danced atop a grand piano during Prince's 2010 Welcome 2 America tour and starred in a Diet Dr Pepper commercial, and, a few days before the *Swan Lake* rehearsal, was featured in a commercial for Under Armour that within a week of its release had more than four million views on YouTube. In the ad, a voice-over reads a rejection letter detailing why "the candidate" is

> Profiles tend to focus on a particular moment in time rather than on a lifetime.

Sputnik/TopFoto

Photographs of the subject of a profile are another common feature of this genre.

the stars of ESPN. Most ballerinas don't have pensions, they rarely dance past the age of forty (injuries often end their careers earlier than that), and a soloist at A.B.T. earns between fifty thousand and a hundred thousand dollars a year. The great Anna Pavlova endorsed Pond's Vanishing Cream. . . .

Copeland grew up in Los Angeles, as one of six children. Her memoir, *Life in Motion*, written with Charisse Jones, portrays her childhood as having been in some ways idyllic: swimming at the beach, a circle of loving and talented siblings, a charismatic and beautiful mother, and a gift for responsibility and leadership. But another version of Copeland's childhood, which also comes through in her memoir, is the hardship tale: not knowing her real father, a succession of differently difficult stepfathers, and uncertainty about whether there would be dinner on any given night.

Profiles typically draw on interviews and observations, and sometimes on published sources such as biographies or news reports, to give readers a thorough understanding of the subject.

not a good fit for ballet — the letter is a fiction, albeit one not unrelated to Copeland's career — while Copeland, who is wearing a sports bra and underwear, slowly rises onto pointe. In chiaroscuro lighting that is usually reserved for boxers' bodies, the camera focuses on Copeland's substantial, sinewy musculature. "I Will What I Want" is the tagline; a billboard in SoHo features a similar muscles-and-determination image. While it is disheartening to be reminded that product endorsement is the strongest measure of mainstream success, it feels good to see a woman who is doing more than being pretty become the kind of idol commonly associated with

As a young girl, Copeland loved dancing to Mariah Carey videos, rewatching a movie about the gymnast Nadia Comaneci, and being very prepared for school, where she was a hall monitor and the class treasurer. She usually showed up an hour early. Until the age of thirteen, she took no gymnastics or dance classes, though she did take and love a woodworking class at the local Boys & Girls Club.

Copeland is considered an unlikely ballerina: she is curvy and she is black, neither of which is a common attribute in the field. But it is her very late beginning and rapid attainment of virtuosity that are arguably without precedent for a female ballerina. (Rudolf Nureyev had a famously late and chaotic start, his early training having been limited by the vagaries of the post–Second World War Soviet Union.) Many professional ballet dancers begin their training around the age of three. Every dancer is a synthesis of givens — height, limb length, natural turnout — and intense effort, but Copeland's late start can exaggerate the tendency we might have to regard a ballerina as simply touched by something divine.

When she was thirteen, and very shy, Copeland followed the lead of her older sister Erica and tried out for the middle-school drill team. She choreographed her own piece, set to George Michael's "I Want Your Sex." The closing move was a split, head held high. The evening after the audition, she received a call saying that she had been named captain of the squad of sixty.

The team's coach, Elizabeth Cantine, was new, and Erica, who had been a drill-team star, told Misty that this was unfortunate; the old coach had led the team to wins all over the state, while Cantine was an unknown, just someone who'd been hired to teach history and English. But Cantine had a background in classical dance, and, after working with Misty for a short time she suggested that she try the ballet class at the Boys & Girls Club. "I wasn't excited by the idea of being with people I didn't know, and though I loved movement, I had no particular feelings about ballet," Copeland said. "But I didn't want to displease Liz."

Cindy Bradley, who taught the class, told me, "I remember putting my hand on her foot, putting it into a tendu pointe, and she was definitely able to go into that position — she was able to go into all the positions that I put her into that day — but it wasn't about that." Bradley said she had a kind of vision, "right then, that first day, of this little girl becoming amazing."

Copeland recalls her first class differently: "I was so embarrassed. I didn't know anything that the other girls in the class knew; I thought I was doing everything wrong."

But she kept attending the class. Copeland had an unusual body: her shoulders were sloped, her legs were long, her knees were hyperextended, and she was effortlessly flexible and strong even as she was very slight. She was in the habit of entertaining her siblings (and slightly weirding them out) by linking her hands together, putting them over her head behind her ears, and then getting her elbows to bend in the wrong direction. She also had a natural ability to quickly memorize and mimic any movement she saw. She began attending ballet classes five days a week, at Bradley's studio in San Pedro. "One day, it just clicked," Copeland told me. "I began to understand what it was."...

Copeland says that eating disorders are not as pervasive among ballerinas as people think. Nearly every woman has at times felt that the shape of her body has determined an overwhelming proportion of someone's response to her; ballet dancers, so much more intimately aware of their bodies' appearance and ability both, might — through professionalism, through necessity — have a healthier way of relating to their bodies than the rest of us. Then again, the stakes are higher. Copeland had never given much thought to her diet, but when it was suggested to her that she needed to "lengthen" — balletspeak for losing weight — she rebelled. This was pretty much the first time in her life that she had done so, and, in the way of a young person, she mostly damaged herself.

"I didn't want to be seen ordering huge amounts of food, but the local Krispy Kreme would do deliveries if the order was large enough," Copeland said. "After practice, I would order two dozen doughnuts and then, alone in my apartment, eat most of them." She felt that her ballet career was getting away from her, that she was far from family, that she was alone. "I was barely over a hundred pounds, but I felt so fat, and even a stranger at a club, when I told him I was a ballerina, said, 'No way,'" Copeland recalled. "It took me about five years to figure out how my body worked, and to understand how to make my muscles more lean."

Even though Copeland now has a more elongated — more classical — physique, and no longer has a double-D chest, she remains more buxom than most ballet dancers, and also more visibly athletic. A significant part of what distinguishes her is her unclassical body. Marie Taglioni, the nineteenth-century ballerina, is thought to have had special appeal because her proportions didn't conform to the ideal; her rounded back made her lean forward a tiny bit, so that she seemed on the verge of losing her balance; her physical limitations ended up shaping what became her definitive style. And it was arguably with Taglioni that ballet — a man's game until a hundred years before, with men "*en travesti*" even playing the roles of women in most serious productions — began to be about ballerinas....

When I visited Copeland backstage after *La Bayadère*, I met a friend of hers, eighty-year-old Raven Wilkinson, an elegant older woman who wore her hair twisted into a topknot. Wilkinson was born in Harlem, and in 1955 joined the

Ballet Russe de Monte Carlo for its American tours. "I had been told not to try out, that they wouldn't take me, because they toured through cities in the South," Wilkinson said to me, when we met for lunch a while later. She has African, Native American, and European ancestors; she is pale, and onstage she wore powder. "But I thought, Well, if I don't even try out I know I'll never have what I want." . . .

The original dream of a uniquely American ballet was of a company that mixed whites and "Negroes" — the term used by George Balanchine, one of the cofounders of New York City Ballet. Balanchine had been influenced by working with Josephine Baker, the black American dancer who became a celebrity in France during the twenties. His vision was only occasionally realized: in his famous *Agon*, he choreographed a pas de deux for Diana Adams and Arthur Mitchell, a white woman and a black man. *Agon* was performed in 1957, to critical celebration, even though it could not be shown on television until 1968. Balanchine also made Maria Tallchief, who was of Osage heritage, an early star of the New York City Ballet. (For a time, he also made her his wife.)

Many black ballet dancers, including Wilkinson, were encouraged to concentrate on "African dance," or maybe modern dance or musical theatre — even if they had spent years training in classical ballet. Virginia Johnson, long a lead ballerina and now the artistic director of Dance Theatre of Harlem, a predominantly African-American ballet company, once said she had been told by someone with good intentions that she could never be a ballerina because there aren't any black ballerinas.

That is not quite true today, but it's in the neighborhood of true. "Let's be honest," Susan Fales-Hill, a writer and a philanthropist who served on the board of A.B.T., says. "Most ballet companies look like an Alabama country club in 1952." There is a small number of Asian-American ballerinas, and a small number of black ones. The reasons usually cited include the holdover of antiquated ideas of beauty, the lack of role models, the preference for a uniform look among the corps dancers in a company, and the high cost of years of training. (Pointe shoes, for example, are around seventy dollars a pair, and a serious dancer can easily go through a pair a week.) Lauren Anderson, a longtime principal dancer with the Houston Ballet, was the first African-American woman to reach the rank of principal ballerina with a major American company other than D.T.H. (Principal is the highest rank for a dancer, above soloist.) She played Odette/Odile a number of times before she retired, in 2006. "When we think of ballerinas, we think of pink and

> In June 2015, less than a year after Galchen's profile was published, Misty Copeland was promoted to principal dancer with the American Ballet Theatre.

pale and fluffy," she told me. "We're not accustomed to thinking of black women's bodies in that context. We're accustomed to thinking of black women as athletic and strong. But all ballerinas are athletic, all ballerinas are strong."...

Copeland acts as a mentor to aspiring dancers, including Makeda Roney, a young woman who wrote Copeland a letter while she was in tenth grade, after seeing her perform. Roney, who was recently accepted into a yearlong program with the Joffrey Ballet, in Chicago, says that she calls or writes to Copeland whenever she feels anxious or discouraged. "She's like a sister to me," Roney said. Copeland has also been a public face for A.B.T.'s recent Project Plié initiative, which provides training and scholarships for kids who live in communities where there is little exposure to ballet.

Copeland's artistic and commercial successes make us all feel good — about ballet, about America — and yet that feeling is somewhat tendentious. It is impossible to distill the current role of race in ballet (or in any field) from one woman's career. Copeland's race makes her immediately distinctive in the ballet world, and this has undoubtedly helped her commercial career, but murmurings, on some online dance-discussion threads, that she has been excessively promoted within A.B.T. because of her race overlook not just her virtuosity but also the many years in which she wasn't a soloist, or even a lead dancer....

In addition to its practice space on Broadway, A.B.T. has a rehearsal space several floors below the stage of the Metropolitan Opera House. One afternoon, I went to see Copeland rehearse a pas de deux with Herman Cornejo for a production of Kenneth MacMillan's ballet *Manon*, which they were to perform for the first time the next day....

I never used to be easily drawn in by the long storybook standards of classical ballet; it was as if the salmon sandwiches and the bubbly rosés served during intermission got in the way. It was easier to access the more immediately legible expressiveness of abstract, modern pieces. But many dancers have told me that they revere the long classical pieces. When I asked why, they talked about how freeing the strict constraints of classical ballet are, from its most basic positions to its thirty-two-fouetté extremes; from other forms of dance, one couldn't transition to classical ballet, but from classical ballet one could do anything.

Dance is not like the other arts. The words in a book stay in place, paintings barely fade, musical performances can be recorded. But watching a recording of dance is about as close to the real thing as reading *Eugene Onegin* in Google Translate. Dancers often restrain themselves, necessarily, during practice, but Cornejo and Copeland seemed to be leaping higher, and moving more articulately, than they did onstage. I had just seen three grand ballet performances in a row, but this harshly lit, uncostumed, and repeatedly interrupted performance was my favorite. It wasn't simply the proximity, the sound of the shoes, the soothingly minor comments — "Your back arm tends to get behind you"; "A little more shoulder at the beginning, so it's not so flat" — it was more the juxtaposition of the mundane and the magnificent: "Be careful when you do the relevé; don't crank her leg too much"; "The second pirouette — did you just do left?"

"People are surprised to hear that I still go to class," Copeland told me. "But that's what dancers do." In a studio class one Thursday morning, there were dancers from all ranks of A.B.T., as well as dancers not yet in the company, stretching, chatting. One dancer asked for a recommendation for a travel agent. Another replied that no one has used travel agents since the eighties. Copeland sat on the floor beside them, in a purple leotard, applying glue to the inside of her pointe shoes. The director of A.B.T.'s studio company, a former dancer named Kate Lydon, called the class to attention: "We'll start with sixteen swings, port de bras forward." The pianist accompanying the class played some Dvořák, then some Bach, then "The Girl from Ipanema." After the barre exercises, there were floor exercises, then jumps, then more exercises moving across the room.

> Because they appear so often in popular periodicals, most profiles are relatively brief.

Starting a Conversation: Thinking Critically about "An Unlikely Ballerina: The Rise of Misty Copeland"

In your writer's notebook, consider Galchen's profile by answering the following questions:

1. In informative writing, the writer generally acts as a reporter or an observer but not as an interpreter. How well does Galchen fulfill this role? Look for specific examples in the essay that demonstrate this role.

2. As a reader of this informative document, what question do you believe Galchen is trying to answer? How well is that question answered? What other information do you need to answer that question?

3. Galchen's profile relies heavily on interviews and on Copeland's own words. Why are firsthand quotations from the subject of the profile important to this piece of writing? Could the piece have worked without as many direct quotes from Copeland? Who else does Galchen quote, and why are these other voices important?

4. **Reflection:** As the title of the article asserts, Copeland's success as a ballerina is considered "unlikely" for many reasons — her race, her physical shape, her background. Have you ever worked toward a goal that seemed "unlikely"? What aspects of Copeland's journey could help you overcome obstacles to your goals?

Newsletter Articles

Illyanna Maisonet
Why Aren't There More Puerto Rican Restaurants . . . in California?

Newsletter articles provide information about an issue, event, or individual, often from a personal perspective. They can be distributed on the web, via email, and in print. Illyanna Maisonet, a Puerto Rican and a cook, writes and publishes a newsletter that focuses on Puerto Rican food and Northern California history. Her article considers why Puerto Rican food is not more popular on the West Coast.

Why Aren't There More Puerto Rican Restaurants . . . in California?

Illyanna Maisonet

> Newsletter articles can be written formally or informally, depending on the newsletter publisher's preference. In this article, Maisonet writes in a first-person voice, cites her sources, and provides support for her points.

My grandparents came to Northern California in 1955. My grandfather packed up my nana, mother and uncle and moved to Sacramento. They knew no one there. Why my grandpa chose the area is unknown to anyone but him. But I'm thankful he did.

Virtually isolated from other Puerto Ricans, my nana continued to cook in the "old-fashioned" style that her mother and aunt taught her, making beans from dried instead of canned, and making sofrito — a paste made from cilantro, tomatoes, peppers, onions and garlic — from scratch.

But because they were the only Puerto Rican family in Sacramento at the time, she quickly made friends with those she could communicate with: her Mexican neighbors. She quickly learned to cook their tortillas, chile rellenos and menudo, and these dishes remained in her cooking repertoire. In 2014, six decades after my grandparents first moved to Sacramento, there were reportedly 11,215 Puerto Ricans in Sacramento — but not a single Puerto Rican restaurant.

Recently, I've been thinking about why Puerto Rican food is not more popular on the West Coast.

Puerto Ricans are U.S. citizens and can come and go freely — if their economic situation allows — to create a life on the mainland. Yet despite more than 30,000 Puerto Ricans in Alameda, Contra Costa, Santa Clara and San Francisco counties, Puerto Rican food isn't popular here. (Although San Jose does have an annual Puerto Rican festival, which takes place this year on June 17.)

According to the Center for Puerto Rican Studies at Hunter College in New York, there were an estimated 200,000 Puerto Ricans living in California in 2014, accounting for just 4 percent of all Puerto Ricans living in the United States. For context, about 84,000 people moved from Puerto Rico to the United States in 2014 alone.

"I've only ever heard of a Puerto Rican community being in Florida and New York," says Paxx Caraballo Moll. Caraballo Moll and partner Audrey Berry are part of a new generation of chefs shepherding a fresh Puerto Rican culinary movement, and recently opened Baoricua, a Puerto Rican–Taiwanese food stand in San Juan, Puerto Rico. So without more Puerto Ricans on the West Coast, maybe that's why the cuisine is not as popular here, Caraballo Moll says.

And as with many Latin American foods, there's a constant comparison to Mexican cuisine.

"The Mexican demographic is huge and they have implanted their culture and food in a unique way that is perceived as Latin food everywhere," says Manolo Lopez of Mofongo, a Puerto Rican pop-up restaurant in New York. "I only know a handful of Puerto Ricans in the West Coast and none are in the food industry. I spent some time in San Francisco and Los Angeles, and our ingredients are also hard to find: recao, platanos, aji dulces, et cetera."

How many Puerto Rican restaurants do you know in Northern California? Yes, there is Sol Food in Marin. Good for you for knowing. But did you know there are more? Well, a few more, at least: Borinquen Soul in Oakland is a take-out restaurant within a liquor store, with great alcapurrias — grated plantain and green banana stuffed with seasoned meat and fried. In San Francisco, Parada 22 has been open in the Haight for seven years,

> Newsletter articles generally identify sources of information in a journalistic manner, most often by citing individuals and organizations by name in the body of the text or by linking to the source. In some cases, sources might be cited in a works cited list or bibliography, but this is rare.

and the Mission's El Nuevo Frutilandia serves both Puerto Rican food and Cuban food. There's El Coqui in Santa Rosa, and, of course, Sol Food's two North Bay locations, which are the mainstream darlings of California–Puerto Rican cuisine. But for the most part, that's it.

It's possible the lack of Bay Area Puerto Rican restaurants is due to a lack of support, and certainly there's the high cost of entry into the restaurant industry. Plus, while a soulful and delicious cuisine, traditional Puerto Rican food is just not sexy-looking; it's double-starch and brown on brown on brown.

With the country's best-known Mexican chef being Rick Bayless and the best-known Thai chef being Andy Ricker, sometimes I also wonder if Puerto Rican food might need, well, a comparable mainland chef to bring it to mainstream status — or even a *Top Chef* competitor like Hawaii's Sheldon Simeon, who showcased the range of Filipino food beyond adobo. He managed to find a balance of re-creating the soulful flavors of his Filipino rustic cuisine but with a refined appearance. Or perhaps we need an Instagram-savvy Puerto Rican to plate carne guisada in a contemporary way utilizing edible flowers.

> Newsletter articles often help readers understand the implications of the information they present.

Maybe we should look to the diaspora for its culinary champions. In Puerto Rico, traditional methods of cooking were once in danger of disappearing in the face of American colonization, due to a complicated import-export relationship, defunct agrarian culture and the introduction of processed foods and fast-food chains, among other challenges. But those of us on the mainland, isolated and trying to salvage our grandmother's recipes via osmosis, cook the most traditional way.

Only recently has a younger culinary generation found its voice on the island, partly thanks to the duo of chefs Jose — Jose Enrique and Jose Santaella — who have incorporated modern (and often Euro-centric) techniques with Puerto Rican ingredients. They have, in turn, cultivated a new generation of young chefs, including Paxx Caraballo Moll, who have tentacled out across the island creating their own culinary endeavors.

Maybe that movement will eventually spread to the mainland. No one seems to know anything about Puerto Rican food here. You'd think it'd be easy bringing the food of Puerto Rico, an island belonging to the United States since 1898, to the West Coast. Now, it just seems like a big order to fill.

"There's simply not enough knowledge outside the community about what (Puerto Rican food) is," says Alicia Kennedy, associate editor of *Edible*

Manhattan. "Even here in New York City, where there are more Puerto Ricans, it's not spreading beyond those who have a connection to the culture."

Lopez, from Mofongo in New York, concurs that education is the first step.

"We just have to get people to know our food for it to be able to expand and be recognized around the world," Lopez says. "The more media (that) write about our pop-ups and collaborations, the more people will know."

Places that serve Puerto Rican fare
Borinquen Soul: 2020 Macarthur Blvd., Oakland [CLOSED]
La Perla: 3409 Fruitvale Ave., Oakland, CA 94602
El Coqui: 400 Mendocino Ave., Santa Rosa
El Nuevo Frutilandia: 3077 24th St., San Francisco
Parada 22: 1805 Haight St., San Francisco
Sol Food: 401 Miller Ave., Mill Valley; and 901 Lincoln Ave., San Rafael

> Maisonet provides addresses for some Puerto Rican restaurants, helping readers learn more about them.

In your writer's notebook, consider how Maisonet addresses her writing situation by answering the following questions:

Starting a Conversation: Thinking Critically about "Why Aren't There More Puerto Rican Restaurants . . . in California?"

1. What question (or questions) does Maisonet answer in this newsletter article? Who is the intended audience? How does Maisonet address this audience in the answer(s) she gives?

2. One of the goals of informative writing is to make connections to contemporary issues. In what ways does Maisonet call attention to the cultural value of Puerto Rican cuisine? How does the article's organization make the connection apparent to the newsletter's reader?

3. Identify the types of evidence that Maisonet uses. What makes this evidence compelling? What impact does it have?

4. Newsletters are typically distributed to a relatively small group of subscribers, even when a newsletter, like Maisonet's, is free and distributed on the web. In what ways might this affect the information she shares and the manner in which she shares it, either positively or negatively? If you were analyzing the effectiveness of a newsletter, what would you consider?

5. **Reflection:** Imagine you are writing a newsletter article about a topic you care about deeply. Which aspects of Maisonet's article would you emulate? Which would you disregard? Explain your choices in detail.

GENRE TALK

Reflective Writing | **Informative Writing** | Analytical Writing | Evaluative Writing | Problem-Solving Writing | Argumentative Writing

Readers of informative documents often have a specific purpose or interest in the subject. Residents of California, scientists, environmentalists, and the general public can benefit from the information presented in this article from NASA about the severity of the wildfires in Southern California. Additionally, writers of informative documents may have certain aspects of the topic that they want to publicize or details they want to share. They may make use of various media, such as images, slide shows, maps, or infographics to share that information most effectively.

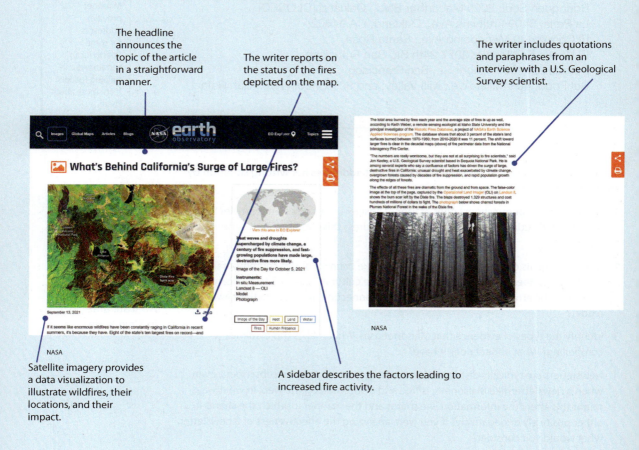

The headline announces the topic of the article in a straightforward manner.

The writer reports on the status of the fires depicted on the map.

The writer includes quotations and paraphrases from an interview with a U.S. Geological Survey scientist.

NASA

Satellite imagery provides a data visualization to illustrate wildfires, their locations, and their impact.

A sidebar describes the factors leading to increased fire activity.

NASA

How Can I Write an Informative Essay?

The first step in writing a successful informative essay is recognizing that you don't have to be an expert on something to write about it — you simply have to know how to learn enough about it to share your findings with your readers. The second step is understanding how to collect and work with information. This doesn't mean that an informative essay needs to look like a research paper. As you've seen throughout this chapter, the amount and type of information used in informative documents can vary widely. What it does mean, however, is that you should understand where you can find information — for example, through interviews, published documents, the web, direct observation, or personal experience — and how to work with it once you've collected it.

This section helps you tune in to the conversations around you and take on the role of reporter as you choose a subject, gather information, prepare your draft, and review and improve your draft. As you work on your contribution to the conversation, you'll draw in particular on the critical thinking skills of remembering, understanding, and creating. As you work on your essay, you'll follow the work of Gabriella Guerrero, a first-year student who wrote an informative essay about the fast fashion industry.

Find a Conversation and Listen In

Informative essays offer a good opportunity to learn more about something that intrigues you and to report what you've learned to readers who share your interest in the subject. To get started on your informative essay, prepare yourself to take on the role of reporter and spend some time thinking about your purpose, your readers, and the context in which your writing will be read (see *What Should I Know about Writing Situations?* in Chapter 1). Look around for a topic of conversation that will interest both you and your readers — and that you can investigate in the time available to you.

- **REFLECT ON YOUR INTERESTS**

Nobody knows everything, but most of us know a little (or a lot) about a few things — especially if they involve us personally or professionally. As you search for ideas for an informative essay, turn to your daily life for inspiration.

In Process

An Informative Essay about Fast Fashion

Gabriella Guerrero wrote an informative essay for her first-year writing course. To learn about her topic, Gabriella read articles about the fast fashion industry and its effects on workers and the environment. She also searched the web for information from agencies such as the Environmental Protection Agency and nonprofit organizations concerned with the issue. Follow Gabriella's efforts to inform her readers in the In Process boxes throughout this chapter.

- **Personal interests and hobbies.** What do you like to do in your spare time? What magazines do you read? What television shows do you like to watch? What makes you happy? Curious? Angry? What frightens you? Amuses you?
- **Academics.** Your major and your favorite classes are rich sources for essay ideas. Think about recent class discussions that interested you, questions that puzzled you, or information that surprised you when you first learned it.
- **Work.** Any past or current job, volunteer activity, or career you hope to enter involves specialized knowledge of some sort, from learning how to fill a soda machine to getting to know the U.S. tax code. Ask yourself whether you would be interested in informing others about this specialized knowledge.
- **Reading.** What have you read recently that interested or surprised you? What annoyed you or made you angry? What have you read that made you think?

Any of these areas can serve as a jumping-off point for generating ideas for an informative essay. Spend some time brainstorming or freewriting about these aspects of your life (see *Generate Ideas* in Chapter 2), and then review your notes to identify the areas that seem most promising. (For additional suggestions, see the writing project ideas at the end of this chapter.) As you think about your ideas, remember that the best subjects are usually out of the ordinary. Instead of writing about the broad issue of capital punishment, for example, you would do better to consider a little-known but potentially important aspect of the subject, such as how inmates on death row spend their last day before execution or the role of DNA testing in overturning convictions. Once you've identified a few possible subjects, select one or two that interest you most, and jot down your thoughts about what you already know and what you need to learn before you start writing.

Working Together: Try It Out Loud

Before you start writing to inform, start a conversation with your classmates about something that interests you. Form small groups and choose a familiar subject (such as sports, family, your hometown, or the work of a favorite artist or musician). Take turns speaking while the other members of the group listen, respond, and ask questions. Your purpose is to inform the rest of the group, so try to present a fair and accurate view of your subject.

When you are finished, take a few minutes to reflect on the exercise. What did you learn about your audience? Did you have to adapt what you said based on their interest level and what they already knew? What kind of questions did they ask? What seemed to interest them the most about the subject?

How Can I Write an Informative Essay? | CHAPTER 08   **207**

In Process

Using the Library Catalog

After considering her assignment and writing situation, Gabriella Guerrero decided to focus on the impact of the fashion industry on the environment. She felt that this focus would allow her to accomplish her purpose of informing her readers about an important issue and believed that it would interest both her and her readers. She knew from her own shopping habits as well as those of her friends that fashions change so quickly that shifts in style often leave perfectly good clothing hanging unused in closets. She decided to learn more about why clothing goes out of fashion so quickly.

To learn more about the issue of fast fashion, Gabriella Guerrero searched her library's catalog for sources that addressed her subject.

[Search box: ALMOST EVERYTHING | "fast fashion" | A-Z Database List | Advanced Search | Research Help | Search Library Website | Off-Campus Access]

Gabriella searched for the phrase *fast fashion*. She placed quotation marks around the phrase.

▲ **Gabriella's search of the library catalog**

Gabriella's searches produced several promising sources, including the following.

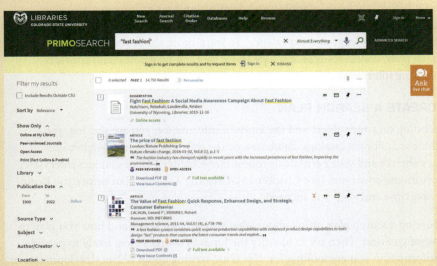

Clicking on the title will show the complete record for the source.

The results show the source's availability, its location, and (if available) a link to full text of the document.

▲ **Results of Gabriella's library catalog search**

- **ASK QUESTIONS ABOUT PROMISING SUBJECTS**

Writers who adopt the role of reporter often find themselves confronted with a seemingly endless amount of information on their subject. Before you begin examining sources closely, narrow your focus by determining which subjects interest you the most and which conversation you want to join. Each of the following questions focuses your attention on a general subject in a different way, and each provides a useful starting point for an informative essay. Depending on the subject, you'll find that some questions are more relevant than others.

- **Importance.** Why is this an important subject? Who believes that it is important? Why do they believe it is important?
- **Process.** How does _____ work? What steps are involved?
- **History.** What is the origin of _____? What recent events are related to it? What are the implications of those events?
- **Limitations.** What is limiting the use of _____? What has kept _____ from succeeding? What must happen before _____ is accepted?
- **Advantages and disadvantages.** What are the advantages of _____? Who benefits? What are the disadvantages? Who, if anyone, is negatively affected?

Gather Information

No matter how much you already know about a subject, you'll want to learn more about it before you begin planning and drafting your essay. Informative essays tend to draw extensively on information from other sources and, to a lesser extent, on personal knowledge and experience. To learn more about your subject, create a search plan, collect sources, evaluate those sources, take notes, and consider conducting interviews.

- **CREATE A SEARCH PLAN**

Depending on your subject and the kinds of information you are seeking, you might search library catalogs, databases, or the web (see Chapter 14); browse library shelves and visit periodicals rooms (see Chapter 14); or conduct interviews, observations, or surveys (see Chapter 15). Creating a search plan before you begin will save time and keep you focused.

To develop a search plan, think about what you need to know and how you plan to use what you find. Then try to identify the types of sources most likely to provide the information you are looking for. If you are writing about recent developments in consumer robotics, for example, you want the most up-to-date information you can find. As a result, you should look in library databases focusing on the subject and search the web. You might also want to interview an expert on the subject, such as a professor of engineering or computer science. In contrast, if you are writing about the influence of Greek culture on the Roman Empire, you would probably focus on books and scholarly journals that you find by searching your library catalog, browsing the shelves, and visiting periodicals rooms.

If you're not sure where to start, a reference librarian can suggest search strategies and relevant resources. You can learn more about creating a research plan and locating and using sources in Part Three.

Working Together: Plan Your Search for Sources

Before you visit the library, search a database, or browse the web, sit down with a group of classmates to generate ideas for a search. To carry out this activity, follow these steps:

1. Explain your subject and discuss your purpose for informing readers. If your readers go beyond the instructor and your classmates, describe your readers and their needs, interests, knowledge, and backgrounds. Talk briefly about specific ideas you have for gathering information on your subject.

2. Once you've explained your subject, the other members of your group should brainstorm ideas about useful resources for locating sources, such as the library catalog, specific databases, useful websites and directories, and relevant field research methods.

3. For each resource that has been identified, the group should brainstorm suggestions for using it effectively. For example, the group might generate a list of specific keywords and phrases to use in your search, create a list of good candidates for an interview and useful interview questions, and make suggestions about what to look for in an observation.

4. At the end of the discussion, ask any questions you have about the resources and search strategies your classmates have suggested.

If you are working face-to-face, take notes on the discussion. If you are using a chat or text messaging program, record a transcript of the session. If you're meeting online, takes notes or ask for permission to record the session so you can review it later. The goal of the session should be to generate as many useful search resources and strategies as possible. Don't rule out any ideas, no matter how trivial or ridiculous they might seem at first. When the exchange is completed, turn to the next writer and repeat the process.

● COLLECT SOURCES

To collect sources, search for them in library catalogs, in databases, and on the web. Visit your library to check out books and government reports, browse the shelves, and use the periodicals room. You can learn more about these activities in Part Three.

● ASSESS AND EVALUATE YOUR SOURCES

Depending on your subject, you might find yourself confronted with a dizzying array of promising sources, or you might find yourself gritting your teeth as one search after another comes up empty. In most cases, you'll collect at least a few useful sources, from books and scholarly articles to websites and blogs to video clips and news articles. Be aware, however, that not all information is created equal and that some sources will be more appropriate for an academic essay than others. Before you decide to use a source, assess its fit with your project and check its credibility. Then evaluate the evidence it provides, the credentials and experiences of its author and publisher, and its timeliness.

Need a refresher on assessing and evaluating sources? See Chapter 4.

● TAKE NOTES

Once you've located enough reliable and credible sources to inform your essay, spend time taking notes on them. Because note taking often involves putting information about a subject into your own words, it can help you learn more about your subject and the writers who have been contributing to the conversation you want to join. Taking notes can also help you identify the most important information in your sources.

By studying a source and noting important information, ideas, and arguments, you'll gain a clearer understanding of the source and your subject. Careful note taking also helps you avoid plagiarism and lays the foundation for drafting your document. You can learn more about taking notes in Chapter 4.

- **CONSIDER FIELD RESEARCH**

Consider using observation, a survey, interviews, or correspondence to collect information you might not be able to locate through other means. Interviews — in which one person seeks information from another — can be particularly useful as you work on an informative document. They provide firsthand accounts of an event, authoritative interpretations of an issue, and thoughts on a subject from the people who have been affected by it. You can conduct interviews face-to-face, over the telephone, via video, and even through a messaging app.

The decision to conduct an interview should be based on the kinds of information you need to support your argument, although it can also be a result of having access to someone who has specific expertise or experience relevant to your subject or issue. As you prepare for an interview, consider your purpose, develop a limited set of main questions, and draft follow-up questions for each main question. If possible, record the interview. In all cases, take notes. (You can learn more about conducting interviews and other forms of field research in Chapter 15.)

Prepare a Draft

Writers of informative essays focus on reporting information to their readers. As you prepare a draft of your informative essay, you'll decide which information, ideas, and arguments to present and how you will share them with your readers.

Your decisions about what to focus on, which points to make, and what evidence to use will influence what your readers learn about your subject and how they are likely to understand it. Although reporters strive for objectivity in their writing, experienced writers recognize the difficulty of presenting information in a completely unbiased manner. They understand that their choices can (and will) lead readers to think about a subject in a particular way. Consider a writer selecting details for an informative essay about the impact of bans on smoking in bars and restaurants. Statistical information about cash register receipts would focus readers' attention on financial implications of the ban for small business owners; a photograph of an asthmatic bartender might encourage readers to consider the positive public health effects of such a ban; and an interview with a smokers' rights advocate could emphasize concerns about eroding personal freedoms. No matter how objectively the writer presents the information, the final mix of statistics, images, and quotations will affect the conclusions readers draw from the document.

It's best to begin by choosing a main point and expressing it as a thesis statement. Then you can decide which supporting points and evidence will most effectively support your main point. During the drafting process, you should also decide whether to include visual information, how to organize your ideas, and how to frame your introduction and conclusion.

Assessing and Evaluating Sources

To gain a more thorough understanding of the impact of the fast fashion industry, Gabriella Guerrero read several articles she found through her library's periodical databases. She also searched the web for up-to-date news and information. Not surprisingly, her searches of the web pulled up several unreliable sources, such as this one.

The site appears to focus primarily on retail sales.

Web page provides no indication of authorship or authority to write on the subject.

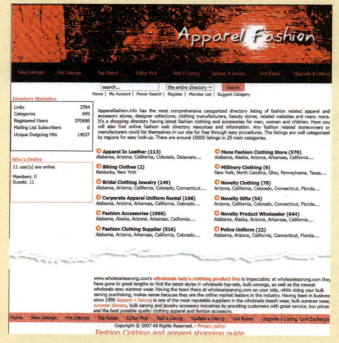

The design of the site and the copyright information suggest it has not been updated since 2007.

▲ An unreliable source

Gabriella's searches of the web also brought her to the website for the U.S. Congress Joint Economic Committee. On that site, she found a report addressing fast fashion. Gabriella bookmarked the website and downloaded the report.

The site indicates that it is associated with a joint committee of the U.S. Congress.

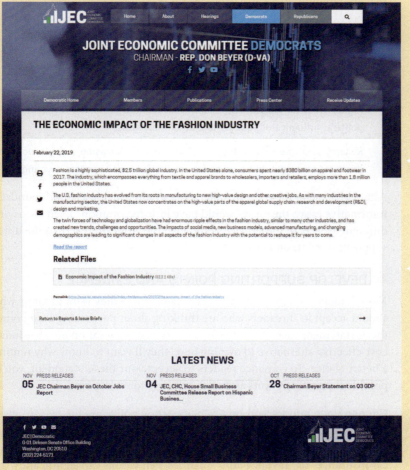

Layout and illustrations are carefully thought out and look professional.

A link to a related file (a report from the committee) is provided.

Contact information is provided.

▲ **A reliable source**
Joint Economic Committee

● PRESENT YOUR MAIN POINT

In an informative essay, the main point is usually presented in the form of a thesis statement. A thesis statement, typically no more than a single sentence, directs readers' attention to what you want them to learn about a subject. Consider how the following thesis statements about voter turnout among younger Americans direct readers' attention in a particular way:

> The high turnout among younger voters in the last presidential election — and in particular in Democratic primaries and caucuses — underscores the growing importance of young Americans on the political scene.

> The growing political commitment of voters under the age of twenty-five has led to higher voter turnout, which, in turn, has reduced the historic imbalance in the relative political influence of younger and older Americans.

> Regardless of the causes, the overall pattern of increasing voter turnout among younger voters should be cause for celebration among voters — young and old alike.

Is your thesis statement focused enough for your purpose? See Chapter 18.

Although each of these thesis statements would provide a sound foundation for an informative essay, the essays would have little in common. Their focus on distinctly different aspects of the subject would lead the writer to rely on quite different supporting points and evidence.

● DEVELOP SUPPORTING POINTS AND EVIDENCE

Most readers want more than a thesis statement — they want to know why they should accept it. If readers who are thinking about purchasing a car come across a thesis statement such as "For many drivers, renting a car on an occasional basis is a cost-effective alternative to owning one," they'll want to know why renting could be a better choice. To convince readers to accept your thesis statement, you'll need to provide supporting points and offer evidence for each point.

Choose your supporting points Supporting points are the reasons you give readers to accept your main point. They are usually expressed as topic sentences in the form of general statements, such as "Renting a car means you can pay less in car insurance" or "If your family qualifies, Pell Grants can significantly reduce the cost of a college education." As you choose your supporting points, keep in mind that they should not only serve as reasons to accept your main point but also be consistent with how you've presented your thesis statement. In short, you should resist the urge to include every idea you've come across. You can find more advice on developing support for a thesis statement in Chapter 18.

Developing Support

For her informative essay about the human and environmental impacts of fast fashion, Gabriella Guerrero identified the following supporting points:

1. The manufacturing process for fast fashion apparel uses significant amounts of power, which contributes to global warming.

2. The manufacturing process contributes to pollution of land, water, and air by releasing toxic chemicals and microplastics into the environment.

3. When fast fashion products are thrown away, they make a sizable contribution to landfills.

4. Workers in apparel factories, mostly in developing countries, suffer from local pollution.

5. Workers are paid low wages and often work in unsafe conditions.

In her first draft, she expressed the first point as a general statement and offered evidence from a source to support it.

> Pollution from this industry includes the fuel used to power factories — typically fossil fuels. Fossil fuels emit toxic chemicals into the atmosphere and are the biggest contributor to global warming (Center for Climate and Energy Solutions, 2022). On its website, the Center reported, "Greenhouse gas emissions from the power sector have fallen dramatically since their peak in 2005, but nonetheless represent a major source in the economy." This underscores how fast fashion corporations are profiting at the expense of our environment.

Gabriella drew on information from a leading environmental think tank.

She used APA in-text citation style to acknowledge her sources.

Gabriella's first supporting point

Identify evidence for each supporting point Without evidence to support them, even the most clearly expressed supporting points will not be enough to inform your readers fully. You need evidence to help them understand why they should accept the reasons you've used to support your thesis statement. In a profile of Misty Copeland (earlier in this chapter), for instance, writer Rivka Galchen uses evidence to illustrate a point about Copeland's unusual status as an African American ballerina:

Virginia Johnson, long a lead ballerina and now the artistic director of the Dance Theatre of Harlem, a predominantly African-American ballet company, once said she had been told by someone with good intentions that she could never be a ballerina because there aren't any black ballerinas.

Writers of informative essays also use information from sources to present ideas and clarify statements. You might draw on a source to define a complex term. You might amplify a statement by providing examples from sources. Or you might qualify a statement by noting that it applies only to specific situations and then use a quotation or paraphrase from a source to back that up.

Working Together: Brainstorm Supporting Points and Evidence

You can use group brainstorming sessions to help generate supporting points and evidence. You can work in person or online (using chat, text messaging, or a threaded discussion forum). To carry out the activity, follow these steps:

1. The writer should describe the writing project, its main point, and ideas for supporting points.
2. Each member of the group should make suggestions about the supporting points the writer mentions.
3. Each member of the group should suggest additional supporting points.
4. Each member of the group should make suggestions about potential sources of evidence to support each point.

If you are working face-to-face, ask one member of the group to take notes on the discussion. If you are using a chat, video conferencing, or messaging program, be sure to record or save a transcript of the session. The goal of the session is to generate as many potential supporting points as possible. Take care not to rule out any ideas, no matter how trivial or ridiculous they might seem at first. When the exchange is completed, turn to the next writer and repeat the process.

As you select information from sources for your essay, consider your writing situation (see Chapter 1). Be sure that the evidence you choose will help you accomplish your purpose and carry out your role; that you provide enough detail and explanation to help readers understand the information, ideas, or arguments you present to them; and that you present the evidence in a way that won't conflict with your readers' values and beliefs.

To identify evidence to support your points, follow these guidelines:

1. List your supporting points.
2. Review your notes to identify evidence for each point.
3. If necessary, review your sources (or find new ones) for additional information.
4. Avoid relying too heavily on one type of information.
5. Avoid relying too heavily on information from a single source.
6. Consider how the evidence fits your writing situation.

● CONSIDER GENRE AND DESIGN

As is the case with other academic essays, the basic design of your informative essay will reflect the formatting requirements of your assignment and the expectations of your readers, particularly your instructor. Typically, those requirements specify the use of wide (one-inch) margins, double-spaced lines, page numbers, and a readable font. These design features make it easier for instructors and classmates to read and comment on the essay.

Other design elements can help you clarify information for your readers and add visual interest to your essay. As you think about how you will present information to your readers, consider the benefits of using visual evidence to support your points, in particular photographs, drawings, charts, graphs, and tables (see *Use Illustrations* in Chapter 22).

You can draw on your sources for visual evidence in two ways. You might borrow an illustration from a print or an online source to help readers understand a complex concept or process, such as the steps involved in cellular respiration. Or you might use data from one or more sources to create an original chart, graph, or table to clarify a point, such as the growth of the Asian American population (see the following chart).

You can read more about document design in Chapters 22 and 23.

Acknowledge the source of any images or numerical information (see Chapter 17).

Illustrations should appear as close as possible to the point where they are mentioned in the text.

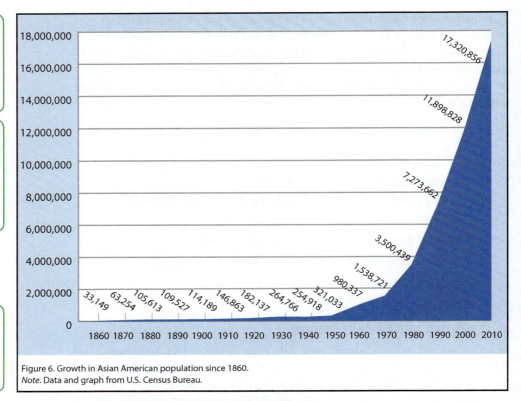

Figure 6. Growth in Asian American population since 1860.
Note. Data and graph from U.S. Census Bureau.

A title or caption should identify or explain the illustration.

▲ A chart converting data from a source into visual evidence

● **FRAME YOUR INFORMATION**

After you've settled on the supporting points you want to make and the evidence you'll use to develop your ideas, spend some time thinking about how you will put everything together for your readers.

Introduction Your introduction sets the tone for your essay and influences how your readers understand and interpret the information that you give them. Most informative essays present the thesis statement in the introduction so that readers will grasp the writer's main idea from the start. Beyond stating your thesis, you can use a range of strategies to introduce your ideas. Two effective options are providing a historical account and asking a question. Historical accounts, such as the one

Illyanna Maisonet provides in the first part of her newsletter article "Why Aren't There More Puerto Rican Restaurants . . . in California?," can help your readers understand the origins of a subject and how the situation has changed over time. Asking a question invites your readers to become participants in the conversation.

Organization The organization of your essay also affects how readers respond to your points. Your organizing strategy should take into account your purposes and your readers' needs and interests, as well as the nature and amount of evidence you've assembled to support your points. To organize your essay, choose an organizing pattern and create an outline or a map. You can use a wide range of organizing patterns in an informative essay, but some are better suited to the genre than others. If you are informing your readers about an event or a series of events, for instance, you might want to use chronological order to structure your essay. If you are providing an overview of competing ideas about an issue, you might choose comparison and contrast. And if you are explaining the defining characteristics of a subject, such as the typical attitudes of college-age voters, description might be a useful pattern to follow.

Learn more about organizing patterns, outlines, and maps in Chapter 19.

Conclusion You've probably read conclusions that simply summarize a document. These summaries can be effective, especially if your essay has presented complex concepts. A conclusion can do more, however, than simply restate your points. If you asked a question in your introduction, for instance, consider answering it in your conclusion. And if you want your readers to continue thinking about your subject after they've finished reading your essay, you might conclude by offering additional insights about what the information you've provided might mean for readers, as featured writer Gabriella Guerrero does in her finished essay later in this chapter.

View strategies for writing introductions and conclusions in Chapter 20.

Review and Improve Your Draft

Writing an informative essay involves juggling information, identifying main and supporting points, providing evidence for those points, and framing your ideas to accomplish your purposes. Any one of these activities can pose a significant challenge to a writer. Add them together and you've created a complex task that is sure to require additional work beyond a first draft. As you review your draft, pay particular attention to how well you've focused your discussion of the main point, the clarity of your discussion, your use of information from sources, and the effectiveness of your introduction and conclusion.

● FOCUS YOUR DISCUSSION

Maintaining a clear focus is one of the most difficult challenges faced by writers of informative essays. Even when dealing with the most obscure subjects, the amount of information available to writers is still likely to be so large that it can be difficult to decide what to use and what to set aside. As you review your essay, make sure that your draft focuses on a single main point, that your thesis statement clearly conveys that point, and that every supporting point is relevant and well defined.

● ENSURE CLARITY

Readers invest time in an informative document because they want to learn about a subject. If the document is unclear or difficult to follow, they'll look elsewhere. Review your essay to ensure that you've discussed your subject as clearly as possible. To ensure clarity, make certain that you use information from sources accurately and that you refer to concepts and ideas consistently. Make your prose as economical as possible, and choose the right words for your purpose, readers, and subject. In addition, vary the structure of your sentences and paragraphs without making them overly complex. You can read more about strategies for ensuring a clear discussion in Chapters 20 and 24.

● REVIEW YOUR USE OF SOURCES

The effectiveness of your informative essay depends heavily on your selection and use of sources. As you revise, ask yourself these questions: Have you chosen the right sources to support your points? Have you used enough sources to make your points effectively? Have you used the right amount of evidence from your sources? Have you clearly differentiated your own ideas from those of your sources? Have you clearly identified the sources from which you've drawn information? Have you provided appropriate citations in both the text and the works cited list? Have you paraphrased accurately and fairly? Have you quoted properly?

You can learn more about using information from sources in Chapter 21. For a fuller discussion of why you should document sources, see Chapter 17. For guidelines on the MLA and APA documentation systems, see Chapters 25 and 26.

● ASSESS YOUR INTRODUCTION AND CONCLUSION

Your introduction and conclusion serve not only as the beginning and end of your essay but also as a means of framing your discussion. Your introduction calls your readers' attention to specific aspects of your subject — while turning their attention away from others — and your conclusion reinforces their understanding of the points you've made in the essay. If your introduction, conclusion, supporting points, and evidence are inconsistent with one another, your essay will be ineffective. To avoid inconsistencies, review your introduction and conclusion, keeping in mind your main point, supporting points, and use of evidence from sources. You can read more about framing your introduction and conclusion in Chapter 20.

- **RESPOND TO FEEDBACK FROM YOUR INSTRUCTOR**

Instructors will sometimes offer feedback on drafts of a writing assignment, particularly if the assignment is a major project for a course. Typically, this kind of feedback focuses on larger issues, such as support for your points, the ways in which you've addressed your readers, or the way you've organized your document. If your instructor has offered feedback on more than one draft, feedback on later drafts might address concerns at the sentence or word levels.

Once you've revised your essay, ask yourself how you might polish and edit it so that your readers will find it easy to read — and ask a friend, relative, or classmate to proofread your final draft to make sure that it is free of distracting errors. For a discussion of editing and proofreading strategies, see Chapter 24.

In Process

Responding to Instructor Feedback

Gabriella received comments from her instructor on the first draft of her essay. After expressing his interest in the topic she was addressing, he suggested that she might be providing far more information than necessary in her introduction — so much, in fact, that it would work against her efforts to frame her essay effectively.

In response, Gabriella shifted some of the information she had included in the first draft of her introduction to later points in the essay. The result was an introduction that readers found easier to follow and that framed their understanding of the topic more effectively.

Peer Review: Improve Your Informative Essay

One of the biggest challenges writers face is reviewing a draft of their own work as a reader rather than as the writer. Because you know what you're trying to say, you find it easy to understand your draft. To determine how you should revise your draft, ask a friend or classmate to read your essay and to consider how well you've adopted the role of reporter.

Purpose	1. Did you find the essay informative? Did you learn anything new?
	2. What questions does the essay answer? Do I need to address any other questions?
Readers	3. Did you find the essay interesting? Why or why not?
	4. Does the information I've included in my essay address my readers' needs, interests, knowledge, and backgrounds?
	5. Does the essay seem fair? Did you detect any bias or agenda in the way I presented information?
Sources	6. Does the information make sense? Can I add, clarify, or rearrange anything to help you understand the subject better? Do you think any of the details are unnecessary?
	7. Do my sources strike you as reliable and appropriate? Does any of the information seem questionable?
Context	8. Is my subject sufficiently narrow and focused? Is my thesis statement clear?
	9. Would any of the information be better presented in visual form?
	10. Is the physical appearance of my essay appropriate? Did you find the font easy to read? Did you have enough room to write down comments?

For each of the points listed above, ask your reviewers to provide concrete advice about what you should do to improve your draft. It can help if you ask them to adopt the role of an editor — someone who is working with you to improve your draft. You can read more about peer review in Chapter 5.

★ Student Essay

Gabriella Guerrero, "Fast Fashion? Not So Fast!"

The following informative essay was written by featured writer Gabriella Guerrero.

Fast Fashion? Not So Fast!   1

Gabriella Guerrero
Colorado State University
Composition 150
Professor Mike Palmquist
May 5, 2022

Fast Fashion? Not So Fast!

People like to look good. They like to be in style. And they like to do so without spending most of a paycheck. Enter fast fashion — an up-and-coming way of producing great looking clothes that are fashionable and affordable. For consumers, fast fashion makes it possible to keep up with the latest fashion trends without draining your bank account. For the companies that produce such apparel, fast fashion makes it possible to meet the needs of consumers while making a tidy profit.

What could go wrong? Plenty. Fast fashion, as an industry, has negative consequences for both the people who produce it and for the environment. Those consequences include exploitive and unhealthy labor practices, environmental damage associated with the manufacturing processes used to produce the fabrics used in fast fashion, and environmental impacts associated with clothing that is designed from the start to be discarded quickly.

Fast Fashion: A Quick Take

Fast fashion has become a global phenomenon, wrote environmental activities and Green Seeds Project founder Chloé Mikolajczak in 2019, with as many as 100 billion new garments created each year. "From crop tops to mum jeans and bombers, fashion trends are making their way into wardrobes around the world faster than ever, thanks to social media, its thousands of influencers, and the enormous business opportunity it represents for brands," she wrote in a post on the UN Development Programme blog. "Being trendy has never been easier!," she continued. "Low-cost online retailers allow fashionistas to renew their wardrobes quickly, and for about the cost of a Starbucks latte."

With global revenues of more than $250 billion in the past year (Market-Watch, 2021), fast fashion represents a sizable consumer market. Purchasing patterns are strongly driven by social media campaigns launched by fast fashion brands as well as social media influencers on platforms such as YouTube,

Fast Fashion? Not So Fast!   2

TikTok, Pinterest, and Instagram. "Fast fashion has been a mainstay of popular culture for decades," wrote Clara Fischer (2021). "From the fabulously wealthy to the wannabe millionaire with expensive taste, people rely on trendy clothing that's accessible to all." Yet, Fischer noted, being in style has come at a cost, with the increasingly rapid shifts in fashion turning fast fashion into "a chic, flashy beast, fashioned from inhumane conditions and gargantuan contributions to greenhouse gas emissions."

The Human and Environmental Costs of Fast Fashion

This "chic, flashy beast" is made possible by an industry that relies on cheap materials such as plastic, palm oil, and toxic textile dye to produce mass quantities of stylish, inexpensive, shoddily made clothing. As lovely as these clothes are, they seem to benefit only the people who wear them. When they are manufactured, they contribute to global warming through the electric power they consume (Center for Climate and Energy Solution, n.d.), and they contribute to pollution of land, water, and air by releasing toxic chemicals and microplastics into the environment (Tobin, 2020). In turn, when fast fashion products are thrown away in favor of newer, trendier apparel, they make a sizable contribution to landfills. According to Rachel Bick et al. (2018), "Approximately 85% of the clothing Americans consume, nearly 3.8 billion pounds annually, is sent to landfills as solid waste, amounting to nearly 80 pounds per American per year" (p. 1).

In addition to environmental costs, the industrial processes used in the fast fashion industry have strong negative effects on workers. These workers, mostly from developing countries, suffer from local pollution produced by the factories in which fast fashion apparel is manufactured. They are also routinely paid low wages and often work in unsafe conditions. In a report on textile workers in India, published in 2019 by the Blum Center for Developing Economies, Siddharth Kara (2021) pointed out that the industry employs 12.9 million workers in factories and millions more in work-from-home settings. Among home workers, the report noted, it is not uncommon to see wages at or below starvation standards: "Indeed, [we] found that home-based garment workers in India consist almost entirely of women and girls from historically oppressed ethnic communities who scarcely manage to earn $0.15 per hour" (p. 5).

Per APA style, the year of publication is put in parentheses after the author.

In APA style, in-text references to sources with three or more authors use the first author's last name followed by "et al." You can also use "and colleagues" or a similar phrase.

When the authors and year are named in a signal phrase, the parenthetical citation provides only the page number.

Brackets are used to modify a quotation.

Fast Fashion? Not So Fast! 3

 The garments produced for the fast fashion industry are overwhelmingly destined for Western, industrialized nations. Kara (2019) reported that 47% of the garments produced in India were exported to the United States and the European Union alone.

 Fast fashion is booming and the people who buy this apparel benefit from affordable, stylish clothing while both the workers who produce it and the environment suffer the consequences.

> The writer explains the challenges posed by fast fashion for workers and the environment.

Responses to the Challenges Posed by Fast Fashion

 As awareness of the challenges posed by fast fashion has increased, numerous groups — from local initiatives to nongovernmental organizations to national governments and the United Nations — have explored options for addressing the problems associated with the increasing (and unnecessary) production of inexpensive, disposable clothing. The most promising options include shifting to sustainable clothing production, with the goal of eliminating many of the labor inequities and environmental impacts of the fast fashion industry.

 Shifting to sustainable clothing production would involve reducing the carbon footprint of the manufacturing processes associated with fast fashion apparel, eliminating the release of toxic chemicals used in manufacturing, and embracing equitable labor practices. All of this would face resistance from an industry that relies on producing goods at the lowest possible costs. The most direct solution involves creating (and enforcing existing) regulations that impose cost penalties on companies that do not follow them. In the United States, the Environmental Protection Agency (EPA) has the power to monitor corporations' greenhouse gas emissions and pollution. The Clean Air Act of 2007, for example, regulates emissions for all industries. By imposing penalties for violators of these laws, agencies such as the EPA can financially punish manufacturers who fail to follow regulations.

 The drawback to relying on laws and regulations is that they work only within national borders. As long as a country allows a factory to dispose of toxic chemicals and other materials unsafely, laws and regulations will be ineffective. One solution might involve ensuring that no goods can be imported unless they are certified as using a sustainable manufacturing process. This could help eliminate ongoing reliance on carbon-based power production and the use of environmentally unsafe manufacturing processes.

Fast Fashion? Not So Fast! 4

> APA does not call for a running head in student essays, but Gabriella's instructor required one.

Sustainable manufacturing processes also involve ensuring that workers are paid a fair wage and are provided with safe working conditions. Once again, government regulation is the most widespread response to these issues. But as with environmental concerns, ensuring equitable practices is limited by national borders, and even those countries that develop such regulations might enforce them unevenly or not at all.

Slowing Things Down: Going Beyond Regulations

The most effective strategy for reducing the impacts of fast fashion on both people and the environment could be a concerted effort by consumers to stop purchasing goods produced in harmful and unsustainable ways. A movement based on the concepts of environmental justice and equitable labor practices has the potential to reshape the fast fashion industry.

> The writer explains another impact of fast fashion.

The EPA defines environmental justice as the "fair treatment and meaningful involvement of all people regardless of race, color, national origin, or income, with respect to the development, implementation, and enforcement of environmental laws, regulations and policies." Environmental justice, then, involves ensuring that anyone interacting with the environment use practices that reduce harm to people, regardless of where those people live or the kind of work they do. The fast fashion industry is frequently found exploiting the people of less wealthy nations by requiring them to perform dangerous jobs that involve toxic substances. Understanding that there is social injustice happening behind the scenes of these mass manufacturers can help consumers understand the impact of their purchases. As Bick and her colleagues have argued, "Extending the environmental justice framework to encompass the disproportionate impact experienced by those who produce and dispose of our clothing is essential to understanding the magnitude of global injustice perpetuated through the consumption of cheap clothing" (p. 2). If more people understood the impact of the manufacturing and labor practices involved with fast fashion, significant reductions in purchases of this clothing could result, leading to changes in how our clothing is produced.

> A partial quotation is integrated into the text.

Consumers are quite familiar with these kinds of movements. In the 1900s, the American Socialist Movement sparked significant changes in labor laws. In the 1960s and 70s, the antiwar movement contributed to the U.S. withdrawal from Vietnam. In the early 2000s and 2010s, efforts to address discrimination against LGBTQ people led to significant changes in

Fast Fashion? Not So Fast! 5

both our understanding of the issue and the laws governing marriage and adoption. These movements prove that "We the People" are more powerful than we know, contributing to change at the government level as well as in society as a whole. As Cory Coglianese (2001) pointed out, "Social movement organizations seek to secure law reform; in turn changes in the law bring about changes in the society" (p. 85). There is something very powerful about a massive group of people all agreeing on an idea and on a way that things should be. Understanding that the negative effects of the processes associated with fast fashion extend beyond environmental issues and into the realms of social injustice and labor inequity can help people stand behind this movement and call for change. Fast fashion uses manufacturing processes that are outdated and unsustainable, creating an incredibly unclear future for generations to come.

    One of the most effective ways to make a change is to start with ourselves. We can support local businesses, recycle old clothes to secondhand apparel stores, ask whether we actually need the items we are thinking about buying, and consider the environmental cost for that product. Groups and organizations, such as Change.org's fast fashion site www.change.org/t/fast-fashion-en-us, are working to fight against the negative impacts of fast fashion. In addition to calling for changes in our laws and regulations, we can also make changes in our everyday lives. We can shop secondhand clothing sellers, upcycle old bags and clothing items to give them a new purpose, buy less, buy high-quality items that we can use for years to come, and take care of the items we already own to reduce the need to buy more. These kinds of simple changes can make a significant impact, especially if they are adopted widely.

    By following a more refined, well thought out routine daily, each of us can fight against the fast fashion industry and all of its negative consequences. The ability to breathe clean air and live in a safe environment is a fundamental human right. By choosing to make changes in our everyday life — whether small or big — we can end the damage inflicted by fast fashion.

    We still have time to remedy the mistakes that we have made in our treatment of the environment. But that time is running short. If we do not make changes, we will fill up our land, water, and air with toxic dyes, chemicals, carbon dioxide, and nondegradable items.

> In her conclusion, the writer reinforces the risks she has identified earlier in her essay.

Fast Fashion? Not So Fast! 6

> In APA style, the references are listed on a separate page, with a centered heading.

References

Bick, R., Halsey, E., & Ekenga, C. C. (2018). The global environmental injustice of fast fashion. *Environmental Health, 17*(92). https://doi.org/10.1186/s12940-018-0433-7

> Digital object identifiers (DOIs, a unique code assigned to specific content) allow readers to view the source on the web.

Center for Climate and Energy Solutions. (n.d.). Regulating power sector carbon emissions. Retrieved April 14, 2022, from https://www.c2es.org/content/regulating-power-sector-carbon-emissions/

Coglianese, C. (2001). Social movements, law, and society: The institutionalization of the environmental movement. *University of Pennsylvania Law Review, 150*(1), 85–118. https://www.jstor.org/stable/3312913

> Sources are alphabetized by the author's last name and are formatted with hanging indents.

Fischer, C. (2021, May 18). Fast fashion's increasingly rapid trend cycles are driving major overconsumption. *The California Aggie,* https://theaggie.org/2021/05/18/fast-fashions-increasingly-rapid-trend-cycles-are-driving-major-overconsumption/

> An article from a scholarly journal.

Kara, S. (2019). *Tainted garments: The exploitation of women and girls in India's home-based garment sector*. Blum Center for Developing Economies. https://humanrights.wbcsd.org/project/tainted-garments-the-exploitation-of-women-and-girls-in-indias-home-based-garment-sector/

> A web source.

MarketWarch. (2021, September 28). Global fast fashion apparel market 2021 industry update and significant growth prospects by 2027. https://www.marketwatch.com/press-release/global-fast-fashion-apparel-market-2021-industry-update-and-significant-growth-prospects-by-2027-2021-09-28

Mikolajczak, C. (2019, September 17). Six things you didn't know about the true cost of fast fashion [Blog post]. *United Nations Development Programme Blog.* https://www.undp.org/blog/six-things-you-didnt-know-about-true-cost-fast-fashion

Tobin, C. (2020, July 30). How plastic pollution is being woven into fast fashion culture [Blog post]. *Wilson Center.* https://www.newsecuritybeat.org/2020/07/plastic-pollution-woven-fast-fashion-culture-2/

Project Ideas

The following suggestions offer ideas for writing an informative essay or another type of informative document.

Suggestions for Essays

1. DESCRIBE A SITUATION TO YOUR CLASSMATES

Inform your classmates about a situation that is likely to affect them. For example, you might report on changes to your school's course registration system, or you might let them know about a proposed increase in student fees. Identify the main point you want to share with your readers. You might, for instance, focus on the likely effects of the situation, the individuals or groups who are supporting it, or the events that led to the situation. Then identify supporting points that you'll share with your readers. If you are looking at a fee increase, you could talk about how the money generated by the fee might be used and how (and how many) students might benefit from the service provided through the fee. You might also look at the impact of not providing the service. In your essay, describe the situation clearly, drawing on personal observation, an interview with someone who is familiar with the situation, or written sources (see Chapters 14 and 15).

2. EXPLAIN HOW SOMETHING WORKS

Explain how something works to an audience of your choice, such as your classmates, other college students, your instructor, your parents, or members of the community. For example, you might explain how a new technology improves the performance of wireless headphones or ear buds or how a new diet supplement affects the health of those who use it. In your essay, identify the key features or processes that allow the subject of your essay to accomplish its purpose, and provide evidence to support your main points. Consider supporting your explanation by using observation, interviews, media sources and web-based video, or written sources (see Chapters 14 and 15).

3. CHRONICLE A SEQUENCE OF EVENTS

Write an informative essay that describes a series of events. You might choose a historical event, such as the first Gulf War or the decision to send manned missions to the moon, or a more recent event, such as the decision to fire the coach of a local professional sports team, a major layoff at a national technology firm, or a recently passed law that has caused some controversy. In your essay, identify the event you will chronicle and lay out the sequence of events that led up to it. Provide information about the event by drawing on sources from experts who have written or spoken about the event, by examining news reports that came before or after the event, and by conducting field research (see Chapter 15) such as interviews, observation, and correspondence (email messages, text messages, social media posts, or letters).

4. WRITE A PROFILE

Select a friend, family member, or public figure and write a profile for a newspaper, magazine, journal, blog, or website. If you are writing about a friend or family member, interview the subject of your profile and, if possible, interview friends or family members who are well acquainted with your subject. Your profile should offer insights into the person's character and contributions.

If you are writing about a public figure, ask for an interview. If you cannot conduct an interview, locate sources that offer information about the person. Your profile should offer insights into your subject's accomplishments, interests, and plans. You should reflect on the person's impact on the community, the region, or society in general. Base the profile on personal experience, information from a published source or an interview with someone who is aware of or acquainted with the person, and your own reasoning.

5. REPORT THE NEWS

Share news of a recent event, discovery, or disaster with an audience of your choice. You might direct your essay to your instructor, your classmates, other college students, your friends, or people from your hometown. Choose a subject that would interest your readers but that they are unlikely to know about. For example, if you are writing to people from your hometown, you might choose to write about something that has occurred at your college or university. If you are writing to your instructor or classmates, you might choose something that recently occurred in your hometown. Provide information about the event by conducting field research (see Chapter 15) such as interviews, observation, and correspondence (email messages, text messages, social media posts, or letters). You should also review and use accounts from news services that had reporters in place at an event or a disaster or that provided information about a new discovery through experts or knowledgeable reporters.

Suggestions for Other Genres

6. CREATE AN INFORMATIVE BROCHURE

Begin working on your brochure by considering your purpose and your readers. Identify the single most important message you want to convey to your readers, and determine how you would like them to react to your message. Then brainstorm the organizing patterns and design strategies you might use to convey that message. Once you've decided on the content, organization, and design of your brochure, create a mockup and ask for feedback from a friend, a classmate, a relative, or an instructor. Keep that feedback in mind as you revise and edit your brochure. Pay attention to the design principles discussed in Chapter 22. In particular, think carefully about how you stage information and how you use illustrations and colors to frame your most important messages and convey a specific mood to readers.

7. DEVELOP AN INFORMATIVE WEBSITE

Begin working on your website by considering your purpose and your readers. Once you've identified the information you want to provide, consider how best to present it. Give some thought to the overall structure of your site — that is, the number of and relations among the pages on your site. Then determine which information you will present on each page, and choose the type of navigation tools you'll provide so that your readers can easily move from page to page.

Once you've worked out the overall structure of the site, spend time developing a consistent look and feel for your pages. Your pages should have a similar design (such as a standard color scheme, consistent placement of navigation tools, consistent fonts for headers and body text, and so on). Finally, decide on the type of illustrations and the nature of communication tools, if any, that you'll use on the site. As you develop your design and create your pages, consider the design principles discussed in Chapter 22. To learn more about designing websites, see Chapter 23.

8. DRAFT AND DESIGN AN INFORMATIVE ARTICLE FOR A PRINT PUBLICATION

As you prepare to write your article, decide whether you want to focus on a particular subject or publish in a particular magazine, journal, or newspaper. If you want to write about a particular subject, search your library's databases and the web for relevant articles (see Chapter 14). This search can also help you identify publications that might be interested in your article. If you want to publish your article in a particular publication, read it carefully to determine the kinds of subjects it normally addresses. Once you've selected a target publication, analyze it to determine its design and writing conventions (such as level of formality and the manner in which sources are acknowledged).

Provide information about the subject of your article by conducting field research (see Chapter 15) such as interviews, observation, surveys, and correspondence (email messages, text messages, social media posts, or letters) and by drawing on written sources published in print and on the web and media sources such as videos on news sites or YouTube. You can learn more about searching for digital and print sources in Chapter 14.

As you learn about your subject and plan, organize, and design your article, keep in mind what you've learned about the writing and design conventions of the articles you've read. Your article should reflect those conventions. You can learn more about design principles in Chapter 22. You can learn about the distinctive design features of articles in Chapter 23.

In Summary: Writing an Informative Essay

★ **Find a conversation and listen in (p. 205).**
- Reflect on your interests (p. 205).
- Ask questions about promising subjects (p. 208).

★ **Gather information (p. 208).**
- Create a search plan (p. 208).
- Collect sources (p. 210).
- Assess and evaluate your sources (p. 210).
- Take notes (p. 210).
- Consider field research (p. 211).

★ **Prepare a draft (p. 211).**
- Present your main point (p. 214).
- Develop supporting points and evidence (p. 214).

- Consider genre and design (p. 217).
- Frame your information (p. 218).

★ **Review and improve your draft (p. 219).**
- Focus your discussion (p. 220).
- Ensure clarity (p. 220).
- Review your use of sources (p. 220).
- Assess your introduction and conclusion (p. 220).
- Respond to feedback from your instructor (p. 221).

09 Writing to Analyze

What is writing to analyze? 233

What kinds of documents are used to present an analysis? 235

Articles 235
- Carly Lewis, *The Writing on the Virtual Bathroom Wall* 235

Issue analyses 240
- Peter C. Baker, *Reform of the Nerds, Starring Arthur Chu* 240

Rhetorical analyses 248
- Brooke Gladstone, *The Goldilocks Number* 248

Videos 252
- Blank on Blank, *Temple Grandin on Her Search Engine* 252

Genre Talk: Analytical Writing 255

How can I write an analytical essay? 256
- Find a conversation and listen in 256
- Conduct your analysis 261
- Prepare a draft 274
- Review and improve your draft 279

✱ **Student Essay** 282
- Kelsey Smith, *Art Theft on the Rise with Social Media* 282

✱ **Project Ideas** 292

What Is Writing to Analyze?

Analytical writing begins with a question: To what extent does government surveillance of suspected terrorists affect the civil liberties of ordinary citizens? How will new environmental regulations affect plans to drill for oil near a state park? Why do animated films from Pixar Studios appeal to so many adults? The types of documents — or genres (see *What Should I Know about Genre and Design?* in Chapter 1) — writers create to share their answers are as varied as the questions they ask. And each document, in turn, reflects aspects of the writing situations in which writers find themselves: their purposes for analyzing a subject, the interests and expectations of their intended readers, the sources used to support the analysis, and the context in which the document will be read.

Analysis involves adopting the role of *interpreter* (see Chapter 6). Writers who adopt this role help readers understand the origins, qualities, significance, or potential impact of a subject. The choices made by writers who adopt this role — choices about interpretive frameworks, sources, and analytical methods — can lead to quite different conclusions about a subject. As a result, analytical documents not only serve as significant contributions to a conversation but also provide a foundation for further contributions to the conversation.

THE WRITER'S ROLE:
Interpreter

When I analyze a topic, I take on the role of **interpreter**.

PURPOSE
- To find patterns of meaning
- To trace causes and effects
- To determine significance

READERS
- Want to understand the subject
- Expect a careful and appropriate use of analytical techniques
- Expect coherent, focused reasons and evidence for the writer's interpretation

SOURCES
- Especially in the case of textual analysis, the subject itself is often the main source.
- Data, background information, and other writers' interpretations are often obtained from published material.
- Field research (interviews, observation, surveys, correspondence) and personal experience can add details and support.

CONTEXT
- Analytical questions, interpretive frameworks, and genres are shaped by reader expectations and disciplinary standards and expectations.
- Interpreters usually need to frame a subject for readers before analyzing it.

CRITICAL THINKING

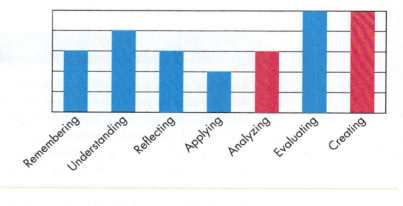
Remembering, Understanding, Reflecting, Applying, Analyzing, Evaluating, Creating

What Kinds of Documents Are Used to Present an Analysis?

Writers share their interpretations of subjects through a strikingly large array of genres. Soldiers and aid workers in the Middle East, Somalia, and Afghanistan, for example, have interpreted the events in which they are involved through books, blogs, and social-networking sites. Commentators analyze the political landscape through columns and editorials. Scholars examine subjects as diverse as Shakespeare's sonnets and the possibility of life on Mars through journal articles and conference presentations. And students are frequently asked to share their interpretations through essays, reports, and presentations.

Regardless of the genre a writer decides to use, most analytical writing begins with an attempt to understand how other writers have approached the challenges of analyzing a particular subject. Examining analytical documents can spark ideas about how to focus an analysis, offer insights into the kinds of interpretive frameworks that have been used to direct past analyses, and provide an understanding of the conclusions other writers have drawn. In the following sections, you'll find examples and discussions of magazine and newspaper articles, rhetorical analyses, and analytical blog posts.

Articles

Carly Lewis
The Writing on the Virtual Bathroom Wall

Magazine and newspaper articles often provide analyses of issues, events, or problems. In "The Writing on the Virtual Bathroom Wall," Carly Lewis explores the increase in "rape list" postings, both online and in the real world. These listings of alleged sexual abusers have been widely controversial. While supporters say that an unreliable legal system leaves no other way for their voices to be heard, critics contend that such postings are defamatory and, as such, illegal. In a careful analysis, Lewis brings a larger issue to light: we do not yet have an effective way to handle sexual assault.

The Writing on the Virtual Bathroom Wall

In the post-Cosby era, women are reviving a controversial tactic: naming names.

Carly Lewis

> Because most articles are written for a specific publication, writers typically have a clear picture of their readers (in terms of age, income, education, hobbies, and so forth) and can target their analysis to the needs and interests of a narrowly defined group. An article about an election, for example, might analyze turnout among younger voters, the campaign of a recently elected senator from the Midwest, or the impact of organizations such as the Teamsters or the National Rifle Association.

> Lewis is a writer whose work has been featured in *Maclean's* (where this article was published) as well as *New York Magazine*, *The Guardian*, *Interview*, *Spin*, the *Globe and Mail*, *Flair*, and the *National Post*, among others.

Last month, a stack of loose papers with the title "s--t list" appeared in the women's washroom of a Toronto concert venue. On the first page was a handful of names, written in black marker, of alleged sexual abusers, most of them well-known figures in Toronto's music and west-end nightlife scenes. One of the people named on the list had been acquitted in two sexual assault cases this year. (In the second trial, the judge noted that the man's testimony and the complainant's were "equally plausible.")

Before social media, the list would have been viewed by a limited contingent of clubgoers. (The venue's capacity is around 1,400.) But the velocity of digital sharing being what it is, a photo of the first page spread via Twitter, Facebook and Instagram. The names of the alleged aggressors were later posted to a dedicated Tumblr page, which featured — for an evening — additional names that had been emailed to the page's creator.

The creator says she was not involved in the bathroom list, but says she started the Tumblr as a way to share its warnings with people who weren't at the concert. She has since removed the site due to fear of legal repercussions. She can't vouch for the accuracy of the list, she acknowledges, but her perspective is simple: she believes the accusers, despite their anonymity, and the absence of other details. "The men on the list are popular, respected members of the community, and I am sick of their actions being excused," she said by email. "The law isn't really on our side. It's important that we look out for each other as best we can."

Post–Jian Ghomeshi — and the highly public allegations against Bill Cosby et al. — it's become impossible to ignore both the reluctance of women to report sexual assault, given the uphill battle they face in the legal system, and the fact that people often know about allegations of abuse for years, even decades before they become public. In the cases of Cosby and Ghomeshi, it took years for accusers' voices to be heard. When they were, it was because they joined forces to amplify one another. These were landmark

> Analyses often focus on a particular facet of an issue, exploring its significance and using it to shed light on a larger problem, trend, or question.

moments: women speaking about sexual assault to media rather than to police, and being heard in the absence of any charges.

Women are also speaking out in "rape lists," such as the one in the Toronto club — and not just between bathroom stalls. There was at least one other Toronto Tumblr that named names and ran accounts of alleged assaults and other aggressive behavior. It, too, was taken down recently. In September 2014, rape lists showed up in women's washrooms at the University of Chicago, and a corresponding Tumblr page that named "people known to commit varying levels of gender-based violence" appeared around the same time. According to *Jezebel*, the Tumblr, which has since been removed, stated that its aim was "keeping the community safe — since the university won't." In 2012, a Kentucky high school student revealed the names of her convicted abusers on Twitter (for which she faced a contempt-of-court charge, later dropped). In 2013, a dating app called Lulu, which allowed users to rate the bad dates they'd gone on, quickly became a space for women to warn other women about creepy or uncomfortable encounters they'd had with men — much the way an Uber driver's low rating functions as a warning to potential customers.

Rape lists, online or off, are a way to help women bypass an unfriendly legal system. They are also "seriously defamatory," says Toronto-based defamation lawyer Peter Downard, senior litigation counsel at Fasken Martineau. It's not unusual for people to take matters into their own hands when official structures fail to protect them. "In the face of that failure, there is going to be great frustration," says Downard, who considers rape lists a form of civil disobedience expressed through vigilantism.

The creator of the Toronto Tumblr page says that, as a survivor of abuse herself, her mission is to warn women. "My intentions are not to incite a witch hunt against the named," she says. "I simply want a safe space for survivors to share information." This strategy echoes a controversial suggestion made by Germaine Greer a few years ago. "I wish there were an online rapists' register, and that it was kept up-to-date, because we know the courts can't get it right," said the well-known feminist academic and author of *The Female Eunuch*.

The legal route comes, undeniably, with serious challenges. Sexual assault survivors who do come forward often face re-traumatization, as well as a legal system perceived to be stacked in favor of the accused. Not surprisingly, Statistics Canada estimated that only around eight percent of sexual assaults in Canada are reported to police.

> Authors of magazine and newspaper articles are less likely than writers in academic or professional settings to use works cited or references lists, although they typically identify their sources in the body of the article.

Hence the prevalence of anonymous rape lists — and all the issues they raise. Women have been plumbing the ethics of underground symposia for decades. In autumn 1990, a list of alleged rapists appeared in a women's washroom at Brown University. At its fullest — the list stayed intact for months — it contained roughly 30 names, some of which had been reported to officials.

A story about the list in the student newspaper alerted the rest of campus. At the time, Brown's executive vice-president of university relations, Robert Reichley, called the list "anti-male" and branded its contributors "Magic Marker terrorists." Custodians were instructed to remove selected graffiti from campus washrooms. "Men who've assaulted me or a woman I know," in the women's washroom was scrubbed away. Meanwhile, misogynistic graffiti remained. Later that year, a new list appeared: "Women who need to be raped." One of the students named on that list was prominent campus feminist Jesselyn Radack.

"If officials had actually listened to what the women graffitists had to say," Radack wrote later in the collection of essays *Just Sex: Students Rewrite the Rules on Sex, Violence, Activism, and Equality*, "they would have realized that the motivation was to protect women in the absence of a judicial board willing to hear complaints of sexual violence."

Today, Radack is better known as a legal adviser to Edward Snowden, as well as a former ethics adviser to the U.S. Department of Justice, and the whistleblower who disclosed what she believed to be a violation of ethics during the FBI's interrogation of enemy combatant John Walker Lindh during America's 2001 invasion of Afghanistan. "Women are going to engage in guerrilla tactics," Radack told *Maclean's*, "but I would much rather have a legal system that adequately [and] confidently handles sexual assault."

Twenty-five years after the Brown controversy, it's hardly better inside the law. "Within a criminal-court context, it is very difficult to get a conviction," says Simona Jellinek, a Toronto-based lawyer whose firm specializes in representing sexual assault survivors. Jellinek argues that false accusations of rape are "absolutely rare." But "if the judge hears both sides and thinks they're both credible, the judge actually has no other option but to acquit, even if the judge believes the survivor."

In May 2014, the names of four alleged assailants appeared in various women's washrooms at Columbia University, a month after 23 students filed a federal complaint in one month against Columbia. "We needed some way to warn people that these people are violent," one of the activists involved told the *Guardian*. (According to the *Guardian*, one student complained that, though her attacker confessed to assaulting her, he was merely suspended for one semester, then returned to school. The paper noted that his father made a financial contribution to Columbia.)

For all the cultural progress we've made, the Sharpie marker — and its online equivalent — remains, somehow, mightier than the law. In fact, the online version of the bathroom wall is even more powerful: It can warn more women faster, but it can also change a person's reputation permanently and without an accuser coming forward.

Of course, it is defamatory to scribble the name of one alleged rapist on a wall; it is defamatory to scribble the names of 30, and it is certainly defamatory to tweet it. That's one reason the Ontario Civil Liberties Association feels defamation should be abolished from Canadian law completely. "Defamation is a tool that the powerful use to silence criticism," says Joseph Hickey, executive director of the non-profit organization. "I would rather see members of society independently assess information they receive, and not feel the need to depend on legal authority to decide whether they approve of someone's reputation or not." That position is considered by many to be extreme. "They would have to remove the Supreme Court of Canada if they wanted to do that," says Downard.

But if preventive measures rely on abuses that have already taken place, and if official institutions are not remedying the problem, women may continue to turn to unofficial watch lists. "It's a matter of ensuring effective measures for bringing [abusers] to justice, so that women don't have to write on bathroom walls," says Radack. "It's such a desperate thing to have to do."

Late last month, the creator of the Toronto Tumblr emailed to say she was no longer in pursuit of a legally sound way to keep the list of names online. "I can't believe how hard it is to speak up about abusers," she says.

"To me, the problem clearly indicates a serious barrier in the way in which we deal with sexual assault," says Downard, of rape lists. "An act like this, if it is emblematic of a dysfunction in our society, it's just the canary in the coal mine."

> The online version of the bathroom wall is even more powerful: It can warn more women faster, but it can also change a person's reputation permanently.

An analysis may speculate on potential outcomes.

Starting a Conversation: Thinking Critically about "The Writing on the Virtual Bathroom Wall"

In your writer's notebook, reflect on Lewis' analysis by responding to the following questions:

1. Consider the tone of "The Writing on the Virtual Bathroom Wall." Does Lewis fairly represent both sides of the issue? Who is not represented, and why?

2. What sources does Lewis use? How does she draw on sources to lend credibility to her argument? Why do you think Lewis chose the sources that she did?

3. Lewis writes, "For all the cultural progress we've made, the Sharpie marker — and its online equivalent — remains, somehow, mightier than the law" (par. 15). How does Lewis support this claim? How does this claim inform Lewis' ultimate analysis?

4. Lewis wrote her essay before the Me Too Movement called attention to the issues of sexual assault and harassment. In what ways, if any, does her argument differ from those made by those involved in the Me Too Movement? Do you think that it is still controversial to name names? In what ways has this debate evolved over the past few years?

5. **Reflection:** In paragraph 2, Lewis remarks on the power of social media: "Before social media, the list would have been viewed by a limited contingent of clubgoers. . . . But the velocity of digital sharing being what it is, a photo of the first page spread via Twitter, Facebook and Instagram." How has digital sharing affected the ways in which we converse about controversial issues like the one Lewis documents in this essay? In this sense, is social media a positive or negative force? Why?

Issue Analyses

Peter C. Baker
Reform of the Nerds, Starring Arthur Chu

Articles and essays that analyze issues often begin with a question, a problematic fact, or a puzzling situation that leads to a question. In this excerpt from a 2015 article published in *Pacific Standard*, Peter C. Baker analyzes the underbelly of "nerd-dom" and Arthur Chu's rising role as a voice of positive change in what's grown to be a contentious, even dangerous culture. Baker chronicles how Chu has become a perhaps surprising advocate for reining in the aggressive, misogynistic culture of the online gaming world. By questioning how nerd culture became so angry, Baker sheds light on the larger issues of gender in gamer culture, self-expression, and the reappropriation of the "nerd."

Reform of the Nerds, Starring Arthur Chu

How a game-show champion became the embattled conscience of American male geekdom.

Peter C. Baker

In January of 2014, I started getting text messages from my college friends asking whether I was following our old classmate Arthur Chu on *Jeopardy!* I wasn't — I hadn't watched the show for years — but I tuned in the next day.

From then on, I watched rapt as Chu racked up what was, at the time, the third-longest winning streak in the show's history, drawing attention not only for the size of his haul (almost $400,000 in the end), but also for his supremely stereotypical nerdiness. He used an unorthodox strategy that drew on both game theory and statistical analysis of the *Jeopardy!* board. He was slightly pudgy, with glasses, and his hair was cut in a harsh horizontal line across his forehead. His shirts were rumpled, his ties poorly knotted. He spoke in a monotone and sometimes interrupted *Jeopardy!* host Alex Trebek, cutting off Trebek's patter so they could move on to the next question.

I had barely known Chu in college, but I loved watching him win. He seemed to simultaneously embody nerd stereotypes and vindicate them — by raking in a fortune. I especially liked his attitude toward his detractors: When people mocked him on Twitter, he re-tweeted their jibes, as if to demonstrate how little they hurt.

After Chu's run ended, I found myself missing it. Several months later, checking his Twitter feed, I saw him announce he would be appearing on a panel at a gaming convention in Maryland called MAGFest, where he would be talking about "the general unpleasantness in the nerd community this year," including "the Gamergate fiasco." This had the ring of familiarity, but I would have been hard pressed to say what any of it meant.

It didn't take much research for me to pick up that 2014 had been a tumultuous year in American nerddom. Long-simmering tensions built into the very concept of "the nerd" had reached a boiling point, with shockingly vicious results: death threats, rape threats, and torrents of online abuse, most of them made by nerds themselves against those perceived to be finding fault with nerd culture.

To my surprise, some of the most interesting and well-circulated analyses of the mayhem had been written by none other than Arthur Chu, who had leveraged his 15 minutes of game-show fame into, of all things, a national platform for his opinions about nerds: What America gets wrong about nerds; what nerds — especially male nerds — get wrong about themselves; and why it matters. In Chu's view, nerd-dom has a toxic, intolerant fringe, one that has gone unchecked in large part because nerds are awful at policing their own subculture, especially online. In an era when the nerds are increasingly ascendant, Chu wants to make nerd culture better — and to stop more of his fellow nerds from getting drawn into the worst of it. . . .

Before *Jeopardy!*, Chu was working as an insurance compliance analyst in Broadview Heights, a small city outside of Cleveland, where he also acted and did improv on the side. Waiting for his *Jeopardy!* episodes, which were pre-taped, to air, he hoped that the publicity might help him get gigs as a voice actor, a side career he's been trying to build for years. (It sounded quixotic to me, until Chu told me he'd had several voice-over gigs already, including a video for Safeway.)

When the *Jeopardy!* episodes were broadcast, they triggered a tsunami of media attention. Chu had never anticipated that people would care so much about his clothes, weight, or way of speaking. It was his introduction to a peculiarly modern form of exposure, one in which you can watch in real time as thousands of people entertain themselves by talking about you as if you weren't there. Some deemed Chu smug; others opted for digs about his weight. ("Looks like he just ate a pizza in bed," tweeted one nonfan.) Many deemed his aggressively money-focused strategy unsportsmanlike. The media started calling him "the *Jeopardy!* villain."

But the notoriety also had more agreeable results. Chu gained fans, many of them Asian Americans happy to see a nerdy Chinese American kicking unapologetic ass on the national stage. TV shows wanted to interview Chu, and reporters wanted to profile him. Chu said yes to almost everything, intrigued by the possibility of finding his way into a new career — something, he told me, "that sort of goes with the rhythm of my interests, instead of getting orders from corporations." He thought it was absurd that a person could get famous from a game show, but — as he puts it in the trailer for *Who Is Arthur Chu?*, an upcoming documentary — "I'd rather be famous for that than for nothing."

Chu also began to find his voice as a writer, as Web publications took an interest in his byline. In May, Chu was asked to review *The Big Bang Theory*, the popular sitcom about nerds, for the *Daily Beast*. It was his fourth assignment for the site (on which his author bio describes him as a "Chinese-American nerd" who is "shamelessly extending his presence in the national spotlight by all available means"). But Chu never wrote the review. On the Friday before it was due, a 22-year-old named Elliot Rodger went on a violent rampage in Isla Vista, California, killing six people and injuring 14 others before committing suicide. On the day of his killings, Rodger had emailed a 141-page manifesto to family and acquaintances that described the violence he was about to commit as revenge on the female gender for ruining his life and on sexually active men for besting him.

When Chu read Rodger's manifesto, he found much of it to be terribly familiar. Except for the parts about murder, it read like a standard-issue litany of complaints by a lonely male nerd blaming women for his loneliness. "It's all girls' fault for not having any sexual attraction towards me," Rodger wrote. Instead of writing a review of *The Big Bang Theory*, Chu stayed up past dawn writing a different piece — an angry one — in which he insisted that, though Rodger was mentally ill, his attitudes toward women were common, especially among aggrieved male nerds. Chu confessed to having spent much of his own life as a lonely nerd and to having contributed to a culture that excused bad behavior. He said he had known nerdy male stalkers, even nerdy male rapists, but to his disgust had never confronted them.

"So, a question, to my fellow male nerds," he wrote. "What the fuck is wrong with us?"

The term "nerd" has come a long way since the 1980s, when it simply denoted an awkward social loser, usually a bespectacled, physically graceless male too book-smart for his own good. Today, it encompasses ever more subtypes: the loser; the intense (or even just mildly intense) fan of this or that pop-culture phenomenon; and the wealthy Silicon Valley coder or CEO wielding power over the American zeitgeist. The idea that "we are all nerds now" is increasingly common: See *The Guardian* in 2003, *New York* magazine in 2005, *Esquire* in 2013, and *The New York Times* last year.

Chu recognizes that many nerds are thriving in the post-industrial economy and that many once-nerdy interests are now mainstream. But he is careful to stress that the more painful variety of nerd-dom, the kind you don't adopt by choice, still exists. He knows there is still such a thing as not fitting in, or being unable to get a date. And he knows how much it sucks, because he's been there himself.

Chu's parents are fundamentalist Christians who immigrated to America from Taiwan. They lived in Rhode Island until Chu was 12, then moved to Boise, and by the time Chu was in high school they had settled in Cerritos, California,

> Writers of issue analyses need to know about and understand the history and significance of their subjects. Depending on the specific publication and writing situation, they might rely on statistical evidence, personal experience, or direct observation.

near Los Angeles. "Growing up evangelical was a real double bind," he says. He didn't accept religion easily, arguing the fine points of C. S. Lewis with his Sunday school teachers, which made him an outsider in the evangelical community. Meanwhile, being an evangelical Christian — not to mention an Asian-American child with an advanced vocabulary and precise diction — marked him as an outsider everywhere else.

"I was the kid who probably spent fully 10 times as many hours reading books at school [as] exchanging words with any of my classmates," he wrote last year in *Salon*. "It was years before I learned to talk something like a normal human being and not an overly precise computerized parody of a 'nerd voice.' People felt uncomfortable around me, disliked me instinctively."

Chu joined a clique of what he calls "bitter angry guys" who desperately wanted female attention and felt antipathy toward women for not giving it to them. Even when Chu managed to get a high school girlfriend, he resented her for being, as he saw it, above him, as an automatic result of being female. He says he and his friends had "tunnel vision" and couldn't understand that "it could suck to be sexually wanted as much as to be sexually invisible."

After high school, he moved east to attend Swarthmore, a Pennsylvania liberal arts college with fewer than 1,600 students. He promptly joined a storied campus club, devoted to science fiction, fantasy, and the general embrace of nerddom, called SWIL — the Swarthmore Warders of Imaginative Literature. Chu felt he'd arrived in utopia: an in-the-flesh version of the online message boards he'd frequented through high school.

But SWIL did not feel so welcoming to all of its members. Chu says several male SWILlies were guilty of behavior that ranged from off-putting (sexist jokes) to predatory (dating a local high school student). A larger group of SWILlies turned a blind eye to it. In Chu's view, this was because of nerd indulgence, born of a reluctance among people who have been ostracized to set standards that might exclude others. What one group of SWILlies viewed as misogyny and harassment got written off by the other group of SWILlies as awkwardness, or autism, or misunderstanding. (Both factions were made up of males and females.)

By his own reckoning, Chu spent most of college as part of the second group. But over time, thanks in part to friendships with some of the female SWILlies who felt uncomfortable, he came to think the club had a problem. Among the issues were club events that attracted creepy alumni — guys who had a habit of, as Chu puts it, "serially sleeping" with freshmen — and, in 2007, a group of reformers within SWIL voted not only to change the club's

> An analysis might draw on narrative or reflective writing as a way of providing supporting evidence.

name (to Psi Phi — get it?) but also to ban alumni from its meetings and parties, an act of nerd exclusion that caused serious rifts among club members. Chu strongly supported the ban, eagerly debating its merits. (Jillian Waldman, who was co-president of SWIL in 2004 and 2005, disputes Chu's characterizations of "old-school SWIL," which she says was the more tolerant club.)

The SWIL civil war coincided with a general unraveling in the rest of Chu's life. Freed from his strict home, Chu was suddenly free to stay up all night playing video games, fine-tuning the SWIL newsletter, writing his campus newspaper column ("Chu on This"), editing Wikipedia articles, and indulging his insatiable appetite for debate on any subject under the sun. He was also spending more and more time in campus theater productions.

Chu's GPA dropped, and he got kicked out of a seminar, setting in motion a chain reaction that made him unable to graduate on time. He spent an extra year living in Philadelphia and taking classes, and another finishing his course work from his parents' house in California. He used the public library there to research his thesis and to try to launch his voice-over career, or, when that didn't work, to just find a job, any job, in the crashing economy. He sank into depression, played too many video games, and wondered how much longer he could go on.

Chu's choice last May to surprise his *Daily Beast* editor with an article about nerds and the Isla Vista killings ended up paying off. Headlined "Your Princess Is in Another Castle," a reference to *Super Mario Bros.*, the article went viral. Chu started getting calls from the media once more. This time, CNN and NPR didn't want to talk about his "Daily Double" *Jeopardy!* strategy. They wanted to hear about "nerd lust."

Chu found himself with a new sense of purpose. Other people had made similar observations about nerd culture before, but thanks to *Jeopardy!*, Chu had a shot at taking the issues to a bigger audience. In the months that followed, he wrote more about the dark currents within nerd-dom. One article discussed nerd power-lust. ("The creepy nerd fantasy that remains alive and well in today's Age of the Nerd Triumphant is not of making peace with the popular kids but taking their throne.") Another called out blockbusters like *Game of Thrones* and *Avatar* for nerd ethnic chauvinism. ("We repeatedly tell stories about a white protagonist who goes on a journey of self-discovery by mingling with exotic brown foreigners and becoming better at said foreigners' culture than they themselves are.")

Then came the controversy dubbed Gamergate, which was to raise Chu's profile even further. To explain Gamergate simply — or at all — is no easy task, but it began last August, when a 24-year-old man named Eron Gjoni posted a rambling, 9,000-plus-word blog post about the game developer Zoe Quinn, an ex-girlfriend whom he accused of cheating on him with a video-game journalist in order to advance her career. Quinn had often criticized the way women are portrayed and treated by mainstream gaming culture, so a contingent of hardcore gamers viewed Gjoni's allegations against her as emblematic of a corrupt journalistic culture that was out to undermine traditional games that were fun but non-PC: too violent, the bad guys too dark-skinned, the women too scantily clad. The angriest of them bombarded Quinn with online harassment, including death and rape threats. Some of Quinn's detractors broke into her accounts for online services like Tumblr, posted nude photos of her, and published her home address, leading her to move out of her residence. Online campaigns also sprang up targeting other female game developers and gaming writers.

> In many cases, writers of issue analyses must explain unfamiliar background material to their readers or interpret complex data for them.

Chu was horrified by the online Gamergate mobs, but also energized. He sparred with Gamergate supporters — meaning those who sided with gamers against people like Quinn — on Twitter, and he wrote articles categorizing Gamergate supporters as part of a "reactionary" movement doomed to eventual failure. If his hope was to become a nerd pundit, here was the ideal cultural moment.

Chu often stressed that he understood firsthand the pain of persistent social and romantic rejection. He assured readers that he, too, loved video games and well knew how powerful a refuge they could provide. But he also insisted that not all injustices merit equal pity. Yes, he wrote, he sympathized with some of the aggrieved feelings out there, but he could not endorse the self-pitying militancy they generated, calling it a "toxic swell of nerd entitlement that's busy destroying everything I love." . . .

In Chu's view, nerds created much of what we love about Internet culture but also much of what we hate about it. Intended as a refuge from real-world hierarchies and prejudices, the Internet has often wound up simply reproducing, even exaggerating, the power dynamics of the "real world," complete with bullying. Chu feels that if nerds were more willing to set some community standards, like the SWILlies did at Swarthmore, and behave with less indifference to the worst of their peers, they could make the world a lot more pleasant and protect the best of nerdiness — the joyful obsessions, the embrace of outsiders, the indifference to convention.

One challenge for Chu's conversion efforts is that he has trouble accounting for his own recovery from nerdy bitterness. When I asked him about this during one of our conversations, he shook his head, looking genuinely mystified. "I don't know," he said. "That's, you know, 'there but for the grace of God.'" But he was quick to point to one development his younger, angrier self could barely have imagined: wedlock.

Chu met his wife-to-be, Eliza Blair, at Swarthmore during his sophomore year; she was one of the SWILlies (a co-president, eventually) who led the reform charge. They didn't hit it off. "He was a huge blowhard jerk and I hated him on sight," she wrote me in an email. "It was all insecurity, immaturity."

Over time, though, Blair became Chu's biggest fan. In 2006, she made drawings of all her SWIL friends, representing their futures. Chu was depicted standing on a podium, speaking to an enthralled audience of thousands. "I knew that under the shitty nerd veneer was a guy with a lot of depth and a lot to say about the way the world works," Blair wrote. "I loved that guy and wanted to give him every chance to succeed.". . .

Chu has seen enough of the world to know he can't convince Gamergate obsessives that their outrage is absurd. Indeed, despite his love of debate, he has only limited faith in argument *per se*, which is one reason he has softened since college on his view of activists, whom he used to disdain because they weren't as committed as he was to exhaustive skeptical argument. If lonely nerds are to be wooed away from defeatism and rage, he believes, they must be reached with camaraderie as much as reason. "You can have someone who wants to be a good role model for you," Chu says, "but if they don't speak the same language, you're just not going to take influence from them."

At the reconvened MAGFest panel, it was clear that people were speaking the same language, reveling in both the debate and the shared obsessions. Chu stayed on stage for two hours more, then announced that he wanted a drink and invited anyone who wanted to keep talking upstairs to a hotel suite. A dozen nerds skipped the video-game hall, the board- and card-game rooms, and the live-action roleplay zone and instead squeezed into an elevator together and headed up to keep debating, college-style, nerd culture's glory and excesses, its past and future. It felt optimistic, passionate, welcoming, and, sure, a little awkward: Chu's ideals made manifest. There was music playing from tiny laptop speakers, and someone had set up a disco ball. The crowd stayed for hours, nerding into the night.

Starting a Conversation: Thinking Critically about "Reform of the Nerds, Starring Arthur Chu"

In your writer's notebook, reflect on Baker's analysis by responding to the following questions:

1. How does Baker establish a brief history of the term "nerd"? At what point in the article does Baker introduce this term? Why might defining terms be an important aspect of analytical writing?

2. *Pacific Standard* is a print and online magazine "for affluent and influential readers interested in working toward forward-looking changes." How is the intended audience for this publication reflected in "Reform of the Nerds"? Consider Baker's tone — how do you think it would change for a different publication?

3. How does Baker connect Chu's personal experiences with the evolution of the larger nerd culture? Why is this connection important? What purpose does it serve in Baker's analysis?

4. **Reflection:** As he nears his conclusion, Baker writes, "Intended as a refuge from real-world hierarchies and prejudices, the Internet has often wound up simply reproducing, even exaggerating, the power dynamics of the 'real world,' complete with bullying." In what ways have you observed or experienced this aspect of online life? Baker describes several of Chu's strategies for confronting this problem in the online gaming world — how could these strategies be applied to other instances of the "exaggerated power dynamics" online?

Rhetorical Analyses

Brooke Gladstone
The Goldilocks Number

Rhetorical analyses take numerous forms, from articles and essays to blogs, web pages, and — as in the case of Brooke Gladstone's graphic analysis — comics. Typically, rhetorical analyses address factors such as the writer's purpose and background, the nature of the audience involved in a particular communication situation, the context in which a particular communication act took place, or the source of the information used in a particular exchange.

"The Goldilocks Number" first appeared in Brooke Gladstone's book *The Influencing Machine: Brooke Gladstone on the Media*, illustrated by Josh Neufeld. It was adapted from a radio segment Gladstone produced for NPR in 2010.

Writers of rhetorical analyses often draw on sources of information that reflect the knowledge and interests of their intended readers. A rhetorical analysis written for a scholarly journal in political science, for example, might rely more heavily on scholarly articles and books than would an analysis directed to a general audience, which might rely more heavily on observation, interviews, and references to news articles or broadcasts.

Gladstone, a journalist and media analyst, calls *The Influencing Machine* a "media manifesto" in which she challenges readers' common assumptions about media. Note how the illustrations enhance Gladstone's analysis and help distinguish her own ideas from those of her sources.

Starting a Conversation: Thinking Critically about "The Goldilocks Number"

In your writer's notebook, reflect on Gladstone's analysis by responding to the following questions:

1. "The Goldilocks Number" begins by inquiring into the story behind a seemingly improbable statistic. What leads Gladstone to question the numbers she keeps hearing? Why do you think she chooses the sources she does to find answers?

2. Gladstone traces her evidence back through several layers in order to find out the truth behind the statistic, and in the last panel of the first page, Neufeld depicts Gladstone in a detective's outfit with a magnifying glass. In what ways does Gladstone's research resemble that of a detective? What questions does she return to as she tracks down each new source? How do those questions — and the answers she finds — shape her analysis?

3. Rhetorical analysis is a specific type of analysis (see *Rhetorical Analysis* later in this chapter). In what ways is Gladstone's analysis of the Goldilocks number a rhetorical analysis? How does she take into consideration the context and audience around her questions?

4. Many of the experts Gladstone cites in her analysis were also cited in a 2006 *National Law Journal* article by Jason McClure that addresses the very same misuse of the number 50,000. How might Gladstone have better acknowledged this article in her work?

5. **Reflection:** Gladstone concludes with the comment, "Sometimes the simplest reasons are the scariest." What do you think she means? In what ways, and to whom, are the "simplest reasons" the most frightening in this situation?

Videos

Blank on Blank
Temple Grandin on Her Search Engine

Web-based videos, such as those found on YouTube and TikTok, can consist of the contributions of a single creator, or they can draw on contributions from a group, a corporation, or an organization. They are frequently used to present information, evaluations, analyses, and arguments. Videos are typically brief, although some will be as long as a Hollywood movie (or longer). The following video from Blank on Blank, which is produced by the nonprofit organization Quoted Studios, presents an interview with Temple Grandin, a professor at Colorado State University who is well-known for her work on both autism and animal behavior. The video provides insights into the cognitive processes Grandin uses to make sense of the world.

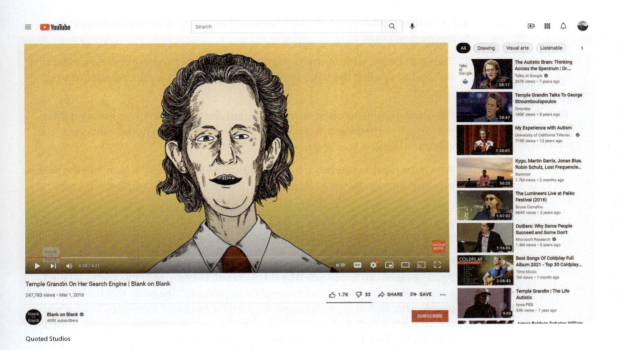

Quoted Studios

Quoted Studios

▲ Scan this code to watch the video in its entirety

Starting a Conversation: Thinking Critically about "Temple Grandin on Her Search Engine"

In your writer's notebook, reflect on Blank on Blank's video by responding to the following questions:

1. The video begins with Grandin's response to questions from an interview by Janet Bishop. Did you find this to be an effective strategy to spark your interest? Why or why not?

2. Analytical documents often identify a pattern and then establish its meaning. What pattern is being explored in this video? Did you find it engaging, off-putting, or confusing? Explain your reaction.

3. Who is the intended audience for this video? How can you tell? How might the analysis provided through the video have differed if it was directed at another audience?

4. Videos often use a more conversational approach than formal analytical essays and articles. Evaluate Grandin's tone in the video. Is it conversational? Scholarly? A mix of the two? How does the approach influence your perception of her analysis?

5. **Reflection:** Grandin observes, "If you got rid of all of the genes that cause autism, you'd be rid of Carl Sagan, you'd be rid of Mozart. Einstein, today, would be labeled autistic. He had no speech until he was three years old." She notes that half of all the people who work in big tech have at least a mild version of Asperger's. In what ways does this encourage us to rethink our understanding of cognitive diversity? In what ways, if any, does it change your thinking about autism?

GENRE TALK

Reflective Writing | Informative Writing | **Analytical Writing** | Evaluative Writing | Problem-Solving Writing | Argumentative Writing

Recent conflicts have seen millions of immigrants fleeing Ukraine, Syria, and Iraq and seeking safety and asylum in Greece, Turkey, Hungary, Poland and other parts of Europe and eventually the United States. Immigrants from the Middle East have added yet another frontier to the conversation about immigration, in addition to the heated debates over the U.S.–Mexican border. Because it is a complicated topic with many vexing issues, immigration is well suited to analytical writing, which aims to answer questions, identify causes and effects, and consider future significance or consequences. Analytical writing on the topic of immigration considers how issues such as personal safety, national security, religious tolerance, cultural assimilation, and moral obligation fit together, overlap, and sometimes contradict each other.

This report from the Pew Research Center analyzes how immigration continues to change American demographics more than fifty years after the 1965 Immigration and Nationality Act. It also examines how the American public views immigrants from various parts of the world and how it values their impact on various aspects of American life, from the economy and crime to food, music, and the arts. Drawing on recent census data and online surveys conducted in English and Spanish of more than three thousand Americans, this report offers a complex portrait of how immigration is shaping the makeup and the attitudes of the country today.

PEW Research Center

The title page clearly lists the title, publication date, and sponsoring organization of the report.

The individual authors and their roles are identified, and contact information is provided.

PEW Research Center

Section headings help organize the information in the report.

Source information is cited at the bottom of each figure.

Figures illustrate census data and survey responses. Figures are labeled, numbered, and set off from the main text with rules.

Color, italics, boldface, and distinct fonts contribute to a formal but eye-catching design.

How Can I Write an Analytical Essay?

Got questions? Got an inquiring mind? Got the discipline to follow up on a question carefully and thoroughly? If you answered "yes" to these questions, you've got what it takes to start writing an analytical essay.

That's not all it takes, of course. Writing an analytical essay also involves refining your question, gaining a fuller understanding of your subject, applying an appropriate interpretive framework, and drafting your response to your analytical question. But the foundation of an analytical essay — and of all analytical documents, for that matter — is developing and responding to a question about a subject.

As you work on your analytical essay, you'll draw on several critical thinking skills, especially remembering, understanding, reflecting, analyzing, and creating. Throughout this chapter, you'll follow the work of Kelsey Smith, who wrote an analysis of the theft of creative work on the internet.

Find a Conversation and Listen In

Analytical essays allow you to share your interpretation of a subject with your readers. Your analysis will reflect not only your analytical question and interpretive framework but also what other writers involved in the conversation about your subject have written and the types of analyses they've conducted. It will also reflect the demands of your writing assignment. To get started on your analytical essay, review your assignment and spend some time thinking about your writing situation (see Chapter 1). Then start generating ideas about the kinds of questions you might ask, find a conversation worth joining, and learn more about it.

- **REFLECT ON YOUR SURROUNDINGS**

Analysis is largely a search for patterns — and searching for patterns is something we do on a daily basis. As we learn to drive, for example, we start noticing the typical behaviors of other drivers as they approach an intersection. It doesn't take long to learn that we can reliably predict whether other drivers are planning to go through the intersection, stop, turn left, or turn right — even when they fail to use turn signals. When we see behaviors that are unusual or unexpected, we go on alert, making sure that we aren't hit by a driver who isn't paying attention. Similarly,

In Process

An Analysis of a Cultural Trend

Kelsey Smith wrote an analytical essay for her introductory composition course. She used analysis to explore different types of art theft online, particularly via social media. Follow Kelsey's efforts to write her analytical essay by reading the In Process boxes throughout this chapter.

Courtesy of Sherri Gandolfi

we look for patterns in everything from playing tennis (noticing, for instance, how a player grips the racket before returning a shot) to reading the newspaper (learning where we can find stories that interest us or how to distinguish news from advertisements).

Humans are quite good at identifying and responding to patterns. But it takes time to notice them and even more time to figure out how they work. Before choosing a specific focus for your analytical essay, identify general topics that might interest you enough to explore in depth. One good way to begin is to brainstorm or freewrite about the objects and events that surround you.

- **Your media.** Scan your collections of music, books, and movies, and think about anything you've listened to, read, or watched that grabbed your attention. You might be rewarded by looking beneath the surface for meaning or themes, or you might find yourself intrigued by a plot line or a style that appears to be part of a larger trend.

- **The daily news.** Whether you follow current events in newspapers, on television, or on your phone, recent and ongoing news stories offer rich opportunities for analysis: Why were some groups offended by a magazine cover? Is third-party health insurance to blame for the high cost of medical care? How do "bad boy" or "bad girl" celebrities influence children's behavior? Be alert to the questions that occur to you as you read, to reactions (other people's and your own) that surprise you, and to themes that seem to pop up from one day to the next.

- **Your leisure activities.** No matter what you do for fun — participate in a sport, play video games, take photographs — you can probably find some aspects of your lifestyle that raise questions or suggest a trend.

- **Your physical environment.** Take a look around you. A favorite poster in your bedroom, for instance, might be a good candidate for interpretation. A new bank in town might inspire questions about interest rates, community service, or architectural style. An overflowing trash bin might suggest an analytical essay on recycling or municipal waste management.

You'll find additional writing project ideas at the end of this chapter.

● **ASK INTERPRETIVE QUESTIONS**

The foundation for analysis is a question that is open to interpretation. For example, asking whether you have enough money to purchase a ticket to the latest Jennifer Lawrence movie would not require an interpretive response. Either you have enough money or you don't. Asking whether Lawrence's performance breaks new ground, however, would require an analysis of her work in the film.

You can generate potential interpretive questions about promising topics by brainstorming, freewriting, or clustering in response to the following prompts. Each prompt focuses your attention on a general topic in a different way, and each provides a useful starting point for an analytical essay. Depending on your topic, you'll find that some prompts are more productive than others.

- **Elements.** Think about the subject in terms of its parts. How does it break down into smaller pieces, or how can it be divided in different ways? Which parts are most important, and which are less significant?

- **Categories.** What groups does the subject belong to? How is it similar to or different from other subjects in a particular group? How can comparing the subject to related subjects help you and your readers understand it in a new way?

- **History.** Look into the origins of the subject. What recent events are related to the subject, and what are the implications of those events? Does your subject build on previous events? Will it continue to have influence in the future, and if so, how will it do so?

- **Causes and effects.** What caused the subject, and why is it the way it is? What are the subject's influences on people, events, and objects? Who or what affects the subject? What effects is the subject likely (or unlikely) to cause in the future?

Working Together: Try It Out Loud

Working in a small group, choose a popular song that everyone in your group likes, or choose one of the top songs of the week on the Billboard Top 100 or on American Top 40. Then use one set of the interpretive question prompts in the previous section to analyze the song. If you are doing this activity during class, the class might choose a single song, and each group might choose a different set of prompts. Take turns asking questions about the song while the other members of the group try to answer them. Record your answers, noting both agreements and disagreements. Your purpose is to interpret, so don't get distracted by whether the song is good or bad; instead, focus on its significance and implications. If you are doing this activity during class, each group should report its results to the class.

When you are finished, take a few minutes to reflect on the activity. What did you learn about different ways of approaching an analysis? Did some interpretive questions produce more useful or interesting results than others? How did examining the song from multiple perspectives affect your interpretation of it?

- **Relationships.** How is the subject connected to other ideas, events, or objects? For example, are changes in the subject related to changes in those ideas, events, or objects?
- **Meaning.** What is the subject's significance and implications? Can different people find different meanings in the subject, and if so, why? Does a close examination of the subject reveal a new way of thinking about it?

As you ponder ways to turn a general topic area into the subject of your analytical essay, spend time learning about other people's answers to the most promising questions you've generated. You can discuss the subject with people you know, skim sources published on the subject, or even observe the subject firsthand. You can learn more about gathering information in Chapter 2 and in Chapters 13 to 15.

SEARCH FOR SOURCES

Once you've identified a promising question, learn whether — and how — other writers have attempted to answer it. Analytical essays tend to draw on information and analyses from other sources in addition to the writer's personal knowledge and interpretation, so even if you already know a great deal about a subject, be sure to review other writers' contributions to the conversation and to look for sources you can use to support your analysis.

To search for sources that have been published on a particular subject or in a particular discipline, turn to databases, your library's catalog, and the web. The sources you find can help you gain an in-depth understanding of your subject, as well as a sense of useful interpretive frameworks, existing interpretations, and unanswered questions. You can read more about searching for sources in Chapter 14.

In Process

Searching Databases

Kelsey Smith used her interpretive question—*What does art theft look like in a digital space?*—to develop search terms for research in her library's databases. She knew from exploring her subject that it had been addressed in newspapers and online publications, so she searched databases such as LexisNexis Academic and Newspaper Source. Because she also wondered whether law and communications studies had been conducted on the subject, she searched the Legal Source, Communication and Mass Media Complete, and Academic Search Premier databases.

Photo: Courtesy of Sherri Gandolfi

Kelsey used the search terms *art, theft, copyright, social media, online,* and *digital*. She searched all fields in the database and used Boolean operators (AND and OR) to require that *art* and either *theft* or *copyright* and either *social media* or *online* or *digital* be present (see Chapter 14).

Courtesy of Sherri Gandolfi

The search produced 620 results, including videos. The database allowed Kelsey to view abstracts (summaries of the sources) and complete reference information.

To narrow her search, Kelsey began applying search limits (see Chapter 14).

Kelsey's database searches produced sources in several scholarly publications. She located one of the articles, which focused on ownership in the age of social media.

Conduct Your Analysis

An analytical essay helps readers understand the origins, qualities, significance, or potential effects of a subject. A successful essay builds on a carefully crafted analytical question, a thorough understanding of the subject, and a rigorous and fair application of an appropriate interpretive framework. It also builds on a clear understanding of your writing situation.

● REFINE YOUR QUESTION

Begin your analysis by reviewing the interpretive questions you generated about your subject (see *Ask Interpretive Questions* earlier in this chapter). Choose one that interests you and will allow you to carry out your assignment. Then review and refine your question. Ask yourself:

- How might I respond to this question? Will my response be complex enough to justify writing an essay about it? Will it be too complex for my assignment?
- Is the question appropriate for the conversation that I'm planning to join?
- Will the question help me accomplish my purposes?
- Will my response interest my readers or address their needs?

A good analytical question is open to interpretation. Questions that focus on factual or yes/no answers seldom provide a strong foundation for an analytical essay. In contrast, questions that lead you to investigate the origins or potential impacts of a subject, to consider its qualities, to weigh its significance, or to explore its meaning are more likely to lead to success. Consider the differences between the following sets of questions.

Questions Leading to Factual or Yes/No Answers	Questions Open to Interpretation
When did the Iraq War end?	What caused the Iraq War?
Has NASA's annual budget kept pace with inflation?	How can NASA pursue its mission on a reduced annual budget?
Who were the villains in the first Indiana Jones movie?	In what ways do the key themes of the first Indiana Jones movie reflect changes in American foreign relations?
Who won the last World Series?	What contributed to the success of the last World Series champions?

You should also consider how a question will direct your thinking about your subject. For example, you might want to understand the potential effects of a proposal to reduce the cost of attending your state's public colleges and universities by increasing class size and laying off faculty and staff. Asking a question about the plan's impact on education might direct your attention toward students and the trade-offs between lower costs and the quality of instruction. In contrast, asking a question about the plan's impact on the state budget might lead you to view the subject through the lens of business concerns and economic forecasts. Although the questions are related, they would lead to significantly different analyses.

● SEEK A FULLER UNDERSTANDING OF YOUR SUBJECT

If you've ever talked with people who don't know what they're talking about but nonetheless are certain of their opinions, you'll recognize the dangers of applying an interpretive framework before you thoroughly understand your subject. To enhance your understanding of your subject, use *division* and *classification*. Division allows you to identify the elements that make up a subject. Classification allows you to explore a subject in relation to other subjects and to consider the similarities, differences, and relationships among its elements.

Division Division breaks a subject into its parts and considers what each contributes to the whole. A financial analyst, for example, might examine the various groups within a company to understand what each group does and how it contributes to the overall value of the company. Similarly, a literary critic might consider how each scene in a play relates to other scenes and how it contributes to the play's major theme. As you use division to examine a subject, keep in mind the following guidelines:

- **Pick a focus.** Division can take place on many levels. Just as you can divide numbers in different ways (100, for example, can be seen as ten 10s, five 20s, four 25s, and so on), you can divide subjects differently. A government agency, for instance, might be considered in terms of its responsibilities, its departments, or its employees. Trying to understand every aspect at once, however, would be difficult and unproductive. Use your analytical question as a guide to determine how best to divide your subject.

- **Examine the parts.** Most subjects can be thought of as a system of interrelated parts. As you divide your subject, determine what role each part plays, individually and in relation to other parts.

- **Assess contributions to the whole.** As you divide a subject, be sure to consider the contributions that each part makes to the larger whole. In some cases, you'll find that a part is essential. In other cases, you'll find that it makes little or no contribution to the whole.

Even though you can divide and reassemble a subject in a variety of ways, always take into account your purpose and your readers' needs, interests, and expectations.

It might be easier to focus on a government agency's departments than on its functions, but if your question focuses on how the agency works or what it does, you'll be more successful if you examine its functions.

Classification Classification places your subject — or each part of your subject — into a category, allowing you to discover how and to what extent your subject or a part of your subject is similar to others in the same category and how it differs from those in other categories. Identifying those similarities and differences, in turn, allows you to consider the subject, or its parts, in relation to the other items in your categories. As you use classification to gain a better understanding of your subject, consider the following guidelines:

- **Choose a classification scheme.** The categories you work with might be established already, or you might create them specifically to support your analysis. For example, if you are analyzing state representatives, you might place them in standard categories: Democrat, Republican, Libertarian, Green, and so on. Or you might create categories especially for your analysis, such as who voted for or against particular types of legislation.

- **Look at both similarities and differences.** When you place an item in a category, you decide that it is more similar to the other items in the category than to items in other categories. However, even though the items in a broad category will share many similarities, they will also differ in important ways. Botanists, for example, have developed a complex system of categories and subcategories to help them understand general types of plants (such as grasses, roses, and corn) as well as to consider subtle differences among similar plants (such as corn bred for animal feed, for human consumption, and for biofuels).

- **Justify your choices.** Your decisions about what to place in a given category will be based on your understanding of categories that have been established by someone else or, if you've created it yourself, your definition of the category. Be prepared to explain why a particular category is the best fit for your subject. If you want readers to accept your classification of Walmart as a mom-and-pop retailer, for instance, you have to explain that your category is defined by origin (not current size) and then inform readers that the chain started as a single discount store in Arkansas.

Classification and division are often used in combination, particularly when you want to consider similarities and differences among different parts of your subject. For example, if you are examining a complex organization, you might use division to analyze each department. You might use classification, in turn, to analyze groups of departments that have similar functions, such as customer service and technical support, and contrast those departments with departments in other categories, such as sales, marketing, and research and development.

● **APPLY AN INTERPRETIVE FRAMEWORK**

An interpretive framework is a set of strategies for identifying patterns that has been used successfully and refined over time by writers interested in a given subject area or a particular field. Writers can choose from specialized frameworks used in disciplines across the arts, sciences, social sciences, humanities, engineering, and business. A historian, for example, might apply a feminist, social, political, or cultural analysis to interpret diaries written by women who worked in defense plants during World War II, while a sociologist might conduct correlational tests to interpret the results of a survey. In a writing course, you'll most likely use one of the broad interpretive frameworks discussed here: trend analysis, causal analysis, data analysis, text analysis, and rhetorical analysis.

By definition, analysis is subjective. Your interpretation will be shaped by the question you ask, the sources you consult, and your personal experience and perspective. But analysis is also conducted within the context of a written conversation. As you consider your choice of interpretive framework, reflect on the interpretive frameworks you encounter in your sources and those you've used in the past. Keep in mind that different interpretive frameworks will lead to different ways of seeing and understanding a subject. The key to success is choosing one that can guide you as you try to answer your question.

Need help with context? See Chapter 1 for more information.

Trend analysis Trends are patterns that hold up over time. Trend analysis, as a result, focuses on sequences of events and the relationships among them. It is based on the assumption that understanding what has happened in the past allows us to make sense of what is happening in the present and to draw inferences about what is likely to happen in the future.

Trends can be identified and analyzed in nearly every field, from politics to consumer affairs to the arts. For example, many economists have analyzed historical accounts of fuel crises in the 1970s to understand changes in fuel prices. Featured student writer Kelsey Smith used trend analysis to explore art theft on social media (see her final essay later in this chapter). To conduct a trend analysis, follow these guidelines:

- **Gather information.** Trend analysis is most useful when it relies on an extensive set of long-term observations. Gathering a large collection of news reports about NASA since the mid-1960s, for example, can tell you whether the coverage of the U.S. space program has changed over time. By examining changes in coverage, you can decide whether a trend exists. You might find, for instance, that the press has become progressively less positive in its treatment of the U.S. space program.

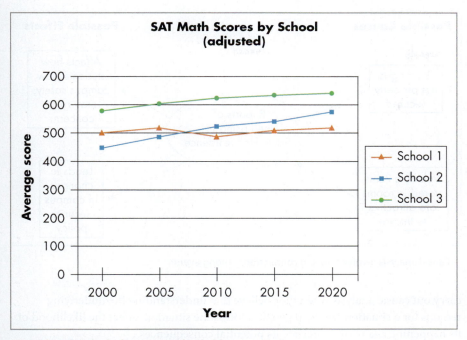

▲ Trend analysis looks for patterns that hold up over time

- **Establish that a trend exists.** Some analysts seem willing to declare a trend on the flimsiest set of observations: when a team wins an NFL championship for the second year in a row, for instance, some sports writers are quick to announce the start of a dynasty. As you look for trends, cast a wide net. Learn as much as you can about the history of your subject and carefully assess how often events related to your subject have moved in one direction or another.

- **Draw conclusions.** Trend analysis allows you to understand the historical context that shapes a subject and, in some cases, to make predictions about the subject. The conclusions you draw should be grounded strongly in the evidence you've collected. They should also reflect your writing situation — your purposes, readers, and context. As you draw your conclusions, exercise caution. Ask whether you have enough information to support your conclusions. Search for evidence that contradicts your conclusions. Most important, on the basis of the information you've collected so far, ask whether your conclusions make sense.

Causal analysis Causal analysis focuses on the factors that bring about a particular situation. It can be applied to a wide range of subjects, such as the Great Recession, the rise of terrorist groups, or the impact of calorie restriction on longevity. Writers

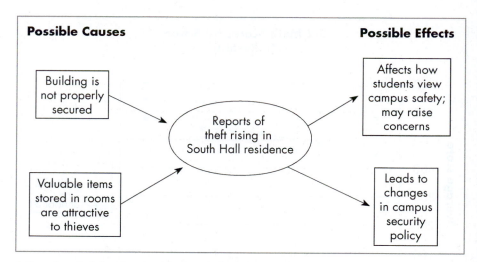

▲ Causal analysis involves tracing connections among events

carry out causal analysis when they believe that understanding the underlying reasons for a situation will help people address the situation, affect the likelihood of its happening again, or appreciate its potential consequences.

In many ways, causal analysis is a form of detective work. It involves tracing a sequence of events and exploring the connections among them. Because the connections are almost always more complex than they appear, it pays to be thorough. If you choose to conduct a causal analysis, keep in mind the following guidelines:

- **Uncover as many causes as you can.** Effects rarely emerge from a single cause. Most effects are the results of a complex web of causes, some of which are related to one another and some of which are not. Although it might be tempting, for example, to say that a murder victim died (the effect) from a gunshot wound (the cause), that would tell only part of the story. You would need to work backward from the murderer's decision to pull the trigger to the factors that led to that decision, and then further back to the causes underlying those factors.

  Effects can also become causes. While investigating the murder, for instance, you might find that the murderer had long been envious of the victim's success, that he was jumpy from the steroids he'd been taking in an ill-advised attempt to qualify for the Olympic trials in weight lifting, and that he had just found his girlfriend in the victim's arms. Exploring how these factors might be related — and determining when they are not — will help you understand the web of causes leading to the effect.

- **Determine which causes are significant.** Not all causes contribute equally to an effect. Perhaps our murderer was cut off on the freeway on his way to meet his girlfriend. Lingering anger at the other driver might have been enough to push him over the edge, but it probably wouldn't have caused the shooting by itself.

- **Distinguish between correlation and cause.** Too often, we assume that because one event occurred just before another, the first event caused the second. We might conclude that finding his girlfriend with another man drove the murderer to shoot in a fit of passion — only to discover that he had begun planning the murder months before, when the victim threatened to reveal his use of steroids to the press just prior to the Olympic trials.

- **Look beyond the obvious.** A thorough causal analysis considers not only the primary causes and effects but also those that might appear only slightly related to the subject. For example, you might consider the immediate effects of the murder not only on the victim and perpetrator but also on their families and friends, on the wider community, on the lawyers and judges involved in the case, on an overburdened legal system, and even on attitudes toward Olympic athletes. By looking beyond the obvious causes and effects, you can deepen your understanding of the subject and begin to explore a much wider set of implications than you might have initially expected.

Data analysis Data is any type of information, such as facts and observations. It is often expressed numerically. Most of us analyze data in an informal way on a daily basis. For example, if you've looked at the percentage of people who favor a particular political candidate over another, you've engaged in data analysis. Similarly, if you've checked your bank account to determine whether you have enough money for a planned purchase, you've carried out a form of data analysis. As a writer, you can analyze numerical information related to your subject to better understand the subject as a whole, to look for differences among the subject's parts, and to explore relationships among the parts.

To begin a data analysis, gather your data and enter the numbers into a spreadsheet or statistics program. You can use the program's tools to sort the data and conduct tests. If your set of data is small, you can use a piece of paper and a calculator. As you carry out your analysis, keep the following guidelines in mind:

- **Do the math.** Let's say you conducted a survey of student and faculty attitudes about a proposed change to the graduation requirements at your school. Tabulating the results might reveal that 52 percent of your respondents were female, 83 percent were between the ages of eighteen and twenty-two, 38 percent were juniors or seniors, and 76 percent were majoring in the biological

Use of Social-Networking Sites	# surveyed	% who use social networking regularly
Gender		
Male	48	56%
Female	42	65%
Age		
16–20	20	85%
21–30	31	71%
31–45	28	46%
45+	11	27%
Education		
Some high school	12	35%
High school graduate	25	56%
Some college	34	65%
College graduate	16	64%
Graduate school	7	62%

▲ Data analysis can involve assessing information from a variety of sources

sciences. You might also find that, of the faculty who responded, 75 percent were tenured. Based on these numbers, you could draw conclusions about whether the responses are representative of your school's overall population. If they are not, you might decide to ask more people to take your survey. Once you're certain that you've collected enough data, you can draw conclusions about the overall results and determine, for example, the percentage of respondents who favored, opposed, or were undecided about the proposed change.

- **Categorize your data.** Difference tests can help you make distinctions among groups. To classify the results of your survey, for example, you might compare responses from full-time and part-time students. Similarly, you might examine differences in the responses between other groups — such as faculty and students; tenure-line and non-tenure-line faculty members; and first-years, sophomores, juniors, seniors, and graduate students. To carry out your analysis, you might look at each group's average level of agreement with the proposed changes. Or you might use statistical techniques such as t-tests, which offer more sensitive assessments of difference than comparisons of averages. You can conduct these kinds of tests using spreadsheet programs, such as Microsoft Excel or Google Sheets, or statistical programs, such as SAS and SPSS.

- **Explore relationships.** Correlation tests allow you to draw conclusions about your subject. For example, you might want to know whether support for proposed changes to graduation requirements increases or decreases according to GPA. A correlation test might indicate that a positive relationship exists — that support goes up as GPA increases. Be cautious, however, as you examine relationships. In particular, be wary of confusing causation with correlation. Tests will show, for example, that as shoe size increases, so do scores on reading tests. Does this mean that large feet improve reading? Not really. The cause of higher reading scores appears to be attending school longer. High school students tend to score better on reading tests than do students in elementary school — and, on average, high school students tend to have much larger feet. As is the case with difference tests, you can use many spreadsheet and statistical programs to explore relationships.

- **Be thorough.** Take great care to ensure the integrity of your analysis. You will run into problems if you collect too little data, if the data is not representative, or if the data is collected sloppily. Similarly, you should base your conclusions on a thoughtful and careful examination of the results of your tests. Picking and choosing evidence that supports your conclusion might be tempting, but you'll do a disservice to yourself and your readers if you fail to consider all the results of your analysis.

Text analysis Today, the word *text* can refer to a wide range of printed or digital works — and even some forms of artistic expression that we might not think of as documents. Texts open to interpretation include novels, poems, plays, essays, articles, movies, speeches, blogs, songs, paintings, photographs, sculptures, performances, websites, videos, television shows, and computer games.

Students enrolled in writing classes often use the elements of literary analysis to analyze texts. In this form of analysis, interpreters focus on theme, plot, setting, characterization, imagery, style, and structure, as well as the contexts — social, cultural, political, and historical — that shape a work. Writers who use this form of analysis focus both on what is actually presented in the text and on what is implied or conveyed "between the lines." They rely heavily on close reading of the text to discern meaning, critique an author's technique, and search for patterns that help them understand the text as fully as possible. They also tend to consider other elements of the wider writing situation in which the text was produced — in particular, the author's purpose, intended audience, use of sources, and choice of genre.

> In the song "What Is New Orleans, Part 2," recorded by Kermit Ruffins and the Rebirth Brass Band, a call-and-response pattern structures both the lyrics ("What is New Orleans? New Orleans is . . .") and also the interaction between Ruffins and the musicians. Frequently, after Ruffins sings a pattern of syllables, the musicians echo or answer him, as though the music itself is to be considered a sufficient response. Meanwhile, the song's lyrics highlight the importance of food in the city's culture by beginning with a list of meals. Each meal is associated with a specific time and day of the week, giving the impression that the rest of the week's events are scheduled around these meals. Ruffins then lists musicians and locations, moving from the specific to the general, from individual lounges to entire neighborhoods.

▲ Text analysis can focus on a wide range of artistic expression

If you carry out a text analysis, keep the following guidelines in mind:

- **Focus on the text itself.** In any form of text analysis, the text should take center stage. Although you will typically reflect on the issues raised by your interpretation, maintain a clear focus on the text in front of you, and keep your analysis grounded firmly in what you can locate within it. Background information and related sources, such as scholarly articles and essays, can support and enhance your analysis, but they can't do the work of interpretation for you.

- **Consider the text in its entirety.** Particularly in the early stages of learning about a text, it is easy to be distracted by a startling idea or an intriguing concept. Try not to focus on a particular aspect of the text, however, until you've reviewed the full text. You might well decide to narrow your analysis to a particular aspect of the text, but lay the foundation for a fair, well-informed interpretation by first considering the text as a whole.

- **Avoid cherry-picking.** "Cherry-picking" refers to the process of using only those materials from a text that support your overall interpretation and ignoring aspects that might weaken or contradict your interpretation. As you carry out your analysis, factor in *all* the evidence. If the text doesn't support your interpretation, rethink your conclusions.

Rhetorical analysis In much the same way that you can assess the writing situation that shapes your work on a particular assignment, you can analyze the rhetorical situation (see Chapter 1) that shaped the creation of and response to a particular document. A rhetorical analysis, for example, might focus on how a particular document (written, visual, or some other form) achieved its purpose or on why readers reacted to it in a specific way.

Rhetorical analysis focuses on one or more aspects of the rhetorical situation.

- **Writer and purpose.** What did the writer hope to accomplish? Was it accomplished and, if so, how well? If not, why not? What strategies did the writer use to pursue the purpose? Did the writer choose the best genre for the purpose? Why did the writer choose this purpose over others? Are there any clear connections between the purpose and the writer's apparent values, beliefs, and experiences?

- **Readers/audience.** Was the document addressed to the right audience? Did readers react to the document as the writer hoped? Why or why not? What aspects of the needs, interests, values, beliefs, and experiences of the audience might have led them to react to the document as they did?

- **Sources.** What sources were used? Which information, ideas, and arguments from the sources were used in the document? How effectively were they used? How credible were the sources? Were enough sources used? Were the sources appropriate?

- **Context.** How did the context in which the document was composed shape its effectiveness? How did the context in which it was read shape the reaction of the audience? What physical, social, cultural, disciplinary, and historical contexts shaped the document's development? What contexts shaped how readers reacted to it?

Rhetorical analysis can also involve an assessment of the argument used in a document. It is common to examine the structure of an argument, focusing on the writer's use of appeals — such as appeals to logic, emotion, character, and so on (see *Appeal to Your Readers* in Chapter 12) — and the quality of the evidence that was provided. In many courses, these appeals are referred to using the classical Greek terms *logos* (logic), *pathos* (emotion), and *ethos* (character). Courses that use these rhetorical concepts might also explore the notion of *kairos*, which refers to timing or opportunity. It is also common, in rhetorical analysis, to ask whether the argument contains any logical fallacies, such as sweeping generalizations or questionable analogies (see *Ensure the Integrity of Your Argument* in Chapter 12). In general, writers who examine an argument will typically connect the analysis to one or more of the major elements of the rhetorical situation. For example, the writer might explore readers' reactions to the evidence used to support an argument. Or, as Brooke Gladstone does in her analysis of the Goldilocks number earlier in this chapter, you might focus on how evidence migrates from one document to another.

Carrying out a rhetorical analysis almost always involves a close reading (or viewing) of the document (see the previous section for a discussion of text analysis). It can also involve research into the origins of the document and its effects on its audience. For example, a rhetorical analysis of the Declaration of Independence might focus not only on its content but also on the political, economic, and historical contexts that brought it into existence; reactions to it by American colonists and English citizens; and its eventual impact on the development of the U.S. Constitution.

As you carry out a rhetorical analysis, consider the following guidelines:

- **Remember that the elements of a rhetorical situation are interrelated.** Writers' purposes do not emerge from a vacuum. They are shaped by their experiences, values, and beliefs — each of which is influenced by the physical, social, cultural, disciplinary, and historical contexts out of which a particular document emerges. In turn, writers usually shape their arguments to reflect their understanding of their readers' needs, interests, knowledge, and backgrounds. Writers also choose their sources and select genres that reflect their purpose, their knowledge of their readers, and the context in which a document will be written and read.

- **If you analyze the argument in a document, focus on its structure and quality.** Rhetorical analysis focuses on the document as a means of communication. It might be tempting to praise an argument you agree with or to criticize one that offends your values or beliefs. If you do so, however, you won't be carrying out a rhetorical analysis. This form of analysis is intended to help your readers understand your conclusions about the origins, structure, quality, and potential impact of the document.

- **Don't underestimate the complexity of analyzing rhetorical context.** Understanding context is one of the most challenging aspects of a rhetorical analysis. Context is multifaceted. You can consider the physical context in which a document is written and read. You can examine its social context. And you can explore the cultural, disciplinary, and historical contexts that shaped a document. Each of these contexts will affect a document in important ways. Because a full analysis of context is likely to take far more space and time than most academic documents allow, focus on the aspects of context that are most relevant to your writing situation.

Applying Interpretive Frameworks

Kelsey Smith used an analysis of a key social-media trend in her essay to address one key aspect of art theft on the internet. After reading widely about the issue, she selected a number of articles, including one by Catherine C. Marshall and Frank M. Shipman from *Communications of the ACM* titled "Who Owns the Social Web?" Kelsey highlighted words and phrases and wrote notes in the margin about her evolving understanding of how communications scholars view ownership on social media.

Photo: Courtesy of Sherri Gandolfi

Who Owns the Social Web?

By Catherine C. Marshall, Frank M. Shipman
Communications of the ACM, May 2017, Vol. 60 No. 5, Pages 52-61
10.1145/2996181
Comments

User-contributed content plays an increasingly important role in the Internet's evolution, overtaking professionally created and curated resources. Sophisticated recording technologies allow non-professionals to produce high-quality photos and videos. Improved editing and sharing applications facilitate other aspects of media creation, including larger-scale collaborative efforts. And social media venues give their users new opportunities to publish, curate, and recommend content. Every phase of the creative process—from recording to editing to publishing—has become more popular and interactive. At the same time, content ownership has become more complicated. Any distinct item may be associated with a virtual web of stakeholders.

Back to Top

Key Insights

- Intellectual property law and social norms concerning content ownership are diverging in conspicuous ways; we find that legally contentious actions (such as downloading and saving content) may seem benign to most Internet users.
- Managing rights relies on content owners' ability to envision plausible reuse scenarios, including commercial reuse of their content as data, and predicting which are most likely.
- Everyday reuse of social media content is opportunistic, pragmatic, and highly contextual; users reason about the fairness of reusing other people's content but do not necessarily trust them to do the same.

> The authors call out social media as a key factor in how complicated ownership is on the internet.

> The authors summarize their opening about why online ownership is complicated: because nothing online exists in a vacuum.

A product review posted on Amazon might attract hundreds of comments that contribute substantively to the review's value and credibility. Videos on YouTube might respond to, excerpt, or satirize one another. Ongoing conversational threads on Twitter are held together by hashtags and @responses. Gamers use their avatars to interact with one another against the backdrop of a virtual universe and, in so doing, create new forms of data that build on the game's commercial content. Moreover, as individuals develop rich personal profiles, they publish new kinds of online representations of themselves.

> Unlike books or movies, which have clear copyright guidelines, the internet creates new data and new publications that don't have rules yet.

Courtesy of Sherri Gandolfi

Prepare a Draft

As you prepare to draft your analytical essay, you'll decide how to present the results of your analysis to your readers. Your draft will reflect not only your conclusions and the results of your application of your interpretive framework but also what others involved in the conversation have written about your subject and the types of analyses they've conducted. As you write, you'll focus on making an interpretive claim, explaining your interpretation, designing your essay, and framing your analysis.

● MAKE AN INTERPRETIVE CLAIM

Your interpretive claim is a brief statement — usually in the form of a thesis statement (see Chapter 18) — that helps readers understand the overall results of your analysis. Essentially, it's a one- or two-sentence answer to your interpretive question. Just as your question should be open to interpretation, your claim should be open to debate. If it simply repeats the obvious — either because it is factually true or because it has long been agreed to by those involved in your written conversation — it will do little to advance the conversation.

Your claim will frame your readers' understanding of your subject in a particular way. It will also reflect the interpretive framework you've decided to use. Consider the differences among the following claims about distance running:

> Evidence collected since the mid-1990s suggests that distance running can enhance self-image among college students.

> Since 2000, distance running has undergone a resurgence in the United States, allowing the country to regain its standing as a leader in the international running community.

> Distance running, when it is addressed at all in contemporary novels, is usually used to represent a desire to escape from the pressures of modern life.

Each of these interpretive claims would lead a writer to focus on different aspects of the subject, and each would reflect a different interpretive framework. The first calls readers' attention to a causal relationship between distance running and mental health. The second directs attention to a trend analysis of increasing competitiveness among elite distance runners. And the third makes a claim about how distance running is treated in literature.

● EXPLAIN YOUR INTERPRETATION

People who read analyses are intelligent, curious people. They want to know more than just what you think of a subject; they want to know how you arrived at your interpretation and why your analysis is reasonable. Your readers won't always agree with your interpretation, and that's fine — but even if you can't persuade them to accept your analysis, you do want to convince them that your take on the subject is insightful and well considered.

Provide relevant reasons for your interpretation Build on your interpretive claim by presenting reasons to accept your analysis. The overall results of your analysis form your main point, and the reasons to accept your analysis become your supporting points.

Look over the results of your analysis, and ask yourself why readers should agree with your interpretation. You might come up with more reasons than you can possibly use — or you might find yourself struggling to find enough reasons to support your claim. Either way, try to generate as many potential reasons as possible, taking care not to rule out any at first, no matter how trivial or ridiculous they might seem.

Once you have generated a substantial list of potential reasons, select the ones that are most directly related to your interpretive claim and framework, and then choose those most likely to convince your readers that your analysis is sound. For example, you might find several reasons to support your analysis of a new novel's significance, among them comments published in literary journals such as *PMLA* and endorsements by celebrities such as Oprah Winfrey and Gwyneth Paltrow. If you are using text analysis as your interpretive framework, you might find commentary offered by authorities in the field of literary studies more useful than celebrity endorsements.

Working Together: Generate Reasons for Your Interpretation

The goal of this collaborative activity is to generate potential reasons supporting your interpretation of your subject. You can work in person or online (using video conferencing, text messaging, a meeting app, or a discussion forum). If you are working face-to-face, one member of the group should take notes on the discussion. If you are using chat, be sure to record a transcript of the session. To carry out the activity, follow these steps:

1. One by one, the members of the group should describe their writing projects, the overall results of their analysis, and the reasons that will be offered to support the analysis.

2. After each writer has spoken, the group should offer feedback on the reasons offered by the writer. Are the reasons sound, appropriate, and credible?

3. Members of the group should also suggest additional reasons each writer might consider.

Support your reasons with evidence No matter which reasons you choose, each of them must be supported by evidence. Analytical essays tend to rely on a mix of evidence from the subject itself (particularly in the case of text analyses and rhetorical analyses), from the writer's reflections and personal experience, and from published or field sources. Evidence can include the following:

- language or images from a text that is being analyzed
- quotations, paraphrases, and summaries from published sources such as reports and journal articles
- illustrations in the form of images, charts, graphs, and tables
- statements from personal interviews
- notes from an observation
- numerical information

You can use evidence to provide examples and illustrations, to define ideas and concepts, to illustrate processes, and to associate particular ideas and concepts with authorities, such as political leaders, subject-matter experts, or people who have been affected by the subject.

You can read more about how to use evidence to support your analysis in Chapter 21.

To organize your evidence, list all the reasons you will use to support your overall analysis, review your notes to find evidence that supports each reason, and then list the evidence below each reason. You might need to review your sources to locate additional evidence or even obtain additional sources. If you are conducting a text analysis, be careful to avoid cherry-picking your evidence (see *Text Analysis* earlier in this chapter). If you are conducting another type of analysis, make sure that you haven't relied too heavily on a single source of evidence.

Establish the context It's quite possible — even likely — that others involved in a conversation will have conducted their own analyses of your subject. Be sure to check for those analyses so that you can place your analysis in a larger context. Ideally, you'll be able to present your interpretation as a contribution to a growing understanding of the subject rather than simply as an isolated set of observations.

As you draft your analytical essay, keep in mind the other interpretations you've encountered. Review the sources you consulted as you learned about your subject and conducted your analysis. If you find reasonable interpretations that support — or contradict — yours, consider how to address them in your essay. You might offer similar interpretations to back up one or more of your reasons, or you might explain why another writer's analysis is less adequate than your own. In either case, you should briefly define significant existing analyses for your readers and explain how your interpretation complicates or improves on what's been said before.

Supporting Reasons with Evidence

Kelsey identified two key reasons for art theft online:

> Reason 1: Social media users online posting and reposting art out of admiration for the work or as a way to gain followers.

> Reason 2: Companies taking an artist's work without their knowledge to make a profit.

Kelsey used these two reasons as the framework for understanding art theft and the available methods for combating it. Here is her preliminary list of evidence to support her second reason, that companies are reproducing the work of independent artists for profit:

- Companies taking an artist's work without their knowledge to make a profit: Online retailers such as Zara creating "near-identical" copies, cited at ShopArtTheft.com.
- The "internet's sharing atmosphere" and the resulting confusion or disregard about copyright implications noted by Jessica Gutierrez Alm in the *Hamline Journal of Public Law & Policy*.
- Court cases such as *Agence France Presse v. Morel*, in which a company was found in violation of the Digital Millennium Copyright Act.

As she drafted her essay, Kelsey used her lists of evidence to remind herself of sources she might turn to while making her points.

Courtesy of Sherri Gandolfi

● **CONSIDER GENRE AND DESIGN**

A well-written analytical essay uses design for three primary reasons: to improve readability, to simplify the presentation of complex concepts and information, and to achieve the writer's goals. As is the case with other academic essays, you'll need to consider the expectations of your readers about design elements such as wide margins, double-spaced lines, page numbers, and a readable body font. But you can also use page layout elements as well as color, shading, borders, and rules to enhance the effectiveness of your essay.

Other design elements — such as illustrations and captions, tables and figures, and bulleted and numbered lists — can also contribute to the effectiveness of your essay. As you consider how best to connect with your readers, reflect on which design strategies will help you accomplish your purpose. Chapters 22 to 23 provide a detailed discussion of document design principles, elements, and strategies.

FRAME YOUR ANALYSIS

The results of your analysis will be strongly influenced by your interpretive question, interpretive framework, and sources of evidence. You can increase the odds that your readers will accept your conclusions if you help them understand your choices.

Introduction Rather than launching immediately into your interpretation, begin by introducing readers to your subject and explaining its significance. Provide enough information about your subject — in the form of a summary or description of a text, an overview of a trend, or a report of a recent event — to help readers understand your focus and follow your line of thinking. Another useful strategy is to start by offering some context about the conversation you've decided to join. Consider, for example, how Peter C. Baker starts his issue analysis, "Reform of the Nerds, Starring Arthur Chu," by narrating how he first came in contact with his subject:

> In January of 2014, I started getting text messages from my college friends asking whether I was following our old classmate Arthur Chu on *Jeopardy!* I wasn't — I hadn't watched the show for years — but I tuned in the next day.
>
> From then on, I watched rapt as Chu racked up what was, at the time, the third-longest winning streak in the show's history, drawing attention not only for the size of his haul (almost $400,000 in the end), but also for his supremely stereotypical nerdiness. He used an unorthodox strategy that drew on both game theory and statistical analysis of the *Jeopardy!* board. He was slightly pudgy, with glasses, and his hair was cut in a harsh horizontal line across his forehead. His shirts were rumpled, his ties poorly knotted. He spoke in a monotone and sometimes interrupted *Jeopardy!* host Alex Trebek, cutting off Trebek's patter so they could move on to the next question.

Conclusion Because analytical essays so often begin with a question, interpreters frequently withhold the thesis statement (the answer) until the end — after they've given readers sufficient reasons to accept their conclusions as reasonable. You might also wrap up your analysis by raising a related question for the reader to ponder, speculating about the future, or contemplating the implications of your interpretation, as Kelsey Smith does in her essay (see her essay later in this chapter):

> When users respect and support the original artist's work, it allows the artist to feel secure in sharing more of their art, which benefits both sides. If these two groups do not take action in preventative measures, art theft will only continue to rise in number and ruin the livelihood and careers of artists using social media.

You can learn more about using your introduction and conclusion to frame the results of your analysis in Chapter 20.

Organization The organization of your essay can also help frame your analysis because it will affect the order in which you present your reasons and evidence. Your choice of organizing pattern should take into account your purposes and your readers' needs and interests. For instance, if you are reporting the results of a trend analysis, you might want to use chronological order as your organizing pattern. If, by contrast, you are conducting a causal analysis, you might use the cause-and-effect organizing pattern. Creating an outline or a map can also help you organize your thoughts, especially if your assignment calls for a relatively long essay, if you are combining interpretive frameworks, or if you expect to present a lot of reasons or evidence to support your interpretive claim. You can read more about organizing patterns and outlines in Chapter 19.

Review and Improve Your Draft

Creating the first draft of an analytical essay is a complex and rewarding process. In the course of learning about a subject, you'll develop an interpretive question, choose an interpretive framework, and conduct an analysis; you'll make and support an interpretive claim; and you'll organize your reasons and evidence and frame your essay. Once you complete your first draft, you should step back and assess its strengths and weaknesses. A careful review — done individually and with the help of others — can help you pinpoint where you should invest additional time in improving your essay.

- **ENSURE THAT YOUR CLAIM IS DEBATABLE**

If your interpretive claim is not debatable (see *Make an Interpretive Claim* earlier in this chapter), it will do little to advance the conversation about your subject. As you review your essay, focus on your interpretive claim, and ask how your readers will react to it. For example, will your interpretive claim lead readers to disagree with you, or will it surprise or shock them? Will it make them think about the subject in a new way? Will it force them to reconsider their assumptions? If you think that your readers might respond by asking "so what?", you should take another look at your claim.

- **CHALLENGE YOUR CONCLUSIONS**

As you review your essay, challenge your findings by considering alternative explanations and asking your own "so what?" questions. Your initial impressions of a subject will often benefit from additional reflection. Those impressions might be refined, or perhaps even changed substantially, through additional analysis. Or they might be reinforced, typically by locating additional evidence.

- **EXAMINE THE APPLICATION OF YOUR INTERPRETIVE FRAMEWORK**

Ask whether you've applied your interpretive framework fairly and rigorously to your subject. If you are carrying out a causal analysis, for example, ask whether you've ruled out the possibility that the causal relationships you are exploring are simply correlations. If you're conducting a text analysis, ask whether you've fully and fairly represented the text and whether you have considered alternative interpretations. Review how you've used your interpretive framework to make sure that you've applied it carefully and evenhandedly to your subject.

- **ASSESS YOUR ORGANIZATION**

When readers can anticipate the sequence of reasoning and evidence that appears in your analytical essay, they'll conclude that the essay is well organized. If an essay is confusing or difficult to follow, however, they'll conclude that it is poorly written

Peer Review: Improve Your Analytical Essay

One of the biggest challenges writers face is responding to a draft of their own work as a reader rather than as the writer. Because you know what you're trying to say, you'll find it easy to understand your draft. To determine how you should revise your draft, ask a friend or classmate to read your essay and consider how well you've adopted the role of interpreter.

Purpose	1.	Is my interpretive claim clear and easy to understand? Is it debatable?
	2.	Have I offered a careful and thorough analysis to support my claim?
Readers	3.	Did the essay help you understand my subject in a new way? Why or why not?
	4.	Does the analysis seem fair to you? Did you notice any cherry-picking? Can you think of any aspects of my subject that I neglected to consider?
Sources	5.	Are the reasons I've offered for my interpretation coherent? Have I provided enough evidence to support each reason? Should I add or drop anything?
	6.	Do my sources strike you as reliable and appropriate? Does any of the evidence I've used seem questionable?
Context	7.	Did I provide enough (or too much) information about my subject to ground the analysis?
	8.	Does the interpretive framework I've chosen seem like an appropriate choice for analyzing my subject? Would a different framework have been more effective?

For each of the points listed above, ask your reviewers to provide concrete advice about what you could do to improve your draft. It can help if you ask them to adopt the role of an editor — someone who is working with you to improve your draft. You can read more about peer review in Chapter 5.

or, worse, that the analysis is flawed. As you review your essay, ask whether your reasons and evidence seem easy to follow. If you find yourself growing puzzled as you try to read your essay, take another look at your choice of organizing pattern. Check, as well, whether your reasons are presented in an order that allows them to build on one another. If you have difficulty figuring out how you've organized your essay, consider creating a backward outline, an outline based on an already written draft. You can read more about organizing your essay and outlining in Chapter 19.

RESPOND TO FEEDBACK FROM YOUR INSTRUCTOR

When instructors offer feedback on early drafts of an analytical essay, they are likely to focus at least some of their comments on the essay's interpretive question and interpretive framework. Their comments might focus on the clarity of your question, the fit between your question and framework, and the conclusions that emerge from your analysis. If those aspects of the essay are strong, instructors are likely to turn to issues such as how well the analysis appears to address its readers and the essay's organization, use of tables and illustrations, and support offered for conclusions. Feedback on later drafts is more likely to focus on the quality and clarity of paragraphs and sentences and perhaps on more subtle issues related to design.

Once you've revised your essay, ask yourself how you might polish and edit your writing so that your readers will find your analysis easy to read. For an overview of editing strategies, see Chapter 24.

In Process

Responding to Instructor Feedback

Kelsey received comments from her instructor on the first draft of her essay. After praising the originality and currency of her interpretive question, her instructor focused primarily on her interpretive framework, asking her in particular to take another look at the conclusions she had drawn and challenging whether she was applying the interpretive framework as rigorously as she might have. For instance, her instructor felt that there were several examples of art theft—such as individuals uploading stolen art to sites where they could create their own T-shirts, pens, and other objects—that did not fit well into either of Kelsey's two central categories.

In response, Kelsey revised her essay to present more clearly the decisions she had made as she applied the framework she had chosen and to streamline her examples, cutting evidence that did not directly support her framework, even if it was valid and tangentially related to her overall analysis. This allowed her to show more clearly how she had come to her conclusions and to offer additional support for them.

Courtesy of Sherri Gandolfi

Student Essay

Kelsey Smith, "Art Theft on the Rise with Social Media"

The following analytical essay was written by featured writer Kelsey Smith. Courtesy of Sherri Gandolfi

---

Smith 1

Kelsey Smith
December 8, 2022
English 1101

Art Theft on the Rise with Social Media

For most people, the term *art theft* conjures the image of a thief stealing priceless masterpieces from a museum, but in today's day and age the term can be applied to a variation of cases. Whether it's copying, reposting, or taking credit for a piece of art, art theft on social media is only growing and increasingly becoming a given result of sharing artwork on the internet. Online art theft can be seen across all social media sites and involves everyone: the social media user, the artist, and companies or businesses. The concern is that social media users are not aware of the implications and consequences art theft could have on them or the artist. This general acceptance of online art theft allows companies to steal designs for their own financial gain, which further damages the livelihood of the artist.

As an artist who utilizes social media for sharing my work, I have noticed multiple cases of art theft across the online art community. I have seen various degrees of theft ranging from reposting the artist's work without attribution, to brands and companies ripping off small independent artist's designs. Personally, I have dealt with, and still am dealing with, the theft of my art in cases that vary in severity. Online theft is no longer unexpected but now *anticipated* if you are an artist using social media. It is only a matter of time. I sincerely hope that my experiences and the materials contained within this essay implore you to be more conscious of the critical issue of art theft on social media and the internet.

There are two distinct kinds of art theft taking place, and the first is committed by social media users. This theft takes place across sites like Instagram, Pinterest, Tumblr, and Facebook.

Commonly, those responsible for these cases are users who most likely are not aware of the effects their actions could have. Their purpose behind

---

Annotations:

- Instead of including this information on a title page, Kelsey's instructor requested this information appear on the first page.
- The opening sentence acknowledges the usual context of art theft before shifting to the specific concern the writer will be analyzing.
- The author acknowledges her own biases and insights as an insider in the community she is analyzing.
- The writer sets up her framework, which will focus on the two key types of online art theft she has identified.

▲ Figure 1: Mike Feehan's reposted work was seen by hundreds of thousands of people across Tumblr and Instagram with credit to the wrong person. (Source: Instagram, 2017; Tumblr, 2017.)

Visuals serve as evidence to support the writer's points.

reposting the work is generally out of admiration or the desire to gain followers and likes for their own account through the post. For instance, Mike Feehan, a professional freelance illustrator, said this about his work being reposted, "this is actually the second or third time it was reposted by someone who wasn't me and then picked up by the Tumblr Radar. From there it was reposted to several Instagram accounts with credit to the individual who reposted it" (personal communication, November 16, 2017).

In APA style, personal communications such as email are cited only in the text of the document and not in the reference list.

These cases tend to not impact the livelihood of the artist, but the unanticipated consequences of reposting work could result in misattribution or lost recognition and work opportunities. Feehan further described his experience with art theft, stating, "Since it [the reposted art] has been up, it's been shared and reposted by several Instagram accounts. . . . I'm a freelance illustrator, it's how I make a living, and social media is a big part of how I find clients and work" (personal communication, November 16, 2017). The indisputable fact is that when an artist's work is shared or reposted without their permission or incorrectly, it encourages the action to take place again until it becomes difficult to find the original creator of the content. This damaging cycle of theft only results in loss for the creator, whether it's a missed job opportunity, revenue, or exposure for their art. While this form of theft is not the most detrimental, it still affects the artist greatly and it is highly applicable to social media users considering its regularity.

▲ Figure 2: **Tuesday Bassen's work being compared to Zara's designs.** (Information from Kurtz, 2016.)

Contrary to these minor incidents, the more severe kind of art theft is when a company or business is taking an artist's work without their knowledge and making profit off of it. The website Shop Art Theft (http://shoparttheft.tumblr.com) has called out fashion retailer Zara and other companies for art theft. It continues to provide shop links to the artist's original designs that were stolen so people can support their work. Several independent artists who are victims of Zara have posted statements on the site, including Adam J. Kurtz, the founder of Shop Art Theft, who wrote, "Our original art has been reproduced as pin and patch sets, embroidered decals and prints on apparel. Though some of the themes may be simple shapes or icons, Zara's replications are near-identical" (Kurtz, 2016).

In this case, Tuesday Bassen and several dozen artists fell victim to the deceitful methods and influence of a large company. The artists were attempting to hold Zara accountable for stealing their designs; however, as of 2017 the infringement case remained unresolved. Kurtz, himself a victim, commented, "When you're doing this on nights and weekends or you're trying to make this full-time creative thing work—which is a huge scary risk—it's extremely disheartening. It tells us that our work is worth nothing" (as quoted in Puglise,

2016, para. 17). When an artist is independent, their income relies on the money they make from their work, so in this case, Bassen and Kurtz have lost thousands of dollars in potential revenue. There are many apparel and home décor companies, including Forever 21, Urban Outfitters, and Hot Topic, which have fallen under accusations of stealing designs from independent artists.

Regardless of the case, these companies know they have a greater legal advantage than independent artists when it comes to disputing infringement claims and continuing to profit off stolen designs. The facilitation of digital art theft is impacting hundreds upon thousands of artists who, in some cases, are unaware that their work is being misused and sold. These severe cases of art theft not only harm an artist's reputation but also their livelihood.

Because art theft has become commonplace on social media, it allows cases of theft to continue and rise in numbers. It has become a major concern for artists worldwide as users share the artist's work on other sites — oftentimes not providing credit or a source, which results in more individuals seeing it while unaware of the authentic creator. Social media sites have become massive facilitators of user-generated content. According to Jessica Gutierrez Alm (2014), "The unprecedented instant transfer of information allows rapid and large-scale infringement. Coupled with the Internet's sharing atmosphere, this has fostered a generation of users who freely disregard copyrights" (p. 104). These disregards of copyright can be seen on any social media site, and given the massive numbers of users per month on sites like Pinterest and Twitter with 317 million, Instagram with 600 million, and Facebook with 1.9 billion, there is a guarantee that content is actively being circulated through various outlets (Hutchinson). Whether the individual claims the content as their own, posts the art without permission from the artist, or does not provide attribution, these kinds of posts are responsible for content being misused and for the impact on the artist's reputation credit. While some aspects for copyrighting original work are not yet adapted to the practices on the internet, Alm (2014) theorized that a court "would likely find social media content to be fixed in tangible form. Therefore, for those works that also meet the originality requirement, this renders at least some user-generated content copyrightable material" (p. 111). Most artwork or original content is copyrighted and therefore should not be misused or stolen, yet online theft still occurs. This means that users do not understand that not all work posted on social media qualifies for "free-use," a commonly accepted belief on the internet. It is crucial that more social media users be made aware of the consequences online theft could have on them or the artist.

There are several misconceptions when it comes to the action of reposting or sharing artwork by social media users. As mentioned earlier, because social media users are often unaware of the harm digital art theft causes to artists and the implications of their actions, digital art theft results in a multitude of cases ranging in severity. Often, the user is under the misapprehension that reposting an image without credit is acceptable since a vast majority of others do it as well. A study conducted by Catherine Marshall and Frank Shipman (2017) examined social norms across social media in regards to sharing images, which was defined as "posting existing user-contributed media on another site or service, possibly without attribution, along with varying degrees of content transformation and varying user intent" (p. 55). Their study revealed that the participants were not able to distinguish whether it was right or wrong to repost or share a piece of work with or without attribution. In other cases, if the user has some awareness of the implications of art theft but is unable or unwilling to search for the source, they'll write: "Artist unknown" or "Credit to Artist" as seen here:

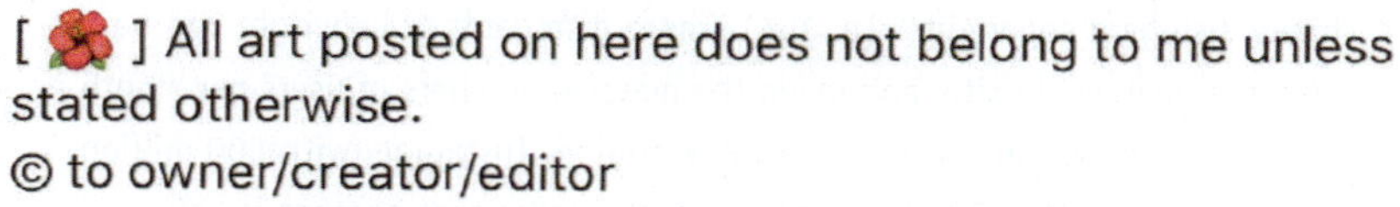

[🌺] All art posted on here does not belong to me unless stated otherwise.
© to owner/creator/editor

▲ **Figure 3: Instance of incorrect attribution.** (Information from Instagram.com, 2017.)

However, this method is ineffective and still causes damage by limiting the exposure the artists could be receiving for their work. These beliefs and misconceptions are leading to the acceptance of "freeuse" on user-generated content, which harms any kind of artist whether it is a musician, photographer, or writer. If users continue not to respect the conditions set by the artist or fail to realize that not all content posted to the internet can be used for the user's own individual or financial gain, artists will no longer feel secure in posting their work. Therefore, individuals should be willing to ask the artist about their policies or locate the source of the piece they would like to repost and search for statements about copyright or usage rights. If they do not do so, they will only further the facilitation of online theft.

To combat online art theft, social media users should know how to recognize stolen/reposted art so they can be sure not to assist in the further theft of an artist's work. One of the first signs they should look for is whether or not there is credit to the artist. They can determine this by checking for the artist's account in the description of the post or see if they are tagged in the image. They should also check whether the image has a poor, grainy quality, filter, or missing watermark/signature. If so, it has most likely been reposted. You can see an example here of my own work:

The writer identifies existing options for addressing the issue she is analyzing.

▲ **Figure 4:** In this case of a repost you can tell the image to the right has been edited and has a poorer quality than the original. Right: original, left: repost. (Information from Instagram.com, 2017.)

Additionally, if the title or description of the work is missing, this usually indicates that the account or user is not the creator of the piece. Finally, if the caption contains promotions or an excessive number of hashtags there is a possibility of it being a repost.

Smith 7

When artwork is shared like this, more individuals are exposed to it through a secondary source, which creates a less direct route to the original artist. If social media users are more attentive to signs of stolen art, they can help artists and disrupt the cycle of reposted artwork.

Another method for preventing reposted or stolen artwork is taking action as a social media user or fan of an artist's work. Artists do not have the number of connections and reach that their followers have and, in most cases, artists hear about the misuse of their work from fans or users who happen to recognize it. Feehan said he "was alerted to the repost case by my followers" (personal communication, November 16, 2017) and Kurtz said he was made aware of the theft of his design when "a European fan tweeted at a few of us whose work was stolen together in a single set of pins available for sale at Zara's store" (as quoted in Gallier, 2015, para. 4). Supporting and respecting the work of artists will allow them to confidently create works knowing they have a community of people looking out for them. Even if alerting the artist seems tedious, you can report the account, which will help the content be removed. Instagram, Pinterest, Tumblr, and Twitter all have their own set of conditions regarding copyright and the DMCA (Digital Millennium Copyright Act) and they have the jurisdiction to proceed in removing posts of copyright infringement or misattribution. An instance of these guidelines being implemented can be seen in the case of *Agence France Presse v. Morel v. Getty Images* (2014): "The court ruled in Morel's favor based on the Twitter terms of service and the news agency's violation of the DMCA" (Tao, 2017, p. 619). Morel sued for the unauthorized use of his work by a news agency that had sold it to multiple news outlets, and due to the DMCA guidelines, he was awarded $1.2 million in damages. These conditions provide artists the rights to protect their work and the security to post their work to a site. Overall, social media users should be mindful of cases of art theft and assist artists in monitoring and defending the use of their work.

> *The writer provides relevant background information for her readers.*

While the Digital Millennium Copyright Act (DMCA) might be effective in some cases, it is lacks new regulations that are applicable to current social media practices. Published in 1998, the DMCA is steadily being criticized for not being relevant to the new ways of the internet. Social media sites like Pinterest that are dependent on the circulation of reposted content, are trying to avoid any drastic changes to the DMCA that might leave them facing

Smith 8

massive legal damages. Craig Carpenter (2013) said Pinterest has prevented this with their terms of service, which "explicitly instruct users to not post images that would violate copyright laws and state that individual users are liable for their own posts" (p. 3). Carpenter also stated, "These steps shelter the host website from most copyright liability under the safe-harbor provisions in the Digital Millennium Copyright Act" (p. 10). Despite such conditions being in place, social media sites allow infringement to occur unless an individual actively monitors or reports the stolen content. In Pinterest's case, 14 million posts are shared every day and 50 billion pins have been posted in total as of 2016 (Lowe). The staggering number of posts cannot be regulated nearly as closely as it should, which results in online theft. It is time for the DMCA to be modified in accordance with current practices on the internet. It needs to be revised so there can be an assurance that content being posted by creators is protected and that users and businesses can actively be held accountable for infringement. Updating the DMCA will limit the amount of online art theft taking place and better defend the use of an artist's work.

Besides involving social media users in reducing art theft, there are methods that artists can utilize that can help prevent the theft of their work. The first is watermarks, which is a way to brand an artist's work and also keep it from being used by other individuals or companies. Several kinds of watermarks can be used, such as the name of your account, a signature, and the location of the post (e.g., Tumblr, Instagram, Twitter, etc.). Some artists place one large watermark placed across the image to prevent any kind of editing to remove it. The kind of watermark depends on the preference of the artist and varies in degrees of protection against theft.

However, in regard to methods to prevent online theft, Feehan wrote, "I know some artists have resorted to putting large watermarks over their images, but as an artist I find that can ruin a piece of art — it's not something I would ever do" (personal communication, November 16, 2017). There are other alternatives when it comes to protecting the work an artist will post online, such as uploading a lower resolution image to ensure that companies cannot use high-resolution files to produce replicas. Unfortunately, this can come at the cost of the quality of the work. Another prevention measure is paying a fee to get a copyright registration for your work. This method, along with hiring a lawyer or attorney to regulate the use of the artist's work, is the most expensive and time consuming. According to Nicolas Wells, a trademark lawyer, "An experienced intellectual property lawyer will typically charge from $250 to $500 to prepare and file your application to register a copyright" (Wells, n.d.). Moreover, in the circumstance you need to hire a lawyer and file a copyright infringement against a company it will cost even more. Tuesday Bassen, a victim of Zara's art theft, stated on Twitter, "I plan to press further charges, but even to have a lawyer get this letter has cost me 2k so far" (2016). There are several options when it comes to preventing online art theft and unfortunately the most reliable methods are the ones that are the most expensive. To artists who do not have the financial means, I would recommend watermarking your work to assert that it belongs to you and using image-tracking resources such as TinEye or reverse Google search to monitor its use. Using these sites, you can track the use of your work and what sites the image appears on, as well as seeing if anyone copied or traced the original piece. Overall, there are reliable measures that can be taken to protect and defend an artist's work and hopefully prevent any cases of theft.

As mentioned, I have seen the online theft of my own art. Time after time, my artwork has surfaced on sites such as Pinterest, Instagram, and Facebook, despite my never having posted it there. In these cases, most of my work is not linked back to me, no credit is given, or it is linked to another person's post. As mentioned earlier, these kinds of posts, which in some cases have accumulated tens of thousands of views, have cost me potential exposure as a young artist. In more severe cases, I have seen my work on product sites like Wish.com, where the company is making profit off my art by selling it on merchandise. In that situation, I very much wanted to remove my work from that site Unfortunately, I could not take any action because I had failed to watermark the image and I did not have the means to send a cease and desist letter. Experiencing the consequences of not protecting and safeguarding my work has only made me more resilient in preventing the theft of my current art. Therefore, I think it is crucial that artists, regardless of their following or skill, should value their work enough to protect it and prevent any kind of theft from taking place.

Art theft is steadily becoming an epidemic among the online art community, and social media users and artists both have the ability to change this. The minor cases of art theft influence the actions of large companies, which furthers the misconception that artwork on the internet can be used

Smith 10

freely. People need to understand that behind every piece of art there is a creator who invested time, money, and resources to create that piece. For individuals and companies to overlook that for their own selfish needs is unacceptable. It is essential that users become more educated in how art theft is detrimental to an artist's name and work, and artists must start taking measures to ensure the protection of their work. When users respect and support the original artist's work, it allows the artist to feel secure in sharing more of their art, which benefits both groups. If these two groups do not take action in preventative measures, art theft will only continue to rise in number and ruin the livelihood and careers of artists using social media.

The conclusion offers two potential outcomes of the problems and solutions that the writer has analyzed.

References

Agence France Presse v. Morel v. Getty Images. No. 1:10-cv-02730-AJN. (S.D.N.Y., 2014, Aug. 12). http://www.loeb.com/-/media/files/publications/2014/08/agence-france-presse.pdf

A legal document found on the web.

Alm, J. G. (2014). "Sharing" copyrights: The copyright implications of user content in social media. *Hamline Journal of Public Law & Policy, 35*(1), 104–131.

An article published in a law journal.

Carpenter, C. C. (2013). Copyright infringement and the second generation social media: Why Pinterest users should be protected from copyright infringement by the fair use defense. *Journal of Internet Law, 16*(7), 1–21.

Gallier, T. (2015, July 26). Independent artists claim high street chain Zara is copying their designs. *BBC*. http://www.bbc.co.uk/newsbeat/article/36884063/independent-artistsclaim-high-street-chain-zara-is-copying-their-designs

The citation for an online article includes the URL.

Hutchinson, A. (2017). Top social network demographics 2017 [Infographic]. *SocialMediaToday*. https://www.socialmediatoday.com/social-networks/top-social-network-demographics-2017-infographic

Kurtz, A. J. (2016). *Shop art theft*. http://shoparttheft.tumblr.com

Lowe, L. (2016). 125 amazing social media statistics you should know in 2016. *SocialPilot*. https://www.socialpilot.co/blog/125-amazing-social-media-statistics-know-2016

Marshall, C. C., & Shipman, F. M. (2017). Who owns the social web? *Communications of the ACM, 60*(5), 52–61. https://doi.org/10.1145/2996181

Puglise, N. (2016, July 21). Fashion brand Zara accused of copying LA artist's designs. *Guardian*. https://www.theguardian.com/fashion/2016/jul/21/zara-accused-copying-artist-designs-fashion

Tao, E. J. (2017). A picture's worth: The future of copyright protection of user-generated images on social media. *Indiana Journal of Global Legal Studies 24*(2), 617–635. https://muse.jhu.edu/article/678127

@TuesdayBassen (2016, July 19). I plan to press further charges, but even to have a lawyer get this LETTER has cost me 2k so far [Tweet]. Twitter. https://twitter.com/tuesdaybassen/status/755555670271795200

Wells, N. (n.d.). How much does a U.S. copyright registration cost? *WellsIpLaw*. Retrieved December 1, 2017, from https://www.wellsiplaw.com/how-much-does-a-u-s-copyright-registration-cost/

Sidenotes:
- Digital object identifiers (DOIs, a unique number assigned to specific content) allow readers to view the source on the web.
- When the source is a social-media site, usernames are acceptable as the author portion of a citation.
- The abbreviation n.d. is used when no publication date is available. A retrieval date is provided for undated sources.

Project Ideas

The following suggestions can help you focus your work on an analytical essay or another type of analytical document.

Suggestions for Essays

1. ANALYZE AN ACADEMIC TREND

Identify a trend in a field of study that interests you. For instance, you might have noticed the increasing use of statistical methods and advanced mathematics in biology courses, a decreasing emphasis on politics and great leaders in history courses, or a growing focus on ethics in business courses. Confirm that the trend exists, through reading, viewing, observing, or interviewing (see Chapter 15). Then choose a main point and express it as a thesis statement (see Chapter 18).

Ask yourself whether the trend has implications for how the field of study addresses issues central to that field and whether it will affect how work is shared with audiences inside or outside the field. To support your analysis, consult scholarly journals, survey instructors in the field, or interview students who are majoring in the field. Provide evidence in the form of quotations, paraphrases, and summaries (see Chapter 21).

2. INTERPRET A RECENT EVENT OR A POPULAR TREND

Interpret a recent event or the rise of a popular trend for an audience of your choice, such as your classmates, other college students, your instructor, your parents, or members of the community. You might focus on an event such as a local ballot initiative, a natural disaster affecting your region, an incident involving law enforcement officers and college students, or anything you've read about in the news that intrigues or worries you. Or you might focus on a trend such as the rise in popularity of a particular kind of music or growing interest in a particular area of study. Like Kelsey Smith (see her essay in the previous section), you might also analyze some potential outcomes of that trend, showing how they impact various groups. In your essay, describe the event or trend and explain why your readers might be interested in it or need to know about it. To support your analysis, draw on published sources (see Chapter 14), or conduct field research using interviews, observations, or surveys (see Chapter 15).

3. ASSESS THE EFFECTS OF A HISTORICAL EVENT

Analyze the long-term consequences of a historical event for an audience of your choice. You might direct your essay to your instructor, your classmates, other college students, your friends, or people working in a particular profession. Choose a historical event that has implications for your audience. For example, if you are writing for people from your hometown, you might choose to write about something that occurred when the town was founded. If you are writing for your instructor or classmates, you might choose something related to education, such as the passage of Title IX, which banned discrimination on the basis of sex in educational programs that receive federal funding, or the Morrill Act, which established public land-grant universities. In your essay, describe the event clearly, identify the sources you used to learn about it, and discuss the implications of the event for your readers.

4. ANALYZE AN ADVERTISEMENT

Write an essay that uses rhetorical analysis to interpret an advertisement. Address your essay to your instructor. Choose an ad that interests you, and develop an interpretive question to guide your analysis. For example, you might ask how ads for a credit card company use appeals to character or logic to elicit a positive response from readers, or you might ask how an ad for a popular brand of beer uses emotional appeals to distinguish the beer from its competitors. If possible, include part or all of the ad as an illustration in your essay. To support your analysis, draw on published sources (see Chapter 14), or conduct field research using interviews, observations, surveys, or correspondence (see Chapter 15).

5. CONDUCT A RHETORICAL ANALYSIS

Write an essay that uses rhetorical analysis to analyze a published source, such as a speech, a video, a television show, or a documentary. You might use elements of the writing situation to analyze how a writer crafted a document — focusing on the writer's purpose, the readers' needs and interests, the context in which the document was read, and the sources used to help accomplish the writer's purpose. Or you might explore how readers of the document or viewers of a media source are likely to react to attempts to achieve the writer's purpose. If you focus on the writer's argument, consider examining the document or media source for use of logical fallacies.

Your essay should show clear links between the points you make in your analysis and relevant passages from the document or media source that is the subject of your analysis. Ideally, you will use quotations, paraphrases, summaries from a written document, or media clips to illustrate the points you make in your essay.

Suggestions for Other Genres

6. DRAFT AND DESIGN A COLUMN FOR A MAGAZINE

Decide whether you want to write about a particular subject or submit your column to a particular magazine. If you have a specific subject in mind, search your library's databases and the web for articles that address it. This can help you identify magazines that might be interested in your column. If you want to publish your column in a particular magazine, read two or three issues cover to cover to determine the kinds of subjects it normally addresses. Once you've selected a target magazine, analyze it to determine its writing conventions (such as the level of formality and the manner in which sources are acknowledged) and design conventions. You can read more about design principles in Chapter 22. As you learn about your subject and plan, organize, and design your column, keep in mind what you've learned about the columns you've read. Your column should reflect those writing and design conventions.

While most columns rely heavily on personal experience, support your analysis by drawing on published sources and, if appropriate, by using observation, interviews, surveys, and correspondence. If you provide evidence from published sources, use the strategies for integrating sources discussed in Chapter 21. As you plan and draft your column, avoid shifting from analyzing your subject to reporting on it. While it will be important — even necessary — to help readers understand that subject, you should focus the majority of your column on analysis.

7. CREATE A NEWS ANALYSIS

Begin working on your news analysis by identifying an event to analyze. Consider whether analyzing this event will help you accomplish your purposes as a writer. Then reflect on whether your readers will want or need to know about the event. Finally, identify the newspaper, magazine, or website where you'd like to publish your news analysis.

Once you've made these preliminary decisions, learn more about the event by using your library's databases to identify relevant news reports and commentaries by other analysts. For more information about using databases, see Chapter 14. Consider using correspondence (see Chapter 15) to reach out to experts on the issue or to contact individuals who might be familiar with the event. Use what you learn about the event to plan, organize, and design your news analysis.

As you plan and draft your news analysis, avoid focusing largely on providing information about the event. While it will be important — even necessary — to help readers understand the event, you should focus most strongly on analysis. To check on your success in providing your analysis, seek feedback on your drafts from other writers (friends, classmates, relatives) and from your instructor.

8. ANALYZE A POEM, SHORT STORY, OR NOVEL

Analyze a poem, short story, or novel that you've read recently. Address your analysis to your instructor and other readers who share your interest in this work of literature. Focus on a clearly stated interpretive question, and use text analysis as your interpretive framework.

As you carry out your analysis, consider which elements of literary analysis you might use. You might focus on common literary elements, such as theme, plot, setting, characterization, imagery, style, and structure. You might also focus on the writing situation in which the author worked. For example, you could explore the social, cultural, political, and historical contexts that shaped the author's efforts. Or you might focus on what you can learn about why the author created the work and how well the author understood how readers would react to it. Base your analysis not only on what is clearly present in the work but also on what can be found between the lines.

Support your analysis by drawing on the work of literature and published reviews or journal articles. In your essay, identify and briefly describe the work you're analyzing. Then offer your interpretation of the work.

In Summary: Writing an Analytical Essay

* **Find a conversation and listen in (p. 256).**
  - Reflect on your surroundings (p. 256).
  - Ask interpretive questions (p. 257).
  - Search for sources (p. 259).
* **Conduct your analysis (p. 261).**
  - Refine your question (p. 261).
  - Seek a fuller understanding of your subject (p. 262).
  - Apply an interpretive framework (p. 264).
* **Prepare a draft (p. 274).**
  - Make an interpretive claim (p. 274).
  - Explain your interpretation (p. 274).
  - Consider genre and design (p. 277).
  - Frame your analysis (p. 278).
* **Review and improve your draft (p. 279).**
  - Ensure that your claim is debatable (p. 279).
  - Challenge your conclusions (p. 279).
  - Examine the application of your interpretive framework (p. 279).
  - Assess your organization (p. 280).
  - Respond to feedback from your instructor (p. 281).

10 Writing to Evaluate

What is writing to evaluate? 297

What kinds of documents are used to share evaluations? 299

Scholarly articles 299
   Thomas Polk, *A Review of the* MLA Handbook, *Eighth Edition* 299

Web-based articles 304
   Marie-Helen Maras, *4 Ways 'Internet of Things' Toys Endanger Children* 304

Media reviews 307
   Justin Kanoya, *Thoughts on* Crazy Rich Asians: *How Representation Impacts Self-Worth* 307

Progress reports 311
   National Cancer Institute, Excerpts from *Cancer Trends Progress Report* 311

Genre Talk: Evaluative Writing 321

How can I write an evaluative essay? 322

Find a conversation and listen in 322
Conduct your evaluation 327
Prepare a draft 331
Review and improve your draft 336

✳ **Student Essay** 339
   Brooke Shannon, *Is* Wicked *All That Wicked?* 339

✳ **Project Ideas** 344

What Is Writing to Evaluate?

As readers, we seek out evaluative documents as much as any other type of writing. We search for reviews of new movies and restaurants; we surf the web to learn about the strengths and weaknesses of products ranging from treadmills to phones to insect repellents; and we read editorials, letters to the editor, and columns in online magazines in the hope that they will help us develop an informed opinion about recent issues and events.

Writing to evaluate involves adopting the role of *evaluator* (see Chapter 6). Writers who adopt this role focus on reaching an informed, well-reasoned conclusion about a subject's worth or effectiveness and clearly conveying their judgments to readers. Their writing is usually balanced, and they generally offer clear reasoning and ample evidence to support their judgments.

Evaluative documents make important contributions not only to our personal lives but also to written conversations. On an individual level, evaluations help us make decisions that can affect everything from the brand of car we drive to how we vote in the next election to where we attend college. Within a written conversation, evaluations provide the basis for making collective judgments about how to move the conversation forward.

THE WRITER'S ROLE:
Evaluator

As an **evaluator**, I write with certain criteria in mind.

PURPOSE
- To determine whether something has succeeded or failed
- To improve or refine something
- To provide a basis for choosing among alternatives

READERS
- Want another person's opinion
- Expect judgments to be based on appropriate criteria and supported with evidence and analysis

SOURCES
- The subject itself is often an important source of evidence.
- Published documents, personal experiences, and, in some cases, interviews and observations provide additional support.
- Reviewing other sources alerts evaluators to alternative opinions and perspectives.

CONTEXT
- Decisions about criteria and evidence reflect a writer's knowledge of readers, of the subject, and of its background and setting.
- Effective evaluations balance positive and negative assessments and acknowledge alternative perspectives.

CRITICAL THINKING

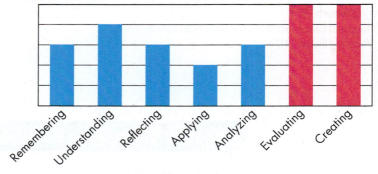

What Kinds of Documents Are Used to Share Evaluations?

Writers can draw on a wide range of documents to share their judgments. Their evaluations might appear in print, as is often the case with articles and editorials, or on the web, which is increasingly home to reviews, many of them posted to discussion boards and electronic mailing lists. In writing and writing-intensive courses, the most frequently assigned evaluative projects include essays, reports, blog entries, and source evaluations.

Evaluative documents make important contributions to conversations that focus on the relative merits of products, media, policies, proposals, and artistic works, and they often stand on their own as assessments, opinions, or advice that readers seek out as they try to form their own judgments. Evaluations can also contribute to broader conversations that focus less on judgment alone and more on problem solving or argument. For example, an evaluative report on a U.S. government program might help a writer support a proposal to change foreign policy. The following sections offer discussions and examples of four of the most common evaluative genres: scholarly articles, web-based articles, media reviews, and progress reports.

Scholarly Articles

Thomas Polk
A Review of the MLA Handbook, *Eighth Edition*

Scholarly articles convey a writer's judgment to readers who share an interest in an academic discipline, such as biochemistry, sociology, or art history. In the following article from the academic journal *Across the Disciplines*, author Thomas Polk evaluates the significant changes made to the Modern Language Association's (MLA) documentation guidelines. Polk's evaluation is positive, although he points out changes that will likely cause concern to scholars who have come to rely on the MLA's guidance on research writing.

A Review of the *MLA Handbook*, Eighth Edition

Reviewed by Thomas Polk
George Mason University

> Thomas Polk is a doctoral candidate at George Mason University.

Modern Language Association of America. (2016). *MLA Handbook* (8th ed.). Modern Language Association of America.

In his 2014 article "References, Please," Tim Parks asks a question that many of us have either heard or asked ourselves: "Are we never going to acknowledge that modern technology has changed things?" *Things*, for Parks, means the landscape of scholarship and its citation practices. While he is partly venting frustration in his article, Parks is also asking an important question: is a rigorous citation style, like that prescribed by the MLA, necessary in the age of Google? Do we need to vex ourselves trying to find the page number for a quote in a book we read electronically when that quote can often be found simply by typing it into a search engine? Does including information about the publisher and its home city really increase the quality of research?

> Polk frames the issue by pointing to questions regarding the usefulness of citation systems.

Probably not. But formal citations do play an important role in scholarship, according to Kathleen Fitzpatrick, the principal writer of the 8th edition of the *MLA Handbook*. In her response to Parks and defense of (MLA's) citation style, "The Future of Academic Style: Why Citations Still Matter in the Age of Google" (2016a), Fitzpatrick argues that citation practice might be *the* thing that centralizes scholarship, even more so than a discipline's "subject matter, its vocabulary, or its syntax. . . . Citations in academic writing . . . are intended to refer the questioning reader back to the sources or precedents for the argument at hand." By which she means, citations are the mechanism through which academic conversations take place. So, while few people outside of the English department and Humanities fields might pay attention to the MLA, the conversations spurring and responding to the most recent changes of its "style Bible" serve as a compelling example of similar conversations that have and will continue to occur throughout academia.

> Polk responds to the question by citing and quoting from another scholarly article. He uses APA style, which is followed in the journal that published his article.

As evidenced by Fitzpatrick's (2016a) response to Parks, the 8th edition of the *MLA Handbook* is shaped by an awareness of the growing disinterest and outright criticism of its rigid style from the digital community and others with similar proclivities. The homegrown attribution approaches of Internet users (replete with their "h/t" and hyperlink) have become too popular for the MLA to ignore. Thus, Rosemary Feal, the Executive Director of the MLA, writes in the "Foreword" to the 8th edition, "We release new editions of the *MLA Handbook* when developments in scholarly research and writing call for changes in MLA style. The eighth edition brings one of our greatest shifts ever" (2016, viii). That shift is rooted in the MLA's interest in focusing not on a prescription of correct form but "on the writer's decision making" (Fitzpatrick, 2016b, xii). And while that shift might not fully attend to Parks' (2014) suggestion to "wipe the slate clean," this new approach does result in a dramatically different, and arguably better, product.

Perhaps, what is most notable about the latest edition of the *MLA Handbook* is not what *is* present but what is *not* present, which is quite a lot. Fitzpatrick and her collaborators ended up with a print edition that is roughly half the size of the previous edition (from 292 pages in the 7th edition down to 146 in the 8th), with a proportional discount in price ($22.00 down to $12.00). That reduction also finds its way into the title, which no longer carries the phrase "for Writers of Research Papers." The loss of the language in the title is especially telling of the attention this latest edition pays to digital communities and the MLA's interest in maintaining contact with current pedagogical practices. Although these reductions might be a welcome change for some readers, they might also irk others who appreciated the depth and breadth of information covered in previous editions.

> Polk describes significant changes to the *Handbook*, pointing to a reduction in coverage of research writing practices. He notes that these changes might cause concern to some scholars.

The most tangible and principal result of the renovated perspective is a citation template almost certainly inspired by a variety of online citation generators. The template is built around nine core elements: author, title, title of container, other contributors, version, number, publisher, publication date, and location. These elements aren't really any different from before, but their presentation is. In the old format, the MLA simply listed the many different formulas and models that writers would use to create citations. In the new presentation, readers first encounter the template graphic listing each element in order followed by the appropriate piece of punctuation that should be used in the works-cited entry. In the following sections of the *Handbook*, each element is explained with depth sufficient enough to include graphics demonstrating where the element may be found in different sources (e.g., a book, an article, or a blog).

This new edition also adopts the word "container" to represent larger media that contain smaller media, such as a database that contains many articles or a video game that contains a book. (Fitzpatrick specifically mentions a question about this kind of source in her article "The Future of Academic Style: Why Citations Still Matter in the Age of Google").

> Polk offers his approval of two changes that will cause concern to some scholars. He refers to two criteria, consistency with existing practices and correctness, neither of which are defined in the review but both of which will be understood by his readers.

Fitzpatrick (2016b) takes care to explain this new concept, which results in the juxtaposition of a citation for an article in *The Georgia Review* found in *JSTOR* next to a citation for an episode of *Pretty Little Liars* viewed through *Hulu*.

Certain to cause conversation (and controversy) are two particular changes: the removal of the long list of model citations and the return of URLs. While the 8th edition does contain a handful of model citations, many educators will undoubtedly lament the fact that they no longer can direct students (or themselves) to a model citation for a variety of sources. However, creating a model citation for all possible sources a writer might reference becomes a Sisyphean effort doomed to fail in the end because of the dynamic nature of information in today's (scholarly) landscape. We are constantly creating new types and combinations of sources, and the result of that creation is an impossibly long list of models that is at best incomplete. Accepting and acknowledging this reality provides the MLA with an opportunity to either double down on its past approach or to reinvent itself. Fortunately, Fitzpatrick (2016b) chooses the latter option and adopts an orientation informed more by practice than correctness.

And certainly, the re-appearance of the URL will cause some aestheticians to cringe. URLs, however, can serve a practical purpose by providing readers access to the same source used by a writer, which becomes important as sources continue to proliferate across the Internet challenging our ability to read the same sources peers used to craft their research. This last point might be what Fitzpatrick (2016a) had in mind when she described citation systems as "future-oriented." She writes, "When a reader searches for a quotation, she is likely to turn up not just the original source of that quotation but also a host of copies, borrowings, and reuses, texts in which that quotation appears but from which it did not originate." The strength of academic citations, Fitzpatrick contends in her response to Parks, lies in their ability to reliably guide a reader to the exact source a writer has used. Of course, we might question the reliability of URLs, and the MLA, aware of their imperfect nature, is not holding fast to their inclusion in the works-cited list. Though the MLA does believe the "location" of a source is a core element, they remain open to omitting URLs altogether based upon an instructor's (or presumably a writer's) preference. They also smartly advise writers to use DOIs or permalinks when available.

> The conclusion offers the overall judgment that the *Handbook* has achieved the goal of keeping pace with changes in the discipline.

Both of these changes, however, are the manifestation of a deeper choice the MLA has made. It will be easy to either celebrate or criticize them, but the shift from prescribing model citations to framing a citation practice is an important advancement and one that is attempting to keep in touch with current pedagogical and assessment practices. The MLAs grappling with the juxtaposition between fixity and fluidity, past and future, denotes a profound soul searching for such a foundational organization and a potentially pivotal moment in the evolution of academic citation style. Fitzpatrick (2016a) hopes that the 8th edition becomes a catalyst for a new movement in citation practice "that makes the academic style guide seem less like a misnomer, and more like a set of natural practices through which scholars can help organize the often unruly publications by which we are increasingly surrounded." Thus, the MLA publishes its "groundbreaking" edition "for the digital age" in its interest in staying, well, *modern*.

References

Feal, Rosemary. (2016). Foreword. In *MLA handbook* (8th ed.) (pp. vii–viii). Modern Language Association of America.

Fitzpatrick, Kathleen. (2016a, March 29). The future of academic style: Why citations matter in the age of Google. *Los Angeles Review of Books.* https://lareviewofbooks.org/article/the-future-of-academic-style-why-citations-still-matter-in-the-age-of-google/

Fitzpatrick, Kathleen. (2016b). Preface. In *MLA handbook* (8th ed.) (pp. ix–xiv). Modern Language Association of America.

Parks, Tim. (2014, September 13). References, please. *The New York Review of Books.* http://www.nybooks.com/daily/2014/09/13/references-please/

An APA style reference list is provided. The journal in which it was published departs from APA style in a few ways, one of which is requiring that first names be spelled out in the reference list.

Starting a Conversation: Thinking Critically about "A Review of the *MLA Handbook*, Eighth Edition"

In your writer's notebook, consider how Polk responds to his writing situation by answering the following questions:

1. Polk frames the issue by pointing to questions regarding the usefulness of citation systems. Why do you think he does this? What does he accomplish by doing so?

2. How does Polk incorporate into the article existing scholarship about documentation systems? Why is this acknowledgment important in a piece of scholarly writing?

3. What criteria does Polk use to evaluate the effectiveness of the *Handbook*? How well does the book measure up to these criteria?

4. In his conclusion, Polk offers a favorable evaluation of the *Handbook*. In making that judgment, what criterion seem to be most important to him? Why do you think he relies on that criterion?

5. **Reflection:** As a current student, what do you think about the value of the changes made to the *Handbook*? Do you find Polk's evaluation reasonable? Why or why not?

Web-Based Articles

Marie-Helen Maras

4 Ways 'Internet of Things' Toys Endanger Children

A number of major magazines, such as *Time*, *The Atlantic*, and *Wired*, offer online versions of their publications, providing electronic copies of print articles along with material written specifically for the web edition. Many magazines, however, publish exclusively on the web. Some of these online publications, such as *Slate* and *Salon*, appeal to a general audience. Others, such as *PC Magazine* (www.pcmag.com) or *Rocky Mountain Bride* (www.rockymountainbride.com), cater to readers with specific interests. In either case, web-based magazines typically offer a mix of traditional articles and essays, blogs, video entries, news feeds, and reader-response forums. This article from *The Conversation*, written by an associate professor at John Jay College of Criminal Justice, analyzes potential hazards in toys that connect to the internet.

4 Ways 'Internet of Things' Toys Endanger Children

By Marie-Helen Maras

As Amazon releases an Echo Dot smart-home device aimed at children, it's entering a busy and growing marketplace. More than one-third of U.S. homes with children have at least one "internet of things" connected toy — like a cuddly creature who can listen to and respond to a child's inquiries. Many more of these devices are on the way, around the world and in North America specifically.

These toys wirelessly connect with online databases to recognize voices and images, identifying children's queries, commands and requests and responding to them. They're often billed as improving children's quality of play, providing children with new experiences of collaborative play, and developing children's literacy, numeric and social skills.

Analytical web-based articles often begin with a question or a problematic fact or puzzling situation that leads to a question. Writers of such articles should know about and understand the history and significance of their subjects.

Online devices raise privacy concerns for all their users, but children are particularly vulnerable and have special legal protections. Consumer advocates have raised alarms about the toys' insecure wireless internet connections — either directly over Wi-Fi or via Bluetooth to a smartphone or tablet with internet access.

As someone with both academic and practical experience in security, law enforcement and applied technology, I know these fears are not hypothetical. Here are four examples of when internet of things toys put kids' security and privacy at risk.

Writers of online articles often embed links to their sources within the text of their documents instead of listing them at the end, allowing readers to jump directly to cited works as they read. When it was published in *The Conversation*, this article included such links as well, providing additional background to support statements such as this one.

1. Unsecured Wireless Connections

Some "internet of things" toys can connect to smartphone apps without any form of authentication. So a user can download a free app, find an associated toy nearby, and then communicate directly with the child playing with that toy. In 2015, security researchers discovered that Hello Barbie, an internet-enabled Barbie doll, automatically connected to unsecured Wi-Fi networks that broadcast the network name "Barbie." It would be very simple for an attacker to set up a Wi-Fi network with that name and communicate directly with an unsuspecting child.

Depending on the specific publication and writing situation, they might rely on statistical evidence, personal experience, or direct observation. In many cases, they must clearly explain unfamiliar background material or interpret complex data for their readers.

The same thing could happen with unsecured Bluetooth connections to the Toy-Fi Teddy, I-Que Intelligent Robot and Furby Connect toys, a British consumer watchdog group revealed in 2017.

The toys' ability to monitor children — even when used as intended and connected to official networks belonging to a toy's manufacturer — violates Germany's anti-surveillance laws. In 2017, German authorities declared the My Friend Cayla doll was an "illegal espionage apparatus," ordering stores to pull it off the shelves and requiring parents to destroy or disable the toys.

Unsecured devices allow attackers to do more than just talk to children: A toy can talk to another internet-connected device, too. In 2017, security researchers hijacked a CloudPets connected stuffed animal and used it to place an order through an Amazon Echo in the same room.

Articles in online magazines can draw on a variety of sources, ranging from interviews, surveys, published studies, and scholarly works to popular culture and personal observation.

2. Tracking Kids' Movements

Some internet-connected toys have GPS like those in fitness trackers and smartphones, which can also reveal users' locations, even if those users are children. In addition, the Bluetooth communications some toys use can be detected as far away as 30 feet. If someone within that range looks for a Bluetooth device — even if they're only seeking to pair their own headphones with a smartphone — they'll see the toy's name, and know a child is nearby.

For instance, the Consumer Council of Norway found that smartwatches marketed to children were storing and transmitting locations without encryption, allowing strangers to track children's movements. That group issued an alert in its country, but the discovery led authorities in Germany to ban the sale of children's smartwatches.

3. Poor Data Protections

Internet-connected toys have cameras that watch kids and microphones that listen to them, recording what they see and hear. Sometimes they send that information to company servers that analyze the inputs and send back directions on how the toy should respond. But those functions can also be hijacked to listen in on family conversations or take photographs or video of children without the kids or parents ever noticing.

Toy manufacturers don't always ensure the data is stored and transmitted securely, even when laws require it: In 2018, toymaker VTech was fined US $650,000 for failing to fulfill its promises to encrypt private data and for violating U.S. laws protecting children's privacy.

4. Working with Third Parties

Toy companies have also shared the information they collect about kids with other companies — much as Facebook shared its users' data with Cambridge Analytica and other firms.

And they can also surreptitiously share information from third parties with kids. One toy company came under fire, for example, in both Norway and the U.S. for a business relationship with Disney in which the My Friend Cayla doll was programmed to discuss what were described as the doll's favorite Disney movies with kids. Parents weren't told about this arrangement, which critics said amounted to "product placement"-style advertising in a toy.

What Can Parents Do?

In my view, and according to consumer advice from the FBI, parents should carefully research internet-connected toys before buying them, and evaluate their capabilities, functioning, and security and privacy settings before bringing these devices into their homes. Without proper safeguards — by parents, if not toy companies — children are at risk, both individually and through collection of aggregate data about kids' activities.

> Commenting functions following evaluative articles encourage readers to respond to writers in a public forum, creating an ongoing written conversation that anyone can join. In these and other ways, analytical discussions usually move forward more quickly and more unpredictably online than they do in print journals.

In your writer's notebook, record your thoughts on "4 Ways 'Internet of Things' Toys Endanger Children" by responding to the following questions:

1. The outcome of the evaluation is clearly stated in the title. Why do you think Maras made this style choice? What impact does it have on the reader?

2. Unlike some evaluations, this piece does not compare similar products. Instead, it analyzes and evaluates an entire market of products (Internet of Things–enabled toys). How does this format affect the content of the evaluation? How does it affect its tone?

3. How does Maras address counterarguments to her analysis? How effectively are the counterarguments addressed? Can you think of any holes in her analysis that have not been addressed at all?

4. What types of evidence are supplied to support the claim of the evaluation? How does Maras use each type of evidence? Did you find the evidence convincing? Why or why not?

5. **Reflection:** What was your opinion of the Internet of Things and other smart technology before reading this evaluation? Did the evaluation change your opinion? What aspect of the evaluation was most persuasive?

Starting a Conversation: Thinking Critically about "4 Ways 'Internet of Things' Toys Endanger Children"

Media Reviews

Justin Kanoya

Thoughts on Crazy Rich Asians: *How Representation Impacts Self-Worth*

Media reviews present an evaluation of a work of art, a song or music album, a television program, a book, a movie or play, a computer game, a DVD, a website, or any of a number of other cultural productions. This review, by DJ and occasional writer Justin Kanoya, evaluates a blockbuster film and applies the criteria of cultural and societal merit to the usual qualifications for a successful movie.

Thoughts on *Crazy Rich Asians:* How Representation Impacts Self-Worth

Justin Kanoya

> The subject of the review reflects the shared interests of the group of writers and readers involved in a written conversation. Author Justin Kanoya focuses on the cultural impact of *Crazy Rich Asians* as a lens for understanding its value.

A few years back, Jon Mertz scribed an article on Thin Difference about principles that lead to a life well lived.

They were these two simple statements:

> What you do in your present matters.
> What you pass forward matters.

This goes along with the idea that, for me, the most important thing we need is positive self-worth. It's not money, not even family . . . but how we feel about ourselves. And of course, how we make others feel about themselves.

The way we go about our days and what we are putting out in the world, are the things that inspire others and sustain for future generations.

How Representation Impacts Self-Worth

This entire thought process has come to mind with the recent release of "Crazy Rich Asians," (CRA) the first motion picture, with an all Asian lead cast, to be released by a major Hollywood studio since "The Joy Luck Club" in 1993. It's worth noting in 2002, the smaller yet still significant MTV Films released "Better Luck Tomorrow," which also included an all Asian cast.

CRA is a really good movie. While I'm not a qualified film critic, there are those that are giving it praise and even the Star Lord himself, actor Chris Pratt, tweeted "Holy crap, what an awesome movie!! Haven't seen a movie that good in a long, long time."

Not that box office receipts translate into Oscar statues, but it did rake in more than $25 million in its opening weekend, so the court of public opinion must also be pretty favorable.

All this fuss over a romantic comedy. It's not a period piece, documentary, or a film with the million dollar special effects. The film is a simple love story, as cliché as Julia Roberts or Meg Ryan, Cameron Diaz or Jennifer Aniston getting the boy, then losing the boy and then getting the boy again.

But what is the difference this time around? It's the actors on the screen — all of them. The leading roles, the extras, even the setting and the city. They are all Asian.

> Because media reviewers expect their readers to understand what's necessary for success in a particular medium, they often do not define their criteria. For example, a movie critic will assume that readers are familiar with the importance of acting, plot, and cinematography. In this review, the author argues that "the court of public opinion" has deemed it a success, regardless of the more accepted critical criteria.

And that is really something special to see.

An entire cast of Asians is carrying a $30 million, big-studio film. You also won't see one scene of kung fu fighting, not one gangster, not one stroll through a red light district. All the typical portrayals of someone of Asian descent on the silver screen.

Representation Matters Because It Inspires

About halfway through the film, I was genuinely moved by what I was seeing, and it had nothing to do with the story. It was the actors — all Asian. They had American, British and Chinese accents.

They were not token characters. They were the movie. Watching a film like this, as an Asian American, is refreshing. Watching it, as a Caucasian, is eye-opening — I would hope.

We've heard of the aspiring black politician who said he was inspired because Barack Obama "looked like me." Or the aspiring Asian American journalist who was inspired because Connie Chung "looked like me."

Constance Wu, who plays the lead female character, said this: "Before CRA, I hadn't even done a tiny part in a studio film," she said. "I never dreamed I would get to star in one because I had never seen that happen to someone who looked like me."

Who knows what a film like "Crazy Rich Asians" will do for aspiring Asian American actors? Or just anyone dreaming of a life better than where they are now.

It's hard to put into words what it was like watching the film and having these thoughts unfold in my mind.

Representation Shapes Opinions and Attitudes

Like it or not, what is put in front of us for our entertainment contributes to the opinions we have of people, places and cultures. When there is a lack of inclusion, there is a lack of empathy.

But inclusion needs to be positive. It cannot mean the same thing over and over: the black teenager in a gang, the Latino drug dealer, the Asian karate teacher or the weak white female.

What happens to our self-worth if we are only exposed to negative portrayals of our culture? What legacies are we passing forward?

A film like CRA is doing what we need in the present exactly. It's doing something that not only matters today, but is likely stamping a significant impact for years to come.

Despite having an all Asian cast, CRA is not an "Asian movie." It's

> What we consume as entertainment contributes to the opinions we have of people, places and cultures.

> The evidence used to determine whether the subject of a review has met the criteria for success is most often drawn from the subject itself and from the reviewer's personal interpretation, although writers sometimes include evidence from interviews, surveys, or published sources to support their evaluations. In this case, the author is deeming the movie successful because of his understanding of its social impact, drawing on quotes from some of the cast and the history of films with all-Asian casts as supporting evidence.

just a good movie. A story about love and how much culture and upbringing factors into the personal decisions these characters make. A cliché storyline? Perhaps. But this time, finally, Asians were telling it.

As noted earlier "Better Luck Tomorrow" and "The Joy Luck Club" were the last films released in America with an all Asian cast. Those were 16 and 23 years ago, respectively.

Hopefully, we won't have to wait so long for the next one. And hopefully a positive portrayal of diversity and inclusion will just be the norm and not the occasional, once every couple decades thing it is now.

Starting a Conversation: Thinking Critically about "Thoughts on *Crazy Rich Asians*: How Representation Impacts Self-Worth"

In your writer's notebook, record your thoughts on Kanoya's review by responding to the following questions:

1. Describe the tone Kanoya uses in his review. Is his writing style formal or casual? What kind of language does he use to describe *Crazy Rich Asians*? How do these descriptions reflect Kanoya's evaluation of the film?

2. Kanoya uses comparison and contrast to explain the ways in which, in his opinion, *Crazy Rich Asians* is different from other successful romantic comedies. To whom or what does he draw the comparison? Why is that comparison significant to Kanoya, and why does he feel that it should be significant to his readers?

3. In the third-to-last paragraph, Kanoya notes that *Crazy Rich Asians* is "not an 'Asian movie.'" What does he mean by an "Asian movie," and why is this significant to his point? Would more explanation of the difference between an "Asian movie" and a movie with an all-Asian cast make Kanoya's argument stronger, or is his target audience likely to understand his distinction?

4. Ultimately, what is Kanoya's position on *Crazy Rich Asians*? How can you tell? Explain in a few sentences why you agree (or disagree) with his review.

5. **Reflection:** Consider times in your life when you have relied on reviews. Perhaps you have consulted reviews during a major event like purchasing a car or even for the more routine question of where to eat dinner. What kind of information is important to you in a review? What makes you trust a review or take its judgment seriously?

Progress Reports

National Cancer Institute
Excerpts from Cancer Trends Progress Report

Progress reports provide an assessment of a project or an initiative. For example, a state environmental agency might issue a report on its efforts to reduce pesticide and fertilizer runoff from farmland into state watersheds. The National Cancer Institute, which compiled this progress report, is a government-run agency working on cancer research. This particular report, housed at progressreport.cancer.gov, is continually updated in order to provide an up-to-date summary of the work of the National Cancer Institute.

INTRODUCTION

The nation's investment in cancer research is making a difference. The rate of death from cancer continues to decline among both men and women, among all major racial and ethnic groups, and for the most common types of cancer, including lung, colon, breast, and prostate cancers. The death rate from all cancers combined continues to decline, as it has since the early 1990s. Many people who have had cancer live longer and enjoy a better quality of life than was possible years ago. This steady improvement in survival reflects progress in diagnosing certain cancers at an earlier stage, improvements in treatment, and the results of public health initiatives encouraging preventative measures and screening.

Still, cancer remains a major public health problem that profoundly affects the more than 1.6 million people diagnosed each year, as well as their families and friends.

- Cancer remains the second most common cause of death in the United States, exceeded only by heart disease, accounting for nearly one in every four deaths.
- The incidence of some cancers, including kidney, thyroid, pancreas, liver, uterus, melanoma of the skin, myeloma (cancer of plasma cells), leukemia, testis and oral cavity and pharynx, is rising.

- The burden of some types of cancer weighs more heavily on some groups than on others. The rates of both new cases and deaths from cancer vary by socioeconomic status, sex, and racial and ethnic group.
- The economic burden of cancer also is taking its toll. As the U.S. population ages and newer technologies and treatments become available, national expenditures for cancer continue to rise and could potentially exceed overall medical care expenditures combined.

Why a Progress Report Is Needed

Since the signing of the National Cancer Act in 1971, our country has vigorously fought the devastating effects of cancer. Now it is time to see how far we have come. The *Cancer Trends Progress Report* is a series of reports that describe the nation's progress against cancer through research and related efforts. The report is based on the most recent data at the time of analysis from the National Cancer Institute, the Centers for Disease Control and Prevention, other federal agencies, professional groups, and cancer researchers.

The *Cancer Trends Progress Report* was designed to help the nation review past efforts and plan future ones. The public can use the report to better understand the nature and results of strategies to fight cancer. Researchers, clinicians, and public health providers can focus on the gaps and opportunities identified in the report, paving the way for future progress against cancer. Policymakers can use the report to evaluate our progress relative to our investment in cancer research discovery, program development, and service delivery.

What's in the Report

The *Cancer Trends Progress Report* includes key measures of progress along the cancer control continuum.

- **Prevention.** The measures in this section cover behaviors that can help people prevent cancer, the most important of which is avoiding tobacco use and secondhand smoke exposure. This section also addresses physical activity, dietary choices and alcohol consumption, and exposure to sun and chemicals in the environment.
- **Early Detection.** Screening tests provide ways to find cancers early, when there is the best chance for cure. This section describes the extent to which

> Report formats vary widely. Government reports, for example, are often distributed as bound documents, as well as in downloadable formats. Reports such as this one, which are made up of entire websites, are more rare. In contrast, reports written for a company or a political group might be distributed to only a small group of readers. Regardless of the number of readers, however, the writers of these documents often put a great deal of effort into the report's design.

people are following recommended screening guidelines to detect breast, cervical, colorectal, lung and prostate cancers.

- **Diagnosis.** We can learn much about our progress against cancer by looking at the rates of new cancer cases (incidence) and cancers diagnosed at late stages. This section reviews both these areas.
- **Treatment.** This section describes common treatment options and measures the rates at which people are undergoing those treatments. It also describes new treatment options emerging from ongoing research and monitoring activities.
- **Life After Cancer.** This section addresses trends in the proportion of cancer patients who are alive 5 years after their diagnosis, the costs of cancer care, and the health behaviors among survivors.
- **End of Life.** This section includes the rate of deaths (mortality) from cancer and the estimated number of years of life lost (person-years of life lost) due to cancer.

Where possible, the *Cancer Trends Progress Report* shows changes in these data over time (trends). This report shows whether the trends are "rising," "falling," or "stable" using standard definitions and tests of the statistical significance of the trends (see Methodology for Categorizing Trends). For some measures, differences in the cancer burden among various U.S. racial and ethnic groups, income groups, and groups by level of educational attainment, are also presented.

Most of the measures for age-adjusted cancer death rates in this report are identical to those presented in Healthy People 2020, a comprehensive set of 10-year health objectives for the nation sponsored by the U.S. Department of Health and Human Services. This enabled us to show the nation's progress relative to cancer-related targets for Healthy People 2020.

How Data Were Selected

In selecting measures that would be meaningful to readers of this report, we relied largely on long-term national—rather than state or local—data collection efforts. (State and local data are available online at State Cancer Profiles). The report includes more measures for prevention than for other segments of the continuum, because preventive measures hold so much potential in positively impacting national progress to reduce the burden of cancer. A substantial proportion of

> Longer reports, particularly those that assess the effectiveness of a project or an initiative, often rely on information gathered by researchers associated with the project. The source of this kind of evidence might include surveys, interviews, testing, observation, and reviews of published sources.

cancers could be prevented by behavioral choices, making prevention a key focus of the report.

The data in the *Cancer Trends Progress Report* come from a variety of systems and surveys with different collection techniques and reporting times, so time periods may vary. The starting point or baseline year against which to measure how well the nation is progressing toward the Healthy People 2020 targets depends on the data available. For example, data for most Diagnosis, Life After Cancer, and End of Life measures are available starting in 1975, while data for most Prevention, Early Detection, and Treatment measures are available beginning in the late 1980s or early 1990s.

TRENDS AT A GLANCE

Last Updated:

February 2018

The Trends-at-a-Glance offers an overview of trend direction measure by measure. Trends noted as stable or non-significant change (NSC) are not changing significantly. The difference between "stable" and "non-significant change" is based on statistical computations described in the Methodology for Characterizing Trends appendix.

The table below provides a snapshot of recent national trends (as characterized by the Average Annual Percent Change [AAPC]) for measures included in this report. Green indicates that the recent trend is moving in the desired direction. Red indicates that the recent trend is not moving in the desired direction. Purple indicates that the recent trend is moving but it is indeterminate whether the direction is desired or not. There is no background color for trends that are stable or show a non-significant change in direction. The column labeled "Recent trend time period" shows the dates associated with each trend. These dates depend upon the recency of available data.

Click on any measure title in the "Measure" column to read more about the measure. For a more complete summary of the measures, including their progress compared with the Healthy People 2020 target (where one exists), see the Summary Tables by topic.

> Because most reports focus narrowly on a subject, they often use criteria that might be unfamiliar to readers, particularly those, such as supervisors and managers, who might not be as well versed in the subject as the specialists who wrote the report. As a result, the criteria used in the evaluation are often defined in detail and, when applied in the report, discussed at length.

Legend:
- green – headed in the right direction
- red – headed in the wrong direction
- purple – indeterminate

Cancer Trends Progress Report – Trends at a Glance			
Measure	Desired Direction	Recent Trend	Recent Trend Time Period
Prevention			
Tobacco Use Initiation (Ages 12–17)			
All tobacco products	Falling ⬇	Falling ⬇	2010–2014
Cigarettes	Falling ⬇	Falling ⬇	2010–2014
Smokeless tobacco	Falling ⬇	Falling ⬇	2010–2014
Cigars	Falling ⬇	Falling ⬇	2010–2014
Youth Tobacco Use			
Cigarettes, Cigars and Smokeless Tobacco	Falling ⬇	Falling ⬇	2011–2015
Cigarettes	Falling ⬇	Falling ⬇	2011–2015
Smokeless tobacco	Falling ⬇	Stable	2011–2015
Cigars	Falling ⬇	Falling ⬇	2011–2015
Adult Tobacco Use			
Cigarettes	Falling ⬇	Falling ⬇	2012–2016
Smokeless Tobacco	Falling ⬇	Stable	2012–2016
Cigars	Falling ⬇	Non-Significant Change	2010–2016
E-Cigarettes	Falling ⬇	Non-Significant Change	2014–2016

National Cancer Institute

CANCER SURVIVORS AND SMOKING

Last Updated: *February 2018*

Additional Information on Cancer Survivors and Smoking

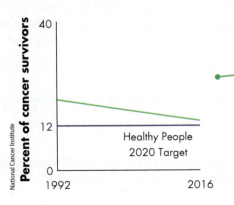

Charts and graphs are common elements in reports because of their ability to present complex data simply for a nonexpert reader.

Introduction

Despite their increased risk for chronic health conditions and premature death, many cancer survivors continue to smoke after their diagnosis. Young survivors (those younger than age 40) may be at particular risk for smoking. To enhance the length and health-related quality of their lives, efforts are needed to identify these individuals and provide them with evidence-based interventions to help them quit smoking and remain tobacco free.

As the population of cancer survivors increases and their expected time of survival lengthens, the health behaviors of these individuals is becoming an important focus of attention. Adoption or maintenance of healthy lifestyles after cancer has the potential to reduce both cancer- and non-cancer-related morbidity. In some cases, lifestyle choices such as smoking may also affect survival. Tracking these behaviors permits evaluation of how well cancer control efforts are working to reduce unnecessary disability and death among those with a history of cancer.

Measure

Rates of smoking among cancer survivors are based on the self-reporting of individuals with a cancer history who are interviewed as part of the annual population-based National Health Interview Survey (NHIS). Participants were asked whether they were a current smoker.

Healthy People 2020 Target

- There is no Healthy People 2020 target for smoking rates among cancer survivors, though it does include a national objective to increase the mental and physical health-related quality of life of cancer survivors. However, it is reasonable to set this at the goal determined for the general population, which is to decrease to 12 percent the proportion of people who smoke.

Healthy People 2020 is a set of goals set forth by the Department of Health and Human Services.

Note: Goals are indicated as blue line on Detailed Trend Graphs.

Data Source

Centers for Disease Control and Prevention, National Center for Health Statistics. National Health Interview Survey, 1992–2016.

Evidence-based Resources

Resources are available to assist cancer control planners, program staff, and researchers to design, implement, and evaluate evidence-based survivorship programs. Visit Cancer Control P.L.A.N.E.T. - survivorship for data on cancer incidence, research syntheses, cancer control plans, research-tested interventions, interactive communities of practice, and other resources.

Additional Information on Cancer Survivors and Smoking

For health professionals

- Tobacco Smoking Cessation in Adults, Including Pregnant Women: Behavioral and Pharmacotherapy Interventions (September 2015). U.S. Preventive Services Task Force.

Scientific reports

- Correlates of continued smoking versus cessation among survivors of smoking-related cancers. Berg CJ, Thomas AN, Mertens AC, Schauer GL, et al. Psycho-Oncology 2013;22:799–806.
- Tobacco use and cessation for cancer survivors: an overview for clinicians. Karam-Hage M, Cinciripini PM, Gritz ER. CA Cancer J Clin. 2014 Jul-Aug;64(4):272-90. doi: 10.3322/caac.21231. Review.
- Cigarette smoking, comorbidity, and general health among survivors of adolescent and young adult cancer. Kaul S, Veeranki SP, Rodriguez AM, Kuo YF. Cancer. 2016 Sep 15;122(18):2895-905.
- Use of Electronic Cigarettes Among Cancer Survivors in the U.S. Salloum RG, et al. Am J Prev Med. 2016 Nov;51(5):762-766.
- Tobacco smoking and the risk of subsequent primary cancer among cancer survivors: a retrospective cohort study. Tabuchi T, Ito Y, Ioka A, Nakayama T, et al. Annals of Oncology 2013; 24(1):2699–2704.

For smokers

- Smokefree.gov. National Cancer Institute.
- SmokefreeTXT. National Cancer Institute.
- Smokefree Women. National Cancer Institute.
- Tobacco. National Cancer Institute.

METHODOLOGY FOR CHARACTERIZING TRENDS

In order to obtain a consistent characterization of population trends in factors related to the prevention, early detection, or treatment of cancer, the joinpoint statistical methodology was used in this report. This methodology characterizes a trend using joined linear segments on a logarithmic scale; the point where two segments meet is called a "joinpoint." The methodology is used to characterize trends in cancer incidence and mortality rates (e.g., in the SEER Cancer Statistics Review).

The Joinpoint software uses statistical criteria to determine:

- The fewest number of segments necessary to characterize a trend
- Where the segments begin and end
- The annual percent change (APC) for each segment. (A linear trend on a log scale implies a constant annual percent change.)

In addition, a 95-percent confidence interval around the APC was used to determine if the APC for each segment differed significantly from zero. Whenever possible, weighted regression lines (utilizing standard errors) were calculated using the Joinpoint software. Using a log response variable, the weight (motivated by the delta method) equals the square of the response variable divided by the square of the standard error. If the standard errors were unavailable, an unweighted regression was used.

Using the results of these analyses, we characterize trends in this report with respect to both their public health importance and statistical significance. If a trend was:

- Changing less than or equal to 0.5% per year ($-0.5 \leq APC \leq 0.5$), and the APC was not statistically significant, we characterized it as **STABLE**
- Changing more than 0.5% per year ($APC < -0.5$ or $APC > 0.5$), and the APC was not statistically significant, we characterized it as **NON-SIGNIFICANT CHANGE**
- Changing with a statistically significant $APC > 0$, we characterized it as **RISING**
- Changing with a statistically significant $APC < 0$, we characterized it as **FALLING**

While these categorizations are somewhat arbitrary, they do provide a consistent method to characterize the trends across disparate measures. However, statistical significance in addition to the absolute value of change for incidence and mortality trends were used to ensure consistency with all major publications on national cancer trends.

To avoid statistical anomalies, a joinpoint segment must contain at least 3 observed data points, and no joinpoint segment can begin or end closer than 3 data points from the beginning or end of the data series. Due to these constraints on the joinpoint models, data series with a smaller set of data points are limited as to where a joinpoint can occur and how many joinpoints can be fit into the series. For example, if there are 4 data points or fewer, only 1 segment and no joinpoints can be fit to the series. For 5 to 7 data points, up to 2 segments and 1 joinpoint can be fit to the series. For 8 to 10 data points, up to 3 segments and 2 joinpoints can be fit. To avoid some of these limitations and allow a degree of flexibility as to where a joinpoint can be placed in a series, we established a set of guidelines on what method to use for calculating the APC of a data series based on the number of estimates that make up the data series:

- 2–6 data points: because of the limited number of data points, Joinpoint was not used, Instead, an APC was calculated between each consecutive data point, and the statistical significance of the APC was calculated using a two-sample test based on the standard errors derived from the survey/data source.
- 7–11 data points: a joinpoint analysis with a maximum of 1 joinpoint.
- 12–16 data points: a joinpoint analysis with a maximum of 2 joinpoints.
- 17–21 data points: a joinpoint analysis with a maximum of 3 joinpoints.
- 22–26 data points: a joinpoint analysis with a maximum of 4 joinpoints.
- 27 or more data points: a joinpoint analysis with a maximum of 5 joinpoints.

In addition to the annual percent change (APC) estimates, this report also presents the <u>average annual percent change</u> (AAPC), a measure which uses the underlying joinpoint model to compute a summary measure of the trend over a fixed pre-specified interval The AAPC is useful for comparing the most recent trend across different groups (e.g., racial groups or gender) when the final joinpoint segments are not directly comparable because they are of different lengths. Regardless of where the joinpoints occur for the different series, the AAPC can be computed over the same fixed interval for all the series (e.g., 2007–2011 to characterize the most recent trend). The AAPC is computed as a weighted average of the APC's from the joinpoint model, with the weights equal to the length of the APC intervals included. When there are seven or fewer data points, the AAPC was computed based on the connected data points, rather than an underlying joinpoint model. The derivation of the AAPC and its standard error based on a series of connected points is presented in a technical report from the Surveillance Research Program.

Measures were age-adjusted to the 2000 U.S. standard population using the direct method of standardization (see the tutorial on Calculating Age-adjusted Rates). Whenever possible, age-adjustment for measures was done using the age-adjustment groups specified for the Healthy People objective that corresponds to the data series.

Starting a Conversation: Thinking Critically about *Cancer Trends Progress Report*

In your writer's notebook, analyze the evaluation presented in the progress report by responding to the following questions:

1. What kinds of sources are included in this report? How does the use of these sources contribute to the credibility of the evaluation?

2. Why is it important to establish credibility in an evaluation?

3. What do you think is the primary reason this progress report includes suggestions for best practices to successfully reduce the incidence of cancer? How does this serve the purpose(s) of the report?

4. Consider the examples and data used to support the progress in fighting cancer. Based on the examples and reasons cited in the report, who do you think is its intended audience? Which examples and reasons lead you to this conclusion?

5. **Reflection:** This excerpt highlights the data surrounding smoking as a risk factor for cancer. Are you or someone you know a smoker? Do you consider smoking to be a concern for your age group? Has reading this excerpt changed your perspective at all? Why or why not?

GENRE TALK

Reflective Writing | Informative Writing | Analytical Writing | **Evaluative Writing** | Problem-Solving Writing | Argumentative Writing

Recent innovations in wearable technology and a growing range of fitness apps have led to a new generation of health-oriented technology tools. As a student, you are likely juggling classes, a job, extracurricular activities, volunteer work, your social life, and maybe even a family, all while trying to stay healthy. Smart watches, monitors, and trackers not only count your steps, measure your heart rate, monitor your sleep, and keep track of your calories but also offer GPS tracking to map your runs or bike rides and integrate smoothly with other fitness apps. This online article evaluates the Microsoft Band 2, a wearable fitness tracker, first defining what the product does ("What is it?"), then listing positive and negative features ("Like" and "Not like"), and finally offering an evaluative judgment ("Should you buy it?").

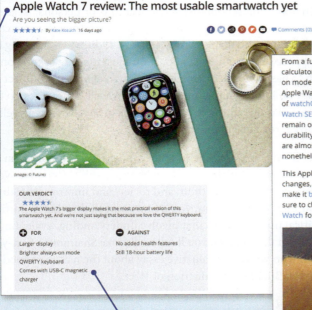

title of article provides an attention-grabbing summary of writer's evaluation of product.

Section headings (not shown) divide the article, providing clear guidance to readers.

The comments section at the end of the article (not shown) invites readers to extend the conversation, share their own experiences, or include links to other reviews or products.

A video provides an alternative way to view the result of the review.

How Can I Write an Evaluative Essay?

If you regularly make purchases online, you've almost certainly run into reviews on sites such as Amazon or Consumer Reports. Chances are also good that you've turned to a local newspaper or searched the web for help deciding which movie to watch or which new restaurant to try. It turns out that product and media reviews are both plentiful and easy to locate. That's not the case, however, for other types of evaluations. For instance, if you're hoping to learn whether it would be better to work an extra ten hours per week or take out a college loan, or if you're trying to determine whether your community should join an electrical power cooperative or start its own wind farm, you're likely to find that the best place to look for answers is in the mirror.

Evaluative essays allow you to address subjects — some as complex as genetic engineering in agriculture and others as seemingly straightforward as deciding how to travel between home and school — that connect to your personal, academic, or professional life. Like other academic essays, they also present some intriguing challenges for writers. In addition to choosing an appropriate subject for evaluation, you must identify criteria on which to base your judgment, learn enough about your subject to make an informed judgment about how well it measures up to your criteria, and convey your judgments in a well-written, well-organized, readable manner.

This section helps you tune in to the conversations around you and take on the role of evaluator as you choose a subject, conduct your evaluation, prepare your draft, and review and improve your draft. As you work on your essay, you'll find yourself drawing in particular on critical thinking skills that involve understanding, evaluating, and creating. In this chapter, you'll follow Brooke Shannon, a first-year student who wrote an evaluative essay about the nature of good and evil in the Broadway production of *Wicked*.

Find a Conversation and Listen In

Evaluative essays allow you to share your judgments with readers who will consider your conclusions seriously and, in many cases, act on your recommendations. Your decision about which conversation to join should reflect your interests and your writing

In Process

An Evaluative Essay about the Effectiveness of a Media Production

Brooke Shannon wrote an evaluative essay for her introductory composition course. Brooke wanted to go deeper than a typical media review, crafting an extended in-depth evaluation of the stage production *Wicked*. Follow Brooke's efforts to write her evaluative essay by reading the In Process boxes throughout this chapter.

Justin Devries Photography

assignment. For example, were you surprised by a new government plan to regulate the banking industry? Are you wondering whether a promising new television show has a future? If so, ask yourself what interests you most about the subject, and then start listening to what others have had to say about it.

● **EXPLORE YOUR NEEDS, INTERESTS, AND CONCERNS**

Evaluative documents are most successful when their subject matches up with readers' needs, interests, or concerns. Readers of *Snowboarding* magazine, for instance, typically view the sport as an important part of their lives and are interested in new developments in equipment and techniques. An evaluation of the latest boards from Burton is likely to address the needs and interests of these readers, many of whom might be in the market for new equipment. Similarly, readers of the magazine might be interested in an evaluation of the effectiveness of conditioning techniques or energy bars.

Readers are also likely to read evaluative documents that address their concerns. Subscribers to *Snowboarding*, for example, might be concerned about the impact of climate change on ski resorts or about plans to allow petroleum extraction in areas near resorts.

As you consider potential subjects for your essay, ask yourself what has caught your attention lately — or better yet, what has long been a matter of interest or concern to you. And be sure to consider your own current needs. To explore potential subjects, use idea-generating strategies such as brainstorming, freewriting, or clustering (see *Generate Ideas* in Chapter 2) to respond to questions like these:

- **Products.** Take an inventory of your personal interests, such as hobbies, outdoor activities, or sports. What new products have been introduced lately? Are you thinking of buying (or have you bought) any of them? Are they truly useful, or has the manufacturer overhyped them? Would you recommend them to others?
- **Media.** What's new and interesting in books, movies, television, music, video games, or the web? What have you read, watched, or listened to that made you think? Have you noticed any developments that trouble you? Have you heard or read criticisms that you think are unfair?
- **Campus life.** Are you thinking about joining a club, team, or group but can't decide if it's worth your time? Do your peers engage in any behaviors that seem dangerous or unhealthy to you? Have you attended a guest lecture or student performance that you felt was overrated or underappreciated? Has a new building or work of public art sparked controversy?

- **Ideas.** Have you been worried or intrigued by a new development you read about in a professional or trade journal? Have you heard an unusual proposal for a new public policy or business incentive? How have you responded to the different teaching methods you've encountered in your high school and college classes? What do you make of conflicting arguments in your course readings?

You'll find additional ideas for evaluative writing projects at the end of this chapter.

● LOCATE SOURCES

Databases and the web are rich sources of information and ideas for writers conducting evaluations. Product and media reviews are among the most popular items on the web, and online editions of newspapers and magazines offer a seemingly endless collection of commentary and critique on everything from the latest diets to pending legislation to new techniques for studying and taking exams. If you're interested in whether professional soccer has a future in the United States, for example, you could find data and opinions on websites such as SoccerTimes.com and USSoccer.com, check out developments reported in the sports sections of newspapers on the web, and read the online versions of magazines such as *SoccerAmerica* and *90:00*.

Similarly, databases provide access to published magazines where reviews can be found. You can also search databases for evaluations published in professional and scholarly journals. To search for information and evaluations for just about any subject that intrigues you, consult general web search sites, media search sites, and databases (see Chapter 14).

Working Together: Try It Out Loud

Before you conduct an evaluation, start a conversation with your classmates about the advantages and disadvantages of majoring in a particular subject. Form small groups and choose a subject area to evaluate, such as English, history, business, psychology, chemistry, math, art, or sociology. As a group, identify the kinds of criteria you will use to evaluate each major, such as personal rewards, academic challenges, skill development, or future employment opportunities. Then take turns applying the criteria to your major (or the major that currently interests you most) while the other members of the group listen, respond, and ask questions. After everyone has had a chance to speak, revisit your criteria. Were they useful in helping you evaluate the majors? Would you consider changing your criteria?

If you are doing this activity during class, share your conclusions about your criteria with other groups. Then, as a class, take a few minutes to reflect on the exercise. Did every group use the same criteria? If not, what might account for the differences?

Searching the Web

Brooke Shannon learned more about the critical reception of *Wicked* by searching for information on the web. _{Justin Devries Photography}

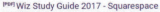

> Brooke used the search terms *Wicked, Broadway*, and *critical thinking guide*. She found a number of resources for students as well as some reviews and culture guides.

Brooke used a search engine to look for websites using keywords such as *Wicked, Broadway, criticism, critical thinking,* and *evaluation*. Her searches allowed her to identify and locate enough sources that she was able to get a good initial understanding of the subject. Because she was particularly interested in a more academic approach to understanding the production rather than a purely aesthetic one, she decided to download an article written by Michael Bowen, an arts and culture writer, who had written a "thinking person's guide to this Broadway spectacle" and who carefully examines the social and political commentary running through *Wicked*.

● **NARROW YOUR FOCUS BY ASKING QUESTIONS**

As you learn about possible subjects for your evaluation, use the following questions to identify which ones capture your interest and best meet the needs of your assignment. Each question focuses your attention on a subject in a different way, and each provides a useful starting point for an evaluative essay. Depending on the subject, you'll find that some questions are more relevant than others.

In Process

Focusing on a Subject

Brooke Shannon brainstormed in response to the questions on the facing page about a subject she was considering for her evaluative essay: a media review on the theater production *Wicked*. As she asked and answered questions, two promising focuses emerged: the importance of productions like *Wicked* for the audiences who love them and the social and political commentary within the production.

Importance:

Not important as in life changing. Important in that media influences us, makes us think about things.

___ Other critics find it important.
___ It touches people and tells important stories.
___ Readers might decide to go see the show or they might understand it in a more meaningful way.

> Brooke used two sets of questions to guide her brainstorming. She generated lists of ideas in response to each approach.

Prevailing opinion:

___ Critics have evaluated the financial success of *Wicked*/how audiences responded.
___ Examined trends and rankings and how much money *Wicked* made.
___ Much less about social and political impact or *why* it was a success with fans.
___ How do artistic decisions make *Wicked* more powerful/successful?
___ What makes *Wicked* so powerful and meaningful?

After reviewing the results of her brainstorming, Brooke decided that while a more typical media review would evaluate how entertaining or financially successful a particular production was, she wanted to explore a different angle. As a result, she chose to focus on how *Wicked* is both a complex and meaningful production by highlighting key artistic decisions and why they connect with the audience.

Justin Devries Photography

- **Importance.** Do you think this is an important subject? If so, why? Who else believes that it's important? Why do they believe that it's important? What would readers do with an evaluation of this subject?
- **Appropriateness.** What aspects of this topic lend themselves to evaluation? Do you have the resources and the time to learn about it and examine it closely?
- **Effectiveness.** Is _____ an effective response to _____? Is it designed well? Is it likely to produce the intended results?
- **Costs/benefits.** What are the benefits of _____? What are the costs? Are the benefits worth the costs?
- **Prevailing opinion.** How have others responded to this subject? How did they reach their conclusions? What have they neglected to consider?

Conduct Your Evaluation

Far too many evaluators tell readers little more than "this is good (or bad or ineffective or the best choice) because I say so." It's as if these writers believe that readers will accept their conclusions without question or doubt.

As a reader, when was the last time you did that?

If you're like most readers, you expect evaluators to provide sound reasoning and appropriate evidence to back up their judgments. As a writer, you should strive to offer the same things to your readers. The judgments you reach in your evaluation should move beyond knee-jerk reactions or general pronouncements. For example, rather than saying a baseball manager should be fired because the team failed to win the division, you should also consider the quality of players available throughout the season, the strength of the competition, and the decisions made during key games.

An effective evaluative essay is based on a clear understanding of your subject, a carefully chosen set of criteria, and well-supported judgments — first, about how well the subject of your evaluation meets each criterion and, second, about the overall results of your evaluation. As you conduct your evaluation, start by choosing a set of criteria that is relevant and clearly defined. Then review what you've learned about your subject, and consider whether you've collected enough evidence to make an informed judgment. Finally, use your criteria and evidence to make your judgments, making an effort to ensure that your evaluation is balanced and fair.

● DEFINE YOUR CRITERIA

Criteria are the factors on which your judgments about a subject are based. In many written conversations, criteria are well established. Movie reviewers, for example, typically base their judgments on plot, characterization, cinematography, editing, and directing, while restaurant reviewers tend to use criteria such as the taste and presentation of the food, the attentiveness and courteousness of the waitstaff, the cleanliness and attractiveness of the restaurant, and the cost of a meal. Similarly, writers of progress reports tend to focus on a fairly consistent set of criteria, most often results, responses to unexpected challenges, and cost-effectiveness.

Even when evaluating well-established subjects, however, writers often depart from the norm. A movie reviewer might focus on the use of product placement in a film, while a music reviewer might draw criteria from poetry or drama to evaluate a new rap album.

Often, you will have the option of choosing among a wide range of evaluative criteria. Consider, for example, the criteria you might use to evaluate competing health plans for employees at a small company:

- overall cost to the company
- cost per employee to participate in the plan
- deductibles
- coverage
- choice of health-care providers
- ease of access to plan information
- access to plan administrators
- required paperwork
- speed of reimbursement to employees

If you chose all these criteria, your evaluation would be quite lengthy. To keep the evaluation brief and to the point — and, of course, useful for readers — you would focus on fewer criteria. If you were creating a brief overview of competing health care plans for managers, you might focus on overall cost to the company, employee costs, coverage, required paperwork, and access to plan administrators. If you were creating a report for employees, on the other hand, your criteria might include employee costs, deductibles, coverage, choice of health-care providers, ease of access to plan information, and speed of reimbursement. The key is to choose those criteria most relevant to your subject, your purpose, and the needs and interests of your readers.

● IDENTIFY EVIDENCE

Evidence provides evaluators with a basis for making their judgments. Evaluative essays tend to rely on a mix of evidence from published sources, observations, and personal experience.

Some evidence is quantitative — that is, it can be measured. For instance, the rate of inflation over the past decade or the number of people participating in a noontime activity program can be found through sources such as public documents or direct observation. Other evidence is qualitative — that is, it is based on the writer's experiences with and reactions to the subject. Music reviewers, for example, usually base their evaluations on the originality of the music, the quality of the performance, and the quality of the recording and production. Some criteria, such as cost, can be judged on both quantitative and qualitative evidence. For instance, you can calculate the amount of money that would be required to pay for a particular program or solution, but you can also view cost in terms of its impact on quality of life or on the environment.

To identify evidence for your evaluation, list the criteria you'll use to conduct your evaluation. Determine whether each criterion will rely on quantitative or qualitative evidence. Then pinpoint potential sources of evidence for your evaluation by reviewing your initial research and any notes you've taken. Next to each criterion, list the evidence on which you'll base your judgments. If you find that you don't have enough evidence to support a thorough evaluation, look for more information.

● MAKE YOUR JUDGMENTS

Once you've identified and organized your evidence, you're ready to determine how well your subject measures up to the criteria you've selected. The quality of your judgments depends not only on the number and kinds of criteria you've defined and the amount and types of evidence you've collected but also on your commitment to being fair and reasonable. If you are applying quantitative evidence to a small number of criteria, making your judgments might be a fairly straightforward process. However, if you are making multiple judgments on the basis of qualitative evidence, it might take significantly more time and effort to complete your evaluation. The challenge you face in making your judgments will also depend on how much impact your decision has on your life or the lives of others. For example, weighing which of three job offers to accept is probably of far greater consequence than comparing the features and costs of two video game systems.

To make judgments about your subject, list your criteria and examine the evidence you've assembled. Write down your judgments in as much detail as possible so that you can draw on them as you draft your essay.

In Process

Making Judgments

For her evaluation of *Wicked*, Brooke Shannon selected five criteria to determine the play's effectiveness: the use of Broadway elements, the emotional impact of the plot, the power of the final lesson, the award-winning casts, and the connection to other cultural matters. To sort through her notes and decide what information would best support her evaluation, she created a table that identified possible evidence for her criteria and made a judgment about whether she had sufficient evidence to support her evaluation. Because she had tried to find some atypical standards for judging the success of *Wicked*, Brooke realized that she had not found a lot of evidence on typical Broadway elements and needed to do some additional research.

Criterion	Evidence	Judgment
Use of Broadway elements	• Powerhouse vocals • Beautiful scenery	Need to find more evidence to support this point
Emotional impact of plot	• Elphaba's awkward youth • Elphaba and Glinda's evolving relationship • Elphaba's transformation into someone "wicked"	Enough evidence
Power of final lesson	• "Don't judge a book by it's cover" • Animal rights • Fighting against discrimination	Enough evidence
Award-winning casts	• Original cast: Idina Menzel and Kristin Chenowyth • Grand Rapids cast: Ginna Claire Mason and Mary Kate Morrissey	Enough evidence
Connection to other cultural things	• *Wicked* book by Gregory Maguire • *The Wizard of Oz*	Enough evidence

Justin Devries Photography

Prepare a Draft

Writers of evaluative essays focus on conveying the results of their evaluation processes to their readers. As you prepare your draft, you'll decide how to convey the overall result of your evaluation, present and define your criteria, share the evidence on which you've based your judgments, design your essay, and frame your evaluation for your readers.

Your draft will be strongly influenced by the purpose of your evaluation. If your intention is to help readers understand whether something has succeeded or failed, for example, consider how your readers will react to your judgments. If you are arguing that a project has failed, you might want to discuss whether the project should be carried out with specific changes or whether it should be abandoned altogether. If you are offering your judgments about which of several options is best, you might want to discuss the trade-offs associated with accepting your judgment. And if you are trying to help readers understand how your subject might be improved or refined, you might want to include guidance about how to put those improvements or refinements into practice.

● STATE YOUR OVERALL JUDGMENT

The goal of an evaluative essay is to share your judgment about a subject, often with the intention of helping readers make a decision. It's usually a good idea, then, to give readers a summary of your overall judgment — your verdict — in the form of a thesis statement. In some cases, you'll want to mention the criteria on which your judgment is based so that readers understand the thinking behind your evaluation. Your thesis statement can also frame your subject in a way that helps achieve your purpose and address the needs and interests of your readers. Consider, for example, how the following thesis statements about locally grown produce set up different expectations among readers.

> Thesis statement 1: Buying your fruits and vegetables at a farmers market might be a little less convenient and a little more expensive than going to the supermarket, but you'll be rewarded with healthier, tastier food.

> Thesis statement 2: Importing fruits and vegetables carries hidden environmental costs that outweigh the benefits of having year-round access to seasonal produce.

> Thesis statement 3: By insisting on produce that has been grown nearby, consumers can support family farms and have a positive impact on their local economies.

Each of these thesis statements focuses on different aspects of the same subject. The first one emphasizes consumer concerns about price, convenience, and quality. The second thesis statement directs attention to the environmental consequences of shipping food long distances. The third one points to the economic benefits of supporting local businesses. These thesis statements would lead to quite different evaluative essays.

Where you place your thesis statement depends largely on your understanding of your readers' needs and interests. Sharing your overall judgment at the beginning of the essay allows readers to follow the logic of your evaluation process and better understand how the criteria and evidence relate to the evaluation's overall result. However, if your overall judgment is likely to be seen as unusual or controversial, it might be best to share it later in the essay, after allowing evidence to unfold in a way that helps readers understand the reasons underlying your conclusions.

Is your thesis statement focused enough? See Chapter 18 for help.

● PRESENT YOUR EVALUATION

To be effective, your evaluative essay must do more than present a straightforward report of criteria, evidence, and judgments. It should help readers understand your subject in a particular way and show them that you've chosen appropriate criteria and evidence. Equally important, your essay should prove to your readers that you've based your judgments on sound and thorough reasoning and that you've conducted a balanced evaluation.

Explain your criteria Criteria are an essential part of any evaluation (see *Define Your Criteria* earlier in this chapter). Your readers should understand not only what your criteria are but also why you've selected them. In some cases, you can rely on general knowledge to supply the rationale for your choice of one or more of your criteria. If you were evaluating an advertising campaign for a new soft drink, for example, you could probably rely on a widespread understanding that sales figures are an important factor in the evaluation.

In most cases, however, you should define your criteria explicitly. For example, if you were evaluating a new state program that encourages high school students to take additional driver education courses after receiving their licenses, you might use criteria such as teenagers' willingness to sign up for the courses and the effectiveness of the program. But how would you define a criterion such as effectiveness? In the context of continuing education courses for newly licensed drivers, it might mean lowering the number of accidents attributable to inexperience, or preventing injuries or deaths associated with teenage drivers, or increasing drivers' awareness of the problems caused by distraction or impatience, or some combination of these factors. Your readers should understand how you've defined your criteria so that they can follow — and, ideally, accept — your evaluation.

Support your judgments with evidence Providing evidence to explain the reasoning behind your judgments helps readers accept your evaluation as valid and carefully thought out. Evidence can also help deepen your discussion of the overall results of your evaluation. In general, you'll want to apply evidence to each of your criteria to show readers how your subject measures up. You can also use evidence to

- introduce your subject
- define your criteria
- provide examples and illustrations
- associate particular ideas and concepts with authorities, such as political leaders, subject-matter experts, or people who have been affected by your subject

In Process

Using Evidence to Support Judgments

Brooke Shannon drew on information and opinions from her sources to support her judgment that *Wicked* unravels important life lessons in an entertaining way.

> *Wicked* pulled on the audience's heartstrings through intense character development, teaching viewers how to look beyond the surface. Glinda "is snooty, haughty, ambitious, conscious of her beauty and initially not interested in befriending the green outcast" (Dawe). However, the relationship between them blooms into a friendship beyond popularity. Glinda shares the secret of her love for Fiyero to Elphaba. This is the start of Glinda's understanding of Elphaba's personality. Glinda decides to look past Elphaba's green skin and discovers the good nature of her heart . . .
>
> Through Glinda's changed perception, the audience is taught that not everything is what it seems. In Michael Bowen's explanation of *Wicked*, Glinda and Elphaba's relationship is assumed to be the reason why Elphaba accepts her differences and, "learns that being an outcast (because of her green skin) isn't necessarily a bad thing" ("Wicked on the Inside"). Elphaba is a commanding character who defies the norm, so audiences are coached to set significance on character, not outer appearances.

> Brooke cites information from an online magazine, identified by the author's name.

> An expert is identified in an attribution.

Justin Devries Photography

Whether you draw your evidence from print, broadcast, or digital sources or from field research, be sure to identify your sources. Evaluative essays typically rely on citation systems such as those provided by the Modern Language Association and the American Psychological Association to identify sources (see Chapters 25 and 26). If you are unsure about which citation system to use, consult your instructor. (You can read more about how to use evidence to support your evaluation in Chapter 21.)

Be fair To be effective, your evaluation must be fair. The notion of fairness is sometimes confused with objectivity. In fact, being truly objective is difficult — and perhaps impossible. Each writer approaches an evaluation with a particular set of experiences, values, and beliefs that leads to a particular outlook on a subject. These differences among writers — even the most disciplined and rigorous — lead to minor and sometimes major differences in their judgments, even when they work with the same criteria and evidence. Being fair and reasonable, as a result, does not necessarily mean coming to the same conclusion as another writer. Instead, it means taking the time to consider different points of view, weighing evidence carefully, and being as consistent in your judgments as possible.

One way to ensure fairness is to provide a context for your evaluation. By making it clear to your readers what you've evaluated, what you've considered during the evaluation process, and how you've approached the evaluation process, you can help them understand how and why you've come to your conclusions. If a reviewer has concerns about the size of a new phone, for example, she might point out that she has small hands or that she prefers to send texts using one hand. By providing context, you'll increase the likelihood that your readers will view your evaluation as sound and well supported.

● **CONSIDER GENRE AND DESIGN**

Like other academic essays, evaluative essays can benefit from thoughtful consideration of design. Bear in mind your readers' expectations about design

---

Working Together: Ask Whether Your Judgments Are Fair

Use feedback from other writers to assess the fairness of your judgments. Describe your subject, briefly define your criteria, present your evidence, and discuss your judgments. The other members of the group should pose reasonable questions about your choice of criteria, selection of evidence, and judgments, paying particular attention to the reasonableness of your judgments. Whenever possible, they should also suggest alternative judgments. Take notes on the doubts expressed by other members of the group so that you can consider them during revision.

elements such as wide margins, double-spaced lines, page numbers, and a readable body font. In addition, consider the benefits of using headings and subheadings and bulleted and numbered lists. Headings and subheadings identify and briefly summarize the sections of your essay, helping readers compare the judgments you've made in different sections of your essay. Numbered and bulleted lists allow you to present evidence or a series of judgments about a subject in a compact form. If you use similar lists — for example, of strengths and weaknesses or of costs and benefits — in different sections of your essay, readers will find it easier to locate and compare the lists.

You can find discussions of document design in Chapters 22 and 23.

● **FRAME YOUR EVALUATION**

The choices you make as you structure your essay will affect how your readers understand and interpret your evaluation. Your strategies for organizing, introducing, and concluding your essay should take into account your purposes — for example, whether you are assessing success and failure or making a recommendation and what you hope readers will do after they've read your essay — as well as your readers' needs and interests. They should also take into account your criteria and the nature and amount of evidence you've assembled to support your judgments.

Organization To decide how to organize your criteria, evidence, and judgments, create an outline or a map (see Chapter 19). Most evaluative essays are organized either according to the items that are being evaluated or by the criteria used to evaluate them. If you are evaluating a single item, such as a proposed change to class registration procedures or the performance of a musical group on a recently released album, you are likely to present your evaluation as a series of judgments, applying one criterion after another to your subject. If you are evaluating more than one item, you can use your criteria to organize your discussion, or you can discuss each item in turn. Evaluative essays can also employ several of the organizing patterns discussed in Chapter 19, such as comparison and contrast, costs and benefits, or strengths and weaknesses.

Introduction Most evaluative essays begin with some explanation of the context and a description of the subject. In some cases, your readers will be unfamiliar with particular aspects of the subject — or even with the subject as a whole. For example, if you are evaluating a new technology for distributing movies online, your readers will probably appreciate a brief discussion of how it works. Once you've established the parameters of your evaluation and decided how to frame your introduction, you can use a range of strategies to put it into words, including asking questions, leading with a quotation, or telling a story. You can read more about strategies for introducing your essay in Chapter 20.

Conclusion Your conclusion offers an opportunity to highlight or even to present the overall results of your evaluation. If you've already presented your overall results in the form of a thesis statement earlier in the essay, you might use your conclusion to reiterate your main judgment or to make a recommendation for your readers. You can also turn to other strategies to conclude your essay, such as linking to your introduction, asking a question, or speculating about the future. Chapter 20 provides more strategies for using your conclusion to frame the results of your evaluation.

Review and Improve Your Draft

Writing a successful evaluative essay depends on choosing an appropriate subject, considering your writing situation, selecting appropriate criteria and evidence, making fair judgments, and deciding how to frame and organize your evaluation. Don't be surprised if your first draft doesn't successfully address all of these challenges: few first drafts do. Instead, take advantage of the opportunity to revise. As you review your draft, pay particular attention to your choice of criteria, your selection of evidence, and the fairness of your judgments.

● REVIEW YOUR CRITERIA

Once you've written a first draft, read it carefully. Then step back and ask questions about your criteria. Ask whether you've used enough — or too many — criteria (generally, evaluative essays include between two and five). Most important, ask whether you've considered the most significant criteria. For example, an evaluation of competing approaches to funding intercollegiate athletic programs that doesn't consider the impact of those approaches on tuition and fees is missing an important criterion.

● RECONSIDER YOUR EVIDENCE

Good criteria and reasonable judgments are the heart of an effective evaluative essay, but they are seldom sufficient to convince readers to accept your point of view. Presenting an evaluation — even a careful one — that lacks well-chosen evidence is like telling your readers, "Look. I'm really smart, and I'm making good judgments. Trust me." Few readers give their trust so easily. As you review your essay, ask whether you've provided enough evidence to support your judgments. Then ask whether you've chosen the right evidence. As you conduct your review, make sure that you haven't relied so heavily on a single source of evidence that it appears as though you're simply borrowing someone else's evaluation. Try to draw evidence from multiple sources, such as published documents and personal experience.

● ENSURE THAT YOUR JUDGMENTS ARE FAIR AND REASONABLE

The most important question you can ask about your evaluative essay is whether your judgments are well grounded and convincing. Individual judgments should reflect the criteria and evidence you've presented to your readers. And your overall conclusion should reflect your judgments as a whole. If your judgments do not line up with your criteria and evidence, your readers will question your conclusions. Similarly, if your judgments are based on poorly chosen criteria or inadequate evidence, your readers will also question your conclusions. On the other hand, if your readers see your criteria as appropriate and your judgments as reasonable and well supported, they'll be far more likely to act on your evaluation.

● RESPOND TO FEEDBACK FROM YOUR INSTRUCTOR

When instructors provide feedback on early drafts of an evaluative essay, they tend to turn their attention first to the writer's choice of criteria, their application of those criteria, and the use of evidence to support the points made in the essay. If the essay is focusing on a common topic, such as a restaurant, a new movie, or a musical album, they'll likely consider whether the essay meets the expectations of readers familiar with evaluations of those kinds of topics. In most cases, instructors will turn to other concerns, such as organization and writing quality, only if they're satisfied that you're doing an effective job of conducting your evaluation.

In Process

Responding to Instructor Feedback

Brooke Shannon received comments from her instructor on the first draft of her essay. After expressing his interest in the subject Brooke was addressing, he asked her to take another look at her choice of criteria. Brooke's instructor suggested that her essay might benefit from a more focused set of criteria. He suggested that Brooke search for some evaluations on similar topics and list the criteria those evaluations used.

In response, Brooke reduced the number of criteria she was using, deleting the two items that seemed to have the least direct connection to the show itself. The result was a more focused evaluation that used criteria that were more relevant to her subject than those she decided to cut.

Justin Devries Photography

Peer Review: Improve Your Evaluative Essay

One of the biggest challenges writers face is reading a draft of their work as a reader rather than as the writer. Because you know what you're trying to say, you find it easy to understand your draft. To determine how you should revise your draft, ask a friend or classmate to read your essay and consider how well you've adopted the role of evaluator.

Purpose
1. What subject does the essay address? Is it a subject that readers will need or want to know about?
2. Does the thesis statement clearly convey an overall judgment?
3. What role does this essay take on? Is it recommending improvements or making a final judgment?

Readers
4. Did you find the essay interesting? Why or why not?
5. Does the evaluation address my readers' needs, interests, and backgrounds?
6. Do the criteria seem appropriate for the subject? Did I use too many criteria? Too few? Should I add or remove any criteria?

Sources
7. Have I provided enough evidence to support my judgments? Too much?
8. Have I relied on a particular source — or a particular type of source — too heavily?
9. Do my sources strike you as reliable and appropriate? Does any of the evidence I've used seem questionable?

Context
10. Have I provided enough information about the subject? About my reasons for evaluating it?
11. Do the judgments made in the essay seem fair? Did you detect any bias or agenda in the way I presented my evaluation? Do you know of any alternative points of view that I should take into consideration?
12. Is the physical appearance of my essay appropriate? Should I consider adding headings or lists?

For each of the points listed above, ask your reviewers to provide concrete advice about what you should do to improve your draft. It can help if you ask them to adopt the role of an editor — someone who is working with you to improve your draft. You can read more about peer review in Chapter 5.

Student Essay

Brooke Shannon, "Is *Wicked* All That Wicked?"

The following evaluative essay was written by featured writer Brooke Shannon. Brooke's essay follows the requirements of the ninth edition of the *MLA Handbook*.   Justin Devries Photography

---

Shannon 1

Brooke Shannon
Professor Jennifer Shinabarger
Comp I
6 November 2017

Is *Wicked* All That Wicked?

Wicked provides several different points of view for the audience to visualize (Faherty). But, what makes *Wicked* unique? Besides the fact the Traveling Broadway show was awarded three Tony Awards in 2004, *Wicked* clearly defines the definition of "good" and evil," and is more than a simple story between two friends.

What Is *Wicked* About?

The *Wicked* posters present mysterious elements that give the impression the play is simply an acted-out explanation of what happened before Dorothy came to Oz. Although this is true, *Wicked* is much more than what the posters sketch. This show, brought to Grand Rapids, Michigan by the Devos Performance Hall, reveals an initial rivalry and a budding friendship between Glinda, the Good Witch, and Elphaba, the Wicked Witch of the West. It, entertainingly, brings fans through a wild journey of Elphaba and Glinda making their way to Emerald City in order to meet the Great Oz and petition for animal rights. Through carefully crafted characters, humorous and musical elements, and supernatural powers, the audience is in for a playful ride with flying monkeys, magic bubbles, and broomsticks, Oh My!

The infamous antagonist in the play is commonly known as the Wicked Witch of the West. However, Elphaba's hardened heart was more of a reaction than an innate concept. According to TJ Dawe, an actor, director, and writer in Vancouver, Elphaba was presented "sympathetically." Born from an affair between a man and her mother, Elphaba's birth father disowns her and her

The heading includes the writer's name, the instructor's name, the course, and the date.

The title is centered per MLA style. While it is not MLA style, bold is used here to call attention to the title and internal headings.

Per MLA style, headings are set flush left.

The writer contrasts the original Wizard of Oz *story with the complexities of the narrative in* Wicked.

green skin is a constant reminder of her unconventional and controversial birth, making her hideous to her father (Faherty). When it was time for her to attend college and tend to her wheelchair bound sister, Nessarose, Elphaba was ecstatic. Unfortunately, excitement plummeted when Elphaba's peers screamed in fear of her green skin, expressing angst over her differences. Elphaba represents the outcast and grabs the hearts of the audience by displaying her relatability. Elphaba's striking personality and Glinda's flimsy nature, together, fulfilled every *Wicked* fan's dream through compelling vocals, a strong set, and a show production worthy of all audiences.

Broadway Elements

Glinda's Popular Performances

Entertaining plots and character development can make, or break, a Broadway show, but *Wicked* does not disappoint in making sure those aspects are delivered. Similarly, vocal performance, stage set up, and costume creativity is equally important. Ginna Claire Mason, as Glinda, and Mary Kate Morrissey, as Elphaba, bring life to the stage as they flip magic wands and fiercely ride wicked broomsticks. Together, they shatter the expectations of the audience with their powerhouse vocals. In the witty vocal performance of "Popular," Mason perfectly demonstrated the vain and bubble headed character with ease as she gracefully flopped across the Devos Center stage. Mason taunted Morrissey with loose and whimsical vocals meant to amuse the audience.

Elphaba's Wicked Vocals

Mason may have commanded attention with her ditzy humor and prom-like dresses, but Morrissey characterized the sarcastic Elphaba equally as accurately. Morrissey showed off the hefty set of lungs she utilized in Act I's, "Defying Gravity." Morrissey displayed Elphaba's emotion passionately during this specific piece through exaggerated facial expressions and heightened vocal performance. These impactful acts allowed the audience to hang onto every word and understand the emotions of the character.

Stages, Costumes, and Personalities . . . If You Care to Find Me!

The choral execution was not the only component that made this Broadway show a hit. The stage setup was unique in its visually appealing

Shannon 3

presentation of Emerald City, consisting of manufactured clocks and a dark green hue. The striking dragon hovering over the creative stage honed in on Elphaba's dark aesthetic. While the stage set up added to the enjoyment, each custom costume brought life to the characters; most notable were the munchkins, the scarecrow, and the tin man. As stated in the article review "*Wicked* Defies Gravity," one scene includes Glinda dressed, "in an unforgettable pink layer-cake party dress" suiting her traditionally girly personality (Cultured.GR). The audience, whether in the front row or the back row, was able to match the costume with the voice, such as Glinda's soprano tone and glittery gowns and Elphaba's angered speech and pointy black hat. The costumes and their distinct colors told the story of the characters in an inventive way. Elphaba's structured black dress, a collection of black and red fabrics, speaks volumes about her true objectives. Elphaba's costume changes signify the character's development. Elphaba starts the play wearing a simple strapped black dress and slowly progresses into the black gown. As for Glinda, her pink, knee-length dresses matched her juvenile innocence while she attended college. But, she soon shocks the audience in her light blue, fluff-filled, sparkle permeated gown as she takes

> A partial quotation indicates that the phrase is taken from the source named in the attribution.

> For online sources that do not include page numbers, only the author or title of the source needs to be included in parentheses.

▲ Elphaba from *Wicked*
Frank Micelotta/Getty Images/Entertainment/Getty Images

her leadership role in Emerald City. Each intrinsic feature was portrayed brilliantly in *Wicked*, making the show a success.

The Importance of *Wicked*'s Plot

For *Wicked*, successful characters and elaborate wardrobes may be necessary, but a successful plot ties the show to audiences. While Elphaba's pathway towards a cold heart was creatively depicted by supernatural powers and flying minions, Glinda's rise to Emerald City fame involved a whole lot of curly blonde hair flips. The audience was shoved around with various emotions from each character, showing the wide variety of well-crafted, purposeful action. For instance, in Act II, Elphaba makes the decision to fake her death and entrusts Glinda to take care of the Grimmerie, a spell-book. In this moment, Elphaba and Glinda perform "the tearjerker, 'For Good'" (Bowen). Through an emotional delivery, Elphaba and Glinda explain the importance of their relationship and how people come into one's life for a reason. Although some may think the plot solely focused on how Elphaba turned wicked, the play brought in an all-too-familiar character who may have stolen a pair of red slippers. Dorothy's tornado incident was soon connected to the death of Nessarose, Elphaba's sister, and explains Elphaba's raging urge to capture Dorothy . . . and her little dog too. Though entertaining, the plot, a two and half hour family fun experience, is the bulk of what teaches core values in the popular Broadway show.

Lesson Learned

Beneath the Surface

Wicked pulled on the audience's heartstrings through intense character development, teaching viewers how to look beyond the surface. Glinda, "is snooty, haughty, ambitious, conscious of her beauty and initially not interested in befriending the green outcast" (Dawe). However, the relationship between them blooms into a friendship beyond popularity. Glinda shares the secret of her love for Fiyero to Elphaba. This is the start of Glinda's understanding of Elphaba's personality. Glinda decides to look past Elphaba's green skin and discovers the good nature of her heart.

> Quotations from professional reviewers are used to support the writer's evaluation.

Shannon 5

Don't Judge a Book by Its Cover

    Glinda's persona eludes to the notion "don't judge a book by its cover." Initially, the Good Witch joined in on the hatred Elphaba was shown by her peers. Elphaba received secret snickers and loud shrieks daily. But, after talking with Elphaba, Glinda gained the understanding that Elphaba was misunderstood. Because Elphaba wore dark clothing and was different, everyone assumed she was evil. However, underneath the green skin and the black clothing lie a caring heart for those who can't fend for themselves, a mindset Glinda never paid attention to developing. Through Glinda's changed perception, the audience is taught that not everything is what it seems. In Michael Bowen's explanation of *Wicked*, Glinda and Elphaba's relationship is assumed to be the reason why Elphaba accepts her differences and, "learns that being an outcast (because of her green skin) isn't necessarily a bad thing." Elphaba is a commanding character who defies the norm, so audiences are coached to set significance on character, not outer appearances.

United or Divided?

    For the duration of the show, Elphaba uses rigid broomsticks and spooky hats to protest for animal rights. Those viewing can take away that humankind is better united. The specific scene in which Elphaba takes demanding, shameless steps to Oz in order to free the flying monkeys shakes the audience as she fights for animal freedom, addressing the issue of discrimination. In one scene, Dr. Dillamond, a professor, is looked at as inferior because he is an animal, specifically a goat. While in class, Dr. Dillamond's animal instincts come ba-ba-back as he goes through the day. Later, people come to capture him because more people were beginning to believe animals belonged in cages without rights. Through Elphaba's passion, the audience learns not to judge others on the color of their skin, or in this case, their fur. In another instance, during class, Dr. Dillamond flipped his chalkboard to see "Animals Should Be Seen And Not Heard." Elphaba shows her support of animals, and comfort, for Dr. Dillamond, by sharing her lunch with him. Scenes such as these add to the positive impressions the audience is left with, allowing observers to see the characters' intentions and to view how the characters adapt to certain events in the play. These basic acts illustrated noticing a person's inside and not just their external presentation.

> The writer offers an interpretation of some of the key scenes in the production.

Shannon 6

Final Act

Through comical characters and a developed storyline, *Wicked* unravels important life lessons to its audience. The public's perception is deterred from a basic Broadway play. The viewer's attention is keyed into the morals and values that are portrayed through laughs, gasps, and applauses. By watching *Wicked,* a general audience of mixed genders, ages, and races are led to the mainstream concept: everyone's journey to acceptance is a complex road, possibly consisting of yellow bricks.

Works Cited

Bowen, Michael. "Wicked on the Inside." *Inlander*, 11 May 2011, https://www.inlander.com/spokane/wicked-on-the-inside/Content?oid=2134990.

Cultured.GR. "'Wicked' Defies Gravity, Expectations with Current Tour's Visit to Grand Rapids." *MLive*, 20 Oct. 2017, https://www.mlive.com/entertainment/grand-rapids/2017/10/wicked_defies_gravity_expectat.html

Dawe, TJ. "Why Wicked Is Important." *Beams and Struts — A Magazine for Hungry Brains and Thirsty Souls*, https://beamsandstruts.com/articles/item/1053-wicked. Accessed 18 Oct. 2017.

Faherty, Allanah. "The Wizard of Oz, Green Skin and Animal Activism: What Is 'Wicked' Actually About?" *Movie Pilot*, 20 Apr. 2017, https://moviepilot.com/p/what-is-wicked-about/4241954.

✱ Project Ideas

The following suggestions provide means of focusing your work on an evaluative essay or another type of evaluative document.

Suggestions for Essays

1. EVALUATE THE EFFECTIVENESS OF AN ELECTED OFFICIAL OR GROUP

Write an essay that evaluates the effectiveness of an elected official or group, such as a mayor, a state legislator, or a city council. Your evaluation might focus on overall performance or on performance related to a specific issue, such as addressing urban growth. Identify and define the criteria you'll use to conduct your evaluation. Collect information from published sources (see Chapter 14). If you can, interview or correspond with the official or a representative of the group (see Chapter 15).

2. EVALUATE A PERFORMANCE

Review a public performance, such as a concert, a play, or a poetry reading, for your classmates. To prepare, read published reviews to familiarize yourself with the criteria that other reviewers have used. In your review, describe the performance and evaluate it, keeping in mind the characteristics of your readers. Take notes and, if possible, interview others who attended the performance. If you can, interview one of the performers. Your review should focus primarily on your personal assessment of the performance. You should draw on your notes and interviews to introduce ideas, illustrate a point, or support your conclusions.

3. EVALUATE A PRODUCT

Select a product you are thinking about purchasing, such as a kitchen gadget, television, laser printer, cosmetic, or piece of athletic equipment. Evaluate it using the criteria of effectiveness, cost, and quality. Provide clear definitions of each criterion in terms of the product you've chosen to evaluate. Your evaluation should draw on written sources, interviews with people who have used the product, and, if possible, your own use of the product.

4. EVALUATE AN ATHLETE OR A COACH

Evaluate the performance of a professional athlete in a team sport, such as a basketball or baseball player, or evaluate the effectiveness of a coach. Select criteria such as the contributions made to the team's success, leadership qualities, entertainment provided to fans, contributions to the community, and so on. In your essay, identify the athlete or coach, explain the contributions the individual has made to their team or sport, identify and define the criteria you are using to evaluate their performance, and present your evaluation to your readers. To support your evaluation, draw on your observations of the athlete or coach, interviews or surveys of other sports fans familiar with the athlete or coach, and published sources that discuss the athlete or coach. If possible, you might also interview the athlete or coach.

5. EVALUATE A PROPOSED SOLUTION TO A PROBLEM

Think of a proposed solution to a problem that you have read or heard about recently. You might focus on proposed legislation for addressing problems with public schools in your state or on a proposal for addressing a foreign policy problem. Alternatively, you might evaluate a new means of dealing with copyright on digital media such as music or videos. Be sure to define the problem, outline the proposed solution, identify and define a set of criteria on which to base your evaluation, and collect information about the problem and its proposed solution by gathering sources or interviewing an expert.

Suggestions for Other Genres

6. POST A MOVIE OR RESTAURANT REVIEW

Review a recently released movie or a new restaurant for the readers of a specific blog or website. To prepare, read reviews that have appeared on the site you have selected, and familiarize yourself with its conventions. If you are reviewing a movie, describe the movie and evaluate it, keeping in mind the interests of your readers. Take notes and, if possible, interview others who have seen the movie. Visit the movie's website to learn about the movie, its director, and its cast. If you are reviewing a restaurant, have a meal at the restaurant with one or more friends. Order a variety of items, examine the decor, and keep track of the quality of the service provided by the waitstaff. After you leave the restaurant, take notes to remind yourself of your impressions of the food, decor, and service. Ask your friends for their reactions, and take note of them as well. In your review, describe the restaurant and evaluate it, keeping in mind the interests of those who read the blog or visit the site.

Your review should focus primarily on your personal assessment of the movie or restaurant. Draw on your notes to introduce ideas, illustrate a point, or support your conclusions.

7. WRITE A PROGRESS REPORT

Write a report that evaluates the progress that a group or organization you belong to has made during a particular period of time, such as the last six months or the last year. To develop the criteria for your progress report, interview key members of the group or organization, or locate any written documents that define its goals. Draw on your personal experience with the group, interviews, and documents (such as funding proposals or a website) as sources of evidence for your evaluation. Your report should define the group's or organization's goals and assess its progress in meeting them. The report might also include recommendations about strategies for enhancing the group or organization's efforts to meet its goals.

8. WRITE A REVIEW OF LITERATURE

A literature review offers your assessment of relevant published sources in a given area, such as the use of social media to support writing instruction or approaches to funding election campaigns. The goal of a literature review is to share your understanding of the range of ideas, information, and arguments you find in a body of published work. For example, you might find that the work you've read about the use of social media in writing instruction focuses on three areas: (1) supporting interaction among members of a given writing class, (2) allowing instructors to share course materials with students, and (3) helping instructors and students share feedback on writing projects.

In your literature review, locate sources using the search strategies discussed in Chapters 13 and 14. Read your sources carefully, identify general approaches to the subject, and provide your judgments about the merits of each approach. Provide an overview of each approach you've identified; then discuss some of the most important or representative sources. Use quotations, paraphrases, and summaries to share information from the sources with your readers. Use in-text citation and a works cited list to identify your sources.

In Summary: Writing an Evaluative Essay

★ **Find a conversation and listen in (p. 322).**
- Explore your needs, interests, and concerns (p. 323).
- Locate sources (p. 324).
- Narrow your focus by asking questions (p. 326).

★ **Conduct your evaluation (p. 327).**
- Define your criteria (p. 327).
- Identify evidence (p. 328).
- Make your judgments (p. 329).

★ **Prepare a draft (p. 331).**
- State your overall judgment (p. 331).
- Present your evaluation (p. 332).
- Consider genre and design (p. 334).
- Frame your evaluation (p. 335).

★ **Review and improve your draft (p. 336).**
- Review your criteria (p. 336).
- Reconsider your evidence (p. 336).
- Ensure that your judgments are fair and reasonable (p. 337).
- Respond to feedback from your instructor (p. 337).

11 Writing to Solve Problems

What is writing to solve problems? 348

What kinds of documents are used to solve problems? 350

Problem-solving articles and essays 350
    Anneke Jong, *Leveling the Playing Field: How to Get More Women in Tech* 350

Proposals 354
    Dave Krepcho, *Grant Proposal for Second Harvest Food Bank of Central Florida* 354

Opinion pieces 363
    Sapna Maheshwari, *Why Elite Female Athletes Are Turning Away from Major Sponsors* 363

Advice 369
    Savannah Peterson, *Advice for Generation Z from a Savvy Millennial* 369

Genre Talk: Problem-Solving Writing 375

How can I write a problem-solving essay? 376
Find a conversation and listen in 376
Develop a solution 379
Prepare a draft 386
Review and improve your draft 391

✳ **Student Essay** 394
    Sophie Kimble, *Sharks for Profit* 394

✳ **Project Ideas** 401

What Is Writing to Solve Problems?

The word *problem* is slippery. When a problem affects us directly, it might take on the dimensions of a crisis: we want to know how to solve it — and the sooner the better. When a problem affects someone else, it might seem, to us, more like an interesting challenge than an imminent disaster. And sometimes a problem is nothing of the sort. It's simply a label for lack of knowledge. For example, when a research scientist talks about work on an interesting problem, it usually involves investigating an intriguing puzzle, which, when solved, will advance our knowledge in a specific area.

Writers who adopt the role of *problem solver* (see Chapter 6) carry out activities such as calling readers' attention to problems, discussing the nature and extent of those problems, or proposing solutions. Whether a writer focuses on defining, discussing, or proposing a solution to a problem depends on how much is known about it. Consider, for example, the evolution of our understanding of the HIV/AIDS epidemic. In the early 1980s, when little was known about HIV — the virus that causes AIDS — it wasn't clear that the growing number of illnesses caused by HIV were related to one another. As a result, the first writers who addressed the problem focused largely on defining the symptoms and arguing that a problem even existed. Later, as more information became available about the origin and effects of the disease, medical researchers began writing reports and scholarly articles that discussed its potential impact on people who carried the virus and on society. As researchers began to understand how the disease was spread and what might be done to prevent infection, they wrote proposals to reduce the spread of HIV. Eventually, as the nature of HIV became better understood, they began proposing programs of medical research that might be carried out to develop a way of preventing, and perhaps even eradicating, the spread of the virus.

THE WRITER'S ROLE:
Problem Solver

Problem solvers like me define a problem and offer possible solutions.

PURPOSE
- To identify or define a problem
- To explain the significance of a problem
- To propose solutions

READERS
- Expect information, ideas, and insights to be presented fairly
- Expect a clear explanation of a proposed solution

SOURCES
- Published information (such as studies, reports, blogs, websites, and news media), personal experience, and field research (including interviews, observation, surveys, and correspondence) help writers define and learn about previous attempts to solve problems.

CONTEXT
- Writers consider what readers are likely to know, assume, and value, and they focus on what readers want or need to understand about the problem.
- Illustrations — such as charts, tables, graphs, and images — can improve readers' understanding.

CRITICAL THINKING

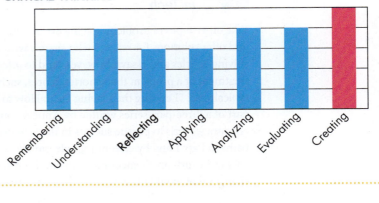

Writers of problem-solving documents are concerned primarily with helping readers understand the nature of and potential solutions to a problem. Sometimes they define and discuss the origins or impact of a problem. Sometimes they reflect on the strengths and weaknesses of potential solutions to a problem. In most cases, however, they analyze a problem and offer readers a thoroughly considered, well-supported solution. In doing so, they play a critical role in advancing our understanding of and response to problems.

What Kinds of Documents Are Used to Solve Problems?

It's rare to spend a day without running across documents that promise to solve a problem: advertisements alert us to solutions for problems (with our health, our love lives, our breath) that we might not know we have; email messages ask us for our help with problems ranging from hunger to funding for the arts; and websites, such as VoteSmart.org and NASA's Global Climate Change Solutions, offer solutions to problems. Unfortunately, the number of unsolved problems far exceeds those with solutions. As a result, writing to solve problems is a common occurrence.

In your work writing a problem-solving essay, you might turn to sources as varied as books, reports, pamphlets, posters, memos, opinion columns, and blog entries — any of which might define a problem or advance solutions to a problem. The following examples illustrate four of the problem-solving documents you're likely to encounter: problem-solving articles and essays, proposals, opinion pieces, and advice.

Problem-Solving Articles and Essays

Anneke Jong

Leveling the Playing Field: How to Get More Women in Tech

Like other types of problem-solving documents, articles and essays can define problems and offer solutions for readers who share a writer's interest in an issue. Problem-solving articles and essays, however, tend to offer a more reflective and comprehensive treatment of a problem than shorter genres, such as advice or opinion columns, typically do. "Leveling the Playing Field: How to Get More Women in Tech" is the final part of a three-part series written by Anneke Jong and published on themuse.com. Jong encourages girls to pursue success in the tech field by exposing them to potential career paths in Part 1 and by celebrating role models in the field in Part 2. Part 3 questions why more girls aren't encouraged to build coding skills and considers the positive changes that would likely result if they were encouraged to develop such skills.

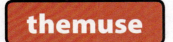

Leveling the Playing Field: How to Get More Women in Tech

By Anneke Jong

> Anneke Jong is the vice president of operations and marketing at Reserve, an online services company. She is also a speaker and tech writer, with several articles featured on themuse.com.

This article is part of a three-part series, "Solving the Pipeline Problem: How to Get More Women in Tech." Check out <u>Part 1: Girls Don't Know What Computer Science Is</u> and <u>Part 2: You Can't Be What You Can't See</u>.

The Problem: Girls Haven't Coded Before

Omosola Obetunde was lucky. Her parents sent her to computer science camp in 8th grade. "I didn't know it was computer science. I just thought it would be cool to make things." Seven years later, she's a computer science major at Stanford University.

Sara Haider's parents also exposed their daughter to technology early — she learned to program at age 9. "I had no idea <u>I could do this for a job</u> until I took computer science in high school and my teacher told me, 'there's a career in this.'" Today, Haider is a software engineer at Twitter, and sees her family's encouragement as a key influencer in her career.

When I talked to women who have decided to pursue a career in computer science, I was surprised to learn that nearly all of them credited early exposure to programming as the greatest factor in their decision to become engineers. Conversely, they cited a lack of early exposure to computer science as the primary deterrent for women who leave — or never join — the field.

> Problem-solving articles are also likely to offer the writer's personal insights into a problem, the situation out of which it emerges, and the reasons why the proposed solution is preferable to competing solutions.

"There's a competitive showiness in the classroom that intimidates some women who don't have experience," says Kathy Cooper, a master's candidate in computer science. "Even in intro classes, the guys seem like they've been programming before."

Cooper's instinct is right: Boys really are more prepared. Although most of the female computer science students I spoke to had taken Advanced Placement (AP) Computer Science classes in high school, they're part of a small minority. According to the most recent reporting from the College Board, female enrollment in AP Computer Science is as low as 14%, making it the most gender-skewed AP class in the country.

> Along with quotes from interviews, Jong cites data from relevant authorities to support her assessment of the problem.

And the uncommon ground starts even before that. "There's an impression that guys start coding when they're little. Boys play with robots, and girls play with dolls," says J. J. Liu, a sophomore computer science major. "[It] feels like the guys have been 'speaking code' for a long time."

This sense that boys have a head start creates a high competence threshold for women in computer science, even those who have prior experience in the field.

"Because of the stereotype that women do worse in computer science, a lot of high-achieving women get a B on their first exam and think they're just not good enough. They feel behind already, so they quit," laments Obetunde.

Angie Schiavoni, who teaches programming to underserved middle school girls, has observed a similar mind-set among her students: "I've seen that girls feel like they have to be super good at something to pursue it."

The Solution: Teach Computer Science to Middle School Girls

So, solving the pipeline problem requires giving our girls the confidence they need to go head-to-head with their male classmates. Unless we put our female and male students on equal footing going into college, young women are at risk of perceiving their efforts as a failure, feeling behind, and quitting early to pursue something else.

> In academic settings, instructors are usually the primary readers, although students are often asked to address a different audience, such as fellow students or the members of a particular community. Professional writers are nearly always addressing a broader audience, or even multiple audiences, as Jong does here — writing for career-builders but also calling on her readers as parents and people with cultural or social influence.

Key to this is getting middle school girls to think programming is cool. As the College Board stats show, reaching girls in high school is too late — at that point, they're already opting out of studying programming. Plus, the earlier they start learning, the better their chance of success in the field will be.

"Kids are like sponges with foreign languages, and programming languages are no different," Schiavoni says. "We can't leave girls behind in an industry that will be the forefront of our economy for years to come."

Silicon Alley venture capitalist and father of two Fred Wilson agrees. On his blog, AVC, he openly called for more computer science curriculum in schools: "We continue to teach our kids French but we don't teach them Ruby on Rails. Which do you think will help them more in the coming years?"

Schiavoni's solution is Code Ed, a program that trains middle school girls to code HTML and build their own websites. "It's inspiring to see how engaged our students are," explains Schiavoni. "The girls jump up and down and cheer when they change the background color."

She wants girls to see programming not as work, but as a creative process to pursue their passions. (Just what kinds of passions do 5th graders pursue? Schiavoni jokes that 90% of her students make Justin Bieber fan sites.)

Say what you will about Bieber, Code Ed works — and girls' opinions on computer science change dramatically after they go through the program. "I used to hear about boys and men doing all the websites," said 12-year-old Taiya Edwards, who went through Code Ed's program in the Bronx. "But now I know that girls can do anything a guy can do."

When asked if she'll make another website, she responded with an emphatic, "Yeah! I'll probably make one with advice for teens."

Code Ed isn't the only organization teaching girls about computer science — there are regional groups like Black Girls Code and Code Now, Microsoft's national Digigirlz program offers high school girls hands-on workshops, camps, and online training in technical topics like building a website, and the UN has launched a Girls in ICT portal. And these are all extremely important efforts. We just need more.

> *In web articles, links are an easy way to provide both support and resources to readers.*

We're All Part of the Solution

Some say that teaching girls to code isn't that important. "Women can always hire someone to code for them," the skeptics say.

But why should women go find someone else to code for them? Relying on someone else to build your ideas means you need to have funding or be willing to give up equity in your company. Knowing how to program means the difference between spending months finding the right technical cofounder and being able to go home and build your idea tonight.

Plus, making investments to improve the pipeline of women in tech doesn't just benefit the next generation of girls, but it primes our economy for a boost in innovation. The female Mark Zuckerberg is out there, and it's within our power to make sure she follows her dream.

> *Readers of problem-solving essays and articles might be part of a broad audience, such as subscribers to a general-interest magazine such as Time or The Atlantic, or they might be part of a more narrowly defined group, such as community college administrators, parents of children with autism, small-town mayors, or members of a particular church. In this article, Jong is writing for an audience of career-builders, calling on them to be part of the solution.*

Starting a Conversation: Thinking Critically about "Leveling the Playing Field: How to Get More Women in Tech"

In your writer's notebook, reflect on the problems and solutions presented in Jong's article by answering the following questions:

1. Identify and evaluate the organizing pattern (see Chapter 19) used in the article. How does the organization of the article reinforce the author's purpose? Would a different organizing pattern have been more effective? Why or why not?

2. Themuse.com is designed to help readers explore different career options. What does the design of the site allow you to infer about its intended audience?

3. What is the "pipeline problem" (par. 10)? What are the causes of this problem? Why does Jong think we need to address this problem?

4. In presenting her solution, how does Jong address potential counterarguments? Does she effectively address roadblocks to achieving her solution? What additional information could have been included? What information, if any, might she have left out? Why do you think she approaches potential opposition to her proposed solution in this manner?

5. **Reflection:** Jong argues that girls need more access to learning coding skills, as well as more opportunities to see coding as "cool." How is coding perceived in your peer group? Do you think your friends, family, and classmates believe that tech has a gender problem? Explore two or three ways that coding could become more accessible or more popular with young girls.

Proposals

Dave Krepcho
Grant Proposal for Second Harvest Food Bank of Central Florida

Proposals offer a plan for solving a specific problem. They are usually presented to groups or individuals who have resources that might be used to address the problem or who can grant permission for putting a plan into effect. The following proposal, written by Dave Krepcho, the CEO of a nonprofit organization, asks that a charitable foundation fund their efforts to provide food for elementary school students.

SECOND HARVEST FOOD BANK OF CENTRAL FLORIDA

411 Mercy Drive
Orlando, FL. 32805
Ph: 407-295-1066

November 5, 2013
Ms. Irene Gray
Application Contact
Leonard C. & Mildred F. Ferguson Foundation
4767 Munson St., NW
Canton, OH, 44718

Dear Ms. Gray:

The Second Harvest Food Bank of Central Florida has remained faithful to the mission of fighting hunger since 1983. Over the past thirty years, more than 350 million pounds of food and grocery items have been distributed to needy people through our "partner agencies" of more than 500 qualified 501(c)(3) nonprofit organizations. By helping to close the gap between our community's need for donated food and the amount of food available through collaborative efforts, it is a mission that touches hundreds of thousands of lives each year.

We achieve the goal of alleviating hunger in several ways, from providing access to food and other grocery products to needy children and families to mobilizing community leaders by bringing visibility to the invisible problem of hunger and poverty. Through the efforts of donors, volunteers, and nonprofit agencies providing emergency food assistance, nutritious food is made available to the hungry neighbors in our community.

One of our feature programs, the Hi-Five Kids Pack Program, exists to serve chronically hungry children by providing them with take home food packs on Fridays. The nutritious meal packs are given to students on Fridays to help keep them nourished over the weekends when they are not in school.

> Proposals typically define a problem, describe a plan for addressing the problem, and argue that the person or group making the proposal has the capacity to carry out the plan.

The Second Harvest Food Bank of Central Florida is requesting a $38,500 grant from the Leonard C. & Mildred F. Ferguson Foundation in order to provide 10,000 food packs to meet the needs of food insecure elementary students. Combined with existing financial support, these monies will be used to equip new Hi-Five elementary school sites in Central Florida with weekend food resources for hungry students, and reading materials to help educators and school administrators identify which students are suffering from hunger and should be invited to participate in the Kids Pack Program.

Enclosed is a grant proposal requesting funds for the Hi-Five Kids Pack Program. Thank you for your consideration.

Sincerely,
Dave Krepcho
President/Chief Executive Officer
Second Harvest Food Bank of Central Florida

SECOND HARVEST OF CENTRAL FLORIDA OVERVIEW

The Second Harvest Food Bank of Central Florida began in 1983 as the vision of concerned citizens that felt a strong need for a local response to the problem of hunger in our community. Since then, the Second Harvest Food Bank of Central Florida has remained faithful to our mission to fight hunger, and as a result, more than 350 million pounds of food and grocery items have reached needy people in Central Florida. Through the collaborative efforts of donors, volunteers, and over 500 501(c)(3) non-profit agencies providing emergency food assistance, nutritious food is made available for people who are hungry.

The Goal of Second Harvest Food Bank is to alleviate hunger. We achieve that goal by:

- providing access to food and other grocery products in order to meet the need of those we serve

- promoting and supporting the development of our partner agencies' ability to fulfill their missions

- mobilizing leaders and communities by bringing visibility to the invisible problem of hunger and poverty
- developing more holistic and county-specific solutions to hunger in the Central Florida region

During the past thirty years, Second Harvest has been actively working to increase its impact in the Central Florida community. Second Harvest's programs seek to close the gap between our community's need for donated food and the amount of food available. We facilitate twelve programs, including Second Helpings, Kids Café, Hi-Five Kids Pack Program, Benefits Connection, and the Second Harvest Culinary Training Program in our Darden Community Kitchen.

In addition to our programs, our brand new facility, the Morgan and Morgan, P.A. Relief Center has expanded our ability to relieve hunger in Central Florida. We conservatively project that our new hunger relief center will bring 644 million pounds of food resources to food insecure Central Floridians over the next twenty years. In addition to our main facility in Orlando, we have warehouse facilities in Brevard and Volusia Counties, which provide those communities with local access to food resources.

STATEMENT OF NEED

For many children, leaving school on Friday afternoon means spending time with friends, attending sporting events, and other fun activities. But if a child is hungry, Friday afternoon often means two days without school breakfast or lunch, and little or no food at home. Sadly, for tens of thousands of at-risk children in Central Florida, Saturday and Sunday mean going hungry.

Florida has one of the highest food insecure rates of children in the United States. Food insecurity for kids under the age of 18 years old ultimately means that they do not know if they will have enough food to eat on any given day, or if they will face a weekend of hunger. Second Harvest Food Bank of Central Florida has been able to study the problem of chronic childhood hunger in our area through information obtained from the Florida Department of Education and data collected from Map the Meal Gap, a study done by Feeding America.

> The structure and general appearance of proposals vary widely and tend to reflect the interests of the intended audience. Often, proposals must follow strict guidelines outlined in grant application instructions or a call for proposals. A statement of need is a common element in proposals requesting nonprofit funding.

For example, according to the Map the Meal Gap study, there are nearly 65,000 food insecure children under 18 years old in Orange County alone. The number of children attending Orange County Public Schools who are receiving free/reduced-cost school lunches has grown from 92,800 in the 2008-2009 school year to over 112,300 in 2012–2013. This difference is an increase of nearly 21%.

Research has shown that undernourished children are sick more often and require more hospitalization than children who are well-nourished. Studies further indicate that underfed at-risk children:

- experience growth and developmental impairments that limit their physical, intellectual and emotional development.
- cannot learn as much, as fast, or as well, because chronic under-nutrition harms their cognitive development during a time of rapid brain growth.
- do poorly in school and have lower academic achievement.
- have more social and behavioral problems because they cannot adapt as effectively to environmental stress.

The epidemic of hunger affects a high number of elementary students in counties throughout Florida. There are thousands of children who wonder if they might not have food to eat after school is over on Fridays. A child should be consumed with learning to tie their shoes, sounding out vowels and syllables as they read, and practicing their addition and subtraction. Their focus on academics should not be distracted by a grumbling stomach and thoughts of when they will have the chance to eat again.

> Some proposals resemble academic essays, or even lab reports, with wide margins, double-spaced lines, headings and subheadings, and limited use of color and illustrations. Others more closely resemble magazine articles or brochures, with heavy use of color, illustrations, columns, and other design elements.

HI-FIVE KIDS PACK PROGRAM DESIGN

Objective

To meet the need of at-risk food insecure elementary students, the Hi-Five Kids Pack Program was developed in 2006. The ultimate objective of the Hi-Five Kids Pack program is to reduce the symptoms of chronic hunger for food insecure children in Central Florida. When undernourished children are provided with proper nutrition for their growing bodies, they are better able to remain focused in school and function at their optimal capacities.

Methods

Hi-Five serves hungry children by providing them with take home food packs to keep them nourished on the weekends when they are not in school and when a cafeteria is not accessible. The easy-to-open packs contain foods that provide nutrients across the spectrum of wholesome meals and help alleviate symptoms of chronic hunger in children. The name "Hi-Five" comes from the positive feeling you get by giving a "high five" and the five healthy food groups, which are both meaningful for children facing hunger.

The program targets schools with a large percentage of the student population eligible for the free or reduced-cost school lunch programs. Hi-Five ultimately aligns with Second Harvest's mission to fight hunger. Since its inception, Hi-Five has distributed 218,000 food packs to cover food insecure children over the weekends. There is great potential for the program to be implemented in new elementary schools, which means reaching more students in counties such as Brevard, Lake, Marion, Orange, Osceola, Seminole, and Volusia.

The Hi-Five program can continue to fight childhood hunger and do so most effectively by receiving funding that will cover additional schools for at least one year. Through joint efforts with partner agencies and schools, the Hi-Five program has helped make it possible for hungry elementary students to access needed food resources on weekends when it is not readily available to them.

In order for our Hi-Five Kids Pack Program to meet its intended purpose and mission, we collaborate with elementary schools and nonprofit children's programs that serve at-risk children. These partners are equipped by Second Harvest with materials that describe symptoms of chronic hunger, and provide details on how to approach students who demonstrate those indications. Consequently, collaborators can identify which children are suffering from hunger, and invite them to participate in the program so that the packs can be distributed.

Each collaborating partner site determines how the food packs will be distributed to the children. A classroom teacher, nurse, or even an administrator may discreetly place the food pack in the child's backpack. Every effort is made to provide the food assistance discreetly, as to not embarrass the child, which can help preserve his/her self-esteem.

The Hi-Five packs are prepared and stored at our distribution center and delivered to the participating partner schools on a monthly basis. The individual items have a shelf life of at least one year, which allows distributions of all pre-pack items well in advance of any expiration date.

Each pack will contain seven or eight nutritious items such as:

Chocolate milk

Beans and franks

Macaroni O's with beef

Cut green beans

Fruit juice

Mac and cheese

Chicken Vienna sausages

Granola bar

The Hi-Five Kids Packs are efficiently assembled at our Hunger Relief Center by our dedicated volunteers. Last fiscal year, nearly 13,000 people volunteered over 40,000 hours in support of our mission to fight hunger.

PROGRAM EVALUATION

Since Second Harvest Food Bank of Central Florida implemented the Hi-Five Kids Pack Program in 2006, we have established twenty-five school distribution sites.

To measure the success of the Hi-Five Kids Pack Program at a new school site, Second Harvest will evaluate accomplishment of the program's objectives by using the same evaluation methods used at our existing sites.

The need for Kids Packs differs for each site because student attendance and the number of students getting free or reduced-cost lunch vary at each school. Based on these numbers, our program manager and volunteer coordinators determine the number of Hi-Five Packs that need to be made, stored, and distributed to schools each month. Typically, we project 3,000 food packs for the year, which equates to about 300 food packs distributed per month for a period of ten months.

Second Harvest also requires each elementary school to keep Hi-Five Pack distribution records. These records simply contain the amount of Hi-Five Kids Packs that are distributed and the date of each distribution. These records are kept by school officials and are reported to Second Harvest's Program Department once a month.

Depending on the numbers reported on these distribution records, as well as the school's enrollment numbers, Second Harvest will adjust the number of Kids Packs that each school receives accordingly.

FUTURE FUNDING

When Second Harvest seeks to open a new Hi-Five site, we want to make sure that we are going to have a lasting impact and be a long-term and consistent presence at that school site. It is important to provide consistent support for food insecure children who might depend on their Hi-Five Kids Packs for one year and not have it the next.

Second Harvest Food Bank of Central Florida has successfully grown our financial support from the local community since we began our service to the community in 1983. During our recent Capital Campaign, we successfully increased our unrestricted support from the community, particularly in our online giving efforts while successfully securing capital campaign support.

When approached by corporate groups wishing to support Second Harvest Food Bank, we offer the Hi-Five Kids Pack Program as an excellent opportunity to support our mission both financially and as a volunteer project.

We will continue to seek foundation funding for the Hi-Five Program. For a number of years, we have had support for this program from two local foundations: the Darden Restaurants Foundation and the Winter Park Health Foundation. However, the numbers of hungry children continue to grow, so our need for support continues to grow.

PROGRAM BUDGET

The funding of the Hi-Five Kids Pack Program is simple. One Kids Pack costs $3.85 to produce, so the $38,500 in the budget below would provide 10,000 Kids Packs.

Budget 2013–2014 Academic Year

Description	Total Budget
Program Staff Salaries	$3,040.00
Payroll Taxes	$266.00
Benefits	$494.00
Food	$34,700
Total	**$38,500**

> Proposals, especially those requesting funding for a particular project or initiative, often include detailed budgets and plans for evaluating the outcome and benefits of the proposed actions.

BENEFITS

The Second Harvest Food Bank of Central Florida has seen the impact that the Hi-Five Kids Pack Program has made on children at our other twenty-five distribution sites. We are very eager to bring the Hi-Five Kids Pack Program to another school because of the difference it will make in the children's lives. Not only will the opening of a new site feed food-insecure children for the weekends, but it will help to improve their long-term learning, development, and growth as well.

Starting a Conversation: Thinking Critically about "Grant Proposal for Second Harvest Food Bank of Central Florida"

In your writer's notebook, evaluate Krepcho's proposal by responding to the following questions:

1. What elements of Krepcho's proposal demonstrate his sensitivity to the concerns of elementary school students? What elements demonstrate his awareness of the concerns of the members of the Leonard C. & Mildred F. Ferguson Foundation?

2. How would you characterize the organization of this proposal? In what ways does the structure — overview, statement of need, program evaluation, and so on — help the writer achieve his purpose?

3. Krepcho addresses possible concerns with the effectiveness of the Hi-Five Kids Pack Program in the section "Program Evaluation." Where else in the proposal does he address potential concerns, and how does he refute them? Can you think of additional possible objections? What questions might remain in readers' minds?

4. At several points in his proposal, Krepcho provides concrete information, such as a sampling of the specific food items often included in the Kids Packs. How do these details support his claims? What important details, if any, are missing?

5. **Reflection:** Think about where you grew up and the support your community provides for students from food-insecure homes. Do you think a proposal like this one would be popular in your community? Do you think it does enough to address the problem? Is there a different concern for elementary school students in your community that you could imagine drafting a proposal to address?

Opinion Pieces

Sapna Maheshwari
Why Elite Female Athletes Are Turning Away from Major Sponsors

Opinion pieces — often in the form of essays, articles, columns, letters to the editor, or guest editorials — present focused arguments supported by analysis and evidence. They usually appear in magazines or newspapers and, to a lesser extent, in journals and on the web. Opinion pieces often advance arguments about a problem or a proposed solution that has been covered elsewhere in the publication. It is common, for example, to find an opinion column in a newspaper responding to an event reported in a front-page story. In the following article, "Why Elite Female Athletes Are Turning Away from Major Sponsors," Sapna Maheshwari provides a clear analysis of changes in the sponsorship deals entered into by leading female athletes in the United States and describes the approaches they have developed to address the inequities and oppression that have sometimes affected them. In the context of her careful reporting and analysis, Maheshwari makes a clear call for change.

nytimes.com

Why Elite Female Athletes Are Turning Away from Major Sponsors

Sapna Maheshwari

> Sapna Maheshwari is a business reporter covering retail for *New York Times*. She was featured on *Time Magazine's* list of "140 Best Twitter Feeds of 2014." She is a graduate of the University of North Carolina at Chapel Hill and a native of East Lyme, Connecticut.

Athleta, the activewear brand for women and girls owned by Gap Inc., had never sponsored an athlete when it approached the six-time Olympic champion sprinter Allyson Felix in 2019, shortly after she took Nike to task for its pay practices for pregnant runners.

The smaller company was interested in supporting Ms. Felix's career, and said it would not penalize her for losing races or choosing to have more children. (Nike changed its policy for pregnant athletes after the criticism by Ms. Felix, whose contract with the company ended in 2017.) She said that she liked that Athleta was led by women and that it appreciated that she was a mother as well as an athlete.

"It's a very pressured situation to be sponsored traditionally in track and field — it's about numbers if you don't perform, reductions and all of these things," Ms. Felix, who will compete in the Tokyo Games, said in an interview. With Athleta, she added, "I felt like I had more value as a person, and that was something I hadn't experienced before."

> The article as published on the *New York Times* website includes several images of female Olympic and international class athletes.

A growing number of top women athletes, including Simone Biles and former Olympians, have been choosing to strike new types of deals with smaller activewear brands instead of traditional sponsors like Nike. Several young female runners say that smaller brands are willing to work with them in different ways, like bringing them on as employees, giving them equity or involving them in new products, and that they are paying more attention to their personal stories and Instagram accounts than their race performance.

Bigger apparel companies like Nike and Adidas are established power players that can often drastically increase an athlete's visibility through marketing. But critics say they do not always put the athletes first. Nike, for

Sapna Maheshwari, "Why Elite Female Athletes Are Turning Away from Major Sponsors," *The New York Times*, July 30, 2021. Copyright © 2021 by The New York Times. All rights reserved. Used under license. https://nytimes.com.

instance, has come under intense scrutiny in recent years for its treatment of pregnant athletes, accusations of bullying and restrictive contracts.

Runners have traditionally been paid by sponsors for achievements like completing a specified number of races per year or attaining certain rankings, medals and times. To some, it felt "very transactional," said Colleen Quigley, a steeplechaser who left Nike this year and is now sponsored by Lululemon. That financial incentive fueled an intense pressure to compete, even if an athlete was struggling or injured, and can have a deleterious psychological impact, she said.

Ms. Biles ended her sponsorship with Nike this year and moved to Athleta, telling the *Wall Street Journal* that with the smaller brand, "it wasn't just about my achievements, it's what I stood for and how they were going to help me use my voice and also be a voice for females and kids." After she dropped out of the Olympic gymnastics team and all-around competitions this week, saying that the pressure she faced had adversely affected her mentally, Athleta issued a statement of support.

"We stand by Simone and support her well-being both in and out of competition," Kyle Andrew, the company's chief brand officer, said in a statement. "Being the best also means knowing how to take care of yourself. We are inspired by her leadership today and are behind her every step of the way."

Female athletes say it has not always been that way.

"As athletes, we're always going to struggle with that sense that we only have value if we can run fast, jump far or throw far," Ms. Quigley said. "It's not true, but it can feel that way really easily."

Platforms like Instagram have become a particular asset for athletes, especially those in sports that typically command major attention only once every four years. They also give athletes a way to be valued by sponsors regardless of their ranking.

Today, "our contracts are incorporating social media more and more," said Alexi Pappas, a former Nike athlete, writer and filmmaker who competed in the 2016 Olympic Games in Rio, and is now sponsored by companies including Champion. "There are other ways to add value, and those can be social media, press appearances, writing blogs and so on."

Nikki Neuburger, Lululemon's chief brand officer, said that it was aiming to work with mindful, well-rounded athletes, and that the brand and its customers cared less about placements and records. (Ms. Quigley withdrew from the U.S. Olympic trials this summer, but if she had gone to

> Compared to other opinion pieces that address problems, such as columns and editorials, articles tend to rely more heavily on evidence from other sources as well as firsthand reporting. In this article, the author has provided links to other articles as well as quotations from athletes and industry figures.

Tokyo, she would have been the brand's first Olympic athlete to compete in track and field.)

"There's still so much tremendous recognition that comes with winning and performing at an elite level," Ms. Neuburger said. "What's changed over time is that in and of itself, that's not what's inspiring people — they want to know the highs and lows of the journey to get there, they want to know what you're doing outside of the track and not just on race day."

The newer sponsorship deals also follow several years of reports about the intense pressure and stringent contracts that can exist between sponsors and elite athletes, and the aggressive tactics industry powerhouses use to keep top performers on their rosters.

In 2016, Nike made headlines when it sued Boris Berian, a star runner at the time, after his contract with the brand expired and he tried to sign with New Balance. Nike claimed it matched New Balance's offer. Mr. Berian's representatives argued that Nike did not in fact match the offer, because the company's proposed contract included "reductions" — clauses that allow sponsors to cut pay when athletes fail to meet certain performance metrics or attend competitions, even if they are injured.

The incident provoked criticism of such punitive clauses and illuminated the powerful negotiating stance of megasponsors. "I think of that as the beginning of this conversation in the running world," Ms. Pappas said.

The unique pressures felt by women athletes have taken center stage more recently. Mary Cain, a former Nike runner who is now employed by Tracksmith and chief executive of Atalanta New York City, a professional women's running team, told the *New York Times* that her Nike coaches urged her to lose so much weight that her body started to break down. Ms. Felix's criticism of Nike's pay policies for pregnant athletes, also in the *Times*, came after two of her former teammates shared their own harrowing experiences of dealing with pregnancy and sponsorships.

Nike said that it standardized a policy in 2018 that waived performance reductions for 12 months for pregnant athletes. It expanded the policy to 18 months in 2019. "We are proud of our current policy and believe it clearly conveys our support for athletes as they start their journey as mothers," Sandra Carreon-John, a spokeswoman for Nike, said.

Restrictive policies around pregnancy were long the norm, though. Sally Bergesen, founder and chief executive of Oiselle, a small running company based in Seattle, said that her brand sponsored the runner Lauren Fleshman when she was pregnant in 2013, and knew at that time that many major sponsors would not sign a track and field athlete who was expecting.

"Up until then and I think still in some contracts, they classified pregnancy as an injury, which has always been as preposterous as it sounds," Ms. Bergesen said.

Ms. Carreon-John noted that more than a third of the U.S. track and field women's roster is made up of Nike athletes. "Individual situations of a handful of athletes are not representative of Nike's support of women's sport," she said, adding, "No footwear, apparel or equipment manufacturer provides the level of support Nike provides to women's sport, period."

To be sure, Nike is a huge company and has supported a sprawling number of athletes for decades. "Nike has done a lot of great things, but sometimes when you're the big brand, there are more opportunities to get things wrong at the end of the day," said Merhawi Keflezighi, founder of HAWI Management, who represented Mr. Berian and manages Ms. Pappas. He commended the company for changing its policies for pregnant athletes and added that since 2016, the industry has become less aggressive about reduction clauses in contracts.

The new sponsorship opportunities are arising as the athletic apparel market continues to grow — a trend further fueled by the pandemic. Athleta and Lululemon were among the rare apparel brands that saw sales soar last year. In the running world, there were five to six brands that were more visible at the U.S. Olympic trials in Eugene, Ore., in June than in the past, Ms. Neuburger of Lululemon said.

"The athletic sportswear and athleisure market is transforming from growth to maturity with newer and rising entrants," said Angeline Close Scheinbaum, associate professor of marketing at Clemson University. "So naturally, a shift in athlete endorsers from the market leader to other brands is occurring."

Dr. Scheinbaum said that she viewed the trend as less of an exodus from established leaders and more about "athletes, especially women, joining a smaller brand that can become synonymous with these star athletes and their platforms and stories."

Indeed, brands that are pursuing elite women athletes are keen to embrace their backgrounds and causes that matter to them. Ms. Cain said that the most famous women athletes have often become household names because they have an "and" tied to their performance — "athlete and activist" or "athlete and mental health advocate," she said.

"Unless you have five different ways to sell yourself, you're just not valued monetarily in the same way as the white dude next to you is," she said. While that dynamic is unfair, she said, it has created a situation where women athletes often have bigger and more engaged followings online, and more brands are starting to take notice of that.

Ms. Andrew, Athleta's chief brand officer, said that corporations were beginning to prize "female values" across the board.

"There are companies that don't need to set up their partnerships in the same way they set them up for male athletes," Ms. Andrew said. "There's ways of supporting athletes in a female-forward way, and I do think it's a change and female athletes are looking for more because like most women, we're not just one thing in our lives."

Athleta and Ms. Felix recently introduced a grant program to help athletes who are mothers cover child care costs while traveling to competitions. The company will also fund a post-Olympic gymnastics exhibition tour organized by Ms. Biles that will be an alternative to U.S.A. Gymnastics, the sport's national governing body. Ms. Cain, working for Tracksmith, has been charged with building the brand's presence in New York City. Oiselle, in order to attract women athletes, has even given some of them equity in the company.

Nike noted that it has pursued initiatives like Play Academy with the tennis star Naomi Osaka, which supports the participation of young girls in sports and focuses on Black, Asian and Latino communities. (The company has also been supportive of Ms. Osaka, who took time away from major tennis tournaments this year to focus on her mental health.)

Ms. Felix, who recently introduced her own sneaker brand, Saysh, said that when she was a teenager, "you had maybe three or four options, and you went a certain route and didn't think about any of the other things because nobody was doing it." She anticipates that changing even more.

Ms. Cain said that she viewed the evolving relationship between sponsors and athletes as a generational shift. Younger athletes are increasingly asking questions about sponsorships and health insurance, career skills and other forms of support that they may not have asked for in the past, she said.

"Gen Z kids are graduating from college and they're signing contracts," Ms. Cain said, adding that at 25, she was at the tail end of the millennial generation. "The difference between what they want and what people older than me wanted is very different. It used to kind of be, how much are you going to give me financially, and now it's much more than that."

In your writer's notebook, record your analysis of Maheshwari's article by responding to the following questions:

1. Consider the opening of this opinion piece. How would you describe its purpose? Is it what you would expect in a problem-solving document? Why do you think Maheshwari begins this way? In what ways is her approach effective or ineffective?

2. The details of corporate athletic sponsorships are not widely understood by the public. How does Maheshwari describe the practices involved in sponsorship? Does the evidence she provides to support her descriptions seem appropriate and convincing? Why or why not?

3. Maheshwari points both to the downsides of traditional corporate sponsorships and the benefits of new sponsorship arrangements. Do you feel she fairly represents the advantages and disadvantages of both new and old sponsorship models? Why or why not?

4. What can you infer about Maheshwari's personal beliefs about changes in how corporations sponsor female athletes? What does this suggest about the beliefs of the intended audience?

5. **Reflection:** It is rare to be successful enough to attract sponsorship from a corporation. While sponsorships certainly can benefit individual athletes, do they also offer benefits for society more generally? Why do you think so?

Starting a Conversation: Thinking Critically about "Why Elite Female Athletes Are Turning Away from Major Sponsors"

Advice

Savannah Peterson
Advice for Generation Z from a Savvy Millennial

Writers offer advice in a variety of forms, from advice columns to speeches and presentations to essays and articles. What distinguishes documents that offer advice is the writer's purpose and role: writers who offer advice believe that a problem exists, that they understand the problem, that their readers have an interest in the problem (and most likely are affected by it), and that their advice — their solution to the problem — is worth sharing. Savannah Peterson — who was selected as one of Forbes 30 Under 30 entrepreneurs — takes a traditional approach, giving advice to the next generation about the choices she feels brought her success. She shared her advice through *Medium* (medium.com), a web-based publishing platform that combines the features of a multi-authored blog, a news aggregator, and a social-networking platform.

Advice for Generation Z from a Savvy Millennial

Savannah Peterson

> Readers can sometimes gain a great deal from the advice of writers and presenters, particularly when the advice is supported by hard-won experience and insights gained through careful reflection and analysis.

I just turned 30. *Cue eye-roll.* I know, to kids I'm old, and to sage adults, I'm young. I'm in the meaty part of the sandwich in-between the wonder bread of youth and the cheese of middle age (yes, that's a dad joke pun). I remember pondering "30" when I was a teenager and always thinking it was "SO old." I skipped third grade, finished college in under four years, and started my first company before I could legally drink. I'm used to being the youngest in the room. Lately, that's started to change. Two weeks ago, I presented to a room of "Emerging Planners" in New Zealand. The "emerging" bit means they were all under 30 . . . a realization I had on stage midway through my presentation. It visibly jarred me, yet I couldn't help my laughter. It was a moment of tragic comedy, like much of life.

Honestly, I wasn't sure I'd get here, 30 felt so far away at times. Starting a company at 20 is *en vogue* now, but was less chic 10 years ago. Early in my career I would let people believe whatever they wanted about my age. Not necessarily lying, but also not denying their over-estimation. When I became a Forbes 30 Under 30 at 27, my age was plastered everywhere.

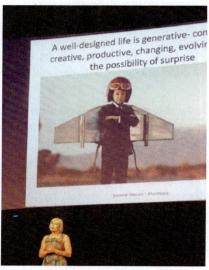

▲ Presenting to the "Emerging Planners Congress" in New Zealand shortly before I realized I was the oldest in the room.

© Savannah Peterson

The secret was out! It was a relief. Three years later I'm proud of my age and where I'm at.

At [Savvy Millennial](), I help solve the needs of diverse communities through innovative new products. I've built an international brand known for connecting people to the future. I get to travel the world inspiring other entrepreneurs, and when I'm lucky, speaking to brilliant young minds like yours. I'm not trying to brag, but it's a super

> To determine whether advice is trustworthy and useful, consider the source. To some extent, you can base your trust on the reputation of the publisher. Well-established publishers — such as reputable magazines, major news channels, and many of the larger book publishers — guard their reputations vigorously, and readers or viewers can expect that the advice they make available will have gone through a careful vetting process.

cool "job." It's also not one I could have written down on my college apps. The world is changing. Two things you should know upfront:

If you work hard, you can achieve your dreams (here's an embarrassing video *of me achieving one thanks to NASA recently.)*

Life is seldom easy; its many moving parts are complicated and you must savor the moments of pure joy.

The following tips are the best I have to offer at this stage to help you on your journey.

Do your best, F the rest. Seriously. It's that simple. My friend Bob shared this with me in my early 20's and he was in his 50's. I was struggling to start my first social media company while waiting tables at a local Italian joint during the evenings. I was afraid of not being "worth the client investment," (as if anyone had a legitimate set of KPIs for social in 2009 . . . or now). He looked me square in the face, and asked if I was prepared to give them my best. I was, and then he imparted probably the best advice I've ever received. Bob reminded me, as long as I do my best, I have nothing to be ashamed of, professionally or personally. You are the only who has to sleep with yourself each night. Life's not fair, and much is out of our control. If you do good, and are good to people, you'll have no remorse. Give this life all you've got. If you take

nothing else from this piece, take (the late and great) Bob's advice.

Let yourself be weird. My mom used to shush me when I would self-identify as a "nerd." Every time I mentioned being one, she'd exclaim, "No you're not. I'm not raising a nerd!" She didn't want me to end up an outcast. I had stick-out ears, memorized all the presidents in a night, and used to read the dictionary with my Student Body girlfriends during lunch. The odds were against her. We spoke recently while I was vlogging for NASA at Kennedy Space Center. Turns out she's come around on the geek squad now. As proof, she texted me after our successful launch, "GOOOOO NEERRRDDSS!!!!" One small step for Savannah, one large step for nerd-kind.

The Millennials were the first generation to really obsess over personalization. We didn't have it all figured out yet, and the internet was still slow, so we blasted brands across our chests and expressed ourselves through rhinestones. We bedazzled, and now you add rainbow AR Snapchat filters to your selfies. It's the same game, but you, Generation Z, get to take it to the next level. This is a good thing. The world is waking up to your individuality. Own it. 3D Print it. And . . . ignore your parents on this one. So what if they were the star quarterback and you like dungeons and dragons. They should thank their lucky stars they don't have to worry about CTE.

> Sources of advice are identified within the text or presentation in relatively general forms, most often by referring to the author or title of the source. Because advice is more informal, sources might be identified more informally as well, as with "My friend Bob . . ." here. Formal, in-text citation and works cited lists are seldom used.

Fail early and often. This is more than just a Silicon Valley cliché. Someone once told me, "no one can make your mistakes for you." They're right. Only you can learn your limits and uncover your passions. My mom taught me the value of work and how to save money. I taught myself how to earn, and spend it young, long before I needed to pay rent. I also tested my boundaries (safely-ish) with various vices before moving 1,200 miles away from parental supervision. I saw the negative impacts on those who lacked balance in both budget and booze early in college. Too much constraint leads to rebellion. Life is one big series of prototypes. The same principle applies to where you live and work. It took a decade of experimental residencies in Seattle, Austin, and New York City before I happily returned to my home state of California. Screw up early, apologize often, and learn something from it. Then get wiser and build toward the life of your (new) dreams.

Resist conformity and love yourself. When you're busy trying to fit in, you never feel comfortable in your skin — because it isn't your skin. The "popular" kids don't end up winning the game of life. You'll grow into the self-conscious bits and pieces of your person, I promise. I was called "dumbo," to which I would proudly retort "smarto!" Witty, I know. I had a gender-neutral bowl cut pre-puberty. I

▲ A smug Polaroid snap just days before moving to Austin in 2011, where I'd last all of 60 days before heading west again.

© Savannah Peterson

even wore my headgear to school. I'm not necessarily advocating you take it that far, but we all blossom. Your perceived "ugly duckling" features will one day swan. Focus on the things that make you feel good versus the things that don't. Time heals/morphs/matures all, annoying as it is. I was obsessed with my body's "imperfections" (who isn't when young) and looking back, this three sport athlete was in great shape. I wish I'd been easier on myself then, so I am now. Furthermore, you can still have abs at 30! My insta proves it. Take a deep breath. Focus on something (or one square inch of your body) you love. And continue believing in yourself. You got this.

Don't betray loyal friends for opportunistic ones. You'll be remorseful later on. I introduced myself to a tall, nervous boy, his first day of third grade 23 years ago, and this past weekend, his

> The evidence and analysis offered as support for advice varies widely. Advice is often based on analysis or personal experience, but it can also include results from studies, statistical analysis of survey data, excerpts from interviews, and reports from observation. In this case, Peterson posts links to her social-media accounts, her website, and to other sources online to provide context and support for her advice.

"first friend" saw him tie the knot. It was easy, stepping back into a familiar familial nest for a night of revelry. I also was invited to officiate the wedding of my dear friend from Stix from college, in Scotland a few years ago. The "tripod" is all now in their 30's, spread across the country, but our WhatsApp group keeps us tight. We make visits happen when we can. Wrapping the comfort of shared history, respect and love around each other in hugs that feel like a blanket. My point is, don't chase every shiny friend object. Stay in touch. Send the text or the snap. Indicate you care somehow despite the distance whether it's across the quad or across the globe. Time may lead you down different paths, but you'll never regret investing in a true friend. Of the things I'm most proud of at 30, my friends are #1. Find your tribe....

Understand what fuels your body and mind. Prototype everything. Read. Try different foods and explore your athletic capabilities. Learn your boundaries. Pay attention to what gives you energy and what depletes it. This applies to activities and nutrients, as well as substances. Part of why I love traveling is I find local customs, particularly those centered on wellness, to be fascinating. Society will throw a lot of fad diets at you, friends will go through dramatic workout phases, and inevitably you will be peer pressured. Ignore anything that doesn't feel right. Wait for time to test methods that sound too good to be true. Eat what makes your body function best. If that's raw kale, great. If it's meat and potatoes, that's cool too.

Wellness is more about consistency and balance than obsessive calorie-counting. I feel my best when I start the day with a trail run (or hike) with my dog, Martini. Others prefer group fitness after work. Regardless, find a way to integrate some form of exercise into your day. Dedicate time each day to being off-screen and still. Wellness is a lifestyle choice it pays to make. Listen to your body. Be well.

Check your judgement. Never side with the bullies. Prejudice is passed down and racism is learned. Block out the subtle adult jokes and jaded remarks you hear and never repeat them. Harsh words make permanent impressions on young minds. I have had many

> I thank you for your attention. Time is the most precious resource you have. All my best on the journey ahead,
> ~Savannah

> You can make judgments about the quality of advice by comparing what is being said with your understanding of the problem and by reflecting on your experiences. If you find that the advice seems applicable, you might have greater confidence in following it. In this case, Peterson's suggestion mirrors our own: be skeptical of advice that you cannot confirm or that does not seem reasonable.

Keeping the peace: Principal Pete Zotovich observes the demonstration.

Let's get circumambi[ulating for] unity. Many other proteste[rs once a] circle had been formed. S[...]

Meet the press: Peace rally organizer sophomore Sa[van]nah Peterson gets interviewed by KSBY reporter Tony C[...]

▲ Here's a snap in the paper from a walkout I led in 2003. I'm sorry we haven't done more yet, but we took a stand then, and we stand with you now.

© Savannah Peterson

less-than-glamorous moments, but I am proud of every time I stood up to a bully. It started on the Kindergarten playground (I told a lunch-thieving menace to back off our smaller peers) and it continues politically (#MeToo.) We all deserve equal rights and equal access to opportunity. Encourage acceptance and equality at home and with your peers. The majority of Generation Z is a minority. Respect it all. We know when we stand on the wrong side of history. The buck stops with us. The young people have had #enough. Your generation is rising. Join them.

Starting a Conversation: Thinking Critically about "Advice for Generation Z from a Savvy Millennial"

In your writer's notebook, record your analysis of "Advice for Generation Z from a Savvy Millennial" by responding to the following questions:

1. Who do you think Peterson's intended audience is? Who else, outside of the intended audience, might this article appeal to? Why?

2. Peterson alternates between direct advice to the reader and personal anecdotes. Why do you think she does this? What effect does it have on her relationship with her readers?

3. How does Peterson build support for her solutions to the problem of finding success and personal happiness? What sort of reasons or examples does she use? How believable are her proposed solutions? If you were writing an article on this topic, what other information would you include?

4. In paragraph 10, Peterson writes, "Don't betray loyal friends for opportunistic ones. You'll be remorseful later on." What do you think *opportunistic* means in this context? How would you paraphrase what Peterson is saying?

5. **Reflection:** Based on your experiences so far (in whatever generation you belong to), do you agree with Peterson's suggestions for finding success? Why or why not? Do you have other solutions to add? Is there anything Peterson proposes that seems unreasonable or unattainable?

GENRE TALK

Reflective Writing | Informative Writing | Analytical Writing | Evaluative Writing | **Problem-Solving Writing** | Argumentative Writing

In recent years, more attention has been drawn to the problem of child labor on cocoa farms. According to the U.S. Department of Labor, more than two million cocoa laborers in Ivory Coast and Ghana are between five and fourteen years old. To harvest the cocoa, laborers must perform extremely hazardous work, including clearing forests with chainsaws, cutting down cocoa bean pods with machetes, and carrying heavy sacks of cocoa beans. Labor analysts and policy researchers have found that many children are trafficked into slavery in the cocoa industry, with little hope of earning their freedom. As global demand for chocolate increases, several fair trade companies have created partnerships with cocoa farmers to pay them a fair wage, allowing them to hire legal adult workers and ensure safe working environments.

These Halloween cards from the International Labor Rights Forum offer hard facts about the problem and ask readers to become part of the solution.

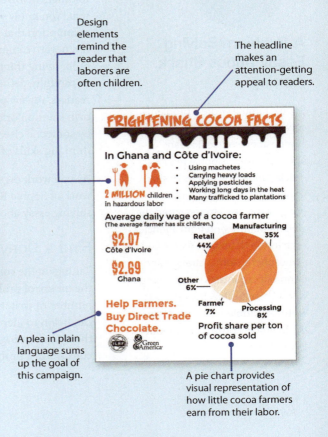

A tag line identifies the dilemma facing consumers.

A point-by-point explanation shows how direct trade companies address the problem of slave labor in the cocoa industry.

A photograph personalizes the plight of cocoa farmers.

Design elements remind the reader that laborers are often children.

The headline makes an attention-getting appeal to readers.

A plea in plain language sums up the goal of this campaign.

A pie chart provides visual representation of how little cocoa farmers earn from their labor.

Both images Courtesy of International Labor Rights Forum and Green America

How Can I Write a Problem-Solving Essay?

We all have problems. Some of us have more than others. You've probably heard someone say, "I've got a problem. My taxes are due" or "I'm about to be evicted from my apartment" or "My hard drive crashed." When people make statements like these, they are assuming that you share their understanding of the problem. Unfortunately, that's not always the case. You might assume that the person who has a problem paying taxes lacks the money to do so and that the best solution is to get a loan or pick up a part-time job. In fact, the problem might be based on a moral objection to how the government uses revenue raised through taxes.

Until people share an understanding of a problem, it can be difficult to develop a solution and put it into effect. A successful problem-solving essay begins with the recognition that explaining a problem to others involves far more than saying, "I've got a problem with that. You know what I mean?" In this chapter, we'll work from the assumption that a problem is best understood as a situation that has negative consequences for an individual, a group, or some other living thing. To address such a situation in writing, you need to carefully define your problem, consider its significance for readers, review past efforts to address it, and either develop your own solution or argue for the adoption of one that's been proposed by someone else. This will involve drawing heavily on the critical thinking skills of understanding, analyzing, evaluating, and creating.

As you work on your own problem-solving essay, you'll follow the work of Sophie Kimble, a first-year student who wrote a problem-solving essay about the impact of shark finning on ocean ecosystems.

Find a Conversation and Listen In

Taking on the role of problem solver requires you to understand the nature of problems — an understanding that a surprisingly large number of writers appear to lack. By learning about problems, you can begin to identify and understand them and even to address them in meaningful ways. Once you gain an understanding of what constitutes a problem, you can begin to look for and learn about

In Process

A Problem-Solving Essay about Shark Finning

Sophie Kimble wrote a problem-solving essay for her introductory composition course. To learn about her topic, Sophie read articles about the causes of shark finning and its effect on ocean ecosystems. She also searched the web for information from agencies such as the National Oceanic and Atmospheric Administration and nonprofit organizations concerned with oceans. Follow her efforts to write her problem-solving essay in the In Process boxes throughout this chapter.

problems that intrigue you. In the process, you'll position yourself to choose a problem to address in your essay.

● EXPLORE DIFFICULTIES

A good problem-solving essay begins with what educational philosopher John Dewey called a "felt difficulty" — the recognition that something isn't right. As you learn about an issue, you might find yourself wondering why something is the way it is, or perhaps you'll say to yourself, "That's not right." Treasure these early moments of recognizing a problem. If you feel that something isn't right, there's a good chance that a problem is near at hand.

As you search for felt difficulties in the world around you, keep in mind the idea that a problem is a situation with negative consequences for someone or something. Your responses to the following sets of questions can help you identify subjects that might serve as the focus for a problem-solving essay. (For additional suggestions, see writing project ideas at the end of this chapter.)

- **Community.** What kind of difficulties have you encountered or noticed in your neighborhood? Have you been stuck in long lines at a bank or post office? Have you volunteered at a food pantry that has been overwhelmed by an influx of new clients? Run across a pothole so deep that it ruined one of your tires? Been bothered by the recent actions of local politicians or law enforcement officials?

- **Economy.** Are any of your friends or relatives having financial difficulties? Have you worried about what the future holds for you? For your parents? For your children?

- **Work.** Do any issues at your workplace need to be addressed? Is the industry in which you work facing any challenges? Have you grown aware, through your course work or general reading, of difficulties facing people in your field of study?

- **News.** What have you read recently that surprised or worried you? What annoyed you or made you angry? What have you read that made you think? What controversies have you noticed on the evening news or on the websites you visit?

To begin turning a felt difficulty into a defined problem, jot down what doesn't feel right and then brainstorm or freewrite about it (see *Generate Ideas* in Chapter 2). As you list ideas or write about your felt difficulty, the problem will begin to come into focus.

● ASK QUESTIONS ABOUT PROMISING SUBJECTS

Even if you think you know a great deal about each of the problems you've identified as potential subjects for your essay, check them out thoroughly before you begin trying to solve one. To learn more about a promising problem, reflect on your own experiences with it, discuss it with others, and find and review relevant published sources through your library or the web. (You can learn more about locating, collecting, and managing information in Part Three.)

Once you've learned about the most promising problems, select those that continue to hold your interest, and then spend a few minutes responding to the following questions. Each set of questions focuses your attention on a problem in a different way, allowing you to think not only about the problem but also about its potential as the focus of your problem-solving essay. Depending on the problem you work with, you'll find that some questions are more useful than others.

- **Relevance.** Is this problem widespread, or does it involve only a small group of people? Who or what is affected by it, and how are they affected? Will my readers think it's important? Can I address it within the limits of my assignment?
- **Definition.** What, exactly, is the problem? How can I explain it? What kinds of information will readers need to understand it?
- **Context.** When and where did this problem begin? How much is known about it? What solutions have been tried? Why haven't they worked?
- **Causes and effects.** What caused this problem? What must happen before it can be solved? What is likely to happen if it isn't solved?

As you consider these questions, remember that the best problems to tackle in an essay are usually highly specific. For example, instead of writing about the general problem of encouraging college students to become teachers, you might focus on how to encourage students in a particular discipline, such as math or biology, to become high school teachers in rural school districts.

● LOCATE RELEVANT SOURCES AND CONDUCT FIELD RESEARCH

As with other types of essays, you might find it useful to locate published sources that address the problem you are investigating. By searching library catalogs, databases, and the web, you can locate sources that will help you understand the problem and its potential solutions more deeply.

Similarly, you might find it useful to collect information firsthand through techniques such as interviews, observations, correspondence, and surveys. Field research allows you to gain insights you might not be able to obtain through published sources. A survey, for example, can help you learn about the beliefs, attitudes, or behaviors of people associated with a problem. Typically, surveys help you answer *what, who,* or *how* questions — such as "What kinds of exercise do you engage in at least once a week?" — rather than more analytical *why* questions. With this in mind, you might use a survey to discover whether the attitudes and beliefs about education differ among students who stay in school and those who drop out. Or you might use a survey to explore whether students who put a high value on community involvement are highly engaged in volunteer activities.

Learn more about searching for sources and conducting field research in Chapters 13, 14, and 15.

Develop a Solution

Once you've identified a promising problem and learned about it, you can begin to develop a solution to the problem. If your problem has already attracted the attention of other writers, the solution you choose might be one that another

Working Together: Ask Whether Your Judgments Are Fair

Before you start working on your problem-solving essay, start a conversation with a small group of your classmates about a minor problem that affects you. Explain the problem as clearly as you can, and tell the members of your group about how you think you might solve it. Ask them whether your preliminary solution seems likely to work and why. Then ask them to suggest additional solutions. Take turns speaking while the members of the group listen, respond, and ask questions.

When you are finished, take a few minutes to reflect on the exercise. What did you learn about your audience? Did they understand the problem right away, or did you have to adapt or expand your initial explanation? How much detail did you have to give them before your solution made sense? Did they think your solution was reasonable? What kinds of solutions did they suggest as alternatives? Did their questions and suggestions help you develop a better understanding of your problem or give you new ideas about how to solve it?

writer has already advanced, or it might be an improved version of someone else's proposed solution. If the problem has remained unresolved for some time, however, you might find it best to develop a new solution. If your problem is relatively new or is one that has not yet attracted the attention of other writers, you might develop your own solution to the problem, or you might look at how similar problems have been addressed and then adapt one of those solutions.

Whatever approach you take, remember that a clear problem definition is the single most important element in a problem-solving essay. Without it, even the most elegant solution won't be convincing. A problem definition enables you to take a problem apart, examine its causes and effects, and understand whom or what it affects. It also influences how your readers understand the problem and how they are likely to react to your solution.

In addition, remember that a solution must be practical. Few readers will be impressed by a solution that costs too much or takes too long to put into effect or that causes even more problems than it solves. As you consider potential solutions to your problem, carefully assess their feasibility and potential consequences.

● DEFINE THE PROBLEM

Some people define a problem with a particular solution in mind. As a result, their solution usually looks good in theory. But a solution based on a weak problem definition seldom works well in practice, and it is unlikely to convince your readers. For this and other reasons, you should define your problem as clearly and accurately as possible.

You can define your problem by exploring situation and effects, focusing on actions, examining severity and duration, and considering goals and barriers.

Situation/effects Explore the effects a problematic situation has on people or things. Ask yourself:

- What is the situation?
- What are its effects?
- Who or what is affected?

Agent/goals/actions/results Focus on actions that have unwanted results. Ask yourself:

- Who or what is the *agent* (the person, group, or thing that acts in a manner that causes a problem)?
- What are the agent's *goals*?
- What *actions* does the agent carry out to accomplish the goals?
- What are the *results* of the agent's actions?

Severity and duration Analyze the severity and duration of the effects of a problematic situation. Ask yourself:

- What is the situation?
- What effects are associated with the situation?
- How severe are the effects?
- What is the duration of the effects?

Goals and barriers Identify goals, and ask what obstacles stand in the way of accomplishing them. Ask yourself:

- What are the goals?
- What barriers stand in the way of accomplishing the goals?

Most of these methods of defining a problem focus on cause/effect relationships, and many involve unintended consequences. However, each one allows you to view a problem from a different perspective. Because your problem definition has powerful effects on the development of a solution to your problem, it can be useful to experiment with different ways of defining the problem.

● CONSIDER POTENTIAL SOLUTIONS

Use your problem definition to weigh potential solutions. If your problem definition focuses on the causes of the problem or barriers to achieving a goal, for example, consider solutions that address those causes or barriers. If your problem definition focuses on actions that have had unexpected or undesired effects, explore solutions that might address those effects. If your problem definition focuses on the duration and severity of a problem, ask yourself how the duration and severity of the problem might be reduced or perhaps even eliminated.

In Process

Developing a Survey

As part of her problem-solving essay about shark finning, Sophie Kimble explored the idea of launching a social-media campaign to raise awareness about the issue. Sophie created a survey to find out more about students' social-media habits. She kept it brief so that more students would respond.

> A multiple-choice question asks respondents to pick one answer.

1. Which social media platform do you use the most? (Check one.)

   ___ Facebook
   ___ Twitter
   ___ Snapchat
   ___ Instagram

> Room is provided for brief comments.

Comment:

2. Which topics do you tend to write about frequently on social media? (Check as many as apply.)

   ___ College life (academics, campus life)
   ___ News and politics (local, state, and national)
   ___ Sports and entertainment (sports, books, music, movies, video games)
   ___ Lifestyle (food, entertaining, pets)
   ___ Science and technology
   ___ Other: _____

> A multiple-choice question asks respondents to pick multiple answers.

Comment:

3. How likely are you to bookmark or retweet a post that you find relevant or informative?

   ___ Very likely
   ___ Somewhat likely
   ___ Neither likely nor unlikely
   ___ Somewhat unlikely
   ___ Very unlikely

> A Likert-scale question asks students to indicate the likelihood that they would retweet a favorite post.

Comment:

As you generate ideas for possible solutions, keep in mind what you've learned about your problem. If you're dealing with a problem that other writers have addressed, pay attention to the solutions they've proposed. Even if those solutions have failed to solve the problem — which is likely, given the continuing existence of the problem — they might have helped address at least some of its effects. Consider the impact of these earlier solutions, weigh their negative consequences, and ask whether you might adapt them — or parts of them — for your own use.

Defining a Problem

Sophie Kimble used the situation/effects questions (discussed earlier in this chapter) to develop her problem definition. In response to her instructor's request for a formal problem definition, she used the situation/effects approach.

What is the situation? Shark finning involves cutting off a shark's fin(s) and throwing the fish back into the ocean to bleed or drown to death. Shark finning is a response to the demand for shark fin soup, which is seen as a symbol of wealth and status, as well as the demand for the use of shark fins in traditional medicines. Even though shark fins add no taste to shark fin soup and there is little evidence of its effectiveness in traditional medicine, more than 100 million sharks are slaughtered every year. Because sharks are seen as dangerous predators, little sympathy exists among the public for preserving sharks.

What are the effects? For sharks, shark finning is a death sentence. They rely on movement in order to circulate oxygen throughout their bodies, so they slowly suffocate. For ocean ecosystems, the results are equally dangerous. As the apex predator of the ocean, sharks are vital to the balance of this already suffering ecosystem.

Who is affected? The ocean ecosystem is in danger due to a lack of balance brought on by a declining shark population. This affects all life in the ocean. It also affects life on land, including people.

Because Sophie was trying to approach the problem of shark finning as a situation with extremely broad effects, the situation/effects questions worked well for her. Since she was also interested in assessing the severity of the problem and its long-term impact, she might also have used the questions that address severity and duration. If she had been trying to identify the causes of the problem, she might have used the agent/goals/actions/results questions.

In your writer's notebook, create a list of potential solutions — both your own and those of other writers — and briefly describe them. Evaluate each solution by answering the following questions:

- How well does this solution address the causes of the problem?
- How well does this solution address the effects of the problem?
- To what extent does this solution address the needs of the people or things affected by the problem?
- What costs would be associated with this solution?
- What advantages does this solution have over other solutions?
- What disadvantages does this solution have?

Review your responses to the questions, and identify your most promising solutions. If you've identified more than one solution, ask whether the best features of each might be combined into a single solution. As you consider each solution, you'll gain a better understanding of the problem itself. Your problem-solving essay will be most effective if you clearly connect your solution to your problem definition, so you might find it useful to revise your definition to reflect the additional thinking you've put into the problem. Remember that your problem definition isn't set in stone. It can be revised and improved throughout the process of writing your essay.

● ASSESS THE PRACTICALITY OF YOUR SOLUTION

Most problems can be solved given unlimited time, vast sums of money, revisions to the laws of physics, or changes in human nature. If your solution requires any or all of these, however, your readers are likely to question its practicality. Before you start drafting your essay, ensure that your solution is feasible by asking whether your solution can be implemented

- in a reasonable amount of time
- with available funding
- with available resources
- given current knowledge and technology
- without causing additional problems

Consider as well how your readers' needs, interests, and backgrounds will affect their responses to your solution. For example, if your readers have strong religious beliefs about the use of birth control, they probably won't react favorably to a proposal to reduce teenage pregnancies by requiring public schools to dispense contraceptives.

Developing a Solution

To begin solving the problem she had defined, Sophie Kimble created a cluster of ideas. She used the situation/effects and severity/duration questions discussed earlier in this chapter to explore causes, effects, severity, and potential solutions to the problem of shark finning.

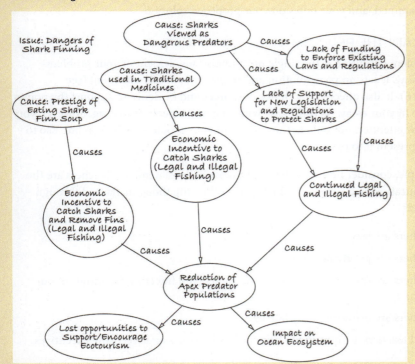

In Process

Sophie placed her issue — the dangers of shark finning — in a bubble at the center of his cluster.

Each cause, effect, level of severity, and solution generated more specific ideas.

Sophie's cluster helped her lay out existing and potential responses to the problem. With that in mind, she used freewriting to generate ideas that might solve both aspects of the problem.

> Sharks are not an animal that people generally feel natural empathy toward such as dogs, pandas, polar bears, etc. And the people participating in the industry are just trying to feed their families, and this industry helps them make money. Previous solutions, such as legislation and regulation, haven't solved the problem. If we look at solutions that involve changing attitudes toward sharks and providing alternative ways for people to make a living, such as ecotourism, we might find a solution that works.

Finally, consider potential objections to your solution. If your solution requires funding or resources that might be used for other purposes, for example, ask whether readers will object to reducing funding for those purposes. You might be able to modify your solution to account for likely objections, or you might want to prepare an argument about why the trade-offs are better than just leaving things as they are.

Prepare a Draft

As you get ready to draft your essay, review your problem definition, the solutions you've examined, and your notes on your proposed solution.

● EXPLAIN THE PROBLEM

Your problem definition is the single most important element of your problem-solving essay. It sets up your solution and shapes your thesis statement (see Chapter 18). It also affects your choice of sources and evidence to support the points you make in your essay. As is the case with so many aspects of writing, however, you should pay attention not only to the content of your problem definition but also to how you present it to readers.

For example, consider how a reader might react to the statement "Teachers are the reason education is in trouble." Which of the following thoughts flashed through your mind?

- Teachers are lazy.
- Teachers are poorly prepared.
- Teachers are spreading left-wing propaganda and infecting the minds of our youth.
- Teachers are extraordinarily boring.
- Good teachers are quitting to become stockbrokers or advertising executives.

All of the above? None of the above? Now substitute "students" or "parents" or "politicians" or "television" or "video games" in the same statement. What flashes through your mind?

Statements like these are unclear because they don't define the problem. They don't explain, for example, what it is about teachers (or anything else) that causes education to be in trouble.

Consider the differences between "Teachers are the reason education is in trouble" and the following problem definitions.

Problem definition 1: The lack of certified science teachers in public schools has limited the development of a general understanding of key scientific concepts among Americans. Without that understanding, it will be difficult to carry out informed debates about policies that rely on an understanding of scientific concepts, such as the development of small-scale nuclear power plants or decisions about how best to deal with pandemics.

Problem definition 2: The relatively low salaries offered to beginning teachers, combined with the growing cost of higher education and the high debt burden incurred by many college graduates, have reduced the attractiveness of pursuing a career as an educator. The result is a growing shortage of qualified teachers in key areas, such as the sciences, mathematics, and the arts. Because of this shortage, students are not receiving the education they deserve.

Each of these problem definitions calls attention to the effects of a particular situation on specific groups or individuals. In the first example, the situation — a lack of certified science teachers — affects Americans' ability to understand and participate in debates about scientific issues. In the second example, the economic situation faced by beginning teachers affects college students' willingness to pursue careers as teachers, which in turn affects the education of students. Through their clarity and detail, both of these problem definitions offer significant advantages over "Teachers are the reason education is in trouble."

As you consider how best to explain your problem definition to your readers, reflect on what they already know about it. If they are already familiar with the problem, you might be able to convey your problem definition in one or two sentences that frame the solution that will follow. If they are unfamiliar with the problem, however, you might need to devote a significant portion of your essay to establishing the existence of the problem and explaining its consequences.

● PROPOSE YOUR SOLUTION

Most problem-solving essays frame the problem in a way that prepares readers to accept the proposed solution. The problem of rising college tuition costs, for example, might be framed so that the best solution would seem to involve more online learning opportunities, while the problem of a growing national debt might be framed so that the best solution would appear to rely on changes in tax laws.

After you introduce a problem to your readers, you can present a thesis statement that summarizes your proposed solution. Your thesis statement should be closely tied to your problem definition, and it should suggest a logical and reasonable means of addressing the problem. Because your thesis statement will frame readers' understanding of your solution in a certain way, it serves as a powerful tool for influencing your readers. Consider the differences among the following thesis statements addressing the problem of low salaries for teachers who leave college with high levels of debt:

> **Thesis statement 1:** If we are to ensure an adequate supply of qualified teachers, we must increase their starting salaries.
>
> **Thesis statement 2:** The most promising approach to ensuring an adequate supply of qualified teachers is paying the tuition and fees for college students who promise to spend at least five years teaching in our public schools.

Each of these thesis statements calls attention to a different solution to the problem. The first focuses on salaries, suggesting that the promise of higher salaries will lead more students to consider a career in teaching and perhaps will encourage those who do become teachers to stay in the profession. The second thesis statement focuses on the cost of attending college, borrowing an approach used successfully to attract new doctors to rural areas. Each thesis statement offers a reasonable solution to the problem as it has been defined, yet each would also lead the writer to produce a significantly different essay.

Is your thesis statement focused enough? See Chapter 18 for help.

● EXPLAIN YOUR SOLUTION

Your solution is what most readers will remember about your essay. Once you've defined the problem and proposed your solution, explain your solution by going into detail, offering support for your ideas, and considering your solution in light of promising alternatives.

Go into detail A surprising number of problem-solving essays spend several pages defining and discussing the consequences of a problem, only to offer a skimpy discussion of a proposed solution. Readers are rarely satisfied with such an approach, so be sure to spend some time identifying the key aspects of your solution. Help your readers understand, in detail, how you would implement the solution, how much it would cost to put into effect, what kinds of effects the solution would have on the problem, and how you would judge its effectiveness in addressing the problem.

Provide support for your points Most problem-solving essays rely heavily on evidence to establish the existence of a problem, support a proposed solution, and dismiss alternative solutions. Your solution should offer a reasonable and thoughtful response to the problem, and it should be clear that your proposed solution is superior to alternatives.

You can use evidence to

- identify and frame your solution
- provide examples and illustrations
- illustrate processes that might be required to put the solution in place
- associate particular ideas and concepts with authorities, such as political leaders, subject-matter experts, or people who have been affected by the problem

To develop support, list the key points you are making about your proposed solution. For each point, review your sources and notes to identify relevant evidence, and then list the evidence below each point. If your sources support your solution, draw on evidence from them to show your readers why your solution is likely to be effective. If your sources do not directly address your solution, consider using personal experience or field research (see Chapter 15). You can read more about how to use evidence to support your points in Chapter 21.

Address promising alternative solutions As you draft your problem-solving essay, be sure to consider alternative solutions that are likely to occur to your readers. In proposing a solution to a problem, you are essentially making an argument that your solution is preferable to others. If your readers can think of alternatives, especially alternatives that might be less expensive or more effective than yours, they might wonder why you haven't mentioned them. To address (and dismiss) alternative solutions, you can do the following:

- Identify the strongest alternative solution, explain why it's the best of several alternatives, and then explain why your solution is better.
- Identify a group of alternative solutions that share the same weakness, such as high cost or impracticality, and explain why this group of solutions is weaker than your solution.
- Identify a group of promising alternatives, and dismiss each solution, one after the other.

You can gain insights into effective strategies for organizing your response to alternative solutions by reading about organizing patterns in Chapter 19.

● CONSIDER GENRE AND DESIGN

Depending on the complexity of the problem you're addressing and the nature of the solution you propose, design can contribute greatly to the overall effectiveness of your essay. As you contemplate design options for your essay, make note of any formatting requirements specified in your assignment (such as margins, spacing, font, and the like). Consider as well the expectations of your readers, particularly your instructor. You might also think about including visual evidence such as figures and images. These illustrations can help readers better understand complex concepts or see trends that would be difficult to discern through textual descriptions alone. Be sure to provide captions to help direct readers' attention to key information in the illustration. And place illustrations near their first mention in the text. You can learn more about figures, images, captions, and other aspects of document design in Chapters 22 and 23.

Providing Support for Key Points

Sophie Kimble identified support for her key points by listing each point, then reviewing her notes to find sources that would support those points. She wrote the relevant sources next to each point.

Key Points	Support
Sharks are endangered, with fins cut off, to provide shark fin soup and traditional medicine treatments.	Liu, Tutton Photograph of Shark Fin Soup
This has a strong impact on ocean ecosystems because sharks are an apex predator essential to ecosystems and sharks have a slow reproductive/maturation cycle.	Scales, Castro
Previous efforts at legislation have proven less effective than needed because of a strong black market.	Animal Welfare Institute, Rogers
There is little sympathy for sharks among the general public.	Knowlton and Benchley, Tsoi et al.
We can change this through social media campaigns, education, and reliance on ecotourism.	Ramsey, Pew Charitable Trusts Screen capture of Ocean Ramsey website

FRAME YOUR ESSAY

Once you've worked out how to define the problem and present your proposed solution, decide how you'll organize, introduce, and conclude your essay.

Organization Most problem-solving essays start with an introduction, then define the problem and explain the proposed solution, and finish with a conclusion. Longer problem-solving essays often make use of the organizing patterns discussed in Chapter 19. For instance, process explanation can offer a helpful outline for explaining the steps involved in implementing a solution. The costs/benefits and strengths/weaknesses patterns provide a practical structure for both analyzing a problem and examining a solution's potential. And problem-solving essays that address several alternative solutions often take advantage of the comparison/contrast pattern.

Introduction Your introduction creates a framework within which you can present your thesis statement and prepare your readers to understand how you've defined your problem. You can draw on a number of strategies to draw your readers in:

- Use an anecdote (a brief story) to personalize the problem.
- Use dramatic statistics, as Sophie Kimble does in her essay, to illustrate the scope of the problem.
- Use quotations from experts, or from people who have been affected by a problem, to make the problem hit home with your readers.
- Draw comparisons between this problem and other, more widely understood problems.

You can read more about strategies for introducing your essay in Chapter 20.

Conclusion In much the same way that you can use your introduction to direct readers toward a particular understanding of a problem, you can use your conclusion to encourage them to accept your ideas for solving it. Most problem-solving essays end with a call to action, in which the writer urges readers to do something specific to help put the solution into effect. Other strategies you can employ to conclude your essay include summarizing your problem definition and proposed solution, circling back to the introduction, and speculating about the future. You can learn more about framing your conclusion in Chapter 20.

Review and Improve Your Draft

The success of your problem-solving essay rests heavily on how well you can define your problem, present your solution, convince readers that your solution is feasible, and consider alternatives and potential objections to your solution. Few writers can manage all these tasks in a first draft, so keep them in mind as you assess your draft and revise your essay.

● REASSESS YOUR PROBLEM DEFINITION

Now that your essay is in draft form, consider how well you present your problem definition and how effectively it leads to your proposed solution. Your problem definition should direct your readers' attention to the problem in a particular way. If not, they'll find it difficult to understand how your definition of the problem is related to your proposed solution. As you draft your essay — and spend additional time thinking about the problem — you will almost certainly deepen your understanding of the problem. Take a few moments now to ask whether your problem definition fully reflects that understanding.

Then ask some harder questions: Have you defined your problem in the best way (with *best* defined in light of the solution you've proposed and the needs, interests, and backgrounds of your readers)? Will your readers accept the problem definition you've developed? If you suspect that they'll object to it or find it inadequate, how can you change it to address their likely concerns?

● REVIEW THE PRESENTATION OF YOUR SOLUTION

When you're in the midst of drafting, it's normal to spend more time on some aspects of your solution than others or to overlook key steps that will be required to put the solution into effect. As you review your draft, take a careful look at how you've presented your solution. Have you explained it logically and clearly? Have you provided your readers with a sufficiently detailed understanding of what the solution involves and how it could work? Have you presented sufficient evidence to support your points?

● CHECK THE FEASIBILITY OF YOUR SOLUTION

When you're caught up in the details of presenting a solution, it's easy to lose sight of whether the solution will actually work. During your review, ask whether the solution you've proposed can be put into practice given the time, funding, and resources that are available. If you suspect that you've proposed a solution that might not be cost-effective — such as solving the problem of rising tuition costs by giving every high school graduate who wants to attend college a $100,000 scholarship, a solution that would cost taxpayers roughly $400 billion each year — you might want to reconsider your solution. Similarly, if the time and resources necessary to achieve a solution are simply not available, take another look at your options.

- **CONSIDER OBJECTIONS AND ALTERNATIVE SOLUTIONS**

Put yourself in the position of your readers, and ask some hard questions. Why is this solution better than another? What are the major drawbacks of your proposed solution? Under what conditions would your solution be likely to fail? Identify the objections your readers might have to your solution, and address them in your essay. Look as well for challenges to your solution that your readers might not consider but that you've become aware of in the course of your reading. Then address each challenge, explaining clearly why your solution is preferable to the alternatives you've identified.

- **RESPOND TO FEEDBACK FROM YOUR INSTRUCTOR**

Unsurprisingly, instructors who provide feedback on early drafts of problem-solving essays tend to focus most of their initial attention on the quality of the problem definition, the solution that is offered, and the support provided for the solution. Given the complexity of most problems, instructors are likely to offer suggestions about strengthening even well-defined problems and well-thought-out solutions. In addition to these major aspects of the essay, they are also likely to comment on how well you've adapted to the needs, interests, and backgrounds of your readers and on the organization of your essay. If your instructor has offered feedback on more than one draft, later drafts might address concerns at the sentence or word levels.

Responding to Instructor Feedback

Sophie received comments from her instructor on the first draft of her essay. Her instructor seemed interested primarily in how she was defining her problem and framing the issue. Noting that Sophie's initial problem definition didn't seem to be well matched to her proposed solution, her instructor asked her to spend more time considering her problem definition.

In response, Sophie focused her problem definition more specifically on her concerns about shifting public attitudes toward sharks. She called attention to the lack of awareness of the importance of sharks in ocean ecosystems and the economic incentives to continue the practice of shark finning. She also called attention to the lack of effectiveness of existing approaches to solving the problem.

Peer Review: Improve Your Problem-Solving Essay

One of the biggest challenges writers face is reading a draft of their own work as a reader rather than as the writer. Because you know what you're trying to say, you find it easy to understand your draft. To determine what you should do to revise your draft, ask a friend or classmate to read your essay and to assess how well you have adopted the role of problem solver by answering the following questions:

Purpose	1. Is my problem definition sufficiently narrow and focused? Is it clear and easy to understand?
	2. Do you believe the problem is significant? Why or why not?
	3. Is my solution clearly presented? Does it seem like a reasonable response to the problem I've defined?
Readers	4. Were you aware of the problem before you read the essay? Are other readers likely to be familiar with it? Do I need to say more about it to help readers understand?
	5. Are you convinced that my solution can work? Does it seem feasible? Why or why not?
	6. Have I presented ideas fairly? Are you aware of any potential objections or alternative solutions that I should have addressed?
Sources	7. Does the evidence I've offered to define the problem and support my proposed solution make sense? Can I add or clarify anything to help you understand the problem and solution better? Do you think any of the evidence is unnecessary?
	8. Do my sources strike you as reliable and appropriate? Does any of the evidence I've used seem questionable?
Context	9. Have I taken my readers' knowledge, assumptions, and values into consideration?
	10. Would any of the information I've drawn on in this essay be better presented in visual form? Could I make changes in page layout, color, shading, or rules to improve the essay's appearance?

For each of the points listed above, ask your reviewers to provide concrete advice about what you should do to improve your draft. It can help if you ask them to adopt the role of an editor — someone who is working with you to improve your draft. You can read more about peer review in Chapter 5.

★ Student Essay

Sophie Kimble, "Sharks for Profit"

The following problem-solving essay was written by featured writer Sophie Kimble.

Kimble 1

Sophie Kimble
Professor Mike Palmquist
Composition 150
May 5, 2022

Sharks for Profit

    Imagine a great white shark swimming in open water. In the minds of most people, this image might elicit more fear than awe. The average person would surely rather find themselves face to face with almost any other predator. Pop culture and primal instincts encourage us to fear these creatures, and their strange appearance and mannerisms cause us to believe they are different, alien, and dangerous.

    The reality is that sharks swim near humans every day, and they rarely attack. In 2020, the International Shark Attack File database reported only 57 unprovoked shark attacks on humans worldwide, and of those only ten involved unprovoked fatalities (Florida Museum of Natural History).

    In contrast, humans may be a shark's biggest nightmare. In the most comprehensive study published on the impact of shark deaths associated with fishing, Boris Worm and his colleagues estimate that approximately 100 million sharks are killed globally each year. One of the major incentives for this is the shark fin trade, which has been a multi-billion dollar industry since the 1980s (Rogers). Shark fins are used in shark fin soup, which is a popular dish in Asia, and often seen as a symbol of status and wealth (Fig. 1). They are also used in traditional medicines (Tutton). According to CNN senior editor Marian Liu, a pound of shark fin can sell for up to $930, and sometimes a bowl of shark fin soup can cost as much as $160. And this is the case despite the fact that it does not add any taste to the dish.

Fig. 1. Shark fin soup.

skaman306/Getty Images

Kimble 2

Shark finning — the practice of removing a shark's fin(s), and letting the shark die a slow and painful death through suffocation, blood loss, or starvation — is the largest cause of shark mortality. "When a shark's fin is sliced off, the animal dies," says Yvonne Sadovy, a professor in the School of Biological Sciences at the University of Hong Kong and lead author of a major report on shark finning. "It cannot move, feed or swim, so it just starves to death on the sea bottom" (qtd. in Liu).

The danger to ocean ecosystems posed by shark finning is clear. Sharks are essential to the health of oceans in their role as apex predators. According to shark biologist Jasmin Graham, "They maintain balance in ecosystems and keep things in order, removing weaker, sicker prey and stopping any single species from exploding in numbers and taking over" (Scales). The mass murder of sharks is especially problematic because sharks are slow to reproduce (Castro et al.). As a result, shark finning is causing a decline in shark populations, and our oceans are losing a vital and essential resource. Nathan Pacoureau and his colleagues in a study published in *Nature* in 2021 estimate that, since 1970, world populations of sharks and rays have declined by more than 70 percent (568). The rate of decline has been steady, they report, at an average of 18.2 percent per decade.

As a result of its damaging impact on ocean ecosystems, shark finning has been banned in the coastal waters of the United States, the European Union, Australia, Canada, and China, as well as in many other countries. Yet the shark fin industry is so lucrative — and so well hidden — that it is difficult to change what is happening. More important, though the act of shark finning is banned, importation of shark fins is often allowed. In the U.S., for example, it was not until 2021 that Congress passed legislation banning the importation of shark fins (Shark Fin Sales Elimination Act of 2021). Similarly, Canada, which had been the second largest importer of shark fins, did not ban the importation of shark fins until 2019 even though shark finning had been banned in its coast waters since 1994 (Cecco). In other countries, particularly in East Asia, shark fin soup remains popular and the importation of shark fins remains legal.

Ending shark finning will require more than legislation. We must reduce the demand for the product and infiltrate the supply chains. To reduce demand for the product, we should turn to social media, marketing campaigns, and

Kimble 3

education. The people who consume shark fin soup and use traditional medicines that include shark fins, as well as the people they interact with, should understand that sharks are not mindless monsters.

Social media campaigns have already proven effective. Influencer Ocean Ramsey (#OceanRamsey), who has more than 1.2 million followers on Instagram, has been a strong proponent of banning both shark finning and the consumption of shark fin soup (Fig. 2). Her posts are frequently reposted, helping to increase awareness of the need to address both the decline in shark populations and the cruelty associated with the practice of shark finning. Influence.co, which lists influencers on Instagram and other platforms, currently lists more than 450 influencers who post about sharks. Increasing awareness through social media has great promise for increasing public awareness — and shifting public attitudes — about the need to protect sharks.

Fig 2. The Instagram section of Ocean Ramsey's web page. Source: Ocean Ramsey (oceanramsey.org)

> The first part of a comprehensive solution is discussed. Sophie uses a key social media influencer's work to indicate how the solution could be implemented.

> The figure caption is set in italic, distinguishing it off from the main body text.

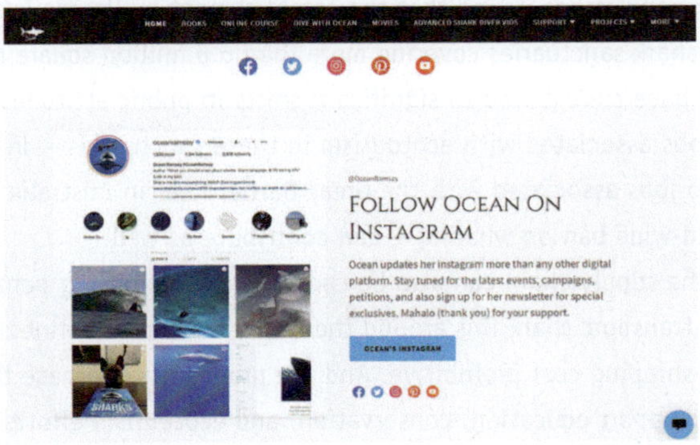

Another way to encourage changes in attitudes about sharks and shark finning is through increasing the visibility of resources that people come across without looking — in short, *marketing*. Broadcast networks such as CBS and NBC, cable television networks such as TNT, and streaming providers such as Netflix and HBO could be given incentives such as tax breaks for including public service ads and educational programming that address the shark finning crisis. Tax breaks could be extended to print and digital media advertisers as well as to the ecotourism industry, with media and ecotourism companies that

> Sophie continues to explain the elements of her solution.

Kimble 4

help spread awareness of the effects of shark finning receiving support for those efforts.

Our public education system also offers a promising means of changing attitudes. The role of sharks is rarely included in school biology and environmental curricula. Increasing understanding of the important role they play in the environment — and the fact that they are seldom a danger to humans — can lead to important shifts in public understanding of their critical contributions to ocean ecosystems.

Finally, we must infiltrate and disrupt the supply chains that are enabling the shark finning industry. The people engaging in these industries are not necessarily evil — many are just trying to feed their families. Instead of punishing people who provide the manual labor of this industry, governments could provide funding to create new jobs devoted to ocean cleanup. This could help people transition out of shark finning to new jobs. Ecotourism can play an important role in efforts to disrupt the supply chain as well. Pew Charitable Trusts, for example, reporting in 2019 on a decade of conservation work focused on shark populations, found that the establishment by Pacific Island nations of eight shark sanctuaries covering more than 6.6 million square miles of ocean habitat have contributed to significant shifts in public attitudes toward sharks. Jobs associated with ecotourism in these sanctuaries — in a manner similar to jobs associated with the Great Barrier Reef in Australia and the (nearly) world-wide ban on whaling — can contribute as well.

[An initiative by the Pew Charitable Trusts is used to show how one element of the solution could be implemented.]

Disrupting the supply chain can also be carried out by imposing penalties on shippers that transport shark fins around the world. Government fines can be used to make shipping cost prohibitive. And the proceeds from these fines could be used to support education, conservation, and ecotourism efforts.

Governments will play a central role in changing attitudes toward sharks and shark finning and disrupting shark finning supply chains. With increased awareness of the benefits of sharks and the commercial benefits associated with ecotourism, eliminating shark fin soup does not need to be seen as a loss, but as a gain. That said, one critical obstacle remains before we can reach this goal. Because of constant efforts to help us become aware of the crises that face us, we are bombarded on a daily basis with images of dead or dying animals, burning forests, and melting icebergs. We have become numb to the destruction of the environment. Complicating efforts even further, the

[Sophie discusses a key obstacle to the success of her solution.]

Kimble 5

voices crying out for change are drowned out by massive corporations whose desire for profits lead them to create advertising campaigns that encourage the environmental crises their products create.

    Nearly 100 million sharks will be murdered this year (Fig. 3). Their fins will be consumed by wealthy people who will probably forget about it a few days later. If change is not made soon, our oceans will continue to deteriorate, and we'll face mounting environmental crises. This is all connected. The loss of sharks, the melting of icebergs, the deterioration of forests, and every other devastation as a result of human industry amplifies the current changes our planet is facing. Sharks affect the ocean, the ocean affects the atmosphere, and the atmosphere affects what we breathe and how we live. It is essential that the public is made aware of the need for change. Shark finning must end. The health of shark populations and our oceans are simply too essential for this problem to be ignored.

> Sophie concludes by emphasizing the consequences of not taking action. She ends her conclusion with a call for action.

Fig. 3. Sharks dumped on a beach after their fins have been cut off.

> An image of dead sharks, victims of shark finning, is used to reinforce Sophie's conclusion.

Mark Conlin/VWPics/Alamy

Works Cited

Castro, José I., Christa M. Woodley, and Rebecca L. Brudek. "A Preliminary Evaluation of the Status of Shark Species." *Food and Agriculture Organization of the United Nations*, 1999, https://www.fao.org/3/x2352e/x2352e00.htm.

> Sources are organized alphabetically by author.

Kimble 6

Cecco, Leyland. "Canada Becomes First G7 Country to Ban Shark Fin Imports." *The Guardian*, 21 June 2019, https://theguardian.com/world/2019/jun/21/canada-bans-shark-fin-imports-sale.

Florida Museum of Natural History. "World Locations with Highest Attack Rates." 2 Feb. 2018, https://www.floridamuseum.ufl.edu/shark-attacks/trends/location/world/.

Liu, Mariann. "Toxic Delicacy of Shark Fin Causes Ecosystem Chaos, and Consumers are Pushing Back." *CNN Health*, 4 Feb. 2019, https://cnn.com/2019/02/04/health/shark-fin-chinese-new-year-hong-kong-intl.

Pacoureau, Nathan, et al. "Half a Century of Global Decline in Oceanic Sharks and Rays." *Nature*, vol. 589, pp. 567–571, 27 Jan. 2021, https://doi.org/10.1038/s41586-020-03173-9.

Pew Charitable Trust. "How the Pacific Region Paved the Path to Successful Shark Conservation." 16 Dec. 2019, https://www.pewtrusts.org/en/research-and-analysis/articles/2019/12/16/how-the-pacific-region-paved-the-path-to-successful-shark-conservation.

Rogers, Michael. "The Shark Fin Soup Industry." *Shark Sider*, 11 Mar. 2022, https://www.sharksider.com/shark-fin-soup/.

Scales, Helen. "Why We Need Sharks: The True Nature of the Ocean's 'Monstrous Villains.'" *The Guardian*, 6 July 2020, https://www.theguardian.com/environment/2020/jul/06/why-we-need-sharks-the-true-nature-of-the-oceans-monstrous-villains.

Tutton, Mark. "Traditional Medicines Continue to Thrive Globally." *CNN*, 2009, https://cnn.com/2009/HEALTH/06/24/traditional.treatment/.

United States, Congress, House. Shark Fin Sales Elimination Act of 2021. *Congress.gov*, https://www.congress.gov/bill/117th-congress/house-bill/2811. 117th Congress, 1st session.

United States, Congress, Senate. Shark Fin Sales Elimination Act of 2021. *Congress.gov*, https://www.congress.gov/bill/117th-congress/senate-bill/1106. 117th Congress, 1st session.

Worm, Boris, Brendal Davis, Lisa Kettemer, Christine Ward-Paige, Demian Chapman, Michael Heithaus, Steven Kessel, and Samuel Gruber. "Global Catches, Exploitation Rates, and Rebuilding Options for Sharks." *Marine Policy*, vol. 40, 2013, pp. 194–204, https://doi.org/10.1016/j.marpol.2012.12.034.

Project Ideas

The following suggestions provide a means of focusing your work on a problem-solving essay or another type of problem-solving document.

Suggestions for Essays

1. DEFINE A PROBLEM AT YOUR SCHOOL

In a brief essay, define a problem at your college or university. You might choose a problem related to your major, your residence hall, a campus neighborhood, an extracurricular activity, or your school's student government. Using one of the sets of problem-definition questions provided in *Define the Problem* earlier in this chapter, describe the problem in as much detail as possible, and define the consequences if it were to be left unaddressed. Use observation, interviews, or a survey of affected students to collect information about the problem (see Chapter 15). If the problem might be common to other institutions, locate and review published sources that address the problem (see Chapter 14).

2. PROPOSE A SOLUTION TO A LOCAL PROBLEM

Identify and define a problem in your community or local school district, and then propose a solution. You might, for example, choose a problem related to conducting local elections or funding local schools. Similarly, you might look at issues such as homelessness in your community or school district. Collect information about the problem from published sources, such as a community newspaper, a local magazine, or a website with a local focus. Conduct research to locate other communities with a similar problem and find out how they've addressed it. If possible, interview or correspond with someone who knows about or has been affected by the problem (see Chapter 15).

3. TRACE THE DEVELOPMENT OF A PROBLEM

Identify a problem that has not yet been solved, and trace its development. Discuss its causes, factors that contribute to its ongoing status as a problem, and factors that have worked against the creation of a successful solution. To support your discussion, locate published sources that have considered the problem. If you can, collect evidence firsthand through observation, surveys, or interviews (see Chapter 15). Although you are not required to offer a solution, consider using your conclusion to suggest directions that might be pursued to solve the problem.

4. EVALUATE PROPOSED SOLUTIONS TO A PROBLEM

Evaluate solutions that have been proposed to solve a problem. In your essay, briefly define the problem, and then discuss the long-term consequences of the problem if it were left unsolved. Then identify approaches that have been proposed to solve the problem. Choose two to four proposed solutions to evaluate. Define your evaluation criteria (see *Define Your Criteria* in Chapter 10), and discuss how well each of the proposed solutions measures up. In your conclusion, offer your assessment of whether the solution you deem most likely to succeed will actually be implemented. To support your discussion, locate published sources that have addressed the problem (see Chapter 14).

5. EVALUATE A SOLUTION THAT HAS GONE WRONG

Identify an attempt to solve a problem that has produced unintended consequences or failed to adequately address the problem. You might find, for example, that mandatory sentencing requirements for possession of alcohol or drugs have led to a significant increase in incarceration, which in turn has harmed otherwise law-abiding citizens and placed a significant burden on the state budget. In your essay, define the problem that gave rise to the solution, explain the intent of the solution, and analyze how it went wrong. Offer an alternative approach to addressing the problem. To support your argument, locate published sources that have addressed the problem (see Chapter 14). If the problem lends itself to field research (see Chapter 15), consider using observation, interviews, surveys, or correspondence to gather information about the problem and the solution that was put into place.

Suggestions for Other Genres

6. DRAFT AND DESIGN A PROBLEM-SOLVING ARTICLE FOR A NEWSPAPER OR MAGAZINE

Begin by deciding whether you want to write about a particular problem or publish in a particular newspaper or magazine. If you want to write about a particular problem, search your library's databases for articles about the problem. This can help you identify newspapers and magazines that have published articles dealing with the problem. If you want to publish your article in a particular newspaper or magazine, read a few issues of the publication carefully to determine the kinds of problems it normally addresses. Analyze its writing conventions (such as level of formality and the manner in which sources are acknowledged) and design conventions. Your article should reflect those writing and design conventions. In your article, define the problem you are addressing, argue for the importance of solving the problem, propose your solution, and consider and dismiss alternative solutions. You should support your argument with evidence from other sources, such as journal and magazine articles, newspaper articles, blogs, and websites (see Chapter 14). You can also interview an expert or correspond with someone who has been affected by the problem (see Chapter 15).

7. WRITE A PROPOSAL TO SOLVE A PROBLEM

Choose an issue of interest to you and define a problem associated with it. Then develop a potential solution and identify an organization or government agency that might provide funding for your solution. Before drafting your proposal, conduct research on the problem and on the organization or agency. In your proposal, frame the issue (see *Frame Your Essay* earlier in this chapter) in a way that helps your potential funder understand the importance of the problem, explain how addressing the problem will support the mission of the organization or agency, and describe how your proposal will solve the problem. Be sure to identify the likely outcomes of implementing your proposed solution. You should draw on published sources (see Chapter 14) and interviews with experts (see Chapter 15) to support your proposal. You should also provide a budget and an evaluation plan. If you have questions about how best to complete the proposal, ask your instructor.

8. WRITE A LETTER OF COMPLAINT

Write a letter that identifies and complains about a problem you've experienced with a product or service. Your letter should be addressed to a person, a group, or an agency that has the capacity to address the problem. To prepare your letter of complaint, conduct research on the problem and on the person, group, or agency (see Chapters 14 and 15). Your letter should be no longer than 1,000 words. It should clearly define the problem, explain why the recipient of the letter is in a position to address the problem, and explain how to address the complaint. If you have questions about how best to compose the letter, discuss them with your instructor.

In Summary: Writing a Problem-Solving Essay

* **Find a conversation and listen in (p. 376).**
  * Explore difficulties (p. 377).
  * Ask questions about promising subjects (p. 378).
  * Locate relevant sources and conduct field research (p. 378).

* **Develop a solution (p. 379).**
  * Define the problem (p. 380).
  * Consider potential solutions (p. 381).
  * Assess the practicality of your solution (p. 384).

* **Prepare a draft (p. 386).**
  * Explain the problem (p. 386).
  * Propose your solution (p. 387).
  * Explain your solution (p. 388).
  * Consider genre and design (p. 389).
  * Frame your essay (p. 391).

* **Review and improve your draft (p. 391).**
  * Reassess your problem definition (p. 392).
  * Review the presentation of your solution (p. 392).
  * Check the feasibility of your solution (p. 392).
  * Consider objections and alternative solutions (p. 393).
  * Respond to feedback from your instructor (p. 393).

12 Writing to Convince or Persuade

What is writing to convince or persuade? 404

What kinds of documents are used to convince or persuade? 406

Argumentative essays 406
  Anu Partanen, *What Americans Keep Ignoring about Finland's School Success* 406

Advertisements 413
  Men Can Stop Rape, Where Do You Stand? 413

Point/counterpoint editorials 418
  Katharina Nieswandt, Point: *Basic Income after Automation? That's Not How Capitalism Works!* 418
  Ben Bloch, Counterpoint: *Tax Robots and Universal Basic Income* 423

Open letters 426
  Angela Nickerson, *An Open Letter to Lands' End* 426

Genre Talk: Argumentative Writing 430

How can I write an argumentative essay? 431
Find a conversation and listen in 431
Build your argument 435
Prepare a draft 445
Review and improve your draft 452

✳ **Student Essay** 455
  Jeremy Alcazar, *Reforming, Not Defunding, the Police* 455

✳ **Project Ideas** 463

What Is Writing to Convince or Persuade?

Some people love a good argument. Others go out of their way to avoid conflict. Regardless of where you stand, it's hard to deny the important role that debate and discussion play in our daily lives. Unfortunately, few of the arguments we encounter on a daily basis are well grounded and fully thought out. Whether you're listening to a talk show, reading the lunatic ravings of a misinformed blogger, or streaming a clever clip on YouTube about the issue of the day, it can be almost comically easy to pick out the flaws in a weak argument.

An effective argument, on the other hand, makes a well-supported, well-considered point about an issue in an attempt to convince or persuade readers. *Convincing* involves gaining readers' agreement that a position on an issue is reasonable and well founded. *Persuading* involves getting them to take action. One writer, for example, might seek to convince readers that the drinking age should be lowered to eighteen, while another might attempt to persuade teenagers to take a vow of sobriety.

Argumentative documents are the means through which many written conversations make progress on an issue. Whether they attempt to convince or persuade, writers who create these documents adopt the role of advocate (see Chapter 6). By stating a claim and providing evidence to support it, advocates help

THE WRITER'S ROLE:
Advocate

As an **advocate**, I write to convince or persuade my readers to see my perspective on a subject.

PURPOSE
- To stake out a position on an issue
- To convince others to agree with the position
- To persuade readers to take action

READERS
- Want thoughtful consideration of an issue that is important to them
- Look for a clearly stated claim supported by ample reasons and reliable evidence
- Expect a fair and reasonable presentation of information, ideas, and competing arguments

SOURCES
- Advocates appeal to readers' reason, emotion, and trust as they present arguments.
- Evidence can come from personal observation, print and digital documents, or field research.
- Supporting information is often presented in visual form.

CONTEXT
- Effective writers consider opposing points of view and choose argumentative strategies that establish common ground with readers.
- Advocates might use color and images to set a mood and often present supporting information in visual forms — such as charts, tables, and graphs — to help readers understand an issue.

CRITICAL THINKING

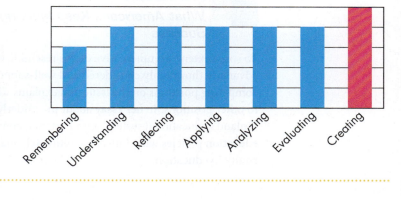

readers understand options for addressing the issue. By pointing out the drawbacks of competing arguments, they help participants in the conversation weigh alternatives. More than any other type of document, written arguments help us decide — individually and as a group — what we should believe and how we should act. In doing so, they have a profound effect on how we live our lives.

What Kinds of Documents Are Used to Convince or Persuade?

Argumentation involves making a claim, supporting it with reasons and evidence, addressing reasonable alternatives, and urging readers to accept or act on the writer's claim. Virtually any type of writing, then, can contain an argument — and even documents that serve primarily to reflect, inform, analyze, evaluate, or solve problems often contain some elements of argumentation.

Understanding the genres that can be used to convince or persuade can help you prepare to write your own argument. In this section, you'll find examples of common argumentative documents: argumentative essays, advertisements, point/counterpoint editorials, and open letters. As you read these documents, reflect on the contexts in which the writers found themselves. Ask, for example, what readers need to know about an issue to be convinced or persuaded. Ask about the kinds of evidence that readers interested in a particular issue might accept — or reject. And ask about the design elements that might influence readers — positively or negatively — as they consider an argument.

Argumentative Essays

Anu Partanen
What Americans Keep Ignoring about Finland's School Success

To some extent, argumentative essays resemble written debates. Writers typically advance a thoroughly considered and well-supported argument that addresses competing positions on the issue and explains why the writer's position is preferable to other positions. In her essay about the underlying causes of the success of Finland's educational system, Anu Partanen compares and contrasts Finland's education policies with America's, ultimately making a compelling claim about equity in education.

What Americans Keep Ignoring about Finland's School Success

by Anu Partanen

Everyone agrees the United States needs to improve its education system dramatically, but how? One of the hottest trends in education reform lately is looking at the stunning success of the West's reigning education superpower, Finland. Trouble is, when it comes to the lessons that Finnish schools have to offer, most of the discussion seems to be missing the point.

The small Nordic country of Finland used to be known — if it was known for anything at all — as the home of Nokia, the mobile phone giant. But lately Finland has been attracting attention on global surveys of quality of life — *Newsweek* ranked it number one last year — and Finland's national education system has been receiving particular praise, because in recent years Finnish students have been turning in some of the highest test scores in the world.

Finland's schools owe their newfound fame primarily to one study: the PISA survey, conducted every three years by the Organization for Economic Co-operation and Development (OECD). The survey compares 15-year-olds in different countries in reading, math, and science. Finland has ranked at or near the top in all three competencies on every survey since 2000, neck and neck with superachievers such as South Korea and Singapore. In the most recent survey in 2009 Finland slipped slightly, with students in Shanghai, China, taking the best scores, but the Finns are still near the very top. Throughout the same period, the PISA performance of the United States has been middling, at best.

Compared with the stereotype of the East Asian model — long hours of exhaustive cramming and rote memorization — Finland's success is especially intriguing because Finnish schools assign less homework and engage children in more creative play. All this has led to a continuous stream of foreign delegations making the pilgrimage to Finland to visit schools and talk with the nation's education experts, and constant coverage in the worldwide media marveling at the Finnish miracle.

This argumentative essay originally appeared in The Atlantic, *a monthly magazine devoted to political, cultural, and literary topics.*

Argumentative essays almost always draw on information from other sources (articles, books, websites, statistics, interviews, and so on) to provide evidence that supports the effort to convince readers of the merits of a particular stance on an issue or to persuade them to take action. Argumentative essays can also draw extensively on a writer's personal experience with an issue. In this essay, Partanen weaves survey data and other concrete evidence into her narrative about Pasi Sahlberg's visit to the United States.

Partanen, a journalist born in Finland and currently based in New York, has written for several American and Scandinavian publications. She is the author of *The Nordic Theory of Everything: In Search of a Better Life*, a book about lessons from Nordic society that can help Americans.

So there was considerable interest in a recent visit to the U.S. by one of the leading Finnish authorities on education reform, Pasi Sahlberg, director of the Finnish Ministry of Education's Center for International Mobility and author of the new book *Finnish Lessons: What Can the World Learn from Educational Change in Finland?* Earlier this month, Sahlberg stopped by the Dwight School in New York City to speak with educators and students, and his visit received national media attention and generated much discussion.

And yet it wasn't clear that Sahlberg's message was actually getting through. As Sahlberg put it to me later, there are certain things nobody in America really wants to talk about.

During the afternoon that Sahlberg spent at the Dwight School, a photographer from the *New York Times* jockeyed for position with Dan Rather's TV crew as Sahlberg participated in a roundtable chat with students. The subsequent article in the *Times* about the event would focus on Finland as an "intriguing school-reform model."

Yet one of the most significant things Sahlberg said passed practically unnoticed. "Oh," he mentioned at one point, "and there are no private schools in Finland."

> Finland's experience shows that it is possible to achieve excellence by focusing not on competition, but on cooperation, and not on choice, but on equity.

This notion may seem difficult for an American to digest, but it's true. Only a small number of independent schools exist in Finland, and even they are all publicly financed. None is allowed to charge tuition fees. There are no private universities, either. This means that practically every person in Finland attends public school, whether for pre-K or a Ph.D.

The irony of Sahlberg's making this comment during a talk at the Dwight School seemed obvious. Like many of America's best schools, Dwight is a private institution that costs high-school students upward of $35,000 a year to attend — not to mention that Dwight, in particular, is run for profit, an increasing trend in the U.S. Yet no one in the room commented on Sahlberg's statement. I found this surprising. Sahlberg himself did not.

Sahlberg knows what Americans like to talk about when it comes to education, because he's become their go-to guy in Finland. The son of two teachers, he grew up in a Finnish school. He taught mathematics and physics in a junior high school in Helsinki, worked his way through a variety of positions in the Finnish Ministry of Education, and spent years as an education expert at the OECD, the World

Writers of argumentative essays must carefully consider readers' needs, interests, backgrounds, and knowledge of an issue. A thorough understanding of readers' familiarity with the issue, their purposes for reading the essay, and the values, beliefs, and assumptions they bring to a reading of the essay can help a writer make thoughtful, strategic choices about how to present and support an argument. Here, Partanen provides useful background information that is likely unfamiliar to her audience.

Bank, and other international organizations.

Now, in addition to his other duties, Sahlberg hosts about a hundred visits a year by foreign educators, including many Americans, who want to know the secret of Finland's success. Sahlberg's new book is partly an attempt to help answer the questions he always gets asked.

From his point of view, Americans are consistently obsessed with certain questions: How can you keep track of students' performance if you don't test them constantly? How can you improve teaching if you have no accountability for bad teachers or merit pay for good teachers? How do you foster competition and engage the private sector? How do you provide school choice?

The answers Finland provides seem to run counter to just about everything America's school reformers are trying to do.

For starters, Finland has no standardized tests. The only exception is what's called the National Matriculation Exam, which everyone takes at the end of a voluntary upper-secondary school, roughly the equivalent of American high school.

Instead, the public school system's teachers are trained to assess children in classrooms using independent tests they create themselves. All children receive a report card at the end of each semester, but these reports are based on individualized grading by each teacher. Periodically, the Ministry of Education tracks national progress by testing a few sample groups across a range of different schools.

As for accountability of teachers and administrators, Sahlberg shrugs. "There's no word for accountability in Finnish," he later told an audience at the Teachers College of Columbia University. "Accountability is something that is left when responsibility has been subtracted."

For Sahlberg what matters is that in Finland all teachers and administrators are given prestige, decent pay, and a lot of responsibility. A master's degree is required to enter the profession, and teacher training programs are among the most selective professional schools in the country. If a teacher is bad, it is the principal's responsibility to notice and deal with it.

And while Americans love to talk about competition, Sahlberg points out that nothing makes Finns more uncomfortable. In his book Sahlberg quotes a line from Finnish writer Samuli Paronen: "Real winners do not compete." It's hard to think of a more un-American idea, but when it comes to education, Finland's success shows that the Finnish attitude might have merits. There are no lists of best schools or teachers in Finland. The main driver of education policy is not competition between teachers and between schools, but cooperation.

Finally, in Finland, school choice is noticeably not a priority, nor is engaging the private sector at all. Which brings us back to the silence after Sahlberg's comment at the Dwight School that schools like Dwight don't exist in Finland.

"Here in America," Sahlberg said at the Teachers College, "parents can choose to take their kids to private schools. It's the same idea of a marketplace that applies to, say, shops. Schools are a shop and parents can buy whatever they want. In Finland parents can also choose. But the options are all the same."

Herein lay the real shocker. As Sahlberg continued, his core message emerged, whether or not anyone in his American audience heard it.

Decades ago, when the Finnish school system was badly in need of reform, the goal of the program that Finland instituted, resulting in so much success today, was never excellence. It was equity.

Since the 1980s, the main driver of Finnish education policy has been the idea that every child should have exactly the same opportunity to learn, regardless of family background, income, or geographic location. Education has been seen first and foremost not as a way to produce star performers, but as an instrument to even out social inequality.

In the Finnish view, as Sahlberg describes it, this means that schools should be healthy, safe environments for children. This starts with the basics. Finland offers all pupils free school meals, easy access to health care, psychological counseling, and individualized student guidance.

In fact, since academic excellence wasn't a particular priority on the Finnish to-do list, when Finland's students scored so high on the first PISA survey in 2001, many Finns thought the results must be a mistake. But subsequent PISA tests confirmed that Finland — unlike, say, very similar countries such as Norway — was producing academic excellence through its particular policy focus on equity.

That this point is almost always ignored or brushed aside in the U.S. seems especially poignant at the moment, after the financial crisis and Occupy Wall Street movement have brought the problems of inequality in America into such sharp focus. The chasm between those who can afford $35,000 in tuition per child per year — or even just the price of a house in a good public school district — and the other "99 percent" is painfully plain to see.

Pasi Sahlberg goes out of his way to emphasize that his book *Finnish Lessons* is not meant as a how-to guide for fixing the education systems of other countries. All countries are different, and as many Americans point out, Finland is a small nation with a much more homogeneous population than the United States.

> Understanding readers' needs, interests, and backgrounds can also help a writer determine how best to acknowledge and argue for the comparative inadequacy of competing positions on the issue. In this case, Partanen points to recent cultural movements in the United States as evidence that the U.S. education system is not working as effectively as it should be.

Yet Sahlberg doesn't think that questions of size or homogeneity should give Americans reason to dismiss the Finnish example. Finland *is* a relatively homogeneous country — as of 2010, just 4.6 percent of Finnish residents had been born in another country, compared with 12.7 percent in the United States. But the number of foreign-born residents in Finland doubled during the decade leading up to 2010, and the country didn't lose its edge in education. Immigrants tended to concentrate in certain areas, causing some schools to become much more mixed than others, yet there has not been much change in the remarkable lack of variation between Finnish schools in the PISA surveys across the same period.

Samuel Abrams, a visiting scholar at Columbia University's Teachers College, has addressed the effects of size and homogeneity on a nation's education performance by comparing Finland with another Nordic country: Norway. Like Finland, Norway is small and not especially diverse overall, but unlike Finland it has taken an approach to education that is more American than Finnish. The result? Mediocre performance in the PISA survey. Educational policy, Abrams suggests, is probably more important to the success of a country's school system than the nation's size or ethnic makeup.

Indeed, Finland's population of 5.4 million can be compared to many an American state — after all, most American education is managed at the state level. According to the Migration Policy Institute, a research organization in Washington, there were 18 states in the U.S. in 2010 with an identical or significantly smaller percentage of foreign-born residents than Finland.

What's more, despite their many differences, Finland and the U.S. have an educational goal in common. When Finnish policymakers decided to reform the country's education system in the 1970s, they did so because they realized that to be competitive, Finland couldn't rely on manufacturing or its scant natural resources and instead had to invest in a knowledge-based economy.

With America's manufacturing industries now in decline, the goal of educational policy in the U.S. — as articulated by most everyone from President Obama on down — is to preserve American competitiveness by doing the same thing. Finland's experience suggests that to win at that game, a country has to prepare not just some of its population well, but all of its population well, for the new economy. To possess some of the best schools in the world might still not be good enough if there are children being left behind.

Is that an impossible goal? Sahlberg says that while his book isn't meant to be a how-to manual, it is meant to be a "pamphlet of hope."

"When President Kennedy was making his appeal for advancing American science and technology by putting a man on the moon by the end of the 1960s, many said it couldn't be done," Sahlberg said during his visit to New York. "But he had a dream. Just like Martin Luther King a few years later had a dream. Those dreams came true. Finland's dream was that we want to have a good public education for every child regardless of where they go to school or what kind of families they come from, and many even in Finland said it couldn't be done."

Clearly, many were wrong. It is possible to create equality. And perhaps even more important — as a challenge to the American way of thinking about education reform — Finland's experience shows that it is possible to achieve excellence by focusing not on competition, but on cooperation, and not on choice, but on equity.

The problem facing education in America isn't the ethnic diversity of the population but the economic inequality of society, and this is precisely the problem that Finnish education reform addressed. More equity at home might just be what America needs to be more competitive abroad.

Starting a Conversation: Thinking Critically about "What Americans Keep Ignoring about Finland's School Success"

In your writer's notebook, record your analysis of Partanen's essay by responding to the following questions:

1. Partanen begins her argument with a question: "Everyone agrees the United States needs to improve its education system dramatically, but how?" What assumptions is Partanen making about her readers? How do you think readers are likely to respond to these assumptions?

2. Partanen notes that when it comes to education, "there are certain things nobody in America really wants to talk about" (par. 6). To what things, specifically, does she refer? Why do you think she says Americans don't want to talk about them?

3. Aside from advocate, what roles does Partanen take on as she presents her argument? How does she signal to her readers when she is changing roles?

4. What counterarguments does Partanen raise in her essay? How does she respond to ideas and information that don't seem to support her argument? How effective would you say her responses are, and why?

5. **Reflection:** Partanen quotes Pasi Sahlberg as saying that his book isn't intended as a "how-to manual" for reforming American education; rather, "it is meant to be a 'pamphlet of hope'" (par. 34). What do you think this statement means? How might a "pamphlet of hope" be a better approach than a "how-to manual"?

Advertisements

Men Can Stop Rape
Where Do You Stand?

Advertisements seek to persuade the people who see or hear them to take a specific action — whether it's purchasing a product, supporting a cause, applying for a job, donating to a nonprofit organization, or voting for a political candidate. The argument usually takes the form of a simple claim, which might be conveyed through a brief slogan, such as "The Best Food in Texas"; through an image, such as a photo of people having a good time while they use a particular product (an adult beverage, for example, or a new sports car); or through an endorsement in which a celebrity extols the virtues of a particular product. The argument might even take the form of a detailed list of features and benefits, such as you might see in a brochure for a phone or a new prescription drug. In some cases, such as political campaigns or the battle between cable, satellite, and streaming television providers, advertisements can also make negative claims.

The advertisements beginning on the next page, developed by the nonprofit organization Men Can Stop Rape for its "Where Do You Stand?" campaign, challenge men to help prevent rape with a mix of imagery and brief passages of text. Representing an effort to model effective intervention strategies, the ads are designed to appear as banners, postcards, and posters. They target young adults on college campuses.

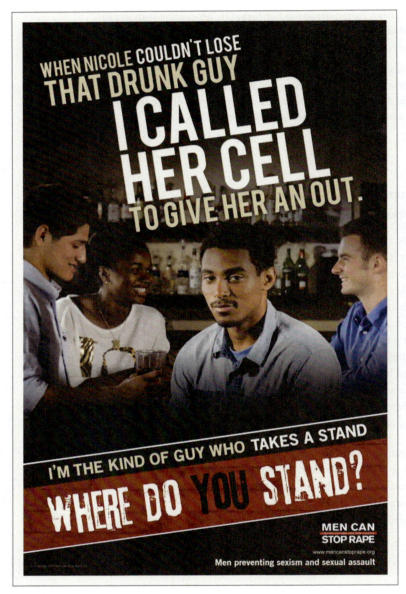

© 2011 Men Can Stop Rape

Few readers seek out advertisements. They usually encounter them as they flip through a magazine, browse the web, watch television, listen to the radio, or drive along a highway studded with billboards. Because most readers don't devote a great deal of time to considering an advertisement, most ads are designed to capture the reader's or viewer's attention and convey their claim as quickly as possible.

Advertisements typically rely on images and limit the amount of written text. For example, the long-running advertising campaign originated by the California Milk Processors Board asks the simple question "Got Milk?" Another, developed by the U.S. Marines and used for more than four decades, encouraged enlistment with the slogan "The few. The proud. The Marines." This series asks "Where Do You Stand?"

© 2011 Men Can Stop Rape

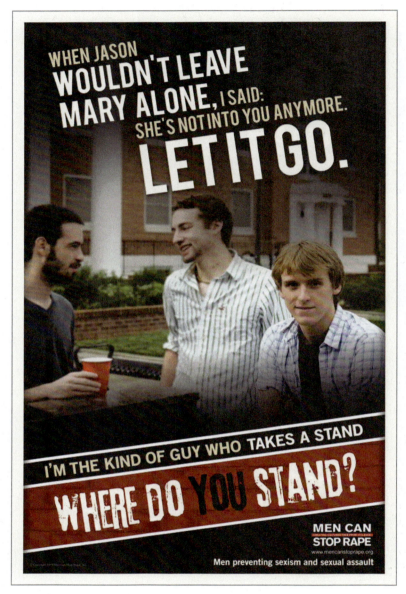

© 2011 Men Can Stop Rape

> The visual composition of an advertisement (such as the decision to have one person directly facing the viewer) is key to its effectiveness. For guidance on design principles, see Chapter 22.

4 THINGS YOU CAN DO TO TAKE A STAND

1. Distraction
Call your friend's cell to ask her a question or suggest it's time to go. You can also distract the guy harassing her: "Hey man, didn't I see you at [fill in the blank]?"

2. Group Intervention
Ask your/her friends to help out with distraction or separation. They can pull her aside to check in. Or they can say to him: "We see what you're doing and it's not okay."

3. Get an authority
Ask the bartender, bouncer, or any other authority figure to help support the intervention.

4. Prepare Yourself
Be aware of the pressures men face not to take a stand and choose what kind of man you want to be.

WHERE DO YOU STAND?

© 2011 Men Can Stop Rape

> Advertisements typically include a concrete action that the author would like the audience to perform.

Starting a Conversation: Thinking Critically about "Where Do You Stand?" Advertisements

In your writer's notebook, record your analysis of the "Where Do You Stand?" advertisements by responding to the following questions:

1. Although the four advertisements are part of the same campaign, their specific messages are different. What particular actions does each advocate? What characteristics do they share?

2. How would you describe the relationship between text and image in these advertisements? What effect does the design of the ads and the images used in them have on their overall message?

3. This campaign was aimed at college students and young adults between the ages of eighteen and twenty-five. How are these ads meant to appeal to that audience? In what ways do the ads reflect the culture and values of their readers?

4. **Reflection:** The "Where Do You Stand?" campaign represents one of many Men Can Stop Rape initiatives. How have you reacted to them? Do you agree with the assumptions they make about college-age men and women? Why or why not?

Point/Counterpoint Editorials

Katharina Nieswandt
Point: *Basic Income after Automation? That's Not How Capitalism Works!*

Ben Bloch
Counterpoint: *Tax Robots and Universal Basic Income*

Point/counterpoint editorials are used by newspapers, magazines, and other news media to illustrate opposing views about an issue. If disagreement exists about a proposed amendment to a state constitution, for example, a newspaper might invite proponents and opponents of the amendment to contribute to a point/counterpoint editorial. The two editorials might be placed side by side on a single page, or, depending on the size of the page and the amount of space given to their writers, they might be placed on facing pages. Alternatively, authors writing for disparate publications may argue about the same issue, as Katharina Nieswandt and Ben Bloch do here, writing for *The Conversation* and *Tech Crunch*, respectively. Because they are addressing the same specific element of an issue — in this case the role of automation in discussions of universal basic income — their arguments are naturally in conversation with each other.

Point: Basic Income after Automation? That's Not How Capitalism Works!

By Katharina Nieswandt

Philosophers, economists and other academics have long discussed the idea of "basic income" — an unconditional monthly check from the government to every citizen, in an amount at least high enough to cover all basic necessities. Recently, this idea has gained some political traction, even among conservative parties — but early tests in both Finland and Canada are shutting down, with officials saying they're too expensive.

One reason this idea has caught politicians' attention is the fear that large-scale automation will soon put many people out of work permanently, even as economic growth continues. (Truck and taxi drivers are currently the most discussed example.) Basic income is seen as a solution to the social problems that the predicted "technological unemployment" will bring.

In the past, the argument goes, there was a lot of work to be done. Hence income had to be earned by working, and government checks had to be reserved strictly for those who were unable to work. Income was deserved, a compensation for the burden of work.

But with less and less work to do, this system comes to resemble a twisted game of musical chairs: In the future, it will be mathematically impossible for everyone who wants a job to find one. We can therefore no longer deny income to those who don't work.

This might be called the "Automation Argument" for basic income. The Automation Argument is extremely popular; countless contemporary newspaper and blog articles take it as a premise. But the Automation Argument is false, and it impedes meaningful economic change.

A false and dangerous argument

Under capitalism, technological progress results in more products, not in more leisure. Factories that improve their efficiency don't shut down and send workers home early — workers keep the same hours and crank out more goods.

True, technological progress can cause temporary unemployment. But a look at history will tell you that, unless we switch to another economic system, there is no reason to fear (or hope) that

> In general, point/counterpoint editorials are designed simply. In some cases, they might include charts, tables, photographs, and other illustrations — should the editors of the newspaper, magazine, or website wish to call attention to the relative importance of the issue being addressed. Most often, however, they do not include illustrations or headings. In this case, neither author uses images, but Nieswandt chooses to use headings, in part because of the complexity of the points she is making.

automation will put people out of work permanently. (Contrary to recent claims, artificial intelligence will not change that point.) The Automation Argument simply misunderstands how our economy works.

Neither does the Automation Argument advocate fundamental economic reforms. It justifies basic income by the need to cushion the effects of automation, and that is the same reason we give for today's conditional welfare payments: The checks are a charity toward those who cannot work. So even if automation did cause widespread and permanent unemployment, a basic income for those affected would not be progressive or emancipatory.

Section 1.01 Robots have never reduced human work-hours

The premise that automation will make human work superfluous flies in the face of all historical evidence. (Economists refer to it as the "Luddite Fallacy.") The dream that machines will some day do most work for us is almost as old as mankind. Since the early 20th century, that dream has seemed within reach, and predictions of the end of work abound.

In 1930, British economist John Maynard Keynes famously predicted that, within 100 years, only 15 hours of work per week would be needed to satisfy one's "absolute needs." In 1980, French philosopher André Gorz suggested a policy that would have increased free time for workers at the pace at which computers were then expected to increase workers' productivity: from a 40-hour workweek to a 35-hour week over the first four years, to 30.5 hours at the end of year eight, and so on.

And yet today, despite all technical progress, we still have to eat our bread in the sweat of our face. How is that possible?

Section 1.02 It's the economy, naturally

The fact that automation never increased leisure time is an inherent consequence of our economic system. Whenever machines let us do something faster, we tend to just plow that extra time into making more, instead of taking that time off.

Imagine a worker in a shoe factory, who produces 100 pairs of shoes in an eight-hour workday. Now suppose that the machine she operates during these eight hours is exchanged for a new model which suddenly cuts production time in half: Our worker now produces 100 pairs of shoes in only four hours. In principle, the factory could keep shoe production constant, in which case the worker would have the rest of her day off.

That is a political choice a society can make. As of yet, however, we have always chosen the opposite: Capitalist societies keep work-hours constant and increase production.

Our exemplary worker continues to work an eight-hour day, but is now expected to produce 200 pairs of shoes during that day (and usually at the same wage). As the tele-teacher in Douglas Adams' "Hitchhiker's Guide to the Galaxy" aptly explains: Until we reach the "Shoe Event Horizon," we will simply produce ever more shoes.

On the way there, technological progress will indeed wipe out some jobs, but new ones will arise in their places.

Section 1.03 Productivity climbs as work-hours stagnate

Take the example of the U.S.: Work productivity — that is, the value produced per work-hour — has quintupled since 1947. On average, every hour that Americans work today yields five times as many (or as valuable) products as an hour worked by their grandparents. At the same time, however, work-hours per person did not decline.

Other industrialized countries have seen similar increases of work productivity without a decline in work-hours. Many European countries recently raised the retirement age, effectively increasing the absolute number of work-hours per life.

Certainly, the past is not always a guide to the future. Some argue that this time it's different because we will soon have artificial intelligence, so robots could take over even high-skill jobs. But it is unclear why that should make a principle difference if we keep our economic system: The principle of production increase over leisure increase applies independently of the type of job in question.

On top of that, the current changes seem rather small in historical perspective. Google or Airbnb might have introduced important new technologies or business concepts, but we are far from the often-predicted new industrial revolution. (And don't forget that the good old Industrial Revolution created more professions than it destroyed — in the high- and low-skill sectors alike.)

Like all new technologies, automated production does not, by itself, improve people's lives. If we want automation to result in more leisure for the average employee, then we need to make serious changes to our mode of production. (Yes, that is a political choice we have.)

Section 1.04 Basic income would not change much

There is a further reason to be critical of the Automation Argument for basic income. At first sight, this argument sounds revolutionary because we no longer need to do anything to deserve income. Let's face it, the argument says, technological development forces us to overhaul some moral beliefs near and dear to us, such as: "If any will not work, neither let him eat."

> Because they tend to address issues of larger public interest, point/counterpoint editorials are more likely than opinion columns or regular editorials to include evidence such as quotations or paraphrases from published sources, quotations from interviews, or statistical data drawn from published studies. In this sense, point/counterpoint editorials and articles are more similar to reports and essays than they are to opinion columns and letters to the editor.

These beliefs might have been reasonable for most of human existence, the Automation Argument concedes. But in a situation where we lack enough tasks to be carried out, it becomes cynical to consider people who don't work free riders.

The Automation Argument hence presupposes that we currently should work eight-hour days, and it presupposes that (at least by and large) each of us currently receives as compensation what we deserve, given our individual contribution.

In reality, incomes mostly reflect social hierarchies — as do beliefs about who deserves income. To see this, just consider the following three features of our income structure and what we think about them:

1. People who live off government transfers like welfare checks even though they could work are widely regarded as free riders. These people live off our work, and if that's not exploitation, then what is? There is no similar public grudge against people who live off our work by other means: by living off dividends and off government transfers like tax exemptions. While welfare recipients form the bottom of our social hierarchy, the idle rich are even admired.

   > Although Bloch addresses the third point below, these two points remain unaddressed. Gaps in coverage such as this are a good reason to do additional research when you are first joining the conversation about a topic. You would need to find additional sources to try to answer the question of whether there are strong rebuttals to these points, or whether they are concerns held by the majority of participants.

2. Work is widely considered a burden, and income is seen as its deserved compensation. In reality, however, there is no correlation between how burdensome and how well-compensated a job is — otherwise, construction workers, cleaners and prostitutes would top the pay scale.

3. An increase in productivity legally belongs to the owner of the new technology, and few of us seem to mind that. In the example of the shoe factory, production doubled. The worker neither got more time off as a result, nor higher pay: The factory owner got more shoes to sell.

Section 1.05 Is income today deserved?

The Automation Argument does not challenge any of these three beliefs:

1. The income it advocates is unconditional, but it is justified in the same way as today's conditional welfare checks: It is a charity toward those who cannot work and have no capital.

2. Everybody else will continue to work and be paid in the same way that they are today. Those of us who still have a job will collect basic income in addition to our

current salaries (a gain partly annulled by the taxes paid to fund basic income). But there will be no fundamental reform of the economy.

3. Those of us who are laid off are not entitled to any of the gains that the new technology produces. The owner of the new technology alone is entitled to its proceeds, while all of our fellow citizens are now responsible to pay for our living (through taxes that fund basic income).

The call for basic income in order to soften the effects of automation is hence not a call for greater economic justice. Our economy stays as it is; we simply extend the circle of those who are entitled to receive public benefits. If we want economic justice, then our starting point needs to be more radical: We need to reconsider our deeply ingrained belief that wages and proceeds today are (usually) deserved.

> Author Ben Bloch counters this point below in "Tax Robots and Universal Basic Income."

Counterpoint: Tax Robots and Universal Basic Income

By Ben Bloch

Technological innovation is moving at an ever-accelerating pace, and this comes with vast benefits and inevitable changes to our way of life. One downside is that machine learning and automation are already replacing jobs, and this will increase rapidly. It also has the potential to replace much of that income with Universal Basic Income (UBI), or government cash handouts to all adult citizens, perhaps starting with covering some element of taxes and rising in the range of $100,000/year per citizen within the next 20 years.

Sound ludicrous? Proponents of UBI include well-known figures such as Mark Zuckerberg, Richard Branson and Elon Musk. Musk stated last year that he believed job loss would be so severe due to automation that some form of UBI will be necessary to support our society. Bill Gates suggested that every time an employee is replaced by a robot, or in most cases software using automation through artificial intelligence or machine learning, that the business owners should have to pay a tax on that, much like the employee would on wages. But to date, most other UBI ideas have involved raising taxes on people with higher earnings. What if the real solution to UBI was through a path of lowering income taxes on all people?

Stanford lecturer and executive director of East Palo Alto-based investment bank Woodside Partners Kartik Gada believes that continued technology deflation will both lead to the need for UBI and a route to fund it, rather than increased government debt. In his ATOM publication, Gada gives a great deal of data supporting his argument. "In response to technological deflation, the central banks of the world will have to create new money in perpetuity, increasing the stream at an exponentially rising rate much higher than is currently assumed," says Gada. "This now-permanent need for monetary expansion, if embraced, can fund government spending more directly. This in turn creates a very robust, dynamic, and efficient safety net for citizens, while simultaneously reducing and even eliminating most forms of taxation by 2025."

Technological deflation is caused by a convergence of rapidly deflating technologies to an ever-rising percentage of the economy. Gada estimates that technology comprises about 2 percent of the world economy currently, and this percentage is on the brink of rising quickly.

For example, in 2007, the iPhone replaced most of the technology in your home, leading to less need for new purchases in that category year to year. The same iPhone 8 that you just bought for $699 will likely cost a quarter of that to buy new in three years, partly due to the release of a newer, faster, more powerful model at the top of the price ladder. Home Internet of Things devices, from Alexa and Ring to Nest, also are replacing and consolidating multiple normal purchases into lower-cost devices.

So while the price of new tools and toys might seem like it is going up on a case by case basis, it's rapidly decreasing versus capabilities, speed, power, number of purchases required, etc. In addition, artificial intelligence and machine learning are driving use of automation up and use of employees for specific roles and functions down.

Amazon reportedly installed 75,000 robots to replace human jobs in 2017. This helps them and other companies drive down costs, which makes it possible to offer lower prices across the board.

These factors, from continued innovation and efficiencies, paired with automation that reduces jobs and prices, has led to fewer consumer purchases and rapid overall declines in aggregate consumer spending—and could lead to serious problems for employment and the overall economy. If this happens, it may be more far-reaching than many realize and will certainly

> Income taxes can be eliminated and an unconditional Universal Basic Income can be funded.

> Discussions of complex information indicate that the audience for Bloch's argument are likely to be highly educated and have an interest in the economy.

be scary for some along the way. Gada believes that we are nearing a point in our economy during which deflation is a more serious threat than inflation as the percentage of technological goods we buy increases and the cost and number of those goods decreases.

To make up for this deflationary pressure, the Federal Reserve first lowered the Fed Funds rate to 0 percent. But when deflation proved to be too much for even that, they had to go even further, and generate all new liquidity above that.

To this end, the Federal Reserve embarked on a program known as Quantitative Easing (QE), relying on the purchase of mortgage-backed securities and treasuries.

Other countries followed suit with similar programs. This has staved off deflation for now, but this may not continue to work in the next crisis without alternate methods of dispersing capital in a more direct, cash-oriented manner.

Eventually, central bank actions like QE will have to be permanent and ever-increasing. Enter the notion of funneling the QE money into a form of UBI. As automation and technology efficiencies increase, this also will create great savings for world governments as they can now deliver services for far less cost. While governments may not lower taxes willingly, competitive pressure between states and nations will rise, forcing them to compete for efficiency of governance. It is in this manner that income taxes can be eliminated and an unconditional Universal Basic Income can be funded.

The key is that as income tax is phased out and technology is monetized to fund government, new jobs are created more quickly, and this offsets the job loss through automation, with the UBI serving as a cushioning mechanism while people transition. Ultimately, Gada believes that the phase-out of income tax combined with UBI will foster a vastly higher degree of entrepreneurship in the economy, and this will be the source of most professional activity in the future.

Under the transition program that Gada has outlined in his publication, the numbers start in the early thousands of dollars each year per citizen, and rise continuously to upwards of $100,000 in the 2030s. That number may seem high, but is not outside of the range of long-term trendlines in world economic growth or the ever-accelerating levels of central bank liquidity actions being done worldwide. Not to be forgotten is the high cost of income tax on productivity and entrepreneurship, and how both will find a greatly enhanced climate when the tax burden on humans is lowered.

Could we be on the brink of an age where a much more advanced version of the #TaxRobots idea that Bill Gates has advocated can indeed be implemented? According to Kartik Gada, this may not be too many years away.

> Here Bloch addresses one of Nieswandt's concerns — that the benefits of automation will remain with the owners of the companies.

> While Bloch (and Gada) see UBI as a transition between the current economy and a more mechanized future economy, Nieswandt (in the previous article) addresses concerns about UBI as a sustainable economic model for the long term. Even when point/counterpoint editorials address the same issue, they will usually include some different angles or information on the topic.

Starting a Conversation: Thinking Critically about Point/Counterpoint Editorials

In your writer's notebook, record your analysis of Nieswandt's and Bloch's articles by responding to the following questions:

1. Briefly summarize each writer's claim. On what major points do Nieswandt and Bloch disagree? On what, if anything, do they agree?

2. Katharina Nieswandt's point editorial appeared in *The Conversation*, whose tagline is "Academic rigor, journalistic flair," while Ben Bloch's counterpoint ran in *Tech Crunch*, a source concerned with "startup and technology news." What types of facts and evidence does each writer use to support the stances of their publications? Are the articles shaped by partisan political debates? How can you tell?

3. What does Nieswandt mean by "the Automation Argument" in paragraph 5? Though Bloch doesn't use the same phrasing, how does he refute Nieswandt's position on "the Automation Argument"? What in her argument does he not successfully refute?

4. **Reflection:** After reading both the point and the counterpoint, which editorial was more convincing? Why? Are you surprised by your reaction?

Open Letters

Angela Nickerson
An Open Letter to Lands' End

Open letters are written to an individual or group of individuals, an organization, a corporation, or a government agency and are published in a public forum, such as a newspaper, magazine, or website. Open letters often respond to an action taken or a decision made (or not made) by the recipient of the letter. Sometimes the letter writers are well-known authors or national figures, sometimes they're representatives of an organization with a stake in an issue, and sometimes they are average citizens who want to voice their opinion on an issue that affects them, such as Amy Nickerson who addresses her letter to Lands' End, a popular clothing brand.

Dear Lands' End,

I have been a customer for years. I like your clothes. They are reliable and good quality. I buy them for myself and for my son.

Today, I am writing to you as a mom and as one of your customers, as a feminist and as a concerned citizen. And I write you as a woman working hard to raise a boy who will be healthy, loving, and an ally and advocate for all.

Your latest kids catalogue arrived this week, and I am disappointed. I need to buy a winter coat and some ski pants for my son, so I looked at your spreads…

It shouldn't surprise me. Your peers do it, too: bright, vibrant colors marketed for girls; black, brown, blue, green, and maybe red for boys.

Why? Do you really think that boys only like primary colors and black or brown? They don't. My son LOVES turquoise, apple green, red, and orange, for example. But look at what you offer for him:

▲ The "Boys' Expedition Down Parka" selections

> The format of an open letter is typically simple, consisting of a salutation (Dear . . .), one or more paragraphs of plain text, and the name of the writer or group (in place of a signature).

> When open letters are published in newspapers or magazines, they usually appear in the form of paid advertising or as public service announcements. In this case, Nickerson's letter appeared online at Medium.com, a site committed to surfacing a variety of perspectives on current topics.

And here's the very same coat marketed to girls:

▲ The "Girls' Expedition Down Parka" selections

> Although brief letters typically provide little in the way of formal evidence to support an argument, longer letters might offer a thorough discussion that is carefully supported by evidence from personal experience, observation, interviews, and published sources. In this case, Nickerson includes images of the Lands' End catalog to support her criticism of their gendered color options for children's clothing.

They are the SAME coat. Why not just call them "Kids' Expedition Down Parkas" and put them all on the same page?

You do the same thing with snow pants.

They are kids! Their bodies are so similar — just call them Kids' Squall Bibs and Pants. Boys can wear all of those colors. Girls, too.

I have gotten away for six years buying "girls" clothes for my son, because they are colors or animals or designs that he likes. But now he can read. And if he picks up a copy of a Lands' End catalogue and finds that the limey green jacket he loves is a girls' jacket, he will never wear it again — not because he won't still love it, but for fear of being teased.

Because here's the thing: despite my best efforts, our culture says that my Viking-loving, Star Wars-obsessed, Lego-playing boy is not allowed to love or wear turquoise or lime green or purple or . . . hot pink (a color he LOVES but thinks it must be in secret). Our culture says that boys and girls must be different from the very beginning — pink and blue, sugar and snips, spice and snails.

But boys and girls are all of those things. There are girls who would love to wear a kelly green jacket and snow pants — but they are locked out of those choices in the same way that you select navy blue for my son.

And even in the seemingly benign marketing of children's winter clothes gender stereotypes are reinforced from an early age. Looking at your current graphic tees for kids, for example: I am glad to see three science-related shirts for girls! But where are the hedgehogs, foxes, or horses for boys? Are boys only interested in cars, dinosaurs — and only T Rex in aggressive stances — or space?

If we are serious about tackling the toxic masculinity which persists in our culture, we must look at the images we market to our children. Boys get dinosaurs that are threatening and aggressive. Girls get sparkly dinosaurs who love each other. What kind of messages do these seemingly innocuous shirts convey? Trust me. My child wouldn't be afraid of wearing something "girly" if he never encountered others who have sneered at his choices. And he is only six years old.

Of course, there are some styles specific for girls. And there are some specific to boys. It is great to celebrate the differences between boys and girls. But we also must celebrate the commonalities. And to reinforce toxic stereotypes of either one is neither healthy nor right.

As a mom, I ask you for some middle ground. Before it gets complicated . . . before their bodies begin to radically differentiate . . . can you just let kids be kids? Let them love what they love. Celebrate their sweetness. Promote harmony. And help move us toward a more open, accepting, peaceful, and loving society.

You may say, "We are just a clothes company." But fashion has a powerful voice in our culture. Use yours for good.

> Open letters are likely to reflect issues covered by the publication or addressed by the website on which the letter appears. In this case, Nickerson is raising the issue of parity in how children's clothing is marketed, something she can expect that parents and socially conscious readers will be interested in.

> Open letters often close with a call to action (or for a particular action to be halted).

In your writer's notebook, record your analysis of "An Open Letter to Lands' End" by responding to the following questions:

1. Why do you think Nickerson uses an open letter format? Why is this structure meaningful in her effort to address both the marketing staff at Lands' End specifically and the larger audience of children's clothing consumers more generally?

2. Nickerson points to specific images in her critique, noting the color differences and the way that characters such as dinosaurs are portrayed. How does the inclusion of these images help to support her point? Would more or fewer images help to strengthen her argument? Why or why not?

3. In paragraph 4, Nickerson specifically mentions her son and his love of "bright, vibrant colors" that Lands' End has reserved for the girls' jackets. What sort of rhetorical appeal is she making here? What other rhetorical appeals does Nickerson make in her open letter? What other details might she include to strengthen these appeals?

4. In the second-to-last paragraph, Nickerson asks Lands' End for "some middle ground." What does she mean by this? Why is the term *middle ground* appropriate in this situation?

5. **Reflection:** At the end of her letter, Nickerson raises a hypothetical objection that Lands' End is "just a clothes company" before calling on the company to use its voice and power for good. After reading this letter, consider your own experiences with fashion brands. Do they seem to be using their influence for good? Why or why not? Have you ever said that you are "just a college student" when faced with a challenging situation? Does this letter help you consider your own power and how you might, as Nickerson suggests, use it for good?

Starting a Conversation: Responding to "An Open Letter to Lands' End"

GENRE TALK

Reflective Writing | Informative Writing | Analytical Writing | Evaluative Writing | Problem-Solving Writing | **Argumentative Writing**

Zara. H&M. Forever 21. These popular clothing retailers are at the heart of "fast fashion," the latest trend in consumer buying habits. Fast fashion retailers price their goods very inexpensively and receive new shipments every day, including knock-offs of high-end designs. The combination of low prices (plus sales that slash the prices even further) and the constant influx of trendsetting goods is hard to resist, so shopping at stores like these can become a habit.

There is a hidden price for such cheap apparel, however. The workers who manufacture these goods are paid meager, often unlivable, wages. They toil for twelve- or fourteen-hour shifts in unsafe working conditions, as the 2012 fire in a Bangladeshi sweatshop illustrated. Our wear-and-toss shopping habits also take an environmental toll, as landfills hold ever-growing piles of discarded clothing.

Slowly, the problem of fast fashion is being brought to light. The documentary film *The True Cost* (2015), an exposé of garment sweatshops and the fashion industry, argues that fast fashion is hardly fun, cheap, or benign.

The navigation menu offers opportunities to learn more about the problem.

A tagline argues the film's main point.

Bright colors grab the viewer's attention.

Viewers can watch the film immediately online.

A brief quotation by a well-known source lends authority to the film.

The True Cost documentary, © 2015 Untold Creative, LLC, www.bullfrogfilms.com

How Can I Write an Argumentative Essay?

Many people believe that an argument is effective only if it's won, that unless they convince or persuade someone, they've failed in their mission to change the world — or their community or the minds of people they hang out with or the people they interact with on social media. In fact, most written arguments aren't so much about winning or losing as about sharing the writer's perspective with others who are interested in an issue. Think of it as exploring alternative ways of thinking, acting, and believing — as advancing a conversation about an issue. If you follow this line of thinking, you'll recognize that the effectiveness of your essay isn't based on whether you win the argument. It is based on your ability to affect the community of readers and writers to whom you direct your argument.

Then again, sometimes winning is all that matters. Application essays for medical or business school, no matter how well written, are seldom considered successful if the writer isn't accepted. The same is true of letters requesting scholarships. And if you're a teenage driver, either you get to borrow the car or you don't.

In this section, you'll learn about the processes and strategies involved in writing an argumentative essay. Given the complex challenges involved in writing effective arguments, you can expect to draw on a wide range of critical thinking skills, including understanding, reflecting, analyzing, evaluating, and creating.

As you work on your essay, you'll follow the work of Jeremy Alcazar, who wrote an argumentative essay about police reform.

In Process

An Argumentative Essay about Police Reform

Jeremy Alcazar wrote an argumentative essay for his composition course. Jeremy learned about his topic by reading magazine articles, newspaper articles, websites, scholarly and professional journal articles, and blogs, as well as through discussions with friends. Follow his efforts to write his argumentative essay in the In Process boxes throughout this chapter.

Find a Conversation and Listen In

Argumentative essays grow out of a belief that a choice must be made, a situation should be changed, or a mistake should be corrected. In general, people don't argue when they're happy with a situation, nor do they argue when they agree with one another. They argue because they believe that someone or something — a person, a group, a movement, a government — is wrong. As you consider possible subjects for your argumentative essay, take stock of the conversations taking place around you. Ask what bothers you. Ask what conflicts affect you, individually or as a member of a community. Look for an issue that matters not only to you but also to the people who might read your essay. Then take on the role of advocate, and reflect on your writing situation — your purpose, your readers, and the contexts in which your writing will be read (see Chapter 1).

● EXPLORE DISAGREEMENTS

Unless they're deeply conflicted, few people carry on extended arguments with themselves. The kinds of arguments that are worth addressing in academic essays revolve around issues that affect a larger community. To identify issues that might interest you and your readers, explore popular, professional, and academic conversations. In almost every case, you'll find points of disagreement and debate

In Process

Generating Ideas about Conversations

The massive Black Lives Matter protests in 2020 led Jeremy Alcazar to explore conversations related to policing.

> One of the main reasons this movement has really picked up momentum is because people are simply tired of civilians getting injured and murdered when that should not be happening at all. The problem is, this will not be the best solution to the problem. To simply remove police forces or defund them and make them less than what they already are would not be a great idea because we need the police force. We just need them to be better and we need to truly feel like they are here to protect us; not bring us down and hurt our communities and target minorities, which is what we continue to see today. Police need more training for the situations they respond to so they can be better about handling situations they encounter in the field. And they need to be held accountable for their actions. This would look like harsher punishments for officers as well as making sure these punishments stick to them in court so they cannot get away with what they do which we continue to see happen a lot now. This is also a big reason people across the nation are frustrated.

Jeremy used the results of his freewriting to explore approaches to addressing police violence. The articles he found in newspapers, in magazines, and on the web helped him learn more about the ideas being proposed to address the issue.

that bring people together in discussions — sometimes polite and sometimes anything but — about the challenges that confront us.

- **Popular conversations.** Visit the news and opinion sections of websites such as CNN.com, Foxnews.com, and NPR.org (National Public Radio's website) to learn about issues that have sparked discussion. Read blogs and opinion columns, view the latest news reports on issues that have spurred popular debate, and view Facebook pages and Twitter feeds.
- **Professional conversations.** Tune in to the conversations taking place in your field of interest. Skim some trade and professional journals to find points of disagreement. Read some blogs that focus on your profession, and notice what people are arguing about. If you're working full- or part-time, listen to what your coworkers are talking about.
- **Academic conversations.** Look for disagreements in course readings, and pay attention to controversies addressed during class discussions and lectures. Ask professors and graduate students what's "hot" in their fields. Scan the tables of contents of recent issues of academic journals. Visit websites that focus on your discipline.

Recognizing ongoing conversations can give you insights into debatable issues that might serve as the basis for your argumentative essay. Try listing issues from one or more of these areas — or from the writing project ideas at the end of this

Working Together: Try It Out Loud

Before you start developing your argument, hold an informal debate with your classmates about an issue that affects all of you. Form small groups, and choose an issue you're familiar with and that lends itself to argument, such as a disagreement affecting your hometown, school, or state. You might scan the school paper or a local publication for current issues worth discussing. Explain your perspective on the issue, and then state your position. Offer reasons and, if possible, evidence from personal experience or readings to support your argument. Ask the other members of your group to identify counterarguments, giving their own reasons and evidence. Take turns speaking while the other members of the group listen, respond, and ask questions.

When you are finished, take a few minutes to reflect on the exercise. What did you learn about presenting an argument? Did you have to adapt what you said based on your classmates' values, beliefs, and concerns? What kind of questions did they ask? What seemed to interest them the most about the issue? How did they react to your argument? What reasoning and evidence did they find most convincing? Least convincing?

chapter — and then explore your thoughts about them (see *Generate Ideas* in Chapter 2). When you've finished, review what you've written to identify the areas that seem most promising, and then select one or two that interest you most. Jot down your thoughts about what you already know and what you would need to learn before you can develop your argument.

● TRACK ONLINE CONVERSATIONS

Issues worth arguing about almost always become a topic of conversation. Often, that conversation takes place online, through blogs and social media. These resources are designed specifically to support exchanges among writers and readers. By following these online conversations, you can not only learn more about your subject but also discover what other writers and readers think about it.

Blogs consist of chronologically ordered entries on a website and most closely resemble entries in a diary or journal. Blogs allow readers to post their responses to entries, so a single blog entry might be accompanied by several — sometimes hundreds — of responses.

Do you know how to locate online sources? See Chapter 14 for help.

Social media venues such as Facebook, Twitter, Instagram, and LinkedIn provide opportunities to identify people who share your interest in an issue. By searching these sites, you can identify individuals who might be knowledgeable about an issue or have been affected by it.

Follow up on what you learn by consulting other resources. Some news sites, such as FoxNews.com, allow readers to comment on their articles, much as blogs allow readers to post replies. You can also locate sources through your library's catalog and databases. If you still have unanswered questions, conduct additional searches, talk to a librarian, or collect information through observations or interviews.

● ASK QUESTIONS ABOUT PROMISING ISSUES

Before you begin constructing an argument, determine which aspect of an issue interests you most. The best written arguments are usually focused and narrow. Be wary of writing about something as broadly defined as climate change or ethics in politics. Instead, try to find a subtopic that you can manage in the space and time available to you. For example, if you're interested in climate change, take a look at issues such as the carbon emissions that result from producing the batteries used in hybrid cars and trucks. Each of the following questions focuses your attention on a general issue in a different way, and each provides a useful starting point for an argumentative essay. Depending on the subject, you'll find that some questions are more relevant than others.

- **Values.** Why is this important to me? What about it will matter to readers? Can I make an argument without letting my emotions run away with me?
- **Definition.** Why do people disagree about this issue? What, exactly, is at stake?
- **Possibilities.** What could be accomplished if this issue is addressed? What might happen if it is not addressed?
- **Positions.** What positions have been taken on this issue? What intrigues me about those positions?
- **Strengths and weaknesses.** What are the strengths of other writers' arguments? What are the weaknesses?

As you narrow your focus, ask yourself one last question: Is your goal to convince your readers to agree with you or to persuade them to act? Be aware that persuading people to act can be a far greater challenge than convincing them to agree with you. For example, it's easy to convince someone that it's a good idea to spend more time studying. It can be far more difficult to persuade that person to set aside two more hours each day to do so. As you consider how you'll focus your argument, remember that it will take a compelling argument to persuade your readers to act.

Build Your Argument

Putting together an effective argumentative essay starts with knowing what you want others to believe or how you want them to act. But that's just the beginning. To build your argument, you must develop a strategy for achieving your goal. Your strategy should reflect not only your overall goal but also a thorough understanding of your readers — their purposes in reading your essay, their knowledge of the issue, and their needs, interests, and backgrounds.

In short, you'll need to figure out how to get your readers to accept your argument. To do so, start by defining your overall claim, and then identify the reasons and supporting evidence that will be most convincing or persuasive to your readers. In addition, consider how opposing positions affect your argument, and make sure that your reasoning is sound.

In Process

Locating Sources

Jeremy Alcazar was interested in learning about historical patterns of police violence. In particular, he was interested in whether trends, such as increasing or decreasing levels of violence, could be found. His web searches led him to a Brookings Institution report by Rashawn Ray and Clark Neily that explored both trends and potential changes in policing—such as a 1400 percent increase in use of SWAT teams since 1980—that might have contributed to increases in violent interactions with police.

Jeremy located an article by Rashawn Ray and Clark Neily on the Brooking Institution website.

A PDF version of the report is available for download.

Extensive references at the end of the report allowed Jeremey to read several related sources.

Jeremy saved a copy of this article. Then he followed the links in it to related materials and saved those as well. Later, he printed a copy and highlighted key passages.

DEFINE YOUR OVERALL CLAIM

It's important to understand precisely what you want your readers to believe or do before you begin drafting. Your overall claim — the heart of the argument you want to make — will serve as a touchstone as you juggle the complexities of crafting an argument. Your claim should take into account your purpose as a writer, the conversation you've decided to join, and the readers you hope to convince or persuade.

You can begin to define your overall claim by brainstorming or freewriting (see *Generate Ideas* in Chapter 2) in response to the following questions:

- What is my position on this issue?
- Which aspects of this issue interest me most?
- Which aspects of this issue do I feel most strongly about?
- What do I want my readers to believe or do as a result of reading my essay?
- What are my readers likely to think about this issue? What will it take to change their minds or get them to act?
- How does my position differ from those advanced by other writers? How is it similar?

Review what you've written. Then try to express, in one or two sentences, your overall claim. Later, your claim can serve as the basis for a thesis statement (see Chapter 18). For now, use it to direct your thinking about the argument you want to formulate.

DEVELOP REASONS TO ACCEPT YOUR OVERALL CLAIM

Few readers will accept "because I'm right" as a good reason to accept your position on an issue. They expect you to explain why you're right. Developing an explanation begins with identifying reasons that are consistent with your own perspective on the issue. At this stage of your writing process, don't worry about whether your readers will be convinced or persuaded by your reasoning. Instead, treat your efforts to develop reasons to accept your overall claim as you would any other form of brainstorming. As you generate a list of potential reasons, you can certainly begin to ask whether the reasons you've identified are well grounded, logical, and consistent with the values and beliefs held by you and your readers. And later, as you draft your essay, you can decide how to present your reasons to your readers. For now, though, your primary goal is to generate as many potential reasons as possible to support your overall claim.

Generate ideas about potential reasons Your understanding of an issue and the conversations surrounding it will provide a framework within which you can develop a set of reasons to support your overall claim. To guide your efforts, ask questions such as the following, and respond to them by brainstorming, freewriting, clustering, mapping, or using sentence starters (see *Generate Ideas* in Chapter 2):

- **Costs.** What costs are associated with not accepting and acting on your overall claim? Are there monetary costs? Will time and effort be lost or wasted? Will valuable resources be wasted? Will people be unable to lead fulfilling lives? Will human potential be wasted? Will lives be lost?

- **Benefits.** What will be gained by accepting and acting on your overall claim? Who or what will benefit if the claim is accepted and acted on? What form will these benefits take?

- **Alternatives, choices, and trade-offs.** What will happen if people don't accept your claim? Are the alternatives to your claim acceptable? Why or why not? Why would someone choose to accept your claim? What would they lose or gain by accepting your claim? By rejecting it?

- **Parallels.** Can you find similarities between the overall claim you are making about this issue and claims made about other issues? Can you argue that, if your claim is accepted and acted on, the outcomes will be similar to those found for other issues? What consensus, if any, exists among experts on this issue about what similar situations have led to in the past?

- **Personal experience.** What does your personal experience tell you is likely to happen if your claim is accepted and acted on? What does it tell you might happen if it is rejected?

- **Historical context.** What does history tell you is likely to happen — or not happen — if your claim is accepted and acted on? What does it tell you might happen if it is rejected? What consensus, if any, exists among experts on this issue about what similar situations have led to in the past?

- **Values and beliefs.** In what ways is your overall claim consistent with your values and beliefs? With those of your readers? In what ways is it consistent with larger societal and cultural values and beliefs? How might it further those values and beliefs?

Examine the list of reasons you've generated to determine which ones fit best with your overall claim, your purpose, and what you know about your readers.

Decide how your reasons support your overall claim Effective arguments make connections (sometimes called *warrants*) between the overall claim and the reasons offered to support it. Sometimes readers accept a connection because they share the writer's values and beliefs or have similar experiences with and knowledge of an issue. In other cases, readers accept a connection because the writer explains it effectively. This explanation (sometimes called *backing*) provides readers with information and analysis that help them understand and accept the connection.

Warrant: Police should be trained to control suspects without inflicting injury while also keeping themselves safe and unharmed.

Backing: Police departments are responsible for providing training to officers. Departments benefit from improved relationships with civilians and reduced payouts for injuries and deaths.

Claim: Integrating Brazilian jiu jitsu into police training reduces the risk of injuries during arrests **Reason:** because it focuses on grappling and controlling rather than striking, as **Evidence:** demonstrated in a recent study conducted with the Marietta, Georgia, police department.

The reasons you choose to support your overall claim should reflect your understanding of the conversation you've decided to join. Your reasons should emerge from careful thought about the information, ideas, and arguments you've encountered in your reading. Your reasons should reflect your purpose and goals. And they should take into account your readers' needs, interests, backgrounds, and knowledge of the issue.

As you consider your reasons, ask how clearly they connect to your overall claim. Ask whether you should explain each connection or leave it unstated. Your answers will depend in part on the extent to which your readers share your values, beliefs, experience, and knowledge of the issue. If your readers' backgrounds and knowledge differ from yours, connections that make sense to you might not be clear to them.

- **CHOOSE EVIDENCE TO SUPPORT YOUR REASONS**

Your argument will be effective only if you back up each of your reasons with evidence. Most readers will expect you to provide some sort of justification for accepting your reasons, and their assessment of your evidence will affect their willingness to accept your argument. The form your evidence takes will depend on your overall claim, the reasons themselves, and your readers' values and beliefs. In general, consider drawing on the following types of evidence to support your reasons:

- textual evidence, in the form of quotations, paraphrases, and summaries
- numerical and statistical data
- images, including photographs and drawings
- media items, including video, audio, and animations
- tables, charts, and graphs
- information and ideas from interviews, observations, and surveys
- personal experience
- expert opinion

Take the following steps to identify evidence to support your reasons:

1. List the reasons you are using to support your overall claim.
2. For each reason, review your notes to identify relevant evidence.
3. List your evidence below each point.
4. Identify reasons that need more support, and locate additional evidence.
5. Consider dismissing or revising reasons for which you don't have sufficient evidence.

Effective arguments typically provide evidence that is both plentiful and varied in type. A writer arguing about the need to improve the U.S. health-care system, for example, might draw on personal experience, interviews with friends and relatives, policy briefs from the American Medical Association, reports issued by government agencies, and articles in magazines and scholarly journals.

As you choose evidence to support your reasons, think about whether — and, if so, how — you will show the connections between reasons and evidence. These connections, often called *appeals*, help readers understand why a reason is appropriate and valid. Common appeals include citing authorities on an issue; using emotion to sway readers; calling attention to shared principles, values, and beliefs; asking readers to trust the writer; and using logic.

You can read more about using appeals later in this chapter. You can read about how to identify evidence to support your reasons in Chapter 18.

How Can I Write an Argumentative Essay? | CHAPTER 12 | **441**

Claim: Integrating Brazilian jiu jitsu into police training reduces the risk of injuries during arrests **because it focuses on grappling and controlling rather than striking,** as demonstrated in a recent study conducted with the Marietta, Georgia, police department.

Appeal: Studies provide data that can be used to inform decisions.

Evidence

In Process

Choosing Evidence

Jeremy Alcazar chose the evidence he would use in his essay by creating a list of reasons to support his overall claim that a comprehensive approach to reforming policing was needed. He reviewed the notes he took on his sources, listing sources next to each reason and deciding whether he needed more or better evidence for each reason. He created a simple table in a word-processing file to keep track of his evidence.

Reason	Evidence/Source	Notes
We need to change police training, starting with the police academies that train new officers and continuing throughout their careers.	Semuels, Alana. "Society Is Paying the Price for America's Outdated Police Training Methods." *Time*, 20 November 2020, https://time.com/5901726/police-training-academies/.	"Many programs at community and technical colleges are taught by retired cops who use a military-style teaching method that incorporates war stories from police work and warns recruits that they will face a choice on the streets: kill or be killed. That differs from the type of training that criminal-justice experts have called for."
We should recruit a more representative police force.	Ray, Rashawn, and Clark Neily. "A Better Path Forward for Criminal Justice: Police Reform." Brookings Institution, April 2021 https://www.brookings.edu/research/a-better-path-forward-for-criminal-justice-police-reform/.	"Police have to be of the people and for the people. Often times, police officers talk about themselves as if they are detached from the community."
Police need to be held accountable for their actions, especially when those actions involve injury or death.	Hindi, Saja. "Colorado among First in U.S. to Pass Historic Police Reforms Following Protests." *The Denver Post*, 13 June 2020, https://denverpost.com/2020/06/13/colorado-police-reform-bill-passes-legislature/.	Recent state legislation in Colorado, Iowa, and New York shows how new laws are being used to address unnecessary use of force by police officers.

• IDENTIFY AND CONSIDER OPPOSING CLAIMS

A critical part of developing and supporting your argument is identifying opposing claims, or counterarguments. You might assume that calling attention to competing positions in your essay will weaken your argument. Nothing is farther from the truth. Identifying opposing claims provides opportunities to test and strengthen your reasons and evidence by comparing them with those put forth by other writers. Considering counterarguments also allows you to anticipate questions and concerns your readers are likely to bring to your essay. And later, as you are writing your draft, your responses to these opposing claims will provide a basis for clearly explaining to your readers why your argument is superior to others.

Remember that you're making an argument about your issue because people disagree about how to address it. If reasonable alternatives to your argument didn't exist, there would be no need for an argument in the first place. As a writer contributing to an ongoing conversation, you have a responsibility to indicate that you're aware of what has been said and who has said it. More important, you have a responsibility to consider carefully how your argument improves on the arguments made by other members of the conversation.

To identify opposing claims, review the sources you encountered as you learned about your issue. Identify the most compelling arguments you found, and ask how the reasons and evidence offered to support them compare to yours. Then ask whether you can think of reasonable alternative positions that haven't been addressed in the sources you've consulted. Finally, talk with others about your issue, and ask them what they think about it.

Working Together: Identify and Consider Opposing Claims

Working with a group of two or more classmates, carry out a "devil's advocate" exercise to identify and consider opposing claims (see *Role Playing* in Chapter 5). First, briefly describe your issue, overall claim, and reasons. Other members of the group should offer reasonable alternative arguments. One member of the group should serve as a recorder, taking careful notes on the exchange and listing opposing claims, reasons supporting those claims, and your response to the claims. Once the exchange (which might last between three and ten minutes) is completed, switch roles and repeat the activity for every other member of the group.

This activity can be carried out face-to-face, online, or on the phone. If you are working on the activity using a chat program or a threaded discussion forum, you can review the discussion later. If you are using a video conferencing app, you can record your exchange.

For each reason you expect to use in support of your overall claim, create a list of opposing points of view, briefly describing each one and noting where you found it. To determine whether you're making the best possible argument, consider each of these opposing claims in turn. Take notes on your response to each one, considering both its merits and its faults. Use what you've learned to reflect on and refine your overall claim and the reasons and evidence you've identified to support it. Later, you can use what you've learned to address counterarguments in your essay (see *Address Counterarguments* later in this chapter).

● ENSURE THE INTEGRITY OF YOUR ARGUMENT

If you're familiar with the "buy this car and get a date with this girl (or guy)" school of advertising, you know that arguments often lack integrity. Although weak arguments might be easier to develop, they usually backfire (setting aside the enduring success of automobile ads filled with attractive people). Readers who recognize errors in reasoning or the use of inappropriate evidence are likely to reject an argument out of hand.

Acquainting yourself with common logical fallacies can help you not only ensure the integrity of your argument but also identify and address counterarguments based on fallacious reasoning and weak or inappropriate forms of evidence. Some of the most common logical fallacies are described below.

Fallacies based on distraction

- **A red herring** is an irrelevant or a distracting point. The term originated with the practice of sweeping a red herring (a particularly fragrant type of fish) across the trail being followed by a pack of hunting dogs to throw them off the scent of their quarry. For example, the question *Why worry about the rising cost of tuition when the government is tapping our phones?* is a red herring (government surveillance has nothing to do with increases in college tuition).

- **Ad hominem attacks** attempt to discredit an idea or argument by suggesting that a person or group associated with it should not be trusted. These kinds of attacks might be subtle or vicious. If you hear someone say that a proposed wind farm should be rejected because its main supporter cheated on her taxes or that school vouchers are bad because a principal who swindled a school district supports them, you're listening to an ad hominem attack.

- **Irrelevant history** is another form of distraction. For example, arguing that a proposal is bad because someone came up with the idea while they were using cocaine suggests that the state of mind of the person who originates an idea has something to do with its merits. It might well be the case that the idea is flawed, but you should base your assessment on an analysis of its strengths and weaknesses. Otherwise, you might as well say that an idea is undoubtedly sound because someone thought of it while they were sober.

Fallacies based on questionable assumptions

- **Sweeping generalizations**, sometimes known as *hasty generalizations*, are based on stereotypes. Asserting that the rich are conservative voters, for example, assumes that everyone who is rich is just like everyone else who is rich. These kinds of arguments don't account for variation within a group, nor do they consider exceptions to the rule.

- **Straw-man attacks** oversimplify or distort another person's argument so it can be dismissed more easily. Just as a boxer can easily knock down a scarecrow, a writer who commits this fallacy might characterize an opposing position as more extreme than it actually is, or might refute obviously flawed counterarguments while ignoring valid objections.

- **Citing inappropriate authorities** can take several forms: citing as an authority someone who is not an expert on a subject, citing a source with a strong bias on an issue, suggesting that an individual voice represents consensus when that person's ideas are far from the mainstream, or treating paid celebrity endorsements as expert opinion.

- **Jumping on a bandwagon**, also known as *argument from consensus*, implies that if enough people believe something, it must be true. The idea of jumping on a bandwagon refers to the practice, in early American politics, of parading a candidate through town on a bandwagon. To show support for the candidate, people would climb onto the wagon. This type of argument substitutes group thinking for careful analysis.

Fallacies based on misrepresentation

- **Stacking the deck** refers to the practice of presenting evidence for only one side of an argument. Most readers will assume that a writer has done this deliberately and will wonder what the writer is trying to hide.

- **Base-rate fallacies** are commonly found in arguments based on statistics. If you read that drinking coffee will triple your risk of developing cancer, you might be alarmed. However, if you knew that the risk rose from one in a billion to three in a billion, you might pour another cup.

- **Questionable analogies**, also known as *false analogies*, make inappropriate comparisons. They are based on the assumption that if two things are similar in one way, they must be similar in others. For example, a writer might argue that global warming is like a fever and that, just as a fever usually runs its course on its own, so too will the climate recover without intervention.

Fallacies based on careless reasoning

- **Post hoc fallacies**, formally known as *post hoc, ergo propter hoc* fallacies ("after this, therefore because of this"), argue that because one event happened before a second event, the first event must have caused the second event. For example, a student might conclude that a low grade on an essay exam was assigned because of an argument with the instructor during class. In fact, the real cause might be poorly written responses to the exam questions.

- **Slippery-slope arguments** warn that a single step will inevitably lead to a bad situation. For instance, one of the most common arguments against decriminalizing marijuana is that it leads to the use of stronger narcotics. Indeed, some heroin, cocaine, or methamphetamine users might have first tried marijuana, but there is no evidence that *all* (or even most) marijuana users inevitably move on to harder drugs.
- **Either/or arguments** present two choices, one of which is usually characterized as extremely undesirable. In fact, there might be a third choice, or a fourth, or a fifth.
- **Non sequiturs** are statements that do not follow logically from what has been said. For example, arguing that drinking a particular brand of vodka will lead to a successful love life is a non sequitur.
- **Circular reasoning**, also known as *begging the question*, restates a point that has just been made as evidence for itself. Arguing that a decline in voter turnout is a result of fewer people voting is an example of circular reasoning.

As you build your argument — and in particular, as you consider counterarguments and check your reasoning for fallacies — you might find that you need to refine your overall claim. In fact, most writers refine their arguments as they learn more about an issue and consider how best to contribute to a conversation.

Prepare a Draft

Drafting involves decisions about how to frame your thesis statement, appeal to your readers, address counterarguments, take advantage of design opportunities, and organize your reasons and evidence.

● MAKE AN ARGUMENTATIVE CLAIM

The overall claim you developed as you built your argument (see *Build Your Argument* earlier in this chapter) provides the foundation for your thesis statement — a brief statement that conveys the main point you want to make about your issue. In an argumentative essay, a thesis statement should be debatable, plausible, and clear.

- **A debatable thesis statement is one with which readers can disagree.** Saying that we should take good care of our children, for example, isn't particularly debatable. Saying that we need to invest more public funding in mandatory immunization programs, however, would almost certainly lead some readers to disagree. Even though your goal in writing an argumentative essay is to convince readers to accept or act on your argument, there's little to be gained in arguing for something with which everyone will agree. An argumentative essay is useful only if it makes people think and, ideally, change their attitudes, beliefs, or behaviors.

- **A plausible thesis statement appears at the very least to be reasonable, and in fact the claim it makes might appear to be convincing or persuasive on its own.** That is, although your claim should be debatable, don't make it so extreme that it comes across as ridiculous or absurd. For example, it's one thing to argue that the news media should pay more attention to political candidates' platforms and leadership qualities than to their personal failings; it's quite another to argue that a candidate's criminal record should be ignored.

- **A clear thesis statement advances a claim that is easy to follow.** It explains what readers should believe or how they should act. Typically, this involves using words such as *should*, *must*, or *ought*. It's important to remember that you are attempting to convince or persuade your readers. Unless you tell them what to believe or how to act, they won't be sure of your position.

An effective thesis statement will shape your readers' understanding of the issue, directing their attention to particular aspects of the issue and away from others. Consider, for example, the following thesis statements about athletes' use of performance-enhancing drugs:

Thesis statement 1: If for no other reason, athletes should avoid the use of performance-enhancing drugs to safeguard their personal health.

Thesis statement 2: National and international governing bodies for sports should engage in a coordinated effort to educate aspiring athletes about ethics and sportsmanship.

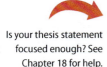
Is your thesis statement focused enough? See Chapter 18 for help.

These thesis statements would lead to significantly different argumentative essays. The first thesis statement directs readers' attention to the health consequences for athletes who use performance-enhancing drugs, while the second focuses attention on the contributions that might be made by what are essentially large corporate and government agencies. Each thesis statement is plausible and debatable, and each one tells readers what they should believe or act on. Yet each leads the reader to view the issue in a significantly different way.

● APPEAL TO YOUR READERS

As you work on your draft, consider the strategies you'll use to convince or persuade your readers to accept your argument. These strategies are essentially a means of appealing to — or asking — your readers to consider the reasons you are offering to support your overall claim and, if they accept them as appropriate and valid, to believe or act in a certain way.

Fortunately, you won't have to invent strategies on your own. For thousands of years, writers and speakers have used a wide range of appeals to ask readers to accept their reasons as appropriate and valid. Much of the work of ancient Greek and Roman thinkers such as Aristotle and Cicero revolved around strategies for presenting an argument to an audience. Their work still serves as a foundation for how we think about argumentation.

Appeals to authority When you present a reason by making an appeal to authority, you ask readers to accept it because someone in a position of authority endorses it. The evidence used to support this kind of appeal typically takes the form of quotations, paraphrases, or summaries of the ideas of experts in a given subject area, of political leaders, or of people who have been affected by an issue. As you consider whether this kind of appeal might be appropriate for your argumentative essay, reflect on the notes you've taken on your sources. Have you identified experts, leaders, or people who have been affected by an issue? If so, can you use their statements to convince your readers that your argument has merit?

Appeals to emotion attempt to elicit an emotional response to an issue. The famous "win one for the Gipper" speech delivered by Pat O'Brien, who portrayed Notre Dame coach Knute Rockne in the 1940 film *Knute Rockne: All American*, is an example of an appeal to emotion. At halftime during a game with Army, with Notre Dame trailing, he said:

> Well, boys . . . I haven't a thing to say. Played a great game . . . all of you. Great game. I guess we just can't expect to win 'em all.
>
> I'm going to tell you something I've kept to myself for years. None of you ever knew George Gipp. It was long before your time. But you know what a tradition he is at Notre Dame. . . . And the last thing he said to me — "Rock," he said, "sometime, when the team is up against it — and the breaks are beating the boys — tell them to go out there with all they got and win just one for the Gipper. . . . I don't know where I'll be then, Rock," he said — "but I'll know about it — and I'll be happy."

Using emotional appeals to frame an argument — that is, to help readers view an issue in a particular way — is a tried-and-true strategy. But use it carefully, if you use it at all. In some types of documents, such as scholarly articles and essays, emotional appeals are used infrequently, and readers of such documents are likely to ask why you would play on their emotions instead of making an appeal to logic (see *Appeals to Logic* on the next page) or an appeal to authority.

Appeals to principles, values, and beliefs rely on the assumption that your readers value a given set of principles. Religious and ethical arguments are often based on appeals to principles, such as the need to respect God, to love one another, to trust in the innate goodness of people, to believe that all of us are created equal, or to believe that security should never be purchased at the price of individual liberty. If you make an appeal to principles, values, or beliefs, be sure your readers share the particular principle, value, or belief you are using. If they don't, you might need to state and justify your underlying assumptions at the outset — or you might want to try a different kind of appeal.

Appeals to character Writers frequently use appeals to character. When politicians refer to their military experience, for example, they are saying, "Trust me. I'm a patriotic person who has served our country." When celebrities endorse a product, they are saying, "You know and like me, so please believe me when I say that this product is worth purchasing." Appeals to character can also reflect a person's professional accomplishment. When scientists or philosophers present an argument, for example, they sometimes refer to their background and experience, or perhaps to their previous publications. In doing so, they are implicitly telling their readers that they have been accurate and truthful in the past and that readers can continue to trust them. Essentially, you can think of an appeal to character as the "trust me" strategy. As you consider this kind of appeal, reflect on your character, accomplishments, and experiences, and ask how they might lead your readers to trust you.

Appeals to logic A logical appeal refers to the concept of reasoning through a set of propositions to reach a considered conclusion. For example, you might argue that a suspect is guilty of murder because police found her fingerprints on the murder weapon, her blood under the murder victim's fingernails, scratches on the suspect's face, and video of the murder from a surveillance camera. Your argument would rely on the logical presentation of evidence to convince jurors that the suspect was the murderer and to persuade them to return a verdict of guilty. As you develop reasons to support your claim, consider using logical appeals such as deduction and induction.

- **Deduction** is a form of logical reasoning that moves from general principles to a conclusion. It usually involves two propositions and a conclusion.

    Proposition 1 (usually a general principle): Stealing is wrong.

    Proposition 2 (usually an observation): John stole a candy bar from the store.

    Conclusion (results of deductive analysis): John's theft of the candy bar was wrong.

Deduction is often used to present arguments that have ethical and moral dimensions, such as birth control, welfare reform, and immigration policy.

- **Induction** is a form of logical reasoning that moves from specific observations to general conclusions, often drawing on numerical data to reveal patterns. Medical researchers, for example, typically collect a large number of observations about the effectiveness and side effects of new medications and then analyze their observations to draw conclusions about the effectiveness of the medications. Induction is based on probability — that is, whether something seems likely to occur in the future based on what has been observed. Three commonly used forms of induction are *trend analysis, causal analysis,* and *data analysis* (see *Apply an Interpretive Framework* in Chapter 9).

Choosing appeals You can use different types of appeals to support your claim. Emotional appeals can be mixed with appeals to character. A coach's address to a team before an important athletic competition often relies not only on appeals to emotion but also on appeals to character, asking the players to trust what the coach has to say and to trust in themselves and their own abilities. Similarly, appeals to principle can be combined with appeals to emotion and logic.

To choose your appeals, reflect on your purpose, readers, sources, context, and overall claim. In your writer's notebook, do the following:

1. Put your overall claim in the form of a thesis statement.
2. List the reasons you will offer to accept your overall claim.
3. Identify the evidence you will use to accept each reason.
4. Ask what sorts of appeals will help you connect each reason to the evidence you have chosen.
5. Sketch out promising appeals. Ask, for example, how you would appeal to authority, or how you would appeal to logic.
6. Ask how your readers are likely to respond to a given appeal.
7. Ask whether each appeal is appropriate in light of your overall argument. An emotional appeal might seem effective by itself, for example, but if the argument you've developed relies largely on appeals to logic and authority, an emotional appeal might surprise your readers.

● ADDRESS COUNTERARGUMENTS

Your readers will expect you to consider and address reasonable alternatives to your overall claim. They'll do so not only because it is appropriate to acknowledge the contributions of other authors who have written about an issue but also because they want to understand why your argument is superior to the alternatives. If your readers are aware of opposing claims but notice that you haven't addressed them, they'll question your credibility. They might conclude that you haven't thought carefully about the issue, or they might wonder whether you haven't addressed opposing claims in your essay because you think the other claims are stronger than yours.

To address counterarguments, review the work you did to identify and consider opposing claims as you built your argument (see *Ensure the Integrity of Your Argument* earlier in this chapter). Consider the strengths and weaknesses of each claim in relation to your argument and in relation to the other opposing claims you identified. Decide whether to concede, refute, or ignore each claim — and then do so respectfully.

Concede valid claims Show your readers that you are being fair — and establish common ground with readers who might otherwise be inclined to disagree with you — by acknowledging opposing points of view and accepting reasonable aspects of counterarguments. For example, if you are arguing that your state government should spend more to repair roads and bridges, acknowledge that this will probably mean reducing funding for other state programs or increasing state taxes.

You can qualify your concession by explaining that although part of a counterargument is sound, readers should consider the argument's weaknesses. You might note, for example, that reducing funding for some state programs could be offset by instituting fees for those who use those programs most.

Refute widely held claims A counterargument might be widely advocated or generally accepted yet still have significant weaknesses. If you identify widely held claims that have weaknesses such as cost, undesirable outcomes, or logical flaws, describe the counterargument, point out its flaws, and explain why your claim or reason is superior. For example, you might note that although it is costly to maintain roads and bridges, allowing them to fall into disrepair will cost far more in the long run — in terms of both funding and loss of life.

Ignore competing claims Don't assume that addressing counterarguments means giving every competing claim equal time. Some counterarguments will be much stronger than others, and some will be so closely related to one another that you can dismiss them as a group. Once you've addressed valid and widely held competing claims, you can safely ignore the rest. Even though your sense of fairness might suggest that you should address every counterargument, doing so will result in a less effective (and potentially much longer) essay.

As you present your discussion of counterarguments, maintain a reasonable and polite tone. You gain little, if anything, by insulting or belittling writers with whom you disagree, particularly when it's possible that some of your readers think a certain counterargument has merit. It is preferable — and generally more effective in terms of winning your argument — to carefully and politely point out the limitations of a particular counterargument.

● CONSIDER GENRE AND DESIGN

A well-written argumentative essay uses design to help readers understand your argument more clearly, usually by clearly presenting reasons and evidence or by setting a mood through the use of carefully selected illustrations. The design of your essay should reflect the formatting requirements of your assignment and the expectations of your readers, particularly your instructor.

In many cases, the appeals you choose to make to your readers will suggest design elements that can enhance your argument. Photographs, for example, can strengthen (or serve as) an emotional appeal. Pull quotes can underscore appeals to values, beliefs, and principles by calling a reader's attention to shared assumptions and important ideas. And tables, charts, and graphs can support appeals to authority.

You can find discussions of document design in Chapters 22 and 23.

● FRAME YOUR ARGUMENT

Most written arguments rely on a well-established set of elements: a clearly expressed thesis statement, a thorough discussion of the reasons and evidence supporting the overall claim, careful consideration of counterarguments, and an introduction and a conclusion. The presentation of these elements, however, is as varied as the issues addressed in argumentative essays and the writers who tackle them.

Organization As you organize your argumentative essay, give some thought to the sequence in which you present your reasons and evidence and discuss counterarguments. If you are drawing heavily on emotional appeals, for example, you might lead with a particularly striking appeal, one designed to outrage or excite your readers — or at least to get them to continue reading your essay. If you are crafting an argument that relies heavily on logical analysis, you should ask whether any of your appeals build on (or logically follow) other appeals. You should also ask whether some appeals are easier to understand and accept than others. If so, be sure to present them before you advance more complex or objectionable appeals. Counterarguments might all be addressed early on, discussed in turn, or withheld until you've established the reasons in support of your overall claim.

See Chapter 19 for advice on organizing your essay.

Introduction and conclusion Your introduction and conclusion not only provide the framework within which your readers will understand the issue you are addressing but

Read more about strategies for introducing and concluding your essay in Chapter 20.

also influence their willingness to accept your argument. In their introductions, writers of argumentative essays frequently rely on strategies such as asking a question, leading with a quotation, and telling a story. In their conclusions, they often use strategies such as speculating about the future, asking a question, and closing with a quotation.

Review and Improve Your Draft

An effective argumentative essay makes its claim in such a manner that readers will understand an issue in a particular way, provides plausible and well-supported appeals to accept that claim, addresses likely counterarguments, and avoids the traps posed by logical fallacies and other forms of argument that lack integrity. Few writers can fully address all these elements in a first draft, so don't expect to produce a finished essay in one sitting. Set aside enough time to review your draft and to revise it at least once. Allowing at least a day or two between completing your draft and reviewing it makes it easier to recognize opportunities for improvement and to clarify your thinking.

● CONSIDER YOUR OVERALL CLAIM

Before you review any other part of your draft, spend some time reassessing your overall claim. Is it presented in such a manner that your readers will understand the issue in a specific way? Have you stated it clearly? Is it possible that your readers might reasonably misinterpret your claim or might think of the issue differently than you do? Finally, is the claim stated in a way that is consistent with how you've framed your introduction and conclusion?

● REVIEW YOUR REASONS, EVIDENCE, AND APPEALS

How you present your overall claim will set up expectations among your readers about how you're likely to support it. For example, if you've said that the city council needs to increase funding for a flood mitigation program, your readers are likely to expect that at least some of your reasons for making the claim will touch on the consequences of failing to fund the program at a reasonable level. As you review your draft, ask whether your reasons make sense individually, and then ask whether they work well together. Most important, ask how your readers are likely to react to each reason and whether you've provided enough evidence to support it.

● EXAMINE YOUR TREATMENT OF COUNTERARGUMENTS

As you review how you've addressed counterarguments, put yourself in your readers' place. Doing so allows you to pose reasonable arguments that contradict your overall claim about the issue. If you believe a counterargument is plausible and likely to be raised by your readers, make sure you've responded to it. Your response need not be lengthy, but it should let readers know that you've considered the counterargument and found it less effective than the argument you're making.

● ENSURE THE INTEGRITY OF YOUR ARGUMENT

Carefully review the reasons and evidence you've offered to support your overall claim. Then review the list of common logical fallacies found earlier in this chapter. Make sure that your argument is free of these fallacies. Even an otherwise strong argument can fail to convince or persuade readers if it relies in part on questionable argumentative strategies.

● RESPOND TO FEEDBACK FROM YOUR INSTRUCTOR

When instructors offer feedback on early drafts of an argumentative essay, they almost always focus on the clarity of the overall claim, the reasons offered to support the claim, and the quality and appropriateness of the evidence to support the reasons. They are also likely to assess the integrity of the argument. If the central argument in the essay is strong, they'll turn to the use of appeals, consideration of counterarguments, and consideration of readers. If feedback is offered on later drafts of an essay, instructors will be more likely to comment on concerns at the sentence or word levels.

In addition, ask whether your readers are likely to accept the kinds of appeals you've used to present your reasons and evidence. Always consider your readers' needs, interests, backgrounds, and knowledge of the issue. You might conclude, for instance, that an emotional appeal will backfire, that your readers will expect more evidence from authorities, or that you could strengthen an appeal to values by explaining an underlying assumption.

In Process

Responding to Instructor Feedback

Jeremy received comments from his instructor on the first draft of his essay. After expressing his interest in the topic he was addressing, Jeremy's instructor suggested that he might provide more information about the issue in his introduction. His instructor expressed concerns that, while many readers would be familiar with the Black Lives Matter protests, some might be less clear about their origins and the nature of the demands for change. He also asked Jeremy to consider expanding his discussion of how best to reform the police and to do a bit more to consider counterarguments.

In response, Jeremy lengthened his introduction, providing additional information that helped him frame the issue more clearly for his readers. The result was an introduction that better prepared readers to accept his overall claim. He also expanded the discussion of his approach and revised his discussion of counterarguments.

Peer Review: Improve Your Argumentative Essay

One of the biggest challenges writers face is reading their own work as a reader rather than as the writer. Because you know what you're trying to say, you'll find it easy to understand your draft. To determine what you should do to revise your draft, ask a friend or classmate to read your essay and to assess how well you have adopted the role of advocate by answering the following questions:

Purpose
1. How do you interpret my purpose for writing? Does my goal seem to be to convince or to persuade?
2. Is my overall claim plausible and debatable? Do you agree with what I am saying? If not, what should I do to convince you?
3. Do the reasons I've offered to support my claim seem sufficient and appropriate?

Readers
4. Do you accept the connections I've made (or have assumed to exist) between my reasons and my overall claim?
5. Do you find the issue significant? Why or why not?
6. Does my reasoning seem sound? Did you catch any fallacies?
7. Have I used argumentative appeals appropriately and effectively? Should I consider making any other kinds of appeals?

Sources
8. Does the evidence I've offered to support my appeals make sense? Can I add or clarify anything to help you understand the argument better? Do you think any of the evidence is unnecessary?
9. Do my sources strike you as reliable and appropriate? Does any of the evidence I've used seem questionable? Have I relied on any sources too heavily?
10. Is it clear which ideas and information are my own and which came from my sources?

Context
11. Have I clearly introduced and effectively handled counterarguments? Did I present them fairly?
12. How familiar were you with this issue before reading my essay? Do I need to provide more (or less) background information or context? Did I fail to include any reasons or evidence that you expected?
13. Could I strengthen any of my appeals by bringing in design elements, such as photographs or tables?

For each of the points listed above, ask your reviewers to provide concrete advice about what you should do to improve your draft. It may help if you ask them to adopt the role of an editor — someone who is working with you to improve your draft. You can read more about peer review in Chapter 5.

Student Essay

Jeremy Alcazar, "Reforming, Not Defunding, the Police"

The following argumentative essay was written by featured writer Jeremy Alcazar.

Alcazar 1

Jeremy Alcazar
Professor Mike Palmquist
Composition 150
May 5, 2022

Reforming, Not Defunding, the Police

In March 2018, Stephon Clark died after being shot seven times by two police officers in the backyard of his grandmother's home in Sacramento, California. Officers Terrence Mercadal and Jared Robinet were investigating a nearby break-in when they saw Stephon holding a black object they thought was a gun. It was his phone. In March 2020, Breonna Taylor, a 26-year-old emergency medical technician whose boyfriend was under suspicion of drug distribution, was shot eight times by police officers who invaded her apartment during a no-knock raid. In May of the same year, George Floyd, arrested because he had allegedly used a counterfeit $20 bill, died at the hands of Minneapolis police officer Derek Chauvin.

On June 6, 2020, less than a month after George Floyd's death, roughly half a million people participated in protests at 550 locations across the United States (Buchanan et al.). By July of that year, Buchanan and his co-authors, pointing to a report from Civis Analytics, reported that as many as 26 million Americans had participated in Black Lives Matter protests (see Fig. 1). The Black Lives Matter movement began in the aftermath of the 2013 acquittal of the vigilante who killed unarmed teenager Trayvon Martin for walking through the wrong neighborhood, and came into national prominence one year later following the killing of teenager Michael Brown in Ferguson, Missouri. It has become the single most important protest movement in the history of the United States. And it is not limited to the U.S. In the summer of 2020, protests of police violence erupted across the globe.

Annotations:

- Information about the writer, class, and submission date is formatted according to MLA guidelines.
- The title is centered.
- Jeremy provides a historical account of some of the Black Americans killed by police officers.
- Jeremy summarizes key findings from a *New York Times* report.
- A reference to a photograph is placed near where the photograph appears in the text.

Stephen Maturen/Getty Images

Fig. 1. Protest in Minneapolis on May 26, 2020.

The reasons for protest are straightforward. A National Public Radio investigation revealed that, since 2015, at least 135 unarmed Black men and women have been killed in the United States by police (Thompson). The risk of dying from encounters with the police is more than twice as high for Black men as it is for White men (Edwards et al.). And few police-involved deaths result in prosecutions, let alone convictions (Thomson-DeVeaux et al.). Rayshawn Ray, in an article published by the Brookings Institution, shared striking numbers — and names — about how White people and Black people fare at the hands of the police:

> Black people are 3.5 times more likely than white people to be killed by police when they are not attacking or have a weapon: George Floyd. Black teenagers are 21 times more likely than White teenagers to be killed by police: Tamir Rice and Antwon Rose. A Black person is killed every 40 hours by police: Jonathan Ferrell and Koryn Gaines. One in every 1,000 Black people are killed by police: Breonna Taylor. And, as sobering as these statistics are, they are improvements to the past.

The Black Lives Matter protests following the death of George Floyd led to calls for massive change in how we police our communities. Some protestors advocated for the complete defunding of the police. Others called for reform that amounted to transforming police departments into community safety organizations. Still others called for reforms in how police are recruited and trained. Almost all called for increased sanctions for police misconduct.

Calls to "defund the police" garnered the most attention from the media (Collins; Henderson and Yisrael). This radical idea became a rallying cry for supporters of the police, who often used it to characterize their political opponents as too liberal and soft on crime. What would happen, they asked, if no one was there to answer your 9-1-1 call? Pointing to the shootings, violence, and vandalism that occurred in Seattle's Capitol Hill Autonomous Zone after the police left the area to protestors, critics argued that the answer was self-evident.

But those exhausted by civilians getting injured or killed during interactions with police feel that a change is vital. Rejecting the complete defunding of the police, some have argued that we can reform policing by replacing police departments with departments of public safety (Beer; Cardi). And in Minneapolis, where George Floyd was murdered, the city council voted to replace their police department with a new model based on that approach (Beer). Interestingly, this is neither a new idea (Illuzzi) nor one that necessarily changes the relationship between police and citizens.

Still others have argued for a range of solutions, including changing how we recruit and train police (Khazan; Lamorena; Marvel; Preston; Ray and Neily; Semuels), changing the reward structures under which police operate (Johnson and Johnson; Santa Maria et al.), and aggressively holding those who violate standards (and laws) accountable for their actions (Ferré-Sadurní & McKinley; Hindi). Considered individually, these solutions amount to little more than band aids. Taken together, however, they hold great promise for transforming policing in the United States.

To simply remove police forces or to defund them and make them less than what they already are is not the best option. For a range of reasons, we need a police force (regardless of whether you call it a police department or a department of public safety). But we also need them to be better and we need to truly feel like they are here to protect us; not to bring us down, hurt our communities and target minorities, which is what we see far too often today. A better solution would be a combination of strategies. *[Jeremy begins to present his three-part plan.]*

First, we need to change police training, starting with the police academies that train new officers and continuing throughout their careers. Alana Semuels, writing for *Time*, points out a critical disconnect in how police academies operate: *[Jeremy introduces the first part of his plan.]*

> Many programs at community and technical colleges are taught by retired cops who use a military-style teaching method that incorporates war stories from police work and warns recruits that they will face a

Alcazar 4

choice on the streets: kill or be killed. That differs from the type of training that criminal-justice experts have called for, which emphasizes de-escalating confrontations, working with and listening to community members and teaching cadets to recognize signs of mental illness.

How police officers are trained varies widely from state to state, but roughly 40 percent of police cadets receive training at two-year, four-year, or technical colleges (Semuels). If we are to improve training, we need to carefully examine how new officers are educated and ensure that the courses they take are up to the task of preparing them for the challenges they will face.

We should also train police officers in how to respond with appropriate levels of force. Brian Manley, Austin, Texas, police chief, points out the challenges associated with current training methods. "Oftentimes, police officers are sent to situations for which we're not always the best trained or the best equipped," he says. "We're just simply the only ones available" (qtd. in McGlinchy). One promising approach, borrowing from mixed martial arts, is the use of Brazilian jiu jitsu (BJJ), a form of martial arts that focus primary on controlling — not striking — a combatant. For more than a decade, the police department in Marietta, Georgia, has used BJJ to increase the range of responses its officers can make when they encounter challenging situations. "BJJ teaches methods to control a suspect and restrain them in various positions, rather than striking them, which reduces the risk of injury to the suspect as well as to the officer," write Marietta police officers Jake King and Clayton Culpepper. Since the training program was implemented, police officers who have participated in it have used tasers at a significantly lower rate than officers who have not received the training and injuries to suspects arrested by BJJ-trained officers are 53 percent lower ("Police Training Reimagined"). More important, officers who have gone through the training are 58 percent less likely to use force.

Training officers in ways that, like using BJJ, allow them to respond with a wider array of strategies can reduce costs to departments due to injuries to officers and those they apprehend. To jumpstart this progress, state and local government could provide funding to jumpstart this extra training cycle.

Second, we should consider how best to recruit a representative police force. Brian Marvel, in an opinion column written for *The Hill*, argues, "We need to invest in programs to recruit minorities into law enforcement while

> Information cited in a source is identified with the words *qtd. in* (for "quoted in").

> Jeremy introduces the second part of his plan.

incentivizing higher education through scholarship and grant programs." Similarly, Rashawn Ray and Clark Neily point out, "Police have to be of the people and for the people. Often times, police officers talk about themselves as if they are detached from the community." In combination, increasing the number of police officers who come from and live in the communities and improving training programs will have strong benefits. Those benefits include building understanding and strong connections with the citizens police serve, increasing the diversity of our police forces, and creating a better-trained workforce.

    Third, police need to be held accountable for their actions, especially when those actions involve injury or death. Recent legislation at the state level in New York, Colorado, and Iowa offer examples of how new laws are being used to address unnecessary use of force by police officers (Hindi). Following the bill's signing by Colorado governor Jared Polis, Denver civil rights attorney Qusair Mohamedbhai said, "This is, in my estimation, the largest single advancement of individual civil rights and liberties for Coloradans in a generation" (qtd. in Hindi). These new laws offer promise not simply because they increase penalties for officers who act violently, although that is a significant benefit, but also because they clarify how officers can and should behave during violent confrontations. They also provide incentives for officers who witness violent confrontations, like those who failed to intervene in George Floyd's death at the hands of Derek Chauvin, to intervene in such confrontations and report colleagues who cross the line.

> Jeremy introduces the third part of his plan.

    Fewer than one percent of officers are ever involved in incidents that result in significant injury or death. Among this group, however, are those who repeatedly cross the line in small or, unfortunately, large ways. An all-too-common response has been that these incidents are the result of a few "bad apples." As Rashwan Ray observes, however, "In policing, people always talk about 'bad apples.' Well, bad apples come from rotten trees — law enforcement agencies imbued with structural racism." Germine Awad, an associate professor at the University of Texas, agrees: "The focus on a few bad apples is misguided at best and dangerous at worst. To root out racism, we need to fix the barrels." Unless the trees (and the barrels) are addressed, change will be difficult to enact and sustain. Police departments must address systemic racism. They must remove officers who engage in unacceptable behaviors. And they must work together to ensure that police officers who are dismissed do not find employment in other departments.

Mary Zerkel, writing for the American Friends Service Committee Blog, observes, "If policing and imprisonment stopped violence, the U.S. would be the most peaceful country in the world. But decades of evidence show us this is not the case." Policing for one is not doing its job like it should and, even worse, our police forces are contributing to the violence in our country. Yet defunding the police will not solve the problem. It would be far better to transform the police by changing how we recruit and train police officers, changing the reward structures under which they operate, and aggressively holding those who violate standards (and laws) accountable for their actions.

Works Cited

Awad, Germine. "Saying 'a Few Bad Apples' Does Not End Systemic Racism in Policing." *UT News*, 22 June 2020, https://news.utexas.edu/2020/06/22/saying-a-few-bad-apples-does-not-end-systemic-racism-in-policing/.

Beer, Tommy. "Minneapolis City Council Unanimously Votes to Replace Police with Community-Led Model." *Forbes*, 12 June 2020, https://forbes.com/sites/tommybeer/2020/06/12/minneapolis-city-council-unanimously-votes-to-replace-police-with-community-led-model/.

Buchanan, Larry, et al. "Black Lives Matter May Be the Largest Movement in U.S. History." *The New York Times*, 3 July 2020, https://nytimes.com/interactive/2020/07/03/us/george-floyd-protests-crowd-size.html.

Cardi, Julia. "Denver's Policing Reform Task Force Releases Recommendations after Nearly Year of Work." *Denver Gazette*, 21 May 2021, https://denvergazette.com/news/local/denvers-policing-reform-task-force-releases-recommendations-after-nearly-year-of-work/article_bc9cf802-ba86-11eb-b191-4ba789854c7c.html.

Collins, Sean. "The Financial Case for Defunding the Police." *Vox*, 23 Sept. 2020, https://vox.com/the-highlight/21430892/defund-the-police-funding-abolish-george-floyd-breonna-taylor-daniel-prude.

Edwards, Frank, et al. "Risk of Being Killed by Police Use of Force in the United States by Age, Race–Ethnicity, and Sex." *Proceedings of the National Academy of Sciences*, vol. 116, no. 34, pp. 16793–16798, https://doi.org/10.1073/pnas.1821204116.

Ferré-Sadurní, Luis, and Jesse McKinley. "N.Y. Bans Chokeholds and Approves Other Measures to Restrict Police." *The New York Times*, 17 June 2020, https://nytimes.com/2020/06/12/nyregion/50a-repeal-police-floyd.html.

Alcazar 7

Henderson, Howard, and Ben Yisrael. "7 Myths about 'Defunding the Police' Debunked." *The Brookings Institution*, 19 May 2021, https://www.brookings.edu/blog/how-we-rise/2021/05/19/7-myths-about-defunding-the-police-debunked/. [Entries for online sources without a DOI include URLs.]

Hindi, Saja. "Colorado among First in U.S. to Pass Historic Police Reforms Following Protests." *The Denver Post*, 13 June 2020, https://denverpost.com/2020/06/13/colorado-police-reform-bill-passes-legislature/.

Illuzzi, Michael J. "Redefining Public Safety: Community Control of the Police Is an Idea That Finally Has Its Day." *Minneapolis Star Tribune*, 10 June 2020, https://startribune.com/redefining-public-safety-community-control-of-the-police-is-an-idea-that-finally-has-its-day/571171042/.

Johnson, Thaddeus L., and Natasha N. Johnson. "Commentary: Departmental Incentive Structures Are the Linchpin to Real Police Reform." *Arizona State University Crime and Justice News*, 9 March 2021, https://crimeandjusticenews.asu.edu/commentary-departmental-incentive-structures-are-linchpin-real-police-reform.

Khazan, Olga. "American Police Are Inadequately Trained." *The Atlantic*, Apr. 2021, https://www.theatlantic.com/politics/archive/2021/04/daunte-wright-and-crisis-american-police-training/618649/.

King, Jake, and Clayton Culpepper. "Teaching Control Tactics with Jiu Jitsu." *Police Law Enforcement Solutions*, 17 Feb. 2020, https://www.policemag.com/543316/teaching-control-tactics-with-jiu-jitsu.

Lamorena, Anthony. "Don't Defund Police, Spend More on Training." *The Crime Report*, 3 June 2021, https://thecrimereport.org/2021/06/03/dont-defund-police-spend-more-on-training/.

Marvel, Brian. "Success on Police Reform Hinges on Funding, Not Defunding Law Enforcement." *The Hill*, 8 Aug. 2021, https://thehill.com/opinion/criminal-justice/566841-success-on-police-reform-hinges-on-funding-not-defunding-law.

McGlinchy, Audrey. "Inside One City's Attempt to Defund the Police." *National Public Radio*. 15 Feb. 2021, https://www.npr.org/2021/02/15/967079446/inside-one-citys-attempt-to-defund-the-police. [A web page without a listed author uses the website publisher as its author.]

"Police Training Reimagined." *Gracie University*, 14 Apr. 2022, https://www.gracieuniversity.com/Pages/Public/Information?enc=kP%2fKbrj0TEbCXXaMIVHTUw%3d%3d. [Since no publication date is available for this online source, the writer includes his date of access.]

Preston, Caroline. "Police Education Is Broken. Can It Be Fixed?" *The Hechinger Report*, 28 June 2020, https://hechingerreport.org/police-education-is-broken-can-it-be-fixed/.

Ray, Rashawn. "What Does 'Defund the Police' Mean and Does It Have Merit?" *The Brookings Institution*, 19 June 2020, https://www.brookings.edu/blog/fixgov/2020/06/19/what-does-defund-the-police-mean-and-does-it-have-merit/.

---. "Bad Apples Come from Rotten Trees in Policing." *The Brookings Institution*, 30 May 2020, https://www.brookings.edu/blog/how-we-rise/2020/05/30/bad-apples-come-from-rotten-trees-in-policing/.

Ray, Rashawn, and Clark Neily. "Police Reform." *A Better Path Forward for Criminal Justice: A Report by the Brookings-AEI Working Group on Criminal Justice*, edited by Rayshawn Ray and Brent Orrell, The Brookings Institution, 2021, pp. 6–15, https://www.brookings.edu/wp-content/uploads/2021/04/Better-Path-Forward_Brookings-AEI-report.pdf.

Santa Maria, Andreas, et al. "Reducing Work-Related Burnout among Police Officers: The Impact of Job Rewards and Health-Oriented Leadership." *The Police Journal: Theory, Practice, Principles*, vol. 94, no. 3, pp. 406–421, https://doi.org/10.1177/0032258X20946805.

Semuels, Alana. "Society Is Paying the Price for America's Outdated Police Training Methods." *Time*, 20 Nov. 2020, https://time.com/5901726/police-training-academies/.

Thompson, Cheryl W. "Fatal Police Shootings of Unarmed Black People Reveal Troubling Patterns." *National Public Radio*, 25 Jan. 2021, https://npr.org/2021/01/25/956177021/ fatal-police-shootings-of-unarmed-black-people-reveal-troubling-patterns.

Thomson-DeVeaux, Amelia, et al. "Why It's So Rare for Police Officers to Face Legal Consequences." *FiveThirtyEight*, 4 June 2020, https://fivethirtyeight.com/features/why-its-still-so-rare-for-police-officers-to-face-legal-consequences-for-misconduct/.

Zerkel, Mary. "6 Reasons Why It's Time to Defund the Police." *American Friends Service Committee*, 15 Oct. 2020, https://www.afsc.org/blogs/news-and-commentary/6-reasons-why-its-time-to-defund-police.

Project Ideas

The following suggestions provide means of focusing your work on an argumentative essay or another type of argumentative document.

Suggestions for Essays

1. ARGUE ABOUT A SOCIAL TREND

Identify and discuss the relevance of a social trend, such as the increasing focus on wellness and healthy lifestyles, changes in home-ownership patterns, or why people are dressing in a particular manner. Then make an argument about (a) the advisability of following the trend, (b) the likely effects — short- or long-term — of the trend on society, or (c) the likelihood that the trend will have a lasting impact. Use evidence from online conversations and your personal observations to support your argument.

2. ARGUE AGAINST A COMMONLY HELD BELIEF

Urge your readers to reject a commonly held belief. For example, you might argue that the widespread belief that writing ability is a gift rather than an acquired skill causes students to give up too easily on efforts to improve their writing. Or you might argue that a particular belief about American families is inaccurate. For example, you might focus your argument on the belief that only children are more likely to be "spoiled," that a woman's life will be less rich if she chooses not to become a mother, or that siblings are friends for life. In your essay, define the belief and make an overall claim about the effects of accepting it. Offer reasons and evidence to support your claim. Base your appeals on logic and on principles, values, and beliefs.

3. URGE READERS TO WIDEN THEIR CULTURAL HORIZONS

Make an argument about the value of attending a play or concert, viewing a movie or watching a television show, attending a poetry reading or an art exhibition, or purchasing a new music album or video game. Your argument should be based on the benefits of appreciating and supporting cultural events, literature, artistic work, music, or games. To support your argument, draw on your observations and interpretations of your subject. You might also use evidence from interviews or surveys and read published work that reviews or analyzes the subject of your essay.

4. ARGUE ABOUT A DEFINITION

Make an argument about a definition, such as how a problem or an issue has been defined or how a particular standard has been developed and applied. For example, you might argue that characterizations of state support for public education as a financial issue are inappropriate and that it would be better to understand the issue as one of ensuring that citizens are well prepared to participate in a democracy. Or you might argue that your state's definition of intoxication (for example, .08 percent blood alcohol content) is inappropriate and that it ought to be higher or lower. Use evidence from published sources to support your argument (see Chapter 14). Depending on the subject of your essay, consider using field research methods such as interviews, observations, surveys, and correspondence (see Chapter 15) to support your argument. Think about the type of evidence you've collected to support your argument and consider which types of appeals are likely to be most effective with your readers.

5. ARGUE ABOUT AN ISSUE IN YOUR AREA OF STUDY

Write an argumentative essay about an issue in a discipline or profession in which you have an interest. For example, if you are interested in human resources, you might argue about the implications of allowing employers to access employees' genetic profiles. The issue you choose should be under debate in the discipline or profession, so be sure to search professional or academic journals and online conversations among members of the discipline or profession for prevailing arguments (see Chapter 14). Depending on the subject of your essay, consider using field research methods such as interviews, observations, surveys, and correspondence (see Chapter 15) to gather information to support your argument. For example, you might locate online discussion forums or subscribe to email lists within your discipline. As you craft your argument, consider the type of evidence you've collected to support your argument and consider which types of appeals are likely to be most effective with your readers.

Suggestions for Other Genres

6. WRITE AN OPINION COLUMN ABOUT A NEW LAW OR REGULATION

In an opinion column, identify a recently passed law or a new regulation (federal, state, or local), and discuss its potential impact. You might, for example, take a look at changes in election laws, such as requirements that state-issued IDs be provided at polling stations. Or you might explore laws that address labeling of genetically modified foods. Offer a brief summary evaluation of the appropriateness or likely effects of the new law or regulation, and then make recommendations to your readers about how to respond. For example, you might argue that a new law is so flawed that it should be repealed. Or you might argue that only by providing adequate funding to a local or state agency can a regulation be enforced effectively. Use evidence from government documents, other published sources, and field research to support your argument.

7. WRITE A BLOG ENTRY ABOUT AN ISSUE RAISED IN ANOTHER BLOG

In a blog, argue about an issue addressed by the author of another blog. For example, you might object to an argument about the economic and political trade-offs of government rescues of failed financial institutions. Or you might argue about the advisability of joining social-networking sites such as Facebook or LinkedIn. Your blog entry should link to the blog entry that raised the issue, as well as to other relevant blogs. Use evidence from blogs and other published sources to support your argument. You should refer to your sources by using phrases such as "in an article published in *The New York Times* on July 30, 2021, Sapna Maheshwari argues" or by linking directly to the source.

8. CREATE A PUBLIC SERVICE ADVERTISEMENT

Create a full-page ad suitable for a magazine or website that urges readers to take action on a social issue, such as adoption or hunger. Your ad should use visual images and only enough text to clearly identify the issue and convey your argument to your readers. For inspiration, examine the ads shown earlier in this chapter.

In Summary: Writing an Argumentative Essay

★ **Find a conversation and listen in (p. 431).**
- Explore disagreements (p. 432).
- Track online conversations (p. 434).
- Ask questions about promising issues (p. 434).

★ **Build your argument (p. 435).**
- Define your overall claim (p. 437).
- Develop reasons to accept your overall claim (p. 437).
- Choose evidence to support your reasons (p. 439).
- Identify and consider opposing claims (p. 442).
- Ensure the integrity of your argument (p. 443).

★ **Prepare a draft (p. 445).**
- Make an argumentative claim (p. 445).
- Appeal to your readers (p. 446).

- Address counterarguments (p. 449).
- Consider genre and design (p. 451).
- Frame your argument (p. 451).

★ **Review and improve your draft (p. 452).**
- Consider your overall claim (p. 452).
- Review your reasons, evidence, and appeals (p. 452).
- Examine your treatment of counterarguments (p. 452).
- Ensure the integrity of your argument (p. 453).
- Respond to feedback from your instructor (p. 453).

**PART THREE
Conducting Research**

13 Focusing Your Search

What should I consider as I develop my research question? 467
Consider your issue and disciplinary context 468
Reflect on your purpose and role 470
Look for gaps in the conversation 472

How can I draft my research question? 473
Generate questions about your issue 473

Select and refine your question 474
Be open to change 476

How can I develop my search plan? 477
Identify relevant types of sources 477
Identify appropriate search tools and research methods 478
Review and refine your plan 479

Given the amount of information available through library collections, databases, and the web, experienced writers are typically less worried about finding *enough* sources than they are about finding the *right* sources. This chapter explores strategies for developing a research question and a plan to collect information for a writing project.

What Should I Consider as I Develop My Research Question?

Focus your efforts to collect, read, evaluate, and take notes on sources by developing a research question — a brief question that asks about a specific aspect of your subject, reflects your writing situation, and is narrow enough to allow you to collect information in time to meet your deadlines.

Researcher questions can vary widely. For example, one writer might want to investigate the origin of a problem, such as the increasing severity of hurricanes in the Caribbean, while another might want to understand the implications of severe hurricanes for insurance policies sold in the southeastern United States. The research questions created by these writers would focus on significantly different aspects of the larger topic of severe hurricanes.

Generating potential research questions draws on many of the strategies used to generate ideas for a topic (see *Generate Ideas* in Chapter 2). Among other strategies, you can brainstorm lists of questions, freewrite, use clustering and mapping, and respond to questions.

To begin developing your research question, consider your issue and context, reflect on your purpose and role, and look for gaps in the conversation.

Consider Your Issue and Disciplinary Context

As you've explored your topic and focused on your issue, you've gained an understanding of some of the most important information, ideas, and arguments shaping the conversation you've decided to join. You might also have had the opportunity to talk with others about your issue and perhaps even to conduct observations. If you're like most writers, your initial thoughts about your topic and issue have changed as you've carried out your investigations.

As you begin considering ideas for a research question, ask whether what you've learned about the issue has changed your understanding of your writing situation. Then ask yourself what you'd like to learn next. As you ask these questions, consider how disciplinary or professional contexts might shape the questions you should ask. If you are writing a report for a biology class, for example, your understanding of the kinds of questions biologists typically ask about issues will come into play. That's true for virtually every discipline and profession — each of which has areas that are of interest to its members, and each of which has particular ways of asking questions about those areas of interest.

Disciplinary Questions

Discipline	Types of Questions	Examples
Humanities	Interpretive questions about literature, music, philosophy, rhetoric, and the arts	How did the acceptance of Manet's painting style open the door for Impressionism?
		What similarities does Toni Morrison's character Amy Denver in *Beloved* share with Twain's character Huck Finn?
Social Sciences	Questions about factors that affect human behavior, including "how" and "why" questions about various events	What is the significance of social media platforms such as Facebook and Twitter in protest movements?
		What factors contribute to a person becoming a mass murderer?
		Why did fascism ultimately fail in Italy in the 1940s?
Sciences	"How" and "why" questions about the natural world, including both the environment and living beings	How can we combat the obesity epidemic among school-age children?
		What are the preventable causes of climate change?

Similarly, consider how your understanding of the kinds of genres typically used to communicate within the discipline or profession — such as articles, essays, and presentations — will shape your work on your research question. Some genres, such as books and longer reports, are well suited to broader questions. Others, because of their comparative brevity (think of poster sessions, conference presentations, reports, and essays), are better suited to highly focused research questions.

Your Turn: Generate Questions with a Disciplinary or Professional Focus

In your writers's notebook, brainstorm or freewrite about how your disciplinary background (for example, your major) or the profession you are in or plan to enter is related to the issue you've decided to pursue. On the basis of your brainstorming or freewriting, create a list of potential questions about your issue.

Reflect on Your Purpose and Role

Your purpose and role are among the most important factors driving your efforts to develop your research question. Think about what you are trying to accomplish and how you plan to relate to your readers.

If you want to...	Then you are adopting the role of...
Consider the significance of a subject or issue	Observer (see Chapter 7)
Convey what is known about a subject or issue	Reporter (see Chapter 8)
Look for similarities and differences among subjects or aspects of a subject, ask what leads to a specific outcome, or ask about a series of events	Interpreter (see Chapter 9)
Share your assessment of strengths and weaknesses, advantages and disadvantages, or appropriateness	Evaluator (see Chapter 10)
Define, understand, or offer a solution to a problem	Problem Solver (see Chapter 11)
Advance an argument about an issue	Advocate (see Chapter 12)

The role you adopt will lead you to formulate your research question in particular ways. Writers who inform their readers, for example, develop strikingly different questions than those who seek to persuade them to take action. A writer seeking to inform readers about the impact of warming ocean waters on tropical storms, for instance, might pursue questions such as the following:

> What are the effects of warming ocean waters on the severity of tropical storms?
>
> How has the popular media characterized the causes of increasingly severe tropical storms?
>
> What have recent scientific research studies indicated about the impact of warming ocean waters on the severity of tropical storms?

Your Turn: Generate Questions Based on Your Purpose and Role

In your writer's notebook, use some of the sentence starters in the table *The Relationship between Roles and Writing Questions* to generate a list of potential questions about your issue. Reflect on and evaluate the questions in your list, and identify two or three promising questions.

In contrast, had the writer sought to advocate a particular approach to the issue, the research questions might have resembled the following:

> In light of recent findings about the impact of warming ocean waters on the severity of tropical storms, should the U.S. government increase subsidies for flood insurance?
>
> Given scientific evidence that warming ocean waters are increasing the severity of tropical storms, should the U.S. government increase FEMA funding to mitigate damage in areas affected by the storms?

The Relationship between Roles and Writing Questions

If you adopt the role of...	Then you might ask questions such as...
Observer	What are the implications of _____?
	How can we learn from the example of an individual or group?
	What can we gain from thinking about [an idea / a work of art / a work of literature / a performance]?
Reporter	What is known — and not known — about _____?
	How might we define _____?
Evaluator	How sound are the assumptions that are shaping current thinking about _____?
	What are the best choices available for addressing _____?
	What are the relative strengths and weaknesses of _____?
Interpreter	What has occurred in the past that is relevant to _____?
	What causes _____?
	What are the effects of _____?
	Does the data suggest that _____ [is / is the result of] a trend?
	What is likely to happen [to / as a result of] _____?
	In what ways is _____ [similar to / different from] _____?
Problem Solver	Why is _____ a problem?
	What is the best solution to _____?
	Why should we adopt _____ as a solution to _____?
	What steps can we take to put this solution in place?
Advocate	What are the origins of this argument?
	Who has made the best arguments about _____?
	What do the writers and readers involved in conversation about _____ want to [see happen / avoid happening]?
	How can we find common ground about _____?

Given the critical need to ensure the safety of residents, what steps should local governments take to address the impact of increasingly severe tropical storms?

Look for Gaps in the Conversation

Consider where you might offer something new to the conversation. You don't need to offer something that is radically new, nor do you need to change the direction of the conversation, but you should offer something of value to your readers. The following table uses an approach to newness developed by David Kaufer, Cheryl Geisler, and Christine Neuwirth.

Filling a Gap with Something New

Forms of Newness	Guiding Questions
Newness by aspect. Contributions related to experience or observation.	How can my personal experiences form the basis for a contribution to this conversation?
	How has my knowledge of this issue prepared me to offer something new?
	How can my investigations of this issue prepare me to share something new?
Newness by analogy. Contributions based on comparison.	In what ways is this issue like a library? Like a church? Like a labor union?
Newness by framework. Contributions based on application of methods from another discipline or profession.	How can an anthropological approach help us better understand this issue? A psychological approach? A legal approach?
Prize-winning newness. The least common form of newness.	What can I share that is truly new, game changing, or so unusual and surprising that it will gain my readers' attention?

Your Turn: Explore Gaps in Your Issue

In your writer's notebook, use freewriting, looping, mapping, or clustering to reflect on potential gaps in your issue. Then reflect on how the types of newness outlined in the table *Filling a Gap with Something New* might allow you to fill a gap in the conversation about your issue.

How Can I Draft My Research Question?

Your research question provides the foundation for developing your position on your issue — the main point you will make about your issue (see *How Can I Develop a Position on My Issue?* in Chapter 18). It also guides your efforts to develop a plan to search for and collect information.

Generate Questions about Your Issue

Most research questions begin with the words *who, what, when, where, why,* or *how*. Some research questions use the words *would* or *could* to ask whether something is possible. Still others use the word *should* to analyze the appropriateness of a particular action, policy, procedure, or decision. These words can be applied to

If you are focusing on . . .	Then you might ask questions such as . . .
Sharing information	What is this? How does this work? Why is this important?
Analyzing a historical event	What happened? When / where / how / why did this happen? Who caused this? Who was affected? Could / would / should this _____?
Exploring assumptions	What do people think they know about _____? When did they start thinking this way? Why do they assume that _____? Should they make other assumptions?
Understanding effects	What / why / when / where will/did _____ happen? Who wants / doesn't want _____ to happen? What could / would happen if _____? What should happen?
Analyzing or advancing a goal	What do people want to see happen? Why do they want to see _____ happen? When is the best time to _____? How can we accomplish _____? Could / should _____ be pursued?
Considering policies	What policies exist? Why do these policies exist? When were these policies created? How are these policies applied? Would / could this policy lead to _____? Should _____ be allowed to happen again?

specific aspects of your issue, allowing you to generate a set of initial questions. By reviewing these questions, you can begin to focus on what interests you most about your issue.

Select and Refine Your Question

Once you have a list of potential research questions, select a question that interests you, is consistent with the role you have adopted, and is appropriate for your writing situation. Then refine your question by referring to shared assumptions and existing conditions, narrowing its scope, and conducting preliminary searches.

● REFER TO SHARED ASSUMPTIONS AND EXISTING CONDITIONS

You can refine your research question by calling attention to assumptions that have been made by the community of writers and readers who are addressing your subject or by referring to existing conditions relevant to your subject. Note the difference among these three versions of featured writer Sophie Kimble's research question about shark finning, the practice of removing shark fins so they can be used in shark fin soup. (See Sophie's essay, "To Spray or Not to Spray in Chapter 7.")

Original Question:

What efforts are being made to reduce or eliminate the impacts of shark finning on shark populations and ocean ecosystems?

Alternative 1:

Given the damaging effects of shark finning on shark populations and the larger ocean ecosystem, why have so many governments been slow to ban the practice?

Alternative 2:

In light of the success of public-relations campaigns to reduce the consumption of shark fin soup in China, what barriers exist to the introduction of similar campaigns in Indonesia, Macau, Thailand, and Vietnam?

As you refine your research question, experiment with using qualifying words and phrases such as the following:

Mix . . .	and Match
Although	we know that . . .
Because	it is uncertain . . .
Even though	it is clear that . . .
Given that	studies indicate . . .
If	recent events . . .
In light of	it has been shown . . .
Now that	the lack of . . .
Since	we cannot . . .
While	why . . .

● NARROW YOUR SCOPE

Early research questions typically lack focus. You can narrow the scope of your question by looking for vague words and phrases and replacing them with more specific words or phrases. The process of moving from a broad research question to one that might be addressed effectively in an academic essay might produce the following sequence:

Original Question:

What is behind the increased concern about how we run our elections?

Refined:

What has led to the increased attention to rules governing mail-in ballots and early in-person voting in our elections?

Further Refined:

How has the Supreme Court's July 2021 ruling on Arizona voting rules—and by extension similar rules in other states—affected voter participation in presidential elections?

In this example, the writer has narrowed the scope of the research question in two ways. First, the writer has shifted the focus from general concerns about how elections are run to two areas of concern — mail-in ballots and early in-person voting in elections. Second, the writer has moved from a general focus on elections to a more specific focus on the effects of a Supreme Court ruling on voter participation in presidential elections.

TECH TIP: CONDUCT PRELIMINARY SEARCHES

One of the best ways to test your research question is to conduct some preliminary searches in an online library catalog or database or on the web. If you locate a vast amount of information in your searches, you might need to revise your question so that it focuses on a more manageable aspect of the subject. In contrast, if you find almost nothing, you might need to expand the scope of your question.

Be Open to Change

As you begin drafting your research question, remember that as you learn more about your subject, you might refine your purpose and role. In turn, that might lead to changes in your research question. If you think of your research question as a flexible guide — as a question subject to revision — you can be open to new ways of thinking about the conversation and your contribution to it.

Your Turn: Draft a Research Question

Drawing on the strategies discussed in this section, draft preliminary research questions, choose a promising question, and refine it.

1. Generate several potential research questions about your issue.
2. Select the most promising question.
3. Refine your question by referring to shared assumptions or existing conditions.
4. Refine your question by narrowing its scope.
5. Test the scope of your question by conducting preliminary searches.
6. If necessary, narrow the questions scope further, and conduct additional preliminary searches.

How Can I Develop My Search Plan?

Once you've created your research question, you'll need to decide how to search for and collect information. Use your research questions and your writing situation to shape your search plan — a brief, informal plan that records your ideas about how to locate and collect information.

Identify Relevant Types of Sources

Writers use information found in a variety of sources — digital, print, broadcast, and field — to support the points they make in their documents. To identify relevant sources for your writing project, consider the scope of the conversation you are joining, the timeliness of your subject, the information you'll need to develop your ideas, and the evidence you'll need to support your points.

- **CONSIDER THE SCOPE OF YOUR CONVERSATION**

If the conversation focuses on a highly specialized issue within a scholarly discipline, such as a discussion of gene splicing in biology, the best sources usually are scholarly books and journal articles. If it addresses a subject that has broad appeal, such as transportation problems in your state or region, you can draw on a much wider range of sources, including newspaper and magazine articles, editorials and opinion columns, blogs, websites, podcasts, YouTube videos, and social media posts.

- **CONSIDER THE TIMELINESS OF YOUR SUBJECT**

Some subjects, such as state funding for higher education or alcohol consumption by college students, tend to be discussed over an extended period of time in a wide range of sources. If your subject focuses on a recent event, however, it might be best to turn to magazine and newspaper articles, the web, blogs, observation, surveys, or interviews.

- **CONSIDER WHAT YOU NEED TO LEARN**

If your subject is unfamiliar to you, look for sources that offer general overviews or discuss important aspects of the subject. Such sources tend to include magazine articles, television and radio programs, professional journal articles, and articles on the web.

● **CONSIDER THE EVIDENCE YOU'LL NEED**

Think about the kind of evidence other writers have used to make their points. Have they used numerical data from scholarly research reports? Have they referred to expert opinion? If so, search for sources that can provide these kinds of evidence.

Identify Appropriate Search Tools and Research Methods

In general, you can use three sets of resources to locate information.

- **Digital search tools**, such as library catalogs, databases, and web search sites, allow you to search and browse for sources using a computer. Digital search tools provide access to publication information about — and in some cases to the complete text of — print and digital sources.

- **Print resources**, such as bibliographies, indexes, encyclopedias, dictionaries, handbooks, almanacs, and atlases, can be found in library reference and periodical rooms. Unlike digital search tools, which typically cover recent publications, many print resources provide information about publications over several decades — and in some cases over more than a century.

- **Field research methods** allow you to collect information firsthand. These methods include conducting observations, interviews, and surveys; corresponding with experts; attending public events and performances; and viewing or listening to television and radio programs.

Your Turn: Develop Your Search Plan

In your writer's notebook, sketch out a plan for your search. It can be as informal as a series of brief notes or as formal as a numbered list of steps with detailed instructions. Your plan should do the following:

- provide a brief overview of your issue
- list your research question
- identify the types of sources you'll search for
- describe the tools and methods you'll use to locate sources, including a list of potential search terms (see Chapter 14) and notes about any field research methods you might use (see Chapter 15)
- provide the schedule you'll follow to complete your research, including start dates and projected completion dates

Featured writer Sophie Kimble, who wrote a problem-solving essay about the use of shark finning (see *Select and Refine Your Question* earlier in this chapter), knew that her topic would require recent sources. As she put together her search plan, she decided to search databases for recent scholarly articles and to look for websites that addressed the issue. To obtain the most up-to-date information, she also scheduled an interview with a professor at her university who had expertise related to her topic.

Review and Refine Your Plan

Your search plan might be an informal set of notes or a list of step-by-step instructions complete with details such as keywords to search, interview questions to ask, and observation forms to fill out. No matter how informal it is, you should write it down. A written plan will help you remember the decisions you've made as you've prepared to collect your sources.

Use your plan to schedule time to search for and collect information. Next to each activity — such as searching a database or conducting an interview — identify start dates and projected completion dates. Creating a schedule will help you budget and manage your time.

Share your plan with your instructor, your supervisor, your classmates, or a librarian. Each might suggest additional search tools, research methods, and shortcuts for your project. Take notes on the feedback you receive and, if necessary, revise your plan.

In Summary: Focusing Your Search

* **Consider your issue (p. 467).**
  * Consider your issue and disciplinary context (p. 468).
  * Consider your purpose and role (p. 470).
  * Look for gaps in the conversation (p. 472).

* **Draft your research question (p. 473).**
  * Generate questions about your issue (p. 473).
  * Select and refine your question (p. 474).
  * Remain open to change (p. 476).

* **Plan your search for sources (p. 477).**
  * Identify relevant types of sources (p. 477).
  * Identify appropriate search tools and research methods (p. 478).
  * Review and refine your plan (p. 479).

14 Locating Sources

How can I locate sources using digital resources? 480
Generate search terms 481
Choose search strategies 482
Search library catalogs 485
Search databases 487
Search the web 489
Search media sites 492

How can I locate sources using print resources? 493
Discuss your search plan with a librarian 494
Visit the library stacks 494
Browse periodicals 495
Check reference works 495

Your research question and search plan prepare you to start collecting sources. In this chapter, you'll learn how to generate search terms; how to use library catalogs, databases, and web search sites; and how to take advantage of the print resources in a library. As you start to locate sources, consider your writing situation and the conversation you've decided to join. Focusing on your purpose, role, readers, and context can help you decide which resources and search techniques to use.

How Can I Locate Sources Using Digital Resources?

Writers can turn to four general sets of digital resources to locate information about their subjects: library catalogs, databases, web search sites, and media search sites. You can search these resources using basic and advanced searches.

Generate Search Terms

Regardless of which digital resource you use, the results of your searches will be only as good as your search terms. Even the best search tools can produce poor results — and all too often that's exactly what happens. To increase your chances of obtaining good results, spend time identifying search terms related to your subject.

You can identify useful search terms by building on your research question (see *How Can I Draft My Research Question?* in Chapter 13) or thesis statement (see Chapter 18) or by using a range of idea-generating techniques, such as brainstorming, freewriting, looping, and clustering (see *Generate Ideas* in Chapter 2). Featured writer Kelsey Smith, for example, used freewriting to generate ideas for her searches. Then she highlighted promising keywords and phrases.

> I know a little bit about my topic from personal experience, but I need more information on ==copyright law==. I know how it applies to things like books, but don't really know what it means for art, or how it changes (or doesn't?) when things are shared on ==social media==. ==What rights do the artists have==? How can they better protect themselves and their work? Also, why do people steal other people's work anyway? I understand people ==re-sharing things online==, even though they don't give ==credit to the artists==. I don't like it, but I understand it. But why do ==corporations== think they can get away with ==art theft==? Yet it seems like they do get away with it. How does that happen?

You can also generate search terms by using your research question or thesis statement (see Chapter 18) as a starting point. Featured writer Sophie Kimble, for example, typed her research question in a word-processing program, formatted the most important words and phrases in color, and then brainstormed a list of related words and phrases.

**What efforts are being made to
reduce or eliminate the impacts of shark finning on shark populations and ocean ecosystems?**

reduce	impacts	"shark finning"	populations	"ocean ecosystems"
eliminate	effects	"fin removal"	species	oceans
limit	consequences	"fin cutting"		"ocean life"
lessen	results			"ocean environment"
lower	outcomes			"ocean biology"
decrease				"sea life"
cut				"ocean biome"
mitigate				

Choose Search Strategies

You'll also increase the likelihood of locating useful sources by learning about the types of searches you might conduct.

● PLAN BASIC SEARCHES

A basic search allows you to look for documents that contain as little as a single word or phrase in the subject, title, or text, or, in the case of databases, in other parts of a database record (see *Search Databases* later in this chapter). These searches can return large sets of results. To find results that will be relevant to your subject, consider refining your basic searches by using additional keywords, exact phrases, and wildcards.

Use additional keywords In most cases, using more than one keyword will reduce the number of results returned by your search. This strategy is especially helpful when searching the web, which tends to produce thousands (sometimes millions) of hits for individual words or phrases.

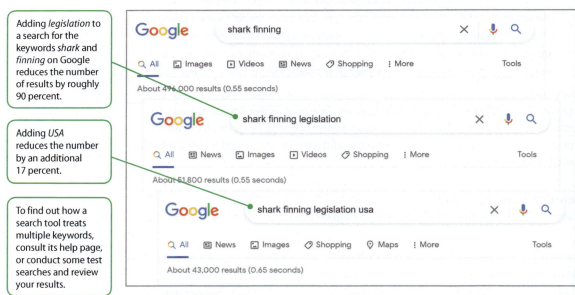

Adding *legislation* to a search for the keywords *shark* and *finning* on Google reduces the number of results by roughly 90 percent.

Adding *USA* reduces the number by an additional 17 percent.

To find out how a search tool treats multiple keywords, consult its help page, or conduct some test searches and review your results.

▲ Planning simple searches

Search for exact phrases Sometimes the best way to locate information is to search for an exact phrase. To further refine your search, you might use *shark finning* as a phrase. This would eliminate sources in which, for example, the words *shark* and *finning* appear but are separated by other words.

▲ A simple search with exact phrases

 TECH TIP: PLAN ADVANCED SEARCHES

You are probably fairly comfortable doing basic searches already, but they can take your research only so far. To obtain more targeted results, use advanced searches. Most library catalogs, databases, and web search sites provide an advanced search page. These pages allow you to focus your searches in powerful ways using *wildcard symbols*, *Boolean operators* (which are used to search for all, some, or none of the words or phrases in a search box), and *search limits* (such as publication date and document characteristics).

Use wildcards Sometimes you might not be sure what form of a word is most likely to occur. Rather than conducting several searches for *legislation*, *legislature*, *legislator*, and *legislate*, for example, you can combine keywords into a single wildcard search. Wildcards are symbols that take the place of letters or strings of letters. By standing in for multiple letters, they allow you to expand the scope of your search.

The following are the most commonly used wildcard symbols:

* usually takes the place of one or more characters, such as *legislat**

? usually takes the place of a single character, such as *sw?m* for swim, swam, or swum

To find out whether wildcard symbols are supported, consult the help section in a library catalog or database or the advanced search page of a web search site.

Focus searches with Boolean operators Boolean operators let you narrow your search by specifying whether keywords or phrases *can*, *must*, or *must not* appear in the results. Some Boolean operators also allow you to search for keywords or phrases that appear next to, before or after, or within a certain distance from one another in a document. A list of commonly used Boolean operators and their functions is provided in the following table.

Boolean Operator	Function	Example
AND/+	Finds sources that include both search terms (either keywords or phrases)	shark AND finning +shark +finning
OR	Finds sources that include either search term	shark OR dogfish
NOT/–	Finds sources that include one search term but not the other	shark NOT whale shark -whale
ADJ (adjacent)	Finds sources in which the search terms appear next to each other	shark ADJ finning
NEAR	Finds sources in which the search terms appear within a specified number of words from each other	shark NEAR finning
BEFORE	Finds sources in which search terms appear in a particular order	shark BEFORE finning
Parentheses ( )	Parentheses are used to group search terms and Boolean operators	(shark ADJ finning) AND (legislation OR law) AND (USA NOT China)

Limit searches Search limits allow you to limit your searches to documents that have particular characteristics. Common limits include publication date (or, in the case of web pages, the date on which a page was last updated), type of document, and the availability of full text (for databases).

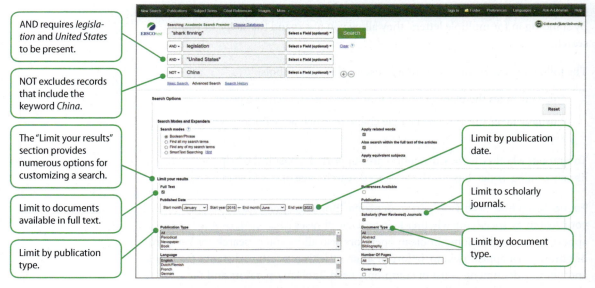

AND requires *legislation* and *United States* to be present.

NOT excludes records that include the keyword *China*.

The "Limit your results" section provides numerous options for customizing a search.

Limit to documents available in full text.

Limit by publication type.

Limit by publication date.

Limit to scholarly journals.

Limit by document type.

▲ Advanced search in a database, using Boolean search terms and limits

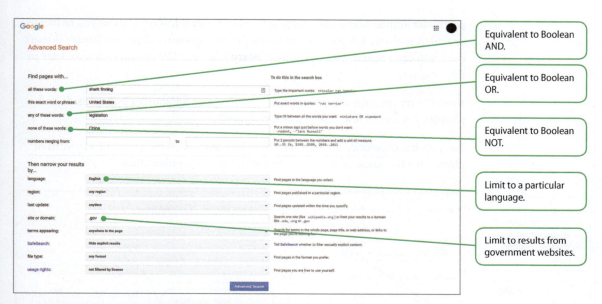

▲ Advanced search on a website, using Boolean search terms and limits

Search Library Catalogs

Online catalogs provide information about the author(s), title, publication date, subject heading, and call number for each source in the library's collection. Typically, they also indicate the location of the source in the library and its availability for checkout. In some cases, library catalogs also support searches of databases (see *Search Databases* later in this chapter) to which the library subscribes.

Library catalogs typically help you locate

- books
- journals owned by the library (although not individual articles)
- newspapers and magazines owned by the library (although not necessarily individual articles)
- documents stored on microfilm or microfiche
- videotapes, audiotapes, and other multimedia items owned by the library
- maps
- theses and dissertations completed by college or university graduate students

In addition to searching your local library catalog, you can also search catalogs available on the web. The Library of Congress catalog (catalog.loc.gov), for example, provides a comprehensive list of publications on a particular subject or by a particular author. Some sites, such as WorldCat (worldcat.org), allow you to locate or search multiple libraries. If you find a promising source that your library doesn't own, you can request it through interlibrary loan (see *Use interlibrary loan* later in this chapter).

Most library catalogs allow you to search or browse for sources by keywords and phrases, author(s), title, subject, and call number.

Search by keyword, author, or title You can search for a specific keyword or phrase, for the name of an author, or for the title of a publication.

▲ Searching by keyword, author, or title

Search by call number or subject heading To locate sources related to a promising result, search by either call number or subject heading.

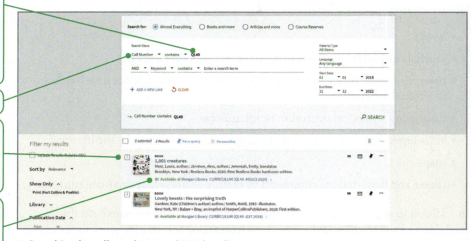

▲ Searching by call number or subject heading

TECH TIP: SEARCH WITH MULTIPLE STRATEGIES

Library catalogs can help you locate sources quickly, especially when you conduct basic searches, such as an author search by last name. If the last name is a common one such as Smith, Garcia, or Chen, however, your search might produce far more results than you would like. In this case, it might help to use the catalog's advanced search form to search with more than one type of strategy — such as author and keyword — at the same time.

Search Databases

While a library catalog allows you to search for publications owned by the library, a database allows you to search for sources that have been published on a particular topic or in a particular discipline regardless of whether the library owns the sources. Although some databases, such as ERIC, Medline, the New York Public Library Digital Collections, and ScienceDirect, are available publicly on the web, most are available only through a library website. Large research libraries often subscribe to hundreds of databases, while smaller libraries might subscribe to only a handful.

Databases supply publication information and brief descriptions of the information in a source; some — but not all — provide electronic copies of the source. Using the citation information provided by the database, you can check your library's catalog for the title of the publication in which the source appears. If your library does not own the publication, you can request it through interlibrary loan (see *Using interlibrary loan* later in this chapter).

● IDENTIFY RELEVANT DATABASES

Databases tend to specialize in particular subject areas and types of sources. To identify databases that might be relevant to your issue, review your library's list of databases or consult a reference librarian. Ask yourself the following questions.

Am I focusing on an issue that is likely to have been addressed in recent news coverage? If so, search *news and information databases* that focus on newspapers and weekly news magazines, such as Alternative Press Index, LexisNexis Academic, Newspaper Source, and ProQuest Global Newsstream.

Am I focusing on a broad area of interest, such as business, education, or government? If so, search *subject databases* that focus on more general issues, such as Academic Search Premier, ArticleFirst, Catalog of U.S. Government Publications, and WorldCat.

Am I focusing on an issue that is related to a particular profession or academic discipline? If so, consult *bibliographies* that focus on that area. Many library websites categorize databases by profession or discipline. For example, if you are interested in an issue related to sociology, you might consult databases such as Arts & Humanities Database, Family & Society Studies Worldwide, and Social Science Abstracts.

Have I already identified sources about my issue? If you have already located promising sources, search *citation indexes* to identify sources that refer to your sources. Depending on your area, you might search Arts & Humanities Citation Index, Science Citation Index, Social Sciences Citation Index, and Emerging Sources Citation Index.

Is the full text of the source available? *Full-text databases* offer the complete source for viewing or download. These databases cut out the middle step of locating the specific periodical that published the article. Databases that offer some of or all of their sources in full text include Academic Search Premier, Black Thought and Culture, ERIC, IEEE Xplore, JSTOR, LexisNexis Academic, and ScienceDirect.

Am I searching for images, video, or audio? If you are seeking nontextual sources, turn to *media databases* such as AccessScience, Artstor, and New York Public Library Digital Collections.

SEARCH WITHIN DATABASE FIELDS

To search for sources using a database, type keywords and phrases in the database's search fields. If you are conducting a basic search, the process will be similar to a search on a web search site (see *Search the Web* later in this chapter). The following illustrations show an advanced search conducted in ProQuest and the results that were returned.

The writer searches within subject headings for sharks and legislation.

The writer uses a Boolean AND search for all three search terms.

Quotation marks signal that the word *United States* should be treated as a phrase.

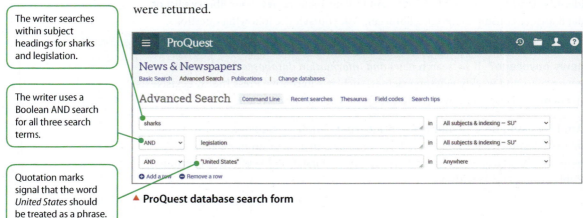

▲ ProQuest database search form

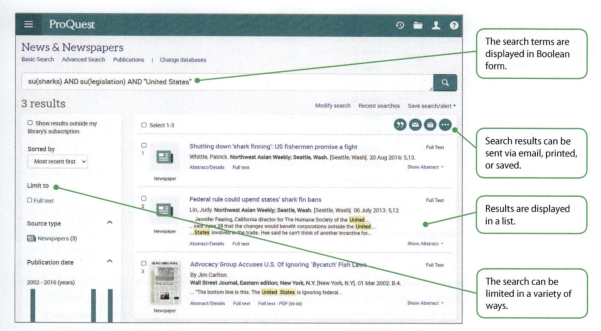

▲ ProQuest database search results

Search the Web

Web search sites can help you sift through the vast amount of information available on the web, including web pages, blogs, social media posts, magazine and journal articles, books, music, photos, and video. While searching the web is one of the easiest and quickest ways to locate information, keep in mind that web-based sources have not been carefully selected by librarians and editors, as is typically the case with the sources found through library catalogs and databases. Instead, sources found on the web can be uneven in quality, ranging from peer-reviewed articles in scholarly journals to blogs created by eighth graders.

To determine which search sites might be best suited to the needs of your writing situation, consider their areas of emphasis and the tools they offer to support searching and working with results.

● USE WEB SEARCH ENGINES

Web search engines keep track of web pages and other forms of information on the internet — including PDF files, PowerPoint files, Word files, blogs, and social media posts — by locating documents on websites and entering them in a searchable database.

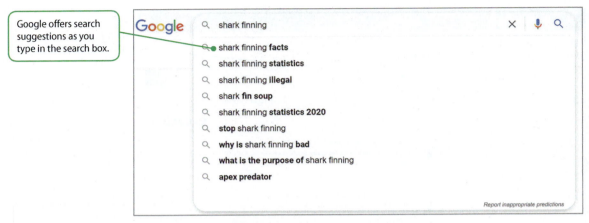

Google offers search suggestions as you type in the search box.

▲ Google search

Leading web search engines include Ask (ask.com), Bing (bing.com), DuckDuckGo (duckduckgo.com), Google (google.com), OneSearch (onesearch.com), Search Encrypt (searchencrypt.com), StartPage (startpage.com), Swisscows (swisscows.com), and Yahoo! (search.yahoo.com).

Keep several cautions in mind as you use web search engines.

- Because the web grows so quickly, search engines struggle to keep up. Some estimates put the number of web pages at more than five trillion. New pages may not be indexed immediately.
- Much of the web is hidden. Most hidden web pages are created on the fly from content stored in databases and as a result are not found by search engines. Other pages are deliberately hidden from web search engines by their owners.
- Web search engines index only a portion of the web — sometimes as much as 20 percent and sometimes as little as 5 percent.
- Some web search sites use other search engines to provide their results. Yahoo's search engine, for example, began using Bing to provide its search results in 2019. Similarly, Startpage uses results from Google.
- Web pages can be moved, deleted, or revised. This means that a search engine's results can be inaccurate.

Ideally, you should use more than one search engine to locate information. If you don't find what you're looking for after using your first choice, you might find it after using another.

TECH TIP: Review privacy policies. You are likely aware of the potential uses and misuses of the information we can reveal through our interactions with social media and search sites. As you consider which search sites to use, review their privacy policies. Some sites, such as Google and Bing, derive their profits from selling ads that reflect the interests revealed through your searches. Others, such as DuckDuckGo, Search Encrypt, Startpage, and SwissCows emphasize the extent to which they protect your privacy.

USE NEWS SEARCH SITES

You can search for news on most major web search sites and directories, such as Bing (bing.com/news) and Google (news.google.com), as well as the sites for news providers such as BBC, CNN, and Reuters. In addition, specialized news search sites allow you to conduct focused searches for current and archived news reports, while social news sites such as Digg (digg.com) allow you to view news stories and videos that have been recommended by other readers.

USE REFERENCE SITES

A reference site allows you to search for information that has been collected in encyclopedias, almanacs, atlases, dictionaries, and other reference resources. Some reference sites, such as Encyclopaedia Britannica Online (britannica.com), offer limited access to information from their encyclopedias at no charge and complete access for a fee. Other sites, such as Information Please (infoplease.com) and Encyclopedia.com, allow unrestricted access to recently published reference works.

One widely used reference site is Wikipedia (en.wikipedia.org), whose articles are collaboratively written by its readers. Because of its comprehensiveness, Wikipedia can serve as a useful starting point for research on a topic. However, because any reader can make changes to most of the pages on the site, it's best to double-check any information you find there.

USE GOVERNMENT SEARCH SITES AND DIRECTORIES

Most government agencies and institutions use the web as the primary means of distributing their publications. USA.gov and Canada.ca, for example, allow you to search the U.S. and Canadian governments' network of online resources, while U.S. Government Printing Office (govinfo.gov) and Government of Canada Publications (publications.gc.ca) provide access to government publications.

- **SEARCH SOCIAL MEDIA SITES**

Social media platforms such as Facebook, LinkedIn, Reddit, Tumblr, and Twitter provide opportunities to locate discussions about the conversation you want to join and to identify people who share your interest in an issue. Most social media platforms include search tools on their main pages as well as on the profile pages for individual and group accounts.

Search Media Sites

The web is home not only to textual information, such as articles and books, but also to a growing collection of other types of media, such as photographs, podcasts, and streaming videos. You can search for media using established search sites, such as Ask, Bing, Google, and Yahoo!, as well as newer search sites that focus on specific media.

- **USE IMAGE SEARCH SITES AND DIRECTORIES**

Image searches have long been among the search tools available to writers. Using Google's image search (images.google.com) or Bing's image search (bing.com/images), for example, you can search for images using keywords and phrases, and you can conduct advanced searches by specifying the size and kind of image you desire. If you are searching for content that is freely available, try Creative Commons Search (search.creativecommons.org). You can also turn to specialized image search engines such as Pexels (pexels.com) and Picsearch (picsearch.com).

TECH TIP: Use visual search tools. While the majority of image search sites rely on keywords and phrases to construct a search, some search sites and apps allow you to search with images. Bing's visual search (bing.com/visualsearch) allows you to upload a file, paste an image, or take a photo and then search for similar images. You can do the same with Google's image search (images.google.com) by clicking on the camera icon in the search bar. On phones, you can use apps such as Bing, Google Lens, and Pinterest to search by image.

- **USE AUDIO SEARCH SITES**

Thinking of the web as the first place to visit for new music has become second nature for many of us. But the audio content available through the web includes more than just music. You can also find radio broadcasts, recordings of speeches, recordings of natural phenomena, and other forms of sound. Sites such as Audio Archive (archive.org/details/audio), FindSounds (findsounds.com), and Freesound (freesound.org) allow you to search for sounds and listen to them before downloading. You can also find curated collections of audio files on sites such as the Library of Congress' Digital Collection (loc.gov/collections).

USE VIDEO SEARCH SITES

Through sites such as YouTube (youtube.com), TikTok (tiktok.com), and Twitch (twitch.tv), as well as video search sites such as Bing Video (bing.com/videos), Google Video (google.com/videohp), and Yahoo! Video (video.searchyahoo.com), web-based video has become one of the fastest-growing parts of the web. You can view everything from news reports on CNN.com to a video about the effects of a recent earthquake to documentaries about efforts related to antiracism. With careful selection and evaluation, you might find video that will help you better understand and contribute to the discussion of your subject.

How Can I Locate Sources Using Print Resources?

Contrary to recent claims, there is life (and information) beyond the web. The print resources available in a library can help you locate a wealth of relevant material that you won't find online. If your writing project has a historical component, for example, bibliographies and indexes can point you toward sources that cannot be located using a database or a web search site. By relying on the careful selections librarians make when adding to a collection, you will be able to find useful, credible sources that reflect your purpose and address your subject.

Your Turn: Record Searches

One of the most important research strategies you can use as you collect information is keeping track of your searches. This will save you time, should you need to search again later, and will help determine which keywords and phrases returned the most promising results.

In your writer's notebook, record the following information for each of your searches:

1. Resource that was searched (for example, a database, library catalog, or search site)
2. Search terms used, such as keywords, phrases, and publication information
3. Search strategies used (for example, basic search, wildcard search, exact phrase search, or Boolean search)
4. Date search was conducted
5. Number of results produced by the search
6. Relevance of the results
7. Notes about the search

To locate information using print resources, discuss your search plan with a librarian, visit the library stacks, browse periodicals, and check reference works.

Discuss Your Search Plan with a Librarian

As you begin collecting information about your subject, use your search plan to capitalize on your library's print resources — and its librarians. Given the wide range of specialized print resources that are available, a few minutes of discussion with a knowledgeable librarian could save you a great deal of time or point you to key resources you might have overlooked.

Visit the Library Stacks

The library stacks — or shelves — house the library's collection of bound publications. By browsing the stacks and checking publications' works cited pages, you can locate related sources. Once you've decided that a source is relevant to your project, you can check it out or request it through interlibrary loan.

One of the advantages of the classification systems used by most libraries — typically the Library of Congress or Dewey decimal classification system — is that they are subject based. Because books on similar subjects are shelved together, you can browse the stacks to look for sources on a topic. For example, if your research takes you to the stacks for books about alcohol abuse, you're likely to find books about drug abuse, treatment programs, and codependency nearby. When you find a publication that seems useful, check the works cited list for related works. The combination of browsing the stacks for sources and checking those sources' works cited lists can lead you to publications relevant to your subject.

You can usually take library books — and some periodicals and media items — home with you to read or view at your own pace. In some cases, a publication might not be available because it has been checked out, reserved for a course, or placed in off-site storage. If a publication has been checked out, you might be able to recall it — that is, ask that it be returned to the library and held for you. If it has been placed on reserve, ask whether you can photocopy or take notes on it. If it has been placed in off-site storage, you can usually request it at the circulation desk.

➤ TECH TIP: USE INTERLIBRARY LOAN

If you can't obtain a particular book, periodical, or media item from your library, use interlibrary loan to borrow it from another library. Most libraries allow you to request materials through the library catalog, and you might be able to check the status of your request or renew interlibrary loan materials through the catalog as well. Because it can take time to process a request, locate a book, and send it to your library, be sure to make an interlibrary loan request well before your writing project due date. To learn how to use interlibrary loan, consult your library's website or ask a librarian.

Browse Periodicals

Periodicals include newspapers, magazines, and academic and professional journals. A periodicals room — or journals room — contains recent issues that library visitors may browse. Many libraries also have a separate room for newspapers published in the last few weeks or months. To ensure everyone's access to recently published issues, most libraries don't allow you to check out periodicals published within the last year, and they usually don't allow newspapers to be checked out at all.

Older periodicals are sometimes placed in bound volumes in the stacks. Few libraries, however, keep back issues of newspapers in paper form. Instead, you can often find back issues of leading newspapers in full-text databases or in microform. *Microform* is a generic name for both *microfilm*, a strip of film containing greatly reduced images of printed pages, and *microfiche*, film roughly the size of an index card containing the same kinds of miniaturized images. You view these images using a microform reader, a projection unit that looks something like a large computer monitor. Many microform readers allow you to print copies of the pages.

In addition to browsing periodicals, use databases to locate specific articles on your subject. Once you've identified an article you want to review, you'll need to find the periodical in which it appears. Conduct a title search for the periodical in the same way you conduct a title search for a book. The library catalog will tell you the call number of the periodical and usually will give information about its location in the library. In addition, some libraries provide a printed list that identifies where periodicals are located. If you have difficulty finding a periodical or judging which publications are likely to be useful for your writing project, ask a librarian for assistance.

Check Reference Works

Reference collections include reliable print resources on a range of topics, from government to finance to philosophy to science. A library's reference collection might be found in a specific area of the library, such as a reference room, or in its stacks. In either case, reference works can be located through your library's catalog.

Although many reference books serve the same functions as databases, others offer information not available in databases. Using reference books to locate print resources has several advantages over using databases.

- **Print resources tend to have longer memories.** Databases typically index sources only as far back as the mid-1980s and seldom index anything published before 1970. Depending on your subject, a database might not include some important sources. If you use a reference book, however, you might be able to locate print resources dating back a century or more.
- **Print resources are more likely to include full-length works such as books.** Many of the print resources in library reference rooms will refer you to books and longer publications as well as to articles in periodicals.
- **Some library reference resources are unavailable in digital form.** While a growing number of print reference books have become available in digital formats, some are available only in print.
- **Entries in print indexes are easier to browse.** Despite efforts to aid browsing, databases support searching far better than they do browsing.

Some of the most important print resources you can consult in a reference collection include bibliographies, indexes, biographies, specialized encyclopedias, handbooks, almanacs, and atlases.

● CONSULT BIBLIOGRAPHIES

Bibliographies list books, articles, and other publications that have been judged relevant to a topic. Some bibliographies provide only citations, while others include abstracts — brief descriptions — of listed sources. Complete bibliographies attempt to list all the sources published about a topic, while selective bibliographies attempt to list only the best sources on a topic. Some bibliographies limit their inclusion of sources by time period, often focusing on sources published during a given year.

Bibliographies can focus on general or specific topics. General bibliographies address a wide range of topics, such as the humanities, the social sciences, or the sciences, in a selective manner. Specialized bibliographies, in contrast, typically provide lists of sources — often annotated — about a specific topic. For example, *A Research Guide to the Ancient World: Print and Electronic Sources* focuses on sources about ancient Egypt, southwestern Asia, and the Mediterranean.

While the information in bibliographies can increasingly be found in databases, those databases are most suited to current topics. If you wish to search for sources from a particular historical period, such as the 1960s, you will have better luck working with print bibliographies from that period.

TECH TIP: To locate bibliographies, indexes, encyclopedias, and other referenced work, consult a librarian or search your library catalog using keywords related to your subject plus *bibliography*, *index*, *encyclopedia*, and so on.

● REVIEW INDEXES

Indexes provide citation information for sources found in a particular set of publications. Many indexes also include abstracts — brief descriptions — that can help you determine whether a source is worth locating and reviewing. The following types of indexes can be found in libraries.

- **Periodical indexes** list sources published in magazines, trade journals, scholarly journals, and newspapers. Some periodical indexes, such as *The Reader's Guide to Periodical Literature*, cover a wide range of general-interest publications. Others, such as *Art Index*, focus on periodicals that address a single subject. Still others focus on a small set of periodicals or even an individual periodical, such as the *New York Times*.

- **Indexes of materials in books** can help you locate articles in edited volumes. Turn to resources such as the *Essay and General Literature Index*, which indexes nearly five thousand book-length collections of articles and essays in the arts, humanities, and social sciences. You might also find indexes that address specific subject areas, such as Asian studies.

- **Pamphlet indexes** list the pamphlets that libraries frequently collect. If you are working with a subject that is likely to be addressed in pamphlets, such as a local voting rights initiative or land-use controversy, ask a reference librarian whether your library has a pamphlet index.

- **Government documents indexes** list publications from federal, state, and local governments. These types of indexes might be found in either the reference room or a separate government documents collection in your library. Ask a reference librarian for help.

● CHECK BIOGRAPHIES

Biographies cover key figures in a field, time period, or geographic region. *Who's Who in America*, for instance, provides brief biographies of important figures in the United States during a given year, while *Great Lives from History* takes a broader view, offering biographies of key figures in world history prior to 2010.

- **BROWSE SPECIALIZED ENCYCLOPEDIAS**

While general encyclopedias, such as the *New Encyclopaedia Britannica*, have moved online and are generally no longer available in print, you can find a great deal of useful information in specialized encyclopedias. General encyclopedias present enough information about a subject to get you started on a more detailed search. Specialized encyclopedias, in contrast, usually cover a field of study or a historical period. Articles in specialized encyclopedias are typically longer than articles in general encyclopedias and offer more detailed coverage of subjects.

- **CONSULT HANDBOOKS**

Like encyclopedias, handbooks provide useful background information about a subject in a compact form. Unlike specialized encyclopedias, most handbooks cover a specific topic area. The entries in handbooks are also much shorter than the articles found in specialized encyclopedias.

- **REVIEW ALMANACS**

Almanacs contain lists, charts, and tables of information of various types. You might be familiar with *The Old Farmer's Almanac*, which is known for its accuracy in predicting weather over the course of a year. Information in almanacs can range from the average rainfall in Australia to the batting averages of the 1927 Yankees to the average income of Germans and Poles before World War II.

- **SCAN ATLASES**

Atlases provide maps and related information about a region or country. Some atlases take a historical perspective, while others take a topical perspective.

In Summary: Locating Sources

* Generate search terms and choose search strategies (p. 481).
* Search your library's catalog (p. 485).
* Search relevant databases (p. 487).
* Use appropriate web search sites and media search sites (p. 489).
* Browse the library stacks (p. 494).
* Examine periodicals (p. 495).
* Check reference works (p. 495).

15 Conducting Field Research

When should I use field research methods? 499

How can I conduct an interview? 500
Plan your interview 501
Conduct your interview 504
Analyze your results 505

How can I conduct an observation? 505
Plan your observation 505
Conduct your observation 507
Analyze your results 508

How can I conduct a survey? 509
Plan your survey 509
Distribute your survey 511
Analyze your results 512

How can I engage in other forms of field research? 513
Engage in correspondence 513
Attend public events 513
Collaborate with others 514

When Should I Use Field Research Methods?

Some writers think of field research as the next best thing to learning about an issue through a published source. If they can't find anything relevant in books, articles, newspapers, social media or the broadcast media, then perhaps field research might be worth considering.

These writers misunderstand the value and power of field research. Far from being a good fallback position, field research is sometimes the best way to learn about an issue or collect information to support a position.

Consider using field research methods if you find yourself in one of the following situations.

- If published sources address your issue from a perspective that you don't find useful, field research can provide another way of approaching the issue. For example, most discussions of gun rights and gun control focus on constitutional arguments. If you want to consider the issue from another perspective, such as differences in how people from rural areas and urban or suburban areas understand the issue, you might find it useful to collect information through interviews, surveys, or correspondence.

- If you are interested in an issue that most people think of as settled, published sources may not include information, ideas, and arguments to help you challenge the conventional wisdom about the issue. Field research, in contrast, can bring new voices into the conversation.
- If the issue you are addressing is so current that little authoritative information is available, field research can provide needed information about it.
- If you come up with a new idea or argument that seems reasonable and obvious but has not yet been addressed by your sources, field research can provide a useful reality check, allowing you to explore your idea or argument through interviews, observation, surveys, or correspondence.
- If your argument can be strengthened by including evidence from primary sources, turn to field research. Information from interviews, correspondence, or observations can bring a document to life, providing your readers with firsthand reports from people who know about or have been affected by an issue. Similarly, information from a survey can allow your readers to see trends and differences among groups that might not otherwise be clear.

Sometimes the decision to use a particular field research method is a natural extension of the kind of work you're doing. For example, a writer exploring the pressures that lead athletes to use performance-enhancing drugs might not only consult published sources but also interview friends and family members who play competitive sports. At other times, writers might use evidence collected firsthand to lend a sense of immediacy to their arguments.

Explore strategies discussed for managing print and digital information in Chapter 16.

Whether you rely primarily on field research or use it in combination with information from published sources, field research methods can be powerful tools for exploring your issue and developing your position.

How Can I Conduct an Interview?

Interviews — in which one person seeks information from another — can provide firsthand accounts of an event, authoritative interpretations of events and issues, and reactions to an event or issue from the people who have been affected by it.

Most interviews follow a question-and-answer format, but some more closely resemble a free-flowing discussion. You can conduct interviews face-to-face, via video conference, over the phone, via email, and even through an instant-messaging program.

Plan Your Interview

The most important things to consider as you plan your interview are whom to interview, what to ask, and how to conduct your interview.

● IDENTIFY INTERVIEW CANDIDATES

Base your decisions on the kind of information you want for your research project.

- If you're trying to better understand a specific aspect of a conversation, interview an expert in the field such as a professor, government official, or member of the business community.
- If you want to learn what people in general think about an issue, interview people who are affected by the issue in different ways.
- If you're hoping to collect quotations from people who are authorities on a subject, interview someone who will be recognized as knowledgeable by your readers.

Once you've decided what sorts of people you want to interview, you'll need to identify and contact interview candidates. If you're working on a writing project for a class, ask your instructor and classmates for suggestions. Then ask whether they can introduce you to the people they suggest. Before you call, email, or text to set up an interview, make some preparations.

- Write a script to help you remember what to say.
- Prepare a list of dates and times that work for you.
- Estimate how much time you'll need to complete the interview.
- Be ready to suggest a location or an online communication venue, such as Google Meet or Zoom, for the interview.
- Leave your phone number or email address so that your interview candidate can get in touch with you if a conflict arises.

● DEVELOP INTERVIEW QUESTIONS

Your interview questions should focus on the issue you want to address in your project. As you prepare your questions, keep the following principles in mind.

- **Consider your research question, the role you are adopting, and the kind of information you want to collect.** Are you seeking background information, or do you want someone's opinion? An answer to the question, "How did this situation come about?" will be quite different from an answer to the question, "What do you think about this situation?"

- **Develop questions that allow for a wide range of responses.** Avoid leading questions that signal what you want to hear so that you're more likely to obtain responses that reflect the views of the person you are interviewing.

- **Ask questions that require more than a yes/no answer.** You'll learn much more from an answer to a question such as "What factors will affect your vote on referendum X?" than from an answer to "Will you vote for referendum X?"

- **Prepare a limited number of main questions and many follow-up questions.** Experienced interviewers know that each question can lead to several follow-up questions, such as "Why do you think this has happened?" or "How did your coworkers react to the new policy?"

- **Be flexible.** Be prepared to tailor your follow-up questions to the interviewee's responses.

● DECIDE HOW TO CONDUCT YOUR INTERVIEW

You can conduct interviews face-to-face, either in person or through video communication programs; over the phone; and through written correspondence such as email, chat, text messaging, or a letter.

- **Face-to-face interviews** conducted in person or through a video conferencing tool such as FaceTime, Google Meet, or Zoom allow you to carry out a nearly normal conversation with the person you are interviewing. As in regular conversations, pay close attention to nonverbal cues, such as facial expressions, body positions, and eye contact. These cues can help you understand whether your questions are clear, welcome, or surprising and can alert you to opportunities to ask useful follow-up questions.

- **Telephone interviews** also let you hold a fairly normal conversation, but they require a setting free of distractions. You won't have visual cues to help you connect with the person you are interviewing, so be sure to listen for pauses, tone of voice, and changes in speaking volume that might indicate surprise, discomfort, or confusion.

- **Written interviews** conducted by email, chat, text messaging, or letter can be a good option if your subject is difficult to reach because of distance or a busy schedule. Written responses to interview questions are generally more precise than spoken responses. Written responses can be reviewed and revised by the person being interviewed to ensure that statements are clear and accurate, while spoken responses are usually more spontaneous.

● DECIDE WHETHER TO SHARE QUESTIONS IN ADVANCE

Sharing questions in advance can have benefits and drawbacks. It can allow the person you'll interview to reflect on your questions and prepare a response. If you are interested in seeing candid reactions to a question, however, or if you worry that seeing the questions in advance might make the interviewee reluctant to go through with the interview, don't share them.

● DECIDE HOW TO RECORD AND TAKE NOTES

Recording or saving a transcript of an interview, along with taking notes, provides you with a complete record of what was said, which helps you ensure the accuracy of quotations, paraphrases, and summaries.

- **Recordings.** If you plan to record the interview, seek permission in advance or at the start of the interview. Some people might be nervous about being recorded, so be prepared to explain how you'll use a recording. Choose initial questions that put interviewees at ease and make them comfortable about the interview process.

- **Transcripts.** If you are conducting an interview via email (or even via a series of text messages), you'll have a written record of all the responses to your questions. Similarly, you can save a transcript from most chat sessions, either by saving a file from the chat program or copying and pasting the transcript into a word-processing file. Transcripts can be used to create accurate quotations, and they make it relatively easy to review responses to your questions.

- **Taking notes.** You should always take notes during an interview. Recordings and transcripts can be lost through technological glitches. More important, taking notes allows you to respond to new information and ideas, to consider how you might use the interview in your document, and to identify important parts for later review.

TECH TIP: You can use several tools to create transcripts from recorded interviews.

- If you have saved a video of your interview, you can upload it to YouTube (setting it as "unpublished" to preserve privacy). YouTube will create close captions and a transcript. After you save the transcript, you can remove the video.

- If you have access to the web version of Word in Microsoft Office 365, you can open the *Dictate* tool on the *Home* ribbon and then choose *Transcribe*. You can drag and drop common audio and video files into the tool and then edit the generated transcript.

- You can use web-based tools — some are free, while some charge a fee — to transcribe your recording. Search the web with the keywords *transcribe recording*.

Conduct Your Interview

Consult the following checklist before you conduct your interview.

Checklist for Conducting Interviews

- ✔ **Arrive early and review your questions.** If you are conducting your interview over the phone or with a computer, review your questions and then contact the person you are interviewing at the agreed-upon time.

- ✔ **Introduce yourself and ask for permission to record the interview.** Explain why you are conducting the interview. Ask for permission to record or generate a transcript and ensure that you will be allowed to use quotes from the interview.

- ✔ **Set up and test your recording equipment or computer.** Ideally, use an audio or video recorder to make a complete record of face-to-face or phone interviews and use the built-in recording or transcript-generating features in online communication tools. At a later time, you can review what was said and create exact quotations from the recording or transcript.

- ✔ **Ask your questions clearly and be ready to respond with follow-up questions.** Allow the person you are interviewing to answer your questions fully and without interruption. Don't insist on strictly following your list of interview questions; if discussion naturally flows in another useful direction, be prepared to shift your line of questioning.

- ✔ **Take notes, even if you are creating a recording or transcript.** Write down key points made during the interview as well as any important ideas that come to mind.

- ✔ **Be alert for related sources mentioned in the interview.** If specific sources that might be relevant to your writing project are mentioned during the interview, ask for copies of those sources or for the exact titles and where you might find them.

- ✔ **End the interview on time.** Show respect for the person you are interviewing by sticking to the agreed-upon time.

- ✔ **Leave your contact information when the interview is over.** Provide a way for the person you interviewed to reach you to change or add anything to their comments.

- ✔ **Send a thank-you note or email message.** Let the person you interviewed know how much you appreciated the opportunity to learn from them.

Analyze Your Results

Treat your interview recording or transcript as you would any other source. Read it, listen to it, or view it critically:

- Look for new information, ideas, and arguments.
- Look for statements that confirm or contradict information from your other sources.
- Look for inconsistencies and contradictions within the interview as a whole.
- Ask whether the information, ideas, and arguments are relevant and credible.
- Determine whether the person you interviewed is as qualified as you'd expected when you planned the interview.
- Look for statements that provide context about the issue.
- Look for statements that might help your readers better understand the issue or view the issue in a particular way.
- Be cautious about reading too much into the responses. Be as fair as possible to the person you interviewed. In short, maintain your integrity.

Then ask whether you can use the information, ideas, and arguments from the interview in your project document. If not, it may help you understand the issue more fully or raise questions that you could investigate in other ways.

How Can I Conduct an Observation?

Like interviewing, observing a setting can provide you with valuable insights you would not be able to find in other sources. Although some observations can involve a significant amount of time and effort, an observation need not be complicated to be useful.

Plan Your Observation

As you plan your observation, keep the following guidelines in mind.

● DETERMINE WHAT, HOW, AND HOW OFTEN TO OBSERVE

If, for example, you've decided to observe the interactions between sales clerks and customers, you'll quickly learn that there are not only many stores in your community but also several different kinds of stores. Observing the interactions between clerks and shoppers at a grocery store won't tell you much about what happens in a high-traffic clothing store. And there's no guarantee that clerks and customers behave the same way with each other on any given day (think Labor Day sales events versus a normal Tuesday afternoon). Should you conduct multiple observations? Should you observe multiple types of stores?

The answers to these questions will depend largely on how you will use the information you collect during your observations. If you want to learn more about the topic but don't need to collect a great deal of information, then you might want to conduct a fairly limited observation. If you decide to use evidence from your observations throughout your project, then you will need to conduct multiple observations, possibly in more than one setting. In this case, as you prepare for each observation, review your observations from previous sessions so that you can focus on the most important aspects of what you've observed so far.

The choices you make about how to record your observations are equally important. Can you make audio or video recordings? Can you do so without disrupting the normal behavior of the subject of your observations or violating their privacy?

Can you take notes unobtrusively, or will doing so draw attention? Would it be better to record your impressions immediately after the observation? And can — or should — you collect any materials during your observation session? The answers to these questions will have important implications for how you decide to conduct your observation.

● DETERMINE WHETHER TO ASK PERMISSION TO OBSERVE

Seeking permission to observe someone can be complicated. People have expectations about privacy, and they can (and often do) change their behavior when they know they are being observed. As you consider whether to ask for permission, imagine yourself in the position of someone who is being observed. If you are still uncertain, ask your instructor for advice.

If you decide to seek permission, be sure to include a clear description of your writing project and explanations of why you believe observation will enhance the project, how you'll use the observations, and how you will ensure the privacy of the individuals, groups, or organization you observe. If you decide to contact the person by telephone, jot down some notes before you call.

In some cases, you might find it useful to use a permission form, such as the one shown below.

Current School / Program Information

Name _____

Address _____

City _____ State _____

Phone _____

Email _____

I, the undersigned, hereby authorize [*observer name*] to observe [*the setting*] for the purposes of completing work on [*name of writing project*]. I understand that I may revoke this authorization, in writing, at any time.

Signature: _____

Date: _____

▲ Sample permission form for observation sessions

Conduct Your Observation

You'll find a number of similarities between collecting information in an interview and collecting information during an observation. The checklist that follows will help you conduct your observation.

Checklist for Conducting Observations

✔ **Arrive early.** Give yourself time to get prepared.

✔ **Review your planning notes.** Remind yourself what you're looking for and how you will record your observations.

✔ **Introduce yourself.** If you have asked for permission to observe a setting (such as a class or a day-care center), introduce yourself before you begin your observation. Use your introduction as an opportunity to obtain signatures or consent forms if you need them.

✔ **Set up your recording equipment.** You'll certainly want to make sure you've got a notepad and pens or pencils. You might also have a laptop computer, a phone or tablet, or an audio or a video recorder (assuming you are legally allowed to make recordings in your city or state). Test whatever you've brought with you to make sure it's working properly.

✔ **Take notes.** As with interviews, take notes during your observation even if you're using an audio or a video recorder. Noting your impressions and ideas while conducting an observation can help you keep track of critical events. If you find yourself in a situation where you can't take notes — such as at a swimming lesson, when you're taking part in the lesson — try to write down your thoughts about what you've observed immediately after the session.

✔ **Leave contact information and send thank-you notes.** If you have asked someone for permission to observe the setting, give the person a way to contact you, and send a thank-you note after you have completed the observation.

Analyze Your Results

Treat your observation notes or recordings — as well as any materials you collected during your observations — as you would any other source. Ask whether you observed the setting thoroughly enough to feel confident about moving forward with an analysis. If so, do the following:

- Identify key features and patterns of behavior.
- Identify key individuals and describe their actions.
- Look for unusual and surprising patterns and actions.
- Ask what you've learned about the issue through observation.
- Look for patterns and actions that provide context about the issue.
- Look for patterns and actions that might help your readers better understand the issue or lead them to view the issue in a particular way.

Then ask whether you can use what you've learned in your project document. If you're unsure, consider whether your analysis can help you generate new questions and whether you should pursue another form of field research.

How Can I Conduct a Survey?

Surveys allow you to collect information about beliefs, attitudes, and behaviors from a group of people. Typically, surveys help you answer *what* or *who* questions — such as "Who will you vote for in the next election?" Surveys are less useful in obtaining the answers to *why* questions. In an interview, for instance, you can ask, "Why did you vote the way you did in the last election?" and get a reasonably well-thought-out answer. In a survey, you're unlikely to collect lengthy, carefully written responses. The strength of surveys lies in sheer numbers. A well-designed survey administered to a sizable group of people can provide insights into an issue that often can't be obtained easily using other methods.

Plan Your Survey

As you plan your survey, take the following steps.

- **IDENTIFY POTENTIAL SURVEY RESPONDENTS**

Consider whom and how many people to survey. For instance, if you're interested in what students in a specific class think about an issue, survey all of them. Even if the class is fairly large (say, one hundred students), you can easily tabulate the results of a brief survey. However, most surveys aren't given to everyone in a group. National polls, for instance, seldom survey more than one thousand people, yet they are used to assess the opinions of everyone in the country. So how will you select your representative sample? One way is to choose people from the group at random. You could search your school's directory for last names beginning with a specific letter (a, b, c, and so on) and select every twentieth name. Another option is to stratify your sample. For example, you could randomly select a specific number of first-year, second-year, third-year, and fourth-year students — and you could make sure that the number of STEM, business, and liberal arts majors is proportional to their enrollment at the school.

- **DECIDE WHAT TO ASK AND HOW TO ASK IT WITH INTEGRITY**

Designing effective surveys can be challenging. Start by considering the strengths and weaknesses of the different kinds of questions typically found on surveys:

- **Yes/no items** divide respondents into two groups.
- **Multiple-choice items** indicate whether a respondent knows something or engages in specific behaviors. Because they seldom include every possible answer, be careful when including them.

- **True/false items** more often deal with attitudes or beliefs than with behaviors or events.
- **Likert scale items** measure respondents' level of agreement with a statement, their assessment of something's importance, or the number of times they engage in a behavior.
- **Ranking items force** respondents to place items along a continuum.
- **Rating items** allow respondents to assess the quality or importance of items in relation to each other.
- **Short-answer items** allow greater freedom of response but can be difficult to tabulate.

View featured writer Sophie Kimble's survey on page 382.

Developing a good survey question is similar to writing an essay. The first drafts of survey questions serve to express your thoughts. Subsequent revisions help clarify questions for survey respondents. Keep your purpose in mind to be sure your questions will elicit the information you need.

Consider how a writer created and refined a question about how students view heavy metal music:

1. Write a first draft of the question:

   Do you listen to heavy metal music and why or why not? *(The question is too analytical. It will take a lot of time to answer and results will be hard to tally.)*

2. Simplify the question:

   Why do you listen — or not listen — to heavy metal music? *(This combines both parts of the previous question ("do you" and "why"), but is still too analytical.)*

3. Consider alternative ways of asking a question — including whether it should be a question:

   When you hear heavy metal bands like Lice and Molten, what do you think? *(The question focuses on respondents' reactions to the music, rather than on their reasons for listening.)*

4. Identify and then clarify key words and phrases:

   List five words to describe music by heavy metal bands like Lice and Molten. *(The question is easy for respondents to answer and provides information that can be tallied.)*

As you create questions, keep in mind the importance of asking questions that do not cue the respondents to answer in a particular way. Ask yourself how you might respond to the following questions:

- Do you support increasing income tax rates to reduce the federal debt?
- Do you support increasing income tax rates to ensure that future generations are not crushed under the burden of a spiraling federal debt?

- Do you support increasing income tax rates to enable the federal government to continue its irresponsible and uncontrolled spending on entitlements?

● DETERMINE WHETHER YOU ARE ASKING YOUR QUESTIONS CLEARLY

Test your survey items before administering your survey by asking your classmates, friends, or family members to read your questions. A question that seems perfectly clear to you might confuse someone else. Rewrite the questions that confuse your "testers," and then test them again. Consider the evolution of the following question.

Original Question:

What can be done about voter turnout among younger voters?

Revised Question:

In your opinion, what can be done to increase turnout among 18- to 24-year-old voters?

> Does "about voter turnout" mean increasing voter turnout, decreasing voter turnout, or encouraging younger voters to be better informed about candidates? Does the phrase "younger voters" mean 18-year-olds or 30-year-olds?

Distribute Your Survey

Surveys are typically distributed via email, the web, or social media. Online surveys are easier to distribute and offer more choices of tools you can use to create surveys (such as Alchemer, Google Forms, and SurveyMonkey). Online survey tools also make tabulating results easier, allowing you to break down responses and create charts from survey data. The disadvantages include low response rates and the likelihood that the people who respond will do so because of a specific interest in the issue. In other words, you might find that most of your respondents have some sort of interest or bias that leads them to want to respond and are not a representative sample of the group you hope to understand.

Paper-based surveys are most useful in situations where you can pass them out to a group, such as students in a class or people attending a meeting. Similarly, if people have access to their devices, web-based surveys can also be administered in face-to-face settings. Surveying people over the phone should be avoided. It tends to result in a low response rate and might be prohibited by laws regarding telephone solicitations.

The sheer number of surveys people are asked to complete these days has reduced the public's willingness to respond to them. In fact, a "good" response rate for a survey can be as low as 30 percent, and many professional pollsters find lower response rates acceptable.

Analyze Your Results

For greatest flexibility, tabulate your survey responses, and then visualize them as charts or graphs. If you used paper surveys or collected results via email, enter your results in a spreadsheet program and use its visualization tools. If you used a web-based survey tool, use its built-in charting and graphing tools. When you analyze your results, look for trends and patterns. For example, ask whether age or experience seems to predict responses or whether groups respond differently to particular questions. Look as well for surprising results, such as unexpectedly high levels of agreement or disagreement with Likert-scale items or striking differences in the responses to short-answer questions.

As you conduct your analysis, keep in mind the need to ensure confidentiality for your respondents. Survey respondents usually expect anonymity. As you review your responses, be careful not to reveal personally identifiable information. A respondent might reveal, for example, that she is the only veteran in a particular writing class. If you find this kind of information, do not include it in your report.

Checklist for Conducting Surveys

- ✔ **Keep it short.** Surveys are most effective when they are brief. Don't exceed one page.

- ✔ **Format and distribute your survey appropriately.** If your survey is on paper, make sure the text is readable and that there is plenty of room to write. For emailed surveys, you can either insert the survey questions into the body of your email message or attach the survey file. If you are distributing your survey on the web, use the formatting options in your web survey tool to test out various layouts for your questions.

- ✔ **Explain the purpose of your survey.** Explaining who you are and how you will use the results of the survey in your writing project can help increase a respondent's willingness to complete and return your survey.

- ✔ **Treat survey respondents with respect.** People respond more favorably when they think you are treating them as individuals rather than simply as part of a mailing list. Address potential respondents by name in email messages or cover letters.

- ✔ **Make it easy to return the survey.** Provide clear directions for submitting completed surveys on the web or via email. If you are distributing the survey to students in classes, provide a large envelope with your name and contact information into which the surveys can be placed.
- ✔ **Make your survey available.** Include a copy of your survey questions in an appendix to your project document.

How Can I Engage in Other Forms of Field Research?

Other common forms of field research include engaging in correspondence and attending public events. In addition, you can often collect more information by collaborating with others.

Engage in Correspondence

Correspondence includes any textual communication — such as letters and email — as well as real-time communication using chat or text messaging. If you use chat or text messaging, be sure to save a transcript of the exchange. You can correspond with experts in a particular area; people who have been affected by or are involved with an issue or event; staff at corporations, organizations, and government agencies; or even journalists who have written about a subject. Always explain who you are, what you are writing about, and why you want to correspond.

Attend Public Events

Public events, such as lectures, conferences, webinars, and public meetings and hearings, often provide writers with useful information. You can take notes or record public events by using a phone or digital recorder (if permitted). If you attend a public event in person or on the web, find out whether a transcript or recording of the proceedings will be available.

Collaborate with Others

Conducting field research can be time intensive. Consider forming collaborative teams with your classmates or coworkers to collect information. You can use one or more of the following strategies.

- If you are conducting an observation or attending a public event, you'll find that a single perspective might limit your ability to see what's happening. If other classmates are also conducting observations, you can help each other out. You might observe at the same time as your classmates so that together you can see more of what is taking place. Or you and your classmates might observe the same setting at different times, increasing the amount of information you can obtain. If you decide to work with one or more of your classmates, consider creating an observation checklist so that each observer will know what to look for.

- If you are conducting an interview, share your interview questions with a few classmates before conducting the interview. Have your classmates role-play the interviewee. Then ask them how you might improve your questions.

- If you are conducting a survey, share drafts of your survey with a few classmates. Ask them to note any questions that seem unclear, irrelevant, or ineffective. If they identify any questions that could be improved, ask them why they found the questions problematic and whether they have any suggestions for revision.

- If you are gathering information through correspondence, ask a classmate to review your letter or message before you send it and to offer suggestions for improving it. Your classmate can follow the guidelines for conducting an effective peer review (see Chapter 5).

In Summary: Conducting Field Research

* Consider reasons for using field research (p. 499).
* Plan and conduct interviews (p. 500).
* Plan and conduct observations (p. 505).
* Design, conduct, and analyze a survey (p. 509).
* Use correspondence to collect information (p. 513).
* Attend public events that are relevant to your issue (p. 513).
* Enlist help in carrying out collaborative projects (p. 514).

16 Managing Your Sources

How can I keep track of print materials? 515

How can I keep track of digital materials? 516
Download sources 517
Copy and paste 518
Use email 518
Take photos, make recordings, and save notes 519

Save bookmarks and favorites in your browser 519
Use web tools 520
Back up your files 520

How can I create a bibliography? 520
List sources in a working bibliography 521
Summarize sources in an annotated bibliography 522

If you've ever forgotten to save a phone number, email address, or password, you know how frustrating it can be to lose something. It can be just as frustrating to lose your interview notes or forget where you found a quotation or fact. Your writer's notebook is a good place to keep track of the information you collect during a writing project. You can also organize and save your sources, create a working bibliography, and create an annotated bibliography.

How Can I Keep Track of Print Materials?

Depending on the scope of your writing project, you might accumulate a great deal of print information, such as the following:

- your written notes (in a notebook, on loose pieces of paper, on sticky notes, and so on)
- printouts from web pages and databases
- printed word-processing documents, such as your outline and rough drafts

- books, magazines, newspapers, brochures, pamphlets, and government documents
- photocopies of articles, book chapters, and other documents
- letters, printed email messages, survey results, and so on

Rather than letting all this material build up in messy piles on your desk, create a filing system to keep track of your print documents. Filing systems can range from well-organized piles of paper labeled with sticky notes to three-ring binders to file cabinets filled with neatly labeled file folders.

Regardless of the approach you take, keep the following principles in mind:

- **Make it easy to locate your print materials.** Decide whether you want to group material by topic, by date, by pro versus con, by type of material (web pages, photocopies, original documents, field sources, and so on), or by author.
- **Stick with your organizing scheme.** You'll find it difficult to locate materials if you use different approaches at different points in your research project.
- **Always include complete publication information.** If a source doesn't contain publication information, write it on your copy of the document. You'll need it later. Publication information includes author, title, publisher, place and date of publication, and — for a web source — sponsoring organization and URL.
- **Write a brief note on each of your print materials.** Indicate how it might contribute to your project.
- **Record the date.** Indicating when you found a source can help you reconstruct what you might have been doing at the time. Dates are also essential for documenting web sources and other online sources (see Chapters 25 and 26).

How Can I Keep Track of Digital Materials?

The single most important strategy for managing digital information is keeping it organized. Save your sources in a folder, and use descriptive file names. Rather than naming a file "Notes 1," for instance, name it "Interview Notes from John Garcia, April 27." If you find that you are storing a large amount of information, use subfolders to group your sources.

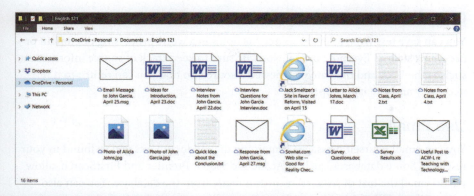

▲ Saving work in folders and subfolders

Download Sources

Downloading digital sources to a hard drive, a flash drive, or a cloud-based service such as Box, Dropbox, iCloud, or OneDrive allows you to open them later in a web browser or word-processing program. Downloading sources can save you time toward the end of your writing project, particularly when you are drafting or revising your document.

Remember that saving a source does not automatically record the URL or the date on which you viewed the source for the first time. Be sure to record that information in your writing log, in your working bibliography (see *List Sources in a Working Bibliography* later in this chapter), or in a document in the folder where you've saved your files.

Learn about backing up your files later in this chapter.

Copy and Paste

You can save text from relevant sources as notes in a word-processing document or programs such as Evernote or OneNote. Be sure to keep track of source information, such as the URL and the date you viewed a source, so that you can return to it if necessary and cite it appropriately.

Use Email

You can email yourself messages containing digital documents you've found in your research. Some databases, such as Academic Search Premier and FirstSearch, allow you to email the text of selected records directly from the database. You can also use email as a "file folder" by sending messages to yourself that include copies of documents in the form of pasted text or attached files. A subject line such as "My Comp 110 Writing Project" enables you to sort your messages or search for the phrase *writing project* and easily view the information you've collected.

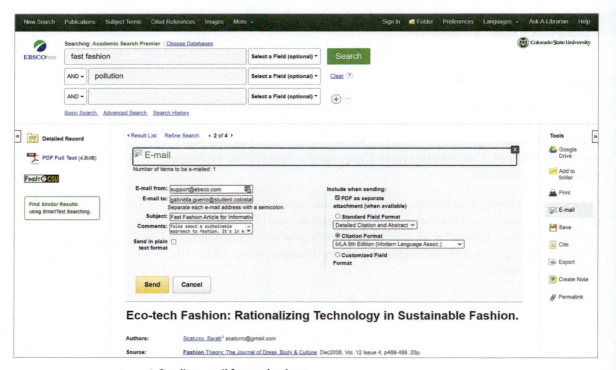

▲ **Sending email from a database**

Take Photos, Make Recordings, and Save Notes

TECH TIP: If you have a phone or tablet, you can use apps to record conversations with others, record voice memos that contain ideas about your project, save video, take photos of sources you find in the periodical room (see *Browse Periodicals* in Chapter 14), and surf the web to locate sources.

As you save information with these tools, keep your work well organized. Use descriptive names, save work in folders or albums, and include notes about where and when you found the information. Talk with other writers about the apps they've found useful, and, if they're free, try them out yourself.

Save Bookmarks and Favorites in Your Browser

You can use a Bookmarks or Favorites list in a web browser to keep track of online sources. Keep these lists organized by putting related items into folders and giving the items on your list descriptive names. If you use this strategy, however, remember that pages on the web can and do change — perhaps even before you finish your

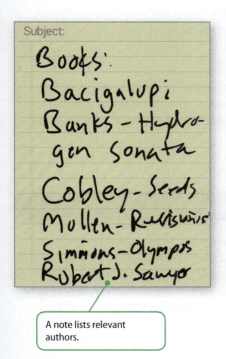

A note lists relevant authors.

A photo records a location.

Voice recording apps can be used to conduct interviews or record ideas.

writing project. Be aware as well that some web pages are generated by database programs, which can result in unwieldy URLs, such as this one:

> http://newfirstsearch.oclc.org/WebZ/FSFETCH?fetchtype=fullrecord
> :sessionid=fsapp2-49320-imjmp9sc-hoge4g:entitypagenum=9:0:recno
> =4:resultset=3:format=FI:next=html/record.html:bad=error/badfetch
> .html:entitytoprecno=4:entitycurrecno=4:numrecs=1

Although this long string of characters starts out looking like a normal URL, the majority of the characters are used by the database program to determine which records to display on a page. In many cases, the URL works only while you are conducting your search. If you add such a URL to your Bookmarks or Favorites list, there's a good chance it won't work later.

Use Web Tools

You can use web clipping and curating tools — which work with your browser as toolbars or "add-ons" (a term used for programs that work within browsers) — to copy all or part of a web page. Leading tools include Diigo (diigo.com), PowerNotes (powernotes.com), and Zotero (zotero.org). In addition to allowing you to save materials from the web, these tools support annotation and often offer additional tools that can help you organize the material you collect.

Back Up Your Files

Whatever strategies you use to save and organize digital materials, replacing lost information takes time and effort. Avoid the risk of lost information by backing up your digital files, saved web pages, email messages, and bookmarks or favorites lists on an external drive or in the cloud.

How Can I Create a Bibliography?

A bibliography is a list of sources with complete publication information, usually formatted according to the rules of a documentation system such as the Modern Language Association (MLA) system (see Chapter 25) or the American Psychological Association (APA) system (see Chapter 26). As you start collecting information, create a working bibliography or an annotated bibliography to keep track of the sources you are using.

List Sources in a Working Bibliography

A working bibliography is a running list of the sources you've explored and plan to use in your writing project — with publication information for each source. The organization of your working bibliography can vary according to your needs and preferences. You can organize your sources in any of the following ways:

- in the order in which you collected your sources
- in categories
- by author
- by publication title
- according to an outline of your project document

The entries in a working bibliography should include as much publication information about a source as you can gather.

Your working bibliography will change significantly over the course of your writing project. As you explore and narrow your topic and, later, as you collect and work with your sources, you will add potentially useful sources and delete sources that are no longer relevant. Eventually, your working bibliography will become one of the following:

- **a works cited or reference list** — a formal list of the sources you have referred to in a document
- **a bibliography or works consulted list** — a formal list of the sources that contributed to your thinking about a subject, even if those sources are not referred to explicitly in the text of the document

Read more about works cited and reference lists in Part Five.

Keeping your working bibliography up-to-date is a critical part of your writing process. It helps you keep track of your sources and increases the likelihood that you will cite all the sources you use in your document — an important contribution to your efforts to avoid plagiarism.

The first six sources from featured writer Sophie Kimble's (see Chapter 11) working bibliography are shown in the next example.

Bhomawat, Dishi. "Shark-Finning: Damage to Global Commons." *Environmental Policy & Law*, vol. 46, no. 1, Jan. 2016, pp. 56–62. https://doi.org/10.3233/EPL-46103.

[DOI (digital object identifier) provided for a scholarly journal article.]

Castro, José l, Christa M. Woodley, and Rebecca L. Brudek. "Biological Characteristics and Reproductive Potential of Sharks." *National Oceanographic and Atmospheric Administration*, 1999, https://www.fao.org/3/x2352e/x2352e06.htm.

Fairclough, Caty. "Shark Finning: Sharks Turned Prey." *Smithsonian*, 14 May 2018, https://ocean.si.edu/ocean-life/sharks-rays/shark-finning-sharks-turned-prey.

"International Shark Finning Bans and Policies." *Animal Welfare Institute*, 3 Mar. 2021, https://awionline.org/content/international-shark-finning-bans-and-policies.

Scales, Helen. "Why We Need Sharks: the True Nature of the Ocean's 'Monstrous Villains'." *The Guardian*, Guardian News and Media, 6 July 2020, https://www.theguardian.com/environment/2020/jul/06/why-we-need-sharks-the-true-nature-of-the-oceans-monstrous-villains.

[Publication date and URL provided for an article on a website.]

▲ Part of Sophie Kimble's working bibliography

Summarize Sources in an Annotated Bibliography

In addition to complete citation information, an *annotated bibliography* provides a brief note — two or three sentences — about each of your sources. Consider your purposes for creating an annotated bibliography, and tailor the content, focus, and length of your annotations accordingly.

- In some writing projects, you will submit an annotated bibliography to your instructor for review and comment. In this situation, your instructor will most likely expect a clear description of the content of each source and some indication of how you might use the source.

- In other writing projects, the annotated bibliography serves simply as a planning tool — a more detailed version of a working bibliography. As a result, your annotations might highlight key passages or information in a source, suggest how you can use information or ideas from the source, or emphasize relationships between sources.

- In still other projects, the annotated bibliography will be the final result of your efforts. In such cases, you would write your annotations for your readers, keeping their purposes, needs, interests, and backgrounds in mind.

Type of Source	Information You Should List
All Sources	• Author(s) • Title • Publication year • Medium consulted • DOI (Digital Object Identifier, if available) • URL (if obtained online and a DOI is not available)
Book	• Editor(s) of book (if applicable) • Publication city • Publisher • Series and series editor (if applicable) • Translator (if applicable) • Volume (if applicable) • Edition (if applicable)
Chapter in an Edited Book	• Publication city • Publisher • Editor(s) of book • Book title • Page numbers
Journal, Magazine, or Newspaper Article	• Journal title • Volume number or date • Issue number or date • Page numbers
Web Page, Blog Entry or Reply, Discussion Forum Post, Email Message, or Chat Transcript	• URL • Access date (the date you read the source) • Sponsoring organization (if listed)
Field Research	• Title (usually a description of the source, such as "Personal Interview with Jessica Lynn Richards" or "Observation of June Allison's Class at Tavelli Elementary School") • Date (usually the date on which the field research was conducted)

An annotated bibliography is a useful tool even if you aren't required to submit it for a grade. By turning your working bibliography into an annotated bibliography, you can remind yourself of each source's information, ideas, and arguments and how the source might be used in your document.

The annotated bibliography that follows provides information that an instructor could use to assess a student's progress on a writing project.

> Entries include all citation information the writer will need for the final document.

Bhomawat, Dishi. "Shark-Finning: Damage to Global Commons." *Environmental Policy & Law*, vol. 46, no. 1, Jan. 2016, pp. 56–62. https://doi.org/10.3233/EPL-46103.

This is an academic journal article about the potential harm to the "global commons" by shark finning. It focuses on the concept of "transboundary harm" and talks about the obligations nations have to address this kind of harm by enforcing international law. This might be useful for building an argument about how we might enact stronger regulations to ban shark finning (or at least reduce the number of nations that allow it).

> Annotations provide brief summaries of the purpose and content of the sources.

Fairclough, Caty. "Shark Finning: Sharks Turned Prey." *Smithsonian*, 14 May 2018, https://ocean.si.edu/ocean-life/sharks-rays/shark-finning-sharks-turned-prey.

This article on the Smithsonian's *Ocean* website discusses the reasons why shark finning is carried out (largely to make money) and why its use as the primary ingredient in shark fin soup — which is "a symbol of status" in Chinese culture — has led to the deaths of roughly 100 million sharks each year. It discusses the impact of shark finning and progress that is being made in eliminating the practice. Because this article is on the Smithsonian website, which is highly respected, it seems like it would be useful in providing background information about the problem.

Scales, Helen. "Why We Need Sharks: The True Nature of the Ocean's 'Monstrous Villains'." *The Guardian*, Guardian News and Media, 6 July 2020, https://www.theguardian.com/environment/2020/jul/06/why-we-need-sharks-the-true-nature-of-the-oceans-monstrous-villains.

> Annotations are intended for the writer and the instructor. They indicate how and where the writer will use the source in the document.

This article in the newspaper *The Guardian* provides background information about the importance of sharks in ocean ecosystems. A key statistic that I might use is that a quarter of all shark species are threatened with extinction. It also offers personal insights from the author about sharks, which might provide some useful quotations in my essay.

▲ Selections from Sophie Kimble's annotated bibliography

In Summary: Managing Your Sources

★ Save and organize print materials (p. 515).

★ Save and organize digital materials (p. 516).

★ Create a working bibliography (p. 521).

★ Consider creating an annotated bibliography (p. 522).

17 Avoiding Plagiarism

What is plagiarism? 526
Unintentional plagiarism 526
Intentional plagiarism 527
Plagiarism in group projects 527
Self-plagiarism 528

What are research ethics? 528

What is common knowledge? 530

What is fair use and when should I ask permission to use a source? 530

How can I avoid plagiarism? 532
Conduct a knowledge inventory 532
Take notes carefully 533
Attribute ideas appropriately 534
Identify sources in your document 534
Understand why writers plagiarize 535

What should I do if I'm accused of plagiarism? 535

Few writers intentionally try to pass off the work of others as their own. However, deadlines and other pressures can lead writers to take notes poorly and to cite sources improperly. In addition, access to documents through the web and full-text databases has made it all too easy to copy and paste work from other writers without acknowledging its source.

Failing to cite your sources, intentionally or accidentally, can lead to serious problems. Your readers will not be able to determine which information, ideas, and arguments are your own and which are drawn from your sources. If they suspect you are failing to acknowledge your sources, they might doubt your credibility and even stop reading your document. More seriously, submitting academic work that does not properly identify sources might result in a failing grade or other disciplinary action.

What Is Plagiarism?

Plagiarism is a form of intellectual dishonesty. It involves either unintentionally using someone else's work without properly acknowledging where the ideas or information came from (the most common form of plagiarism) or intentionally passing off someone else's work as your own (the most serious form of plagiarism).

Plagiarism is based on the notion of *copyright*, or ownership of a document or an idea. Like a patent, which protects an invention, a copyright protects an author's investment of time and energy in the creation of a document. Essentially, it assures authors that, when they create a document, someone else won't be able to steal ideas from it and profit from that theft without penalty.

In this sense, plagiarism in academic writing differs in important ways from the kind of mixing and remixing that can take place in popular culture. The expectations of readers of source-based documents differ, for instance, from those of people who listen to music. While listeners enjoying a song on the radio might not be surprised to hear part of another song added to a mix, readers of an article in *Time* magazine or an academic journal might be alarmed to read an unattributed passage that they recognize as the work of another writer. Context matters, and in this case the context of academic writing differs significantly from that of popular culture.

Unintentional Plagiarism

In most cases, plagiarism is unintentional, and most cases of *unintentional plagiarism* result from taking poor notes or failing to use notes properly. You are plagiarizing if you

- quote a passage in a note but neglect to include quotation marks and then later insert the quotation into your document without remembering that it is a direct quotation
- include a paraphrase that differs so slightly from the original passage that it might as well be a direct quotation
- don't clearly distinguish between your ideas and ideas that come from your sources
- neglect to list the source of a paraphrase, quotation, or summary in your text or in your works cited list

Although unintentional plagiarism is, by definition, something that the writer hasn't planned to do, it is nonetheless a serious issue and, when detected, is likely to have consequences. Some instructors might require that an assignment be rewritten; others might impose a penalty, such as a lowered grade or failure on the assignment.

Intentional Plagiarism

Intentional plagiarism can lead to academic penalties ranging from a reduced grade on an assignment to failure of a course to expulsion. Intentional plagiarism includes the following:

- engaging in "patchwork writing," which involves piecing together passages from two or more sources without acknowledging the sources and without properly quoting or paraphrasing
- creating fake citations to mislead a reader about the sources of information used in a document
- copying or closely paraphrasing extended passages from another document and passing them off as the writer's original work
- copying an entire document and passing it off as the writer's original work
- purchasing a document and passing it off as the writer's original work

Plagiarism in Group Projects

Peer review and other collaborative activities raise important, and potentially confusing, questions.

- If another writer suggests changes to your document and you subsequently incorporate them into your document, are you plagiarizing?
- What if those suggestions significantly change your document?
- If you work with a group of writers on a project, do you need to identify the parts that each of you wrote?
- Is it okay to list yourself as a coauthor if another writer does most of the work on a collaborative writing project?

The answers to these questions will vary from situation to situation. In general, it's appropriate to use comments from peer reviewers in your document without citing them. If the comments are particularly helpful, you might acknowledge the reviewer's help in your document, perhaps in a footnote, an endnote, or an acknowledgments section. It is usually appropriate to list coauthors on a collaboratively written document without individually identifying the text that was written by each, although some instructors ask that individual contributions be noted in the document or on a cover page. If you are uncertain about what is appropriate, ask your instructor.

Self-Plagiarism

Reusing an assignment for more than one class, often referred to as *self-plagiarism*, is generally frowned upon by writing instructors. If you wrote a term paper in one class and then turned it in for a grade in another, you wouldn't learn anything new about conducting research, developing an argument, considering your readers, and so on.

On the other hand, if you have written previously about a topic that still intrigues you, you might ask your instructor if you could build on your earlier work. Similarly, if you are working on a new topic that is relevant to two of your current classes, you might talk with your instructors about completing a more ambitious project for both classes.

Self-plagiarism is also frowned on in published writing and can cause significant problems, including charges of copyright violation — especially if your writing is published by different publishers, such as on multiple websites or in more than one journal or magazine.

TECH TIP: TRANSLATION TOOLS

Translation tools such as Google Translate (translate.google.com) can convert text from one language to another. They can be helpful if you've written a document in one language and want to share it in another. Using these tools might seem to differ little from using the spelling and grammar tools in word-processing programs and on the web. But be cautious. If a course is designed to improve your writing skills in one language, but you've written your document in another and then used a translation program, you might be working against the goals of the course. It's best, as a result, to ask your instructor for advice.

What Are Research Ethics?

Research ethics are based on the notion that writing — and, in particular, research writing — is an honest exchange of information, ideas, and arguments among writers and readers who share an interest in an issue. As a writer, then, you'll want to behave honestly and ethically. In general, you should do the following:

- Acknowledge the sources of the information, ideas, and arguments you use in your document. By doing so, you show respect for the work that others have done before you.

- Accurately and fairly represent the information, ideas, and arguments from your sources to ensure that you do not misrepresent other writers' work to your readers.

- Provide citation information for your sources. These citations help your readers understand how you have drawn your conclusions and where they can locate those sources should they want to consult them.

These three rules are the essence of research ethics. Ultimately, failing to act ethically — even when the failure is unintentional — can reflect poorly on you and your document. If your readers suspect that you have acted unethically, they will question the accuracy and credibility of the information, ideas, and arguments in your document. If they suspect you've sacrificed research ethics altogether, they'll probably stop reading your document.

By engaging in ethical research practices — acknowledging your sources, representing them fairly, and citing them accurately — you can earn the trust of your readers and increase the chances that they'll pay attention to your argument. The example from a rough draft of featured writer Gabriella Guerrero's essay about fast fashion demonstrates a writer's adherence to research ethics.

Fast fashion relies on producing inexpensive clothing that follows the latest fashion trends. It involves the use of cheap materials, such as plastic, palm oil, and toxic textile dye — to produce mass quantities of clothing. Rachel Bick and her coauthors point out that "approximately 85% of the clothing Americans consume, nearly 3.8 billion pounds annually, is sent to landfills as solid waste, amounting to nearly 80 pounds per American per year" (2). Understanding the gravity of the situation is critical because the lifestyle we live today is more consumption-driven than it has ever been before. Another major aspect adding to the pollution generated by this industry is its reliance on fossil fuels — which contribute to global warming — to power its factories. While those emissions have decreased by 40 percent since 2005, according to Spencer Nelson, the senior research director at ClearPath, they nonetheless remain a major source of concern (2).

> An attribution identifies the source of an idea.

> A parenthetical citation indicates a paraphrase, identifies the author and his credentials, and provides the page number.

Bick, R., Halsey, E., & Ekenga, C. C. (2018). The global environmental injustice of fast fashion. *Environmental Health, 17*(92), https://doi.org/10.1186/s12940-018-0433-7

Nelson, S. (2021, Aug.) Clear path to a clean energy future 2021: The role of utility commitments on the path to 2050." *ClearPath*, https://static.clearpath.org/2021/08/clear-path-to-a-clean-energy-future-2021-8-21.pdf

> Complete source information is included in the works cited list.

> Sources are cited in APA style.

▲ Adhering to research ethics

What Is Common Knowledge?

Although crediting other authors for their work is important, you almost certainly won't need to document every fact and idea used in your document because some of the information you'll use falls under the category of *common knowledge*. Common knowledge is information that is widely known, such as the fact that the Declaration of Independence was signed in 1776. Or it might be the kind of knowledge that people working in a particular field, such as petroleum engineering, use on a regular basis.

If you're relatively new to your topic, it can be difficult to determine whether information in a source is common knowledge. As you explore your topic, however, you will begin to identify what is generally known. For instance, if three or more sources use the same information without citing its source, you can assume that the information is common knowledge. If those sources use the information and cite the source, however, make sure you cite it as well.

What Is Fair Use and When Should I Ask Permission to Use a Source?

The concept of *fair use* deals with how much of a source you can borrow or quote. According to Section 107 of the Copyright Act of 1976 — the fair use provision (available at www.copyright.gov/title17/) — writers can use copyrighted materials for purposes of "criticism, comment, news reporting, teaching (including multiple copies for classroom use), scholarship, or research." In other words, writers generally don't need to seek permission to use brief quotations from a source or to summarize or paraphrase a source.

➤ TECH TIP: SEEKING PERMISSION

If you are working on an assignment for a course — and do not plan to publish the assignment on the web or in print — you generally can use material from another source without seeking permission. Remember, however, that in all cases you must still cite the source of the material you use.

Writers who plan to publish their work should seek permission to use material from a source if they want to quote a lengthy passage or, in the case of shorter works such as poems and song lyrics, if they want to quote a significant percentage of the source.

Dear Ms. Jackson:

I am a student and am writing an essay for my writing class, English Composition 200, at Colorado State University. The essay will be used only for educational purposes and will be distributed on our class website, which is available only to my instructor and members of my class, for a period of three weeks during April and May of this year.

I would like to include in my essay the following image, which is displayed on your site at www.westernliving.org/images/2302a.jpg, and would greatly appreciate your permission to do so:

> Or ". . . on the web at www.myschool.edu"

> Insert or describe the passage or image. For example, use a phrase such as "paragraphs 3 to 5 of the article," a thumbnail of the image, or the URL of a document or an image on the web.

If you are able to grant me the requested permission, please respond to this email message. My deadline for completing my project is April 22. I appreciate your quick response.

> Or ". . . sign the enclosed copy of this letter and return it to me."

If you are not the copyright holder or do not have authority to grant this request, I would appreciate any information you can provide concerning the current copyright holder.

Thank you for considering this request.

Sincerely,
Sara Petrovich
Sara.Petrovich@students.colostate.edu
(970) 555-1515

> Provide contact information, such as name, address, email address, phone number.

▲ **Sample permission request**

If you seek permission to use a source, explain why and how you want to use it. Many authors and publishers allow academic use of their work but frown on commercial uses. When you contact an author or a publisher, include your name and contact information, the source you wish to use, the purpose for which you will use the source, and the time during which it will be used (see the figure *Sample Permission Request*).

If you contact an author or a publisher by mail, include a self-addressed, stamped envelope. It saves the author or publisher the cost of responding by mail, indicates that you are serious, and perhaps most important, shows good manners.

How Can I Avoid Plagiarism?

In most cases, writers who plagiarize do so unintentionally. You can avoid unintentional plagiarism by learning how to

- conduct a knowledge inventory
- take notes carefully
- distinguish between your ideas and those drawn from your sources
- cite sources in the text and in a works cited or reference list (see Chapters 25 and 26)
- recognize misconceptions about intentional plagiarism

Conduct a Knowledge Inventory

You can avoid unintentional plagiarism by ensuring that you have a clear understanding of your issue. When you are just beginning to learn about an issue, you might find it difficult not only to express your own ideas clearly and effectively but also to restate or reframe the information, ideas, and arguments you've encountered in your sources. The result might be a document composed of passages that have been copied without attribution or paraphrased too closely. To prevent these difficulties, conduct a knowledge inventory by answering three questions:

- What do you already know about the subject?
- What don't you know?
- What do you want to know?

Your answers can serve as a starting point for brainstorming, collecting and working with sources, and planning. They can also serve as a guide for discussing the subject with others. Once you've completed your knowledge inventory, meet with your instructor, consult a librarian, or talk with people who are knowledgeable about the subject. Ideally, these discussions will help you determine the most productive way to learn more about your subject.

Take Notes Carefully

Unintentional plagiarism occurs most often when a writer takes poor notes and then uses information from those notes in a document. Notes might contain direct quotations that are not surrounded with quotation marks, paraphrases that differ in only minor ways from the original passage, and summaries that contain original passages from a source. Taking notes accurately and appropriately is the first — and arguably the most important — step in avoiding unintentional plagiarism.

To avoid plagiarizing as you take notes, keep the following guidelines in mind:

- Surround every quotation with quotation marks.
- Ensure that every paraphrase differs in both wording and sentence structure from the original passage.
- Avoid creating summaries that are little more than a patchwork of sentences pulled from the original source.
- Include publication information — in particular, author information and the location of passages that are quoted or paraphrased — about the source on every note.
- Double-check your notes to be sure that they are accurate and do not include problems that might lead to unintentional plagiarism when you integrate source information into your project document.

For more guidance on quoting, paraphrasing, and summarizing, see *How Can I Take Notes?* in Chapter 3. To learn more about integrating quotations, paraphrases, summaries, numerical information, and illustrations into your document, see Chapter 21.

Your Turn: Conduct a Knowledge Inventory

In your research log, answer the following questions about the issue you've decided to address in your project document:

1. What do I already know about the issue?
2. What don't I know?
3. What do I want to know?

Review your answers, and then identify the concepts that, if you understood them more fully, would allow you to work on your assignment more effectively. Learn about those concepts by discussing them with your instructor, a librarian, or someone who knows about or has been affected by the issue.

Attribute Ideas Appropriately

To distinguish between your ideas and those obtained through your sources, use attributions — words and phrases that alert your readers to the source of the information or ideas you are using. To avoid plagiarizing as you integrate information from your notes into your document, use these guidelines:

- **Look for notes that differ from your usual style of writing.** More often than not, if a note doesn't sound like your own writing, it isn't. If you find a note that might be a direct quotation, a close paraphrase, or a patchwork summary, double-check the note against the original source, and make the changes necessary to avoid plagiarizing that source.

- **Use author attributions to clearly distinguish information, ideas, and arguments drawn from your sources.** Failing to do so is likely to lead your readers to incorrectly think the information, ideas, and arguments are your own. To avoid this problem, attribute source information using phrases such as "according to Jessica Richards" and "Asao Inoue argues."

You can learn more about using attributions to identify the origin of quotations, paraphrases, and summaries in Chapter 21.

Identify Sources in Your Document

Include a complete citation for each source you refer to in your document. The citation should appear both in the text of the document (as in-text citation) and in a works cited or reference list.

In the following examples, the writer includes MLA-style parenthetical citations that refer readers to a list of works cited at the end of the document. Note that both MLA style and APA style use a combination of attributions and parenthetical information to refer to sources (see Chapters 25 and 26).

> Jessica Richards argues, "We need to develop an efficient, cost-effective means of storing electricity from alternative energy sources" (322).

> "We need to develop an efficient, cost-effective means of storing electricity from alternative energy sources" (Richards 322).

If page or paragraph numbers are provided, be sure to cite them for paraphrased and summarized information as well as for direct quotations. (For web sources with sections, provide the relevant section.) The following paraphrase of Jessica Richards' comments about energy needs includes the page number of the original passage in parentheses.

Jessica Richards argues that we need to create an "efficient, cost-effective" system for storing electricity from alternative energy sources (322).

To learn more about identifying sources in your document, see Chapter 21. To learn how to document sources using the MLA and APA documentation systems, see Chapters 25 and 26.

Understand Why Writers Plagiarize

Although most plagiarism is unintentional, some student writers do plagiarize deliberately. The causes of intentional plagiarism in writing assignments range from running out of time to seeing little value in a course. The most common reasons offered to explain intentional plagiarism — and steps you can take to avoid falling victim to its temptation — are listed below.

What Should I Do If I'm Accused of Plagiarism?

If your instructor expresses concerns about the originality of your work or the manner in which you've documented information, ideas, and arguments from your sources, ask for a meeting to discuss the situation. To prepare for the meeting, follow the list on page 537.

Your Turn: Check Your Draft for Unintentional Plagiarism

Unintentional plagiarism is the use of another writer's work without properly acknowledging the source of the ideas or information. Unintentional plagiarism is often the result of rushed work on a project. It typically results from inadequate research writing skills or honest mistakes. To avoid unintentional plagiarism, follow these steps:

1. Check for a works cited or reference list.
2. Identify each quotation, paraphrase, and summary.
3. Check for appropriate attributions.
4. Check for appropriate in-text citation.
5. Ensure that each source is included in your works cited or reference list.
6. Check for changes in writing style. If you find changes, check your notes to identify the source of the passage and ensure that you haven't neglected to include quotation marks or paraphrased too closely.

Plagiarism Myths versus Facts

Myths	Facts
✘ "It's easier to plagiarize."	✔ Some believe it takes less work to cheat than to create an original document. That may be true in the short term, but if you are pursuing a college degree, the odds are high that your profession will require writing ability or an understanding of how to work with information. When you're assigned a report or a proposal down the road, you might regret not taking the time to hone your writing and research skills.
✘ "I ran out of time."	✔ Most writers occasionally find themselves wondering how they can possibly complete an assignment on schedule. If you find yourself in this situation, contact your instructor about a revised deadline. You might face a penalty for turning in work late, but that penalty will almost certainly be less severe than a penalty for intentional plagiarism.
✘ "I couldn't care less about this assignment."	✔ It's not unusual to put off assignments that don't interest you. Rather than avoiding the work, try to approach the assignment in a way that interests you (p. 36), or contact your instructor to see if you can customize the assignment so that it better aligns with your interests.
✘ "I'm no good at writing."	✔ A lot of people have doubts about their ability to write well, and some students convince themselves that plagiarizing is a reasonable alternative to writing their own documents. If you lack confidence, seek assistance from your instructor, a campus writing center, a tutoring center, or a friend or family member. You're likely to find that, even with only modest support, you'll be able to do well.
✘ "I didn't think I'd get caught."	✔ Some students believe — and might even have experiences to support their belief — that they won't get caught plagiarizing. Most writing instructors, however, become familiar with their students' writing styles and might become suspicious if they notice a sudden change in style or encounter varying styles in the same document. Plagiarism detection software used by instructors also increases the likelihood that plagiarism will be discovered.
✘ "Everybody cheats."	✔ Some people plagiarize because they believe that many of their classmates are doing so and fear that not doing so will put them at a competitive disadvantage. The reality is that few students plagiarize intentionally, and those who do still tend to earn lower grades than their peers.
✘ "This course is a waste of my time."	✔ If you view a course as little more than a box that needs to be checked, it might seem reasonable to check that box with as little effort as possible. Turning in work that isn't your own, however, can backfire. If you are caught plagiarizing, you'll most likely receive a reduced — or failing — grade for the assignment or the course. Instead of plagiarizing, talk with the instructor or an academic adviser about your lack of interest. You might find that the course actually has some relevance to your interests and career plans.

- Review your document to identify passages that might have raised suspicions.
- Collect the materials you used in your writing project, such as copies of your sources, responses to surveys, interview transcripts, and so on.
- Collect materials you wrote during the project, such as the results of brainstorming and freewriting sessions; any outlines, clusters, or maps; and drafts of your document.
- Reflect on your writing process.

During the meeting, listen to your instructor's concerns before responding. It's natural to feel defensive, but you'll probably be more comfortable if you take notes and try to understand why your instructor has questions about your document. Once your instructor is finished expressing their concerns, think carefully about what has been said and respond as clearly as possible. Your instructor might ask follow-up questions, most likely about the sources you've used, your writing process, and the document you've written.

If you find that you have engaged in unintentional plagiarism, ask your instructor for guidance about how to avoid it in the future, and ask what sort of penalty you will face. If your instructor determines that you have plagiarized intentionally, ask what consequences you will face.

If you and your instructor are unable to resolve the situation, you might face a disciplinary process. To prepare for that process, learn as much as you can about the academic integrity policies at your institution.

In Summary: Avoiding Plagiarism

★ Understand the definition of plagiarism and the concept of copyright (p. 526).

★ Understand and follow research ethics (p. 528).

★ Understand what is meant by common knowledge (p. 530).

★ Understand the concept of fair use and, when necessary, seek permission to use sources (p. 530).

★ Conduct a knowledge inventory (p. 532).

★ Take notes carefully (p. 533).

★ Use attributions to distinguish between your ideas and those drawn from your sources (p. 534).

★ Cite and document your sources (p. 534).

★ Resist temptations to plagiarize intentionally (p. 535).

★ Know what to do if you are accused of plagiarism (p. 535).

PART FOUR
Crafting and Polishing Your Contribution

18 Developing Your Thesis Statement

How can I develop my position on an issue? 539
Review your notes 540
Consider your writing situation 540

How can I draft my thesis statement? 541
Consider your genre 541
Identify important information, ideas, and arguments related to your position 542

Draft alternatives 543
Focus your thesis statement 543

How can I support my thesis statement? 544
Choose reasons to accept your thesis statement 544
Select evidence to support your reasons 545

Your thesis statement provides a clear, focused expression of the position you've developed on your issue or subject. It is an important tool for sharing your best thinking about the conversation you've decided to join. Thesis statements emerge from your position on an issue — your reactions to what you've learned so far.

How Can I Develop My Position on an Issue?

Writers take a position when they react to what they've learned about an issue or subject, form opinions about it, or decide to take actions because of it. When you're new to a conversation, your position is likely to be tentative and incomplete. As you learn more, your position will become more clearly defined and well thought out.

As you take a position on the issue or subject you've been reading about, review what you've learned and consider your writing situation. You need not express your position in writing, but you'll find that reflecting on how you are approaching the conversation will prepare you for the work of developing your thesis statement and, eventually, your contribution to your conversation.

Review Your Notes

As you consider taking a position, reread your notes and think about what you learned as you evaluated your sources. During your review, do the following:

- List important information, ideas, and arguments that you've come across in your reading.
- Ask what interests you most about the information, ideas, and arguments you've identified in your notes.
- Review and elaborate on the ideas and arguments that you've come up with as a result of your own thinking about the subject.

When you complete your review, identify the ideas you would most like to address in your document.

Consider Your Writing Situation

Use the following questions about your writing situation to develop your position:

- How have the sources you've consulted changed your thinking about the subject?
- Have your purposes — the reasons you are working on this project — changed since you started the project? If so, how do you view your purpose now?
- Has your role as a writer — for example, to inform or to solve a problem — changed since you started your project? If so, how do you view your role now?
- Will focusing on a particular idea help you address your readers' purposes, needs, interests, and backgrounds?
- Can you address this idea given the requirements and limitations of your writing project?

After you've answered these questions, draft some position statements. Treat these position statements as you treated the brainstorming you did early in your writing project. You don't need to write more than a sentence or two and you don't need to edit your position carefully. Focus, instead, on your overall take on the conversation and what you might want to say to the other readers and writers involved in it.

Quinn Jackson (see *Skim for an Overview* in Chapter 3), for example, wrote several draft position statements for the essay she planned to write about preparing teachers to teach writing:

> Teachers should have more classes about writing theory and classroom practice and more professional development on the job.
>
> No matter how much they learn about teaching writing in college (and that's not nearly enough), new teachers will have too many students and not enough time.
>
> Future teachers should have more classes on writing.
>
> Teachers should be writers.
>
> Students won't improve as writers unless they get good feedback.

These position statements are written in a casual manner.

The focus is on ideas and not on grammar or style.

These position statements provided a basis for the thesis statement Quinn eventually used in her essay:

> Because the feedback that teachers provide has a strong impact on students' development as writers, teacher training programs should incorporate best practices for responding to student writing.

Learn more about writing situations in Chapter 1.

How Can I Draft My Thesis Statement?

To develop your thesis statement, think about how your position relates to the type of document you will write and to the information, ideas, and arguments you want to include. Then try out different ways of phrasing your thesis statement. As you develop each new version, try to predict how your readers will react to it.

Consider Your Genre

An effective thesis statement will reflect the genre you plan to use (see *What Should I Know about Genre and Design?* in Chapter 1). Readers of an academic essay will expect a calm, clearly written statement of what you want them to learn, believe, or do. Readers of a newspaper article will expect to see information presented in a balanced and seemingly unbiased manner. Readers of an opinion column will expect you to be more assertive and perhaps even more entertaining about your position on an issue. Consider how the following thesis statements, all addressing problems with the recruitment of athletes at a university, reflect the type of document the writer plans to draft.

Argumentative Academic Essay

- The university should ensure that its recruiting practices are in full compliance with NCAA regulations.

A strong but formal assertion

Informative Newspaper Article

- The university is taking steps to bring its recruiting practices in line with NCAA regulations.

A seemingly unbiased statement of fact

Opinion Column

- The university's coaches need to get their act together before the NCAA slaps them with sanctions.

An informal tone

Identify Important Information, Ideas, and Arguments Related to Your Position

Begin developing your thesis statement by identifying important information, ideas, and arguments related to your position. When you first explored a conversation (see Chapter 2), you asked questions to learn about your subject. Review those questions and examine them for key words and phrases. Then look through your notes to see how your sources address those questions or use those key words and phrases. Consider the following example, which shows a list of Quinn Jackson's initial questions and the important information, ideas, and arguments she found in sources.

Quinn circled key words and phrases in her initial questions about her subject and then identified which sources address those key words and phrases.

Questions about how writing teachers respond to student work:

- What are the ways that (teachers) give (students) (feedback) on their (written work)?

  Have different (approaches) common to (writing feedback) been studied? Are any proven to be more (successful) than others?

  Is (written feedback) more effective than (verbal feedback)?

  What is the (goal) of feedback on (student writing)?

  Does the feedback students receive vary with the (audience) they are writing for?

What my sources say:

Feedback that makes observations is more valuable than feedback that evaluates whether writing is good or bad, successful or unsuccessful (Johnston 56).

Teacher feedback encourages students to do more than just improve their sentences; it helps them develop important habits of mind (Sommers 35).

What goes on in a successful classroom is far more than just "teaching writing"; it extends to what students learn about being citizens of the world (Sommers 36).

You can use the key words and phrases you've identified in your questions and notes in the various versions of thesis statements that you try out.

Draft Alternatives

An effective thesis statement can invite your readers to learn something new, suggest that they change their attitudes or beliefs, or argue that they should take action of some kind. Consider how the following thesis statements reflect these three ways of focusing a position statement.

Position Statement

Teachers should have more classes about writing theory and classroom practice and more professional development on the job.

Thesis Statement: Asking Readers to Learn Something New

Recent research on how teachers give feedback has identified students' most common writing problems and teachers' most common responses.

Thesis Statement: Asking Readers to Change Their Attitudes or Beliefs

When teachers give feedback to students on written work, they are communicating values and ideals that go beyond the classroom.

Thesis Statement: Asking Readers to Take Action

Parents should demand that school districts provide more research-based guidance for responding to student writing.

Experiment with different approaches to determine which one works best for your writing situation. The thesis statement you choose should convey your position in a way that addresses your purpose and your readers' needs, interests, backgrounds, and knowledge of a subject. For example, if you're focusing on the causes of a problem, your thesis statement should identify those causes. If you're advocating a particular solution to a problem, your thesis statement should identify that solution.

Focus Your Thesis Statement

A broad thesis statement does not encourage your readers to learn anything new, change their attitudes or beliefs, or take action. The following thesis statement is too broad.

Broad Thesis Statement

> The feedback that teachers provide on written work has a big impact on students' development as writers.

There's no conversation to be had about this topic because few people would argue with such a statement. A more focused thesis statement would define what should be done and who should do it.

Focused Thesis Statement

> Because the feedback that teachers provide has a strong impact on students' development as writers, teacher training programs should incorporate best practices for responding to student writing.

To focus your thesis statement, ask what your readers would want to know about your subject, what attitudes should be changed, or what action should be taken. Consider their likely responses to your thesis statement, and attempt to head off potential counterarguments or questions.

How Can I Support My Thesis Statement?

Presenting your thesis statement effectively involves far more than knowing what you want others to understand or believe or how you want them to act. You must develop a strategy to accomplish your goal. Developing your strategy involves reflecting on your purposes, your role, your readers, and the conventions typically used in the type of document you plan to write.

Choose Reasons to Accept Your Thesis Statement

In longer documents, such as essays, reports, and websites, writers usually present readers with several reasons to accept their thesis statement. The kinds of reasons will vary according to the types of documents they are writing. In informative documents (see Chapter 8), for example, writers might focus on the three or four most important aspects of the subject they want readers to understand. In analytical documents (see Chapter 9), they might choose points that help readers understand the results of the analysis. In argumentative documents (see Chapter 12), writers usually offer a series of claims that will lead readers to accept their arguments.

To choose the reasons you'll offer to support your thesis statement, consider brainstorming, freewriting, looping, or clustering (see *Generate Ideas* in Chapter 2).

As you generate ideas, reflect on your purpose, your role as a writer, the type of document you intend to write, and your readers.

- **Writing to reflect.** Which of your observations are most significant? What kind of impression do you want to create? (See Chapter 7.)
- **Writing to inform.** What do you want to convey to your readers? What are they most likely to want to know about the subject? (See Chapter 8.)
- **Writing to analyze.** How will you present the results of your analysis? What questions might your readers have about each part of your analysis? (See Chapter 9.)
- **Writing to evaluate.** What is the best way to present your criteria and the results of your evaluation? (See Chapter 10.)
- **Writing to solve problems.** How will you define the problem, and how will you present your solution? What questions do you think your readers will have about your problem definition, proposed solution, and alternative solutions? (See Chapter 11.)
- **Writing to convince or persuade.** How can you convince your readers to accept your thesis statement? How do you think they might respond to your argument? What sort of counterarguments might they propose? (See Chapter 12.)

Select Evidence to Support Your Reasons

For each reason you offer to support your thesis statement, you'll need evidence—such as details, facts, personal observations, and expert opinions—to back up your assertions and help your readers understand your ideas. The evidence you choose plays a central role in gaining your readers' acceptance of your thesis statement.

You can draw evidence from your sources in the form of quotations, paraphrases, summaries, numerical data, and visual images. You can also gather evidence firsthand by conducting interviews, observations, and surveys or by reflecting on your personal experience (see Chapter 15). Chapters 7 to 12 offer detailed suggestions for locating and choosing evidence for specific purposes.

Learn how to locate sources in Chapters 13, 14, and 15.

Use the following prompts to identify evidence to support your reasons:

1. List the reasons you are using to support your thesis statement.
2. Identify relevant evidence from your sources, personal experience, or field research, and then list that evidence below each reason. You might need to review your sources to locate additional evidence or even obtain additional sources.

Learn more about developing reasons and selecting evidence in *Build Your Argument* in Chapter 12.

3. Determine whether you are relying too heavily on information from a single source or on one type of evidence.

As you select supporting evidence, consider the genre of your document. Genre conventions (see *What Should I Know about Genre and Design?* in Chapter 1) often determine how and how much evidence is used in a document. Articles in magazines, newspapers, and websites, for example, are more likely to rely on interviews, observation, and illustrations as primary sources of evidence than are academic essays, whose writers tend to draw information from published sources found in a library or database. Multimodal essays, in contrast, are likely to use not only textual information and images but also audio, video, and animation.

In Summary: Developing Your Thesis Statement

* Take a position on your issue (p. 539).
* Draft your thesis statement (p. 541).
* Choose reasons to accept your thesis statement (p. 544).
* Select evidence to support your reasons (p. 545).

19 Organizing Your Ideas

How can I choose an organizing pattern? 547
Understand the types of organizing patterns 548
Reflect on your writing situation 549

How can I arrange my ideas? 550
Labeling 550
Grouping 551
Clustering 551
Mapping 551

How can I create an outline? 554
Create an informal outline 554
Create a formal outline 556

What if I'm not ready to organize my ideas? 558
Create a zero draft 558
Create an outline or a map from a zero draft 559

A well-organized document allows a reader to predict what will come next. Choose an appropriate organizing pattern by reflecting on your writing situation, genre, thesis statement, reasons, and evidence. With your organizing pattern in mind, use labeling, grouping, clustering, and mapping to arrange your argument, and use informal and formal outlining strategies to organize your document. If you're not ready to use these strategies, consider creating a *zero draft* — a form of freewriting — and then use what you've written to start organizing your ideas.

How Can I Choose an Organizing Pattern?

Organizing patterns provide an overall principle for arranging the information, ideas, and arguments in your document. The pattern you choose should help you organize your document in a manner that your readers can follow easily. It should also help you achieve your purpose and adapt to your readers and context.

Understand the Types of Organizing Patterns

Common organizing patterns include the following.

Chronology reflects the order in which events occur over time. For example, you might focus on a sequence of events in a recent election or during someone's life. Biographies and memoirs, for instance, are often organized chronologically, portraying early events first and moving forward in time.

Description provides a point-by-point account of the physical attributes of a subject. For example, you might focus on what you see as you walk the streets of a city. Description is best for documents that address physical spaces, objects, or people — things that we can see and observe — rather than theories or processes that are not visible.

Definition lays out the distinguishing characteristics of a subject and then provides examples and reasoning to explain what differentiates it from other subjects. For instance, an essay defining *pride* might begin by stating that it is an emotion and then move on to explain why that particular emotion is not as harmful as many people believe.

Cause/effect patterns focus on the factors that lead to (cause) an outcome (effect). For example, you might identify the reasons behind a recent strike by grocery store employees or the health risks that contribute to heart disease.

Process explanations outline the steps involved in doing something or explain how something happens. For example, you might help readers understand the stages of nuclear fission or teach them what to do to prepare for a hurricane.

Pro/con organizing patterns present arguments made for (pro) and against (con) a particular position. For example, you might consider the arguments for and against increased reliance on wind power.

Multiple perspectives organizing patterns arrange information, ideas, and arguments according to a range of perspectives about a subject. Writers who use this pattern frequently provide an analysis supporting one perspective. For example, a writer addressing the use of tidal power as an alternative energy source might present the perspectives of utility companies, environmentalists, oceanographers, legislators, and waterfront residents and ultimately favor one perspective over the others.

Comparison/contrast patterns can help you explore similarities and differences among the information, ideas, and arguments relevant to a subject. A writer analyzing a policy initiative to decriminalize marijuana possession, for example, might consider how current drug laws are like or unlike alcohol prohibition. Another writer might compare and contrast medical and recreational uses of marijuana.

Strengths/weaknesses patterns can help you examine positive and negative aspects of a subject, such as increasing federal funding for health care by instituting a national lottery, or the overall quality of life in a particular city. Writers who choose this organizing principle typically work toward a conclusion where one or two considerations outweigh the others.

Costs/benefits organizing patterns present the trade-offs associated with a subject, usually a choice or proposal of some sort. For example, the writer of an evaluative essay might discuss why the expenses associated with implementing a particular educational initiative are justified (or not) by the potential for improved learning outcomes.

Problem/solution organizing patterns involve defining a problem and discussing the appropriateness of one or more solutions. If multiple solutions are proposed, the writer usually argues for the superiority of one over the others. For instance, an informative article might explain the problem of "brain drain," in which highly educated and skilled workers move out of state, and then argue in support of a proposal to retain and attract more skilled workers.

Reflect on Your Writing Situation

Your choice of organizing pattern will reflect your purpose and the role or roles you adopt as a writer (see Chapters 6 to 12). Consider which pattern will help you achieve your goals as a writer, meet the needs and interests of your readers, adapt to your context, and be consistent with the genre you've chosen. An organizing pattern should also highlight the reasons and evidence you offer to convince readers to accept your thesis statement.

Keep in mind that a writer may use more than one organizing pattern in a document. For instance, a process explanation often works in tandem with chronology, since both present steps in a sequence. Similarly, a document presenting multiple perspectives might use the strengths/weaknesses pattern to evaluate the merits of each perspective.

How Can I Arrange My Ideas?

Once you have selected an organizing pattern, you can use strategies such as labeling, grouping, clustering, and mapping to determine how to present your information, ideas, and arguments. These strategies will also help you later as you develop an outline for your document.

Labeling

Labeling can help you understand at a glance how and where you will use your evidence. For example, you might label notes or sources containing the evidence you want to use in your introduction with "Introduction," those that you plan to use to define a concept with the name of that concept, and so on. Digital notes and sources can be labeled by changing a file name or editing the document text. Print notes and sources can be labeled with pen or pencil or with sticky notes.

Once you've labeled your notes and sources, you can organize them into groups and put them in order.

Label at the top of a note in a word-processing file.

MLA style calls for including URLs in works cited lists.

Annotation captures the main point of the source.

Attempts to Defund Police

McGlinchy, Audrey. "Inside One City's Attempt To Defund The Police." *NPR*. 15 Feb. 2021. https://www.npr.org/2021/02/15/967079446/inside-one-citys-attempt-to-defund-the-police.

NPR segment that focuses on attempts to defund the police in Austin, Texas.

Key Quotes:

"Oftentimes, police officers are sent to situations for which we're not always the best trained or the best equipped. We're just simply the only ones available." (Police Chief Brian Manley)

"But it's unclear if Austin's decision to cut its police budget could ever happen again. Texas Governor Greg Abbott has promised to sign a bill making it almost impossible for cities to reduce their police department budgets." (Reporter Audrey McGlinchy)

▲ **Labeling digital notes and sources**

Grouping

Grouping involves categorizing the evidence you've obtained from your sources. Paper-based notes and copies of sources can be placed in related piles or file folders; sources and notes in word-processing files or on a phone can be saved in larger files or placed in folders; items in bookmarks or favorites lists can be sorted by category. Placing things that are similar in groups allows you to locate the evidence you've collected more easily and helps you understand the range of evidence you might use to support a particular point.

▲ Grouping digital notes and sources in a browser

Clustering

You can use clustering to explore the relationships among your thesis statement, reasons, and evidence. Clustering involves arranging these elements visually on a sheet of paper or on a computer, phone, or tablet screen (using a word-processing program or an app such as iThoughts).

Mapping

Mapping allows you to explore sequences of reasons and evidence. For example, you might use mapping to create a timeline or to show how an argument builds on one reason after another. Mapping can be particularly effective as you begin to think about organizing your document, and it often relies on the organizing patterns discussed earlier in this chapter, such as chronology, cause/effect, comparison/contrast, costs/benefits, and problem/solution.

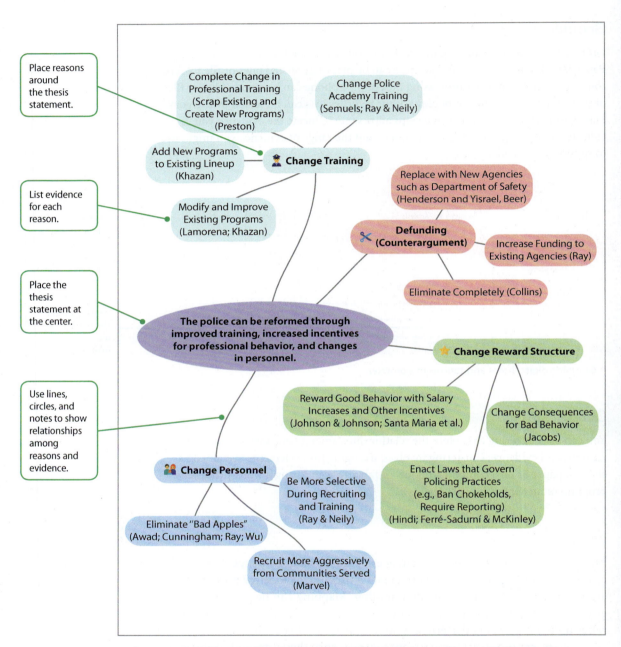

▲ The cause-and-effect map Jeremy Alcazar created on a tablet (see his essay in Chapter 12)

The Dangers of Fast Fashion

Consumerism, and more specifically a desire for fast fashion, has become an increasingly normalized way of life, contributing to exploitive labor practices and unsustainable manufacturing processes.

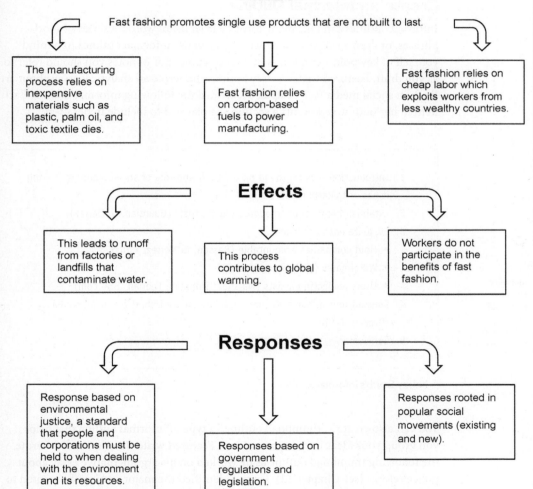

▲ A map of Gabriella Guerrero's informative essay (see her essay in Chapter 8)

How Can I Create an Outline?

Not all documents require an outline, but creating one will usually help you put your thoughts in order. As you develop an outline, you'll make decisions about the sequence in which you'll present your reasons and the evidence you'll use to back them up.

Create an Informal Outline

Informal outlines can take many forms: a brief list of words, a series of short phrases, or even a series of sentences. You can use informal outlines to remind yourself of key points to address in your document or of notes you should refer to as you draft. Featured writer Kelsey Smith, who wrote an analytical essay about art theft on social media (see Chapter 9), created the following informal outline. Each item in her outline represents a section she planned to include in her essay.

1. Introduction — background on art theft and role of social media in making it easier to carry out
2. Establish approaches to addressing art theft (Guardian, Gutierrez)
3. Evaluate each approach
    - Hold companies accountable (Bassen, Gutierrez, Wells)
    - Watermarks (@Meyoco, Feehan)
    - Users respecting artists (Marshall/Shipman, Feehan, BBC.com)
4. Speculations about prospects for addressing art theft on social media (Bassen, Feehan)
5. Conclusion

Kelsey identified sources she could use in each subsection.

▲ **Kelsey Smith's informal outline**

You can also create a "thumbnail outline," a type of informal outline that helps you group your ideas into major sections. Featured writer Jeremy Alcazar wrote the following thumbnail outline as he worked on his argumentative essay about police reform (see Chapter 12). Jeremy identified the major sections he wanted to include in his essay and noted which sources he could use to provide background information and to support his argument.

Introduction

Following the death of George Floyd at the hands of Minneapolis police officers, protests swept the nation, calling for police reform. Some protesters called for the complete elimination of police departments (Collins). Others argued for shifting police services to other agencies (Henderson and Yisrael, Beer). Still others argued for fundamental changes in the recruitment and training of police officers (Preston, Khazan, Lamorena, Ray & Neily; Semuels).

Thesis Statement

Police need to be drawn from the communities they serve, better trained to meet the challenges they encounter, and held accountable for their actions.

Police should be members of the communities they serve

Reform must include recruiting police from the communities in which they work (Marvel). Police are often seen as outsiders and too often they act like it. We need to address the "us versus them" mentality head on.

Police should receive better training

We need more rigorous police academies (Ray & Neily, Semuels), more relevant training (Khazan, Preston), and more intensive training (Khazan, Lamorena, Preston).

Police should be held accountable for their actions

Police should be subject to lawsuits (RerHindi, Jacobs). We need to eliminate bad apples (Awad, Cunningham, Ray, Wu). Police culture should be changed to ensure bad behavior is not tolerated and good behavior is rewarded (Johnson & Johnson, Maria et al).

Conclusion

Efforts to "defund" the police are misguided (Beer, Collins, Henderson & Yisrael). We need to increase funding to improve recruitment, reform training, and hold police accountable. Circle back to introduction to point out that so many people would be alive today if these changes had already been made, and so many more lives will be saved if they are put into practice now.

▲ Jeremy Alcazar's thumbnail outline

Create a Formal Outline

A formal outline provides a complete and accurate list of the points you want to address in your document. Formal outlines use Roman numerals, letters, and Arabic numerals to indicate the hierarchy of information. An alternative approach, common in business and the sciences, uses numbering with decimal points.

Writers use formal outlines to identify the hierarchy of arguments, ideas, and information. You can create a formal outline to identify

- your thesis statement
- the reasons you offer to support your thesis statement
- the sequence in which your reasons should be presented
- evidence to support your reasons
- the notes and sources you should refer to as you work on your draft

The most common types of formal outlines are topical outlines and sentence outlines.

Topical outlines Topical outlines present the topics and subtopics you plan to include in your document as a series of words and phrases. Items at the same level of importance should be phrased in parallel grammatical form. In her topical outline for her problem-solving essay about shark finning (see Chapter 11), featured writer Sophie Kimble used a system of Arabic numbers, letters, and Roman numerals to introduce her issue, define the problem, consider past solutions, and present her solution.

Thesis Statement: We must address the consequences of shark finning for sharks and the larger ocean ecosystem.

1. What is shark finning and what are the problems associated with it?
   a. Sharks are endangered, with fins cut off, to provide:
      i. Shark fin soup (Liu)
      ii. Alternative medicine treatments (Tutton)
   b. Impact on ocean ecosystems:
      i. Sharks are an apex predator essential to ecosystems (Graham, quoted in Scales)
      ii. Sharks have slow reproductive/maturation cycle (Castro et al.)

▲ Sophie Kimble's topical outline

2. What has been done to stop this and why hasn't it worked?
    a. Regulations in Asia and America (Animal Welfare Institute)
    b. But black markets in shark fins persist (Rogers)
3. Why has this problem continued? Lack of empathy for sharks:
    a. Issue is greater in scale than many other issues that receive far more attention
    b. "Jaws Factor" (Knowlton and Benchley)
    c. Not taught in most environmental courses (Tsoi et al.)
4. Potential counterarguments/alternative solutions
    a. Policies and Regulations
    b. Too big of an issue to be fixed
5. How can we change this? (Solutions)
    a. Education
        i. Reconstructing the way people view sharks
            1. Sharks have complex relationships
            2. Very unlikely to ever attack people (Florida Museum)
            3. Vital to ecosystems (Ramsey)
        ii. Shark Week
            1. Needs to become more informative and less about scaring people
            2. Portrayals of sharks in pop culture contribute to negligence
        iii. Funding
            1. Tax breaks to ecotourism industries?
            2. Incentives provided to companies who increase education about shark finning (NGOs)
    b. Efforts to increase empathy for sharks
        i. Ocean influencers (Ramsey)
        ii. Whaling ban and public perception changes over time
        iii. Ecotourism
            1. Sharks are more valuable alive than served in soup (PEW Charitable Trusts)
            2. Tax breaks can spur tourism and support education
6. Conclusion

▲ **Sophie Kimble's topical outline** (*continued*)

Sentence outlines Sentence outlines use complete sentences to identify the points you want to cover. Sentence outlines begin the process of converting an outline into a draft of your document. They can also help you assess the structure of a document that you have already written.

Using her topical outline as a starting point, Sophie Kimble wrote a sentence outline to test her ideas. Part of her sentence outline is shown here.

Thesis Statement: We must address the consequences of shark finning for sharks and the larger ocean ecosystem.

1. Shark finning
    a. Shark finning is the practice of removing a shark's fin(s), and letting the shark die a slow and painful death as a result of suffocation or blood loss. Despite the fact that it does not even add any taste to the dish, millions of sharks continue to be killed for their fins.
        i. Shark fins are used in shark fin soup, which is a popular dish in Asia, and often seen as a symbol of status and wealth (Liu).
        ii. Shark fins are also an important ingredient in traditional medicines in Asia. They are viewed as contributing to general well being and are even touted as being useful for treating cancer (Tutton).

▲ Part of Sophie Kimble's sentence outline

What If I'm Not Ready to Organize My Ideas?

Even after you've read about an issue carefully and thoughtfully, it's completely natural to stare at a blank screen or a piece of paper and think, "What am I supposed to do with this?" If you find yourself at this point, consider writing a *zero draft*.

Create a Zero Draft

A zero draft is a form of extended freewriting (see *Generate Ideas* in Chapter 2). The goal is to write everything you can think of about your subject without worrying about whether you have a good introduction or conclusion, whether the ideas are being listed in any sort of order, or whether the sentences you're writing are well formed and thoughtful. In other words, you can think of it as a knowledge dump.

As you prepare to create a zero draft, give yourself some guidelines. First, try to write for an extended period of time without stopping. You might set a timer for thirty minutes, forty-five minutes, or an hour or more, and then write until the alarm goes off. Second, avoid censoring yourself. There's no need to form your thoughts completely as you write. You should do your best to let the words flow. Third, be creative. As odd as it might sound if you are facing a deadline, you should try to have some fun with your zero draft. Remind yourself that you'll be the only person who will ever see what you write.

Create an Outline or a Map from a Zero Draft

When you've finished your zero draft, set it aside before you look at it again. When you decide to start reading it, use the draft to identify ideas, reasons, and evidence that you might use later as you start working on the first draft of your document. You might, as MacKenzi McQuide suggested in a post on the University of Nevada, Reno, University Writing Center blog, highlight ideas, reasons, and evidence in your zero draft and then list them in the order that seems to make the most sense. At the end of this process, you'll have an informal outline that you can use as you begin to write your first draft (see the discussion of outlines earlier in this chapter). If you're more visually oriented, or if you truly detest outlines, you could also create a map of the ideas in your zero draft and then use it as you write your first draft.

In Summary: Organizing Your Ideas

* ★ Choose an appropriate organizing pattern (p. 547).
* ★ Use labeling, grouping, clustering, and/or mapping to organize your information, ideas, and arguments (p. 550).
* ★ Create an informal or formal outline (p. 554).
* ★ Write a zero draft (p. 559).

20 Drafting Your Document

How can I use my outline or map to write a first draft? 561

How can I draft an effective document? 562
Create paragraphs that focus on a central idea 562
Create paragraphs that use appropriate organizing patterns 563
Integrate information from sources effectively 563
Write clearly and concisely 564
Engage your readers 566
Use details to capture your readers' attention 566
Create transitions within and between paragraphs 567

How can I help readers follow my ideas? 569
Let readers know where your document is taking them 569
Keep related ideas together 570
Keep the flow of your document moving forward 570
Say things just once 571

How can I draft my introduction? 571
Frame your introduction 572
Select an introductory strategy 573

How can I draft my conclusion? 577
Reinforce your points 577
Select a concluding strategy 578
Reinforce your efforts to frame your subject or issue 581

As you've learned about your subject, you've encountered new information, ideas, and arguments. In response, you've considered how to craft your own contribution to the conversation you are joining. How you frame your contribution—that is, how you organize your document, construct your paragraphs, introduce and conclude your document, and design your document—can have a profound effect on readers' understanding of your subject and on their willingness to accept your main idea. This chapter offers guidance on how to use what you've learned to draft an effective contribution to the conversation you've decided to join.

How Can I Use My Outline or Map to Write a First Draft?

Your outline or map provides a framework you can use to draft your document. A well-developed formal outline or a complex map might include your thoughts about

- the points you will include in your document
- the order in which you will make your points
- the amount of space you plan to devote to each point

As you review your purpose and your outline or map, check that you have organized your document in a way that will allow you to achieve your purpose, adopt your role, and address the needs and interests of your readers.

If you have listed information about the sources you will use to support your points, you can check whether you are

- providing enough evidence to support your points
- relying too heavily on a small number of sources
- relying too heavily on support from sources that favor just one side of the conversation

If you created an informal outline or a relatively simple map, you can begin to flesh it out by translating key points within it into sentences or paragraphs. If you created a formal outline, you can turn major headings in the outline into headings or subheadings in your draft and then use the points under each heading as the basis for topic sentences for paragraphs. If your outline or map is highly detailed, you can use minor points as the basis for supporting sentences within each paragraph.

Make sure that you use your notes and review the paraphrases, summaries, and quotations you wrote down. Take advantage of the time you spent thinking about which sources are most appropriate for a particular section of your document. Most important, think of your outline or map as a flexible guide rather than a rigid blueprint.

How Can I Draft an Effective Document?

Effective documents contribute to the conversation in a way that reflects and adapts to your writing situation. Your document should help you accomplish your purpose, address your readers effectively, and help you take advantage of — or work within — the contexts in which it will be read. Deepening your understanding of those contexts — physical, social, cultural, and disciplinary (see *Writing Takes Place in Context* in Chapter 1) — can lead to important changes in how you frame your main idea for your readers and how you support it with reasons and evidence.

Few first drafts measure up to the standards writers set for themselves. In fact, most writers create several drafts before deciding that a document is ready to share with readers. As you draft, be open to change. You might decide to reorganize your ideas or frame your main point in a different way. You might think of new reasons to support your main point. You might launch a search for new information. You might gain a fuller understanding of the contexts in which your document will be read. And you might experiment with different examples or word choices in an effort to show respect for the backgrounds and interests of your readers. As you draft, keep the following observations and ideas in mind.

Create Paragraphs That Focus on a Central Idea

Writers use paragraphs to present and develop a central idea. Depending on the complexity of your thesis statement and the type of document you are writing, a single paragraph might be all you need to present a supporting point and its associated reasoning and evidence — or it might play only a small role in conveying your thinking about your subject. You can draft a more effective document by creating paragraphs that are focused, organized, and well developed and by using transitions that clearly signal the relationships among paragraphs.

Each of your paragraphs should focus on a single idea. Paragraphs often have a topic sentence in which the writer makes an assertion, offers an observation, or asks a question. The rest of the sentences in the paragraph elaborate on the topic sentence. Consider the following paragraph, drawn from Rivka Galchen's profile of the ballet dancer Misty Copeland (see *An Unlikely Ballerina: The Rise of Misty Copeland* in Chapter 8).

> [The central idea of the paragraph is provided in the opening clause, and details about Copeland support it.] Copeland is considered an unlikely ballerina: she is curvy and she is black, neither of which is a common attribute in the field. [The second sentence analyzes why the central idea is significant.] But it is her very late beginning and rapid attainment of virtuosity that are arguably without precedent for a female ballerina.

(Rudolf Nureyev had a famously late and chaotic start, his early training having been limited by the vagaries of the post–Second World War Soviet Union.) Many professional ballet dancers begin their training around the age of three. Every dancer is a synthesis of givens — height, limb length, natural turnout — and intense effort, but Copeland's late start can exaggerate the tendency we might have to regard a ballerina as simply touched by something divine.

> The third sentence offers evidence by way of an exception to the rule, while the fourth sentence provides further information that illustrates why Copeland is "unlikely."

> The fifth sentence builds on the second, extending the analysis of Copeland's fame.

Create Paragraphs That Use Appropriate Organizing Patterns

Effective paragraphs follow an organizing pattern, often the same one that the document as a whole follows, such as chronology, description, or costs/benefits (see *How Can I Choose an Organizing Pattern?* in Chapter 19). These common patterns help readers anticipate what you'll say. Readers who recognize a pattern, such as process explanation, will find it easier to focus on your ideas and argument if they understand how you are organizing your paragraph. Note how the following paragraph from featured student writer Brooke Shannon's analytical essay about *Wicked* (see Chapter 10) uses the sequence of events in the play to convey its point.

> *Wicked* pulled on the audience's heartstrings through intense character development, teaching viewers how to look beyond the surface. Glinda "is snooty, haughty, ambitious, conscious of her beauty and initially not interested in befriending the green outcast" (Dawe). However, the relationship between them blooms into a friendship beyond popularity. Glinda shares the secret of her love for Fiyero to Elphaba. This is the start of Glinda's understanding of Elphaba's personality. Glinda decides to look past Elphaba's green skin and discovers the good nature of her heart.

> The paragraph introduces a key part of the analysis: the role of character development in the show.

> A reputable source is quoted, providing a description of a central character.

> The final sentence describes the outcome of the sequence of events.

Integrate Information from Sources Effectively

Information from sources can be used to introduce an important concept, establish the strength of your argument, and elaborate on the central ideas in your document. Writers frequently state a point, offer a reason to accept it, and support their reasoning with evidence from a source, typically in the form of quotations, paraphrases, and summaries. In the following example, a quotation and a paraphrase are used to support a point introduced in the first sentence of the paragraph.

> We appear to have reached a turning point in the fight to reduce emissions from coal-fired power plants. "Spending on coal projects dropped to its lowest level in a decade

in 2019," wrote New York Times reporters Somini Sengupta and Rick Gladstone in September 2021. "And over the past 20 years, more coal-burning power plants have been retired or shelved than have been commissioned." Sengupta and Gladstone note that countries that had planned to build new coal-fired power plants have cancelled or are reconsidering those plans and that newly built plants in other countries are facing significant funding challenges. In India, for example, Sengupta and Gladstone report that "existing coal plants are running far below capacity and losing money." Meanwhile, in the United States, they point out, coal-fired plants are being shut down at a rapid rate.

Quoting a reporter from a well-known newspaper, the *New York Times*, lends strength to the argument. The quotation, along with subsequent paraphrases and a quotation of information found later in the article, serves as evidence to support the point. (See Chapter 21 for more about integrating information from sources.)

Write Clearly and Concisely

Readers don't want to work any harder than necessary to understand and engage with the information, ideas, and arguments in a document. They get unhappy if they have to put in extra effort to read a document — so unhappy, in fact, that they'll often give up.

To keep your readers engaged with your document, write clearly and concisely. Consider the following passages.

> Please join me, Dr. Watson. I have concluded that I am in a situation in which I require your assistance.
>
> Mr. Watson, come here. I want to see you.
>
> Help!

The second example, reputed to be the first words ever spoken on a telephone, was spoken by Alexander Graham Bell after he'd spilled battery acid on his pants. Had he spoken the first sentence instead, he might have wasted crucial time while he waited for his assistant to figure out what he was being asked to do. The simple exclamation "Help!" might have been even more effective and would certainly have taken less time to utter. Then again, it might have been too vague for his assistant to figure out just what sort of help was required. In general, if two sentences provide the same information, the briefer sentence is usually easier to understand.

The following three techniques can help you write with economy.

- **Avoid unnecessary modifiers.** Unnecessary modifiers are words that provide little or no additional information to a reader, such as *fine, many, somewhat, great, quite, sort of, lots, really,* and *very*.

EXAMPLE SENTENCE WITH UNNECESSARY MODIFIERS

The Volvo S90 serves as a really excellent example of a very fine performance sedan.

REVISED EXAMPLE

The Volvo S90 serves as an excellent example of a performance sedan.

- **Avoid unnecessary introductory phrases.** Avoid phrases such as *there are, there is, these have, these are, here are, here is, it has been reported that, it has been said that, it is evident that, it is obvious that,* and so on.

EXAMPLE SENTENCE WITH UNNECESSARY INTRODUCTORY PHRASE

It goes without saying that drinking water should be clean.

REVISED EXAMPLE

Drinking water should be clean.

- **Avoid stock phrases.** Search your document for phrases that you can replace with fewer words, such as the following.

Stock Phrase	Alternative
as a matter of fact	in fact
at all times	always
at that point in time	then
at the present time	now/currently
because of the fact that	because
by means of	by
due to the fact that	because
in order to	to
in spite of the fact that	although/though
in the event that	if

EXAMPLE SENTENCE WITH STOCK PHRASE

Call the security desk in the event that the alarm sounds.

REVISED EXAMPLE

Call the security desk if the alarm sounds.

Engage Your Readers

As you draft your document, consider how you'll keep your readers' attention. One of the easiest things you can do is to write your sentences in *active voice*. A sentence written in active voice specifies an actor — a person or thing — who carries out an action.

ACTIVE VOICE

Juan took an exam.

The tornado leveled the town.

Nikola Jokic scored the game-winning basket with 0.2 seconds remaining in overtime.

In contrast, a sentence written in passive voice indicates that something was done, but it does not necessarily specify who or what did it.

PASSIVE VOICE

The exam was taken by Juan.

The town was leveled.

The game-winning basket was scored by Nikola Jokik with 0.2 seconds remaining in overtime.

In general, sentences written in active voice are easier to understand and provide more information.

Passive voice, however, can be effective when active voice requires unnecessary information. For example, many scientific experiments are conducted by large teams of researchers. Few readers would want to know which members of the team carried out every task. Rather than using active voice (for example, "Heather Landers, assisted by Shirley Guitron and Shaun Beaty, anesthetized the mice, and then Stephanie Moreira and Justin Switzer examined their eyes for lesions"), you can use passive voice ("The mice were anesthetized, and their eyes were examined for lesions") for a sentence that is clearer, easier to understand, and free of unnecessary information.

Passive voice is also useful if you wish to emphasize the recipient of the action, rather than the actor. Police reports, for example, often use passive voice ("The suspect was apprehended at the corner of Oak and Main Streets").

Use Details to Capture Your Readers' Attention

An effective document does more than simply convey information — it provides details that bring a subject to life. Consider the differences between the following versions of a passage from featured writer Caitlin Guariglia's essay on her family trip to Italy (see Chapter 7).

EXAMPLE 1: MINIMAL DETAILS

The next morning we met our tour guide. He was full of life. He took us to the main historical sites that day. They were spectacular, but I enjoyed listening to Marco more than anything we saw.

EXAMPLE 2: EXTENSIVE, CONCRETE DETAILS

The next morning we met our tour guide Marco. A large, sturdy man who looked like my grandmother cooked for him, he was confident and full of life. He took us to the main historical sites that day: the Vatican, the Colosseum, the Pantheon, the Roman Forum. While all that was spectacular, I enjoyed listening to Marco more than anything we saw. He was a true Roman, big, proud, and loud. The Italian accent made it seem like he was singing everything he said, making it all seem that much more beautiful.

Both examples convey the same main idea. The first example, however, does little more than state the facts. The second example, by providing details about the tour guide's physical appearance, personality, and voice, gives readers a more concrete and more intimate understanding of the subject. (For advice about integrating details from your sources effectively, see Chapter 21.)

Create Transitions within and between Paragraphs

Transitions help readers understand the relationships among sentences, paragraphs, and even sections of a document. Essentially, they smooth the way for readers, helping them understand how information, ideas, and arguments are related to one another. Transitions are most effective when they don't call attention to themselves, but instead move the reader's eye along to the next sentence, paragraph, or section. Consider the following examples of the steps involved in preparing fish.

NO TRANSITIONS

Catch the fish. Clean the fish. Filet the fish. Cook the fish. Eat the fish. Catch another fish.

INCONSISTENT TRANSITIONS

First, catch the fish. Secondly, clean the fish. When you've done that, filet the fish. Next, cook the fish. Fifth, eat the fish. After all is said and done, catch another fish.

CONSISTENT TRANSITIONS

> First, catch the fish. Second, clean the fish. Third, filet the fish. Fourth, cook the fish. Fifth, eat the fish. Finally, catch another fish.

Transitions frequently appear as words and phrases, such as those used in the previous example. Transitional sentences, such as the following, often link one paragraph to the next.

> The results of the tests revealed a surprising trend.

> Incredibly, the outcome was far better than we could have hoped.

Transitional paragraphs, such as the following example, call attention to a major shift in focus within a document.

> In the next section, we explore the reasons behind this surprising development. We focus first on the event itself. Then we consider the reasons underlying the event. Our goal is to call attention to the unique set of relationships that made this development possible.

Section headings and subheadings can also act as transitions by signaling to the reader, through formatting that differs from body text, that a new section is beginning. You can read more about formatting headings and subheadings in Chapter 22.

As you create transitions, pay attention to the order in which you introduce new information and ideas in your document. In general, it is best to begin a sentence with a reference to information and ideas that have already been presented and to introduce new information and ideas at the end of the sentence.

Common transitions and their functions are presented below.

To Help Readers Follow a Sequence	To Compare
furthermore	similarly
in addition	in the same manner
moreover	like
next	as in
first/second/third	by the same token

To Elaborate or Provide Examples	To Contrast
for example	however
for instance	on the other hand
such as	nevertheless
in fact	nonetheless
indeed	despite
to illustrate	although/though

To Signal a Concession	To Introduce a Conclusion
I admit that	as a result
of course	as a consequence
granted	because of
certainly	therefore
it's true that	thus
I will concede that	for this reason

How Can I Help Readers Follow My Ideas?

As you draft your document, think about how your readers will follow your line of argument. Surprises can be pleasant, but few readers will be able — or willing — to follow a complex argument without at least a general sense of where you plan to lead them. Clue your readers in right from the start and provide useful guidance throughout your document about its overall organization. A well-organized document will provide an introduction that states or suggests your purpose, gives enough organizational cues to help your readers follow your argument, makes them want to keep reading, and does so as concisely as possible.

Let Readers Know Where Your Document Is Taking Them

You can use several strategies to give your readers a sense of where your document is going to take them. The most direct strategy, and one that's common in most genres of academic writing, is to provide a "map" — a preview of your main point and supporting points. You can also take advantage of commonly used organizing patterns, such as pro/con or cause/effect, that readers will understand easily.

- **GIVE READERS A MAP**

  Think of maps as promises to your readers that help establish their expectations and convey your purpose for writing. If you are working on an informative document, you might promise to explain the details of a complex issue to your readers. If you define a problem in your introduction, that definition serves as a promise to present a solution by the end of your document. As you draft and revise your document, keep your eyes open for unfulfilled promises.

- **BUILD ON READERS' EXPERIENCES**

  Like you, your readers will be familiar with some of the more commonly used organizing patterns, such as pro/con, cause/effect, or comparison/contrast. Let that familiarity work to your advantage. If you've presented the pro side of an argument, for instance, you can be fairly confident that your readers will expect to read the con side before long. By anticipating and meeting your readers' expectations, you'll increase their confidence in you.

Keep Related Ideas Together

Structure your document logically, with related ideas presented in a sequence that readers will be able to follow. For example, if a particular idea needs to be explained so that readers can understand the rest of your argument, start with that idea. As you think about how to organize a complex set of ideas, ask what idea your readers are likely to expect to learn about next.

As you introduce your idea, ask what your readers already know about it. If it's an unfamiliar idea, you'll need to help them understand it. But you'll want to do so in a way that doesn't detract from your argument. For example, explaining complicated background information just when your readers are expecting you to launch into your new idea can make your document seem unorganized. You can solve this problem by signaling to your readers why you're providing background information before moving on to your next major point.

Keep the Flow of Your Document Moving Forward

You're pursuing a specific purpose and adopting a particular role — for example, to inform your readers about an emerging style of music, to evaluate a travel destination, or to argue against new local regulations. So far, you've met expectations and even built them up, so that your readers are coming along with you gladly. Don't frustrate them now. Keep moving forward.

If you're relating something chronological, use a chronological organizing pattern (see *How Can I Choose an Organizing Pattern?* in Chapter 19). If you've provided a map early in your document, you can simply refer to it. You don't have to say anything as obvious as "The third point to be made is…." Instead, connect one point to the next with transition words or a transitional sentence (see *Create Transitions within and between Paragraphs* earlier in this chapter).

You can also use your readers' expectations to show them how you're moving forward. If, for instance, you're developing a pro/con argument, readers will expect you to make a claim, present evidence to support the claim, present evidence against it, and so on. Simply by following this standard sequence, you'll maintain your readers' momentum.

Be wary of cramming material in somewhere just because you can't think of a better place to put it. This can stop your readers from moving forward. If you think you might be doing this, ask whether your readers will need to know the information to understand your main point. If the answer is no, consider leaving it out. If it's necessary but seems to be slowing down your readers, study your draft to determine whether it might fit better somewhere else.

Say Things Just Once

Writers frustrate their readers when they repeat themselves. Sometimes writers do this because they think the idea or information is important and they want to emphasize it. Unfortunately, readers are more likely to view the repetition as a waste of their time rather than as a helpful reinforcement of a key idea.

As you write, watch out for ideas that seem a little too familiar. That feeling of familiarity probably means that you're repeating yourself. When you find a familiar passage, check your outline, decide on a logical place to make the point, and make it there definitively. Then either get rid of the repetitive passage or change it so that it refers to your main discussion of the point.

How Can I Draft My Introduction?

All readers expect documents to include some sort of introduction. Whether they are reading a home page on a website or an opening paragraph in a research report, readers want to learn quickly what a document is about. As you begin to draft, consider strategies to frame and introduce your main point. Many writers find that crafting an effective introduction is the most challenging part of drafting. If you run into difficulties, put your introduction aside and come back to it after you've made more progress on the rest of the document. There's no law that says you have to write the introduction first.

Frame Your Introduction

Your introduction provides a framework within which your readers can understand and interpret your main point. By calling attention to a specific situation, by asking a particular question, or by conveying a carefully chosen set of details, you can help your readers view your subject in a particular way.

You can frame your discussion by calling attention to

- the agent: a person, an organization, or a thing that is acting in a particular way
- the action: what is being done by the actor
- the goal: what the actor wants to achieve by carrying out the action
- the result: the outcome of the action

Consider, for example, how two introductions to an essay about Facebook are framed.

INTRODUCTION 1

In the wake of revelations by whistleblower Frances Haugen that Facebook "harms children, sows division and undermines democracy in pursuit of breakneck growth and `astronomical profits,'" (Allyn), U.S. citizens from across the political spectrum called on Congress to address the potential harm caused by the social media giant. Americans watched intently as congressional hearings were held, with Haugen serving as a star witness. As was the case with earlier scandals, #DELETEFACEBOOK began once again to trend on Twitter. And many more flocked to Twitter, LinkedIn, Instagram, and Facebook itself to share their take on the hearings. Congress, unsurprisingly, was slow to follow up on the hearings. Americans were not. Their verdict on the hearings was clear: social media — and Facebook in particular — was now viewed with far greater skepticism than it had been before Haugen blew her whistle.

INTRODUCTION 2

In the wake of revelations by whistleblower Frances Haugen that Facebook "harms children, sows division and undermines democracy in pursuit of breakneck growth and `astronomical profits,'" (Allyn), the U.S. government explored a wide range of legislative

_____ Agent
- - - - - Action
======= Goal
.... Result

and regulatory actions to govern the safety and security of social media users. Senators Amy Klobuchar and John Thune, who have both sponsored bills addressing the impact of social media on privacy and public safety, once again called for action. "Instead of expecting the industry to make societal decisions that belong to legislators, it's time for Congress to act," said Thune. Even Facebook itself called for legislation governing the internet. Yet long after the committee hearings had ended, and as has been the case with previous efforts, no bills had advanced out of committee.

———— Agent
- - - - Action
════ Goal
········ Result

The first introduction frames the issue as the impact of Haugen's revelations on Americans' perceptions of Facebook and their willingness to engage with it. The second introduction frames the issue as a failure by legislators to take action on an issue of importance. Even though each introduction draws on the same basic information, and even though both do a good job of introducing the essay, they focus attention on different aspects of the issue.

Your framing of your subject or issue is a key rhetorical decision (see *What Should I Know about Writing Situations?* in Chapter 1). By calling attention to what you think is most important, you can lead your readers to see what you are writing about in a particular way. Most important, you lead them away from seeing it in ways that you think are less useful or productive. In this sense, framing is an act that is far from objective. It reflects your attempt to accomplish your purpose and role as a writer and to address the needs and interests of your readers.

Select an Introductory Strategy

The ability to frame your readers' understanding of a subject is a powerful tool. By directing their attention to one aspect of a subject, rather than to others, you can influence their beliefs and, potentially, their willingness to take action.

Your introduction offers perhaps the best opportunity to grab your readers' attention and shape their response to your ideas. You can introduce your document using one of several strategies.

● **STATE THE TOPIC**

Tell your readers what your subject is, what conversation you are focusing on, and what your document will tell them about it. In the following example, drawn from the scholarly journal *College Student Journal*, Eileen Ferrer and her colleagues announce the topic of their scholarly journal article in a straightforward manner.

> The goal and purpose of this study was to examine the role of music as a potentially stress-alleviating therapy among college students.

● ESTABLISH THE CONTEXT

In some cases, you'll want to give your readers background information about your subject or an overview of the conversation that has been taking place about it. Notice, for example, how Alice Park and Sean Gregory set up their feature article on Simone Biles' decision to withdraw from the 2020 Olympics (see Chapter 8).

> Around 9 p.m. on July 27, as Simone Biles soared high above the vault at the Tokyo Olympics, she lost herself. You could see the confusion in her eyes, which darted sideways instead of locking onto the ground as she made her way back to earth. She would later reveal that she was suffering from a frightening mental hiccup, known as "the twisties," that left her unsure of her whereabouts in midair.
>
> As the Greatest of All Time (GOAT) in a sport that captivates the globe every four years, Biles is all about control. Her life is dedicated to micromanaging every possible element — her diet, her training, her sleep — that goes into performing, so when the lights are brightest, and the stakes highest, little is left to chance. But for Biles, control isn't just about winning; it can be the difference between life and death. She now has four skills named after her, each a breathtaking combination of daring flips and twists. Avoiding disaster requires a constant, firm grip on mental acuity.*
>
> *Alice Park and Sean Gregory, "TIME 2021 Athlete of the Year: Simone Biles," TIME, December 9, 2021. Copyright © 2021 by TIME USA LLC. All rights reserved. Used under license. https://time.com

● STATE YOUR THESIS

If your essay urges readers to accept an argument, an evaluation, a solution, or an interpretation, use your introduction to get right to your main point. In an analytical post published in the *Scientific American* blog (blogs.scientificamerican.com), Scott Barry Kaufman begins by challenging a widespread belief about creativity.

> It's a great myth that creative geniuses consistently produce great works.
>
> They don't. In fact, systematic analyses of the career trajectories of people labeled geniuses show that their output tends to be highly uneven, with a few good ideas mixed in with many more false starts. While consistency may be the key to expertise, the secret to creative greatness appears to be doing things differently — even when that means failing.

DEFINE A PROBLEM

If your purpose is to propose a solution to a problem, you might begin your document by defining the problem. The students at one university use this strategy to introduce their essay proposing more bike lanes around campus:

> Surprisingly, despite the large number of students who bike to classes and work, Main Campus is severely lacking in bike lanes. We have noted with alarm the increase in motor vehicle accidents involving bikers along Stanhope Street, Broadway, and Central Street. This proposal calls for painted bike lanes, increased signage, and focused marketing efforts to ensure the safety of everyone on campus, regardless of their choice of transportation.

MAKE A SURPRISING STATEMENT

Grab your readers' attention by telling them something they don't already know. It's even better if the information is shocking, unusual, or strange. Consider, for example, how Salvatore Scibona opens a literacy narrative he published in *the New Yorker*.

> I did my best to flunk out of high school. I failed English literature, American literature, Spanish, precalculus, chemistry, physics. Once, in a fit of melancholic vanity, I burned my report card in the sink of the KFC where I worked scraping carbonized grease from the pressure cookers. I loved that job the way a dog loves a carcass in a ditch. I came home stinking of it. It was a prudent first career in that I wanted with certainty only one thing, to get out of Ohio, and the Colonel might hire me anywhere in the world. The starting wage was $3.85 an hour. I was saving for the future.

ASK A QUESTION

Asking a question invites your readers to become participants in the conversation. In the second paragraph of his introduction, Salvatore Scibona uses this technique to encourage readers to take an interest in his struggles as a writer.

> But wasn't it far-fetched, this notion of a future, when I could hardly get through eleventh grade? I always showed up at that job; why couldn't I show up at the desk in my room and write a C-minus summary of the life of Woodrow Wilson? The television stayed on day and night, singing like a Siren in the crowded house. "Come sit by me and die a little," it said.

TELL A STORY

Everyone loves a story, assuming that it's told well and has a point. You can use a story to introduce a subject to your readers, as featured writer Caitlin Guariglia does for her reflective essay about a trip to Italy (see Chapter 7).

Crash! The sound of metal hitting a concrete wall is my first vivid memory of Rome. Our tour bus could not get any farther down the tiny road because cars were parked along both sides. This, our bus driver told us, was illegal. He did not tell us, exactly; he grumbled it as he stepped out of the bus. He stood there with his hands on his hips, pondering the situation. Soon, people in the cars behind us started wandering up to stand next to the bus driver and ponder along with him. That, or they honked a great deal.

● PROVIDE A HISTORICAL ACCOUNT

Historical accounts can help your readers understand the origins of a situation and how the situation has changed over time. One writer compares the days of Henry Ford with the drivers of today to introduce her informative essay about moving toward a hydrogen economy.

> In the early twentieth century, the products of Henry Ford's assembly lines introduced Americans to the joys of the open road. Large, powerful automobiles quickly became a symbol of wealth and success. With record-high temperatures and rising tides, Americans today are being forced to take a good, long look at their choices. The SUVs, trucks, and minivans that continue to be popular are increasingly being viewed as symbols of excess and environmental irresponsibility, and a growing number of consumers prefer fuel-efficient hybrid or fully electric vehicles, like the successful Toyota Prius and the Tesla Model 3. In fact, some drivers have become so determined to escape their dangerous dependence on fossil fuels that they've begun to seek out alternative energy sources.

● LEAD WITH A QUOTATION

A quotation allows your readers to learn about the subject from someone who knows it well or has been affected by it. Anneke Jong, in her problem-solving article about how to help more women find careers in technology fields (see Chapter 11), quotes a computer science major at Stanford.

> Omosola Obetunde was lucky. Her parents sent her to computer science camp in 8th grade. "I didn't know it was computer science. I just thought it would be cool to make things." Seven years later, she's a computer science major at Stanford University.

● DRAW A CONTRAST

Drawing a contrast asks your readers to make a comparison.

> There was a time when telephones were single-purpose devices. If the phone rang, you answered. If you needed to call someone, you dialed their number. Text messages

and information at your fingertips were sci-fi speculation (and pretty wild speculation at that). Watching video? That was reserved for movie theaters, television, and home movies. Reading books? That was for libraries and bookstores. Directions? That was for maps — the kind that fold. (Remember those things?) Today, our telephones have become the answer to all of our questions. If you don't believe me, just ask Alexa, or Google, or Siri, or even Bixby.

- **PROVIDE A MAP**

The most direct way of signaling the organization of your document is to provide a map, or preview, of your supporting points in your introduction.

> This report will evaluate three approaches to treating attention deficit disorder in elementary school students: stimulant medications, training in organizational and time management skills, and a gluten-free diet.

How Can I Draft My Conclusion?

Your conclusion provides an opportunity to reinforce your message. It offers one last chance to achieve your purposes as a writer and to share your final thoughts about the subject with your readers. It also offers an opportunity to reinforce the way in which you've framed your main point.

Reinforce Your Points

At a minimum, your conclusion should sum up the major reasons you've offered to support your thesis statement. You might also want to restate your thesis statement (in different words) to reinforce your main point. If you didn't include an overt thesis statement in your introduction, consider stating your main point in your conclusion. Ending with a clear indication of what you want someone to think, believe, understand, or do as a result of reading your document gives you one final opportunity to influence your readers.

In her essay, featured writer Gabriella Guerrero summarizes the information she has provided in her informative essay about fast fashion (see Chapter 8).

> By following a more refined, well thought out routine daily, each of us can fight against the fast fashion industry and all of its negative consequences. The ability to breathe clean air and live in a safe environment is a fundamental human right. By choosing to make changes in our everyday life — whether small or big — we can end the damage inflicted by fast fashion.

We still have time to remedy the mistakes that we have made in our treatment of the environment. But that time is running short. If we do not make changes, we will fill up our land, water, and air with toxic dyes, chemicals, carbon dioxide, and non-degradable items.

Select a Concluding Strategy

Conclusions that summarize a document, like the one above, are common — and sometimes effective, especially when the writer has presented complex concepts. But a conclusion can do much more than simply restate your points. It can also give your readers an incentive to continue thinking about what they've read, to take action about the subject, or to read more about it.

As you draft, think about what you want to accomplish. You can choose from a range of strategies to write an effective conclusion.

● OFFER ADDITIONAL ANALYSIS

Extend your discussion of a subject by supplying additional insights. In her analysis essay about approaches to reducing art theft online, featured writer Kelsey Smith summarizes and reflects on the implications of inaction among the groups most involved in the issue (see Chapter 9).

> Art theft is steadily becoming an epidemic among the online art community and social media users and artists both have the ability to change this. The minor cases of art theft influence the actions of large companies, which furthers the misconception that artwork on the internet can be used freely. People need to understand that behind every piece of art there is a creator who invested time, money, and resources to create that piece and for individuals and companies to overlook that for their own selfish needs is unacceptable. It is essential that users become more educated in how art theft is detrimental to an artist's name and work, and artists must start taking measures to ensure the protection of their work. When users respect and support the original artist's work, it allows the artist to feel secure in sharing more of their art, which benefits both sides. If these two groups do not take action in preventative measures, art theft will only continue to rise in number and ruin the livelihood and careers of artists using social media.

● SPECULATE ABOUT THE FUTURE

Reflect on what might happen next. Justin Kanoya speculates about the role of Asian actors in future films in his review of *Crazy Rich Asians* (see Chapter 10).

Hopefully, we won't have to wait so long for the next one. And hopefully a positive portrayal of diversity and inclusion will just be the norm and not the occasional, once every couple decades thing it is now.

CLOSE WITH A QUOTATION

Select a quotation or paraphrase that does one of the following:

- offers deeper insight into the points you've made in your document
- points to the future of the subject
- suggests a solution to a problem
- illustrates what you would like to see happen
- makes a further observation about the subject
- presents a personalized viewpoint from someone who has experienced the subject you are portraying

Journalist Carly Lewis concludes her analytical article about publicizing the names of rapists (see Chapter 9) with a quotation from a victim whose story she had discussed earlier.

> Late last month, the creator of the Toronto Tumblr emailed to say she was no longer in pursuit of a legally sound way to keep the list of names online. "I can't believe how hard it is to speak up about abusers," she says.
>
> "To me, the problem clearly indicates a serious barrier in the way in which we deal with sexual assault," says Downard, of rape lists. "An act like this, if it is emblematic of a dysfunction in our society, it's just the canary in the coal mine."

CLOSE WITH A STORY

Tell a story about the subject you've discussed in your document. The story might suggest a potential solution to the problem, offer hope about a desired outcome, illustrate what might happen if a desired outcome isn't realized, or simply paint a picture of the issue. For instance, author Peter C. Baker concludes his analytical article (see Chapter 9) with a story that captures the essence of "nerd culture."

> At the reconvened MAGFest panel, it was clear that people were speaking the same language, reveling in both the debate and the shared obsessions. Chu stayed on stage for two hours more, then announced that he wanted a drink and invited anyone who wanted to keep talking upstairs to a hotel suite. A dozen nerds skipped the video-game hall, the board- and card-game rooms, and the live-action roleplay zone

and instead squeezed into an elevator together and headed up to keep debating, college-style, nerd culture's glory and excesses, its past and future. It felt optimistic, passionate, welcoming, and, sure, a little awkward: Chu's ideals made manifest. There was music playing from tiny laptop speakers, and someone had set up a disco ball. The crowd stayed for hours, nerding into the night.

● CLOSE WITH A QUESTION

Questions provide an effective means of inviting readers to consider the implications of the ideas explored in an essay. Reflecting on her childhood as an upper-class African American growing up in the Chicago suburbs in the 1950s, Margo Jefferson contrasts herself and her sister with another pair of African American girls, the daughters of their family's cleaning woman, Mrs. Blake. Jefferson closes the first chapter of her memoir with a compelling question about the impact of the wealthier girls' hand-me-down clothing (see Chapter 7).

> [The daughters] had the same initials we did. Mildred and Diane. Margo and Denise. Mother brought us to the front door to exchange hellos with them. Sometimes Mrs. Blake left carrying one or two bags of neatly folded clothes. Did Mildred and Diane enjoy unfolding, surveying, and fitting themselves into our used ensembles and separates?

● CALL YOUR READERS TO ACTION

Make a recommendation or urge your readers to do something specific. For example, you might ask them to participate in solving a problem by donating time, money, or effort to a project. Or you might ask them to write to someone, such as a politician or corporate executive, about an issue. Calls to action ask readers not just to accept what you've written but to do something about it, as entrepreneur Anneke Jong does in her problem-solving article about how to help more women find careers in technology fields.

> Plus, making investments to improve the pipeline of women in tech doesn't just benefit the next generation of girls, but it primes our economy for a boost in innovation. The female Mark Zuckerberg is out there, and it's within our power to make sure she follows her dream.

● LINK TO YOUR INTRODUCTION

This technique is sometimes called a "bookends" approach because it positions your introduction and conclusion as related ends of your document. The basic idea is to turn your conclusion into an extension of your introduction.

- If your introduction uses a quotation, end with a related quotation or respond to the quotation.
- If your introduction uses a story, extend that story or retell it with a different ending.
- If your introduction asks a question, answer the question, restate the question, or ask a new question.
- If your introduction defines a problem, provide a solution to the problem, restate the problem, or suggest that readers move on to a new problem.

Reinforce Your Efforts to Frame Your Subject or Issue

As you consider your choice of concluding strategy, keep in mind your main point and the manner in which you've chosen to frame it in your introduction and throughout your document. Your conclusion offers a final opportunity to reinforce your readers' understanding of your subject or issue. It allows you to highlight particular reasons for accepting your main point. And it allows you to direct their attention to the aspects of your subject or issue that you view as most important. A strong conclusion will leave your readers with a clear understanding of what you, as a writer, are contributing to the conversation.

In Summary: Drafting Your Document

★ Use your outline or map to begin drafting your document (p. 561).

★ Write clearly and effectively (p. 562).

★ Draft your introduction (p. 571).

★ Draft your conclusion (p. 577).

21 Using Sources Effectively

How can I use sources to accomplish my purposes as a writer? 583
Introduce a point 583
Contrast ideas 584
Provide evidence 585
Align yourself with an authority 585
Define a concept, illustrate a process, or clarify a statement 586
Set a mood 587
Provide an example 587
Amplify or qualify a point 587

How can I integrate sources into my draft? 588
Identify your sources 588
Quote strategically 590

Paraphrase information, ideas, and arguments 595
Summarize sources 596
Present numerical information 598
Use images, audio, and video 598

How can I ensure I've avoided plagiarism? 601
Quote, paraphrase, and summarize accurately and appropriately 601
Distinguish between your ideas and ideas in your sources 601
Check for unattributed sources in your document 603

How should I document my sources? 603
Choose a documentation system 603
Provide in-text references and publication information 604

Using evidence from sources can strengthen your document and show how knowledgeable you've become about the conversation you're joining. In this chapter, you'll learn how to integrate sources into your document and how to work with numerical information, images, audio, and video.

Much of the information in this chapter is based on MLA style, which is commonly used in the humanities (see Chapter 25). See Chapter 26 for guidelines on APA style, which is used in many social sciences.

How Can I Use Sources to Accomplish My Purposes as a Writer?

Your sources can help you introduce ideas, contrast the ideas of other authors with your own, provide evidence for your points, align yourself with an authority, define concepts, illustrate processes, clarify statements, set a mood, provide examples, and qualify or amplify a point. You can present information from sources in several ways:

- as a quotation, paraphrase, or summary
- as numerical information
- as illustrations such as images, audio, video, and animations

As you draft your document, consider how your use of sources might lead your readers to view your issue in terms that are most favorable to your purposes. By selecting source information carefully, you can make your points more directly than you could in your own words. Calling opponents of a proposal "inflexible" and "pig-headed," for example, might signal your biases too strongly. Quoting someone who uses those terms, however, allows you to get the point across without undermining an otherwise even and balanced tone.

The following are some of the most effective ways to use information, ideas, and arguments from sources as you contribute to a written conversation about a subject.

Introduce a Point

You can use a quotation, paraphrase, or summary to introduce a point to your readers.

QUOTATION USED TO INTRODUCE A POINT

"When I came around the corner, a black bear was standing in the middle of the trail," said Joan Gibson, an avid hiker. "We stared at each other for a moment, wondering who would make the first move. Then the bear looked off to the right and shambled up the mountain. I guess I wasn't worth the trouble." Joan Gibson's story, like those of most hikers who encounter bears in the woods, ends happily. But the growing encroachment of humans on rural areas once left largely to wildlife is causing difficulties not only for people who enjoy spending time in the wide-open spaces but also for the animals that make those spaces their home.

PARAPHRASE USED TO INTRODUCE A POINT

A *New York Times* article recently reported that human-bear encounters in Yosemite National Park, which had been on the decline during most of the last decade, have more than doubled in the past year (Spiegel A4). Although no humans have been injured and only one incident resulted in a decision to destroy a bear, park officials point to the uptick in encounters as a warning sign that . . .

Your choice of a quotation or paraphrase will frame the point you want to make, calling your readers' attention to a specific aspect of an idea or argument and laying the groundwork for a response. Think about how the following quotation leads readers to view a public debate about education reform as a battle between reformers and an entrenched teachers union.

> "The teachers union has balked at even the most reasonable proposals for school reform," said Mary Sweeney, press secretary for Save Our Schools, which has sponsored a referendum on the November ballot calling for funding for their voucher plan. "We believe the November election will send a wake-up call about the need to rethink their obstructionist behaviors."
>
> If Sweeney and supporters of Referendum D are successful, the educational landscape in . . .

Phrases such as "balked at even the most reasonable proposals" and "their obstructionist behaviors" place the blame for the problem on the teachers union.

In contrast, note how the following quotation frames the debate as a question of how best to spend scarce education funds.

> "In the past decade, state and local funding of public education in real dollars has declined by 7.2 percent," said Jeffrey Allister, state chair of the governor's Special Commission on Education Reform. "Referendum D, if passed, would further erode that funding by shifting state dollars to private schools." As the state considers the merits of Referendum D, which would institute a statewide voucher program, opponents of the measure have . . .

Phrases such as "funding of public education in real dollars has declined" and "further erode that funding" call attention to the financial challenges faced by schools.

Contrast Ideas

When you want to indicate that disagreement exists on a subject, you can use source information to illustrate the nature and intensity of the disagreement. The following example uses partial quotations (see *Use Partial, Complete, or Block Quotations* later in this chapter) to highlight differences in proposed solutions to a problem.

> Solutions to the state's higher education funding shortfall range from traditional approaches, such as raising taxes, to more radical solutions, among them privatizing state colleges and universities. Advocates of increased taxes, such as Page Richards of the Higher Education Coalition, argue that declines in state funding of higher education "must be reversed immediately or we will find ourselves in a situation where we are closing rural community colleges and only the wealthiest among us will have access to the best education" (A4). Those in favor of privatizing higher education

suggest, however, that free-market approaches will ultimately bring about "a fairer situation in which the poor, many of whom have no interest in higher education, are no longer asked to subsidize higher and higher faculty salaries and larger football stadiums" (Pieters 23).

Base your choices about how to contrast ideas on the clarity and length of your sources and on the effects you hope to achieve. If you want to express complex ideas as concisely as possible, you might use paraphrase and summary. If you want to convey the emotional qualities of an author's position on a subject, use quotations.

Provide Evidence

Documents that consist of a series of unsupported assertions amount to little more than a request for the reader's trust. Even when the writer is eminently trustworthy, most readers find such documents easy to dismiss. In contrast, providing evidence to support your assertions increases the likelihood that your readers will accept your main point. Note the differences between the following passages.

UNSUPPORTED ASSERTION

> Given a choice between two products of comparable quality, reputation, and cost, American consumers are far more likely to purchase goods that use environmentally friendly packaging. Encouraging the use of such packaging is a good idea for America.

No evidence is provided to support the writer's assertion.

SUPPORTED ASSERTION

> Given a choice between two products of comparable quality, reputation, and cost, American consumers are far more likely to purchase goods that use environmentally friendly packaging. A recent study by the High Plains Research Institute found that the shelf life of several biodegradable plastics not only exceeded the shelf life of the products they were used to package but also cost less to produce (Chen and Lohann 33). In addition, a study by the Consumer Products Institute found that, when made aware that products were packaged in environmentally friendly materials, consumers were more likely to buy those products (271).

Summaries of the results of two studies provide evidence for the assertion made in the first sentence.

Similarly, visual sources can lend support to an assertion. An assertion about the unintended consequences of military action, for example, might be accompanied by a photograph of a war-torn street or a wounded child (see *Use Images, Audio, and Video* later in this chapter).

Align Yourself with an Authority

Aligning yourself with an authority — such as a subject-matter expert, a scientist, a politician, or a religious figure — allows you to borrow someone else's credibility and status. Start by making an assertion and follow it with supporting information from a source, such as a quotation, paraphrase, or summary.

New developments in computers and robotics promise to bring about significant changes in both the workplace and daily life. "We are nearing the point where computers and robots will be able to see, move, and interact naturally, unlocking many new applications and empowering people even more," said Bill Gates, cofounder and former chairman of Microsoft Corporation (as quoted in Fried).

> *The quotation was found in an article by Ina Fried.*

Giving Credit to the Source

According to Joel Levine and Lawrence May, authors of *Getting In*, entrance exams are an extremely important part of a student's college application and carry a great deal of weight. In fact, they claim that a college entrance examination is "one of the two most significant factors" in getting into college (the other, unsurprisingly, is high school grades).

> *The attribution "they claim" credits the source of the information to Levine and May.*
>
> *Quotation marks are used to indicate a partial quotation.*

Examples of Attribution in MLA Style

According to Scott McPherson . . .

Jill Bedard writes . . .

Tom Huckin reports . . .

Kate Kiefer observes . . .

Bob Phelps suggests . . .

In the words of William Hochman . . .

As Shirley Guitron tells it . . .

Shaun Beaty indicates . . .

Jessica Richards calls our attention to . . .

> *If you are using APA style, use past tense or present perfect tense to make attributions.*

Define a Concept, Illustrate a Process, or Clarify a Statement

Writers commonly turn to information from sources when that information is clearer and more concise than what they might write themselves. For example, to define a concept, you might quote or paraphrase a dictionary or an encyclopedia. To help readers understand a complex process, such as the steps involved in cellular respiration, you might use an illustration.

Writers also use information from sources to clarify their statements. A writer might explain a point by providing examples from sources or by using quotations or paraphrases to back up an assertion.

> Studies have found connections between weight loss and coffee intake. This doesn't mean that drinking a couple of cups of coffee each day leads to weight loss. However, three recent studies reported that individuals who increased their coffee intake from fewer than three cups to more than eight cups of coffee per day experienced weight losses of up to 7% over a two-month period (Chang; Johnson and Salazar; Neiman). "It may be that increased caffeine intake led to a higher metabolic level, which in turn led to weight loss," noted John Chang, a senior researcher at the Centers for Disease Control. "Or it might be that drinking so much coffee depressed participants' appetites" (232).

Set a Mood

You can also choose quotations and illustrations with an eye toward establishing an overall mood for your readers. The emotional impact of images of a celebration at a sporting event, an expression of grief at a funeral, or a calming mountain vista can lead your readers to react in specific ways to your document. Similarly, a striking quote, such as "The screams of pain coming out of that room will stay with me as long as I live," can evoke a particular mood in your readers.

Provide an Example

It's often better to show with an example than to tell with a general description. Examples provide concrete evidence in your document. Featured writer Caitlin Guariglia uses an example from a well-known film to illustrate a point in her essay about her family's relationship with food (see her essay in Chapter 7).

> And the obsession with eating! My grandmother feeds us constantly. My dad and I always laugh at that scene in Goodfellas where the mobsters show up at two in the morning after killing someone, and one mobster's mother whips up a full pasta meal for them. We know that my grandmother would do the same thing: "Are you hungry? Here, sit, eat!" Grandma holds interventions over pasta. If she is unhappy with something someone in the family is doing, she invites everyone over for pasta, and we hash it out together.

Amplify or Qualify a Point

You can use amplification to expand the scope of a point. In an argumentative essay written for a first-year composition course, for example, a writer draws on information from a source to broaden the discussion of the dangers of puppy mills.

> Several other states have adopted laws that cap the number of puppies living in any one location, a moderate solution that at the very least remediates the mistreatment of animals in these facilities due to overcrowding (Widner 235).

Qualifications, in contrast, allow you to narrow the scope of a statement, reducing the possibility that your readers might misunderstand your meaning. The same writer makes it clear that the existing law does not require sufficient inspections of puppy mill breeders.

> Unfortunately, the AWA is poorly defined and difficult to enforce. First, as a federal law designed to regulate interstate transactions, it requires inspections of animal dealers — breeders who sell to pet stores or other outlets — only. Puppy mills who sell directly to the public circumvent these inspections (Burger 263).

How Can I Integrate Sources into My Draft?

You can integrate information, ideas, and arguments from sources into your draft by quoting, paraphrasing, summarizing, presenting numerical information, and using illustrations. As you do so, be sure to distinguish your ideas and information from those found in your sources.

Identify Your Sources

You should identify the sources of information in your document for several reasons. First, doing so fulfills your ethical obligation to document your sources. Second, it allows you (and your readers) to recognize the boundaries between your ideas and those borrowed from sources. Third, it can help you strengthen your document by calling attention to the qualifications or experiences of the person whose ideas you are incorporating.

- **USE ATTRIBUTIONS AND IN-TEXT CITATIONS**

Whenever you quote, paraphrase, or summarize, distinguish between your ideas and the information you obtained from your sources by using attributions — brief comments such as "according to" or "as the author points out" — to alert your readers that the point is not your own.

Writers who use the MLA or APA documentation system also provide citations — or acknowledgments of source information — within the text of their documents to indicate where borrowed material ends. These citations, in turn, refer readers to a list of works cited or a list of references at the end of the document.

Note the following examples, which use attributions and in-text citations.

MLA Style

Ellen Page argues, "Education reform is the best solution for fixing our public schools" (22).

"Education reform is the best solution for fixing our public schools" (Page 22).

APA Style

Ellen Page (2021) has argued, "Education reform is the best solution for fixing our public schools" (p. 22).

"Education reform is the best solution for fixing our public schools" (Page, 2021, p. 22).

> Attributions identify the author of the quotations.

> MLA-style in-text citations include the author's name and exact page reference.

> APA-style in-text citations include the author's name, publication date, and exact page reference.

When you acknowledge material you've borrowed from sources, try to vary the wording of your attributions. Be aware, however, that the verbs in attributions can convey important shades of meaning. For example, saying that someone "alleged" something is quite different from saying that someone "confirmed" something.

Keep in mind that the form your attributions take will depend on your citation style. MLA recommends present tense ("the author points out"), while APA recommends past tense ("the author pointed out") or present perfect tense ("the author has explained"). These examples follow the MLA recommendations.

Some Common Attributions in MLA Style

according to	claims	expresses	remarks
acknowledges	comments	inquires	reports
affirms	confirms	interprets	says
alleges	declares	muses	states
asks	denies	notes	suggests
asserts	describes	observes	thinks
assumes	disputes	points out	wonders
believes	emphasizes	recalls	writes

> To use these attributions in a document that follows APA style, put them in past or present perfect tense.

You can learn more about in-text citations in Chapter 25 (MLA style) and Chapter 26 (APA style).

● PROVIDE A CONTEXT

Skilled writers know the importance of providing a context for the source information they include in their documents. It's not enough to simply put text within two quotation marks and move on. Such "orphan quotations" — quotations dropped into a paragraph without any introduction — are confusing. Worse, paraphrases and summaries inserted without context can easily be mistaken for plagiarism.

To provide a clear context for your source information, establish why the quotation, paraphrase, or summary is reliable by identifying the source's credentials. In addition, indicate how it relates to your main idea and what it contributes to the point you are making. If you don't, readers will wonder why it's there.

> Description of the findings

> Attribution identifies the source as experts.

> The writer follows MLA style; a parenthetical citation identifies the page number where the quotation was found.

However, Wechsler et al. analyzed trends at schools using social norms marketing and revealed that the campaigns did not necessarily decrease student drinking; in some cases, schools even reported higher alcohol consumption, according to seven criteria that measured whether students drank, how much, and how often. The team from the Harvard School of Public Health's College Alcohol Study suggested that because social norms marketing was first developed at a small school that wasn't very diverse, it might not be as suitable for schools with many different kinds of people. As the researchers explained, "Individual students' drinking behaviors align more closely to the drinking behaviors of their immediate social group rather than to the overall student population at a given school" (492).

Quote Strategically

A well-chosen quotation can have a powerful impact on your readers' perception of your main point and on the overall quality of your document. Quotations can also add a sense of immediacy by bringing in the voice of someone who has been affected by a subject or can lend a sense of authority to your document by conveying the words of an expert. Quotations can range in form from brief partial quotations to extended block quotations. As you integrate quotations, you might need to modify them to suit your purpose and to fit the flow of your sentences. When you do, be careful to punctuate them properly.

Learn more about quoting from sources in *How Can I Take Notes?* in Chapter 4.

● USE PARTIAL, COMPLETE, OR BLOCK QUOTATIONS

Quotations can be parts of sentences (partial), whole sentences (complete), or long passages (block). When you choose one type of quotation over another, consider the length and complexity of the passage as well as the obligation to convey ideas and information fairly.

Partial quotations can be a single word, a phrase, or most of a sentence. They are often used to convey a well-turned phrase or to complete a sentence using important words from a source, as in the following example.

> Weitzman notes that by changing the "contextual forces," such as the availability of alcohol, that encourage students to drink, this approach more strongly emphasizes policies that directly put a stop to excessive drinking — unlike the social norms marketing approach, which relies on influencing individual behavior (187).

Quotation marks indicate the borrowed phrase.

Source information, including the page number containing the quotation, is clearly identified.

Complete quotations are typically one or more full sentences and are most often used when the meaning of the passage cannot be conveyed adequately by a few well-chosen words, as in the following example.

> I smiled when I read Elizabeth Gilbert's memoir Eat, Pray, Love. Gilbert writes, "The Neapolitan women in particular are such a gang of tough-voiced, loud-mouthed, generous, nosy dames, all bossy and annoyed and right up in your face just trying to friggin' help you for chrissake, you dope — why they gotta do everything around here?" (78).

Block quotations are extended quotations (usually four or more typed lines) that are set off in a block from the rest of the text. In general, use a colon to introduce the quotation, indent the entire quotation one inch from the left margin, and include source information according to the documentation system you are using (such as MLA or APA). Since the blocked text indicates that you are quoting directly, you do not need to include quotation marks.

> Instead of cutting education funding, states should provide more money for schools, especially now when jobs are scarce and even trained workers are eager to return to school. Patrick Callan, president of the National Center for Public Policy and Higher Education, observes:
>
> > When the economy is good, and state universities are somewhat better funded, we raise tuition as little as possible. When the economy is bad, we raise tuition and sock it to families, when people can least afford it. That's exactly the opposite of what we need. (qtd. in Lewin)

Parenthetical citation indicates that this material was quoted in another source. In block quotations, the citation information is placed after the period.

● MODIFY QUOTATIONS APPROPRIATELY

You can modify quotations to fit your draft. It is acceptable, for example, to delete unnecessary words or to change the tense of a word in a partial quotation so that it fits your sentence. Keep in mind, however, that writers have an obligation to quote sources accurately and fairly. You should indicate when you have added or deleted words, and you should not modify quotations in a way that distorts their meaning. The most useful strategies for modifying quotations include using an ellipsis mark (. . .) to indicate deleted words, using brackets ([ ]) to clarify meaning, and using "sic" to note errors in a source.

Modify a direct quotation using ellipsis marks. When only part of a passage relates to your writing project, you might want to quote only that part in your document. To indicate that you have changed a quotation by deleting words, use three spaced periods, called an ellipsis mark (. . .). If you don't, your readers will assume that the quotation you are presenting is identical to the text found in the source.

ORIGINAL PASSAGE

[A]s a result of the skyrocketing costs of his programs, particularly the war, Johnson came under pressure to find funds. The conservative coalition of southern Democrats and Republicans on Capitol Hill, led by Ways and Means Committee Chairman Wilbur Mills, insisted that he cut social programs if he wanted the tax increase. Their strength had been bolstered by the midterm elections that cut into the liberal majorities born in November 1964. Johnson, who hesitated as long as possible to ask for a tax increase, finally bit the bullet in January 1967 and made his request to Congress . . .

Source: Julian E. Zelizer. "Blowing Up the Deficit Is Part of the Plan." The Atlantic. December 19, 2017. https://www.theatlantic.com/politics/archive/2017/12/blowing-up-the-deficit-is-part-of-the-plan/548720/

Quotation Modified Correctly Using Ellipsis Marks

"[A]s federal coffers started to dwindle as a result of the skyrocketing costs of his programs, particularly the war, Johnson came under pressure to find funds," wrote Julian E. Zelizer in *The Atlantic* in 2017. "The conservative coalition of southern Democrats and Republicans on Capitol Hill . . . insisted that he cut social programs if he wanted the tax increase. . . . Johnson, who hesitated as long as possible to ask for a tax increase, finally . . . made his request to Congress based on the rising deficits and the inflationary pressure they brought" (par. 6).

> Three periods indicate that material was deleted from within a sentence.

> Four periods indicate the deletion of one or more full sentences.

Modify a direct quotation using brackets. To modify a direct quotation by changing or adding words, use brackets ([ ]). If you don't, readers will assume that the quotation you are presenting is identical to the text found in the source.

The following example shows the use of brackets to change the tense of a verb in a partial quotation.

ORIGINAL QUOTATION

"They treated us like family and refused to accept a tip."

MODIFIED QUOTATION

It's a place where the staff treats you "like family and refuse[s] to accept a tip," said travel writer Melissa Ancomi.

[Brackets indicate that the tense of a word has been changed.]

Modify quotations using "sic." If a passage you are quoting contains a misspelled word or an incorrect fact, use the word "sic" in brackets to indicate that the error occurred in the original passage. If you don't, your readers might think that the mistake is yours.

QUOTATION MODIFIED CORRECTLY USING "SIC"

"Former President Tump's [sic] interest in economic initiatives strongly shaped his foreign policy agenda" (Vincent 221).

● PUNCTUATE QUOTATIONS CORRECTLY

Use the following rules for punctuating quotations:

- Use double quotation marks (" ") around partial or complete quotations. Do not use quotation marks for block quotations.
- Use single quotation marks (' ') to indicate quoted material within a quotation.

    "The hotel manager told the guests to 'make yourselves at home.' "

- Place commas and periods inside quotation marks.
- Place question marks and exclamation points outside quotation marks if the punctuation pertains to the entire sentence rather than the quotation. In the following example, the original quotation is not a question, so the question mark should be placed after the quotation mark.

    But what can be gained from following the committee's recommendation that the state should "avoid, without exceptions, any proposed tax hike"?

- Place question marks and exclamation points inside quotation marks if the punctuation pertains to the quotation itself.

    Dawn Smith asked a critical question: "Do college students understand the importance of avoiding running up the debt on their credit cards?"

- Place colons and semicolons outside quotation marks.

  > Many college students consider themselves "free at last"; all too often, however, they find that freedom has its costs.

- When citation information is provided after a partial or complete quotation, place the punctuation mark (comma, period, semicolon, colon, or question mark) after the parenthetical citation.

  > "Preliminary reports have been consistent," Yates notes. "Without immediate changes to current practices, we will deplete known oil supplies by mid-century" (335).

- At the end of a block quotation, place the final punctuation before the parenthetical citation (see *Quote Strategically* earlier in this chapter).

- Use three spaced periods (an ellipsis mark) to indicate an omission within a sentence.

  > According to critic Joe Robinson, Americans are overworked: "Ask Americans how things are really going and you'll hear stories of . . . fifty- and sixty-hour weeks with no letup in sight" (467).

- Place a period before the ellipsis mark to indicate an omission at the end of a sentence.

  > The most recent information indicates, says Chen, that "we can expect a significant increase in costs by the end of the decade. . . . Those costs, however, should ramp up slowly" (35).

Checklist for Quoting

✔ **Identify the source of the quotation.**

✔ **Punctuate the quotation appropriately.**

✔ **Use ellipsis marks, brackets, and "sic" as necessary.**

✔ **Check each quotation against the source** to be sure you aren't introducing errors or misrepresenting the source.

✔ **Use transitions and attributions** to integrate the quotation effectively into your draft.

✔ **Ensure that the source is cited in your works cited (MLA) or reference (APA) list.**

Paraphrase Information, Ideas, and Arguments

A paraphrase is a restatement, in your own words, of a passage from a source. Paraphrases can be used to illustrate or support a point you make in your document or to illustrate another author's ideas or argument about a subject. Writers choose to paraphrase rather than quote when a paraphrase would present the point more clearly or concisely than would a quotation from a source. Writers also choose to use paraphrases to add variety to a document — particularly when a large number of quotations have already been used — or when they find that the original passage would alter the tone or style of their document. For example, a writer of an article about a band that was purposefully pushing the boundaries of contemporary music might want to note that an important music reviewer had written, "I found this 'concert' to be a complete waste of my time." If the writer had already quoted more compelling statements from several other reviewers, however, the writer might use a paraphrase to indicate that the reviewer had found little in the band's most recent concert to recommend their music.

Learn more about paraphrasing in *How Can I Take Notes?* in Chapter 3.

● ENSURE THE ACCURACY AND FAIRNESS OF EACH PARAPHRASE

Your notes are likely to include a number of paraphrases of information, ideas, and arguments from your sources. Before you integrate a paraphrase into your document, make sure that it is an accurate and fair representation of the source. Reread the source and double-check your paraphrase against it. Then revise the paraphrase as necessary so that it fits the context and tone of your document. Be sure not only that you have conveyed the meaning of the passage fairly and accurately but also that the wording and sentence structure differ from those in the original passage.

● INTEGRATE EACH PARAPHRASE INTO YOUR DOCUMENT

Use author attributions and transitions to help readers distinguish your ideas, information, and arguments from those drawn from your sources. Be sure to cite the source in the text and in your works cited list or references list (see Chapters 25 and 26).

In the following example, note how readers can see where the writer's statement ends and where the support for the statement, in the form of a paraphrase, begins.

> As digital music and video gained popularity, inventors assumed that the same rules would apply to the new hardware and software they developed for digital files. Instead, the Digital Millennium Copyright Act let music, computer, gaming, and other companies restrict technology and research that could have been used to get around their restrictions — including research that would have helped address computer security (Electronic Frontier Foundation).

The writer's idea

Source of paraphrase (in this case, a web document) is cited per MLA style.

> **Checklist for Paraphrasing**
>
> ✔ **Identify the source of the paraphrased material.**
>
> ✔ **Compare the original passage with your paraphrase.** Make sure that you have conveyed the meaning of the passage but that the wording and sentence structure differ from those in the original passage.
>
> ✔ **Use transitions and attributions** to integrate the paraphrase smoothly into your draft.
>
> ✔ **Ensure that the source is cited in your works cited (MLA) or reference (APA) list.**

Summarize Sources

A summary is a concise statement, written in your own words, of the information, ideas, and arguments found in a source. When you integrate a summary into your draft, review the source to make sure your summary is an accurate and fair representation of the source. In addition, be sure to identify the source in the text and include a citation in your works cited or reference list.

Learn more about summarizing sources in *How Can I Take Notes?* in Chapter 4.

You can summarize an entire source, part of a source, or a group of sources to support your ideas.

● SUMMARIZE AN ENTIRE SOURCE

Writers frequently summarize an entire work. In some cases, the summary might occupy one or more paragraphs or be integrated into a discussion contained in one or more paragraphs. In other cases, the summary might be as brief as a single sentence.

In an analytical essay about the health risks faced by overweight athletes, a student writer offers a brief, "nutshell" summary of another source.

> In an editorial in the medical journal *Neurosurgery*, three sports-medicine specialists noted that after a 1994 federal law exempted dietary supplements from regulation by the Food and Drug Administration, heat-related injuries among football players began to rise (Bailes et al., 2002).

The writer uses APA style, which includes the publication year.

The entire source is summarized; because it is a summary, not a direct quotation, page numbers are not necessary.

● SUMMARIZE SPECIFIC INFORMATION AND IDEAS FROM A SOURCE

You can also use summaries to convey key information or ideas from a source. In the following example, the writer of an essay summarizes a section of a book about college admissions. The summary is highlighted.

Bill Paul, author of *Getting In: Inside the College Admissions Process*, a book that tells the stories of several students applying to an elite Ivy League institution, shares three suggestions for students who want to get into a college. Paul bases these suggestions on his discussions with Fred Hargadon, a former dean of admissions at Princeton. Hargadon suggested that the best way students can enhance their chances for acceptance into the college of their choice is to read widely, learn to speak a second language, and engage in activities that interest and excite them and that also help them develop their confidence and creativity (235–49).

Summary is introduced with the author of the book, title, and specific source of the ideas.

Per MLA style, exact pages are cited.

● SUMMARIZE A GROUP OF SOURCES

In addition to summarizing a single source, writers often summarize groups of sources. Such collective summaries (often introduced by phrases such as "Numerous authors argue . . ." or "The research in this area seems to indicate that . . .") allow you to establish a point briefly and with authority. They are particularly effective at the beginning of a document, when you are establishing the nature of the conversation you are joining, and can serve as a transitional device when you move from one major section of the document to another.

When you summarize a group of sources, separate the citations with a semicolon. MLA guidelines require including author and page information, as in the following example.

> Several critics argue that the Hemingway code hero is not always male (Graulich 217; Sherman 78; Watters 33).

In APA style, the author and the date of publication must be included.

> The benefits of early detection of breast cancer have been well documented (Page, 2018; Richards, 2017; Vincent, 2018).

Checklist for Summarizing

✔ **Identify the source of the summarized material.**

✔ **Ensure that you have summarized the source in your own words.** Make sure that you do not merely string together a series of close paraphrases of key passages.

✔ **Use transitions and attributions** to integrate the summary smoothly into your draft.

✔ **Ensure that the source is cited in your works cited (MLA) or reference (APA) list.**

Present Numerical Information

If it suits your subject, you might use numerical information, such as statistics, in your document. You can present this information within sentences. Or you might use tables, charts, or graphs.

If you use tables, charts, or graphs, you still need to accurately and fairly present the numerical information in your document and clearly identify the source of the data, just as you would for textual information. For more information about using tables, charts, and graphs, see *Use Illustrations* in Chapter 22.

Use Images, Audio, and Video

Including images in your print document or adding images, audio, or video files to your electronic document can enhance its effectiveness. Use caution, however, when taking images and audio or video files from other sources. Simply copying a photograph or an audio or video clip into your document might be a form of plagiarism (see Chapter 17).

One student writer carefully documented the source of an image used in an informative essay. Because the writer was composing an academic essay — rather than a document intended for publication and wide distribution — the writer did not seek permission to use it. (In contrast, the publisher of this book sought and received permission to publish that image.)

If you are creating an electronic document, such as a web page or a multimedia presentation, use the following guidelines to integrate digital illustrations:

- Make a link between your document and a document that contains an image, a sound clip, or a video clip — rather than copying the illustration and placing it in your document.
- If it isn't possible or appropriate to create a link to another document, contact the owner of the image, sound clip, or video clip for permission to use it.
- If you cannot reach the owner, review the fair-use guidelines discussed in Chapter 17 for guidance about using the material.

As you would for any sources you cite in your document, make sure you fairly present images, audio, or video and identify the author or creator.

Only by investing in educating their citizens during hard economic times will states see the benefits of having educated workers and business owners—and higher-earning taxpayers—in the state during better times. For this reason, higher education should be a top priority in even trimmed-down state budgets so that students and their families won't face drastic increases in tuition.

At the same time, students still ultimately bear the responsibility for finding the best path to an affordable college education. Students and their families are a necessary part of the solution. They should be willing to apply to a variety of schools, including those they can afford more easily without financial aid. Many students and their families are now considering less expensive routes to a college degree, such as enrolling in public universities or community colleges in their home states (Saleh). Out of eighty-seven college freshmen surveyed at Colorado State University, 80% were likely to recommend community college to a sibling or friend concerned about tuition costs (Tillson). When asked about the benefits of attending community college, students responded that they saw it as "easier to afford" and appreciated that it "makes it easier to work and attend school at the same time" (see Fig. 1). The survey shows that students today are giving community colleges serious thought as an alternative to a four-year university.

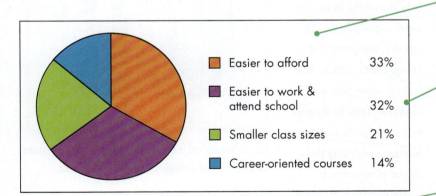

Fig.1: The perceived benefits of choosing a community college. Based on survey data from Tillson.

▲ A chart presenting information in an essay

the most promising alternatives in development is hydrogen—an abundant fuel that is environmentally safe, is far more versatile than gasoline or diesel, can be used to create electricity and fuel internal combustion engines, and produces no waste. Because of these attributes, some experts have argued that a hydrogen economy—an energy system that uses only a hydrogen-oxygen reaction to create energy and electricity—could solve many fuel-related problems, from global warming to America's dependence on foreign oil (Crabtree, Dresselhause, and Buchanan 39). At first glance, hydrogen appears to be the perfect choice. However, three barriers stand in the way of widespread hydrogen usage: as a fuel, it is expensive to produce, difficult to store, and complicated to distribute.

The key to a hydrogen economy is the fuel cell, which uses hydrogen gas and oxygen to produce electricity. In a way, a fuel cell is like a battery, but it never requires charging and it produces only electricity, heat, and water vapor (see Fig. 1). The U.S. Department of Energy (DOE) explains that hydrogen fuel cells use electrode plates to separate hydrogen's protons and electrons, diverting the stream of electrons to create electricity. A "stack" of fuel cells is scalable, so the same basic structure has many different uses ("Hydrogen Fuel"). In theory, stacks of hydrogen fuel

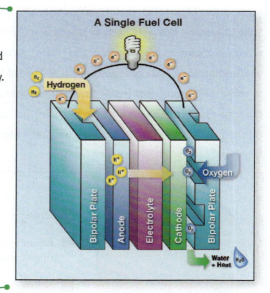

Fig.1: Simplified model of a fuel cell. United States Department of Energy, "Hydrogen Fuel Cells."

▲ An image providing an overview of a complex process

How Can I Ensure I've Avoided Plagiarism?

Because plagiarized material will often differ in style, tone, and word choice from the rest of your document, your readers are likely to notice these differences and wonder whether you've plagiarized the material — or, if not, why you've written a document that has so many stylistic inconsistencies. If your readers react negatively, it's unlikely that your document will be successful.

You can avoid plagiarism by quoting, paraphrasing, and summarizing accurately and appropriately; distinguishing between your ideas and ideas in your sources; and identifying sources in your document.

Learn more about understanding and avoiding plagiarism in Chapter 17.

Quote, Paraphrase, and Summarize Accurately and Appropriately

Unintentional plagiarism usually occurs when a writer takes poor notes and then uses the information from those notes in a document. As you draft, do the following:

- Look for notes that differ from your usual style of writing. More often than not, if a note doesn't sound like your own writing, it isn't.
- Place quotation marks around any direct quotations, use ellipsis marks and brackets appropriately (see *Punctuate Quotations Correctly* earlier in this chapter), and identify the source and the page or paragraph number of the quotation.
- Make sure that paraphrases differ significantly in word choice and sentence structure from the passage being paraphrased, and identify the source and page or paragraph number from which you took the paraphrase.
- Make sure that summaries are not just a series of passages or close paraphrases copied from the source.

Distinguish between Your Ideas and Ideas in Your Sources

Failing to distinguish between your ideas and ideas drawn from your sources can lead readers to think other writers' ideas are yours. Examine how the following passage fails to distinguish the writer's ideas from those of Joel Levine and Lawrence May, authors of a source used in the essay.

FAILING TO CREDIT IDEAS TO A SOURCE

According to Joel Levine and Lawrence May, authors of *Getting In*, entrance exams are an extremely important part of a student's college application and carry a great deal of weight. In fact, a college entrance examination is one of the two most significant factors in getting into college. The other, unsurprisingly, is high school grades.

Because the second and third sentences fail to identify Levine and May as the source of the information about the second important factor affecting admissions decisions — high school grades — the passage implies that the writer is the source of that information.

As it turns out, the writer actually included the necessary attribution in the essay.

GIVING CREDIT TO THE SOURCE

According to Joel Levine and Lawrence May, authors of *Getting In*, entrance exams are an extremely important part of a student's college application and carry a great deal of weight. In fact, **they claim** that a college entrance examination is **"one of the two most significant factors"** in getting into college (the other, unsurprisingly, is high school grades).

> The attribution "they claim" credits the source of the information to Levine and May.

> Quotation marks are used to indicate a partial quotation.

You can use attributions to distinguish between your ideas and those obtained from your sources. As you draft your document, use the name of an author or the title of the source you're drawing from each time you introduce ideas from a source.

Examples of Attribution in MLA Style

According to Scott McPherson . . .

Jill Bedard writes . . .

Tom Huckin reports . . .

Kate Kiefer observes . . .

Bob Phelps suggests . . .

In the words of William Hochman . . .

As Shirley Guitron tells it . . .

Shaun Beaty indicates . . .

Jessica Richards calls our attention to . . .

> If you are using APA style, use past tense or present perfect tense to make attributions.

Check for Unattributed Sources in Your Document

Writers sometimes neglect to identify the sources from which they have drawn their information. You should include a complete citation for each source you refer to in your document. The citation should appear in the text of the document (as an in-text citation, footnote, or endnote) and in its works cited (MLA) or reference (APA) list. If you used a source to gain an understanding of the issue, but do not cite the source in the text of your document, you may also include it in a bibliography.

The following examples use MLA style for citing sources; more detailed information about the sources appears in a list of works cited at the end of the document. In the first example, the writer uses a combination of attribution and parenthetical information; in the second example, the writer provides only a parenthetical citation.

> Reid Vincent argues, "We must explore emerging energy technologies before we reach a peak oil crisis" (322).
>
> Some critics argue that "we must explore emerging energy technologies before we reach a peak oil crisis" (Vincent 322).

MLA-style in-text citations include the author's name and exact page reference.

How Should I Document My Sources?

In addition to citing your sources within the text of your document, you should provide complete publication information for each source you've used. Fully documenting your sources can help you achieve your purposes as a writer, such as establishing your authority and persuading your readers. Documenting your sources also helps you avoid plagiarism, gives credit to others who have written about a subject, and creates a record of their work that your readers can follow and build on.

Choose a Documentation System

The documentation systems most commonly used in academic disciplines are the following:

- **MLA.** This style, developed by the Modern Language Association, is used primarily in the humanities — English, philosophy, linguistics, world languages, and so on. See Chapter 25.

- **APA.** Developed by the American Psychological Association, this style is used mainly in the social sciences — psychology, sociology, anthropology, political science, economics, education, and so on. See Chapter 26.
- *Chicago.* Developed by the University of Chicago Press, this style is used primarily in history, journalism, and the humanities. See chicagomanualofstyle.org.
- **CSE.** This style, developed by the Council of Science Editors (formerly the Council of Biology Editors), is used mainly in the physical and life sciences — chemistry, geology, biology, botany, and so on — and in mathematics. See writing.colostate.edu/guides/guide.cfm?guideid=12 and writing.colostate.edu/guides/guide.cfm?guideid=13.

Your choice of documentation system will be guided by the discipline or field within which you are writing and by any documentation requirements associated with your writing project. If your project has been assigned to you, ask the person who assigned it or someone who has written a similar document which documentation system you should use. If you are working on a project for a writing class, your instructor will usually tell you which documentation system to follow.

Your choice of documentation system will also be guided by the genre you have chosen for your document. For example, while academic essays and articles appearing in scholarly journals typically use a documentation system such as MLA or APA, newspaper and magazine articles often do not; instead, they identify sources in the main text of the document rather than in a works cited or reference list. If you write a digital document that cites other online sources, you might simply link to those sources.

Provide In-Text References and Publication Information

The specific format of your in-text citations will depend on the documentation system you are following. If you use MLA or APA style, you will refer to sources in the text of your document using a combination of attributions and parenthetical information and will include a list of sources at the end of your document. The works cited list (MLA) or reference list (APA) includes the following key publication information about each source:

- author(s) and/or editor(s)
- title
- publication date
- publisher (for books)
- periodical name, volume, issue, and page numbers (for articles)
- DOI (digital object identifier) or URL and access date (for online publications)

Each documentation system creates an association between in-text citations and the works cited or reference list. See Chapters 25 and 26 for documentation models.

In Summary: Using Sources Effectively

★ Use sources to support your points (p. 583).

★ Indicate the boundaries between source material and your own ideas (p. 588).

★ Modify direct quotations carefully (p. 591).

★ Use paraphrases to present ideas more clearly or concisely than is possible through direct quotation (p. 595).

★ Revise paraphrases to fit your tone and style (p. 595).

★ Summarize entire sources, parts of sources, or groups of sources (p. 596).

★ Integrate numerical information appropriately (p. 598).

★ Integrate images, audio, and video responsibly (p. 598).

★ Check for unintentional plagiarism (p. 603).

★ Document your sources (p. 603).

22 Designing Your Document

How can I design my document? 606
Understand design principles 607
Design for a purpose 609
Design for your readers 610
Design to address genre conventions 611

What design elements can I use? 612
Use fonts, line spacing, and alignment 612
Use page layout elements 612
Use color, shading, borders, and rules 615
Use illustrations 615
Use navigation tools 617

Many writers think document design comes at the end of the writing process after drafting, revising, and editing are complete. In fact, design can be a powerful tool during the planning and drafting stages. By considering design as you plan and work on your draft, you can create a document whose appearance helps you achieve your purpose, address your readers effectively, and take advantage of the context in which it will be read.

How Can I Design My Document?

Your decisions about the design of your document — from choosing appropriate fonts to presenting information in charts and tables to selecting compelling illustrations — can have powerful effects on how you shape and present your ideas and how your readers understand and react to your document. Understanding design principles and elements, as well as the design conventions of documents typically assigned in college courses, can help you craft a unique and substantial contribution to a conversation.

Understand Design Principles

Before you begin formatting text or inserting illustrations, consider how the design principles of *balance, emphasis, placement, repetition, consistency,* and *accessibility* can help you accomplish your goals as a writer.

Balance is the vertical and horizontal alignment of elements on your pages (see examples later in this section). Symmetrical designs create a sense of rest and stability and lead readers' eyes to focus on a particular part of a document. In contrast, asymmetrical — or unbalanced — designs suggest movement and guide readers' eyes across the page.

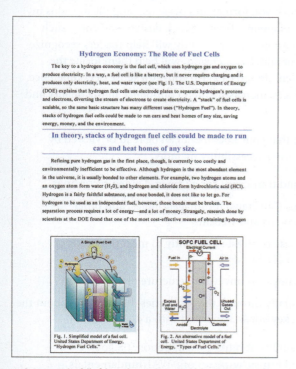 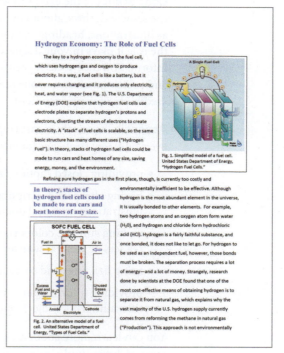

▲ Symmetrical (left) and asymmetrical (right) layouts
Copyright © Macmillan Learning

Emphasis is the placement and formatting of elements, such as headings and subheadings, so that they catch your readers' attention. You can emphasize an element in a document by using a color or font that distinguishes it from other elements; by inserting a border around it and adding a shaded background; or by using an illustration, such as a photograph, drawing, or graph.

Placement is the location of elements on your pages. Placing elements next to or near each other suggests that they are related. An illustration, for example, is usually placed near the passage in which it is mentioned.

Repetition is the use of elements, such as headers and footers, navigation menus, and page numbers, throughout the pages in your document. As readers move from page to page, they tend to expect navigation elements, such as page numbers, to appear in the same place. In addition, repeated elements, such as a logo or website navigation menu, help establish a sense of identity across the pages in your document.

Consistency is the extent to which you format and place text and illustrations in the same way throughout your document. Treating each design element — such as illustrations, headings, and footnotes — consistently will help readers recognize the role it plays in your document and, by extension, will help them locate the information they seek. A consistent design can also convey a sense of competence and professionalism to your readers, increasing their confidence in the quality and credibility of your document.

Accessibility involves ensuring that your document can be read or viewed by everyone. Key strategies for ensuring accessibility include

- providing closed captions and transcripts for audio and video recordings
- having alternate descriptions ("alt" tags) for images, tables, and other illustrations in digital documents and websites
- making sure the colors you use contrast sufficiently to meet the needs of readers or viewers who are color-blind
- using headings and subheadings to convey the structure of a document
- providing information — usually through the Properties dialog box — about the title, author(s), subject, and keywords associated with a document

You can learn more about accessibility at https://www.section508.gov/create/, https://webaim.org/, and https://www.w3.org/WAI/fundamentals/accessibility-intro/.

Keep two other principles in mind: *simplicity* and *moderation*. An overly complex design can obscure important ideas and information. Using design elements moderately to create a simple yet effective design is the best approach.

TECH TIP: CHECK ACCESSIBILITY

Many composing tools are designed to accommodate the needs of readers or viewers who have low or no vision. Microsoft Word and PowerPoint, for example, allow you to check a document for accessibility (see the Review tab). If the tool you've chosen lacks this functionality, consider searching the web for the name of the tool and the keyword *accessibility*.

Design for a Purpose

A well-designed document presents your information, ideas, and arguments in a manner that helps you accomplish your purposes.

▲ **Using images to create an emotional impact**
Justin Lewis/Getty Images

You might use design to achieve any of the following goals.

- **Setting a tone.** One of the most powerful tools writers have for accomplishing their purpose is establishing an emotional context for their readers. You can set a tone by using a particular color scheme, such as bright, cheerful hues, or by selecting photographs or drawings with a strong emotional impact.

- **Helping readers understand a point.** Design your document so that your main and supporting points are clear and easy to understand. Headings or pull quotes can call your readers' attention to central ideas and information. To introduce a main point, you might use a contrasting font or color to signal its importance. To highlight a definition or an example, you might enclose it inside a border or place the passage in a pull quote. You can also help readers understand a point by using illustrations.

- **Convincing readers to accept a point.** The key to convincing readers is providing them with appropriate, relevant evidence. Drawing on the principles of emphasis and placement, you can use illustrations, marginal glosses, pull quotes, and bulleted lists to highlight that evidence.
- **Clarifying complex concepts.** Sometimes a picture really is worth a thousand words. Rather than attempting to explain a complex concept using text alone, add an illustration. A well-chosen, well-placed photograph, flowchart, diagram, or table can define a complex concept such as photosynthesis in far less space, and in many cases far more effectively, than a long passage of text can. Bulleted and numbered lists can do the same.

Design for Your Readers

A well-designed document helps readers understand its organization, locate information and ideas, and recognize the function of its different parts. It is also easy on your readers' eyes: readers working with a well-designed document will not have to strain to read the text or discern illustrations. Use document design to do the following.

Help readers understand the organization of a document Use headings and subheadings to signal the content of each part of the document. Keep in mind the design principles of emphasis and consistency: format your headings in a consistent manner that helps them stand out from other parts of the document.

Help readers locate information and ideas Many longer print documents use tables of contents and indexes to help readers find key points. Websites and multimodal essays (see Chapter 23) typically provide a mix of menus and navigation headers and footers to help readers find their way through a document. You can distinguish these navigation aids from the surrounding text by using bordered or shaded boxes or contrasting fonts or colors.

Help readers recognize the function of parts of a document If you include passages that differ from the main text of your document, such as sidebars and "For More Information" sections, help readers understand their function by designing them to stand out visually. Using emphasis, you might design a sidebar with a shaded or colored box or format a list of related readings or web links in a contrasting font or color.

Use of a contrasting font and color helps readers understand the document's organization.

▲ Headings and subheadings in an essay

Design to Address Genre Conventions

Genres are characterized not only by distinctive writing styles, types of evidence, and organizing patterns but also by distinctive types of design. An article in a magazine such as *Time* or *Rolling Stone*, for example, is characterized by the use of columns, headings and subheadings, pull quotes, and illustrations, while an academic essay is characterized by wide margins, double-spaced lines, and comparatively restrained use of color and illustrations. Your readers will expect your document to be similar in design to other examples of that genre. This doesn't mean that you can't depart from those conventions should the need arise, but it does mean that you should take readers' expectations into account as you design your document.

What Design Elements Can I Use?

Understanding the design elements available to you will enable you to decide which of these options to use as you design your document. These elements include fonts, line spacing, and alignment; page layout strategies; color, shading, borders, and rules; illustrations; and navigation tools.

Use Fonts, Line Spacing, and Alignment

Font, line spacing, and alignment choices are the most common design decisions that writers make. They are also among the most important, since poor choices can make a document difficult to read. The examples that follow provide an overview of the key features of fonts as well as the uses of fonts, line spacing, and alignment.

Use Page Layout Elements

Page layout is the placement of text, illustrations, and other objects on a page or screen. Successful page layout draws on a number of design elements, including white space, margins, columns, headers and footers, page numbers, headings, lists, captions, marginal glosses and pull quotes, and sidebars. Three figures in this chapter — *Using fonts, line spacing, and alignment*; *Using page layout elements*; and *Using color, shading, borders, and rules* — illustrate these design elements.

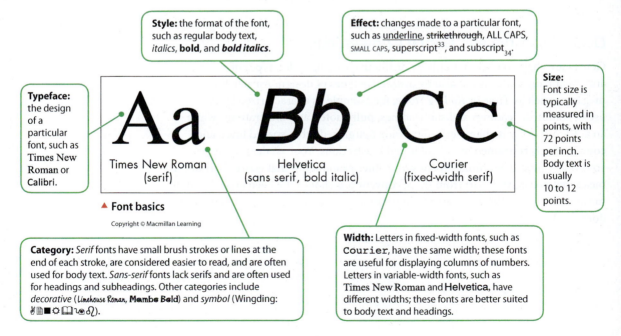

▲ Font basics

Copyright © Macmillan Learning

Line spacing refers to the amount of space between lines of text. Larger line spacing appears easier to read, so you'll often find increased line spacing in introductory paragraphs, executive summaries (which provide an overview of a longer document), and sidebars (see the figure *Using page layout elements*).

When text is crammed together vertically, it is difficult to read and to add comments. Keep this in mind if you are creating a document such as an essay on which someone else might write comments.

Alignment refers to the horizontal arrangement of text and illustrations (such as photos and drawings). You can select four types of alignment.

- **Left alignment** has a straight left margin and a "ragged" right margin; it is typically the easiest to read.
- **Right alignment** has a straight right margin and a ragged left margin.
- **Centered alignment** is seldom used for body text but can make headings stand out.
- **Justified alignment** has straight alignment on both the left and right margins. It adds a polished look and can be effective in documents that use columns — but it also produces irregular word spacing and hyphenation, which can slow the reading process.

Fonts are a complete set of type of a particular size and typeface. As you choose fonts, consider the following:

- **Select fonts that are easy to read.** For body text, avoid decorative fonts and italics.
- **Select fonts that complement each other.** A serif body font, such as Times New Roman or Garamond, works well with a sans-serif heading font, such as Arial, Helvetica, or Calibri.
- **Exercise restraint.** Generally, use no more than four different fonts in a document.

The U.S. Experience

"The Department vigorously enforces our nation's laws that protect working Americans. Fully enforcing the laws deters bad actors from willfully and repeatedly ignoring their responsibilities under the law. This makes American workplaces safer."

—Secretary of Labor Alexander Acosta

The United States remains strongly committed to the elimination of the worst forms of child labor, and showed this commitment when it ratified ILO Convention 182 on the Worst Forms of Child Labor in 1999. The U.S. Department of Labor (USDOL) is the sole federal agency that monitors child labor and enforces child labor laws. For the past 80 years, the Fair Labor Standards Act (FLSA) has governed the permissible employment of child workers. The FLSA's child labor provisions are designed to protect the educational opportunities of youth and prohibit their employment in jobs that are detrimental to their health and safety. The FLSA and its implementing regulations generally restrict the hours and times of day that youth under age 16 can work and lists hazardous occupations too dangerous for young workers to perform. USDOL's Wage and Hour Division (WHD) gives the highest priority to the enforcement of FLSA's child labor provisions.

Protecting the health and safety of young workers, while helping them enjoy positive work experiences, remains a high priority for several other agencies within USDOL. The Occupational Safety and Health Administration (OSHA) enforces the Occupational Safety and Health Act and related regulations, which ensure workplace safety for all employees, regardless of age. The Office of Disability Employment Policy (ODEP) works to improve transition outcomes for youth and young adults with disabilities toward successful employment and adulthood, and the Department's YouthRules! initiative seeks to promote positive, safe work experiences for young workers. The Employment and Training Administration (ETA) also sponsors many programs to provide training opportunities and job placement assistance for America's youth. In addition, the Bureau of Labor Statistics, which serves as a statistical resource to USDOL, gathers statistics on various subjects, including those related to child labor.

The Federal Minimum Ages for Work

The FLSA and its implementing regulations—

- Set a minimum age of 14 for most employment in non-hazardous, non-agricultural industries, limits the times of day and the number of hours that 14- and 15-year-olds may work, and limits the tasks that they may perform.
- Establish a minimum age of 18 for employment in occupations governed by the Department's 17 non-agricultural Hazardous Occupations Orders (HOs).
- Provide different standards for agricultural employment. For example, the FLSA does not restrict the type of work that 16- and 17-year-olds are permitted to perform in agricultural employment. The FLSA also permits 12- and 13-year-olds, with parental approval, to work outside of school hours in nonhazardous agricultural employment.
- Provide exceptions from some or all of these child labor rules for youth who are employed by their parents or persons standing in place of their parents in both agricultural and nonagricultural work. The statute also includes exceptions from the child labor rules for specific types of work, such as newspaper delivery and performing in theatrical productions.

There were 1,747,000 youth ages 16 to 17 employed in the United States in 2016, and 2,237,000 employed in 2017.[13] Despite the restrictions and limitations placed on their work, in 2016, the most recent year for which data are available, there were 17 fatal occupational injuries among youth ages 16 to 17, and 13 fatal occupational injuries among youth below age 16 in the United States.[14]

FIGURE 20

Wage and Hour Division Rigorously Enforces the Fair Labor Standards Act, including Child Labor Laws

748
Number of Cases Where Child Labor Violations Were Found

240
Number of Cases Where Hazardous Order Violations Were Found

491
Number of Minors Employed in Violation of Hazardous Orders

More information about these cases is available in the WHD's enforcement database at https://ogesdw.dol.gov/views/search.php and the WHD website at https://www.dol.gov/whd/data/datatables.htm#panel1.

▲ **Using fonts, line spacing, and alignment**
U.S. Department of Labor

614 CHAPTER 22 | Designing Your Document

Pull quotes (see an example in the figure *Using fonts, line spacing, and alignment*) highlight a passage of text — frequently a quotation — through the use of borders, white space, distinctive fonts, and contrasting colors.

Numbered and bulleted lists (not shown) display brief passages of related information using numbers or symbols (usually round "bullets"). The surrounding white space draws the eye to the list, highlighting the information for your readers, while the brief content in each entry can make concepts or processes easier to understand.

Sidebars (lower left) are brief discussions of information related to, but not a central part of, your document. Sidebars simplify the task of integrating related or supporting information into the body of the article by setting that information off in a clearly defined area.

White space — literally, empty space — frames and separates elements on a page.

Columns generally appear in newspaper and magazine articles — and, to a growing extent, in articles published on the web. Essays, on the other hand, are typically formatted in a single column. Columns can improve the readability of a document by limiting the eyes' physical movement across the page and by framing other elements.

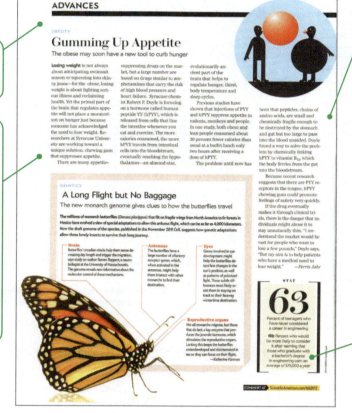

Margins are the white space between the edge of the page or screen (top, bottom, right, and left) and the text or graphics in your document.

Headings and subheadings identify sections and subsections, serve as transitions, and allow readers to locate information more easily.

Marginal glosses are brief notes in a margin or in a space following an article that explain or expand on text in the body of the document.

▲ Using page layout elements

Headers, footers, and page numbers (not shown) appear at the top or bottom of the page, set apart from the main text. They help readers find their way through a document; they provide information, such as the title of the document, its publication date, and its author; and they frame a page visually.

Captions (not shown) describe or explain an image, such as a photograph or chart.

Reproduced with permission. Copyright © 2012 Scientific American, a division of Nature America, Inc. All rights reserved. Photo credits (butterfly) Don Farrall/Photodisc/Getty Images; (gum) Thomas Fuchs

Use Color, Shading, Borders, and Rules

Color, shading, borders, and rules (horizontal or vertical lines) can make your document more attractive, call attention to important information, help readers understand the organization of your document, clarify the function of specific passages of text, and signal transitions between sections. Exercise restraint when working with these design elements. Avoid using more than three colors on a page, unless you are using a photograph or work of art. Be cautious, as well, about using multiple styles of rules or borders in a document.

Use Illustrations

Illustrations — charts, graphs, tables, photographs and other images, animations, audio clips, and video clips — can expand on or demonstrate points made in the text of your document. They can also reduce the amount of text needed to make a point, help readers better understand your points, and increase the visual appeal of your document.

- **PHOTOGRAPHS AND OTHER IMAGES**

Photographs and other images such as drawings, paintings, and sketches, are frequently used to set a mood, emphasize a point, or demonstrate a point more fully than is possible with text alone.

- **CHARTS AND GRAPHS**

Charts and graphs represent information visually. They are used to make a point more succinctly than is possible with text alone or to present complex information in a compact and more accessible form. They frequently rely on numerical information.

- **TABLES**

Tables, like charts and graphs, can present complex information, both textual and numerical, in a compact form.

- **OTHER DIGITAL ILLUSTRATIONS**

Other digital illustrations can also be used, allowing you to include a wider range of media, including audio, video, and animations, which bring sound and movement to your document.

As you work with illustrations, keep the following guidelines in mind.

- **Use an illustration for a purpose.** Illustrations are best used when they serve a clear function in your document. Avoid including illustrations simply because you think they might make your document "look better."

Signal the organization of a document. In a longer print document, headers, footers, headings, and subheadings might be formatted with a particular color to help readers recognize which section they are reading. On a website, pages in each section could share the same background or heading color.

Be consistent. Use the same colors for top-level headings throughout your document, another color for lower-level headings, and so on. Use the same borders and shading for sidebars. Use rules consistently in pull quotes, headers, and footers. Don't mix and match.

Signal the function of text. A colored or shaded background, as well as colored type, can be used to differentiate captions and pull quotes from body text. Rules can also separate columns of text on a page or screen.

Call attention to important information. Color, borders, and shading can subtly yet clearly emphasize an illustration, such as a table or chart, or an important passage of text, by distinguishing it from the surrounding body text.

THE WELL-BEING BALANCING ACT
Pleasure and purpose work together

EVEN THE MOST ardent strivers will agree that a life of purpose that is devoid of pleasures is, frankly, no fun. Happy people know that allowing yourself to enjoy easy momentary indulgences that are personally rewarding—taking a long, leisurely bath, vegging out with your daughter's copy of *The Hunger Games*, or occasionally skipping your Saturday workout in favor of catching the soccer match on TV—is a crucial aspect of living a satisfying life. Still, if you're primarily focused on activities that feel good in the moment, you may miss out on the benefits of developing a clear purpose. Purpose is what drives us to take risks and make changes—even in the face of hardship and when sacrificing short-term happiness.

Working to uncover how happy people balance pleasure and purpose, Colorado State's Steger and his colleagues have shown that the act of trying to comprehend and navigate our world generally causes us to deviate from happiness. After all, this mission is fraught with tension, uncertainty, complexity, short bursts of intrigue and excitement, and conflicts between the desire to feel good and the desire to make progress toward what we care about most. Yet overall, people who are the happiest tend to be superior at sacrificing short-term pleasures when there is a good opportunity to make progress toward what they aspire to become in life.

If you want to envision a happy person's stance, imagine one foot rooted in the present with mindful appreciation of what one has—and the other foot reaching toward the future for yet-to-be-uncovered sources of meaning. Indeed, research by neuroscientist Richard Davidson of the University of Wisconsin at Madison has revealed that making advances toward achievement of our goals not only causes us to feel more engaged, it actually helps us tolerate any negative feelings that arise during the journey.

Nobody would pretend that finding purpose is easy or that it can be done in a simple exercise, but thinking about which activities you found most rewarding and meaningful in the past week, what you're good at and often recognized for, what experiences you'd be unwilling to give up, and which ones you crave more time for can help. Also, notice whether your answers reflect something you feel that you ought to say as opposed to what you truly love. For example, being a parent doesn't necessarily mean that spending time with your children is the most energizing, meaningful part of your life—and it's important to accept that. Lying to yourself is one of the biggest barriers to creating purpose. The happiest people have a knack for being honest about what does and does not energize them—and in addition to building in time for sensory pleasures each day, they are able to integrate the activities they most care about into a life of purpose and satisfaction. **PT**

TODD B. KASHDAN is a psychologist at George Mason University and the author of *Mindfulness, Acceptance, and Positive Psychology*. **ROBERT BISWAS-DIENER** is the author of *The Courage Quotient*. Together they are coauthoring a book on a new approach to well-being in the business world.

HAPPINESS BY THE NUMBERS

.62 Distance from home, in miles, at which point people's tweets begin declining in expressed happiness (about the distance expected for a short work commute).

40 The percentage of our capacity for happiness that is within our power to change, according to University of California, Riverside researcher Sonja Lyubomirsky.

85 Number of residents out of every 100 who report feeling positive emotions in Panama and Paraguay, the most positive countries in the world.

20 The percentage of the U.S. population wealthy enough that their feelings of happiness are not affected by fluctuations in Americans' income equality.

Sources: The University of Vermont, The How of Happiness, Gallup, Psychological Science

THERAPISTS: Interested in receiving Continuing Ed credit for reading this issue? Visit NBCC.org

July/August 2013 Psychology Today 59

▲ Using color, shading, borders, and rules
Psychology Today © Copyright 2013 www.Psychologytoday.com

- **Place illustrations near the text they illustrate.** In general, place illustrations as close as possible to the point where they are mentioned in the text. If they are not explicitly mentioned (as is often the case with photographs), place them at a point in the document where they are most relevant to the information and ideas being discussed. If the illustration does not take up the full width of the page, consider "wrapping" text around it. In Word and many other word-processing and presentation programs, you can access the Wrap Text command by right clicking on the image or opening the Format ribbon or menu.

- **Include a title or caption that identifies or explains the illustration.** The documentation system you are using, such as MLA or APA, will usually offer advice on the placement and format of titles and captions. In general, documentation systems suggest that you distinguish between tables and figures (which basically amount to all other illustrations), number tables and figures in the order in which they appear in the document, and use compound numbering of tables and figures in longer documents (for example, the second table in Chapter 5 would be labeled "Table 5.2"). Consult the documentation system you are using for specific guidelines on illustrations (see Chapters 25 and 26).

Use Navigation Tools

Longer documents — and in particular digital documents such as multimodal essays, websites, and blogs — often include navigation tools that allow readers to move quickly from one part of the document to another.

- **Next and Previous buttons or links** allow readers to move from one part of a document to another.
- **Internal links** help readers move from one page to a related page.
- **External links** help readers open related documents.
- **Tables of contents** allow readers of longer multimodal essays (or print documents presented in digital formats, such as PDF or ePub) to move directly to a particular part of the document.
- **Document maps** help readers visualize the document as a set of concepts, sections, or pages. You can click on part of the map to navigate to a particular point within the document.
- **Menus** can appear on each page, listing major sections within the document.
- **Headers and footers** provide information about the document, helping readers recognize which part they are reading and providing access to links to, for example, a works cited list and an "About" page.

In Summary: Designing Your Document

★ Understand the design principles of balance, emphasis, placement, repetition, and consistency (p. 607).

★ Design to achieve your purposes (p. 609).

★ Design to address your readers' needs, interests, values, and beliefs (p. 610).

★ Design to address genre conventions (p. 611).

★ Use design elements — such as fonts, line spacing, alignment, page layout, color, shading, borders, rules, illustrations, and navigation tools — to increase the readability and effectiveness of your document (p. 612).

23 Working with Genres

How can I choose the right genre? 619
Analyze your assignment 619
Reflect on your purpose, role, readers, and context 620
Consider your writing resources 620

What should I consider as I design an academic essay? 621
Consider how design can help you achieve your goals 621
Consider reader expectations 622
Consider your context 622
View an essay 623

How can I write and design an article? 625
Analyze your target publication 625
Develop and organize your argument 627
Collect and work with sources 627
Draft, design, and review your article 628
View an article 628

How can I create a multimodal essay? 630
Build on your experiences writing academic essays 630
Develop and organize your argument 630

Collect and work with sources 631
Choose composing tools 633
Develop a consistent design 634
View a multimodal essay 635

How can I create a website? 637
Plan your site 637
Design your site 638
Create your site 639
Publish your site 639
View web pages 639

How can I make a presentation? 641
Consider your speaking situation 642
Plan your presentation 642
Create a multimedia presentation 645
Engage with your audience 648
If necessary, present virtually 649
View a presentation 649

You might have the opportunity to decide which genre you'll use to contribute to a conversation. Or you might be asked to adapt the contents of an academic essay for presentation in another genre, such as a brochure or website. As you consider your choices, you'll find you can use a wide array of documents to reach your readers. This chapter discusses how to draft and design some of the most important print and digital genres as well as the presentations that might accompany them or stand in their place.

How Can I Choose the Right Genre?

Experienced writers base their choice of genre on three primary factors: their purpose and role, the expectations of their readers, and the context in which their document will be written and read. One of these factors will probably be more important than the others. For example, if your readers are unlikely to treat your document seriously unless it is presented in a particular genre, such as a scientific journal article, then you would be foolish to choose another genre. To select an appropriate genre, analyze your assignment, reflect on your writing situation, and consider the resources you can draw on as you compose your document.

Analyze Your Assignment

If you are writing in response to an assignment for a class, determine whether your assignment restricts your choice of genre. If your assignment contains a statement such as *write an essay* or *create a website*, then you'll know that your instructor has a specific genre in mind.

If you find no mention of a particular genre, you should look for statements that can help you choose an appropriate genre.

- **Look for statements about your purpose and role.** Most assignments offer guidance on what you should attempt to accomplish. Words such as *inform* and *report*, for example, suggest that your purpose is to write an informative document. In contrast, words such as *convince* and *persuade* indicate that you should write an argumentative document. Although you'll find that some genres — such as essays, articles, and blog posts — can be used to accomplish both purposes, some are better suited to one purpose than to another. Opinion columns, for example, are typically used to advocate an argumentative position, while reports are used primarily to inform.

- **Look for statements about your readers.** Your assignment might provide information about the characteristics of your readers, such as their ages, their educational backgrounds, and their interests. You might be asked, for example, to address the members of a particular academic discipline. If so, identify genres that are commonly used in that discipline.

- **Look for statements about your context.** If your assignment indicates the format in which your document should be submitted, use that information to help determine which genres might be appropriate. If you are expected to submit a printed document, for example, you'll be more likely to choose an essay, a report, or an article than a website, a blog post, or a multimodal essay. Look as well for any statements that indicate where your document might be read, such as references to particular types of publications (newspapers, magazines, websites, and so on).

- **Look for statements about limitations.** Many assignments provide information about word limits or page length. You'll also find guidance about due dates, deadlines for rough drafts or annotated bibliographies or outlines, and the type of documentation system you should use. Use this information to choose your genre. Length limitations are particularly useful, since many genres would be too long for an assignment that asked for a document of no more than five hundred words. Similarly, some documents, such as a multimodal essay, would be difficult to complete in a short period of time.

Learn more about analyzing an assignment in Chapter 2.

Reflect on Your Purpose, Role, Readers, and Context

If you are not given a detailed assignment, use your understanding of your writing situation to choose your genre.

- **Spend time thinking about your purpose and role**, and then ask yourself which genres might best help you accomplish your goals. If you are writing an article about a complex problem, for example, you'll want to read widely about the problem's origins and effects. You'll also want to find out as much as you can about how the problem has been defined, what solutions have been offered, and which solutions have been tried so far. As you learn more about the problem, you're likely to become interested in a particular solution and to want to advocate for that solution in your article. Whether you move into the role of advocate will depend on the nature of the publication.

- **Reflect on the knowledge, interests, purposes, and backgrounds of your readers**, and then ask what this might tell you about appropriate genres. Try to understand what your readers are likely to expect from you and what they might find familiar and easy to read. A well-written scientific report, for example, might be less effective than an informative essay or article simply because your readers might be unfamiliar with the scientific-report genre.

- **Reflect on the context in which your document will be read.** If you know that your readers have easy access to computers, tablets, or phones, you'll have more options than if you know that they can read documents only in print.

Consider Your Writing Resources

In addition to your assignment and your writing situation, think about the tools you can use to write and design your document. In some cases, you might lack the tools necessary to create a particular genre, such as a multimodal essay or a website. If you don't have the right software or a computer or tablet powerful enough to run that software, it's probably best to choose another genre. Similarly, lack of access to a color printer might work against creating a colorful brochure or flyer.

Your choice of genre might also be influenced — in a more positive way — by what you know how to do. If you have experience using desktop publishing programs such as Microsoft Publisher or Adobe InDesign, you'll have far more options for creating a polished print or digital document. Similarly, you can create a website if you know how to use a web-editing program such as Adobe Dreamweaver or are familiar with online website creation tools such as Google Sites, Weebly, Wix, or WordPress.

As you consider your writing resources, keep in mind the wide range of documents that can be created using word-processing and presentation tools such as Word, Pages, Keynote, and PowerPoint. These programs include templates that you can use to create a variety of genres.

What Should I Consider as I Design an Academic Essay?

Some writers might be surprised to see the terms *design* and *academic essay* used in the same sentence. They might be aware that they should use wide margins, readable fonts, and double-spaced lines, and they generally understand that these elements help readers — typically instructors — read and respond to their work. Beyond these elements, however, many writers think of design as having little or no role in their essays.

They're wrong. Thoughtful design can help you achieve your goals, address your readers' expectations, and adapt to the context in which your essay will be written and read.

Consider How Design Can Help You Achieve Your Goals

Traditionally, essay assignments have focused on the written expression of ideas and arguments. As a result, writers have tended to use images sparingly, if at all, and to make limited use of design elements such as color, shading, borders, and rules in their academic essays. Writers have also tended to avoid the use of tables and charts, perhaps thinking that these kinds of design elements are more appropriate for genres such as reports and professional articles.

Yet these design elements can help you present complex information and ideas more clearly, distinguish between items considered in an evaluation, illustrate the aspects of a particular problem, or frame your argument by calling readers' attention to particular information and ideas. As you draft your essay, consider how the wide range of design elements discussed in Chapter 22 might help you accomplish your goals as a writer. As you consider your options, keep in mind your instructor's preferences regarding the use of these elements. If you are uncertain about your instructor's preferences, ask for guidance.

Consider Reader Expectations

Readers approach an essay with a set of writing and design conventions in mind, so consider how you can build on those expectations to accomplish your goals as a writer. Readers expect you to follow generally accepted conventions, such as the guidelines provided by the MLA and APA documentation systems (see Chapters 25 and 26). Your assignment is also likely to provide guidance on how to format an academic essay. If you have questions, you can consult your instructor.

As you design your essay, you can use design elements such as fonts, color, shading, and borders to help readers anticipate and more easily follow the organization of your essay. You can use tables, charts, and figures to let your readers view, understand, and analyze the information you include in your essay. If you are distributing your essay in digital form, you can link to or embed related information — such as video clips, audio clips, and data sets, or you can embed these materials directly in your essay. You can read more about how these design elements can help you in Chapter 22.

Consider Your Context

The context in which your essay is written and read can affect your design decisions in important ways. Think carefully about the resources you can use to write and design your essay. Do you own a computer or tablet? Do you have access to computers at your college or university? Do you have access to color printers? What kind of software programs or web-based resources can you use, and how well do you know them? If you are working on a deadline, you might have limited time to learn how to use a new software program or an ePortfolio tool. Perhaps the time required to use these resources would be better spent on collecting additional sources or revising and editing your draft.

Think equally carefully about how you will submit your essay. Will you deliver your essay to an instructor in printed form, send it as an email attachment, or submit it through a course management system? Will it be included in a print or digital portfolio along with your other work? Will it be available on a blog or web page?

Finally, consider how and where your essay will be read. Will it be read in print in a quiet office or perhaps on a bus or train during a commute? Will it be "required reading" — that is, will it get the careful attention an instructor provides during grading? Or is it something that can be put aside in favor of something else, as might happen if it were being read by a visitor to a website or blog?

Good document design can help you adapt to the contexts in which your essay will be written and read. You can read more about using design elements to adapt to particular contexts in Chapter 22.

View an Essay

The following pages are from an essay written by college freshman Gaele Lopez for his composition class. They reflect his awareness of his instructor's expectations about line spacing, margins, documentation system, page numbers, and a title page.

For another sample essay formatted in MLA style, see the last section of Chapter 25. For a sample essay formatted in APA style, see the final section of Chapter 26.

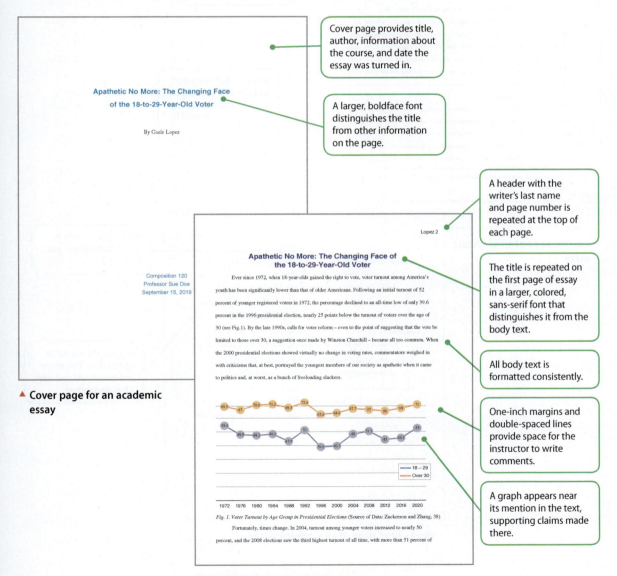

▲ Cover page for an academic essay

▲ First page for an academic essay

▲ **Interior page of an academic essay**

Lopez 3

those under 30 voting. This nearly matched the 1972 turnout, when anger and frustration over the Vietnam war resulted in the largest turnout to date among younger voters.

While turnout among younger voters declined slightly in the 2012 and 2016 elections, it showed significant growth in the 2018 midterm elections, when it increased by 79 percent over turnout in that age group over 2014 numbers (Misra). While still lower than the turnout for voters over 65, these figures suggest that younger voters are likley to play a key role in the 2020 presidential election and may see turnout levels that rival those of 1972 and 2008.

Factors Contributing to the Changes in Voting Behaviors

Why these changes? Is it as sudden as it appears? Analysts Mark Hugo Lopez, Emily Kirby, and Jared Sagoff, writing after the 2004 presidential elections, pointed to "the confluence of extensive voter outreach efforts, a close election, and high levels of interest in the 2004 campaign" as factors that drove turnout among younger voters to "levels not seen since 1992" (1). They cautioned, however, that it was unclear whether the 2004 results were indicators of a significant change or simply an aberration. Indeed, while voter turnout increased again in 2008, in the historic election of America's first Black president, they declined in both 2012 and 2016 (see Fig. 1).

It would appear, despite the declines in turnout among younger voters in the 2012 and 2016 elections, that the trend is toward higher involvement by younger voters in local, state, and national politics. In its report on record turnout in the 2008 primaries and caucuses, which was correlated with increased in the 2008 presidential election by younger voters, the Pew Charitable Trust notes,

> The research showed that college students are deeply concerned avbout issues, inovled personally as volunteers and ready to consider voting. But they want political leaders to be positive, to address real problems and to call on all Americans to be constructively involved. (par. 5)

As we look toward the fall 2020 elections, it seems clear that younger voters will not only play

Callouts:
- A heading, formatted in blue and using a sans-serif font that differs from the serif body font, calls attention to a shift in Gaele's argument.
- Block quotation is set off by indenting the margins on both sides. Quotation marks are not needed for block quotations.

▲ **Works cited page of an academic essay**

Lopez 7

Works Cited

Desliver, Drew. "Millennials, Gen X increase their ranks in the House, especially among Democrats." *Pew Research Center*, 21 Nov. 2018, www.pewresearch.org/fact-tank/2018/11/21/millennials-gen-x-increase-their-ranks-in-the-house-especially-among-democrats/.

File, Thom. "Voting in America: A Look at the 2016 Presidential Election." *U.S. Census Bureau*, 10 May 2017, www.census.gov/newsroom/blogs/random-samplings/2017/05/voting_in_america.html.

Lopez, Mark Hugo, Emily Kirby, and Jared Sagoff. "Fact Sheet: The Youth Vote 2004." *The Center for Information and Research on Civic Learning and Engagement*, 22 July 2005, www.civicyouth.org.

McDonald, Michael P. "Voter Turnout Demographics." *United States Election Project*, www.electproject.org/home/voter-turnout/demographics, Accessed 23 Nov. 2018.

Misra, Jordan. "Voter Turnout Rates Among All Voting Age and Major Racial and Ethnic Groups Were Higher Than in 2014." *America Counts*, 23 Apr. 2019, https://www.census.gov/library/stories/2019/04/behind-2018-united-states-midterm-election-turnout.html.

Vincent, Reid. Personal Interview. 28 Nov. 2018.

Zackerson, Lynn, and Shuting Zhang. "U.S. Presidential Election Voting Patterns: Analyzing Turnout by Age." *Journal of Participatory Democracy*, vol. 6, no. 1, April 2017, pp. 36-47.

Callouts:
- The reference page is titled "Works Cited" per MLA style.
- MLA format is used to cite sources. Entries are double-spaced and have a hanging indent.

> **Checklist for Designing Academic Essays**
>
> ✔ **Consider your writing situation.** Reflect on how design can help you accomplish your purpose and carry out your role as a writer. Consider how design can help you address reader expectations. Think about how the context in which you write your essay will affect your design decisions.
>
> ✔ **Consider genre conventions.** Be aware of the design conventions associated with academic essays, including the following:
>
> - a cover page or an essay header, depending on your instructor's preferences or the formatting requirements of the documentation style you are following
> - a readable body font (such as 12-point Times New Roman or Calibri)
> - double-spaced lines
> - wide margins, one inch or larger
> - consistent use of the documentation system you are following
> - headers and footers in a readable font distinct from the body font
> - if used, headings and subheadings in fonts and colors that distinguish them from the body text and show the relative importance of different heading levels
> - if used, illustrations labeled and placed either within the text near relevant passages or in an appendix, according to your instructor's preferences

How Can I Write and Design an Article?

Articles appear in a wide range of publications, including newspapers, magazines, scholarly and professional journals, and websites. Articles rely heavily on information obtained from sources such as books, websites, government reports, interviews, surveys, and observation. You should consider several factors as you plan, draft, design, revise, and edit an article: the target publication's audience, its typical subjects, its general style and tone, and its overall design.

Analyze Your Target Publication

Analyzing a publication involves asking questions about its readers, the subjects its articles address, its writing conventions, and its design. To locate a print publication, visit your library's periodicals room (see *Browse Periodicals* in Chapter 14) or consult a reference librarian. You can also search for information about the publication on the web (see *Search the Web* in Chapter 14) or in databases (see *Search*

Databases in Chapter 14). To locate information about a digital publication such as *Slate*, visit its website, conduct database searches, or consult a reference librarian.

Readers Examine the publication as a whole to learn what you can about its readers.

- Can you find a letters-to-the-editor or comments section? If so, reading the letters and any responses from the editors and other readers might give you insights into who reads the publication and why they read it.

- If the publication contains advertisements that seem to address its readers (as opposed to personalized ads directed to you online), do they tell you anything about the readers? Who advertises in the publication? What products or services do they offer, or what issues or problems do they address?

- What can you learn about the readers from the range of subjects or issues addressed in articles and other parts of the publication?

- Can you find any information about the publisher? Can you tell whether it is a commercial enterprise, a government agency, a nonprofit organization, a scholarly or professional organization, or an individual? Does the publication have a mission statement? Does the publication describe its purpose or goals, the audience it hopes to reach, or its origins?

Subjects Look at recently published articles in the publication. You can often find them in tables of contents, article indexes, and digital archives. Depending on the publication, you might also be able to search a full-text database (see *Search Databases* in Chapter 14) or search the web for archived articles.

- What issues and subjects do the articles address?

- How long are the articles? Which are the shortest? Which are the longest? Where do they fall on average?

- What do you think is the purpose of the publication? Is its goal to inform, to advocate, to address problems? Or does it address a range of purposes?

Writing Conventions Study the articles in the publication to learn about its writing conventions.

- How would you characterize the style and tone of the articles? Is the tone generally formal, informal, or somewhere in between? Are contractions (*can't, won't, isn't*) used? Are individuals identified by their full names and titles ("Dr. Shaun Beaty")?

- How are sources identified? Do the articles use an in-text citation system, such as MLA or APA (see Chapters 25 and 26)? Do they use footnotes or endnotes? Do the articles link directly to the source? Do they identify sources by name or organization, as is commonly done in news articles?

- What do the authors of articles seem to assume about their readers? Do they use specialized language (or jargon)? Do they expect you to know a great deal about the subject? Do you think the authors expect you to be an expert in the field to understand their articles?

Design To gain an understanding of your readers' expectations about the design of your article, scan articles in the publication, read a few carefully, and take notes.

- Would you characterize the articles as heavy on text? Or are images, tables, charts, figures, and other illustrations used liberally? If the articles are published in a digital format, do they include audio clips, video clips, animations, or interactive tools?
- How is color used in the articles, if at all? Do the articles make use of borders, rules, and shading?
- Do the articles use headings and subheadings? If so, how are they formatted? What kinds of fonts are used? Is there much variety in the fonts?
- How are the articles laid out? Do they use columns? Sidebars? Block quotes?

Even the most narrowly focused publication is likely to display quite a bit of variety. Understanding your potential readers and the subjects they seem to care about, however, can help you compose an article that is well suited to your target publication.

Develop and Organize Your Argument

Your line of argument should reflect your understanding of the issues and subjects addressed in your target publication and the needs, interests, and knowledge of its readers. As in other types of documents, you should develop a main point, select reasons to accept it, and choose evidence to support your reasons (see Chapter 18). Then you should choose an organizing pattern that is consistent with your purpose and role and create a map or an outline of your argument (see Chapter 19).

Collect and Work with Sources

The sources you choose to provide evidence in your article should reflect your understanding of the types of sources typically found in other articles in the publication. Some publications, particularly those focused on news and current events, depend heavily on personal experience and field research — primarily interviews, observation, and correspondence (see Chapter 15). Others, such as professional and scholarly journals, rely primarily on published work and, in some cases, original research. For a successful article, make sure that your sources are consistent with those you've identified during your publication analysis.

Draft, Design, and Review Your Article

The process of writing, designing, revising, and editing an article is similar to that used for academic essays (see Chapter 20, the chapters in Part Two, and the discussion of designing an essay earlier in this chapter). You'll find some differences in the areas of word choice, design, and source documentation. Your choice of language should be consistent with that of the other articles in the publication. In particular, pay attention to the level of formality (including the use of contractions and slang), the use of specialized terminology (jargon), and references to the work of other authors. Review your publication analysis to determine how you should address these issues.

The design of your article should also build on what you learned through your publication analysis. It is generally not necessary to design your article so that it mimics the layout used in the publication; the publication's editors and design staff will handle that. It can be helpful, however, to draft your article with particular design elements in mind. By placing images, tables, charts, and figures in your draft, you can gain a sense of how the article will appear to readers. By creating sidebars or setting up pull quotes (see *Use Page Layout Elements* in Chapter 22), you can determine which points will be highlighted for your readers. Similarly, you can format your headings and subheadings in ways that mirror how they are formatted in the publication and use colors to set a particular mood or to highlight key information. Using design as a composing element can help you view your article as your readers will, allowing you to anticipate how they are likely to understand and respond to it.

As you revise and edit, be sure to ask for feedback from people you trust. Ask them to put themselves in the role of a reader of your target publication. If they are unfamiliar with the publication, share the results of your publication analysis with them. Depending on your purpose and role, you might choose one of the peer-review activities in the chapters in Part Two. You can also review the advice for effective peer review in Chapter 5.

View an Article

For more examples of articles, see Chapters 3, 7, 8, 9, 10, 11, and 12.

The articles that follow were published in the *Tufts Daily*, the independent student newspaper published at Tufts University. Paired with photos, the articles make use of font formatting and visual elements to set a mood, call attention to key points, and convey information.

▲ Front page of a student newspaper

The Tufts Daily

> **Checklist for Writing Articles**
>
> ✔ **Consider your writing situation** and in particular your purpose and role.
>
> ✔ **Analyze your target publication**, focusing on its readers, the subjects and issues addressed in the publication, typical writing conventions, and typical design conventions.
>
> ✔ **Develop and organize your argument.**
>
> ✔ **Collect information** to support your argument.
>
> ✔ **Draft, design, and review your article**, keeping in mind the results of your publication analysis.

How Can I Create a Multimodal Essay?

Learn about making your multimodal essay accessible in *Understand Design Principles* in Chapter 22.

Multimodal essays are characterized by their essayistic form and their use of multiple types of media. As essays, they present information in a linear sequence, one idea after another. As multimodal documents, they combine text with images, animation, sound, video, and/or interactive tools to establish a line of argument and support the writer's points.

To create a multimodal essay, build on your understanding of how to compose an academic essay and then use digital composing tools to accomplish your writing goals and address your readers' expectations.

Build on Your Experiences Writing Academic Essays

The processes writers typically use to compose a multimodal essay are similar to those used to compose academic essays. After you've listened in and reflected on the conversation you've decided to join, you'll consider what to say and how best to say it. Your choice of a multimodal essay will likely reflect your purpose and role, your readers' needs and interests, the nature of the conversation, and the kinds of sources used in documents that have been added to the conversation.

Develop and Organize Your Argument

As with most documents, you'll need to spend time choosing a main point, selecting reasons to accept your main point, choosing appropriate evidence, and making decisions about organization. With the exception of issues related to digital media, these decisions are nearly identical to those you'll face as you work on various types of academic essays. You can read more about the composing strategies associated with particular writing roles in Part Two.

Collect and Work with Sources

Multimodal essays, by definition, rely on sources such as images, animations, video clips, audio clips, and data files. Like academic essays, they also draw on information, ideas, and arguments from written sources, field research, and your personal experience. As you work on your multimodal essay, your first concern should be identifying sources that can be used to support your main point and illustrate the positions and approaches taken by other writers. Then consider how you can use those sources to bring your essay to life.

● CHOOSE YOUR SOURCES

As you consider the sources you might include in your essay, give some thought to the effect each type of source will have on your ability to achieve your writing goals, address the expectations of your readers, and adapt to the context in which your document will be read. Think about the differences, for example, between presenting a written transcript of an interview, linking to an audio clip of the interview, and embedding a video clip of the interview into your essay. Each has its advantages. A written transcript can be skimmed, while readers will need to spend more time opening and listening to an audio or video clip. In contrast, the audio and video clips would allow the reader to pick up on the speaker's tone of voice or facial expressions, neither of which can be conveyed clearly through a transcript.

Similarly, consider the trade-offs between presenting a concise, well-designed table and embedding a spreadsheet containing raw data that a reader could open and work with. Better yet, think about the advantages of including the table *and* the spreadsheet — you'll not only allow your readers to view your conclusions as you've presented them in the table but also give them a chance to work with the data and come to their own conclusions.

● PLACE AND STAGE YOUR SOURCES

Consider how your sources will appeal to your readers and how your readers might interact with them. If your readers are actively engaged with your essay — navigating its contents, viewing images and other illustrations, following links to related sources, and so on — they are more likely to find themselves intrigued with and influenced by your line of argument.

Focus on where you'll place each media source and how you'll call attention to it. In most cases, you'll want to introduce the source before the reader encounters it in the text. In this sense, placing media sources follows the general guidelines for placing illustrations, found in *Use Illustrations* in Chapter 22. You should refer to the source in the body of the text, position the source near where it is mentioned, and provide some sort of caption or figure title to help readers see the connection between it and its mention in the text.

Focus as well on how you'll call attention to a media source — that is, how you'll stage it. If a media source is a critical part of your essay, you'll want to ensure that your readers pay attention to it. A video source might be placed so that it takes up the complete width of the page, and a detailed caption or figure title might provide information that would lead the reader to view or listen to it. If the source provides only modest support, however, then you need not call your readers' attention to it. A photograph of a speaker, for example, might do little more than allow readers to connect a face to a name. In this case, the photo might simply be set off in the margin of the document or aligned along the right side of a paragraph.

● IMPORT OR LINK TO MEDIA SOURCES

Multimodal essays can include complete files downloaded from media sources, as would be the case if you placed a photograph in your essay, or they can link to media sources, as you might do if you wanted your readers to play a YouTube video. When you import a file into your essay, the file is saved within your essay. In contrast, you can link to material elsewhere on the web by using *embed codes*, such as those provided by YouTube. Readers can then choose whether to view the media within your essay or open the site on which it resides. You can also use links to send your readers to the site or network location where the link exists, much as you would with a link to a web page.

Your decisions about importing, embedding, or linking to a source will depend on factors such as design, the length of time you want your essay to be available, concerns about file size, the software you will use to create your essay, and copyright restrictions (see *What Is Fair Use and When Should I Ask Permission to Use a Source?* in Chapter 17).

Consider the following factors as you decide whether to import, embed, or link to a media source.

- **Design.** Importing sources gives you the highest degree of control over the appearance and behavior of the media source, while embedding and linking allow you to minimize the file size of your essay and often allow you to ensure that all media elements will play properly when they are opened.

- **Availability.** If your essay will continue to be available to readers for a lengthy period of time, as might be the case if you are publishing it on a website or in a blog, you need to ensure that your media sources will be available even if they disappear from the site where you found them. In this case, importing the media source would be the best choice.

- **File size.** If you import a video file, your essay might become so large that it would be impossible to send as an email attachment or upload to a course management system. In contrast, if you embed or link to your media sources, the overall size of your essay can be smaller, making it easier to distribute.
- **Context.** If you know that your readers are likely to be reading your essay on a phone rather than on a computer or tablet with a larger screen and faster connection, you might choose an audio clip or an image rather than a video clip because it will open more quickly.

Choose Composing Tools

The composing tool you'll use to create your multimodal essay will affect not only *what* you can do in terms of composing, designing, and distributing your essay but also *how you think about* the essay itself. The capabilities of a particular software program allow you to envision particular types of documents. For example, if you decide to use a multimedia presentation program such as Apple Keynote, Google Slides, or Microsoft PowerPoint, you'll most likely think of your essay as a series of pages that readers will move through in a linear manner, rather than jumping around as they might on a website. In contrast, if you choose a graphics program such as Adobe Photoshop or a multimedia presentation program such as Prezi, the idea of distinct pages might not be a consideration. In this sense, as rhetorician Kenneth Burke has written, a way of seeing is a way of not seeing. The features of a particular composing tool will direct your attention to some possibilities even as they obscure others.

Keep Burke's observation in mind as you consider the wide range of software programs that can be used to create a multimodal essay:

- word-processing programs, such as Apple Pages, Google Docs, Microsoft Word, or Apache OpenOffice Writer
- multimedia presentation programs, such as Apple Keynote, Google Slides, Microsoft PowerPoint, Microsoft Sway, Adobe Spark, Prezi, or Apache OpenOffice Impress
- web-development tools, such as Adobe Dreamweaver, Google Sites, WordPress, or Wix

- publishing tools, such as Adobe InDesign or Microsoft Publisher
- graphics programs, such as GIMP, Adobe Illustrator or Photoshop, CorelDRAW or Corel PHOTO-PAINT, Google Drawings, or Apache OpenOffice Draw

As you choose your composing and design tools, consider how their distinctive features will help you accomplish your goals as a writer. A word-processing program might be a better choice than a multimedia presentation program if, for example, you plan to rely more heavily on text than on images and video. In contrast, a multimedia presentation program offers more options for including multimedia elements than do most word-processing or web-development programs.

TECH TIP: Microsoft PowerPoint and other multimedia presentation programs, such as Apple Keynote, Google Slides, Microsoft Sway, Adobe Spark, and Apache OpenOffice Impress, offer a set of tools that are well suited to integrating multimedia sources with text. The Insert ribbon in PowerPoint, for example, allows you to add images, audio, video, and other media sources along with tables, text boxes, and links. To get started, create a new presentation, and then click on the Insert menu in the command ribbon.

▲ PowerPoint Insert ribbon

Using a multimedia presentation program to create a multimedia essay invites you to think of the essay not as a set of bulleted slides, but as a group of pages that can be filled with various types of media. If you look at each page as a blank canvas, you can design an essay with pages like those you might find in a magazine or on the web.

Develop a Consistent Design

If your multimodal essay uses pages, ensure that they are designed in a way that helps your readers view each page as part of a larger essay. If you've watched a PowerPoint presentation, you've probably seen this idea in action. Even though each page might have different content — a bulleted list of information on one page, a video on another, and an image on yet another — they use the same color scheme, headers and footers, fonts, and background colors.

Regardless of the composing tool you choose, ensure a sense of continuity across your essay by using a consistent color scheme and font scheme, using background images consistently (or not at all), and placing recurring information, such as page numbers and navigation tools (see *Use Navigation Tools* in Chapter 22), in the same place on each page.

▲ Text, a video, and images used on a multimedia presentation slide

View a Multimodal Essay

The following examples are drawn from a multimodal essay written by five first-year seminar honors students at Columbia College Chicago: Jack Dorst, Joe Erwin, Sarah Lemcke, Lia Miller, and Izzy Ruta. The students developed their essay using WordPress, a free website-development program that requires no knowledge of coding. Note their use of text, illustrations, color, headings and subheadings, and navigation menus to clearly convey their argument about what we can do to reduce food waste.

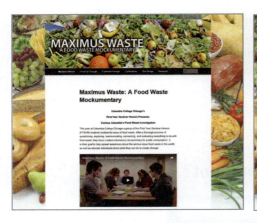

Maximus Waste: A Food Waste Documentary http://www.foodwaste.ccwriting.org/Jack Dorst, Joe Erwin, Sarah Lempke, Lia Miller, Carson Ruta

A consistent look and feel (see *Develop a Consistent Design* in this chapter) are provided through a common color scheme, font scheme, page layout, and page background image.

The pages are designed in an attractive, uncrowded manner, similar to a magazine article.

A menu appears in the same location on each page.

Checklist for Creating Multimodal Essays

✔ **Use your experiences writing academic essays** as a foundation for your work on a multimodal essay.

✔ **Choose your composing tools**, keeping in mind their appropriateness for your writing situation and their tendency to drive design decisions in particular directions.

✔ **Develop an appropriate and consistent design** for your document, paying attention to

- consistent use of fonts, colors, shading, borders, and rules
- larger fonts for headings and subheadings (such as 16-point Times New Roman or Verdana)
- readable body font designed for on-screen reading (such as 11-point Calibri or Georgia)

- placement of titles, text, and illustrations, with illustrations labeled and located near relevant text passages
- if used, transitions between pages (dissolves, page flips) that are quick and not distracting
- if used, background images and sounds that are chosen to enhance rather than obscure or distract from the elements on each page

✔ **Create navigation tools** such as Next and Previous buttons, links, menus, and tables of contents (see *Use Navigation Tools* in Chapter 22).

How Can I Create a Website?

Websites can engage readers in ways that print documents cannot — they can link directly to related sites, allow visitors to access video and audio files, and support communication among the site's readers and writers. This wealth of organization, navigation, and design options, however, carries significant planning, composing, and design challenges, such as keeping your readers focused on your website instead of following links to other sites.

Plan Your Site

The most important concerns to pay attention to during planning include content — the words, images, and other elements you'll include on each page — and the links and other navigation tools your readers will use to find their way to related pages elsewhere on your website.

Learn about making your website accessible in *Understand Design Principles* in Chapter 22.

● CREATE CONTENT

Web pages can include textual information, images, audio, video, animations, linked files, and applications, among other types of material. As you consider your purpose and role, think about what you want your readers to know, do, or believe after they've visited your site. Your decisions about the content and ways to create it should reflect your understanding of your writing situation.

● **CHOOSE NAVIGATION TOOLS**

Your choice of navigational tools (see *Use Navigation Tools* in Chapter 22) will depend on the size and complexity of your site. To help readers navigate a website, developers typically create menus that appear on each page, and they often provide page headers, page footers, breadcrumbs, site maps, tables of contents, and search tools. They also consider how extensively to rely on internal links and links to external websites.

Design Your Site

Many websites are designed in a manner similar to that of magazines, with a heavy use of images and other illustrations. Typical design considerations include choosing a consistent color scheme, formatting headings and subheadings consistently across pages, and using borders, shading, and rules in a manner similar to that of many print publications. In addition, writers who develop websites must also address the placement and appearance of navigation menus and digital illustrations, such as audio and video clips, animations, embedded applications, and downloadable files.

Keep the following principles in mind as you design your site.

- **Simple is better.** Less is more. Don't try to cram too much on a single page or add too much text to a single region on a scrolling page.

- **Place the most important information at the top of each page.** Readers often jump to another website if they don't easily find what they're looking for.

- **Avoid overuse of graphics.** Large images can increase the time it takes for a browser to open a web page. More important, research suggests that readers of web pages are drawn to textual information as opposed to graphical information—a behavior that is strikingly different from readers' typical behavior with print documents. Perhaps because so many websites use images largely as decoration rather than as sources of information (for example, news photographs, diagrams, and charts), readers typically look first at text on a web page.

As you begin to design your website, browse the web for sites that attempt to accomplish a purpose similar to your own. Evaluate their page designs, making note of features and layouts that you might want to use.

Create Your Site

Web developers create websites using a variety of software tools. The easiest and most straightforward options are free online tools such as Google Sites (sites.google.com), Weebly (weebly.com), Wix (wix.com), WordPress (wordpress.com), and Yola (yola.com). You can also use word-processing programs, such as Microsoft Word, which allow you to save documents in the HTML format used by web pages. If you know HTML and CSS — the coding language and style definition specifications used to create websites — you can also create your site with tools ranging from simple text-editing programs such as Notepad and TextEdit to specialized web-editing programs such as Dreamweaver.

Publish Your Site

If you've created your website using a tool such as Google Sites or Wix, your site is already online. If you've used Dreamweaver or a word-processing program, you will need to upload your page files and any associated media files. You will find guidance, usually in the form of help pages, from the website provider that is hosting your site.

Once your website is live, test it. Make sure that your pages open and display properly, that links work, and that media elements open properly on different computers and devices. If you are satisfied with the results of your work, share the URL with the people you want to view your site. In a few days, you'll also find that it will be available through search sites such as Google and Bing.

View Web Pages

The following figures show pages from a website that Quinn Jackson created for future writing teachers. The site was created at Wix.com, which offers free websites and an easy-to-use set of authoring tools.

640 CHAPTER 23 | Working with Genres

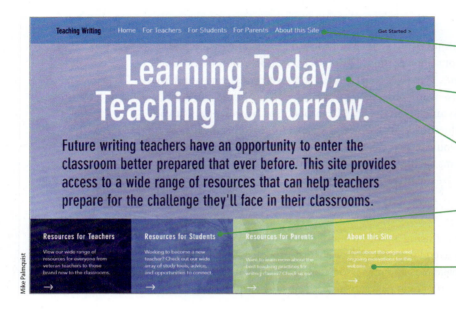

- A navigation bar provides links to major sections.
- The background color remains the same within each section, creating a consistent design.
- The heading identifies the issue addressed by the site.
- The site is highly visual, with easy-to-find links to its main sections.
- An "About this Site" link provides contact information, an email list, and social-networking sites.

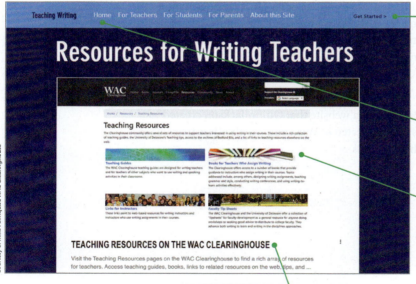

- The navigation bar's background color remains the same, creating a consistent design.
- A link to the home page is provided on all other pages.
- An image of the listed resource draws the eye.
- A heading is set in boldface and uppercase font to distinguish it from the body text.

> **Checklist for Developing Websites**
>
> ✔ **Reflect on your writing situation**, paying particular attention to your purpose and role as well as your readers' expectations.
> ✔ **Plan your site.** Focus on its content and navigation tools.
> ✔ **Design your site.** Pay attention to the following:
>   - a readable body font designed for on-screen reading (such as 11-point Calibri or Georgia)
>   - headings and subheadings formatted in fonts and colors that distinguish them from body text and show the relative importance of levels of headings
>   - labels, captions, and pop-up flags (titles) used to help readers understand links and images
>   - use of alt tags and descriptions for images and other illustrations to ensure accessibility for all readers
>   - information presented in brief, readable chunks, using bulleted and numbered lists whenever possible
>   - color used to set a mood, highlight information, and help readers understand the function of text and illustrations on the site
>   - illustrations placed near the passages that refer to them
>   - images kept as small (in kilobytes) as possible, while being clear and easy to see
> ✔ **Create your site.** Choose a web-development tool such as Google Sites or Wix, a dedicated web-editing program such as Dreamweaver, or a word-processing program.
> ✔ **Publish your site.**
> ✔ **Test your site.**
> ✔ **Distribute the site's URL.**

How Can I Make a Presentation?

Writers frequently make presentations, lead discussions, or share their thoughts through speaking rather than writing. The ability to present your ideas orally is an important skill that you'll use not only in your courses but also throughout your professional and personal life.

Making and giving a presentation involves considering your writing (in this case, *speaking*) situation, planning your presentation, and (optionally) creating a multimedia presentation.

Consider Your Speaking Situation

Making an effective presentation involves much more than simply taking what you've written and reading it aloud. When you share your ideas in person, you connect with your audience through your words, your physical appearance, and your tone of voice. You rely on gestures and other forms of nonverbal communication, as well as your ability to maintain eye contact. That said, it's not simply how you say something. The success of your presentation depends on your audience's ability to follow your argument. Remember that most people find it easier to read (and reread) something than to hear it explained a single time. Listening to the presentation of complex information, ideas, and arguments can be challenging. As you plan and deliver your presentation, be sure to focus on helping your readers follow your points and establishing yourself as credible.

As you plan your presentation, remember that your most important goals are engaging your audience and keeping them interested in your ideas. Ask what you want to accomplish, what your audience expects to hear, and how you can balance your purpose with their needs and interests. The answers to these questions will shape everything in your speech from language choices to visual aids.

Plan Your Presentation

● CREATE A BARE-BONES OUTLINE

Once you've developed a focus for your presentation and determined its main point and general organization, you can create an outline (see Chapter 19). It's a good idea to begin with a basic outline that includes the following:

- an opening line that captures the attention of your audience
- a statement of your main point — typically in the form of a thesis statement
- a sentence establishing your credibility and purpose so that your audience can see that they can trust what you have to say and that you care about and understand the issue, either through personal experience or through research
- two to four key points
- evidence to support your key points
- transition statements to guide your audience through your talk

- a conclusion that reinforces your audience's understanding of the main ideas they should take away from your talk
- a closing line or an invitation to ask questions that makes it clear to your audience that you have finished your presentation

CONSIDER YOUR WORDS

Through your choice of words, metaphors, imagery, and turns of speech, you'll engage your listeners in your argument and ideas. Keep your purpose and role in mind as you decide how to address your audience. For example, if you are attempting to solve a problem, your goal might be to engage your audience personally with the problem. You might talk about how the problem affects "us" and ask listeners to consider what "we" should do to address it.

As you consider your language choices, bear in mind that spoken language is usually more casual than written language. If you adopt the formal tone of an academic research essay, you might sound stiff and unnatural. Remember as well the power of repetition in speeches and other oral presentations. You'll help your audience follow your line of argument by stating important points more than once and in different ways. Finally, consider the role of emotional appeals in your presentation (see *Appeal to Your Readers* in Chapter 12). To connect personally with your audience and to engage your audience with your issue, explore the use of vivid descriptions, anecdotes, and humor. Don't rely too heavily on emotional appeals, however. To maintain your credibility, you'll want to balance pathos with logic by presenting sound reasoning and support for your argument.

Learn more about developing an argument in Chapter 12.

PREPARE SPEAKER'S NOTES

Although some speakers write their presentations word for word, this strategy seldom produces outstanding results. It's better to create notes to prompt yourself as you present your points. Using notes will force you to speak directly to your listeners rather than read from a script. Many seasoned speakers use note cards for their speaker's notes, as they are easy to hold in one hand and are not as distracting as fluttering paper. As you prepare your notes, make sure that the text is large and easy to read so that you can view your next point with a quick glance. Your speaker's notes should include the following information:

- your opening line, written out in full, to get you started in case your mind goes blank because of nervousness
- your preview statement
- any statements that you need to give word for word, such as carefully worded statements about a controversial point or clear descriptions of a complex concept

- your supporting points and reminders of important evidence, including direct quotes, statistics, and names of important people
- transition sentences from one part of the presentation to the next
- memory prompts for any parts of your presentation that you've found yourself forgetting as you practice
- reminders about when to use a visual aid, such as a chart
- brief notes about sources you might want to consult during a question-and-answer session following your talk

The following speaker's notes are from an oral presentation on the use of steroids by adolescent girls involved in sports.

> *Include nonverbal cues in your note cards as a reminder to interact with your audience.*

> *Use short phrases to cue your thoughts.*

1. Intro
   Barry Bonds, A-Rod, Marion Jones, Lance Armstrong — what do all of these big names have in common? *(pause, wait for audience response)*
   - All accused of using performance-enhancing drugs
   - Used to seeing athletes break records, find out later about steroid use
   - Happening for younger athletes — including young women

> *Use brief reminders about nonverbal communication. Format your nonverbal cues in a different color so you don't accidentally speak them out loud.*

> *Write your preview statement word for word in your notes.*

2. Establish credibility & preview
   - My background as an athlete
   - Explain why I care about the topic

   SLOW DOWN!

   Preview:
   (1) First, I am going to talk about the positive impact that competitive athletics can have on young women.
   (2) Then, I'll go over some of the negative consequences of competitive athletics on these young women, including steroid use.
   (3) Finally, I want to talk about what parents and coaches can do to help create a positive athletic experience for these young women.

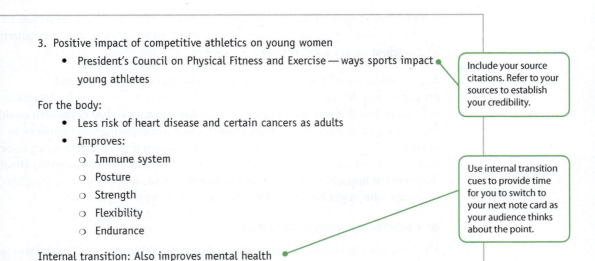

Create a Multimedia Presentation

Many speakers choose to develop a multimedia presentation to accompany their words. In some cases (see *If Necessary, Present Virtually* later in this chapter), it can even take the place of an oral presentation. If it supplements an oral presentation, your multimedia presentation should highlight your points without stealing the show. You've probably seen more than your fair share of presentations in which speakers have read their slides aloud and offered little or nothing beyond the words on the slide. It is far more effective to use your slides to expand on or illustrate — not simply repeat — what you are saying out loud.

Learn about making your multimodal presentation accessible in *Understand Design Principles* in Chapter 22.

CHOOSE MEDIA SOURCES

The distinguishing feature of a multimedia presentation is the wide array of sources you can use to engage with your audience. The sources you choose should support your points or allow you to distinguish your ideas from those advanced by others.

As you would do with a multimodal essay (see *How Can I Create a Multimodal Essay?* earlier in this chapter), consider how the differences among various types of sources — such as images, audio clips, video clips, tables, and charts — can help you achieve your purpose. For example, an image projected onto a screen while you talk is likely to complement your spoken words more than a video clip will, particularly a video clip that has a sound track.

Keep in mind as well the needs, interests, knowledge, values, beliefs, and experiences of the members of your audience. Choose sources carefully. Images and video clips that one audience might view without a great deal of concern could be offensive to another. If your subject matter requires exposing your audience to disturbing images or explicit language, as might happen if you are addressing issues such as gun violence or censorship, warn your audience. If you are uncertain about the potential impact of a source, consult your instructor, a librarian, or a friend or classmate who might be similar to the audience you are trying to reach.

● **CHOOSE COMPOSING TOOLS**

The program you choose to create your multimedia presentation will have a strong effect on its organization and design. Conventional multimedia presentation programs — such as Apache OpenOffice Impress, Apple Keynote, Google Slides, Microsoft PowerPoint, and Microsoft Sway — organize presentations as a collection of slides ordered in a linear sequence from a cover slide to a closing slide. If you don't specify a particular layout, these programs use default slides consisting of a heading and a bulleted list. In contrast, other types of multimedia presentation programs, such as Prezi (prezi.com), organize presentations as one canvas that you can pan and zoom around on, while Emaze (emaze.com) uses three-dimensional effects and zooming to engage an audience. These zooming presentations can be useful for creative purposes such as digital storytelling.

Learn about importing, embedding, and linking to media sources in *How Can I Create a Multimodal Essay?* earlier in this chapter.

As you decide which tools to use, look for program features that can help you during a presentation. The Presenter view in conventional presentation programs allows you to see information that is not projected on the screen, such as notes on the current slide and small images of upcoming slides. During your presentation, these tools can remind you of important ideas that are related to but not displayed on the slide and can help you keep track of where you are in your presentation. Essentially, they serve the same function as the speaker's notes discussed above.

▲ **Presenter view in PowerPoint**

● DEVELOP A CONSISTENT DESIGN

Over the past two decades, audiences in settings ranging from business meetings to lecture halls have been subjected to more poorly designed multimedia presentations than there are drops of water in the ocean. Perhaps you, too, have been subjected to some of these presentations. If so, you'll be aware of the benefits of the following design guidelines.

- **Choose a color scheme that reflects the purpose and tone of your argument.** Use bright colors, for example, for a lighthearted topic. Use neutral colors for a serious presentation.
- **Be consistent in your choice of fonts, colors, and page layout.**
- **Use readable fonts, such as 44-point Corbel for headings and 28-point Calibri for body text.** Avoid elaborate script fonts, which are often unreadable from a distance, or overly playful fonts like Curlz, which can come across as unprofessional.
- **Keep text to a minimum:** some general rules include six words per bullet point, six bullet points per slide, and no more than six slides of all text in a row.
- **To enhance the readability of slides, use either a light background with dark text or a dark background with light text,** and use a minimum of text effects (such as shadows or flashing text). Consider using a contrast checker such as the one found at https://webaim.org/resources/contrastchecker/.

- **Use audio, video, and animation with moderation.** Generally, clips should run no longer than one minute each.
- **Avoid slow or overly complex transitions** (such as dissolves or page flips) between slides.
- **Avoid distracting sound effects** on slides or during slide transitions.

● **PREPARE FOR CHALLENGES**

In most cases, presenters who use multimedia presentations experience few problems. Technical difficulties can occur, however, so it is important to be prepared. You might plan to use a slide clicker, which is similar to a computer mouse, to advance your slides. If it fails, be prepared to stand close enough to your computer or tablet to advance the slides manually. Prepare a backup plan for equipment failure — for instance, if a laptop loses power or an LCD display fails to work properly. You might bring printouts of your presentation, for example, or create a handout summarizing your points.

Engage with Your Audience

When you give a presentation, getting your message across relies almost as much on *how* you say something as on *what* you say. The following techniques will help you polish your delivery.

- **Maintain eye contact with your audience.** Eye contact communicates that you know your topic and that you care about making sure the audience understands your arguments.
- **Vary the pitch of your voice.** Speaking in a monotone is the fastest way to put your audience to sleep. When you mention a startling statistic, raise your pitch. To demonstrate weight and importance, go to a lower register in your voice. Practice using vocal variety to make sure that you sound natural.
- **Project your voice.** You might feel as though you're yelling, but members of the audience will let you know (by looking surprised) if they think you are too loud. Speakers rarely are.
- **Articulate every word clearly.** Even though consonants are often dropped in casual conversation, try to pronounce them more clearly than you would in normal speaking.
- **Slow down.** Most presenters speak too quickly. Slow down your normal rate of speaking to give the audience time to process your words. As you practice, note where you tend to speed up, and add a comment (such as "Slow down!") to your speaker's notes. If you can, record a practice session to double-check your speed.

- **Face your audience as you make your presentation.** If you are using a multimedia presentation, it can be tempting to face the screen. Avoid this temptation.
- **Ensure that presentation slides are readable.** Before you make your talk, preview your presentation on a screen similar in size to the one you will be using during your talk.
- **Point out relevant information on your slides.** Use your multimedia presentation to advance your line of argument.
- **Be prepared to share your slides.** It is common for members of an audience to request the file that contains a multimedia presentation. Be prepared to share it via email, the web, or the cloud.

If Necessary, Present Virtually

TECH TIP: In some cases, you might find that the best way to present to your audience is through a recording or a stand-alone multimedia presentation. If so, you can choose from a range of options.

- **Record your presentation.** You can record your presentation either in front of a live audience or on a video conferencing tool such as Google Meet, Microsoft Teams, or Zoom. If the conferencing tool allows you to record your session, you can save the video file (usually in MP4 format) and share it via the cloud or through a video platform such as YouTube. If you can't present before a live audience, present to yourself. You can share your multimedia presentation on your screen as you deliver your talk.
- **Create a stand-alone multimedia presentation.** In some cases, you might find it most effective to let your multimedia presentation do the talking for you. If so, be sure that you've provided enough information on your slides to convey your points and ensure that your slides display properly on computers, tablets, and phones. Then make sure that you've removed any notes that you don't want your audience to see; check that the format in which you've saved the file can be read on a wide range of computers, tablets, and phones; and choose a means of distributing the file. You can distribute a file by placing it on a website, uploading it to a blog or social-networking site, attaching it to an email message, sharing it through Google Drive or a service such as Dropbox, or saving it on a flash drive and giving it to people you want to view it.

View a Presentation

The following figures show slides from a multimedia presentation designed by Quinn Jackson, a first-year student whose writing project focused on how to prepare future teachers to teach writing.

CHAPTER 23 | Working with Genres

- Title is formatted in a clear, eye-catching font.
- The name of the presenter is clearly identified.
- Fonts are large and easy to read.
- A video clip provides visual interest and an expert's voice to support the presentation.

How Can I Make a Presentation? | CHAPTER 23 | 651

FEEDBACK ON WRITING

- Determine Your Goals for the Assignment
- Choose Your Feedback Methods
- Define the Role of Peer Feedback
  - Develop Rubrics for Peer Feedback
  - Choose the Review Method
  - Establish Ground Rules
- Create a Schedule
  - Make Sure You Can Give Feedback in a Timely Manner

The speaker uses the slides to support her presentation rather than to take its place.

PEER REVIEW ACTIVITIES

- Share Your Goals for Each Activity
  - Global Concerns?
  - Supporting an Argument?
  - Clarity and Style?
- Develop Clear Guidelines
  - Guiding Questions
  - Role as Development Editor
  - Review of Comments by Teacher
- Provide Clear Feedback
  - To Writers
  - To Reviewers

A multilevel bulleted list conveys a strategy for developing peer-review activities.

An illustration supports a key point.

Checklist for Preparing and Delivering Presentations

✔ **Consider your speaking situation.** Review your purpose and role, consider your readers' interests and background, and consider the context in which your presentation will be delivered.

✔ **Plan your presentation.** Narrow your presentation's scope to between two and four key points, create a bare-bones outline of your presentation, and prepare speaker's notes that you can read easily and quickly. Consider how the size and physical arrangement of the room will affect your ability to interact with your audience.

✔ **Optionally, create a multimodal presentation.** Consider the types of sources you will use, choose composing tools, consider accessibility, and develop a consistent design.

✔ **Practice.** Practice your presentation, and ask for feedback from your practice audience.

✔ **Be on time.** Arrive early to ensure adequate time for setup.

✔ **Be prepared.** Anticipate potential problems, and be ready to address them.

✔ **Engage with your audience.** Observe and respond to your audience. Vary the pitch of your voice, speak loudly, and clearly articulate your words.

In Summary: Working with Genres

★ Draft and design an essay (p. 621).

★ Write an article (p. 625).

★ Create a multimodal essay (p. 630).

★ Create a website (p. 637).

★ Make a presentation (p. 641).

24 Revising and Editing

What should I focus on when I revise? 653
Consider your writing situation 654
Consider your argument and ideas 654
Consider your use, integration, and documentation of sources 655
Consider the structure and organization of your document 656
Consider genre and design 656

What strategies can I use to revise? 657
Save multiple drafts 657
Highlight your main point, reasons, and evidence 657
Challenge your assumptions 659
Scan, outline, and map your document 659
Ask for feedback 661

What should I focus on when I edit? 662
Focus on accuracy 662
Focus on economy 662
Focus on consistency 663
Focus on style 663
Focus on spelling, grammar, and punctuation 663

What strategies can I use to edit? 664
Read carefully 664
Mark and search your document 664
Use spelling, grammar, and style tools with caution 665
Ask for feedback 666

When writers revise and edit, they evaluate the effectiveness of their drafts and work to improve them. Although the two processes are related, they focus on different aspects of a document. Revising involves assessing how well a document responds to a specific writing situation, presents a main point and reasons to accept that point, and uses evidence. Editing includes evaluating and improving the expression — at the sentence and word levels — of the information, ideas, and arguments in the document.

What Should I Focus on When I Revise?

Revising involves rethinking and reenvisioning what you've written. It focuses on such big-picture issues as whether the document you've drafted is appropriate for your writing situation; whether your thesis statement is sound and well supported; whether you've properly integrated sources into your document; whether you've organized and presented your information, ideas, and arguments clearly and effectively; and whether you've made appropriate decisions about genre and design.

Consider Your Writing Situation

As you revise, ask whether your document helps you achieve your purposes (see *Writing Has a Purpose* in Chapter 1) and adopt your role (see Chapter 6). If your assignment directed you to inform readers about a particular subject, for instance, consider whether you've provided appropriate information, whether you've offered enough information, and whether that information is presented clearly. If your purpose is to convince or persuade your readers, ask whether you have chosen appropriate reasons and evidence and presented your argument as effectively as you can. You'll find revision suggestions for specific types of assignments in Chapters 7 to 12.

In addition, review your readers' needs, interests, backgrounds, and knowledge of the subject. During revision, imagine how your readers will react to your document by asking questions such as these:

- Will my readers trust what I have to say? How can I establish my credibility?
- Will my readers have other ideas about how to address this subject? How can I convince them that my ideas are worth considering?
- Will my readers find my evidence appropriate and accurate? Is my selection of evidence consistent with their values, beliefs, and experiences?

Finally, identify your requirements, limitations, and opportunities (see *Note Requirements, Limitations, and Opportunities* in Chapter 2). Ask yourself whether you've met the specific requirements of the assignment, such as length and number of sources. Evaluate your efforts to work around limitations, such as lack of access to information. Think about whether you've taken full advantage of your opportunities and any new ones that have come your way.

Consider Your Argument and Ideas

As you revise, ask how well you are conveying your argument and ideas to your readers. First, check the clarity of your thesis statement. Is it phrased in a way that is compatible with the needs and interests of your readers? Second, ask whether your reasons will help your readers understand and accept your thesis statement. As you make this assessment, keep in mind your primary role as a writer — such as advocate, reporter, or interpreter.

- **Writing to reflect.** Have you created a dominant impression of your subject or indicated the significance of your observations for readers? (See Chapter 7.)

- **Writing to inform.** Is the level of detail you've provided consistent with your readers' knowledge of the subject? Have you clearly defined any key concepts and ideas? (See Chapter 8.)

- **Writing to interpret or analyze.** Are your analyses clear and accurate? Have you provided appropriate and sufficient background information to help your readers follow your reasoning? (See Chapter 9.)

- **Writing to evaluate.** Have you clearly described the subject, defined your evaluative criteria, and provided a clear rationale for your judgments? (See Chapter 10.)

- **Writing to solve problems.** Have you clearly defined the problem, considered alternative solutions, and discussed your proposed solution? (See Chapter 11.)

- **Writing to convince or persuade.** Have you made a clear overall point, provided reasons, and presented evidence to support your reasons? Have you appealed to your readers effectively? (See Chapter 12.)

Learn more about adopting roles in Part 2.

Consider Your Use, Integration, and Documentation of Sources

Think about how you've used source information in your document. Review the amount of evidence you've provided for your points and the appropriateness of that evidence for your purpose and readers. If you are arguing about an issue, determine whether you've identified and addressed reasonable opposing viewpoints.

As you do so, determine whether you've presented information, ideas, and arguments from your sources accurately and fairly. Be sure that quotations are accurate and appropriately documented. Ensure that paraphrases and summaries represent the source reasonably and fairly. Although fairness can be difficult to judge, ask whether you've achieved it. For example, writing that an author "ridiculed" a particular idea might enhance the impact of a passage. If the author was only raising questions about the idea, however, using that term would be unfair to your source, to your readers, and to the idea itself.

Learn more about integrating sources into your document in Chapter 21.

Ask yourself, as well, how effectively you've introduced the work of other authors. Begin by considering your use of attributions in terms of your purpose and role.

By characterizing the contributions particular sources are making to the overall conversation, you can frame their arguments — and yours — in a way that helps you achieve your goals. You can also show how particular sources approach your issue, helping your readers better understand how your contribution advances the conversation.

Then consider the relationship you are trying to establish with your readers. Readers appreciate clear identification of the source of a quotation, paraphrase, or summary. Readers also appreciate some variety in how evidence from sources is introduced. To make your writing stand out, vary the words and phrases that identify the sources of the information, ideas, and arguments you use in your document.

Common Attributions	More Specific Attributions
The author writes . . .	The author expresses the opinion that . . .
The author says . . .	The author denies this, noting . . .
The author states . . .	In response, the author observes that . . .

It's also important to review your works cited or reference list for completeness and accuracy. Remember that lack of proper documentation can reduce your document's effectiveness and diminish your credibility. You can learn more about integrating sources in Chapter 21. For guidelines on documenting your sources, see Chapters 25 and 26.

Consider the Structure and Organization of Your Document

Your readers should be able to locate information and ideas easily. As you read your introduction, ask whether it clearly and concisely conveys your main point and whether it helps your readers anticipate the structure and organization of your document. Reflect on the appropriateness of your organizing pattern (see *How Can I Choose an Organizing Pattern?* in Chapter 19) for your purpose and readers. If you've used headings and subheadings, evaluate their effectiveness.

Make sure your document is easy to read. Check for effective paragraphing and paragraph structure (see *How Can I Draft an Effective Document?* in Chapter 20). If you have several small paragraphs, you might combine paragraphs with similar ideas. If you have a number of long paragraphs, break them up and add transitions. Finally, ask whether your conclusion leaves your readers with something to think about. The most effective conclusions typically provide more than just a summary of your argument.

Consider Genre and Design

Consider both the genre — or type — of document that you are writing and your use of design principles and elements (see Chapter 22). If your assignment gave you a choice of genre, ask whether the genre you've selected is appropriate, given your purpose and readers (see Chapter 23). For example, would it be more effective to reach your readers via an informative website, an opinion column, or a brochure?

Would it be more effective to publish your document as a blog entry or as a letter to the editor of a magazine or newspaper? Regardless of the type of document you're writing, make sure that you've followed the conventions associated with it, such as level of formality, accepted sources of evidence, and organization.

Take a careful look, as well, at how you've designed your document (see Chapters 22 and 23). Does it resemble what your readers will expect? For example, if you're writing an academic essay, have you double-spaced your lines, used a readable font, and set wide margins? If you're creating a website, have you made it easy for your readers to find their way around it? Have you ensured that it's accessible (see *Understand Design Principles* in Chapter 22)? Have you consistently formatted your headings and subheadings? Have you used design principles and elements to achieve your purpose and consider your readers?

What Strategies Can I Use to Revise?

You can draw on several strategies for reviewing and improving your document. As you use them, keep track of your ideas for revision by writing comments on sticky notes or in the margins of print documents, by using the Comments tool in word-processing documents, or by creating a to-do list in your writer's notebook.

Save Multiple Drafts

You might not be happy with every revision you make. To avoid wishing that you hadn't made extensive revisions to a draft of your document, save a new copy of your draft before every major revising session. You can add a number to your drafts' file names, such as *Draft1*, *Draft2*, and so on; add the date, such as *Draft-April6* and *Draft-April10*; or use some other naming system that works for you. What's important is that you save multiple versions of your drafts in case you don't like the changes you've made.

TECH TIP: If you save your work in the cloud, you might be able to recover an earlier version of a file. Google Docs allows you to recover previous versions of a file saved in the past thirty days (or up to one hundred versions). Dropbox also allows you to recover versions saved in the past thirty days. Be cautious as you use these tools, since they replace the most recent version.

Highlight Your Main Point, Reasons, and Evidence

As you revise, make sure that your main point (usually expressed as a thesis statement), reasons, and evidence are fully developed. An effective way to do this is to identify and examine each element in your draft, both individually and as a group of related points. If you are working with a printed document, use a highlighter, colored pens or pencils, or sticky notes. If you are working on a digital document, use a highlighting tool to mark the text. You might use different colors to highlight your main point, reasons, and evidence. If you are focusing solely on the evidence in your document, use different colors to highlight evidence from different sources (to help you check whether you are relying too heavily on a single source) or to differentiate the types of evidence you are using (such as quotations, paraphrases, summaries, and numerical data).

Main point — *Wicked* provides several different points of view for the audience to visualize (Faherty). But, what makes *Wicked* unique? Besides the fact the Traveling Broadway show was awarded three Tony Awards in 2004, *Wicked* clearly defines the definition of "good" and evil," and is more than a simple story between two friends.

What is *Wicked* about?

The *Wicked* posters present mysterious elements that give the impression the play is simply an acted-out explanation of what happened before Dorothy came to Oz. Although this is true, *Wicked* is much more than what the posters sketch. This show, brought to Grand Rapids, Michigan by the Devos Performance Hall, **Reasons** — reveals an initial rivalry and a budding friendship between Glinda, the Good Witch, and Elphaba, the Wicked Witch of the West. It, entertainingly, brings fans through a wild journey of Elphaba and Glinda making their way to Emerald City in order to meet the Great Oz and petition for animal rights. **Evidence: Analysis** === Through carefully crafted characters, humorous and musical elements, and supernatural powers, the audience is in for a playful ride with flying monkeys, magic bubbles, and broomsticks, Oh My!

The infamous antagonist in the play is commonly known as the Wicked Witch of the West. However, Elphaba's hardened heart was more of a reaction than an innate concept. According to TJ Dawe, "a Vancouver based **Evidence: Quotations** ······ writer, performer, and director of new theatre pieces," Elphaba was presented "sympathetically" ("Why Wicked"). Born from an affair between a man and her mother, Elphaba's birth father disowns her and her green skin is a constant reminder of her unconventional and controversial birth, making

▲ **Highlight main point, reasons, and evidence**

When you have finished highlighting your draft, review it to determine whether your reasons support your main points as effectively as you had hoped and whether the evidence you've provided to support your reasons is sufficient and varied. If you have relied too heavily on a particular source, for example, your readers might wonder why they shouldn't simply read that source and ignore your document. If you've provided too little evidence, they'll question the basis for your conclusions.

Challenge Your Assumptions

It's easy to accept ideas and arguments that you've worked so hard to develop. But what would a reader with a fresh perspective think? Challenge your main point, reasons, and evidence by using one of the following strategies. Keep track of your challenges by using the Comments tool in your word-processing program.

- **PUT YOURSELF IN THE PLACE OF YOUR READERS**

As you read, try to imagine one of your readers — or, if you're ambitious, a group of readers. Ask questions they might ask. Imagine concerns they might bring to their reading of your document. A reader interested in solving a problem might ask, for example, whether a proposed solution is cost effective, is more appropriate than alternative solutions, or has unacceptable side effects. As you revise, take these questions and concerns into account.

- **PLAY DEVIL'S ADVOCATE**

A devil's advocate raises reasonable objections to ideas and arguments (see *Role Playing* in Chapter 5). As you review your document, identify your key claims, and then pose reasonable objections to them. Make note of these potential objections, and take them into account as you revise.

- **PLAY THE "SO WHAT?" GAME**

As you read your document, ask why readers would care about what you are saying. By asking "So what?" questions, you can gain a better understanding of what your readers are likely to care about and how they might respond to your arguments and ideas. Make note of your responses to these questions, and consider them as you revise.

Scan, Outline, and Map Your Document

Use the strategies in the figure *Scanning, outlining, and mapping your document* to review the structure, organization, and design of your document. As you review the organization and structure of your document, reflect on whether it is appropriate given your purpose, readers, argument, and available information.

Wicked provides several different points of view for the audience to visualize (Faherty). But, what makes *Wicked* unique? Besides the fact the Traveling Broadway show was awarded three Tony Awards in 2004, *Wicked* clearly defines the definition of "good" story between two friends.

What is *Wicked* about?

The *Wicked* posters present mysterious play is simply an acted-out explanation came to Oz. Although this is true, *Wicked* posters sketch. This show, brought to G Performance Hall, reveals an initial riva between Glinda, the Good Witch, and E West. It, entertainingly, brings fans thro Glinda making their way to Emerald Cit petition for animal rights. Through care and musical elements, and supernatural playful ride with flying monkeys, magic

The infamous antagonist in the play is c Witch of the West. However, Elphaba's reaction than an innate concept. Accord writer, performer, and director of new t "Why Wic haba's birth f er unconventi

Elphaba represents the outcast and grabs the hearts of the audience by displaying her relatability. Elphaba's striking personality and Glinda's flims nature, together, fulfilled every *Wicked* fan's dream through compelling vocals, a strong set, and a show production worthy of all audiences.

Glinda's Popular Performances

Entertaining plots and character development can make, or break, a Broadway show, but *Wicked* does not disappoint in making sure those aspects are delivered. Similarly, vocal performance, stage setup, and costume creativity is equally important. Ginna Claire Mason, as Glinda, and Mary Kate Morrissey, as Elphaba, bring life to the stage as they flip magic wands and fiercely ride wicked broomsticks. Together, they shatter the expectations of the audience with their powerhouse vocals. In the witty voca performance of "Popular," Mason perfectly demonstrated the vain and bubble-headed character with ease as she gracefully flopped across the Devo Center stage. Mason taunted Morrissey with loose and whimsical vocals meant to amuse the audience.

Elphaba's Wicked Vocals

Mason may have commanded attention with her ditzy humor and prom dresses, but Morrissey characterized the sarcastic Elphaba equally as accurate. Morrissey showed off the hefty set of lungs she utilized in A "Defying Gravity." Morrissey displayed Elphaba's emotion passionate during this specific piece through exaggerated facial expressions and heightened vocal performance.

Scan headings and subheadings. If you have used headings and subheadings, they can help you track the overall flow of your ideas. Ask whether the organization they reveal is appropriate for your writing situation and your role as a writer.

Scan the first sentence of each paragraph. A quick reading of the first sentence of each paragraph can reveal points at which your ideas shift. As you note these shifts, think about whether they are appropriate and effective.

Map your document. On paper, in a graphics program, or in mind mapping program (see *Mapping* in Chapter 19), draw a map of your document. Like an outline, a map can help you identify the organization of your points and the amount of evidence you've used to support them.

Outline your document. Create a topical or sentence outline of your document (see *How Can I Create an Outline?* in Chapter 19) to assess its structure and organization. This strategy helps you identify the sequence of your points and the amount of space you've devoted to each topic. If you are viewing your document in a word-processing program, use the Styles tool to assign levels to headings in your document; then view it in Outline view.

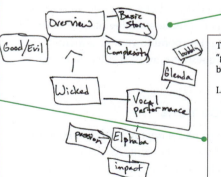

Thesis Statement: *Wicked* clearly defines the definition of "good" and evil," and is more than a simple story between two friends.

I. About Wicked
    a. Before Dorothy came to Oz
    b. Budding friendship between Glinda, the Good Witch, and Elphaba, the Wicked Witch of the West
    c. Origins of Elphaba's hardened heart

▲ Scanning, outlining, and mapping your document

Ask for Feedback

After spending long hours on a project, you might find it difficult to identify problems that your readers could have with your draft. You might read the same paragraph eight times and still fail to notice that the evidence you are using to support a point actually contradicts it. Or you might not notice that your document's organization could confuse your readers. You can ask for feedback on your draft from a friend, relative, colleague, or writing center tutor. It's generally a good idea to ask for help from someone who will be frank as well as supportive. You should also be specific about the kinds of comments you're looking for. Hearing "it's just fine" from a reviewer will not help you revise. You can learn more about engaging in peer review in Chapter 5.

Checklist for Revision

✔ **Review your writing situation.** Does your document help you achieve your purposes and adopt your role? Does it address your readers' needs, interests, knowledge, and backgrounds? Is it well adapted to the context in which it will be read?

✔ **Consider your writing assignment.** Does your document address the writing assignment's requirements? Does it effectively work around limitations and take advantage of opportunities?

✔ **Evaluate the presentation of your ideas.** Does your document provide a clear and appropriate thesis statement? Do your reasons and evidence support your thesis statement, and are they consistent with your primary role as a writer?

✔ **Assess your use, integration, and documentation of sources.** Have you offered adequate support for your points, considered reasonable opposing viewpoints, integrated and acknowledged your sources, and distinguished between your work and that of other writers? Have you used variety in your introduction and attribution of sources? Have you documented your sources appropriately?

✔ **Examine the structure and organization of your document.** Is the introduction clear and concise, does it convey your main point, and does it help your readers anticipate the structure of your document? Is the organization of the document easy to follow? Are paragraphs easy to read? Are transitions effective? Does the conclusion provide more than just a summary of the document?

✔ **Evaluate genre and design.** Does the genre you've chosen help you accomplish your purpose? Have you followed the style and design conventions associated with the type of document you've created?

What Should I Focus on When I Edit?

Editing involves assessing the effectiveness, accuracy, and appropriateness of the words and sentences in a document. Before you begin to edit, remember that editing focuses on your document's words and sentences, not on its overall structure or ideas. If you're uncertain about whether you've organized your document as effectively as possible or whether you've provided enough support for your argument, deal with those issues first. In the same way that you wouldn't start painting a house until you've finished building the walls, hold off on editing until you're confident that you've finished revising.

Focus on Accuracy

You risk damaging your credibility if you provide inaccurate information in your document. To reduce this risk, do the following.

- **Check your facts and figures.** Your readers might think that you're deliberately misleading them if you fail to provide accurate information. As you edit, return to your original sources or your notes to check any facts and figures.

- **Check every quotation.** Return to your original sources or consult your notes to ensure that you have quoted each source exactly. Make sure that you have noted any changes to a quotation with ellipsis marks or brackets and that those changes haven't altered the original meaning of the passage (see *Quote Strategically* in Chapter 21). Be sure to cite each source both in the text and in a works cited or reference list (see Chapters 25 and 26).

- **Check the spelling of every name.** Don't rely on electronic spelling checkers, which provide the correct spelling for only the most common or prominent names.

Focus on Economy

Editing for economy involves reducing the number of words needed to express an idea or convey information. Often you can achieve greater economy in your writing by removing unnecessary modifiers, removing unnecessary introductory phrases such as *there are* and *it is*, and eliminating stock phrases (see *Write Clearly and Concisely* in Chapter 20). Editing for economy generally makes it easier for your readers to understand your meaning, but you should use care; your readers still need to understand the point you are trying to make.

Focus on Consistency

Editing your document for consistency helps you present information and ideas in a uniform way. Use the following techniques to edit for consistency.

- **Treat concepts consistently.** Review your document for consistent treatment of concepts, information, ideas, and definitions.
- **Use numbers consistently.** Check the documentation system you are using for its guidelines on the treatment of numbers. You might find, for instance, that you should spell out the numbers zero through nine and use Arabic numerals for numbers larger than nine.
- **Treat your sources consistently.** Avoid referring to some sources using first names and to others using honorifics, such as *Dr.*, *Mr.*, or *Ms*. Also check that you have cited your sources appropriately for the documentation style you are using, such as MLA or APA (see Chapters 25 and 26). Review each reference for consistent presentation of names, page numbers, and publication dates.
- **Format your document consistently.** Avoid any inconsistencies in your use of fonts, headings, and subheadings and in your placement and captioning of images, tables, charts, and other illustrations (see Chapter 22).

Focus on Style

Your readers will judge you — and what you have to say — not only on what you say but also on how you say it. Edit for matters of style by choosing the right words, using active and passive voice appropriately, adopting a consistent point of view, rewriting complex sentences, varying your sentence length and structure, providing transitions, and using language that is free of bias and stereotyping.

Focus on Spelling, Grammar, and Punctuation

Poor spelling doesn't necessarily affect your ability to get your point across — in most cases, readers will understand even the most atrociously spelled document — but it does affect what your readers think of you. If you ignore spelling errors in your document, you'll erode their confidence in your ability to present ideas or make an argument. The same goes for grammar and punctuation. If your sentences have subject-verb agreement problems or don't use punctuation appropriately, readers might not trust that you have presented your facts correctly. As you put the finishing touches on your document, keep a dictionary and good grammar handbook close by.

What Strategies Can I Use to Edit?

Thorough editing involves making several passes through your document to ensure that you've addressed accuracy, economy, consistency, style, spelling, grammar, and punctuation. The following tips can make that process both easier and more productive.

Read Carefully

As you've worked on your document, you've become quite familiar with it. As a result, it can be easy to read what you *meant* to write instead of what you actually wrote. The following strategies can help you read with a fresh perspective.

- **Set your document aside before you edit.** If time permits, allow a day or two to pass before you begin editing your document. Taking time off between revising and editing can help you see your document more clearly.
- **Pause between sentences for a quick check.** Avoid getting caught up in the flow of your document by stopping after you read each sentence. Slowing down can help you identify problems with your text.
- **Read aloud.** Reading your document aloud can help you find problems that might not be apparent when it's read silently.
- **Read in reverse order.** To check for problems with individual sentences, start at the end of your document and read the last sentence first, and then work backward through the document. To check for problems at the word level, read each word starting with the last one in the document. Disrupting the normal flow of your document can alert you to problems that might not stand out when you read it normally.

Mark and Search Your Document

🕐 **TECH TIP:** Use the following marking and searching strategies to edit for accuracy, economy, consistency, and style.

- **Mark your document.** As you read, use a highlighter pen or the highlighting tool in your word-processing program to mark errors or information that should be double-checked. Consider using different colors to highlight specific types of problems, such as biased language, language with stereotypes, or inconsistent use of formal titles.
- **Use the Find and Replace tools.** Use your word-processing program to edit concepts, names, numbers, and titles for consistency and accuracy. Once you've identified a word or phrase that you'd like to check or change, you can

search for it throughout your document. If you are referring to sources using a parenthetical citation style, such as MLA or APA, use the Find tool to search for an opening parenthesis. If you discover that you've consistently misspelled a word or name, use the Replace tool to correct it throughout your document.

- **Use the Split Window tool.** Some word-processing programs allow you to split your window so that you can view different parts of your document at the same time. Use this tool to ensure that you are referring to a concept in the same way throughout your document or to check for consistent use of fonts, headings, subheadings, illustrations, and tables.

Use Spelling, Grammar, and Style Tools with Caution

TECH TIP: Most word-processing programs provide tools to check spelling, grammar, punctuation, and style. Used with an awareness of their limitations, these tools can significantly reduce the effort required to edit a document.

Spelling checkers have two primary limitations. First, they can't identify words that are spelled correctly but misused — such as *to/two/too, their/they're/there,* and *advice/advise.* Second, spelling checkers are ineffective when they run into words they don't recognize, such as proper names, technical and scientific terms, and unusual words. To compound this problem, spelling checkers often suggest replacement words. If you accept suggestions uncritically, you might end up with a document full of incorrect words and misspelled names.

The main limitation of grammar, punctuation, and style checkers is inaccurate advice. Although much of the advice they offer is sound, a significant proportion is not. If you are confident about your knowledge of grammar, punctuation, and style, you can use the grammar- and style-checking tools in your word-processing program to identify potential problem areas in your document. These tools can point out problems you might have overlooked, such as a subject-verb agreement problem that occurred when you revised a sentence. However, if you don't have a strong knowledge of grammar, punctuation, and style, you can easily be misled by inaccurate advice.

If you have any doubts about advice from your word-processing program's spelling checker, consult an up-to-date dictionary. If you have concerns about the suggestions you receive from the grammar-, punctuation-, and style-checking tools, or if you have questions about the advice you receive from a grammar website, consult a good handbook.

Ask for Feedback

One of the biggest challenges writers face is reading a draft of their own work as a reader rather than as the writer. Because you know what you're trying to say, you'll find it easy to understand your draft. And because you've read your document so many times, you're likely to overlook errors in spelling, punctuation, and grammar. After you've edited your document, ask a friend, relative, or classmate to proofread it and to make note of any problems.

Checklist for Editing

- ✔ **Ensure that your document is accurate.** Check facts and figures, quotations, and the spelling of names.
- ✔ **Edit for economy.** Strive to express your ideas and argument concisely yet clearly.
- ✔ **Ensure that your document is consistent.** Use concepts, numbers, and source information consistently. Check your document for consistent use of formatting and design.
- ✔ **Improve your style.** Strive for economy, use appropriate words, check your verbs, rewrite overly complex sentences, vary sentence length and structure, and use language that is free of bias and stereotyping.
- ✔ **Check for correct spelling, grammar, and punctuation.** Use your word-processing program's spelling, grammar, punctuation, and style tools cautiously; consult a grammar handbook and a dictionary; and ask someone to proofread your draft.

In Summary: Revising and Editing

★ Focus on the big picture when you revise by keeping your writing situation, argument, sources, organization, genre, and design in mind (p. 653).

★ Revise more effectively by saving multiple drafts; highlighting; challenging your assumptions; scanning, outlining, and mapping your document; and asking for feedback (p. 657).

★ Focus on accuracy, economy, consistency, style, spelling, grammar, and punctuation when you edit (p. 662).

★ Take advantage of editing strategies (p. 664).

PART FIVE
Documenting Sources

25 Using MLA Style

How do I cite sources within the text of my document? **669**

How do I prepare the list of works cited? **672**

Modern Language Association (MLA) style, used primarily in the humanities, emphasizes the authors of a source and the pages on which information is located in the source. Writers who use the MLA documentation system cite, or formally acknowledge, source information within their text using parentheses, and they provide a list of sources in a works cited list at the end of their document.

The following student essays are formatted and documented in MLA style:

- Caitlin Guariglia, *Mi Famiglia*
- Brooke Shannon, *Is Wicked All That Wicked?*
- Sophie Kimble, *Sharks for Profit*
- Jeremy Alcazar, *Reforming, Not Defunding, the Police*

For more information about MLA style, consult the *MLA Handbook*, Ninth Edition. Information about the *MLA Handbook* can also be found at mla.org.

Using MLA Style

CITATIONS WITHIN YOUR TEXT

1. Basic format for a source named in your text 669
2. Basic format for a source not named in your text 669
3. Entire source 669
4. Corporate, group, or government author 670
5. Unknown author 670
6. Two or more works by the same author 670
7. Two or more authors with the same last name 670
8. Two authors 670
9. Three or more authors 670
10. Literary work 671
11. Work in an edited collection or anthology 671
12. Sacred text 671
13. Two or more works cited together 671
14. Source quoted in another source 671
15. Source without page numbers 671

ENTRIES IN YOUR WORKS CITED LIST

● BOOKS

16. One author 673
17. Two authors 673
18. Three or more authors 673
19. Corporate or group author 673
20. Unknown author 674
21. Two or more books by the same author 674
22. Editor(s) 674
23. Author(s) with an editor or a translator 674
24. Book in a language other than English 674
25. Edition other than the first 674
26. Republished book 674
27. Book with more than one publisher 675
28. Multivolume work 675
29. Book in a series 675
30. Book with a title within the title 675
31. Work in an edited collection or anthology 675
32. Foreword, introduction, preface, or afterword 677
33. Published proceedings of a conference 677
34. Screenplay 677
35. Graphic narrative or illustrated work 678
36. Sacred text 678
37. Dissertation or thesis 678

● SOURCES IN JOURNALS, MAGAZINES, AND NEWSPAPERS

38. Article in a journal 678
39. Article in a monthly or bimonthly magazine 681
40. Article in a weekly or biweekly magazine 681
41. Article in a newspaper 681
42. Unsigned article 681
43. Article that skips pages 681
44. Article with a quotation in the title 682
45. Article in a special issue 682
46. Editorial 682
47. Letter to the editor 682
48. Review 682
49. Published interview 682

● REFERENCE WORKS

50. Encyclopedia, dictionary, thesaurus, handbook, or almanac 683
51. Entry in an encyclopedia, dictionary, thesaurus, handbook, or almanac (including a wiki) 683
52. Map or chart 683
53. Government publication 683
54. Brochure or pamphlet 684

● FIELD SOURCES

55. Personal interview 684
56. Unpublished letter 684
57. Lecture or public address 684

● MEDIA SOURCES

58. Film or video 684
59. Television or radio program 685
60. Sound recording, audio clip, or podcast 685
61. Musical score 686
62. Work of art, photograph, or other image 686
63. Advertisement 686
64. Cartoon 687
65. Live performance 687

● OTHER DIGITAL SOURCES

66. Entire website 687
67. Academic course or department website 687
68. Short work from a website 687
69. Message posted to a newsgroup, electronic mailing list, or online discussion forum 688
70. Blog 688
71. Email message 688
72. Facebook post or comment 688
73. Twitter post (tweet) 690
74. Instagram post 690
75. Computer software, app, or video game 690
76. Other sources 690

How Do I Cite Sources within the Text of My Document?

MLA style uses parentheses for in-text citations to acknowledge the use of another author's words, facts, and ideas. When you refer to a source within your text, provide the author's last name and the specific page number(s) if the source is paginated. Your reader can then go to the works cited list at the end of your document to find a full citation.

1. Basic format for a source named in your text Most often, you will want to name the author of a source within your sentence rather than in a parenthetical citation. By doing so, you create a context for the material (words, facts, or ideas) that you are including, and you indicate where the information from the author begins. When you are using a direct quotation, paraphrase, or summary from a source and have named the author in your sentence, place only the page number in parentheses after the borrowed material. The period follows the closing parenthesis.

> According to Tattersall, when early humans emerged from the dense forests to the adjacent woodlands, their mobility and diet were forced to change dramatically (45).

When you are using a block (or extended) quotation, the parenthetical citation comes after the final punctuation and a single space (see *How Can I Integrate Sources into My Draft?* in Chapter 21).

If you continue to refer to a single source for several sentences in a row within one paragraph — and without intervening references to another source — you may place your reference at the end of the paragraph. However, be sure to include all relevant page numbers.

2. Basic format for a source not named in your text If you have not mentioned the author in your sentence, you must place the author's name and the page number in parentheses after the quotation, paraphrase, or summary. Again, the period follows the closing parenthesis.

> It would have been impossible for early humans to digest red meat, as their stomachs lacked the necessary acids to break down the muscle and tissue before delivery to the intestines (Tattersall 46).

3. Entire source If you are referring to an entire source rather than to a specific page or pages, you do not need a parenthetical citation.

> Author Jhumpa Lahiri adapted the title for her book of stories *Unaccustomed Earth* from a line in the first chapter of Nathaniel Hawthorne's *The Scarlet Letter.*

4. Corporate, group, or government author Cite the corporation, group, or government author as you would an individual author. You may use abbreviations for the source in subsequent references if you add the abbreviation in parentheses at the first mention of the name. In a parenthetical citation, use a brief version of the name.

> The Social Security Administration (SSA) estimates that a twenty-year-old has a three in ten chance of becoming disabled before reaching retirement age (4). If a worker does become disabled, SSA assigns a representative to review the case individually (7).

5. Unknown author If you are citing a source that has no known author, such as the book *A Woman in Berlin*, use a brief version of the title in the parenthetical citation.

> The narrator pays particular attention to the culture of rape in Berlin during World War II, calling it a "collective experience" and claiming that German women comforted one another by speaking openly about it — something they never would have considered during peacetime (*Woman* 147).

6. Two or more works by the same author For references to authors with more than one work in your works cited list, insert a short version of the title between the author and the page number, separating the author and the title with a comma.

> (Sacks, *Hallucinations* 77)

> (Sacks, *Mind's Eye* 123)

7. Two or more authors with the same last name Include the first initial and last name in the parenthetical citation.

> (F. McCourt 27)

> (M. McCourt 55)

8. Two authors Include the last name of each author in your citation.

> In the year following Hurricane Katrina, journalist and activist Jane Wholey brought together a group of twenty New Orleans middle schoolers in an effort to reimagine their school system's food environment from the ground up (Gottlieb and Joshi 2).

9. Three or more authors Use the last name of the first author and the abbreviation "et al." (Latin for "and others"). If you mention the authors in a signal phrase, use "and colleagues" instead of "et al."

> (Johnson et al. 17)

10. Literary work Along with the page number(s), give other identifying information, such as a chapter, scene, or line number, that will help readers find the passage.

> One prominent motif introduced at the opening of *Beloved* is bestiality, exemplified in Sethe's being described as "down on all fours" at the first appearance of her dead daughter's ghost (Morrison 27; ch. 1).

11. Work in an edited collection or anthology Cite the author of the work, not the editor of the collection or anthology. (See also item 31.)

> In his satirical essay "A Presidential Candidate," Mark Twain outlines his plan to thwart the opposition, insisting that "if you know the worst about a candidate, to begin with, every attempt to spring things on him will be checkmated" (3).

12. Sacred text Give the name of the edition you are using, along with the chapter and verse (or their equivalent).

> It is still very sage advice to "withhold not good from them to whom it is due, when it is in the power of thine hand to do it" (*King James Bible*, Prov. 2.27).

> The Qur'an points to the bee and its natural ability to produce honey as proof of God's existence ("The Bees" 16.68).

13. Two or more works cited together Use a semicolon to separate entries. Entries do not need to be alphabetized.

> Byron Bancroft Johnson founded the American League in 1901 by raiding the National League for its best players, offering them competitive salaries to jump leagues (Appel 3; Stout and Johnson 8).

14. Source quoted in another source Ideally, you should be able to find the original source of the quotation. If you must use a quotation cited by another author, use the abbreviation "qtd. in" (for "quoted in") when you cite the source.

> When Henry Ford introduced the Model T, he insisted on making it a practical and affordable family car, maintaining that "no man making a good salary will be unable to own one — and enjoy with his family the blessing of hours of pleasure in God's great open spaces" (qtd. in Booth 9).

15. Source without page numbers Give a section, paragraph, or screen number, if numbered, in the parenthetical citation.

> First-time American mothers and fathers both have aged an average of three to four years since 1970 (Shulevitz, par. 4).

If no numbers are available, list only the author's name in parentheses.

> It is adults, not children, who present the greatest challenge in gift giving, as adults tend to long for intangibles — like love or career success — that are harder to pin down (Rothman).

How Do I Prepare the List of Works Cited?

MLA-style research documents include a reference list titled "Works Cited," which begins on a new page at the end of the document. If you wish to acknowledge sources that you read but did not cite in your text, you may include them in a second list titled "Works Consulted." In longer documents, the list of works cited may be given at the end of each chapter or section. In digital documents that use links, such as a website, the list of works cited is often a separate page to which other pages are linked. To view works cited lists in MLA style, see the featured student essays in Chapters 7, 10, 11, and 12.

The list is alphabetized by author. If the author's name is not given, alphabetize the entry using the title of the source. If you cite more than one work by the same author, alphabetize the group under the author's last name, with each entry listed alphabetically by title (see item 21).

All entries in the list are double-spaced, with no extra space between entries. Entries are formatted with a hanging indent: the first line of an entry is flush with the left margin, and subsequent lines are indented one-half inch. Unless otherwise noted, use commas to separate items within each entry. Titles of longer works, such as books, journals, or websites, are italicized. Titles of short works, such as articles or chapters, are enclosed in quotation marks. MLA generally indicates the "container" of the source — the larger object, if any, in which the source can be found. Some sources may have multiple levels of containers, such as a periodical article that is accessed via a database. Occasionally, sources may be identified by a descriptive label (editorial, map, letter, photograph, and so on).

Since sources today can often be found in both print and digital form — for instance, you can easily access a *New Yorker* article in the print magazine or on the magazine's website — the source types that follow include model citations for both media. The section on digital sources (see items 65 through 74) features source types that are native to digital formats, such as blogs or social media platforms.

Books

16. One author List the author's last name first, followed by a comma and the first name. Italicize the book title and subtitle, if any. List the publisher (abbreviating University Press as UP), then insert a comma and the publication year. End with a period.

> Page, Scott E. *The Model Thinker: What You Need to Know to Make Data Work for You.* Basic Books, 2018.

Cite an online book as you would a print book, providing the website and DOI (digital object identifier, a unique number assigned to specific content). If a DOI is not available, provide a stable URL. It is optional whether to include http:// or https:// in a URL, but it should be included with the DOI as shown below.

> Seo, S. Niggol. *Climate Change and Economics: Engaging with Future Generations with Action Plans.* Springer, 2021.

> Inoue, Asao B. *Above the Well: An Antiracist Argument from a Boy of Color.* The WAC Clearinghouse/Utah State UP, 2021. https://doi.org/10.37514/PER-B.2021.1244.

Cite an e-book as you would a print book, and then provide the name of the e-reader.

> Bauer, Shane. *American Prison: A Reporter's Undercover Journey into the Business of Punishment.* Kindle ed., Penguin Press, 2018.

17. Two authors List both authors in the same order as on the title page, last name first for only the first author listed. Use a comma to separate authors' names.

> Muthu, Subramanian Senthilkannan, and Miguel Ángel Gardetti. *Sustainability in the Textile and Apparel Industries: Consumerism and Fashion Sustainability.* Springer, 2020.

18. Three or more authors Provide the first author's name (last name first), followed by a comma, and then the abbreviation "et al." (Latin for "and others").

> Gershenson, Seth, et al. *Teacher Diversity and Student Success: Why Racial Representation Matters in the Classroom.* Harvard Education Press, 2021.

19. Corporate, group, or government author Write out the full name of the corporation or group, omitting any articles at the beginning (such as *The*), and cite the name as you would an author. This name is often also the name of the publisher.

> Staff of *The Late Show with Stephen Colbert. Whose Boat Is This Boat? Comments That Don't Help in the Aftermath of a Hurricane.* Simon & Schuster, 2018.

20. Unknown author When no author is listed on the title or copyright page, begin the entry with the title of the work. Alphabetize the entry by the first word of the title other than *A*, *An*, or *The*.

>   *Horses and Foals*. Kingfisher, 2018.

21. Two or more books by the same author Use the author's name in the first entry. Thereafter, use three hyphens followed by a period in place of the author's name. List the entries alphabetically by title.

>   Roberts, Andrew. *Churchill: Walking with Destiny*. Viking, 2018.
>
>   ---. *Napoleon: A Life*. Penguin Books, 2015.

22. Editor(s) Use the descriptive label "editor" or "editors" after the editors' names.

>   Pandey, Anita, and Avinash Sharma, editors. *Extreme Environments: Unique Ecosystems — Amazing Microbes*. CRC Press, 2021.

23. Author(s) with an editor or a translator Start with the author's name, then give the title. Include the label "Edited by" or "Translated by" and the name of the editor or translator, first name first.

>   Horta, Paulo Lemos, editor. *Aladdin*. Translated by Yasmine Seale, Liveright, 2018.

24. Book in a language other than English Provide a translation of the book's title in square brackets.

>   Márquez, Gabriel García. *Del amor y otros demonios* [Of Love and Other Demons]. Vintage Books, 2010.

25. Edition other than the first Include the number of the edition and the abbreviation "ed." (meaning "edition") after the title.

>   Bacon, Nora. *The Well-Crafted Sentence: A Writer's Guide to Style*. 3rd ed., Bedford/St. Martin's, 2019.
>
>   Nadakavukaren, Anne. *Our Global Environment: A Health Perspective*. 8th ed., Waveland Press, 2020.

26. Republished book Indicate the original date of publication after the title. Include any information relevant to republication, such as a new introduction. For online books, give the URL.

>   Harris, Muriel. *Teaching One-to-One: The Writing Conference*. 1986. The WAC Clearinghouse, 2015. https://wac.colostate.edu/books/landmarks/harris/.

Rothfuss, Patrick. *The Name of the Wind: 10th Anniversary Deluxe Edition (Kingkiller Chronicle)*. 2007. Illustrations by Dan Dos Santos, DAW, 2017.

27. Book with more than one publisher If more than one publisher is shown on the book's copyright page and they appear to have equal responsibility for publishing the book, list the publisher names in the order they are shown, separated by a forward slash (/). If one publisher appears to have primary responsibility, list only that publisher.

Inoue, Asao B. *Above the Well: An Antiracist Argument from a Boy of Color*. The WAC Clearinghouse/Utah State UP, 2021. https://doi.org/10.37514/PER-B.2021.1244.

28. Multivolume work End with the total number of volumes and the abbreviation "vols."

Plath, Sylvia. *The Letters of Sylvia Plath: Volume I: 1940–1956*. Edited by Peter K. Steinberg and Karen V. Kukil, vol. 1, Harper, 2017. 2 vols.

If you have used only one of the volumes in your document, include the volume number after the title. List the total number of volumes after the publication information.

Stark, Freya. *Letters: New Worlds for Old, 1943–46*. Edited by Lucy Moorehead, vol. 5, Compton Press, 1978. 8 vols.

29. Book in a series If a series name and/or number appears on the title page, include it at the end of the citation, after the date.

Trindade, Luís, editor. *Narratives in Motion: Journalism and Modernist Events in 1920s Portugal*. Berghahn, 2016. Remapping Cultural History 15.

30. Book with a title within the title Do not use italics for the title within the title.

Stuckey, Sterling. *African Culture and Melville's Art: The Creative Process in* Benito Cereno *and* Moby-Dick. Oxford UP, 2009.

31. Work in an edited collection or anthology Give the author, then the title in quotation marks. Follow with the title of the collection in italics, the label "edited by," and the names of the editor(s) (first name first), the publication information, and the inclusive page numbers for the selection or chapter.

Sayrafiezadeh, Saïd. "Paranoia." *New American Stories*, edited by Ben Marcus, Vintage Books, 2015, pp. 3–29.

How Do I Cite Books Using MLA Style?

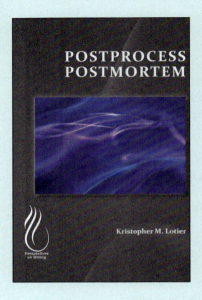

When citing a book, use the information from the title page and the copyright page (typically after the title page), not from the book's cover or a library catalog. See items 16 through 37 for complete models for citing books.

Lotier, Kristopher M. *Postprocess Postmortem*. The WAC Clearinghouse/UP of Colorado, 2021. https://doi.org/10.37514/PER-B.2021.1268.

- A — author
- B — title
- C — publisher
- D — year
- E — DOI or URL

A **The author.** Give the last name first, followed by a comma, the first name, and the middle initial (if given). Omit titles such as "MD," "PhD," or "Sir"; include suffixes after the name and a comma (O'Driscoll, Gerald P., Jr.). End with a period.

B **The title.** Italicize the title and subtitle. Capitalize all major words. End with a period.

C **The publisher.** Provide the publisher's name as listed on the book's title page, but abbreviate "University Press" as "UP" (for example, abbreviate "Oxford University Press" as "Oxford UP"). Do not include the words "Publisher" or "Inc." Follow with a comma.

D **The year of publication.** Use the most recent copyright date. End with a period.

E **DOI or URL.** If available, provide the DOI (digital object identifier), preceded by https://doi.org/. If the book is available online but lacks a DOI, provide the URL. End with a period.

If you are using multiple selections from the same anthology, include the anthology itself in your list of works cited, and cross-reference it in the citations for individual works.

>Eisenberg, Deborah. "Some Other, Better Otto." Marcus, pp. 94–136.

>Marcus, Ben, editor. *New American Stories*. Vintage Books, 2015.

>Sayrafiezadeh, Saïd. "Paranoia." Marcus, pp. 3–29.

32. Foreword, introduction, preface, or afterword Begin with the author of the part you are citing and the name of that part. Add the title of the work; "by" or "edited by" and the work's author or editor (first name first); and publication information. Then give the inclusive page numbers for the part.

>Pollan, Michael. Foreword. *Salt, Fat, Acid, Heat: Mastering the Elements of Good Cooking*, by Samin Nosrat, Simon & Schuster, 2017, pp. 1–4.

If the author of the foreword or other part is also the author of the work, use only the last name after "by."

>Olson, Gregory Allen. Introduction. *Landmark Speeches on the Vietnam War*, by Olson, Texas A&M UP, 2010, pp. 1–12.

If the part has a title, include the title in quotation marks directly after the author.

>Sullivan, John Jeremiah. "The Ill-Defined Plot." Introduction. *The Best American Essays 2014*, edited by Sullivan, Houghton Mifflin Harcourt, 2014, pp. xvii–xxvi.

33. Published proceedings of a conference Provide information as you would for a book. Do not include information about the sponsors, date, and location of the conference. Do include the publisher and date of publication.

>Mueller, Dawn M., editor. *Ascending into an Open Future: The Proceedings of the ACRL 2021 Virtual Conference*. Association of College and Research Libraries, 2021. https://www.ala.org/acrl/conferences/acrl2021/papers.

34. Screenplay Provide information as you would for a book.

>Cholodenko, Lisa, and Stuart Blumberg. *The Kids Are All Right: The Shooting Script*. Newmarket Press, 2011.

35. Graphic narrative or illustrated work List the primary author/illustrator in the first position.

> Ellis, Adam. *Super Chill: A Year of Living Anxiously*. Andrews McMeel Publishing, 2018.
>
> Ahmed, Saladin. *Abbott*. Illustrated by Sami Kivela, BOOM! Studios, 2018.
>
> Smith, Lane. *A Perfect Day*. Roaring Brook Press, 2017.

36. Sacred text Include the title of the version as it appears on the title page. If the title does not identify the version, place that information before the publisher.

> *The Oxford Annotated Bible with the Apocrypha*. Edited by Herbert G. May and Bruce M. Metzger, Revised Standard Version, Oxford UP, 1965.
>
> *The Qur'an: Translation*. Translated by Abdullah Yusuf Ali, Tahrike Tarsile Qur'an, 2001.

37. Dissertation or thesis Cite as you would a book (see item 16). Add the year the dissertation was accepted and the school, followed by a label such as "dissertation" or "thesis."

> Havig, Jenna S. *Advantages and Disadvantages of Flexible Seating*. 2017. Minot State University, thesis.

Sources in Journals, Magazines, and Newspapers

38. Article in a journal Enclose the article title in quotation marks. Italicize the journal title, then list the volume number, issue number, month or season (if applicable) and year of publication, and inclusive page numbers.

> Schechter, Laura. " 'On the Outside Facing the Wooded Ridge': Close Reading Translations and Interpretive Diversity." *Pedagogy*, vol. 18, no. 1, Jan. 2018, pp. 51–68.

For an article available online, provide the print information, if given, and end with the DOI or URL.

> Levy, Ronna J. "Literature Circles: Access to Texts." *Open Words: Access and English Studies*, vol. 12, no. 1, Dec. 2019, pp. 88–109. https://doi.org/10.37514/OPW-J.2019.12.1.05.

For an article from a database, cite the database name before the DOI or URL.

> Woyach, Jennifer A., et al. "Ibrutinib Regimens versus Chemoimmunotherapy in Older Patients with Untreated CLL." *New England Journal of Medicine,* Dec. 2018, *PubMed,* https://doi.org/10.1056/NEJMoa1812836.

How Do I Cite Articles from Periodicals Using MLA Style?

Tutorial

Periodicals include journals, magazines, and newspapers. This tutorial gives an example of a citation for an article in a scholarly journal. See items 39 through 49 for models for citing articles from other types of periodicals.

If you need to cite a periodical article you accessed through a database, consult the guidelines in the following tutorial.

McCracken, Krista, and Skylee-Storm Hogan. "Community First: Indigenous Community-Based Archival Provenance." *Across the Disciplines*, vol. 18, no. 1/2, 2021, pp. 22–32, https://doi.org/10.37514/ATD-J.2021.18.1-2.03.

A **The author.** Give the last name first, followed by a comma, the first name, and the middle initial (if given). Omit titles such as "MD," "PhD," or "Sir"; include suffixes after the name and a comma (O'Driscoll, Gerald P., Jr.). End with a period.

B **The article title.** Give the full title and the subtitle (if any), separated by a colon. Enclose the title and subtitle in quotation marks, and capitalize all major words. Place a period inside the closing quotation mark.

C **The periodical title.** Italicize the periodical title, including the article "The"; capitalize all major words; and insert a comma.

D **The date of publication.** For journals, give volume number, issue number, and the month or season (if applicable) and year of publication. For monthly magazines, give the month and year. For weekly magazines and newspapers, give the day, month, and year, in that order. Abbreviate the names of all months except May, June, and July. Follow the year with a comma.

E **Inclusive page number(s).** Use the abbreviation "p." or "pp." For numbers 100 and above, give only the last two digits and any other preceding digits if different from the first number (322–28, 402–10, 1437–45, 592–603). Include section letters for newspapers, if relevant. End with a period.

F **DOI or URL.** If available, provide the DOI (digital object identifier). If the article is available online but lacks a DOI, provide the URL.

679

Tutorial

How Do I Cite Articles from Databases Using MLA Style?

Libraries subscribe to services such as Lexis-Nexis, ProQuest, InfoTrac, and EBSCOhost that provide access to databases of digital texts. The databases provide publication information, abstracts, and the complete text of documents in a specific subject area, discipline, or profession. (See *Search Databases* in Chapter 14.)

⎯ A ⎯ ⎯ B ⎯ ⎯ C ⎯
Lydenberg, Robin. "Reading Lessons in Alison Bechdel's *Fun Home: A Family Tragicomic*." *College Literature*,
⎯ D ⎯ ⎯ E ⎯ ⎯ F ⎯ ⎯ G ⎯ ⎯ H ⎯
vol. 44, no. 2, spring 2017, pp. 133–65. *Project MUSE*, https://doi.org/10.1353/lit.2017.0008.

A **The author.** Give the last name first, followed by a comma, the first name, and the middle initial (if given). Omit titles such as "MD," "PhD," or "Sir"; include suffixes after the name and a comma (O'Driscoll, Gerald P., Jr.). End with a period.

B **The article title.** Give the full title; include the subtitle (if any), preceded by a colon. Enclose the full title in quotation marks, and capitalize all major words. Place a period inside the closing quotation mark.

C **The periodical title.** Italicize the periodical title, including the article "The." Capitalize all major words.

D **The volume number and issue number if appropriate.** Use the abbreviations "vol." and "no." to indicate the volume number and issue number.

E **The date of publication.** For journals, give the month or season (if applicable) followed by the year of publication. For monthly magazines, give the month and year. For weekly magazines and newspapers, give the day, month, and year, in that order. Abbreviate the names of all months except May, June, and July. Follow the year with a comma.

F **Inclusive page number(s).** Use the abbreviation "p." or "pp." For numbers 100 and above, give only the last two digits and any other preceding digits if different from the first number (322–28, 402–10, 1437–45, 592–603). Include section letters for newspapers, if relevant. End with a period.

G **The name of the database.** Italicize the name of the database, followed by a comma.

H **The DOI or URL.** If available, provide the DOI (digital object identifier). If the article is available online but lacks a DOI, provide the URL.

39. Article in a monthly or bimonthly magazine After the author's name and title of the article, list the title of the magazine in italics, the date (use abbreviations for all months except May, June, and July), and inclusive page numbers.

> Blackmore, Susan. "Decoding the Puzzle of Human Consciousness: Why Us?" *Scientific American*, Sept. 2018, pp. 48–53.

40. Article in a weekly or biweekly magazine Give the exact date of publication in day-month-year order.

> Grossman, Lev. "A Star Is Born." *Time*, 2 Nov. 2015, pp. 30–39.

Cite online articles the same as you would a print article, and then give the URL.

> Covert, Bryce. "Where 'Defund' Isn't Dead." *The Nation*, 29 Nov. 2021, https://www.thenation.com/article/society/police-reform-defund/.

41. Article in a newspaper If the newspaper is not a national newspaper (such as *Wall Street Journal*, *Christian Science Monitor*, or *Chronicle of Higher Education*) or if the city of publication is not part of its name, add the city in square brackets after the name of the newspaper: "[Chisholm, MN]." List the date in day-month-year order, followed by the page numbers (use the section letter before the page number if the newspaper uses letters to designate sections). If the article does not appear on consecutive pages, include only the first page number and a plus sign (+), with no space between.

> Schmelzer, Elise. "State AG to Force Reform." *The Denver Post*, 16 Sept. 2021, pp. A1+.

For newspaper articles found online, cite as you would a print article and give the URL.

> Lin, Liza. "Yahoo Pulls Out of China, Ending Tumultuous Two-Decade Relationship." *The Wall Street Journal*, 2 Nov. 2021, https://www.wsj.com/articles/yahoo-pulls-out-of-china-ending-tumultuous-two-decade-relationship-11635848926.

42. Unsigned article Begin with the title of the article. Alphabetize by the first word other than "A," "An," or "The."

> "I Am Part of the Resistance Inside the Trump Administration." *The New York Times*, 5 Sept. 2018, https://www.nytimes.com/2018/09/05/opinion/trump-white-house-anonymous-resistance.html.

43. Article that skips pages Give only the first page number and a plus sign (+), with no space between.

> Mahler, Jonathan. "The Second Coming." *The New York Times Magazine*, 15 Aug. 2010, pp. 30+.

44. Article with a quotation in the title Enclose the quotation in single quotation marks within the article title, which is enclosed in double quotation marks.

> Díaz, Isabel González. "Enriching the 'Rags-to-Riches' Myth." *The Black Scholar*, vol. 43, no. 1–2, spring 2013, pp. 43–51.

45. Article in a special issue After the author and the title of the article (in quotation marks) include the title of the special issue (in italics), and then write the words "special issue of" before the regular title of the periodical.

> Redd, Steven B., and Alex Mitz. "Policy Perspectives on National Security and Foreign Policy Decision Making." *2013 Public Policy Yearbook*, special issue of *Policy Studies Journal*, vol. 41, no. 1, Apr. 2013, pp. S11–S37.

46. Editorial Include the word "Editorial" after the page number(s) or URL.

> "Keep Toilet Paper Off Your Shopping List This Black Friday (and Beyond)." *The Baltimore Sun*, 25 Nov. 2020, https://www.baltimoresun.com/opinion/editorial/bs-ed-1127-toilet-paper-pandemic-20201125-4u4t6civ7rflbof27xkv2h6zii-story.html. Editorial.

47. Letter to the editor If there is no title, use "Letter to the Editor" as the title.

> Ashton-Williams, Amy. "Measure 110 Has Us on the Right Path." *East Oregonian* [Pendleton, OR], 13 Nov. 2021, A5.

48. Review Start with the author and title of the review, then the words "Review of" followed by the title of the work under review. Insert a comma and the word "by" or "edited by" (for an edited work) or "directed by" (for a play or film) and the name of the author or director. Continue with publication information for the review. Use this citation format for all reviews, including books, films, and video games.

> Cicchino, Amy. "Review." Review of *Oral Communication in the Disciplines: A Resource for Teacher Development and Training*, edited by Deanna P. Dannels, Patricia R. Palmerton, and Amy L. H. Gaffney. *The WAC Journal*, vol. 30, no. 1, 2019, pp. 108-30, https://doi.org/10.37514/WAC-J.2019.30.1.05.

49. Published interview Begin with the person interviewed. If the published interview has a title, give it in quotation marks. If not, write the word "Interview by" followed by the name of the interviewer. Then supply the publication information.

> Musk, Elon. "Interviewing Elon Musk." Interview by David Gelles. *The New York Times*, 19 Aug. 2018, p. A2, https://www.nytimes.com/2018/08/19/insider/elon-musk-interview.html.

Reference Works

50. Encyclopedia, dictionary, thesaurus, handbook, or almanac Cite as you would a book (see item 16).

51. Entry in an encyclopedia, dictionary, thesaurus, handbook, or almanac (including a wiki) Unless the entry is signed, begin your citation with the title of the entry in quotation marks, followed by a period. Give the title of the reference work, italicized, the edition (if available), the publisher, and year of publication. If there is no date of publication, include your date of access.

> "Absence Makes the Heart Grow Fonder." *The American Heritage Dictionary of Idioms*. 2nd ed., Houghton Mifflin Harcourt, 2013.

Cite an online entry as you would a print entry, then give the URL.

> "House Music." Wikipedia, 8 Nov. 2021, https://en.wikipedia.org/wiki/House_music.

52. Map or chart Generally, treat a map or chart as you would a book without listed authors (see item 20), listing its title and publication information. For a map in an atlas or other volume, give the map title (in quotation marks), followed by publication information for the atlas and page number(s) for the map. If the creator of the map or chart is listed, use the creator's name as you would an author's name.

> "The Transatlantic Slave System." *Ways of the World: A Brief Global History*. 4th ed., Bedford/St. Martin's, 2019, p. 411.

For a map or chart found online, cite as you would a print source, then give the URL.

> "Africa." *Worldatlas.com*, 15 Nov. 2021, https://www.worldatlas.com/webimage/countrys/af.htm.

53. Government publication In most cases, cite the government agency as the author. If there is a named author, editor, or compiler, provide that name after the title. Do not abbreviate "Congress," "Senate," "House," "Resolution," or "Report."

> National Oceanic and Atmospheric Administration. *2017 Shark Finning Report to Congress*. U.S. Department of Commerce, 26 Feb. 2019. https://www.fisheries.noaa.gov/resource/document/2017-shark-finning-report-congress.

When documenting a bill, report, or resolution of the United States Congress, include the number and session of Congress from which it emerged.

> United States, Congress, House, Medicaid Extenders Act of 2019. 116th Congress, 1st session, House Resolution 259, Public Law No. 116–3, https://www.congress.gov/bill/116th-congress/house-bill/259.

54. Brochure or pamphlet Format the entry as you would for a book (see item 16).

> *This Is Edinburgh Information Pack: Summer/Spring 2018*. Edinburgh.org, 2018, https://edinburgh.org/media/1297024/This-is-Edinburgh-Press-Information-Pack-2018.pdf.

Field Sources

55. Personal interview Place the name of the person interviewed first, followed by words to indicate how the interview was conducted ("Personal interview," "Telephone interview," or "E-mail interview") and the date. (Note that MLA style is to hyphenate "e-mail.")

> Halseth, Annie. Personal interview. 11 Apr. 2021.

56. Unpublished letter If the letter was written to you, give the writer's name, the words "Letter to the author" (no quotation marks), and the date the letter was written.

> Witham, Lyle. Letter to the author. 6 May 2021.

If the letter was written to someone else, give that person's name rather than "the author."

57. Lecture or public address Give the speaker's name and the title of the lecture (if there is one). If the lecture was part of a meeting or convention, identify that event. Conclude with the event information, including venue, city, and date.

> Biden, Joseph R., Jr. "Address to the Joint Session of Congress." United States Capitol, Washington, DC, 28 Apr. 2021. https://www.youtube.com/watch?v=jsWt76I8Tmg.

> Smith, Anna Deavere. "On the Road: A Search for American Character." National Endowment for the Humanities, John F. Kennedy Center for the Performing Arts, Washington, D.C., 6 Apr. 2015.

Media Sources

58. Film or video Generally begin with the title of the film or recording. Always supply the name of the director, the distributor, and the year of original release. You may also insert other relevant information, such as the names of the performers or screenplay writers, before the distributor.

> *Black Panther*. Directed by Ryan Coogler, written by Ryan Coogler and Joe Robert Cole, Walt Disney Studios Motion Pictures, 2018.

If you want to emphasize an individual's role in the film or movie, such as the director or actor, list that name first.

> Olivier, Laurence, director and performer. *Hamlet*. Paramount, 1948.

For media other than film (such as videotape and DVD), cite it as for a film, unless you are discussing supplementary material found on the DVD, in which case your entry should refer to the DVD.

> "Sweeney's London." Produced by Eric Young. *Sweeney Todd: The Demon Barber of Fleet Street*, directed by Tim Burton, DreamWorks, 2007, disc 2.

For videos found on the web, give the URL after the publication information. If no publication date is given, include the access date at the end of the citation.

> "Watch a Lion Fall from a Tree during Rescue from a Wire Snare Injury." *National Geographic*, video4, Dec. 2018, https://www.nationalgeographic.co.uk/video/tv/watch-lion-fall-tree-during-rescue-wire-snare-injury.

59. Television or radio program If the program has named episodes or segments, list those in quotation marks. Then include the title of the program or series (italicized), the producer, and the date that the program first aired. If there are relevant persons to name (such as an author, a director, a host, a narrator, or an actor), include that information after the title of the program or series. If the material you're citing is an interview, include the word "Interview" and, if relevant, the name of the interviewer.

> "New Frontiers." *Alaska: The Last Frontier*, Episode 8-1, Discovery, 7 Oct. 2018.

> "All Things Considered for Thursday, November 11, 2021." *All Things Considered*, hosted by Audie Cornish, Ailsa Chang, Mary Louise Kelly, Michel Martin, and Ari Shapiro, NPR, 11 Nov. 2021, https://www.npr.org/programs/all-things-considered/2021/11/11/1054644343?showDate=2021-11-11.

60. Sound recording, audio clip, or podcast Begin with the name of the person whose work you want to highlight: the composer, the conductor, the performer, or the host. Next list the title, followed by the names of other artists (composer, conductor, performers). The recording information includes the manufacturer and the date.

> Bizet, Georges. *Carmen*. Performances by Jennifer Larmore, Thomas Moser, Angela Gheorghiu, and Samuel Ramey, Bavarian State Orchestra and Chorus, conducted by Giuseppe Sinopoli, Warner, 1996.

If you wish to cite a particular track on the recording, give its performer and title (in quotation marks), and then proceed with the information about the recording.

For live recordings, include the date of the performance between the title and the recording information.

> Adele. "Easy on Me." *30*. Melted Stone and Columbia Records, 2021.

For audio clips accessed on the web, add the URL after the publication information.

> Goldbarth, Albert. "Fourteen Pages." *The Poetry Foundation*, 15 Apr. 2016, https://www.poetryfoundation.org/podcasts/89129/fourteen-pages.

61. Musical score Give the composer, title, and date. Italicize the title unless it identifies the composition by form ("symphony," "suite"), number ("op. 39," "K. 231"), or key ("E-flat").

> Beethoven, Ludwig van. Symphony no. 5 in C Minor, op. 67. 1807.

If you are referring to a published score, provide publication data as you would for a book. Insert the date of composition between the title and the publication information.

> Minchin, Tim. *Roald Dahl's Matilda: The Musical*. 2012. Wise-Music Sales, 2013.

62. Work of art, photograph, or other image Give the name of the artist; the title of the work (italicized); the date of composition; the name of the collection, museum, or owner; and the city. If you are citing artwork published in a book, add the publication information for the book.

> Cattelan, Maurizio. *Untitled (for Parkett, no. 100/101)*. 2017, Museum of Modern Art, New York.
>
> Husni-Bey, Adelita. *The Council*. 2018, Museum of Modern Art, New York.

For online visuals, including charts or graphs, include the website (italicized), and the URL.

> Goodbye, Cassini. *Al Jazeera*, 14 Sept. 2017, https://www.aljazeera.com/economy/interactive/2017/9/14/goodbye-cassini.

63. Advertisement Provide the name of the product, service, or organization being advertised, followed by the usual publication information. For advertisements found online, include the URL.

> Advertisement for Corley's Albuquerque Lincoln. *Albuquerque Journal*, 8 Nov. 2021, p. Z20.

Advertisement for Hewlett Packard Wolf Security. *The New York Times,* 12 Nov. 2021, https://www.nytimes.com/2021/11/12/business/media/coronavirus -misinformation-radio-podcasts.html.

64. Cartoon Treat a cartoon like an article in a newspaper or magazine. Give the cartoonist's name, the title of the cartoon if there is one (in quotation marks), and the publication information for the source.

Weyant, Christopher. "Inflation's Financial Squeeze." *The Boston Globe,* 11 Nov. 2021, https://www.bostonglobe.com/2021/11/11/opinion/inflations-financial-squeeze.

65. Live performance Generally, begin with the title of the performance. Then give the author and director; the major performers; and the theater, city, and date.

Hamilton. By Lin Manuel-Miranda, directed by Thomas Kail, CIBC Theater, Chicago, 19 Oct. 2016.

Other Digital Sources

66. Entire website For a website with no author, provide the name of the site in italics, followed by the sponsor or publisher, the copyright date or the most recent update date, and the URL. A date of access is not required for web sources if a copyright or recent update date is provided.

The Newton Project. U of Oxford, 2021, https://www.newtonproject.ox.ac.uk.

67. Academic course or department website For a course page, give the name of the instructor, the course title, the institution in italics, the year, and the URL. For a department page, give the department name, a description such as "Department home page," the institution in italics, the date of the last update, and the URL.

Palmquist, Mike. CO150: College Composition, *Colorado State University,* 2021, https://colostate.instructure.com/courses/118371.

English. Department home page. *St. Olaf College,* 2021, https://wp.stolaf.edu /english/.

68. Short work from a website Provide the name of the author; the title of the work in quotation marks; the title of the website, italicized; the date of publication; and the URL.

Martin, Amy. "As Greenland's Ice Sheet Melts, Scientists Want to Know 'How Fast.'" *Pulitzer Center on Crisis Reporting,* 4 Dec. 2018, pulitzercenter.org/reporting /greenlands-ice-sheet-melts-scientists-want-know-how-fast.

> Fiscutean, Andrada, and Ashira Morris. " 'Danger Unites Us': Coalminers on the Frontline of Clean Energy." *Pulitzer Center*, 11 Nov. 2021, https://pulitzercenter.org/stories/danger-unites-us-coalminers-frontline-clean-energy.

If there is no author given, begin the citation with the title of the work and proceed with the rest of the publication information. If the title of the website does not indicate the sponsoring organization, list the sponsor before the URL. If there is no date of publication, give the date of access after the URL.

> "Social and Historical Context: Vitality." *Arapesh Grammar and Digital Language Archive Project*, Institute for Advanced Technology in the Humanities, https://www.arapesh.org/socio_historical_context_vitality.php. Accessed 14 Nov. 2021.

69. Message posted to a newsgroup, electronic mailing list, or online discussion forum Cite the name of the person who posted the message and the title (from the subject line, in quotation marks); if the posting has no title, add the phrase "Online posting." Then add the name of the website (italicized), the sponsor or publisher, the date of the message, and the URL.

> Fink, Lisa. "Last Week of NCTE Verse!" *NCTE Connects*, National Council of Teachers of English, 23 Apr. 2021, https://connect.ncte.org/communities/community-home/digestviewer/viewthread?GroupId=31&MessageKey=862b6cb1-06c6-4036-aed8-53f779dc414f.

70. Blog To cite an entry or a comment on a blog, give the author of the entry or comment (if available), the title of the entry or comment in quotation marks, the title of the blog (italicized), the sponsor or publisher, the date the material was posted, and the URL.

> Sedita, Joan. "The Science of Reading Comprehension." *Literacy Lines*, Keys to Literacy, 3 Oct. 2021, https://keystoliteracy.com/blog/the-science-of-reading-comprehension/.

71. Email message Start with the sender of the message. Then add "E-mail to" and the recipient of the message. Finally, provide the date of the message.

> Page, Ellen. "E-mail to Reid Vincent." 20 Oct. 2021.

72. Facebook post or comment Follow the general format for citing a short work on a website.

> Bedford English. "Today we are recognizing Veterans Day with a list of writers who have served." *Facebook*, 11 Nov. 2021, https://www.facebook.com/BedfordEnglish/.

How Do I Cite Works from Websites Using MLA Style?

Tutorial

Scan the website to find as much of the citation information as you can. If you cannot find a publication date, provide the date you accessed the website. Remember that the citation information you provide should allow readers to retrace your steps to locate the sources. Consult items 66 through 75 for additional models for citing digital sources.

Kelderman, Eric. "Free College IS Dead in Congress, But It's Alive and Well in the States." *The Chronicle of Higher Education*, 3 Nov. 2021, https://www.chronicle.com/article/free-college-is-dead-in-congress-but-its-alive-and-well-in-the-states.

- A — above "Kelderman, Eric."
- B — above the title
- C — under "The Chronicle of Higher Education"
- D — under "3 Nov. 2021"
- E — under the URL

A **The author of the work.** Give the last name first, followed by a comma, the first name, and the middle initial (if given). Omit titles such as "MD," "PhD," or "Sir"; include suffixes after the name and a comma (O'Driscoll, Gerald P., Jr.). Insert a period. If no author is given, begin with the title.

B **The title of the work.** Give the full title; include the subtitle (if any), preceded by a colon. Enclose the title and subtitle in quotation marks, and capitalize all major words. Place a period inside the closing quotation mark.

C **The title of the website.** Give the title of the entire site, italicized. If there is no clear title and it is a personal home page, use "Home page" without italicizing it. If the sponsoring organization is different than the title of the website, list that information next. Follow with a comma.

D **The date of publication or most recent update.** Use the day-month-year format; abbreviate all months except May, June, and July. End with a comma. (If no publication date is given, provide the date of access at the end of the entry. After the URL, insert the word "Accessed" and the date you accessed the work.)

E **The URL.** Give the URL for the article, and end with a period.

73. Twitter post (tweet) Follow the general format for citing a short work on a website, but provide the entire tweet in place of the title, and include the time after the date. If the name of the poster is not provided, use the twitter handle (e.g., @AsaoBInoue). If the name is provided, include the handle in brackets.

> Inoue, Asao [@AsaoBInoue]. "Often our models of good writing are not really the standard for how we expect our students to write. They are models for what we want our students to read and appreciate. . . ." *Twitter*, 27 Oct. 2021, https://twitter.com/AsaoBInoue/status/1453401766783901701?s=20.

74. Instagram post Begin with the account owner's last name and first name. If names are not available, begin with the account owner's username, and include any other contributors. Follow with the photo title in quotation marks or a description if the title isn't available. End with the date the photo was published and the URL.

> National Geographic [@insidenatgeo]. Paul Salopek, photographer. Photo of the Gaoligong range near the old Silk Road trading town of Tengchong. *Instagram*, 10 Nov. 2021, https://www.instagram.com/p/CWG6rWAvjsF/.

75. Computer software, app, or video game Cite computer software as you would a book (see item 16).

> *SimpleMind Pro*. ModelMaker Tools, 2021, https://simplemind.eu/.

76. Other sources For other online sources, adapt the guidelines to the medium. Include as much information as necessary for your readers to find your source as easily as possible. The examples below are for a podcast of a radio program and a historical document available in an online archive.

> Constitution of the United States. 1787. *America's Founding Documents,* US National Archives and Records Administration, https://www.archives.gov/founding-docs/.

> Goff, Phillip Atiba. "How Can Communities Reimagine Their Approach to Public Safety?" *TED Radio Hour,* National Public Radio, 12 Nov. 2021, https://www.npr.org/2021/11/12/1054858000/phillip-atiba-goff-how-can-communities-reimagine-their-approach-to-public-safety.

26 Using APA Style

How do I cite sources within the text of my document? 693

How do I prepare the reference list? 696

American Psychological Association (APA) style, used primarily in the social sciences and in some of the natural sciences, emphasizes the author(s) and publication date of a source. Writers who use the APA documentation system cite, or formally acknowledge, information within their text using parentheses and provide a list of sources, called a reference list, at the end of their document.

To see student essays formatted and documented in APA style, use one of the following examples in Part Two:

- Gabriella Guerrero, *Fast Fashion? Not So Fast!*
- Kelsey Smith, *Art Theft on the Rise with Social Media*

For more information about APA style, consult the *Publication Manual of the American Psychological Association*, Seventh Edition. Information about this publication can be found on the APA website at apa.org.

Using APA Style

CITATIONS WITHIN YOUR TEXT

1. Basic format for a source named in your text 693
2. Basic format for a source not named in your text 693
3. Two authors 693
4. Three or more authors 694
5. Corporate, group, or government author 694
6. Unknown author 694
7. Two or more works cited together 694
8. Two or more works by authors with the same last name 695
9. Two or more works by the same authors(s) in the same year 695
10. Source cited in another source 695
11. Source with no page numbers 695
12. Email, letters, and other personal communication 695
13. Website 696
14. Document from a website 696
15. Common computer software and mobile apps 696

ENTRIES IN YOUR REFERENCE LIST

BOOKS

16. One author 697
17. Two or more authors 697
18. Corporate, group, or government author 697
19. Unknown author 697
20. Two or more books by the same author(s) 697
21. Two or more books by the same author(s) in the same year 698
22. Translated book 698
23. Multivolume work 698
24. Book in a series 698
25. Book in an edition other than the first 698
26. Republished book 698
27. Book with more than one publisher 699
28. Authored book with an editor 699
29. Edited book 699
30. Selection in an anthology or edited book 699
31. Foreword, introduction, preface, or afterword 699
32. Published proceedings of a conference 699
33. Paper published in the proceedings of a conference 700
34. Sacred or classical text 700
35. Published dissertation or thesis 700
36. Unpublished dissertation or thesis 700

SOURCES IN JOURNALS, MAGAZINES, AND NEWSPAPERS

37. Article in a journal 702
38. Article in a magazine 702
39. Article in a newspaper 702
40. Unsigned article 703
41. Editorial 703
42. Letter to the editor 703
43. Review 703
44. Published interview 703

REFERENCE WORKS

45. Encyclopedia, dictionary, thesaurus, handbook, or almanac 705
46. Entry in a reference work (including a wiki) 705
47. Government publication 705
48. Brochure or pamphlet 705

FIELD SOURCES

49. Personal interview 705
50. Unpublished survey data 706
51. Unpublished letter 706
52. Lecture or public address 706

MEDIA SOURCES

53. Film or video 706
54. Television or radio program 706
55. Sound recording, audio clip, or podcast 707
56. Work of art, photograph, or other image 707

OTHER DIGITAL SOURCES

57. Nonperiodical web document 707
58. Email message or real-time communication 708
59. Article posted on a wiki 708
60. Message posted to a newsgroup, email list, or online discussion forum 708
61. Blog post or comment 708
62. Facebook page, post, or status update 709
63. Twitter post (tweet) 709
64. Instagram post 709
65. File obtained online 709
66. Computer software, video game, or mobile app 709

OTHER SOURCES

67. General advice about other sources 711

How Do I Cite Sources within the Text of My Document?

APA uses an author-date form of in-text citation to acknowledge the use of another writer's words, facts, or ideas. When you are summarizing or paraphrasing, provide the author's last name and the year of publication either in the sentence or in parentheses at the end of the sentence. You may include a page or chapter reference if it would help readers find the original material in a longer work. When you are quoting a source, the citation in parentheses should include the page(s) on which the quotation can be found. For sources that do not have pages, provide paragraph numbers. Note that while APA requires page or paragraph numbers only for direct quotations, your instructor might prefer that you include a page or paragraph number with every source you cite in your document. If you're not certain of the requirements for your project, ask your instructor for guidance.

1. Basic format for a source named in your text Place the publication year in parentheses directly after the author's last name. Include the page number(s) (with "p." for "page" or "pp." for "pages") in parentheses after a direct quotation.

> Inoue (2021), having explored the importance of rethinking how best to address racism, argued, "To make something else or make something in a different way, we have to dismantle the machine and build a new machine" (p. 16).

Note that APA style requires using the past tense or present perfect tense to introduce the material you are citing: "Jennings argued" or "Jennings has argued."

2. Basic format for a source not named in your text Insert a parenthetical note that gives the author's last name and the year of the publication, separated by a comma. For a quotation, include the page or paragraph number(s) of the source.

> Psychoneuroimmunology explores the interactions among psychological factors, such as stress and behavior, and various physical systems in the human body, such as the immune system, the neural system, and the endocrine system (Ehrlich, 2019).

> Psychoneuroimmunology, a relatively new field of medicine, explores "the interplay among psychological factors (e.g., behavior, relationships, cognitions, stress), neural and endocrine systems, and the immune system" (Ehrlich, 2019, p. 96).

3. Two authors List the last names of both authors in every mention in the text. If you mention the authors' names in a sentence, use the word *and* to separate the last names, as shown in the first example. If you place the authors' names in the parenthetical citation, use an ampersand (&) to separate the last names, as shown in the second example.

> Similarly, Ray and Neily (2021) pointed out, "Police have to be of the people and for the people. Often times, police officers talk about themselves as if they are detached from the community" (p. 12).

> Still others have argued that we must change how we recruit and train police (Ray & Neily, 2021).

4. Three or more authors In all references to the source, give the first author's last name followed by "et al."

> Finken et al. (2018) studied the causes and consequences of children born with small size for their gestational age.

5. Corporate, group, or government author In general, cite the full name of the corporation, group, or government author the first time it is mentioned in your text. If you add an abbreviation for the name in square brackets the first time you cite the source, you can use the abbreviation in subsequent citations.

> An international treaty to help combat the illicit trade of tobacco products is now in effect (World Health Organization [WHO], 2018). This protocol not only establishes a global tracing system to reduce and eliminate illicit tobacco trade but also will play an important role in protecting people around the world from a serious health risk (WHO, 2018).

6. Unknown author Sources with unknown authors are listed by title in the reference list (see item 19). In your in-text citation, shorten the title as much as possible without introducing confusion. Add quotation marks to article titles, and italicize book titles.

> While women have long outlived men, contributing to a gender gap in longevity, data suggests that the gap is closing ("Life Expectancy," 2019).

If a source identifies its author as "Anonymous," use that word to cite the author of the source.

> The rise in coastal water levels has been referred to as a national crisis (Anonymous, 2021).

7. Two or more works cited together List the sources in alphabetical order by author last name and separate them with semicolons. If you are referring to two or more sources by the same author, order those sources chronologically and separate them with commas; give the author's last name only once ("Gharib, 2017, 2019").

> Rather than encourage exploration into more difficult and inaccessible energy stores, our new awareness of the finite nature of the earth's resources should incite a change

in lifestyle that no longer strains the limits of our environment (Dietz & O'Neill, 2017; Klare, 2016).

8. Two or more works by authors with the same last name Use the authors' initials in each citation.

> While both R. Cohen (2019) and L. Cohen (2021) have presented stark and sincere biographies free of bias, L. Cohen has introduced a new concept to the genre by chronicling three worthy subjects at once.

9. Two or more works by the same author(s) in the same year After organizing the works alphabetically by title, insert a lowercase letter after the publication year ("2022a" or "2022b").

> Garfield (2022b) noted that our evolution as a society is consistently reflected in how we map our world: from the origins of triangulation and the fixing of longitude to aerial photography and, now, GPS and satellite navigation.

10. Source cited in another source Ideally, you should track down the original source of the information. If you cannot find the original, mention its author and indicate where it was cited.

> Slater posited that the rise in online dating services has led to a decrease in commitment, as this technology fosters the notion that one can always find a more compatible mate (as cited in Weissmann, 2022).

11. Source with no page numbers Many visual documents, such as brochures, and digital sources, such as websites and some full-text articles from databases, lack page numbers. If the source has numbered paragraphs, indicate the paragraph number using the abbreviation "para." If the paragraphs are not numbered, include the section heading and indicate which paragraph in that section contains the cited material.

> Zerfas (2021) examined the rise in tactical urbanism, a kind of city planning that employs "small-scale, often temporary projects" to repurpose small bits of unusable public space as parks, gardens, and other areas designed for public use ("What is tactical urbanism?").

12. Email, letters, and other personal communication Give the first initial(s) and last name of the person with whom you corresponded, the words "personal communication," and the date. Don't include personal communications in your reference list.

> (J. M. Rifenburg, personal communication, January 22, 2021)

13. Website For an entire website, give the URL in parentheses in your text, and don't include it in your reference list.

> The Library of Congress (http://loc.gov) offers extensive online collections of manuscripts, correspondence, sound recordings, photographs, prints, and audiovisual materials spanning decades of American history.

14. Document from a website Include the document in your reference list and cite as you would another source. To cite a quotation from a website, give the paragraph number or section heading and include the source in your reference list.

> The Environmental Protection Agency (2016) combats climate change by evaluating policy options that "range from comprehensive market-based legislation to targeted regulations to reduce emissions and improve the efficiency of vehicles, power plants and large industrial sources" (para. 2).

15. Common computer software and mobile apps Refer to the software or app by name, and include the version number, if available, in parentheses. Don't include the software or app in the reference list.

> Students used Adobe Photoshop (version 23.0.1) to complete their photo essays.

How Do I Prepare the Reference List?

The reference list contains publication information for all sources that you have cited within your document, with two exceptions. Personal communications, such as email messages, letters, and interviews, are cited only in the text of the document.

Begin the list on a new page at the end of the document, and center the title "References" at the top. Organize the list alphabetically by author (if the source is an organization, alphabetize it by the name of the organization; if the source has no known author, alphabetize it by title). All of the entries should be double-spaced with no extra space between entries. Entries are formatted with a hanging indent: the first line is flush with the left margin, and subsequent lines are indented one-half inch. Only the initial word and proper nouns (names of people, organizations, cities, states, and so on) in a source title and subtitle are capitalized.

In longer documents, a reference list may be given at the end of each chapter or section. In digital documents that use links, such as websites, the reference list is often a separate page to which other pages are linked.

For examples of reference lists in APA style, see the student essays in Chapters 8 and 9.

Books

16. One author List the author's last name followed by a comma and the first initial. Insert the date in parentheses and italicize the title. Follow with the publisher.

>Engeln, R. (2017). *Beauty sick: How the cultural obsession with appearance hurts girls and women.* HarperCollins.

Cite an e-book as you would a print book. If the book was found on the web and it has a DOI (digital object identifier, a unique number assigned to specific content), provide the DOI at the end of the citation and precede it by "https://doi.org/". Otherwise, provide the URL. Do not end the DOI or the URL with a period.

>Kilby, P. (2019). *The green revolution: Narratives of politics, technology and gender.* Routledge. https://doi.org/10.4324/9780429200823

17. Two or more authors List the authors in the same order that the title page does, each with last name first. Use commas to separate authors and use an ampersand (&) before the final author's name. List every author up to and including twenty; for a work with twenty-one or more authors, give the first nineteen names followed by three ellipsis dots and the last author's name. (Do not use an ampersand in such cases.)

>Sutherland, J., & Hislop, S. (2018). *The Connell guide to Virginia Woolf's* Mrs. Dalloway. Connell Publishing.

18. Corporate, group, or government author Write out the full name of a corporate or group author. If the corporation is also the publisher, use "Author" for the publisher's name. For works by government agencies, list the most specific organization as the author.

>Linguistic Society of America. (2021). *The state of linguistics in higher education: Annual report, 2020.* Author.

19. Unknown author When no author is listed on the title or copyright page, begin the entry with the title of the work. Alphabetize the entry by the first significant word of the title (not including *A*, *An*, or *The*).

>*Diary of an oxygen thief.* (2016). Gallery Books.

20. Two or more books by the same author(s) Give the author's name in each entry and list the titles in chronological order.

>Sanders, B. (2016). *Our revolution: A future to believe in.* Thomas Dunne Books.

Sanders, B. (2018). *Where we go from here: Two years in the resistance*. Thomas Dunne Books.

21. Two or more books by the same author(s) in the same year List the books alphabetically, and include lowercase letters (*a*, *b*, and so on) after the dates.

Sanderson, B. (2018a). *Legion: The many lives of Stephen Leeds*. Tor Books.

Sanderson, B. (2018b). *Skyward*. Delacorte Press.

22. Translated book List the author first, followed by the year of publication, the title, and the translator (in parentheses, identified by the abbreviation "Trans."). Place the original date of the work's publication at the end of the entry.

Sartre, J. P. (2019). *Being and nothingness* (S. Richmond, Trans.). Washington Square Press. (Original work published 1943).

23. Multivolume work Include the number of volumes in parentheses after the title.

Delbanco, N., & Cheuse, A. (Eds.). (2010). *Literature: Craft and voice* (Vols. 1–3). McGraw-Hill.

If you have used only one volume in a multivolume work, identify that volume by number and by title.

Delbanco, N., & Cheuse, A. (Eds.). (2010). *Literature: Craft and voice: Vol. 1. Fiction*. McGraw-Hill.

24. Book in a series Provide the name of the series, capitalizing all important words, a colon and a volume number (if any), a period, and the title.

Fidell, E. R. (2016). *Very short introductions: 227. Military justice*. [Series]. Oxford University Press.

25. Book in an edition other than the first Note the edition ("2nd ed.," "Rev. ed.") after the title.

Palmquist, M. (2021). *The Bedford researcher* (7th ed.). Bedford/St. Martin's.

26. Republished book Provide the most recent date of publication. Identify the original publication date in parentheses following the publisher information.

Freud, S. (2010). *The interpretation of dreams* (J. Strachey, Ed. & Trans.). Basic Books. (Original work published 1955).

27. Book with more than one publisher If more than one publisher is shown on the book's copyright page, list the publisher names in the order they are shown, separated by semicolons.

> Inoue, Asao B. (2021). *Above the well: An antiracist argument from a boy of color.* The WAC Clearinghouse; Utah State University Press. https://doi.org/10.37514/PER-B.2021.1244.

28. Authored book with an editor Include the editor's name and the abbreviation "Ed." in parentheses after the title.

> Wilson, M. (2019). *A true child of Papua New Guinea: Memoir of a life in two worlds* (R. Henry, Ed.). McFarland.

29. Edited book Include "Ed." or "Eds." in parentheses.

> Ávila Reyes, N. (Ed.). (2021). *Multilingual contributions to writing research: Toward an equal academic exchange*. The WAC Clearinghouse; University Press of Colorado. https://doi.org/10.37514/INT-B.2021.1404

30. Selection in an anthology or edited book Begin with the author, publication date, and title of the selection (not italicized). Follow with the word "In," the names of the editors (initials first), the abbreviation "Ed." or "Eds." in parentheses, the title of the anthology or collection (italicized), inclusive page numbers for the selection (in parentheses, with the abbreviation "pp."), and the place and publisher.

> Bazerman, C. (2021). The value of empirically researching a practical art. In N. Ávila Reyes (Ed.), *Multilingual contributions to writing research: Toward an equal academic exchange* (pp. 103–124). The WAC Clearinghouse; University Press of Colorado. https://doi.org/10.37514/INT-B.2021.1404.2.04

31. Foreword, introduction, preface, or afterword Treat as you would a chapter in a book.

> Joli, F. (2016). Foreword. In J. Arena, *Legends of disco: Forty stars discuss their careers* (pp. 1–2). McFarland.

32. Published proceedings of a conference Cite information as you would for a book (see item 16).

> Mayor, J., & Gomez, P. (Eds.). (2014). *Computational models of cognitive processes: Proceedings of the 13th neural computation and psychology workshop*. World Scientific Publishing.

33. Paper published in the proceedings of a conference Treat a conference paper as you would a selection from an edited collection.

> Jacobs, G. M., & Toh-Heng, H. L. (2013). Small steps towards student-centered learning. In P. Mandal (Ed.), *Proceedings of the international conference on managing the Asian century* (pp. 55–64). Springer.

34. Sacred or classical text Treat these texts as you would a book (see item 16), including the title of the edition, the translator's name and/or editor's name (if any), and any other information about the version you used.

> Smith, J., & Reorganized Church of Jesus Christ of Latter Day Saints. (1948). *The book of Mormon*. Board of Publication of the Reorganized Church of Jesus Christ of Latter Day Saints.

35. Published dissertation or thesis If a published dissertation or thesis is available through a commercial database, give the author, date, title, publication number or order number in parentheses, and description in square brackets ["Doctoral dissertation" or "Master's thesis,"] and the institution name]. Then give the database name.

> Hyson, A. R. (2021). *Pushing boundaries: Young people's experiences developing and expressing intersecting identities* (Order No. 28646416). [Doctoral dissertation, University of Minnesota]. ProQuest Dissertations & Theses Global.

If the dissertation or thesis was posted online by the granting university, include the university archive, department, or library in the source position. Provide the URL.

> Degli-Esposti, M. (2019). *Child maltreatment and antisocial behaviour in the United Kingdom: Changing risks over time* [Doctoral dissertation, University of Oxford]. Oxford University Research Archive. https://ora.ox.ac.uk/objects/uuid:6d5a8e55-bd19-41a1-8ef5-ef485642af89

36. Unpublished dissertation or thesis Format as you would a book, replacing the publisher information with a phrase such as "Unpublished doctoral dissertation" in parentheses, followed by information about the college or university.

> McQueen, J. Y. (2013). *On the road of phonological treatment: Paths of learning* (Unpublished honors thesis). Indiana University, Bloomington.

How Do I Cite Books Using APA Style?

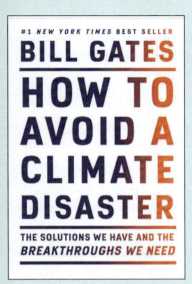

Penguin Random House, LLC.

When citing a book, use the information from the title page and the copyright page (typically after the title page), not from the book's cover or a library catalog. Consult items 16 through 36 for additional models for citing books.

```
  ┌─ A ─┐ ┌─ B ─┐ ┌──────────── C ─────────────
  Gates, B. (2021). How to avoid a climate disaster: The solutions we have and the
  ──────── C ────────┐  ┌──────── D ────────┐
  breakthroughs we need. Penguin Random House.
```

A   **The author.** Give the last name first, followed by a comma and initials for first name and, if any, middle name. Separate initials with a space (Leakey, R. E.). Separate the names of multiple authors with commas; use an ampersand (&) before the final author's name.

B   **The year of publication.** Put the most recent copyright year in parentheses, and end with a period (outside the closing parenthesis).

C   **The title and, if any, the subtitle.** Give the full title; include the subtitle (if any), preceded by a colon. Italicize the title and subtitle, capitalizing only the first word of the title, the first word of the subtitle, and any proper nouns or proper adjectives. End with a period (unless the title ends with a question mark or exclamation point).

D   **The publisher.** Give the publisher's name. Omit words such as "Inc." and "Co." Include and do not abbreviate such terms as "University," "Books," and "Press." End with a period.

E   **DOI or URL (not shown).** If available, provide the DOI (digital object identifier), preceded by https://doi.org/. If the book is available online but lacks a DOI, provide the URL. Do not end with a period.

Sources in Journals, Magazines, and Newspapers

37. Article in a journal After the author and publication year, provide the article title, the journal title, the volume number (italicized), the issue number (if the journal is published in issues), and the inclusive page numbers.

> Ashton, M. (2018). Getting rid of stupid stuff. *The New England Journal of Medicine, 379*, 1789–1791.

> Garicano, L., & Rayo, L. (2016). Why organizations fail: Models and cases. *Journal of Economic Literature, 54*(1), 137–192.

If a DOI is available, include it at the end of the citation and precede it by "https://doi.org/". Do not end the DOI with a period. You do not need to provide a retrieval date or database name.

> Du, S., Liew, S. S., Li, L., & Yao, S. Q. (2018, November). Bypassing endocytosis: Direct cytosolic delivery of proteins. *Journal of the American Chemical Society, 140*, 15986–15996. https://doi.org/10.1021/jacs.8b06584

If the article is obtained online but no DOI is provided, give the exact URL for the article (or for the home page of the journal, if access requires a subscription). Do not end the URL with a period.

> Skinnell, R. (2021). Teaching writing in the (new) era of fake news. *College Composition and Communication, 72*(4), 546–559. https://library.ncte.org/journals/ccc/issues/v72-4/31441

38. Article in a magazine Give the publication date as year and month for monthly magazines and as year, month, and day for weekly or biweekly magazines. Place the issue number, if any, in parentheses directly after the volume number. Include all page numbers. For articles accessed on the web, end with the URL of the magazine's home page.

> Ball, M. (2018, November 19). Nation divided: The midterms delivered a split decision that primes both parties for battle. *Time, 192*(21), 28–36.

> Chodosh, S. (2018, November 28). Siberian unicorns lived alongside humans, and they were so much cooler than the mythical version. *Popular Science*. https://www.popsci.com/siberian-unicorns

39. Article in a newspaper Give the publication date as year, month, and day. Next give the article title followed by the name of the newspaper (italicized). Include all page numbers. If you accessed the article online, end with the URL. (Lengthy URLs may be shortened through a site like bitly.com.)

Hindi, S. (2020, June 13). Colorado among first in U.S. to pass historic police reforms following protests. *The Denver Post*. https://www.denverpost.com/2020/06/13/colorado-police-reform-bill-passes-legislature/

Rouan, R. (2021, November 11). Public transit systems pin hopes on Biden plan. *USA Today*, A2.

40. Unsigned article Begin with the article title, and alphabetize in the reference list by the first word in the title other than *A*, *An*, or *The*.

I am part of the resistance inside the Trump administration. (2018, September 5). *The New York Times*, A23. https://www.nytimes.com/2018/09/05/opinion/trump-white-house-anonymous-resistance.html

41. Editorial Include the word "Editorial" in square brackets after the title.

Keep toilet paper off your shopping list this Black Friday (and beyond) [Editorial]. (2020, November 25). *The Baltimore Sun*. https://www.baltimoresun.com/opinion/editorial/bs-ed-1127-toilet-paper-pandemic-20201125-4u4t6civ7rflbof27xkv2h6zii-story.html

42. Letter to the editor Include the words "Letter to the editor" in square brackets after the title of the letter or, if the letter is untitled, in place of the title.

Ashton-Williams, A. (2021, November 13). Measure 110 has us on the right path [Letter to the editor]. *East Oregonian*, A5.

43. Review After the title of the review, include the words "Review of the book . . ." or "Review of the film . . ." and so on in square brackets, followed by the title of the work reviewed. If the reviewed work is a book, include the author's name after a comma; if it's a film or other media, include the year of release. If the review is untitled, give the bracketed information in place of the title.

Cicchino, A. (2021). Review [Review of *Oral communication in the disciplines: A resource for teacher development and training*, D. P. Dannels, P. R. Palmerton, & A. L. H. Gaffney]. *The WAC Journal, 30*(1), 108–130. https://doi.org/10.37514/WAC-J.2019.30.1.05

44. Published interview Cite a published interview like a periodical article (see items 37–39).

Massondo, A. (2010, July). Yellow-card journalism [Interview by C. Barron]. *Harper's, 321*(1921), 17–18.

Tutorial

How Do I Cite Articles from Periodicals Using APA Style?

Periodicals include journals, magazines, and newspapers. This tutorial gives an example of a citation for an article in a scholarly journal. Models for citing periodical genres can be found in items 37–44.

Freud, E., Culham, J. C., Namdar, G., & Behrmann, M. (2019, March). Object complexity modulates the association between action and perception in childhood. *Journal of Experimental Child Psychology*, *179*, 56–72. https://doi.org/10.1016/j.jecp.2018.11.004

- A = Freud, E., Culham, J. C., Namdar, G., & Behrmann, M.
- B = (2019, March).
- C = Object complexity modulates the association between action and perception in childhood.
- D = *Journal of Experimental Child Psychology*,
- E = *179*,
- F = 56–72.
- G = https://doi.org/10.1016/j.jecp.2018.11.004

A **The author.** Give the last name first, followed by a comma and initials for first and middle names. Separate the names of multiple authors with commas; use an ampersand (&) before the final author's name. End with a period.

B **The date of publication.** Give the year in parentheses. For magazines and newspapers, include month and, if relevant, the day (2019, August 4). End with a period.

C **The article title.** Give the full title; include the subtitle (if any), preceded by a colon. Do not underline, italicize, or put the title in quotation marks. Capitalize only the first word of the title, the first word of the subtitle, and any proper nouns or proper adjectives. End with a period (unless the article title ends with other punctuation).

D **The periodical title.** Italicize the periodical title, and capitalize all major words. Insert a comma.

E **The volume number and issue number.** For magazines and journals with volume numbers, include the volume number, italicized. For magazines and for journals that start each issue with page 1, include the issue number in parentheses, not italicized. Insert a comma.

F **Inclusive page number(s).** Give all the numbers in full (248–254, not 248–54). For newspapers, include the abbreviation "p." or "pp." for page and section letters, if relevant (p. B12). End with a period.

G **The DOI or URL.** If the article has a DOI (a unique digital object identifier), provide it, preceded by "https://doi.org/". If there is no DOI, include the words "Retrieved from" and the URL. Do not end the DOI or URL with a period.

Reference Works

45. Encyclopedia, dictionary, thesaurus, handbook, or almanac Cite a reference work, such as an encyclopedia or a dictionary, as you would a book (see item 16).

> Priest, S. H. (Ed.). (2010). *Encyclopedia of science and technology communication* (Vols. 1–2). Sage.

46. Entry in a reference work (including a wiki) Begin your citation with the name of the author or, if the entry is unsigned, the title of the entry. Proceed with the date, the entry title (if not already given), the title of the reference work, the edition number, and the pages. If the contents of the reference work are arranged alphabetically, omit the volume and page numbers.

> Ray, S., & Schwarz, H. (2016). Globalization. In *Encyclopedia of postcolonial studies*. Wiley-Blackwell.

If the entry was found online, provide the URL. Because the material on a wiki is likely to change, include a retrieval date as well.

> House music. (2021, November 8). *Wikipedia*. Retrieved November 12, 2021, from https://en.wikipedia.org/wiki/House_music

47. Government publication Give the name of the department, office, agency, or committee that issued the report as the author. If the document has a report or special file number, place that in parentheses after the title. If the publication was found online, provide the DOI or URL.

> National Oceanic and Atmospheric Administration. (2019). *2017 shark finning report to Congress*. U.S. Department of Commerce. https://www.fisheries.noaa.gov/resource/document/2017-shark-finning-report-congress

48. Brochure or pamphlet Format the entry as you would a book (see items 16–35); insert "n.d." if there is no publication date. If you found the undated document online, provide a retrieval date.

> *This is edinburgh information pack: Summer/spring 2018*. Edinburgh.org, 2018, https://edinburgh.org/media/1297024/This-is-Edinburgh-Press-Information-Pack-2018.pdf.

> UNESCO. (n.d.). *The world heritage brochure*. UNESCO World Heritage Center. Retrieved November 14, 2021, from https://whc.unesco.org/en/documents/124632

Field Sources

49. Personal interview Treat unpublished interviews as personal communications, and include them in your text only (see item 12). Do not cite personal interviews in your reference list.

50. Unpublished survey data Give the title of the survey first, followed by the date the survey was distributed, and the words "Unpublished raw data."

> The University of Iowa graduation exit survey. (2017, April 19). Unpublished raw data.

51. Unpublished letter Treat unpublished letters as personal communications, and include them in your text only (see item 12). Do not cite unpublished letters in your reference list.

52. Lecture or public address Provide the name of the speaker, followed by the full date of the presentation and the title of the speech if there is one. End the entry with a brief description of the event and its location.

> Warren, E. (2019, September 16). Senator Elizabeth Warren speech in Washington Square Park [Speech video recording]. C-SPAN. https://www.c-span.org/video/?464314-1/senator-elizabeth-warren-campaigns-york-city
>
> Wolin, P. (2016, May 3). Descendants of light: American photographers of Jewish ancestry. 92nd Street Y, New York, NY.

Media Sources

53. Film or video List the director and producer (if available), the date of release, the title, the medium in square brackets ("Motion picture," "DVD," or "Blu-ray disc"), the country where the film was made, and the studio or distributor.

> Lanthimos, Y. (Director). (2018). *The favourite* [Motion picture]. Fox Searchlight Pictures.

For videos found on the web, include the words "Video file" in square brackets after the title and give the URL after the publication information. If there is no author's name, list the screen name provided.

> Fateh, A. (2018, November 9). *WATCH: Video shows camp fire burning through Paradise, California* [Video file]. YouTube. https://www.youtube.com/watch?v=qLMb4IS0jaY

54. Television or radio program Cite as you would a chapter in a book. For a television program, list the director (if available), the broadcast date, and the title, followed by "Television broadcast" or "Television series episode" in square brackets. Then add information on the series, location, and station.

> Waller-Bridge, P. (Writer), & Bradbeer, H. (Director). (2019, March 18). The provocative request (Season 2, Episode 3) [TV series episode]. In P. Waller-Bridge, H. Williams, & J. Williams (Executive Producers), *Fleabag* [TV series]. Two Brothers Pictures; BBC.

For a radio program, the title should be followed by "Radio broadcast" or "Radio series episode" in square brackets. If you accessed the program on the web, include the URL.

> Cornish, A., Chang, A., Kelly, M. L., Martin, M., & Shapiro, A. (Hosts). (2021, November 11). "Thursday, November 11, 2021" [Radio series episode]. *All Things Considered*. NPR. https://www.npr.org/programs/all-things-considered/2021/11/11/1054644343?showDate=2021-11-11

55. Sound recording, audio clip, or podcast Name the author of the song, the date, and the song title, followed by "On," the recording title in italics, the medium (in square brackets), and the production information.

> Yorke, T. (2018). Unmade. On *Suspiria (Music for the Luca Guadagnino Film)* [CD]. London, England: XL Recordings.

For audio clips or podcasts accessed on the web, add the URL after the publication information.

> Mahnke, A. (Host). (2018, November 26). Episode 102: Devil in the details. *Lore* [Audio podcast]. https://www.lorepodcast.com/episodes/102

56. Work of art, photograph, or other image Cite as you would a recording. Include the artist and publication date, if known. If the artist is unknown, begin with the title of the work. If the date is unknown, use "n.d." for "no date." Indicate the medium in square brackets. Identify the city and gallery or publisher.

> Vermeer, J. (1665). *Girl with a pearl earring* [Oil painting]. Mauritshuis. The Hague, Netherlands.

If the source is found online, include the URL.

> Jet Propulsion Laboratory. (2014). *Opportunity's southward view of "McClure-Beverlin Escarpment" on Mars* [Photograph]. NASA. http://photojournal.jpl.nasa.gov/jpeg/PIA17943.jpg

Other Digital Sources

57. Nonperiodical web document Cite as much of the following information as possible: author, publication date, document title, and URL. If the format is noteworthy, include a description of the material in square brackets after the title. Use "n.d." and include a retrieval date before the URL only when the original publication date is unknown. Include the publisher in the retrieval statement if it is not listed as the author.

> USA.gov. (2019, February 13). *Saving and investment options*. https://www.usa.gov/saving-investing
>
> Song, J. (n.d.) *Average cost of college in America*. ValuePenguin. Retrieved November 14, 2021, from https://www.valuepenguin.com/student-loans/average-cost-of-college

For a chapter or section within a web document, identify the section title as well as the main document.

> Mayo Clinic. (2021, September 25). Dental care. In *Adult Health*. https://www.mayoclinic.org/healthy-lifestyle/adult-health/basics/dental-care/hlv-20049421

58. Email message or real-time communication Because email messages and real-time communications, such as text messages, are difficult or impossible for your readers to retrieve, APA does not recommend including them in your reference list. You should treat them as personal communications and cite them parenthetically in your text (see item 12).

59. Article posted on a wiki Include a retrieval date only if the material does not include a specific publication date.

> Sensory deprivation. (2021, October 17). In *Wikipedia*. https://en.wikipedia.org/wiki/Sensory_deprivation

60. Message posted to a newsgroup, email list, or online discussion forum List the author, the posting date, and the title of the post or message subject line. Include a description of the message or post in square brackets. End with the URL where the archived message can be retrieved. Include the name of the group, list, or forum if it's not part of the URL.

> Fink, L. (2021, April 23). Last week of NCTE Verse! [Online discussion list post] NCTE Connects, National Council of Teachers of English. https://connect.ncte.org/communities/community-home/digestviewer/viewthread?GroupId=31&MessageKey=862b6cb1-06c6-4036-aed8-53f779dc414f

61. Blog post or comment To cite an entry on a blog, give the author (or screen name, if available), the date the material was posted, and the title of the entry. Include the description "Blog post" or "Blog comment" in square brackets, and provide the URL.

> Sedita, J. (2021, October 3). The science of reading comprehension [Blog post]. Literacy Lines, Keys to Literacy. https://keystoliteracy.com/blog/the-science-of-reading-comprehension/

62. Facebook page, post, or status update Start with the author's name exactly as it appears and the date of the post. Include up to the first twenty words of the post and a description of the entry in square brackets ("Status update," "Video") and the retrieval URL.

>Bedford English. (2021, November 11). Today we are recognizing Veterans Day with a list of writers who have served [Status update]. Facebook. https://www.facebook.com/BedfordEnglish/

63. Twitter post (tweet) Use the author's real name, if possible, followed by the screen name in square brackets. If the real name is not known, provide only the screen name without brackets. Provide the date, the complete text of the tweet in italics, followed by "Tweet" in square brackets, and the retrieval URL.

>Klobuchar, A. (2021, November 14). *You know what is a big deal? The major investments to make sure our communities are resilient to climate change included in the Bipartisan Infrastructure Bill* [Tweet]. Twitter. https://twitter.com/amyklobuchar/status/1460021525420072965

64. Instagram post Use the account holder's last name and first name, separated by a comma, followed by the username in square brackets. If names are not available, begin with the username, without brackets. If the post has no date, use "n.d." in parentheses. Include the title or caption (up to forty words) in italics. If the post does not have a title, use a description of the post in square brackets. End with the URL.

>National Geographic [@insidenatgeo]. (2021, November 10). [Photograph by Paul Salopek of the Gaoligong range near the old Silk Road trading town of Tengchong.] Instagram. https://www.instagram.com/p/CWG6rWAvjsF/

65. File obtained online Cite as you would a nonperiodical web document (see item 57). Identify the medium in square brackets after the title.

>Jessedee. (n.d.). 5 presentation lessons from *The King's Speech* [PowerPoint slides]. Retrieved November 15, 2021, from https://www.slideshare.net/jessedee/presentation-lessons-from-the-kings-speech-6551851

66. Computer software, video game, or mobile app If a person is named as having rights to the program, software, or language, list that person as the author. Otherwise, begin the entry with the name of the program and "Computer software" in square brackets.

>Microsoft Office 365 [Computer software]. Microsoft.

Tutorial

How Do I Cite Works from Websites Using APA Style?

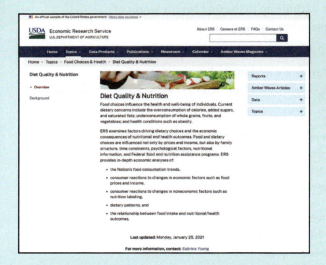

Scan the website to find as much of the citation information as you can. Remember that the citation information you provide should allow readers to retrace your steps to locate the sources. For additional models for citing sources from the web, see items 57–66.

Young, S. (2021, January 25). Diet quality & nutrition. Economic Research Service, U.S. Department of Agriculture. https://www.ers.usda.gov/topics/food-choices-health/diet-quality-nutrition/

    A — Young, S.
    B — (2021, January 25).
    C — Diet quality & nutrition. Economic Research Service, U.S. Department of Agriculture.
    D — https://www.ers.usda.gov/topics/food-choices-health/diet-quality-nutrition/

A   **The author of the work.** Give the last name first, followed by a comma and initials for first and middle names (if any). Separate the names of multiple authors with commas; use an ampersand (&) before the final author's name. If no author is provided, list the title first and follow it with the date.

B   **The date of publication.** Put the year, month, and day in parentheses, if available. If there is no date, use "n.d." in parentheses. End with a period after the closing parenthesis.

C   **The title of the work.** Give the title and subtitle (if any), separated by a colon. Capitalize only the first word of the title, the first word of the subtitle, and any proper nouns or proper adjectives. Italicize the title unless the work is found in a section of the website.

D   **The name of the website.** List the website after the title, unless it is the same as the author.

E   **Retrieval information.** Insert the URL of the work. If the material is likely to be changed or updated, or if it lacks a set publication date, include a retrieval date. (Because this report has a set publication date, the retrieval date is not necessary.)

Other Sources

67. General advice about other sources For citing other types of sources, APA suggests that you use as a guide a source type listed in its manual that most closely resembles the type of source you want to cite.

PART SIX
Handbook

27 Style: Writing Confidently

Write clear, logical sentences 714
Choose the right sentence structures 714
Write in complete sentences 717
Avoid run-ons and comma splices 720
Use parallel structures to help readers understand your ideas 722
Let readers know where your sentence is going 724
Avoid dangling words and phrases 728

Choose language that will earn you respect 730
Match your style to your writing situation 730
Use language that is free of bias and stereotyping 732

Avoid exaggeration 733
Use only words you know 734

Choose lively, concise phrasing 735
To be vivid, be specific 735
Give every word a job to do 735
Favor the active voice 736
Look for alternatives to forms of the verb *to be* 737
If you want to use figures of speech, invent your own 738
Pay attention to relationships among words 738
Avoid using too many *-tion*, *-ing*, and *-ly* endings 740
Make a habit of stating things in an affirmative way 741

How you write is a lot like how you dress: it reveals something about your personality, and it changes depending on your situation. You'd probably wear quite different outfits to attend a job interview, to go camping, and to go out dancing at your favorite club on Friday night. But your sense of style — something your friends would recognize as distinctively yours — will shape your choices. Good writing style — a good idea clearly presented, an interesting turn of phrase — makes your writing more enjoyable to your readers even as it helps readers understand who you are as a writer.

In this chapter, you'll find advice on how to express your ideas effectively at the sentence and word level. You'll find a range of strategies for writing clearly, concisely, and effectively.

Write Clear, Logical Sentences

Like entire documents and single paragraphs, individual sentences can be well or badly organized. They're well organized if readers can readily make sense of them and can understand how they relate (or don't relate) to the sentences before and after them.

Choose the Right Sentence Structures

Sentences come in many flavors. Depending on what you want to convey to your reader, choose among the following sentence types to offer one single idea, to give equal weight to two ideas, or to emphasize one idea over another. In this section, you'll find some terminology that might be unfamiliar. Although it's not necessary to understand this terminology fully to write good sentences, there are benefits to learning what the terms mean. Just as you can watch a football game without knowing specialized terms such as *blitz* or *sack*, you can write clear, concise, and effective sentences without knowing the meaning of terms such as *independent clause* and *subordinate clause*. If you'd like to discuss writing in greater detail, however, it helps to know the terminology.

- **PUT YOUR MAIN IDEAS IN MAIN CLAUSES**

The idea of the **clause** is fundamental. A clause almost always contains a subject and a verb, and most clauses contain other elements as well. A **main clause** is a clause that can stand alone as a sentence:

> I play in a band.

Simple ideas can be expressed simply. If the ideas are powerful, simple phrasing will only strengthen them by making clear that the power doesn't come from fancy wording but from the idea itself.

All the same, a series of simple main clauses, one after the other, sheds no light on any relationships that you, the writer, perceive among the ideas or information you are sharing. To show relationships among ideas and information, it helps to have the full array of sentence structures at your command.

- **TO GIVE MULTIPLE IDEAS EQUAL WEIGHT, USE A COMPOUND SENTENCE**

When you join two or more main clauses in a single sentence, the result is a **compound sentence**. Compound sentences are good for presenting two or more related ideas and giving them equal emphasis:

```
       ┌─MAIN CLAUSE─┐  ┌────────MAIN CLAUSE────────┐
```
I play in a band, and I volunteer at the school radio station.

Be sure to put a comma between the main clauses of a compound sentence, and use a **coordinating conjunction** between them or between the last two of them:

> I love both activities, but I need to give one of them up.
>
> I could quit the band, or I could quit the radio station.
>
> I don't have enough time to study, I never see my old friends, and I'm not even making money.

These are the coordinating conjunctions:

and   but   for   nor   or   so   yet

A compound sentence without any conjunctions or commas is likely to be an incorrect, hard-to-follow run-on (see *Avoid Run-ons and Comma Splices* later in this chapter):

> ✗ I don't have enough time to study I never see my old friends I'm not even making money.

A compound sentence with commas but without a conjunction is likely to be an incorrect comma splice:

> ✗ I don't have enough time to study, I never see my old friends, I'm not even making money.

If you don't want to include a conjunction in a compound sentence you've written, a correct option is to put semicolons (see *Use a Semicolon* later in this chapter) between the clauses:

> ✔ I don't have enough time to study; I never see my old friends; I'm not even making money.

- **TO EMPHASIZE ONE IDEA OVER ANOTHER, USE A COMPLEX SENTENCE**

A **complex sentence** contains a main clause plus one or more **subordinate**, or **dependent**, **clauses**. Like a main clause, a subordinate clause contains a subject and a verb. But unlike a main clause, a subordinate clause doesn't amount to a complete thought and so cannot stand on its own as a sentence. It is subordinate to, or dependent on, a main clause. Complex sentences are good for indicating which of two or more ideas is your focus.

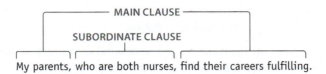

My parents, who are both nurses, find their careers fulfilling.

The focus of this sentence is on how the writer's parents feel about their careers. The subordinate clause (*who are both nurses*) adds information that will give readers a fuller understanding of the main clause (*My parents find their careers fulfilling*).

The same information could be conveyed in a compound sentence, like this:

My parents are both nurses, and they find their careers fulfilling.

But the emphasis is different. This version gives equal emphasis to the fact that the writer's parents are both nurses and the idea that they find their careers fulfilling.

To place one idea in the background of another, you may be able to subordinate the clause with one of these relative pronouns:

that   which   who   whom   whose

For more on *who* and *whom*, see Use Who *for Subjects and* Whom *for Objects* in Chapter 28.

Another kind of subordinate clause contains a main clause but begins with a **subordinating conjunction**:

> *I think about my future could stand on its own as a sentence, but the subordinating conjunction* when *relegates it to a supporting role in this sentence.*

⎾── SUBORDINATE CLAUSE ──⏋ ⎾── MAIN CLAUSE ──⏋
When I think about my future, I don't see myself as a nurse.

> *The subordinating conjunction* because *turns* I love music *into a subordinate clause.*

⎾── MAIN CLAUSE ──⏋ ⎾── SUBORDINATE CLAUSE ──⏋
I hope to be a music critic because I love music.

The most common subordinating conjunctions are these:

after	because	since	when
although	before	so that	whenever
as	even though	than	where
as if	if	that	whereas
as long as	in order to	though	wherever
as soon as	once	unless	whether
as though	provided that	until	while

A sentence that consists only of a subordinate clause feels incomplete and is an incorrect fragment (see *Write in Complete Sentences* below):

✗ Though I would love to make at least as much money as my parents do.

Usually, a fragment can be corrected by attaching it to the sentence before or after it:

✓ I hope to be a music critic, though I would love to make as much money as my parents do.

✓ Though I would love to make as much money as my parents do, I do not love the idea of becoming a nurse.

- **COMBINE COORDINATION AND SUBORDINATION IN A COMPOUND-COMPLEX SENTENCE**

A sentence with more than one main clause and at least one subordinate clause is called a **compound-complex sentence**:

The healthiest food is expensive ┃ MAIN CLAUSE ┃ because it is fresh, ┃ SUBORDINATE CLAUSE ┃ but

people need healthy food ┃ MAIN CLAUSE ┃ whether or not they are rich. ┃ SUBORDINATE CLAUSE ┃

It won't improve your writing to make a habit of constructing elaborate sentences. But it is good to be skilled at turning a group of short, closely related ideas into one compound-complex sentence. In the example above, the writer uses one closely knit sentence to present a problem, give an explanation, and take a stand on an issue.

Write in Complete Sentences

Fragments are parts of sentences that the writer has punctuated as if they were complete sentences. The idea they're trying to express is incomplete:

✗ We start getting everybody up at six in the morning. Even the nursing-home residents who want to keep sleeping.

✗ I saw the band Vogon Soup about three years ago when they were playing at Hooper's. And again the next year, when they put on a spectacular show.

Such careless use of fragments makes the writer seem unskilled. Often, all the writer needs to do to correct the problem is attach the fragment to the previous or next sentence:

✔ We start getting everybody up at six in the morning, even the residents who want to keep sleeping.

In other cases, it's easier or clearer (or both) to change the wording of the fragment so that it stands on its own as a sentence:

✔ I saw the band Vogon Soup about three years ago when they were playing at Hooper's. I saw them again the next year, when they put on a spectacular show.

It is true that everyday speech is full of fragments, particularly in answer to questions — fragments like *Not me*, *Over here*, and *Because I said so!* Since fragments are conversational, you'll find them in dialogue in news writing and fiction, and you'll see and hear them in advertising as well. But in academic and professional writing, fragments suggest that the writer either doesn't know what a proper sentence is (see *Choose the Right Sentence Structure* earlier in this chapter) or hasn't read and revised the document.

● **WATCH OUT FOR SUBORDINATE CLAUSES POSING AS SENTENCES**

Subordinate clauses (see *To Emphasize One Idea over Another, Use a Complex Sentence* earlier in this chapter) contain subjects and verbs, so some of them are easily mistaken for sentences. But they also contain a signal — a subordinating conjunction (see the following discussion of complex sentences) or a relative pronoun (see *Use Pronouns to Help Readers* in Chapter 28) — that they aren't intended to be fully understood by themselves. They depend on a main clause for some of their meaning:

✗ ⎯⎯ SENTENCE ⎯⎯ ⎯⎯ FRAGMENT ⎯⎯
Dinner is served at five sharp. Because the kitchen workers go off duty at six.

Because, a subordinating conjunction, makes sense only if it's understood in relation to the previous sentence. It turns the second word group into a fragment. One way to correct the fragment is to connect the subordinate clause to the previous sentence:

✔ ⎯⎯ MAIN CLAUSE ⎯⎯ ⎯⎯ SUBORDINATE CLAUSE ⎯⎯
Dinner is served at five sharp because the kitchen workers go off duty at six.

✗ Vogon Soup has two alpha males. Who are the lead guitarist and the drummer.

✔ Vogon Soup has two alpha males, who are the lead guitarist and the drummer.

> For *who*, a relative pronoun, to make sense here, it needs to be attached to something outside the clause. When it's unattached, it creates a fragment.

> The fragment is fixed by joining the two clauses.

Write Clear, Logical Sentences | CHAPTER 27   **719**

In the preceding examples, a comma between the clauses indicates that the information in the subordinate clause is not essential to the main point of the sentence (see *To Emphasize One Idea over Another, Use a Complex Sentence* earlier in this chapter).

Another way to correct fragments like these is to delete or change the wording that requires them to connect to another clause:

✔ Dinner is served at five sharp. The kitchen workers go off duty at six.

✔ Vogon Soup has two alpha males. They are the lead guitarist and the drummer.

● **WATCH OUT FOR VERBALS POSING AS VERBS**

Verbals are infinitives (*to sleep, to dream*) and *-ing* verb forms (*sleeping, dreaming*) that may look like verbs but are actually functioning as nouns or modifiers:

✘ We put out snacks in the evening. To keep the residents from going to bed hungry.

✔ We put out snacks in the evening to keep the residents from going to bed hungry.

> *To keep* ... doesn't express a complete idea; it's the reason the snacks are put out.

> The writer's main point is that the staff members don't want the residents to go to bed hungry, so a comma has not been placed between the clauses.

✘ All eyes were on Gordie. Prancing back and forth onstage as he played his guitar.

✔ All eyes were on Gordie prancing back and forth onstage as he played his guitar.

> *Prancing* ... should be modifying *Gordie*. Notice how incomplete the highlighted phrase feels without the previous sentence.

If you correct a fragment by attaching it to the previous or next sentence, make sure you haven't just turned it into a dangling modifier (see *Avoid Dangling Words and Phrases* later in this chapter):

✘ Prancing back and forth onstage, the audience couldn't take their eyes off Gordie.

✔ The audience couldn't take their eyes off Gordie as he pranced back and forth onstage.

> The point is that Gordie's prancing riveted the audience, so the writer has not used a comma before the modifier.

● **WATCH OUT FOR FRAGMENTS THAT BEGIN WITH PREPOSITIONS**

If you begin a sentence with a prepositional phrase, be sure that you finish the sentence:

✘ After eating dinner so early. The residents have a long evening ahead of them.

✔ After eating dinner so early, the residents have a long evening ahead of them.

> In the corrected example, the fragment is attached to the adjacent sentence.

When you attach a fragment to the sentence that follows, you should usually put a comma after it to help readers find the beginning of the main clause.

- **WATCH OUT FOR FRAGMENTS CONSISTING OF EXAMPLES**

  ✗ Vogon Soup plays some covers of other bands' music. Such as "Here Comes the Sun."

  ✓ Vogon Soup plays some covers of other bands' music, such as "Here Comes the Sun."

Generally, set examples off with a comma or a dash (see Chapter 29).

Avoid Run-ons and Comma Splices

Run-on sentences and comma splices consist of two or more main clauses (each containing a subject and a verb and able to stand alone as a sentence) joined in a way that makes them ungrammatical and hard to follow. In a run-on sentence, the main clauses are just stuck together:

        —————— MAIN CLAUSE —————— ┐ ┌—————— MAIN CLAUSE ——————

✗ The band has just three other members they play different instruments on different tracks.

In a comma splice, a comma — and only a comma — comes between the main clauses:

        —————— MAIN CLAUSE —————— ┐ ┌—————— MAIN CLAUSE ——————

✗ The band has just three other members, they play different instruments on different tracks.

Run-ons and comma splices make the writer look sloppy. If you are prone to writing run-ons or comma splices, you may want to review the discussion of standard sentence structures at the beginning of this chapter. To avoid problems with run-ons and comma splices, you need to be able to recognize main clauses. Once you can pick them out, solving the problems is simple. You have four options.

- **USE A COMMA AND A COORDINATING CONJUNCTION**

This option works well when the ideas in the clauses are roughly equal in importance. To fix a run-on, add a comma and a coordinating conjunction — *and, but, for, nor, or, so,* or *yet* — to a run-on. Add a conjunction after the comma in a comma splice:

    The band has just three other members, but they play different instruments on different tracks.

- **USE A SEMICOLON**

This option also works well when the two clauses are of equal importance. In a run-on, add a semicolon. In a comma splice, replace the comma with a semicolon:

> The band has just three other members; they play different instruments on different tracks.

To clarify the relationship between the ideas in the two clauses, consider adding a transition word or phrase (see *Create Transitions within and between Paragraphs* in Chapter 20), such as *in contrast* or *meanwhile*, to the second clause, followed by a comma:

> The band has just three other members; however, they play different instruments on different tracks.

- **BREAK THE SENTENCE IN TWO**

This option works well if the two clauses are long. If they are relatively short, as in the following example, the result can sound choppy and disjointed:

> The band has just three other members. They play different instruments on different tracks.

Sometimes, however, two sentences are the best option to fix a run-on or comma splice that is lengthy or complex.

> ✗ The band has just three other members, Steve, Buzz, and Eliot, and they play different instruments on different tracks.

> ✓ The band has just three other members — Steve, Buzz, and Eliot. They play different instruments on different tracks.

- **SUBORDINATE ONE OF THE CLAUSES**

This option works well if you decide that the idea in one of the clauses is more important than the idea in the other. Put the more important idea in the main clause and the less important one in the subordinate clause (see *To Emphasize One Idea over Another* earlier in this chapter):

> The band has just three other members, who play different instruments on different tracks.

The writer's main point here is that the band has just three other members. The subordinate clause starting with who *presents a less important idea.*

Use Parallel Structures to Help Readers Understand Your Ideas

Parallelism means putting similar ideas or elements of a sentence in similar form. When you're presenting a series of items or making comparisons among them, the items should be of the same kind, and each of them should connect seamlessly to the rest of the sentence.

- **WHEN YOU WRITE A SERIES, MAKE ALL THE ELEMENTS IN IT PARALLEL**

Many sentences contain series — lists of similar things, actions, or people:

> The nursing-home residents' eyes light up when we set out chips, cookies, or brownies.

Series go wrong when the items in the list are mismatched — that is, not parallel:

> ✗ The residents talk with each other, crossword and jigsaw puzzles, and some of them read books.

> *The residents' activities (highlighted) are not parallel. One is a verb phrase (talk with each other), one is a noun phrase (crossword and jigsaw puzzles), and one is a main clause (some of them read books).*

To correct a mismatched series, make all the elements serve the same function in the sentence:

> ✓ The residents talk with each other, do crossword and jigsaw puzzles, and read books.

> *The revised sentence lists the residents' activities in parallel form. Verb phrases beginning with the verbs talk, do, and read now describe them all.*

Sometimes items in a series are connected by *either . . . or* or *neither . . . nor*. These items should also take a parallel form:

> ✗ Many prefer either playing cards or to watch movies.

> *Playing is not parallel with to watch.*

Either form is correct; what's incorrect is the lack of parallelism. The sentence can be revised in either of two ways:

> ✓ Many prefer either playing cards or watching movies.

> ✓ Many prefer either to play cards or to watch movies.

- **COMPARE LIKE WITH LIKE**

When you make a comparison, present the items you're comparing in parallel form:

> ✗ That store's food prices are as expensive as eating in a gourmet restaurant.

> *Prices is not parallel with eating.*

> ✓ Food shopping in that store is as expensive as eating in a gourmet restaurant.

> ✓ That store's food prices are as expensive as the prices in a gourmet restaurant.

> *The revised sentences match shopping with eating and prices with prices.*

Comparisons can also fall short when a writer fails to notice what she's actually comparing:

✗ Our state's food prices are higher than most of the nation.

This sentence doesn't make sense, because it compares *prices* with *most of the nation*.

✓ Our state's food prices are higher than prices in most of the nation.

✓ Food prices are higher in our state than they are in most of the nation.

> The revised sentences compare *prices* with *prices* and *in our state* with *in most of the nation*.

● CONNECT ELEMENTS IN A SERIES TO THE REST OF THE SENTENCE

Even a perfectly grammatical sentence can go wrong if the ideas don't align just right. This problem comes up when the wording that connects a series of parallel items to the rest of the sentence doesn't apply to all of them:

✗ I listen to music before, during, and after I study.

I listen to music before I study is fine, *I listen to music after I study* is fine, but *I listen to music during I study* is garbled.

✓ I listen to music before, while, and after I study.

I listen to music while I study is fine.

✗ Sometimes we discover residents eating fries, subs, slices of pizza, milkshakes, beer, and wine that family members have smuggled in.

> People don't *eat* milkshakes, beer, and wine, so either the word *eating* or the series needs correction.

One way to solve a problem like this is to change the connection point so that all the items do make sense with it:

✓ Sometimes we discover residents with fries, subs, slices of pizza, milkshakes, beer, and wine that family members have smuggled in.

Another option with a long series like that one is to break it into two or more, each with its own connection point. Add a conjunction to the first series to show readers where it ends, and add another conjunction before the second or last series to show where it begins:

✓ Sometimes we discover residents wolfing down fries, subs, and slices of pizza and gulping milkshakes, beer, and wine that family members have smuggled in.

> *Wolfing down* applies to the food, and *gulping* applies to the drinks.

The principle that words must connect properly applies even to a series of just two:

✗ I like music as much or more than my friends do.

✓ I like music as much as or more than my friends do.

✗ We try to make sure family members have a clear understanding and obey the rules.

✓ We try to make sure family members have a clear understanding of and obey the rules.

Or, even better than the previous sentence, because it's easier to follow:

✓ We try to make sure family members clearly understand and obey the rules.

Let Readers Know Where Your Sentence Is Going

● USE CONJUNCTIONS AND TRANSITION WORDS AS SIGNPOSTS

As you do at the paragraph level, use conjunctions and transition words (see *Create Transitions within and between Paragraphs* in Chapter 20) as signposts to indicate where your sentences are continuing along a straight path of thought and where they're heading in a new direction.

Put your signposts, particularly ones that signal a change, where they'll be most helpful — before your readers have started to lose their way:

✗ I love reading the band's tweets, checking out their links, and sharing them with friends. Some of my friends tell me that they like to just listen to the music and use their phones to send their own tweets and photos, however.

By the time readers get to the signposting word *however*, they will have had to figure out for themselves that there is a difference in how the writer responds to the band and how the writer's friends do.

✓ . . . Some of my friends, however, tell me that they like to just listen to the music and use their phones to send their own tweets and photos.

Putting the signpost earlier signals readers that a change in direction is under way. Coming after *Some of my friends*, which follows a first-person sentence, the transition word *however* further suggests that the change has to do with a difference between the writer's response to the band and the writer's friends' responses.

Give readers information at the beginning of the sentence that they will need to make sense of what follows. Long sentences are the most likely to leave readers feeling lost or misled. Suppose, for instance, a long sentence describes something that could have happened in your town yesterday but ends with the information that the event took place in Australia 150 years ago. Readers will probably wish they'd known that from the start.

Make sure, too, that readers will have no trouble understanding what any pronouns you use are referring to. Pronouns that come before their antecedents (see *Make Pronouns Agree with Their Antecedents* in Chapter 28) are likely to be confusing:

✗ At every performance, when **they** jump onstage and start dancing as if they can't help themselves — as if their lives depended on dancing — **fans** show how the band energizes them.

> Who are *they*? We don't find out until the last part of the sentence.

✓ At every performance, when **fans** jump onstage and start dancing as if they can't help themselves — as if their lives depended on dancing — **they** show how the band energizes them.

> The revision puts *fans* at the beginning so we know who's jumping onstage.

● **KEEP RELATED IDEAS TOGETHER**

Except in special circumstances, it would probably never occur to anyone to write anything like this:

✗ Mary, a nursing-home resident I like a lot, was born in August. Her birthday is on the 18th of the month, and the year she was born was 1920.

A clear-thinking person would write, instead:

✓ Mary, a nursing-home resident I like a lot, was born on August 18, 1920.

Sometimes, however, writers scatter bits of related information all over a sentence. In most cases, the result is not good:

✗ Mary founded the women's studies department after becoming a professor at Central University, but earlier, before she was married, she was a professional dancer and earned a degree in music in hopes of being a concert pianist.

Putting the different parts of Mary's life in chronological order will certainly help straighten this sentence out. Readers expect chronological events to be presented in time order. But even after the time order is straightened out, a couple of problems remain:

✗ As a young woman, Mary was a professional dancer and earned a degree in music in hopes of being a concert pianist, but after she married, she became a professor at Central University, founding its Women's Studies Department.

First, most of the sentence is about Mary's professional life, so the mention of her marriage introduces an idea that's not closely related to the other ideas — or if it is, we haven't been told how it's related. The sentence would be better off without the mention of the marriage. Second, the sentence seems to say that she danced in hopes of being a concert pianist. The flip side of keeping related ideas together is keeping unrelated ideas apart:

✔ As a young woman, Mary was a professional dancer, and she earned a degree in music in hopes of being a concert pianist, but ultimately she became a professor at Central University, founding its Women's Studies Department.

Chronology is, of course, not the only possible organizing pattern (see *How Can I Choose an Organizing Pattern?* in Chapter 19). In the following draft of the sentence about Mary, the writer is focusing on relationships between *ideas* (which led the writer to decide to add new information and leave out unrelated facts):

✔ Mary was born the same month and day the United States ratified the Nineteenth Amendment to the Constitution, which gave women the right to vote — and this coincidence, she says jokingly, must have inspired her career at Central University as a professor and the founder of the Women's Studies Department.

Keep related ideas together all the way down to the micro level. Put modifiers next to what they're modifying. Dropping them in carelessly looks just that — careless. Misplaced modifiers can even mislead readers.

Limiting modifiers such as *almost, barely, hardly, merely, nearly, only,* and *simply* are particularly liable to make trouble. Compare these sentences:

He almost lost all his friends.

He lost almost all his friends.

The first sentence says he didn't lose his friends; he *almost lost* them. The second sentence says he did lose *almost all* his friends.

Only I thought we needed money.

I only thought we needed money.

I thought we needed only money.

The first sentence means that no one but the writer thought money was needed. The second sentence means that the writer merely imagined the need for money. The third sentence means that the writer thought that nothing but money was needed.

● KEEP THE FLOW OF THE SENTENCE MOVING FORWARD

A good sentence, like a good musical composition, builds toward its conclusion. The second most emphatic place in a sentence is the beginning. This is the natural spot to establish the connection, if there is one, between what you just said and what you are starting to say now:

> Forensic linguistics is the science of analyzing words to determine whether the person who spoke or wrote them committed a **crime**. One famous **criminal** who was caught with the help of forensic linguistics is Ted Kaczynski, the Unabomber, who from 1978 to 1995 killed three people and injured twenty-three.

The word criminal *here ties in with* crime, *which ended the previous sentence.*

Don't wait too long to get around to something that could possibly hold the reader's interest:

✗ On August 18, 1920, the day when a resident of my nursing home whose name is Mary was born, it also happened that . . .

✓ Women got the right to vote on August 18, 1920 — the very day when . . .

If your sentence contains a series, either make the series move forward chronologically (or backward chronologically, if there's a reason for doing so) or build it conceptually from smaller to bigger, from less to more impressive:

> On seemingly random occasions, for reasons they've never explained, the band turns up onstage in costumes — a cape, a Viking helmet, and even a rubber horse's head, which Gordie soon yanks off and tosses into the crowd.

The most emphatic place in a sentence is the end — the sentence's destination. So if you have something you especially want your readers to notice, try to put it at the end.

Do not end a sentence by trailing off into inessential detail:

✗ . . . the constitutional amendment that gave women the right to vote was ratified, making it the nineteenth constitutional amendment.

✓ . . . when the nineteenth constitutional amendment was ratified.

If you succeed in starting your sentences strong and ending them stronger, sometimes you'll find that you've piled a lot of obstacles in the reader's way in the middle.

> ✗ Bob, everybody's favorite nursing-home resident, not just because he's outgoing and friendly but also because he still practices, for us, the craft with which he earned his living for three-quarters of a century, was a professional magician.

Often, a problem like that results from trying to pack too many ideas into one sentence. The writer is trying to tell us both how Bob earned his living and why he is everybody's favorite resident. However, presenting the two ideas together, at the level of detail the writer has provided, overburdens the sentence:

> ✓ Bob, everybody's favorite nursing-home resident, earned his living for three-quarters of a century as a professional magician. We love him not just because he's outgoing and friendly but also because he still practices his craft for us.

Now the first sentence ends with the interesting fact that Bob has long been a magician. The second sentence begins with *We love him*, referring back to *everybody's favorite resident* in the first sentence, and it ends with the information that Bob still practices magic.

Avoid Dangling Words and Phrases

Everything within a sentence should be clearly connected. Sometimes words will connect themselves in ways that you didn't intend. Or they won't come out as neatly tied together as they might be. These problems can undermine you and what you're trying to accomplish.

● AVOID DANGLING MODIFIERS

The connections between the parts of a sentence can go wrong if a phrase is not near what you intended it to modify. (This is the same principle that applies to limiting modifiers like *almost*, *merely*, *nearly*, *only*, and *simply*, which are discussed in the previous section.)

Here *we*, the staff, seem to be sneaking those illicit treats:

> ✗ When sneaking illicit treats, we notice that the residents look guilty.

This mistake goes by the name of **dangling modifier** or **dangler**. To correct a dangling modifier, you usually have two options. First, you can revise the main clause so that the modifier comes just before the subject:

✔ When sneaking illicit treats, the residents look guilty.

Second, you can revise the modifier so that it includes a subject and verb of its own:

✔ We notice that the residents look guilty when they are sneaking illicit treats.

Writers often make a subtler version of that mistake by trying to connect a modifier to a possessive noun, like *Mary's* in this example:

✘ Born on August 18, 1920, Mary's life took many turns.

✔ Born on August 18, 1920, Mary lived a life that took many turns.

> *The revision makes it clear that the residents are the ones sneaking the illicit treats.*

> *The modifier, which has been moved to the end of the sentence, now includes the subject they and the verb are sneaking.*

> *This sentence says that Mary's life was born in 1920 — not what the writer meant.*

> *The revision says clearly that Mary was born in 1920.*

● **AVOID DANGLING PREPOSITIONS**

Little words like *at*, *for*, *in*, *on*, and *with* are often **prepositions**, which attach a noun, pronoun, phrase, or subordinate clause to the rest of the sentence. In a first draft, writers are liable to place these awkwardly at the end of the clause:

✘ Bob showed us the set of silk scarves that he once entertained the queen of England with.

If you find prepositions at the ends of clauses in your writing, consider whether a different word order would be more graceful. You may also need to change *that* to *which* to accommodate the revision:

✔ Bob showed us the set of silk scarves with which he once entertained the queen of England.

In many cases, though, you'll find that the little word at the end actually belongs there. Sometimes there is no more graceful word order. Then, too, the same words that function as prepositions can also serve as **particles**, or bits of phrasal verbs, and when this is their role, they must follow the main part of the verb:

He urged us, "Try them on. That's what they're here for."

> *Try on is a phrasal verb. For is serving as a preposition, but That's for what they're here is much more awkward than the original wording. Besides, the sentence is in a quotation and should represent the speaker's words accurately — see Quote Strategically in Chapter 21.*

Choose Language That Will Earn You Respect

Academic writers earn respect not only by having good ideas and doing solid research but also by choosing language that suits their purposes and shows them to be fair-minded, trustworthy, and confident. Writers with such characteristics are particularly valued in fields like business, public administration, and journalism.

Match Your Style to Your Writing Situation

In written conversations, most of us express ourselves differently on different occasions and to different people, just as we might plan different menus for a backyard barbecue, a wedding, and a working lunch. Your readers will be more inclined to give you a respectful hearing if you use the kind of language that's customary for your genre.

A dictionary can help you choose the right words.

● **CHOOSE THE RIGHT LEVEL OF FORMALITY**

In text messaging and email to your friends, anything goes. In more formal writing, readers expect to be treated as colleagues, not pals. And they expect to see well-considered, grammatical sentences and well-chosen vocabulary.

Words that an up-to-date dictionary has tagged *slang*, *used in email*, or the like probably do not belong in writing intended for anyone except close friends. The same goes for words or uses of words that feel informal but aren't in the dictionary at all. These are probably too new or too far from the mainstream to use in most kinds of writing:

✗ The Gates Foundation gets no props for its work on malaria.

✔ The Gates Foundation gets no respect for its work on malaria.

✗ It's a dis to local farmers growing healthy food that agribusiness receives way more federal subsidies than they do.

✔ It's an insult to local farmers growing healthy food that agribusiness receives considerably more federal subsidies than they do.

Words tagged *colloquial* or *informal* do not belong in research papers or any other equally formal writing:

✗ According to Gates Foundation statistics, 85 percent of those who die of malaria are ==kids== under the age of five.

✓ According to Gates Foundation statistics, 85 percent of those who die of malaria are ==children== under the age of five.

Informal language can, however, enliven personal essays, journalism, and similar kinds of semiformal writing:

Even little ==kids== like some tracks by the band Vogon Soup.

● AVOID UNNECESSARILY TECHNICAL LANGUAGE

Jargon lies at the other end of the language spectrum. Jargon is made up of terms that hardly ever come up in general conversation — for instance, *pathogens* and *antimicrobial agents* — but are familiar to people who work in a particular field or share a particular interest. It is fine to use the jargon of a field you're writing about if the term is more exact than any general-vocabulary term you know and if it seems to be widely used in that field.

Don't get carried away with jargon, though:

✗ The epidemiology of pathogenic resistance to antimicrobial agents warrants careful scrutiny.

Unless you're confident that your readers already understand the specialized terms you want to use, introduce them gradually or avoid them:

✓ Now that some disease-causing microbes can survive treatment with the drugs and other substances that were developed to kill or control them, it is important to study how and where the resistant microbes are spreading.

> *Microbes* is on the borderline of jargon; the writer chose it because it covers bacteria, viruses, and fungi. *Resistant* is borderline, too; the context makes clear that it refers to resisting treatment.

General-purpose dictionaries aren't much help with jargon. They rarely tag words *jargon* the way they tag other words *informal*. The dictionary may give words that are jargon a tag like *medicine*; in other cases, it may give no tag or may leave the words out. If you need to use specialized terms and want to make sure you're using them accurately, check a special-purpose resource like a medical dictionary.

Use Language That Is Free of Bias and Stereotyping

No one with a well-developed sense of fairness enjoys insulting people or seeing them insulted. Instead, we tend to sympathize with whoever's been insulted and to dislike the person who's responsible. Insults can be direct, or they can take the form of assumptions — for instance, that a woman is less powerful than a man, that an old person must be forgetful, or that a member of a certain political group must be narrow-minded. Unless you are presenting definite evidence to the contrary, do not state or imply that any person or group is inferior or superior to others, and do not state or imply that particular members of a group have stereotypical traits.

Be especially sensitive in how you write about anything that touches on these human characteristics:

age	physical attributes and abilities
citizenship	political opinions
gender	race/ethnicity
health status	religion
intelligence	sexual orientation
mental health	socioeconomic status

When you're writing about groups of people or members of those groups, try to use the words they themselves prefer. For example, mental-health agencies and advocates tend to say *people with schizophrenia* and *people with autism* rather than *schizophrenics* and *autistics* or *people suffering from schizophrenia or autism*. A little research will help you find the right terms.

Similarly, although it was once considered technically correct to use male pronouns (such as *he, him,* and *his*) when the gender of a noun (such as *doctor* or *nurse*) is not known, most readers will object if you do so. Readers are even more likely to object if you make the mistake of referring to representatives of particular professions using gender-specific pronouns:

✗ When describing your symptoms to a doctor, be sure to tell him everything that's relevant. Similarly, when a nurse is taking your blood pressure, feel free to let her know how you feel.

By implying that all doctors are male and all nurses are female, the writer of this passage plays into common stereotypes. The result is that many readers will form a negative opinion of the writer.

To avoid biased language, you can recast your sentences so that generic references (such as a *doctor*) are plural (*doctors*):

> Doctors who pursue advanced specializations might need to spend as many as fifteen years of study before they can go into practice on their own.

Alternatively, you can use *they* to refer to individuals whose gender is not specified. While some readers might object to this, it has become a widely accepted practice:

> A doctor who pursues an advanced specialization might need to spend as many as fifteen years of study before they can go into practice on their own.

Or you can get rid of the pronoun:

> A doctor who pursues an advanced specialization might need to spend as many as fifteen years of study before starting a practice.

Similarly, avoid using gender-specific words for generic roles. Instead, use a gender-neutral form such as the following:

Sexist	Nonsexist
businessman	businessperson
chairman	chair
congressman	representative, member of Congress
mankind	humanity, humankind
policeman	police officer
salesman	salesperson
stewardess	flight attendant
waiter/waitress	server

Avoid Exaggeration

In social conversation, it's normal to say things like "Those were the most beautiful strawberries I've ever seen!" and "I could eat a truckload of them!" But when you're writing for readers who don't know you well, it's important to show that you're reliable. Readers have a sense of what the world is like. Exaggerations tend to affect them much the way insults and biased language do: they begin to mistrust the writer. Avoid stating opinions or conclusions that are more than the facts will bear out, and when possible, present the information that's the basis for your opinion or conclusion so that readers can evaluate it for themselves.

> The highlighted words in this passage are exaggerations.

✗ The biggest problem facing us is that unhealthy food is available everywhere, and anyone can easily afford it. In contrast, healthy food is impossible to find, and it is priced out of almost everyone's reach. The catastrophic result is that everybody in the country is constantly making poor eating choices.

> When the exaggerations are removed, it is easier to agree with the point the writer is making.

✓ Unhealthy food is convenient to buy, and most people can easily afford it. In contrast, healthy food can be difficult to find, and it can be more expensive. The unfortunate result is that many people are regularly making poor eating choices.

Use Only Words You Know

As you polish your writing, you'll probably want to use a thesaurus or dictionary to find exactly the words you need. Don't assume, however, that all the choices a reference website or book offers you are equally good. If you used the word *terrible* but want to make it clear what kind of *terrible* you mean, don't choose *atrocious* or *egregious* or *vile* unless the word is already familiar to you and you know it has the shade of meaning you want.

Of course, it's great to learn new words and use them confidently. If you suspect but don't know that a word is the one you want, check out some of its online uses in sources such as Google News (news.google.com) or Google Scholar (scholar.google.com), and see how these compare with the use you have in mind.

Whenever you have a choice between a simple word and a longer, fancier one that seems to have the same shade of meaning, choose the simple word.

Ornate	Simple
assist	help
employment	job
expeditious	fast
frequently	often
identical	same
individual	person
initiate	start
purchase	buy
reside	live
sufficient	enough
terminate	end
utilize	use

✗ The utilization of monosyllabic locutions is recommended as preferable.

✓ Words of one syllable are best.

Choose Lively, Concise Phrasing

Lively phrasing gives readers — and probably the writer, too — pleasure. Concise phrasing is clear and shows respect for readers' time.

To Be Vivid, Be Specific

A writer might jot down a note like "Climate change really urgent" as they read about and become more familiar with a topic. After some time spent planning and researching, the writer might decide to begin drafting by sketching the setting in which that inspiration came up:

> The building I live in has been standing for more than 150 years, but its roof was no match for the three blizzards in a row that hit us last winter. After the first blizzard, melted snow, turned brownish from the roof's insulation, began leaking into my apartment. The filthy-looking water trickled down the white walls and through the ceiling of my bedroom — onto the dresser, the TV, and eventually my bed. Where I set out buckets to catch the drips, the liquid hit the plastic with a bang. Bang! Bang! Bang! This went on at a rate of about once a second for sixteen days.
>
> Last winter was the snowiest that my city has experienced in its recorded history, and living through it brought home to me how destructive and upsetting abnormal weather can be. The great majority of scientists who study the earth's climate agree that climate change is occurring.

Now readers can also see, vividly and specifically, what led the writer to begin thinking about the situation. Details can bring a scene to life or make an idea persuasive; details that have little to do with the point the writer wants to make, however, are best omitted.

Give Every Word a Job to Do

Writing in a detailed, specific way might seem like a recipe for going on and on. In a first draft, it's fine to write without censoring yourself. As you edit, however, look for words and phrases that aren't carrying their weight and cut or change them. When you see a bland phrase, consider whether you might change it to something livelier that's as clear or clearer. When you see a long-winded phrase, think about what you mean and how you might *say* that. Using a thesaurus to look up words you've written but don't like can often provide inspiration — as long as you understand and feel comfortable with the word (see *Use Only Words You Know* in the previous section).

✗ The dripping into the plastic buckets made a surprisingly loud noise.

✓ The liquid hit the plastic with a bang.

✗ There has never been a winter when more snow fell in my city since people began keeping records of annual snowfalls.

✓ Last winter was the snowiest that my city has experienced in its recorded history.

Favor the Active Voice

In the **active voice**, the subject of the sentence is the actor:

Malaria threatens us.

In the **passive voice**, the subject of the sentence is acted upon:

We are threatened by malaria.

Ordinarily, when you use the active voice, your writing will be more direct and forceful:

✗ More than 200 million people a year are sickened by malaria.

✓ Malaria sickens more than 200 million people a year.

> If *malaria* is the subject instead of *people*, the verb can take the active form *sickens* rather than the passive form *are sickened by*.

To make a passive sentence active, you don't always need to turn it around the way we did in the pair of examples above. Sometimes you can simply change the verb:

✓ More than 200 million people a year contract malaria.

> In this sentence, *people* remains the subject, but the verb *contract* is active.

The passive voice is fine in situations in which you do not want to identify the actor or in which the actor is not important. Here, for example, it's beside the point to say who uses the insecticides:

Insecticides are used in bed nets and sprays to kill mosquitoes.

The passive voice can also be useful when it allows you to start or end a sentence in a way that flows smoothly from the previous sentence into the next one. For instance, compare these two passages:

Malaria poses a serious problem for public health. A parasite causes malaria, and mosquitoes spread it. Killing the parasite, the mosquitoes, or both combats the disease.

Malaria poses a serious problem for public health. It is caused by a parasite, which is spread by mosquitoes. It can be combated by killing the parasite, the mosquitoes, or both.

Although all the verbs in the first passage are in the active voice, the train of thought seems disorganized, jumping from malaria to the parasite and back to malaria, to the mosquitoes and back to malaria, and to killing the parasite and the mosquitoes and back to malaria. In the second passage, malaria is the subject of all three sentences, making it clear that the passage is consistently about the disease.

Look for Alternatives to Forms of the Verb *To Be*

Don't write like this:

✗ Harriet Tubman was a remarkable American. She was born an enslaved person in the 1820s (the exact year is not known) in Maryland. In 1849 she was able to escape to Philadelphia, in the free state of Pennsylvania. She was not satisfied to live comfortably as a free woman, however, when there were so many others who were still enslaved. There was a series of trips that she made back south, guiding her parents, several of her brothers and sisters, and about sixty other people to freedom. In the Civil War, she was at first a cook and a nurse for the Union Army, then an armed scout and spy. She was the first woman to lead an armed expedition in the war, and a raid she was in charge of liberated 700 enslaved people in South Carolina.

Instead, find some verbs that will work harder for you:

✓ Harriet Tubman won renown as a remarkable American. She was born an enslaved person in the 1820s (the exact year is not known) in Maryland. In 1849 she escaped to Philadelphia, in the free state of Pennsylvania. She refused to live comfortably as a free woman, however, when so many others remained enslaved. She made a series of trips back south, guiding her parents, several of her brothers and sisters, and about sixty other people to freedom. In the Civil War, she at first worked as a cook and a nurse for the Union Army, then as an armed scout and spy. She became the first woman to lead an armed expedition in the war, and a raid she led liberated 700 enslaved people in South Carolina.

Although the verb *be* in its various forms — *am, are, is, was, were* — is versatile and sometimes even irreplaceable, often it does only part of the job that a more substantial verb could do. For example, *escaped* is a stronger, more direct way of saying *was able to escape*, and *refused* is stronger and more concise than *was not satisfied*. Furthermore, placeholders such as *there was* and *there were* are notoriously weak ways to begin a sentence or a clause.

If You Want to Use Figures of Speech, Invent Your Own

Figures of speech are words and phrases not intended to be taken literally. Most familiar ones — *weak as a kitten, plenty of fish in the sea, stubborn as a mule* — have been used for so long that all connection to their literal sense has been lost. They don't bring a vivid image to mind. They're clichés. Avoid them.

If your goal is to make readers see something or understand something the way you saw or understood it, stop and think: How does it strike you? Was that filthy-looking water leaking through the ceiling *like a miniature mudslide*? Did those sixteen days *feel like a practical joke gone horribly wrong*?

Don't force it. It's better to do without figures of speech than to write foolish ones:

> *As sick as a dog* is a cliché, and it conveys almost nothing about what it feels like to have malaria.

✗ Malaria makes a person as sick as a dog.

> This is a bit more original, but it is overworked.

✗ Malaria makes people feel as if they were being plunged into a tub of freezing water and having the water heated to nearly boiling, and then back again.

> This conveys the feeling of *fever and chills* more vividly than the purely factual phrase would.

✓ Malaria feels like arctic cold or hellish tropical heat — back and forth, one or the other.

Pay Attention to Relationships among Words

Writing is closely related to sound and imagery. As readers encounter your words, sounds and images will pop into their minds. Writing conveys ideas, too, of course. As a writer, you should work to control the sounds, images, and ideas your words bring to mind.

Controlling the sounds readers will hear often involves using words that have similar sounds:

> Few climate scientists would attempt to predict the weather for specific places at specific times. Using temperature data, however, climate science can make confident predictions about global trends.

The word forms themselves help tie *climate scientists* to *climate science* and *predict* to *predictions*.

✗ We react in one way to weather-related disasters that affect individuals on the other side of the world and in another to catastrophes that happen to people we know.

Here, is the writer trying to draw some distinction between *disasters* and *catastrophes*? Between *individuals* and *people*? It's unclear.

✔ We react in one way to weather-related disasters that affect people on the other side of the world and in another to disasters that happen to people we know.

Disasters and *people* now repeat, helping to establish clearly that the writer is presenting a difference between things that happen at a distance and similar things that happen closer to home.

Making words sound similar is important. It can even be required in some situations (see *Use Parallel Structures* earlier in this chapter). But repetition must be used with care. It can work for you — or against you. Avoid unintentional repeats or echoes, particularly ones that are close together:

✘ It's not so odd that all prime numbers except 2 are odd; all other even numbers are multiples of 2.

Ideas, like sounds, can repeat in undesirable ways:

✘ Recently, Bob has been writing an autobiography of his life.

> An *autobiography* is the story of the writer's life; *of his life* is repetitive.

This blunder is called **redundancy**. So many turns of phrase can be redundant that it would be impossible to list them all. Here are some of the more notorious redundancies:

added bonus	end product	reason is because
advance notice	end result	reason why
advance planning	final outcome	return back
advance reservation	free gift	revert back
advance warning	future plans	same exact
armed gunman	general public	successful achievement
both alike	HIV virus	total annihilation
both . . . different	mutual cooperation	total destruction
both the same	overexaggerate	total extinction
collaborate together	past history	true fact
consensus of opinion	PIN number	unconfirmed rumor

> The *V* in *HIV* stands for *virus*.

> The *N* in *PIN* stands for *number*.

As for the images in readers' heads, beware of **mixed metaphors** — figures of speech that call to mind confused jumbles of images:

✗ The water came pouring in like a freight train, dirtying everything it touched.

> Do trains *pour in*? Do they *dirty* everything they touch? This sentence may be lively, but it's confused and confusing.

Similarly, avoid using words that have more than one meaning in a context that's likely to bring the wrong image or meaning to mind:

✗ Inmates are forbidden to use cell phones.

> Mobile phones? Phones in their cells?

Avoid Using Too Many *-tion, -ing,* and *-ly* Endings

Be particularly suspicious of the ending *-tion*. It makes almost everything it touches abstract — and the more abstract an idea is, the less vivid it will be:

✗ The solution to the problem must include government reprioritization and subsidization of climate research.

Here, the writer tried to load too much meaning into nouns (*solution, reprioritization, subsidization*), stringing them together with a flabby verb (*must include*). Solve the problem by changing some of the nouns to verbs (like *solving, focus,* and *fund*):

✔ Solving the problem will require the government to focus on and fund climate research.

The ending *-ing* isn't as bad, but a sentence full of *-ing*s that are not intended to be parallel (see *Use Parallel Structures* earlier in this chapter) will sound sing-songy. What's more, the parallel word forms suggest that the ideas the words convey have more in common than they do:

✗ Improving weather forecasting and revising the goals of urban planning may be helping.

For ideas that are not parallel, variety in word forms is best:

✔ Improvements in weather forecasting and revisions to the goals of urban planning may help.

Not all adverbs end in -ly, but most words that end in -ly are adverbs. Too many -ly endings, like too many -ings, will give a sing-songy effect. Worse, they are a tip-off that you're filling up your writing with adverbs (see Use Adjectives and Adverbs in Chapter 28):

✘ Unfortunately, the U.S. government currently spends billions of dollars annualy simply to repair damage that natural disasters routinely cause.

You can often cut some -ly adverbs, and you may be able to replace others with synonyms:

✔ The U.S. government now spends billions of dollars a year to repair damage that natural disasters cause.

Make a Habit of Stating Things in an Affirmative Way

Negative statements, which negate the verb, usually make your readers work harder than they would like. They force readers to turn your ideas around to understand what you *are* saying when you are *not* saying something else. This extra work robs your writing of force and directness. Look for affirmative ways to make your points:

✘ Climate change is not just a minor, distant problem.

✔ Climate change is a serious, immediate problem.

A sentence can include a negative word like *no* without being a negative statement:

> No one who has lived through a natural disaster wants to repeat the experience.

The verb is wants, *not* does not want. *The statement contains a negative word, but the statement itself is affirmative.*

If you write affirmative statements habitually, an occasional negative statement will stand out and become forceful:

> Much progress has been made in weather forecasting and in construction techniques to minimize damage from storms. It would be wonderful if research into reversing climate change were making similar progress, but this is not the case.

In Summary: Style: Writing Confidently

* Write clear, logical sentences (p. 714).
* Choose language that will earn you respect (p. 730).
* Choose lively, concise phrasing (p. 735).

28 Grammar: Writing Skillfully

Make verbs work for you 743
Match the number of a verb to the number of its subject 743
Use verb tense and mood to convey timing and possibility 748

Use pronouns to help readers 757
Match subject pronouns with subjects and object pronouns with objects 757
Make pronouns agree with their antecedents 761
Avoid vague or ambiguous pronoun references 762

Use adjectives and adverbs to clarify your ideas 766
Use adjectives to modify nouns and pronouns 766
Use adverbs to modify verbs, adjectives, and adverbs 767
Know when to use *good*, *well*, *bad*, and *badly* 768
Use *-est*, *most*, or *least* only when comparing three or more items 769
Watch out for adverbs with absolute concepts 769

Few things can undermine a good idea or derail a powerful argument as completely as an obvious grammatical error. It isn't that the error is all that important in the larger context. Your argument will still be powerful. Your idea will still be good. But a grammatical error will almost always get your readers' attention.

Unfortunately, it's the wrong kind of attention. Grammatical errors — and to a lesser extent odd but correctly written phrases — can make readers stop reading. In most cases, it's a brief stop, a moment in which they might mutter, "Really?" before they continue. If they've come across several errors, however, they may simply give up, set your work aside, and turn to something else, such as a document that's easier to read.

For this reason alone, anything that makes readers stop reading — and in particular anything that makes it hard to understand your argument or ideas — should be avoided. Writing skillfully, however, has an even more important role in accomplishing your writing goals. A powerful verb can bring your argument to life. A thoughtfully placed pronoun can smooth your readers' passage through the explanation of a complex issue. A well-chosen adjective or adverb can highlight specific aspects of an idea.

In this chapter, you'll learn how writing skillfully can keep your readers' attention focused on your ideas and argument. By exploring some of the most important areas of grammar — using verbs correctly and effectively, using pronouns appropriately, and choosing adjectives and adverbs wisely — you'll learn not only how to avoid errors but also how to enhance your effectiveness as a writer.

Make Verbs Work for You

Without verbs, English would be just a great big pile of stuff — a heap of nouns, noun phrases, and connecting parts unable to move, change, affect one another, or do anything else, because doing is the province of verbs. We may lose sight of that fact after reading one too many verbs like *incentivize*, *prioritize*, and *signify* — verbs that merely suggest abstract concepts. The best verbs show some life. They conquer and comfort, praise and disparage, live and breathe.

Match the Number of a Verb to the Number of Its Subject

Number means singular or plural, one or more than one. Number is not generally an issue if you're writing in the first person (that is, if your subject is *I* or *we*) or the second person (*you*) because the verbs use the simple **base form**, with no ending: *I throw. You catch. We play.*

Most of your writing, though, including nearly all the academic writing you do, will be in the third person, and here number does matter. The verb for a singular subject needs an *-s* or *-es* ending: *She throws. He catches.* The verb for a plural third-person subject uses the base form, with no ending: *They play.*

An important exception to this pattern is the highly irregular verb *be*: *I am. You are. He is. She is. We are. You are. They are. It is.*

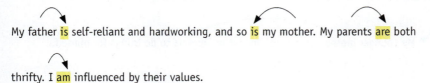

My father is self-reliant and hardworking, and so is my mother. My parents are both

thrifty. I am influenced by their values.

All of that information about verb forms and number seems simple until you start writing real sentences about real topics. Then number can cause trouble in a variety of situations.

● WATCH OUT FOR WORDS THAT COME BETWEEN THE SUBJECT AND VERB

Mistakes with number are especially common when something with a different number from the subject pops up to throw the writer off track:

✗ Committee members at the nursing home *proposes* a staff appreciation day.

✓ Committee members at the nursing home *propose* a staff appreciation day.

> The subject is *members*, not *committee* or *nursing home*.

✗ The trouble they have taken to provide for members of their families in two countries *inspire* me.

✓ The trouble they have taken to provide for members of their families in two countries *inspires* me.

> The subject is *trouble*, not *they* or *members* or *families* or *countries*.

● TREAT MOST COMPOUND SUBJECTS AS PLURAL

A **compound subject** is made up of two or more things, which, taken together, call for a plural verb:

My *mother* and my older *brother are* champion networkers, so they have plenty of friends to fall back on.

If the two nouns are really one, though, use a singular verb:

My *best friend and roommate thinks* my family is old-fashioned.

> *Thinks* is correct here only because the best friend is also the roommate.

Note that the parts of a compound subject are joined by *and*. Words that come after *along with*, *as well as*, *besides*, *in addition to*, *together with*, and similar words and phrases don't actually become part of the subject of a sentence. These additions are usually set off with commas, dashes, or parentheses.

My younger *brother*, along with my father, *prefers* to do things for himself.

> The subject is only *my younger brother*. It is not compound, so the verb needs to be singular.

- **MATCH THE NUMBER OF THE VERB TO THE NEARER OR NEAREST OF ALTERNATIVE SUBJECTS**

Alternative subjects are connected by *or* or *nor*:

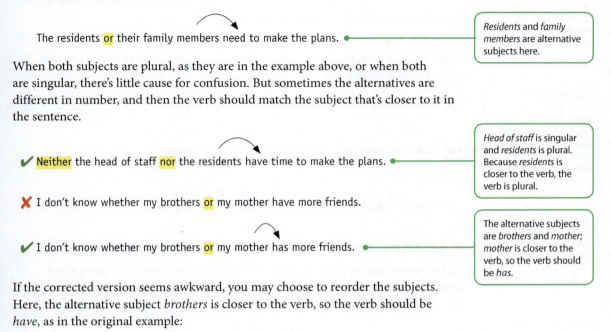

The residents or their family members need to make the plans.

> *Residents* and *family members* are alternative subjects here.

When both subjects are plural, as they are in the example above, or when both are singular, there's little cause for confusion. But sometimes the alternatives are different in number, and then the verb should match the subject that's closer to it in the sentence.

✔ Neither the head of staff nor the residents have time to make the plans.

> *Head of staff* is singular and *residents* is plural. Because *residents* is closer to the verb, the verb is plural.

✘ I don't know whether my brothers or my mother have more friends.

✔ I don't know whether my brothers or my mother has more friends.

> The alternative subjects are *brothers* and *mother*; *mother* is closer to the verb, so the verb should be *has*.

If the corrected version seems awkward, you may choose to reorder the subjects. Here, the alternative subject *brothers* is closer to the verb, so the verb should be *have*, as in the original example:

✔ I don't know whether my mother or my brothers have more friends.

- **MAKE THE SUBJECT AND VERB AGREE, EVEN WHEN THE VERB COMES FIRST**

Not all sentences put the subject before the verb. In fact, all sentences whose main clauses begin with *there is* or *there are*, and some sentences that begin with *it is*, put the subject after the verb.

✘ In sum, there is many people who are on our side, even without taking paid specialists into account.

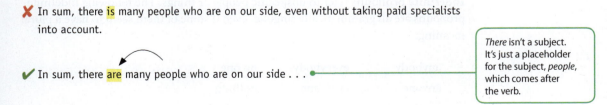

✔ In sum, there are many people who are on our side . . .

> *There* isn't a subject. It's just a placeholder for the subject, *people*, which comes after the verb.

It's often better to turn *there is* and *there are* sentences around (see *Look for Alternatives to Forms of the Verb To Be* later in this chapter):

- In sum, many people are on our side . . .

> Now the subject is in its usual position before the verb, the placeholder is not needed, and the number of the verb is clear.

Other kinds of sentences, too — often ones whose verb is a form of *be* — put the subject after the verb:

- ✗ Especially deserving of appreciation is the night workers.

- ✓ Especially deserving of appreciation are the night workers.

> This sentence is equivalent to *The night workers are especially deserving of appreciation*, so the verb form must match the subject, *workers*.

- ✓ Among those who have helped us the most is our neighbor.

> This sentence is equivalent to *Our neighbor is among those who have helped us the most*.

● **DO NOT CONFUSE THE SUBJECT WITH A NOUN COMPLEMENT**

A **noun complement** is not an object of the verb — not something being acted upon. It is being equated with the subject. Only certain verbs — most commonly *be* — take complements.

- ✓ My parents' fallback, when no one in the family is able to help them, is friends.

> The subject of the sentence is *fallback*, so the verb is singular.

- ✗ The only problem with strategies like theirs are unreliable friends.

- ✓ The only problem with strategies like theirs is unreliable friends.

> The subject is not *strategies* or *friends* but *problem*.

● **USE SINGULAR VERBS WITH SINGULAR INDEFINITE PRONOUNS**

Indefinite pronouns refer to unspecific people or things. The following indefinite pronouns are all grammatically singular, even if some of them seem to have a plural meaning:

anybody	everybody	no one
anyone	everyone	nothing
anything	everything	somebody
each	neither	someone
either	nobody	something

✔ **Anyone** whose relatives emigrated from other countries probably **knows** what I am talking about.

✘ **Each** of my family members **are** that way — except me.

✔ **Each** of my family members **is** that way — except me.

Note that when *each* follows a plural pronoun or noun, it is not an indefinite pronoun but a modifier, and the verb should be plural.

✔ **They** each **have** an independent streak. •───── The subject of this sentence is the plural pronoun *they*, so it takes the plural verb *have*.

✘ **Neither** of my parents **like** to ask strangers for help.

✔ **Neither** of my parents **likes** to ask strangers for help. •───── Even though *parents* is plural, the subject of the sentence is the singular pronoun *neither*, so it takes the singular verb *likes*.

Note that when *neither* is paired with *nor* — as in "Neither my mother nor my brothers ask for help" — these words are not indefinite pronouns but modifiers of alternative subjects (see *Match the Number of the Verb* earlier in this chapter). The number of the verb should match the number of the subject closer to the verb.

● **USE THE RIGHT VERB FORMS WITH COLLECTIVE NOUNS**

Collective nouns gather up multiple people or things and treat the group as a unit. Examples of collective nouns include *army, band, bunch, committee, family, group,* and *team*, but there are many more. Collective nouns are usually treated as singular:

My **family eats** dinner every night at six.

The **band has** five members.

Collective nouns are often followed by phrases that specify what the group consists of: *an army of ants, a band of brothers, a bunch of grapes.* When a noun phrase of this pattern — "a singular of plurals" — is a subject, the verb is still usually singular:

An **army** of ants **swarms** into the house.

The exception is when the members of the group are acting as individuals rather than as a unit:

My band of brothers all volunteer at the homeless shelter.

● **WATCH OUT FOR NOUNS THAT LOOK PLURAL BUT ARE NOT**

Not all nouns that end in *-s* are plural:

Economics is my favorite subject.

Some nouns ending in *-s* are never plural. Others are sometimes singular and sometimes plural, depending on the meaning:

> As a field of study, *statistics*, like *economics*, is singular.

Statistics makes me think.

> When the word *statistics* refers to facts or items of data, it is plural.

The statistics make the point.

Nouns ending in *-s* that are singular include these:

acoustics	gymnastics	physics
biceps	lens	politics
blues (music)	linguistics	robotics
crossroads	mathematics	series
economics	news	statistics

If you're unsure about the number of a particular word in a particular context, check a dictionary.

Use Verb Tense and Mood to Convey Timing and Possibility

Unless you give some indication to the contrary, readers will assume that you're narrating chronological events in time order, presenting causes before effects, explaining problems before solutions, and so on. In these cases, a simple past (or present or future) tense may be all you need. Sometimes, though, you'll want to start in the middle of a sequence. Then verb tenses can help you make clear what came before what, either logically or chronologically.

Consider this paragraph:

> My father responded to the world more openly before September 11, 2001. Since then, even though my family is Hindu, not Muslim, we have at times been targets of ethnic discrimination — people making hateful remarks or vandalizing our property. This has hit my father especially hard, because he had believed in America as a land of freedom and opportunity for people like us. And in 2001, my brothers and I were young. I'm sure my father didn't want us to grow up to be either fearful or angry.

The paragraph starts by dividing the writer's father's world into pre- and post-9/11. It goes on to talk about things that have happened since 9/11, circles back to how the writer's father felt before 9/11, points out something that was the case at the time of 9/11, and ends with an observation about what at that time the writer's father wanted for the future. In this paragraph, the verb tenses help readers stay with the writer the whole way.

The charts that follow demonstrate the verb tenses you have at your disposal.

Simple tenses for regular verbs

The **simple tenses** are generally used for facts (*The earth revolves around the sun*), states of being (*I felt great*), and recurring actions (*I will walk to school every day*).

	Formula	Example
simple present	verb with no ending (first- and second-person singular and plural, and third-person plural); or	Today I/you/we/they smile. Today I/you/we/they watch.
	verb + -s or -es (third-person singular)	Today he/she smiles. Today he/she watches.
simple past	verb + -d or -ed	Yesterday I/you/he/she/we/they smiled. Yesterday I/you/he/she/we/they watched.
simple future	will + verb	Tomorrow I/you/he/she/we/they will smile. Tomorrow I/you/he/she/we/they will watch.

Perfect tenses for regular verbs

The **perfect tenses** are formed with a helping verb or verbs plus a past participle. For regular verbs, the past participle is the same as the simple past. The present perfect places the action in the past (and sometimes continuing into the present). The past perfect places the action in a past earlier than another past time frame. And the future perfect places the action in the future earlier than another future time frame.

	Formula	Example
simple present perfect	*have/has* + past participle	I/you/we/they <u>have watched</u> the show many times. She/he <u>has watched</u> the show many times.
past perfect	*had* + past participle	I/you/she/he/we/they <u>had watched</u> the show before you called.
future perfect	*will have* + past participle	I/you/she/he/we/they <u>will have watched</u> the show ten times by next month.

Progressive tenses for regular verbs

The **progressive tenses** are formed with a helping verb or verbs plus a present participle. For regular verbs, the present participle is the *-ing* form of the verb. Progressive tenses are used for actions that continue over time.

	Formula	Example
present progressive	*am/are/is* + present participle	I <u>am watching</u> the show right now. We/you/they <u>are watching</u> the show right now. She/he <u>is watching</u> the show right now.
past progressive	*was/were* + present participle	I/she/he <u>was watching</u> the show last night. We/you/they <u>were watching</u> the show last night.
future progressive	*will be* + present participle	I/you/she/he/we/they <u>will be watching</u> the show when you call.
present perfect progressive	*have/has been* + present participle	I/you/we/they <u>have been watching</u> the show since I was twelve. She/he <u>has been watching</u> the show since she was twelve.
past perfect progressive	*had been* + present participle	I/you/she/he/we/they <u>had been watching</u> the show for two years before it won an award.
future perfect progressive	*will have been* + present participle	I/you/she/he/we/they <u>will have been watching</u> the show for nine years next year.

As shown in the verb tense charts and as discussed in the section on the subjunctive mood (see *Use Verbs in Special Moods in Special Cases* later in this section), helping verbs are used along with main verbs to create tenses and moods. A helping verb can be a form of *have, do,* or *be*:

have, has, had

do, does, did

be, am, is, are, was, were, being, been

Or it can be one of nine modal auxiliaries:

can	might	should
could	must	will
may	shall	would

Can, may, shall, and *will* all signal more definite possibilities than *could, might, should,* and *would*. For instance, *I can check the bus schedule* implies that the writer is likely to do so; *I could check the bus schedule* is more like an idle thought or an offer to check the schedule if requested. *I may go to the party* is a shade more definite than *I might go.*

Could is also the past tense of *can,* so *I could check the bus schedule* might alternatively be in the past: *Yesterday I realized I could check the bus schedule.* Similarly, *might* is the past tense of *may, should* of *shall,* and *would* of *will.*

● DON'T GET TRIPPED UP BY IRREGULAR VERBS

If you give your verbs a workout with sequences that travel forward and back in time, you'll need to keep in mind that some verbs, including many of the most common ones, have irregular past tenses and past participles.

As noted in the verb charts in the previous section, the past and perfect tenses of regular verbs are easy to create:

Yesterday we **watched** the show.

> The simple past tense of a regular verb is formed by adding *-d* or *-ed.*

They **have watched** the show many times.

> The present perfect tense of a regular verb is formed by combining a form of *have* with the past participle, which for regular verbs is the same as the simple past.

For irregular verbs, the simple past and past participle forms are less predictable:

Yesterday I **rode** the bus into town.

> The verb *ride* is irregular, so the simple past (*rode*) must be used.

> Unlike regular verbs, irregular verbs often have past participles that are different from the simple past tense. Here, instead of *have rode*, the correct verb form is *have ridden*.

✔ I have ridden the bus every day this week.

✘ I seen the show on television.

✔ I saw the show on television.

✔ I have seen the show on television.

✘ It had broke.

✔ It broke.

✔ It had broken.

✘ It costed plenty.

✔ It cost plenty.

If you aren't sure of the past tense or past participle for a verb, check the base form of the verb in a dictionary. If no irregular forms are given in the entry, the verb is regular.

The following irregular verbs can give writers trouble:

Base form of verb	Past tense	Past participle
arise	arose	arisen
be	was, were	been
become	became	become
begin	began	begun
bend	bent	bent
bite	bit	bitten, bit
blow	blew	blown
break	broke	broken
bring	brought	brought
build	built	built
burst	burst	burst

Base form of verb	Past tense	Past participle
catch	caught	caught
choose	chose	chosen
come	came	come
cost	cost	cost
dive	dived, dove	dived
do	did	done
draw	drew	drawn
drink	drank	drunk
drive	drove	driven
eat	ate	eaten
fall	fell	fallen
fight	fought	fought
fly	flew	flown
forget	forgot	forgotten
freeze	froze	frozen
get	got	gotten, got
give	gave	given
go	went	gone
grow	grew	grown
have	had	had
hear	heard	heard
hide	hid	hidden
hurt	hurt	hurt
keep	kept	kept
know	knew	known
lay (= place [something] on a surface)	laid	laid
lead	led	led
let	let	let
lie (= rest)	lay	lain
prove	proved	proven, proved

(*continued*)

Base form of verb	Past tense	Past participle
read	read	read
ride	rode	ridden
ring	rang	rung
rise	rose	risen
run	ran	run
see	saw	seen
send	sent	sent
set (= place [something] on a surface)	set	set
shake	shook	shaken
shoot	shot	shot
shrink	shrank	shrunk
sing	sang	sung
sink	sank	sunk
sit (= take a seat)	sat	sat
slay	slew	slain
speak	spoke	spoken
spring	sprang	sprung
stand	stood	stood
steal	stole	stolen
sting	stung	stung
strike	struck	struck, stricken
swear	swore	sworn
swim	swam	swum
swing	swung	swung
take	took	taken
throw	threw	thrown
wake	woke, waked	waked, woken
wear	wore	worn
write	wrote	written

USE VERBS IN SPECIAL MOODS IN SPECIAL CASES

Statements, exclamations, and questions are all in the **indicative mood**. Here are indicative clauses of three types:

Statement

My parents don't expect strangers to be on their side.

Exclamation

They won't even ask for help!

Question

Would it cross my father's mind to ask a waiter for a napkin?

Usually, statements do the work, and exclamations and questions provide special effects. Make it a habit to phrase your thoughts as statements.

Expressing commands, or the **imperative mood**, is easy — as long as you remember that the subject is always *you* and that it's implied, rather than actually appearing in the sentence. Here a command is addressed to the writer's parents:

Speak up for yourselves! That's what I want to say to them.

The tricky mood is the **subjunctive mood**, used for things that are not, or aren't necessarily, true, including wishes, most *as if* comparisons, and some *if* and *that* statements. In sentences of these kinds, use the past tense to describe the untrue condition or wish:

She wishes that she had a million dollars.

She is acting as if she had a million dollars.

If she had a million dollars, she would buy more books.

> When the subjunctive (*had*) is used in an *if* clause, the same mood (*would*) is also used in the main clause.

Do not use the subjunctive mood in *as if* comparisons and *if* statements when they describe something you believe is true or is likely to come true:

Her financial trouble is serious. She is acting as if she has barely enough money to live on.

If she has enough money at the end of the week, she will buy books.

The switch to the past tense of verbs in subjunctive clauses is simple with every verb except *be* because all verbs except *be*, regular and irregular, have only one past-tense form:

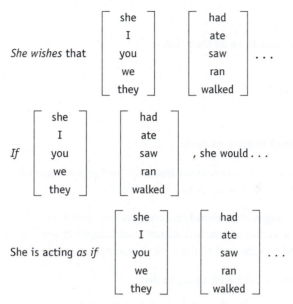

The past tense of *be*, however, has two forms: *was* and *were*. In the subjunctive mood, only *were* is used, even for singular subjects:

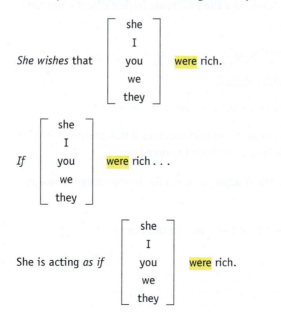

A present-tense version of the subjunctive mood, in which the verb appears in its base form, also exists. Use this for suggestions, requests, and orders:

I have suggested that my father **speak** up in public.

My father requested that the waiter **bring** a napkin.

> Because this is just a wish and the writer's father does not actually speak up, the verb is the subjunctive *speak*, not the indicative *speaks*.

> Because this is a request, the verb is the subjunctive *bring*, not the indicative *brings*.

Use Pronouns to Help Readers

Pronouns stand in for nouns. Reading would be awkward without them:

✗ The band **Vogon Soup** has been together long enough that **Vogon Soup** knows **Vogon Soup's** strengths.

Once readers know what the topic is, pronouns become a shorthand way to refer to it. Reading a name, or any noun, again and again is tedious. And because most pronouns are shorter than the nouns they replace, they save readers — and writers — time:

✓ The band **Vogon Soup** has been together long enough that **it** knows **its** strengths.

Most pronouns cause little or no trouble. The ones that are most likely to go wrong are discussed here. Misusing them is likely to confuse or irritate readers as much as failing to use them at all.

Match Subject Pronouns with Subjects and Object Pronouns with Objects

These are **subject pronouns**, suitable for use as the subjects of clauses — the agents performing the actions:

I
you
he, she, it
we
you
they

These are **object pronouns**, suitable for use as objects — the agents being acted upon:

> me
> you
> him, her, it
> us
> them

● WATCH OUT WHEN USING SUBJECT OR OBJECT PRONOUNS TOGETHER OR WITH A NAME

Hardly anyone gets subject and object pronouns wrong in simple sentences:

> I report for work three evenings a week.

> The members of Vogon Soup invited me to lunch a few weeks ago.

Most people use pronouns like these correctly, without even thinking about it. But some writers get thrown off when a name or second pronoun is added:

> ✗ Me and a nurse named Sally often work the evening shift.

> ✗ The members of Vogon Soup invited her and I to lunch a few weeks ago.

When you're using a pronoun paired with a name or another pronoun, mentally omit the other person to make sure you've used the correct pronoun:

> ✗ Me often work the evening shift.

> ✔ I often work the evening shift.

> ✔ Sally and I often work the evening shift.

> ✔ She and I often work the evening shift.

> ✗ The members of Vogon Soup invited I to lunch a few weeks ago.

> ✔ The members of Vogon Soup invited me to lunch a few weeks ago.

> ✔ The members of Vogon Soup invited her and me to lunch a few weeks ago.

If any of the correct examples above startled you, practice making the mental omissions when you find paired pronouns in your writing. Soon you'll be choosing the correct pronouns without even having to think about it.

• USE *WHO* FOR SUBJECTS AND *WHOM* FOR OBJECTS

In relative clauses (clauses that begin with a relative pronoun, such as *who*, *whose*, *which*, or *that*) and in questions, *who* and *whoever* are used as subject pronouns and *whom* and *whomever* are used as object pronouns. *Whom* and *whomever* might sound formal or even stilted, but that's not so bad in formal academic writing, especially if the alternative flouts the rules of grammar:

✘ Whom deserves our respect? — *If the sentence read He/she deserves our respect, it would be obvious that a subject pronoun is needed. The object pronoun whom is wrong.*

✔ Who deserves our respect? — *Who is the subject of the verb deserves.*

✘ Who does the public respect? — *The public is the subject of the verb does respect, and whom is the object, as him or her would be in The public does respect him/her. The subject pronoun who is wrong.*

✔ Whom does the public respect?

When, however, the object is actually a whole subordinate clause (see *To Emphasize One Idea Over Another, Use a Complex Sentence* in Chapter 27) and the pronoun is the subject of that clause, use a subject pronoun, *who* or *whoever*:

✘ Bob, the magician, performs for whomever is around. — *In Bob performs for them, them is an object pronoun. But whoever is around is a subordinate clause. Although this clause is the object of the sentence, whoever is its subject—so whoever is correct.*

✔ Bob, the magician, performs for whoever is around.

• USE REFLEXIVE PRONOUNS TO REFER TO THE SUBJECT OF THE SENTENCE OR CLAUSE

Myself, yourself, himself, herself, itself, ourselves, yourselves, and *themselves* are reflexive pronouns. Use them when you have an object that's the same as the subject or another word that comes before it in the clause:

Bob will sometimes perform for himself. — *If the sentence used him instead of himself, the audience of one would seem to be someone else. Himself makes clear that Bob is both performer and audience.*

Do not use reflexive pronouns as subjects, and do not use them as objects when the subject is someone or something else:

✘ Bob and myself were in the common room. — *The reflexive pronoun myself cannot serve as a subject; it must be replaced with I.*

✔ Bob and I were in the common room.

✘ Bob performed for the nurses and myself. — *The reflexive pronoun myself cannot serve as an object when someone other than I is the subject (in this case, the subject is Bob), so myself must be replaced with me.*

✔ Bob performed for the nurses and me.

● CHOOSE THE RIGHT PRONOUNS IN COMPARISONS

Use a subject pronoun in a comparison when you're comparing the person or thing with the subject of a sentence:

> Horace is taller than Gordie.

> ✘ Horace is taller than him.

> ✔ Horace is taller than he.

> *Horace* is the subject of the sentence, so someone being compared with Horace should be referred to with a subject pronoun — not an object pronoun.

If a sentence with that pattern seems artificial to you, try adding another word or two:

> ✔ Horace is taller than he is.

Object pronouns in *as* or *than* comparisons are not always wrong. Consider this sentence:

> Horace likes Eliot even more than me.

This sentence means that Horace likes Eliot even more than Horace likes me. If, however, the writer meant that Horace likes Eliot even more than the writer does, the sentence would need a subject pronoun.

> ✔ Horace likes Eliot even more than I do.

> ✔ Horace likes Eliot even more than he likes me.

● USE A SUBJECT PRONOUN FOR A SUBJECT COMPLEMENT

Subject complements are not objects of the verb: they're not being acted upon. They name something that is being equated with the subject in some way. So a pronoun that is used as a subject complement should be a subject pronoun. Subject complements usually follow a form of *be*:

> ✘ The most popular player in the band is him.

> ✔ The most popular player in the band is he.

> The subject is *player*, and the pronoun at the end is its complement. So *him* is wrong; the subject form is *he*.

> ✘ Is that her knocking on the door?

> ✔ Is that she knocking on the door?

> The subject is *that*, and the pronoun is its complement.

Often when subject complements are used correctly, they sound strange. If the sentences above were spoken in an everyday conversation, no doubt the speakers would use the incorrect object pronouns. In writing, where you have time to consider what you've written, you don't have to choose between sounding stilted or being ungrammatical. Find a revision that sounds natural to you and that demonstrates your knowledge of grammar:

> He is the most popular player in the band.
>
> Is she knocking on the door?

Make Pronouns Agree with Their Antecedents

An **antecedent** is the noun (or other pronoun) that a pronoun refers to and stands in for.

> Gordie is surprisingly short. He is five foot six. Dramatic costumes look good on him.

Gordie is the antecedent for *he* and *him*.

Antecedent/pronoun pairs like *Gordie/he*, *guitar/it*, and *drums/they* are quite straightforward, but a few kinds of antecedents are likely to trip writers up.

● WATCH OUT FOR INDEFINITE PRONOUNS

Words like *anybody* and *everyone* are singular **indefinite pronouns**. (For a list of all the singular indefinite pronouns, see *Use Singular Verbs with Singular Indefinite Pronouns* earlier in this chapter.) If you know the gender of the individual to whom you are referring, these words can serve as antecedents for simpler pronouns like *him* and *her*. However, you may prefer to use *they* or *their* in place of a singular indefinite pronoun (see *Use Language That Is Free of Bias and Stereotyping* in Chapter 27).

> ✔ Everyone who wants to sit at the concert should bring their own chair.

If that sounds artificial to you or if you are writing to readers who might not accept the use of *they* or *their* to refer to an individual, look for a natural-sounding, correct alternative. Consider whether you can get your idea across without using pronouns that must agree with an antecedent:

> ✔ Everyone who wants to sit at the concert should bring a chair.

Or revise your sentence to make the subject plural:

> ✔ People who want to sit at the concert should bring their own chairs.

WATCH OUT FOR COLLECTIVE NOUNS

Collective nouns refer to multiple people or things as a unit. Collective nouns should usually be treated as singular, so pronouns that refer to them should be singular as well:

✘ The band has been together for four years, and they have played at Hooper's six times.

✔ The band has been together for four years, and it has played at Hooper's six times.

When members of a group are acting individually, however, a collective noun can be treated as plural:

The band wrote their autographs on a poster for me.

The audience set their chairs on the floor.

If you want to avoid having to treat the collective noun as a plural, you can reword the sentence:

All the band members autographed a poster for me.

The fans who brought chairs set them on the floor.

When a collective noun is treated as singular in one part of the sentence, don't treat it as plural elsewhere in the same sentence:

✘ The band, which has been together for four years, wrote their autographs on a poster for me.

✔ The band, which has been together for four years, autographed a poster for me.

> The singular verb *has*, in a subordinate clause about the band, tells us that *band* is being treated as singular, as is usual. The plural pronoun *their* incorrectly treats the same use of the word *band* as plural.

Avoid Vague or Ambiguous Pronoun References

Pronouns refer to nouns or noun phrases — their **antecedents**. Readers generally expect to have read these nouns and phrases before they get to the pronoun:

The guitar is a special one. It was made entirely by hand in Spain.

Researchers are looking into the question of whether the use of bed nets to combat malaria is causing mosquitoes to hunt for food earlier in the day, before people are in bed. They are trying to answer it as soon as possible.

> The antecedent for *it* is *guitar*.

> The antecedent for *they* is *researchers*, and the antecedent for *it* is *question*.

- **WATCH OUT FOR PRONOUNS WHOSE ANTECEDENTS ARE WHOLE CLAUSES OR SENTENCES**

✗ Although malaria primarily infects the populations of developing countries, it is a problem of global significance. This is apparent in statistics about the disease.

> Does *this* mean that statistics show that malaria infects people in developing countries or that it's a global problem or both — or something else?

If you find such sentences in your writing, look for a noun or phrase that will clarify what *this* means and put it after *this*, turning *this* into an adjective:

✔ Although malaria primarily infects the populations of developing countries, it is a problem of global significance. This problem is apparent in statistics about the disease.

No doubt statistics do also bear out that malaria infects people in developing countries. But if the statistics the writer wants to introduce back up only the point about global significance, it's best to bring that point into sharp focus.

Let's say, though, that the writer does want to share statistics both about developing countries in particular and about the world as a whole. In this case, it would be better to present the situations in coordinate clauses (see *Combine Coordination and Subordination* in Chapter 27) and to change the singular adjective *this* to the plural *these*:

✔ Malaria primarily infects the populations of developing countries, but it is a problem of global significance. These problems are apparent in statistics about the disease.

Occasionally pronouns precede what they refer to:

This is true: malaria kills millions.

This word order reverses the sequence that readers expect, so it can get confusing, and annoying, too, if readers have to wait too long to find out what a pronoun refers to. Use pronouns before their antecedents only for an occasional special effect.

In the example above, the antecedent for the pronoun *this* is not a noun but a whole clause. Some readers object when the pronouns *this, that, these, those,* and *which* are used to refer to clauses rather than to nouns and noun phrases.

- **AVOID USING THE SAME PRONOUN WHEN REFERRING TO DIFFERENT THINGS**

Over the course of a long document, pronouns like *it* and *they* will turn up all over the place and carry many different meanings. This is fine. What isn't fine is using the same pronoun to refer to two different antecedents within a sentence or short passage:

✗ Gordie and Horace were jamming, trying to figure out the chorus to a new song. They could hardly be heard over their instruments because they were so loud.

The first *they* refers to Gordie and Horace, and the second *they* refers to the instruments, but readers are likely to be confused for a moment before they puzzle that out for themselves. It's better to repeat a noun than to repeat a pronoun referring to different things:

✓ . . . They could hardly be heard over their instruments because the instruments were turned up so loud.

- **AVOID USING A PRONOUN WHEN IT MIGHT REFER TO MORE THAN ONE THING**

✗ Gordie and Horace were jamming, trying to figure out the chorus to a new song. Steve, Buzz, and Eliot joined in, and they finally got it to sound right.

In this example, who are *they*?

Maybe the writer meant this:

. . . Steve, Buzz, and Eliot joined in, and Gordie and Horace finally got it to sound right.

Or perhaps the writer meant this:

. . . Steve, Buzz, and Eliot joined in, and the three of them finally got it to sound right.

Or possibly this:

. . . Steve, Buzz, and Eliot joined in, and the five of them finally got it to sound right.

Any of these sentences is fine, as long as it says what the writer meant.

- **USE THE PRONOUN *YOU* ONLY WHEN YOU MEAN YOUR READERS**

Do not use *you* in formal writing to refer to people in general:

✗ Malaria is caused by a parasite, which is spread by mosquitoes. You can combat the disease by killing the parasite, the mosquitoes, or both.

> The writer is not expecting readers to go out and kill parasites or mosquitoes. The word *you* doesn't belong here.

You in such contexts is much worse than using the passive voice (see *Favor the Active Voice* in Chapter 27).

✔ Malaria is caused by a parasite, which is spread by mosquitoes. The disease can be combated by killing the parasite, the mosquitoes, or both.

● USE *THEY* ONLY TO REFER TO PARTICULAR PEOPLE OR THINGS

They needs an antecedent. If you haven't already specified to whom the pronoun refers, don't use *they*:

✘ They say that bed nets have saved countless lives and could save many more.

✔ Public health officials say that bed nets have saved countless lives and could save many more.

● USE THE PLACEHOLDER PRONOUN *IT* SPARINGLY

The pronoun *it* is unusual in that it doesn't always need an antecedent. The rules of English allow it to occupy the place where the subject of a sentence would ordinarily be, so that the real subject can come at the end of the clause:

It complicates the problem that malaria poses its greatest threat in tropical regions.

The sentence above is grammatically equivalent to this one:

That malaria poses its greatest threat in tropical regions complicates the problem.

When you've written a sentence that ends with its subject, look at it critically. In the pair of examples above, the sentence that starts with the true subject is more direct and forceful, and the writer would be better off using that version unless the ideas being presented just before and after this sentence make the *It* sentence fit in more naturally.

Most constructions that cause a sentence to start with *it* — *It is well known that*; *It is worth noting that*; *It may surprise many to learn that*; and so on — do no real work and should be cut.

Do not use *it* without an antecedent, like this:

✘ On the foundation's website, it shows a running tally of malaria deaths.

Usually with this pattern, you can find the true subject of the sentence nearby:

✔ The foundation's website shows a running tally of malaria deaths.

Use Adjectives and Adverbs to Clarify Your Ideas

Adjectives and adverbs add detail to the nouns and verbs that are the pillars of writing. There's a big difference between a *thin white* sandwich and a *greasy, overstuffed* one. (For a discussion of comma use with adjectives, see *Use Commas to Keep Your Sentences Organized and Readable* in Chapter 29.) When someone cries, is that person crying *softly, angrily,* or *hysterically*? Again there's a big difference.

Because nouns and verbs give writing its structure, try to build as much meaning into them as you can. For instance, someone might *whimper, howl,* or *bawl* — and do it without the help of any adverbs. (For more about limiting your use of modifiers, see *Write Clearly and Concisely* in Chapter 20.) Still, you'll often need adjectives and adverbs. Just make sure they clarify rather than clutter your writing.

Use Adjectives to Modify Nouns and Pronouns

Not only do adjectives add coloration and detail to nouns and pronouns, but they also provide extra information. They tend to answer the questions that naturally do come up in relation to nouns: Which one? What kind? How many? How much?

Often, adjectives come before the nouns they modify:

The summer when I was six years old and ready to start school, we moved to a new town, Springfield.

Six modifies *years,* and *new* modifies *town.*

Adjectives can also come after the noun:

My family is Chinese American, and we looked different from most people in Springfield.

In the clauses above, a **linking verb** connects the adjective to the noun: *is* (a form of *be*) connects the adjective *Chinese American* to the noun *family,* and *looked* connects the adjective *different* to the pronoun *we.* Linking verbs — for instance, *feel, seem, believe,* and *think* — express an attitude or a state of being. Note that a verb may function as a linking verb in some cases but not in others:

Use Adjectives and Adverbs to Clarify Your Ideas | CHAPTER 28 **767**

We look different, but I feel confident.

> In this sentence, the verbs *look* and *feel* are linking verbs, connecting the adjectives *different* and *confident* to the pronouns *we* and *I*.

We look at it differently, and I feel strongly about my choice.

> In this sentence, the verbs are not linking verbs. Rather than connecting nouns and adjectives, the verbs *look* and *feel* are being modified by the adverbs *differently* and *strongly*.

Groups of words can function together as adjectives.

Our new house had been on the market for months.

Our next-door neighbor, who never once said a word to us, had a reputation for being unfriendly. The tone of his voice was threatening.

> *On the market for months* modifies *house*; *who never once said a word to us* modifies *neighbor*; *for being unfriendly* modifies *reputation*; and *of his voice* modifies *tone*.

Phrases, clauses, and words that look similar — or identical — to the ones in the examples above aren't always adjectives. Everything depends on how you are using the words in the sentence and what other words they are modifying.

Use Adverbs to Modify Verbs, Adjectives, and Adverbs

Adverbs help answer the questions that nouns and their modifiers cannot: How? When? Where? Why? Under what conditions? To what degree?

Adverbs can modify verbs:

We quickly learned that his reputation was well deserved.

> The adverb *quickly* modifies the verb *learned*.

Adverbs can modify adjectives:

Starting on our very first day in Springfield, I was excruciatingly uncomfortable there.

> The adverb *very* modifies the adjective *first*, and the adverb *excruciatingly* modifies the adjective *uncomfortable*.

Adverbs can modify other adverbs:

I was so excruciatingly uncomfortable that summer.

> The adverb *so* modifies the adverb *excruciatingly*.

And groups of words can function together as adverbs:

I was desperate **to start first grade**. **As my mother packed my lunch on the first morning of school**, she put in a bowl of my favorite comfort food, sesame noodles.

> The phrase *to start first grade* modifies the adjective *desperate*, and the subordinate clause *As my mother packed my lunch on the first morning of school* modifies the verb *put*.

Know When to Use *Good*, *Well*, *Bad*, and *Badly*

Many people have these words mixed up in their minds, in part because they've heard *good* and *bad* said informally in situations where more formal language would call for *well* and *badly*. When you're reaching for one of these words to use as an adverb, always use *well* or *badly*.

✗ My mother cooked really **good**.

✔ My mother cooked really **well**.

> The modifier describes how she cooked. Both the idea that it answers the question *How?* and the fact that it is modifying a verb indicate that the adverb *well* is needed.

✗ I wanted that bowl of noodles **bad**.

✔ I wanted that bowl of noodles **badly**.

The result is better yet if the adverb is placed next to the verb it modifies:

✔ I **badly** wanted that bowl of noodles.

> Here the questions associated with adjectives and adverbs aren't much help, since either *How much?* or *How?* might apply. What is clear is that the word is modifying the verb *wanted*—not *I* and not *noodles*—so the adverb *badly* is needed.

(For more about the placement of modifiers, see *Keep Related Ideas Together* in Chapter 27.)

When you want an adjective, *bad* is always right—unless, of course, you mean *good* or *well*. The fact that *well* can be an adjective and an adverb adds to the confusion between *good* and *well*.

• I feel **good** about my major.

> This statement is correct if you're describing a positive general state of mind. *Feel* is being used as a linking verb to connect the subject with a *good* feeling.

• I felt sick yesterday, but thankfully I feel **well** today.

> This sentence indicates that the writer feels healthy; here *well* is also an adjective, meaning "in good health."

Use -est, Most, or Least Only When Comparing Three or More Items

Superlative adjectives — like *biggest, smallest, hungriest, most peculiar,* and *least desirable* — announce that you're ranking at least three things. **Comparative** adjectives — like *bigger, smaller, hungrier, more peculiar, less desirable* — do the job when you're ranking only two things.

This rule doesn't apply to comparisons with *than*:

✘ Do you like noodles or sandwiches best?

✔ Do you like noodles or sandwiches better?

> Only two choices are offered, so *better* is correct.

✘ I was the more enthusiastic of all the kids when lunchtime started.

✔ I was the most enthusiastic of all the kids when lunchtime started.

> The writer is comparing herself with all the other kids, so *most* is correct.

✘ I was the most enthusiastic than all the other kids when lunchtime started.

✔ I was more enthusiastic than all the other kids when lunchtime started.

> The word *than* creates a comparison between one person or thing and the whole group of other people or things.

As for whether to give an adjective an -er or -est ending (as in *tastier, tastiest*) or use *more* or *less* or *most* or *least* with an adjective (as in *more delicious, most delicious*), use the ending if you know the adjective has one. Most short adjectives do. If you're not sure, check a dictionary. If it doesn't show -er and -est endings for the adjective, then use the additional word.

Watch Out for Adverbs with Absolute Concepts

My decision is completely final! is badly phrased. If a decision is final, it's final, end of story. There's no *completely* about it. Are-they-or-aren't-they properties like this are called **absolute concepts**. Intensifying adverbs (like *completely, very,* and *highly*), comparatives (*more* and *less*), and superlatives (*most* and *least*) are generally illogical with absolute concepts.

A few other examples of absolute concepts are *destroyed* (and other verbals, verbs, and nouns that describe ruin), *perfect*, *round*, *straight*, and *unique*.

✗ The other kids thought my lunch was very unique.

✓ The other kids thought my lunch was unique.

> *Unique* means "one of a kind," so "very one of a kind" is confusing.

Limiting adverbs (see *Keep Related Ideas Together* in Chapter 27) are usually fine with absolute concepts. For example, the word choice in *My decision is not quite final* or *It is almost unique* is easy to defend.

In Summary: Grammar: Writing Skillfully

★ Use verbs to ensure accuracy and clarity (p. 743).

★ Use pronouns to help readers follow your ideas more easily (p. 757).

★ Use adjectives and adverbs to clarify your ideas (p. 766).

29 Punctuation and Mechanics: Giving Your Readers Direction

Use commas to keep your sentences organized and readable 772

Use a comma and a coordinating conjunction to separate two main clauses 772

Use commas to set off introductory elements 773

Use commas to set off detours 773

Use commas in series 775

Use commas to set off most quotations 776

Use commas in other places where readers expect them 776

Use periods, question marks, and exclamation points correctly 777

End most sentences with periods 777

Reserve question marks for actual questions 777

Use exclamation points sparingly 778

Use quotation marks when you borrow words 778

Put quotation marks around direct quotations 778

Put quotation marks around new terms and words used as words 779

Put quotation marks around the titles of short works 779

Place quotation marks correctly with other punctuation 780

Use apostrophes in contractions and possessives 780

Use apostrophes in contractions 780

Use apostrophes to show possession 781

Distinguish among possessives, adjectives, and attributive nouns 781

Give possessive pronouns special treatment 782

Use colons to point to what comes next 782

Use semicolons between equivalent elements 783

Use other punctuation marks in specific situations 783

Use hyphens mainly to help readers understand relationships between adjacent words 783

Use dashes for breaks in thought that are larger than commas suggest 785

Use parentheses for explanatory and other minor asides 786

Use brackets inside parentheses and quotations 787

Use ellipsis marks to indicate omissions 787

Use a slash when quoting poetry or song lyrics and sparingly for alternatives 788

Use sentence mechanics to help readers follow your ideas 788

Use capitalization to mark beginnings 788

Use italics for titles of substantial works, for foreign words, and sparingly for emphasis 790

Use abbreviations and acronyms to help, not frustrate, readers 791

For such tiny symbols, punctuation marks convey a lot of information. They announce endings, turn statements into questions, point readers from one idea to the next, and group ideas together or keep them apart. Similarly, capital letters, italics, and acronyms — the components of sentence mechanics — draw attention to beginnings, add emphasis, and save time for you and your readers.

This chapter explores how writers use punctuation and mechanics when sharing their information, ideas, and arguments with their readers.

Use Commas to Keep Your Sentences Organized and Readable

Commas separate parts of a sentence. Sometimes they help make clear the structure of the sentence, and sometimes they give other clues about what you mean. A joke that turns up on T-shirts and coffee mugs illustrates this point. It goes like this:

> Let's eat Grandma.
>
> Let's eat, Grandma.
>
> Commas save lives!

Use a Comma and a Coordinating Conjunction to Separate Two Main Clauses

When you join two clauses that could each stand on its own as a sentence, put a comma and a conjunction (*and*, *but*, *for*, *nor*, *or*, *so*, and *yet*) between them:

———————— MAIN CLAUSE ————————
Forensic linguistics is a developing science, so

———————— MAIN CLAUSE ————————
many police departments are not yet familiar with it.

Note that a conjunction doesn't always signal the start of a new clause and therefore doesn't need to be preceded by a comma. Do not put a comma in front of a conjunction that's just introducing another part of the same clause:

- The history of DNA evidence suggests a parallel and may be useful to this discussion.

> Here the conjunction *and* joins the verbs *suggests* and *may be*, but the two verbs share one subject, so no comma is needed.

Not . . . but sentences, in particular, tempt writers to put commas where they don't belong:

✗ DNA evidence is not an end in itself, but a tool.

✓ DNA evidence is not an end in itself but a tool.

> This sentence has one subject and one verb, and its main point is that DNA evidence *is* a tool. So it's unhelpful to set the phrase *but a tool* off from the rest of the clause.

For more on this subject, see *Choose the Right Sentence Structures* and *Avoid Run-ons and Comma Splices* in Chapter 27.

Use Commas to Set Off Introductory Elements

When a sentence begins with a subordinate clause (see *Choose the Right Sentence Structures* in Chapter 27), a comma is usually needed to separate it from the main clause:

─────SUBORDINATE CLAUSE─────
If a person is wrongfully accused of a crime,

──────MAIN CLAUSE──────
forensic linguistics may help establish the person's innocence.

Confusion can arise when the comma is left out:

✗ Even when DNA evidence was new police labs used it not just to convict but also to exonerate.

✓ Even when DNA evidence was new, police labs used it not just to convict but also to exonerate.

> The comma not only helps readers find the beginning of the main clause but also prevents them from reading *new police labs* as a connected phrase.

In some cases, such as short introductory elements that can't connect to the next word or words in a misleading way, the use of a comma is a judgment call. In general, however, using a comma will help readers find the beginning of the main part of the sentence.

In England in the 1980s, DNA evidence proved that a man who had confessed to killing a teenager was innocent and that another man was guilty.

Similarly, principles behind forensic linguistics led a U.S. appeals court to overturn the 1963 conviction of Ernesto Miranda.

Use Commas to Set Off Detours

Once you've gotten a sentence started, use commas — or, in special situations, dashes (see *Use Dashes for Breaks in Thought That Are Larger than Commas Suggest* later in this chapter) or parentheses (see *Use Parentheses for Explanatory and Other Minor Asides* later in this chapter) — to set off elements that amount to detours from the main point, additions of background information, or asides. Use commas on both sides of such elements when they're in the middle of a sentence. Use a single comma when the element comes at the end.

Police officers, **furthermore,** have read suspects their "Miranda rights" ever since.

The FBI**, which put a great deal of money and effort into trying to catch the Unabomber,** had no success for years.

> *Furthermore*, a transition word, suggests how the information in this sentence relates to what came just before; it is thus a detour from the point of this sentence.

> The FBI's lack of success is the main point of this sentence. What the FBI did to try to catch the Unabomber is a detour.

This principle doesn't mean that the information or ideas you set off with commas are inessential to your overall point. But any sentence or main clause should have a point of its own. Material that detours from that point should be set off.

Many good writers also make a distinction between *that*, with no comma, and *which*, preceded by a comma, to give their readers one more clue about whether they consider an element essential to the point of the sentence. In the example below, the writer considers the subordinate clause beginning with *that explained* essential:

The Unabomber threatened to kill more people unless major newspapers published a 35,000-word manifesto **that explained** his ideas about society.

> Readers won't know what the manifesto was unless the writer tells them a bit about it, so this characterization is essential.

In the next example, the clause beginning with *which are* is inessential:

The *New York Times* and the *Washington Post***, which** are two of the country's most influential newspapers**,** published the manifesto in 1995.

> The main point of the sentence is that the *Times* and the *Post* published the manifesto in 1995. The material in the *which* clause is an aside, because the writer just wants to point out that the papers met the Unabomber's requirement.

Who, *when*, and *where* can be used either like *that*, without a comma, if they're necessary to the main point of the sentence, or like *which*, after a comma, if they're not.

A man **who** was the brother of Ted Kaczynski**, who** ultimately pleaded guilty to the bombings, tipped off the FBI that the person they were looking for was Ted.

> The first *who* clause is essential because it identifies the man as Kaczynski's brother. The second *who* clause contains valuable information, but it's not essential to the main point of the sentence.

Bear in mind that readers can find it frustrating to be sent on too many detours, even if these are correctly signaled with commas:

✗ A man who was the brother of Ted Kaczynski, who ultimately pleaded guilty to the bombings, and the brother's wife, having recognized the writing style and ideas, tipped off FBI agents that the person they were looking for was Ted.

One more decision about detour-related commas comes up with proper names. Do not set off proper names that are essential to the sentence and the point it is making:

FBI Supervising Special Agent **Joel Moss** conducted linguistic analysis on writing related to the Unabomber case.

> *Joel Moss* is the subject of the sentence and is therefore essential, so it is not set off with commas.

Do set off names when the meaning would be clear and the sentence structure smooth without them:

> The brother's wife, Linda Kaczynski, helped her husband get through the ordeal of turning Ted in.

The name of the brother's wife is not essential to the meaning of the sentence, so it is set off with commas.

Use Commas in Series

Commas separate the elements in series of three or more:

> Ransom notes, spoken or written threats, emergency calls, online scams, and police interrogations all provide forensic evidence.

When you've written a series, look it over to make sure its elements are parallel (see *Use Parallel Structures* in Chapter 27).

Not all writers use the **serial comma** — the one that comes before *and* and the final element of a series. You don't need to if you find it more natural to leave it out. Omitting a serial comma, however, can lead to confusion:

> ✗ I interviewed Jack Hitt, a forensic linguist and a convicted criminal.

Does the writer mean that Jack Hitt is a forensic linguist and a criminal, or did the writer interview three people?

Make a habit of using serial commas, so you and your readers won't need to think about such issues whenever you write a series.

As with nouns presented in a series, two or more adjectives or adjective phrases require commas between them if they modify the noun separately:

> Detectives are only beginning to make sophisticated, effective use of language to clear the innocent and catch the guilty.

You can test whether adjectives are separate by mentally replacing the comma with *and* or *but*:

> Detectives are only beginning to make sophisticated and effective use of language to clear the innocent and catch the guilty.

If one of these replacements has minimal effect on the meaning, use a comma. If, however, the second adjective is an integral part of the noun, don't use a comma:

> But scientific forensic linguistics has tremendous untapped potential.

Here it's forensic linguistics that's being called scientific, and the untapped potential that's being called tremendous. (You wouldn't say *scientific and forensic linguistics* or *tremendous and untapped potential*.)

Use Commas to Set Off Most Quotations

Use commas, or sometimes a colon (see *Use Colons to Point to What Comes Next* later in this chapter), to set off a direct quotation that is complete in itself:

> The Unabomber's manifesto begins, "The Industrial Revolution and its consequences have been a disaster for the human race," and goes on to condemn modern society.

But don't use a comma before a quotation that's part of the flow of your sentence:

> Kaczynski goes on at length about the "industrial-technological system" and what's wrong with it.

For more information on punctuating quotations, see *Use Quotation Marks When You Borrow Words* later in this chapter.

Use Commas in Other Places Where Readers Expect Them

It is conventional to use commas in the following contexts.

IN PLACE NAMES AND ADDRESSES:

> The mailing address for FBI headquarters is 935 Pennsylvania Avenue NW, Washington, DC 20535-0001.

Commas are not placed between states and zip codes

IN DATES:

> On September 10, 1995, newspapers published the Unabomber's manifesto.

IN NUMBERS (EXCEPT YEARS, ZIP CODES, AND STREET NUMBERS) OF FOUR OR MORE DIGITS:

> DNA testing is conducted on only small sections of the human genome, which is about 3,200,000,000 base pairs long and contains 20,000–25,000 genes.

BETWEEN TWO WORDS THAT WOULD OTHERWISE BE MISREAD:

> ✗ He changed his mind completely because of the evidence presented.

Did he change his mind completely (in which case, put a comma after completely)? Or was it completely because of the evidence that he changed his mind (in which case, put a comma after mind)?

WHEN DIRECTLY ADDRESSING SOMEONE:

> Let's eat, Grandma!

WITH *YES* OR *NO*, UNLESS THAT WORD IS MODIFYING ANOTHER WORD:

Yes, please, let's stop discussing commas. No, thanks, I don't want to read any more about them. No thanks to me, this may have gone on too long.

Use Periods, Question Marks, and Exclamation Points Correctly

The period, the question mark, and the exclamation point are the three end punctuation marks, though periods have other uses as well.

End Most Sentences with Periods

A sentence can end with a question mark or an exclamation point, but those are special cases for special effects. Most of the sentences you write should end with periods.

Cap-and-lowercase abbreviations (such as *Dr.* and *Jr.*) also end with periods, but most all-cap abbreviations are written without them (see *Use Abbreviations and Acronyms to Help, Not Frustrate, Readers* later in this chapter for more on abbreviations). If an abbreviation that ends with a period also ends the sentence, use only one period:

> I once met Henry Louis Gates Jr.

But if such an abbreviation concludes a sentence that ends with another punctuation mark, use both the period and the other mark:

> Have you ever met Henry Louis Gates Jr.?

Periods are also used in numbers, as decimal points (*2.0*), and in URLs, or web addresses (*www.macmillanlearning.com*).

Reserve Question Marks for Actual Questions

Use question marks for questions, of course:

> Will my mother ever change?

Put the question mark at the end of the question, not necessarily at the end of the sentence:

> ✗ Will my mother ever change, I ask myself?
>
> ✓ Will my mother ever change? I ask myself.

The question here is not I ask myself *but* Will my mother ever change, *as in the previous example.*

> This is a statement, not a question. The writer is stating that she wonders about something.

✗ I wonder if my mother will ever change?

✓ I wonder if my mother will ever change.

Do not use a question mark for a sentence that has the form of a question but is actually a polite request or is otherwise not intended to elicit an answer:

> The mother is not expecting to be told yes or no; she is making a request.

She, on the other hand, wonders if I will ever learn to hold my tongue. "Would you please stop embarrassing me," she will say.

Use Exclamation Points Sparingly

Social email, texts, and ads use lots of exclamation points to show warmth and enthusiasm. But this convention does not carry over to more formal writing. In most academic writing, exclamation points should be used rarely.

✗ But then a salesperson will be rude, or someone we know will share an opinion that I find offensive, and I'll find myself speaking up before I even realize what I'm doing!

Use Quotation Marks When You Borrow Words

Quotation marks are essential in any document that draws passages directly from sources (see Chapter 21 to learn more about making direct quotations). But quotation marks have several other uses as well, including setting off terms that will be new to your readers, signaling that you are referring to a word itself and not in a normal sense, and identifying a source by title.

Put Quotation Marks around Direct Quotations

> In the first sentence, there is no comma after the word *phrase* because the quotation is part of the flow of the sentence.

By repeating the phrase "Ain't I a woman?" in her speech at the 1851 women's convention, Sojourner Truth exposes the double bind of black women in antebellum America.

Use single quotation marks only to set off a quotation within a quotation.

As one literary critic wrote, "The command 'Look at me! Look at my arm!' calls attention to both the cause of Sojourner Truth's slavery (her black skin) and its effect (her muscled physique)."

For a fuller discussion of attributing and punctuating quotations, see Chapter 21.

Put Quotation Marks around New Terms and Words Used as Words

Use quotation marks to set off new terms that you're introducing:

> Although she agitated for abolition, Sojourner Truth did not participate in the "Underground Railroad," the loose network of people who secretly helped enslaved individuals who had escaped to reach freedom in the North.

After you've introduced a new term, it is no longer new to the reader, so if you use it again, you should not put quotation marks around it.

When you use a word as a word — rather than using it in the usual way, to refer to something else — you can put quotation marks around it:

> The use of "ain't" in Truth's speech intentionally emphasizes her lack of schooling.

Another correct option is to put words that are used as words in italics (see *Use Italics* later in this chapter):

> The use of *ain't* in Truth's speech is intentional.

Whichever format you choose, follow it consistently.

Do not use quotation marks for common expressions or to call attention to ordinary words:

> ✗ Though grammatically incorrect, the word "ain't" has become "part and parcel" of African American dialect.

Put Quotation Marks around the Titles of Short Works

Use quotation marks to set off the titles of articles, songs, short stories, poems (except book-length ones), episodes of television series, and other short works (see Chapters 25 and 26 for a fuller discussion of citing articles):

> "Words on Trial," by Jack Hitt, in the July 23, 2012, issue of *The New Yorker* discusses forensic linguistics.
>
> My favorite song by Vogon Soup is "Paula Nancy Millstone Jennings."

For the titles of longer works, use italics (see *Use Italics* later in this chapter) instead of quotation marks.

Place Quotation Marks Correctly with Other Punctuation

When you use quotation marks, put periods and commas inside the closing quotation mark:

> Sojourner Truth's speech is famous for its repeated use of "ain't."

Make an exception to this rule when you are citing a quotation:

> According to the *New Yorker* article, an FBI forensic linguist cracked the Unabomber case "by analyzing syntax, word choice, and other linguistic patterns" (25).

Put question marks and exclamation points inside the quotation marks only if they're part of the quotation itself:

> Sojourner Truth commands the audience, "Look at my arm!"

> Are you surprised that the Unabomber's manifesto includes the words "chimerical" and "anomic"?

For more on citing sources, see Chapters 25 and 26.

Use Apostrophes in Contractions and Possessives

Although the same key is used to type an apostrophe and a single quotation mark, the two have different uses and should be used with care.

Use Apostrophes in Contractions

Some readers of formal academic writing object to **contractions** — shortened forms that leave out some characters of the original (for example, *you're* is a contraction of *you are*, and *don't* is a contraction of *do not*). If you think your readers won't mind contractions and you do include them in your writing, use an apostrophe to indicate where letters (or numbers) are missing:

> I can't help thinking that my parents were naïve in the '90s, but I'll never get them to agree with that.

Note that when an apostrophe comes at the beginning of a word or number, your word-processing software will probably turn it into an open single quotation mark, which faces the wrong way. To get it right, add a second apostrophe, which the software will turn into a close single quotation mark, and then delete the first one.

Use Apostrophes to Show Possession

Possessives are a grammatical form that indicates possession, or ownership:

> my parents' house
>
> my mother's mother

Use an apostrophe plus *s* to form the possessive of a singular noun or a plural noun that does not end in *s*:

> the interviewer's questions
>
> children's memories

Many writers prefer to add an apostrophe plus *s* to form the possessive of a singular noun ending in *s*, although it is not strictly required. Ask your instructor how to handle these words, or if you are writing for a particular publication, such as a newspaper or journal, look at how the publication handles possessives:

> the class's assignment
>
> the class' assignment

Use an apostrophe alone to form the possessive of a plural noun that ends in *s*:

> bloggers' points of view
>
> Americans' attitudes

Distinguish among Possessives, Adjectives, and Attributive Nouns

Adjectives and **attributive nouns** — nouns that are being used as adjectives — do not use apostrophes, so it's important to be able to tell these forms apart from possessives.

singular possessive	an American's rights under the law
plural possessive	Americans' rights
adjective	the American legal system
attributive noun	the United States legal system

Give Possessive Pronouns Special Treatment

Confusingly, **possessive pronouns** do not use apostrophes.

> my, your, his, her, its, our, their
>
> mine, yours, hers, ours, theirs

This difference is doubtless the reason so many people have trouble distinguishing between *its* and *it's* in particular. You wouldn't add an apostrophe to *my* or *mine* or *his* or *her* or *hers* — so anywhere you could substitute one of these other possessives (not for meaning but to see whether the structure seems all right), use the apostrophe-free possessive *its*. Anywhere you could substitute *it is*, use the apostrophe-containing contraction *it's*.

> *It's* is a contraction that could be replaced with *It is*, so it has an apostrophe. The second *its* is possessive (equivalent to *the country's*), and it cannot be replaced with *it is*, so it should not contain an apostrophe.

> It's a great country, and its legal system, though hardly perfect, is widely admired.

The difference between *its* and *it's* may seem trivial — hardly worth bothering with. But many people who are accustomed to making the distinction see this the other way around: once a person understands the principles of using apostrophes, the effort it takes to get them right is trivial.

Use Colons to Point to What Comes Next

Text followed by a colon often introduces examples or a list of bullet points or some other series that does not look like ordinary paragraphed writing:

> Sojourner Truth's speech mentions the following experiences:
>
> - Plowing and planting
> - Being struck by a lash
> - Bearing thirteen children

Colons can also be used in a similar way within paragraphs and sentences. The text before or after a colon can be, but does not need to be, a complete sentence:

> This is worth remembering: patience is a virtue.

Do not use a colon where the words alone make the meaning clear:

> ✗ The members of the class include: Drina, Gabriela, Phil, Roger, and Sandra.

When you introduce a quotation of two or more full sentences, it is best to use a colon:

> Frederick Douglass said: "If there is no struggle, there is no progress. Those who profess to favor freedom, and yet depreciate agitation, are men who want crops without plowing up the ground."

Use Semicolons between Equivalent Elements

You may use a semicolon instead of a comma and a conjunction between the clauses of a compound sentence (see *Choose the Right Sentence Structure* in Chapter 27):

> My father's father talks to strangers; my mother's mother does too.

Do not, however, use semicolons between clauses just because you can. If the sentence seems equally good with a conjunction, use a comma and the conjunction. If the sentence is long, consider making each clause a separate sentence.

Semicolons can also impose order on an unruly series. If one or more of the elements in a series contains a comma, use semicolons to separate the elements:

> My father grew up in Mumbai, India; my mother grew up in Delhi; and my brothers and I grew up here.

Use Other Punctuation Marks in Specific Situations

Several other forms of punctuation can be used to help convey your ideas and argument to your readers. These include hyphens (-), dashes (—), parentheses (), brackets [], ellipses (. . .), and slashes (/).

Use Hyphens Mainly to Help Readers Understand Relationships between Adjacent Words

English often combines two or more words, or a word and a combining form, to make a compound word—but it doesn't do it in a consistent way.

Some compounds are closed:

> bookstore, coworker, daylight, fatherland, fireball, nationwide, nonsmoking, steelworker

Some compounds are open:

> book club, day labor, mass media, mother ship, non sequitur, steel wool

And some compounds use hyphens:

> co-owner, father-in-law, fire-eater, mass-produce, mother-of-pearl, nation-state, self-governing

To make things worse, words that are not compounds may need to be hyphenated when you use them together as an adjective that comes before a noun.

● CHECK A DICTIONARY

Dictionaries give entries for closed, open, and hyphenated compound words. So when you don't know whether a compound is written with a space, a hyphen, or neither, look it up. If you don't find an entry for the compound, check the entries for the parts of the compound.

● USE HYPHENS TO MAKE COMPOUND ADJECTIVES

In addition to hyphens in compounds that you find in the dictionary, you'll need to use hyphens between words that function together as an adjective before a noun.

> a large-scale manhunt
>
> a 17-year-long campaign of terror

When such a combination comes after the noun, do not hyphenate it unless it is likely to be misread:

> a manhunt on a large scale

Avoid assembling long strings of words that need hyphens to be understandable:

> ✗ a federal-government-funded crime-control initiative
>
> ✓ a crime-control initiative funded by the federal government

Do not put a hyphen between an adverb and an adjective. Remember that most words that end in *-ly* are adverbs.

> a federally funded initiative to control crime
>
> a completely new problem set

● DO NOT ADD HYPHENS TO INTERNET ADDRESSES

When you need to divide a URL or an email address between two lines, do not add a hyphen. Break it before a period or *after a slash*:

> https://www.macmillanlearning.com/college/us/
> discipline/English

● HYPHENATE BETWEEN SYLLABLES AT THE END OF A LINE

Any word that's more than a few letters long may need to be hyphenated for the sake of a line break — if, that is, the layout of your document requires the word to begin on one line and end on the next.

When you need a line break, always make it between syllables. If you're not sure where a word's syllables begin and end, check a dictionary. Most dictionaries use dots to show where the syllable breaks are.

Avoid adding an end-of-line hyphen to a compound that already contains a hyphen:

> ✗ a govern-
> ment-funded initiative

If you don't see an easier way to correct a clumsy line break like the one above, revise the sentence:

> ✓ an initiative
> funded by the government

Use Dashes for Breaks in Thought That Are Larger than Commas Suggest

You can use dashes to add an aside or a comment on the material in the main part of a sentence. Put the aside after one dash at the end of the sentence or between a pair of them in the middle. Dashes add emphasis to what comes after or between them:

> The Unabomber case was one of the FBI's most expensive investigations — which is saying a lot.

The writer is stepping outside the role of reporting on the Unabomber case to inject an opinion, so a dash works well here.

Use no more than two dashes in any sentence. A sentence littered with dashes can leave readers struggling to keep straight which phrases you intended to be the main part of the sentence and which you intended as detours.

> ✗ Other targets of major FBI investigations over the years have included the Ku Klux Klan, Nazi agents — during World War II — Communist agents — during the Cold War — and, outrageously, Dr. Martin Luther King Jr.

These two pairs of dashes are likely to leave the reader confused. The material between them is not crucially important, so two pairs of parentheses would work better.

Use Parentheses for Explanatory and Other Minor Asides

Parentheses are always used in pairs. They tend to de-emphasize the material within them and suggest that this material is not necessary for understanding your overall point:

> The Unabomber case went to trial (Kaczynski's brother and mother sat in the front row), but Kaczynski soon pleaded guilty to all charges.

The detail about Kaczynski's brother and mother is irrelevant to the writer's larger point: the outcome of the trial.

Avoid putting essential information or ideas in parentheses:

> ✗ In his manifesto, Kaczynski writes about the "industrial-technological system" (and how harmful it is).

The idea that Kaczynski considered the industrial-technological system harmful adds essential meaning to the sentence, so this idea should not be in parentheses.

You can enclose whole sentences in parentheses, and when you do, in order to get the rest of the punctuation and the capitalization correct, you'll need to decide whether the contents are parenthetical to the sentence or to the larger idea you're exploring in the paragraph.

> Principles behind forensic linguistics led a U.S. appeals court to overturn the 1963 conviction of Ernesto Miranda. (Police officers have read suspects their "Miranda rights" ever since.) But the same principles have also led to many convictions (see page 6 of this report).

The information in the first parenthetical statement digresses from the writer's larger point. It can stand on its own, so the writer has placed it outside the previous sentence. The remark in the second pair of parentheses relates specifically to that one sentence in which it appears, so the writer has placed that parenthetical statement inside the related sentence.

Use parentheses around acronyms (see *Use Abbreviations and Acronyms* later in this chapter) that you are introducing:

> Information technology (IT) can be used to record and analyze language exactly.

Also use parentheses around the numbers in enumerations:

> The handbook is divided into three sections: (1) style, (2) grammar, and (3) punctuation and mechanics.

Use Brackets inside Parentheses and Quotations

You can use brackets as parentheses within parentheses (a pair of parentheses inside another pair of parentheses is confusing and incorrect):

> The name Unabomber comes from the designation that the FBI used for the case (UNABOM [an acronym for "UNiversity and Airline BOMber"]) before it was solved.

Also use brackets to add information within a quotation or to clarify something that might be confusing or ungrammatical when taken out of its original context:

> According to the report, "Analysis of the data demonstrated that each [subject in the experiment] exhibited a unique word-use pattern."

In the report itself, the previous sentences discussed the experimental subjects, so the meaning of each *was clear. Here the word is unclear unless what it refers to is specified.*

> The researcher reported that he "compare[s] word-use patterns using software that [he] developed."

The researcher's original wording was I compare *and* I developed. *Minor changes are needed to make the wording fit the current writer's sentence.*

For more information on using brackets when modifying quotations, see *Punctuate Quotations Correctly* in Chapter 21.

Use Ellipsis Marks to Indicate Omissions

Use ellipsis marks in quotations to indicate where you have omitted words or whole sentences. For omissions within a sentence, replace the omitted words with a three-point ellipsis mark (. . .):

> "When in the Course of human events, it becomes necessary for one people to dissolve the political bands which have connected them with another, . . . a decent respect to the opinions of mankind requires that they should declare the causes which impel them to the separation."

If a comma comes right before the material you omit, leave it in if you think it will help the reader follow the sentence.

For omissions of whole sentences, add the period (or other end punctuation mark) to the end of the ellipsis marks to indicate the omission:

> "We hold these truths to be self-evident, that all men are created equal. . . . The history of the present King of Great Britain is a history of repeated injuries and usurpations, all having in direct object the establishment of an absolute Tyranny over these States."

See *Punctuate Quotations Correctly* in Chapter 21 for more detailed information about using ellipsis marks.

In social email, people often use ellipsis marks to trail off or to show hesitation or shyness. Do not do that in more formal writing.

Use a Slash When Quoting Poetry or Song Lyrics and Sparingly for Alternatives

When you quote poetry, song lyrics, or the like, use a slash (with a space on either side) to show the line endings in the original:

> The song begins like this: "Paula Nancy Millstone Jennings / At her table poetry penning / Loved to tell of dying swans. / Now her poetry's gone, all gone."

Alternatives like *Mr./Ms.* and *and/or* are graceless and should be avoided if possible. Certain alternatives, such as *pass/fail* and *Jekyll/Hyde personality*, are acceptable; do not add a space before or after the slash. Avoid constructions such as *he/she* in favor of more inclusive language (see Use Language That Is Free of Bias and Stereotypes in Chapter 27).

Use Sentence Mechanics to Help Readers Follow Your Ideas

Sentence mechanics — capitalization, italics, abbreviations, and acronyms — help readers understand the information you are sharing with them. Understanding some basic guidelines about sentence mechanics can help you convey information clearly and concisely.

Use Capitalization to Mark Beginnings

The capital letter that starts a sentence, together with the punctuation mark that ended the previous sentence, signals to the reader that a new thought is under way. Similarly, capital letters in the middle of a sentence mark the beginnings of proper names, of the words in a title, or of other special uses of language.

- **CAPITALIZE PROPER NAMES**

People, places, organizations, branded products, and creative works like articles, books, movies, and songs all have names, and (unless they or the creators of, say, a product have a well-known preference to the contrary) you should begin these names with capital letters:

> Last year my brother Steven visited our grandparents in Mumbai, India, and brought them an Apple iPad as a gift from our parents.

- **CAPITALIZE TITLES THAT IMMEDIATELY PRECEDE A PERSON'S NAME**

> Steven told our grandparents that Prince William has the same tablet.

If you need so much as a comma between the title and the name, do not capitalize the title:

> Steven told our grandparents that the duke of Cambridge, William, has the same tablet.

(See *Use Commas* earlier in this chapter for information about when to set off names with commas.)

Do not capitalize descriptions that aren't actually titles:

> The Vogon Soup guitarist Gordie Jones has an Apple tablet, too.

- **CAPITALIZE ADJECTIVES DERIVED FROM PROPER NAMES**

    > The Indian way of life is different from the American way of life.

- **CAPITALIZE MOST WORDS IN THE TITLES OF WORKS**

The major words in the titles of short works that you enclose in quotation marks (see *Use Quotation Marks* earlier in this chapter) and in the titles of substantial works that you italicize (see *Use Italics for Titles of Substantial Works* later in this chapter) should be capitalized.

Do not capitalize articles (*a*, *an*, *the*), conjunctions (for example, *and*, *but*, *so*), or prepositions (*between*, *in*, *on*, *over*) unless they are the first or last word of the title or subtitle:

> I gave Steven the phrase book *Say It in Hindi* to take with him.

Capitalize *is* and *are*. Even though they're short words, they are verbs, which should be capitalized in titles:

> He played "While My Guitar Gently Weeps," "I Me Mine," and "All You Need Is Love" for our grandparents.

- **FOLLOW THE SPECIALIZED CAPITALIZATION STYLE OF ORGANIZATIONS AND BRANDS**

The person, company, or organization whose name it is gets to decide, within limits, how the name should be written:

> My parents bought the iPad on eBay.

However, when you begin a sentence with a name that starts with a lowercase letter, capitalize the letter to mark the beginning of the sentence:

> EBay sells all kinds of things.

While this might be correct, it might be better to revise the sentence so that *EBay* is not the first word:

All kinds of things are sold on eBay.

If an organization or a product spells its name in all caps — or in all lowercase letters — do not follow that style unless you are being paid as an advertiser. For personal names, however, retain the preferred styling of the individual.

✗ My VISA card was declined, so I ended up spending the evening at home alone, on reddit, where I read about Bell Hooks.

Capitalize just the initial letter:

✓ My Visa card was declined, so I ended up spending the evening at home alone, on Reddit, where I read about bell hooks.

Use Italics for Titles of Substantial Works, for Foreign Words, and Sparingly for Emphasis

● ITALICIZE THE TITLES OR NAMES OF SUBSTANTIAL WORKS

Use italics for the names of books, journals, magazines, newspapers, websites, plays, movies, radio and television programs, symphonies, ballets, albums, paintings, and sculptures:

The *International Journal of Speech, Language, and the Law* presents research in and analysis of forensic linguistics.

The author was interviewed on *Slate* and NPR's *Fresh Air*.

● ITALICIZE FOREIGN WORDS

English has adopted words from many other languages and made them ours. *Bagel, curry, espresso,* and *salsa* all come from other languages and cultures; now, however, they are included in English dictionaries, so there is no need to italicize them. Italicize foreign words that do not appear in the dictionary:

Steven's *Daadi* and *Dada* — that's Hindi for "Grandma" and "Grandpa" — loved their gift and asked Steven to use it to take a photograph of them to send to our family.

● USE ITALICS FOR EMPHASIS

"That's the *best* idea I've ever heard!" he told them.

When your emphasis will likely be obvious to the reader or when you've already added a word for emphasis, do not italicize. The word *do* in sentences like this one, for example, is inherently emphatic:

✗ I *do* hope my grandparents will be able to figure out how to use the iPad.

To decide whether italics are useful or overkill, take them out, read the sentence aloud or in your mind, and see whether the natural emphasis is the same as (or better than) the emphasis with the italics.

If for design reasons you choose to italicize certain elements, remove the italics from the words that you would ordinarily italicize:

> The author is a frequent contributor to the Central University Sentinel.

This note about the author is italicized. The Sentinel *is a publication, so its name would ordinarily appear in italics. To make the same distinction in italicized text, un-italicize the name.*

Use Abbreviations and Acronyms to Help, Not Frustrate, Readers

● **USE STANDARD ABBREVIATIONS**

Abbreviations of titles like *Mr., Ms., Dr., Rev.,* and *Prof.* before names are common in documents, as are abbreviations like *Jr., MD, DDS,* and *PhD* after names.

The abbreviations *a.m.* and *p.m.* (meaning "morning" and "afternoon"), *BCE* and *CE* ("before the common era" and "common era"), and °F and °C ("degrees Fahrenheit" and "degrees Celsius") are in standard use in references to specific times, years or periods, and temperatures:

> 10:00 a.m.
>
> the sixth century BCE
>
> 78 CE
>
> 70°F (or 21°C)

Few other abbreviations, apart from acronyms, belong in academic and business documents. However, abbreviations like *Mon.* and *Tues., Jan.* and *Feb., St.* and *Rd.,* and *m.p.h.* are fine in tables and other places where space is tightly limited.

Use the postal abbreviations for states (*AL, AR,* and so on) in mailing addresses, but spell out state names elsewhere. If you use abbreviations, use them consistently.

Do not use texting abbreviations like *btw* and *YOLO* in formal writing.

● USE ACRONYMS TO SIMPLIFY AND CLARIFY

Acronyms are abbreviations made up of the initial letters of words. Most of them are written in all caps without periods: *AAA*, *HMO*, *ISP*, *USPS*. A few exceptions, like *U.S.* and *U.N.*, are typically written with periods after the initials to keep readers from being tempted to read them as words. Check a dictionary or an organization's website if you have doubts about how to write an abbreviation.

Generally, to introduce an acronym, give the full name immediately followed by the acronym in parentheses. When giving the words the acronym stands for, you don't have to capitalize them merely because they are capitalized in the acronym:

- the Association of Southeast Asian Nations (ASEAN) *[This is the organization's proper name, so the capital letters are correct.]*
- an application programming interface (API) *[This is a generic term, so the words should not be capitalized.]*

The convention of introducing acronyms in parentheses is intended to alert readers that from then on you will be using the acronym instead of the name. With this in mind, include the acronym only if you refer to it later in your document.

If you use the acronym just once or twice, consider whether your writing might be more readable without the acronym. You can either repeat the full name or use a generic phrase, like "the association" or "the interface."

If you think that a particular acronym will be familiar to readers and feel that it needs no introduction—for instance, *DNA*, the *FBI*, and *NASA*—you may use the acronym instead of the full name the first time you refer to the thing or organization.

In Summary: Punctuation and Mechanics: Giving Your Readers Direction

* Use commas to ensure readability (p. 772).
* Use periods, question marks, and exclamation points appropriately (p. 777).
* Use quotation marks to show what you've borrowed from others (p. 778).
* Use apostrophes in contractions and possessives (p. 780).
* Use colons to point to what comes next (p. 782).
* Use semicolons between equivalent elements (p. 783).
* Use hyphens, dashes, parentheses, brackets, ellipsis marks, and slashes effectively (p. 783).
* Use sentence capitalization, italics, abbreviations, and acronyms to convey information to your readers clearly and concisely (p. 788).

Acknowledgments

Peter C. Baker, "Reform of the Nerds," *Pacific Standard Magazine*, May 4, 2015, pp. 44–53. Copyright © 2015 Grist Magazine. Used with permission. All rights reserved.

Ben Bloch, "Tax Robots and Universal Basic Income," *TechCrunch*, July 17, 2017. Copyright © 2017 Ben Bloch. Used with permission.

Hunter Brimi, Ed.D, "Teaching Writing in the Shadow of Standardized Writing Assessment: An Exploratory Study," *American Secondary Education* 41.1 (Fall 2012). Copyright © 2012 The Dwight Schar College of Education, Ashland University. Used with permission.

Sandra Cisneros, "Only Daughter" from *Latina: Women's Voices from the Borderlands*. Edited by Lillian Castillo-Speed. Copyright © 1990 by Sandra Cisneros. First published in GLAMOUR, November 1990. By permission of Susan Bergholz Literary Services, New York, NY and Lamy, NM. All rights reserved.

Rivka Galchen, "An Unlikely Ballerina," *The New Yorker*, September 22, 2014. Copyright © 2014 Condé Nast. Used with permission. All rights reserved.

Brooke Gladstone, "The Goldilocks Number," from *The Influencing Machine: Brooke Gladstone on the Media*, pp. 49–51. Illustrated by Josh Neufeld. Copyright © 2011 by Brooke Gladstone and Josh Neufeld. Used by permission of W. W. Norton & Company, Inc., and by permission of SLL/Sterling Lord Literistic, Inc. All rights reserved.

International Networks Archive, Princeton University, The Magic Bean Shop and The Fries That Bind Us, infograph. Copyright © 2003 INA - www.Printceton.edu/-INA. Map design by Flaming Toast Productions.

Margo Jefferson, "Are We Rich?" from *Negroland: A Memoir* by Margo Jefferson. Copyright © 2015 by Margo Jefferson. Used by permission of Pantheon Books, an imprint of the Knopf Doubleday Publishing Group, a division of Penguin Random House LLC. All rights reserved.

Peter Johnston, "Guiding the Budding Writer," from the September 2012 issue of *Educational Leadership*, 70(1), Alexandria, VA: ASCD. © 2012 by ASCD. Reprinted with permission. All rights reserved.

Anneke Jong, "Leveling the Playing Field: How to Get More Women in Tech," *The Muse*. Copyright © The Muse. Used with permission.

Justin Kanoya, "Thoughts on *Crazy Rich Asians:* How Representation Impacts Self-Worth," August 21, 2018. Copyright © 2018 by Thin Difference. All rights reserved. Used with permission.

Scott Barry Kaufman, "Why Creativity Is a Numbers Game," *Scientific American*, December 29, 2015. Reproduced with permission. Copyright © 2015 by SCIENTIFIC AMERICAN, a Division of Nature America, Inc. All rights reserved.

Eric Kelderman, "Free College Is Dead in Congress, but It's Alive and Well in the States," November 3, 2001. Copyright © 2001 by The Chronicle of Higher Education. Republished with permission of the Chronicle of Higher Education, permission conveyed through Copyright Clearance Center, Inc. Used with permission. All Rights reserved.

Dave Krepcho, Grant Proposal for Second Harvest Food Bank of Central Florida, November 5, 2013. Reprinted by permission.

Carly Lewis, "The Writing on the Virtual Bathroom Wall." Originally published in *Maclean's Magazine* on November 2, 2015. Copyright © 2015. Used by permission of the author.

Sapna Maheshwari, "Why Elite Female Athletes Are Turning Away from Major Sponsors," *The New York Times*, July 30, 2021. Copyright © 2021 by The New York Times. All rights reserved. Used under license. https://nytimes.com.

Illyanna Maisonet, "Why Aren't There More Puerto Rican Restaurants . . . ," eatgordaeat.substack.com, July 13, 2021. Copyright © 2021 by Illyanna Maisonet. Used with permission. All rights reserved.

Marie-Helen Maras, "4 Ways 'Internet of Things' Toys Endanger Children," *The Conversation*, May 10, 2018, https://theconversation.com/4-ways-internet-of-things-toys-endanger-children-94092. This article is licensed under Creative Commons Attribution-No Derivatives 4.0 International Public License (https://creativecommons.org/licenses/by-nd/4.0/).

Krista McCracken and Skylee-Storm Hogan, "Community First: Indigenous Community-Based Archival Provenance," *Across the Disciplines*, November 8, 2021, 18 (1/2), 23–32. Copyright © 2021 by Krista McCracken and Skylee-Storm Hogan. Used with permission. All rights reserved.

James Mollison, Where Children Sleep. Copyright © 2010 by James Mollison. Used with permission.

Angela Nickerson, "An Open Letter to Lands' End," *Medium.com*, October 31, 2017. Copyright © 2017 by Angela Nickerson. Reprinted by permission.

Katharina Nieswandt, "Basic Income after Automation? That's Not How Capitalism Works!," *The Conversation*, August 6, 2018, https://theconversation.com/basic-income-after-automation-thats-not-how-capitalism-works-65023. This article is licensed under Creative Commons Attribution-No Derivatives 4.0 International Public License (https://creativecommons.org/licenses/by-nd/4.0/).

Alice Park and Sean Gregory, "TIME 2021 Athlete of the Year: Simone Biles," *TIME*, December 9, 2021. Copyright © 2021 by TIME USA LLC. All rights reserved. Used under license. https://time.com.

James Parker, "An Ode to Not Being a Morning Person," *The Atlantic*, September 2021. Copyright © 2021 by The Atlantic Monthly Group, Inc. All rights reserved. Distributed by Tribune Content Agency, LLC.

Anu Partanen, "What Americans Keep Ignoring about Finland's School Success," *The Atlantic*, December 29, 2011. Copyright © 2011 by Anu Partanen. Used with permission.

Savannah Peterson, "Advice for Generation Z from a Savvy Millennial," *Medium.com*, April 9, 2018. Copyright © 2018. Reprinted by permission of the author. All rights reserved.

Thomas Polk, "A Review of the MLA Handbook, Eighth Edition," *Across the Disciplines*, September 6, 2016, 13(2). Copyright © 2016 by Thomas Polk. Used with permission. All Rights reserved.

Salvatore Scibona, "Where I Learned to Read," *The New Yorker* (June 13 & 20, 2011, issue). Copyright © 2011 by Salvatore Scibona.

Nancy Sommers, "Living Composition" from *Teaching English in the Two-Year College* 43.1 (September 2015). Copyright 2015 by the National Council of Teachers of English. Reprinted with permission.

Index

A

Abbreviations, 4, 777, 791
Absolute concepts, 769–770
Academic connections, exploring, 30
Academic course websites, in MLA style, 687
Academic culture, 13–14
Academic essays/writings
  design of, 21, 611
  online writing *vs.*, 4
  plagiarism in context of, 526
  purpose of, 10
  thesis statement in, 541–542
Academic trend, analyzing, 292–293
Accessibility
  in design, 608–609
  of multimedia presentations, 652
AccessScience, 488
Accuracy, of source representation, 528–529, 595, 596, 601, 655, 662
Acronyms, 786, 792
Active reading, strategies for, 51–63
Active voice, 566, 736–737
Ad hominem attacks, 443
Adjectives
  bad/badly use, 768
  capitalization of, 789
  commas with, 775–776
  comparative, 769
  compound, 784
  good/well use, 768
  as modifiers, 766–767
  possessives and attributive nouns *vs.*, 781
  superlative, 769
Adverbs
  with absolute concepts, 769–770
  avoiding excessive use of, 740–741
  bad/badly use, 768
  comparative, 769
  good/well use, 768
  intensifying, 769
  limiting, 770

  as modifiers, 767–768
  superlative, 769
Advertisements
  analysis of, 293–294
  argumentative writing in, 413–418, 465
  design of, 416
  in MLA style, 686–687
  public service, 465
"Advice for Generation Z from a Savvy Millennial" (Peterson), 369–374
Advice writing, 369–374
Advocate(s), 8, 405–406, 470, 473
  writing role as, 123, 124, 127
Affirmative statements, 741
Afterword, author of
  in APA style, 699
  in MLA style, 677
Agent/goals/actions/results
  framing introduction toward, 572–573
  in problem-solving writing, 381
Agreement
  agree/disagree responses, 73
  pronoun-antecedent, 761–762
  subject/verb, 743–748
Alcazar, Jeremy, 431, 432, 436, 441, 453, 552, 554–555
  "Reforming, Not Defunding, the Police," 455–462, 667
Alignment, in design, 612–614
Almanacs
  in APA style, 705
  in MLA style, 683
  searches of, 478, 491, 496, 498
American Psychological Association style. *See* APA style
Analogies, false/questionable, 444
Analysis
  of academic trend, 292–293
  analytical writing, 157, 233–296, 544
  analytic responses, 73–74
  in argumentative writing, 405, 406
  of assignment, 32–36, 619–620, 654
  causal, 264, 265–266, 267, 279–280
  conclusion offering additional, 578

  conducting, for analytical writing, 261–273
  critical thinking and, 27, 61, 234, 256
  data, 267–269
  in evaluative writing, 298
  of genre, 21
  graphic, 248–251
  in informative writing, 182
  of interview results, 505
  of observation results, 508
  in problem-solving writing, 350, 370, 372, 374
  of reflective writing topic, 162–163
  rhetorical, 248–251, 271–272, 293–294
  sentence starters for, 43
  of survey data, 96, 267–268, 512
  of target publication, for articles, 625–627
  text, 269–270, 276
  trend, 257, 279, 292–293
  of writing situation, 15, 248–251, 269, 271, 272, 292–293
Analytical writing, 233–296
  analytical blog posts as, 235, 269
  causal analysis in, 264, 265–266, 267, 279–280
  collaboration on, 258, 276
  conclusion in, 278, 290–291
  conducting analysis for, 261–273
  context for, 234, 235, 252, 264, 265, 269, 271, 272, 276, 278, 280, 294
  conversations on topic for, 258
  critical thinking in, 234, 256
  data analysis in, 267–269
  definition and description of, 233–234
  design of, 241, 277
  division of topic in, 262–263
  drafting, 274–279
  essays as, 157, 256–294
  explanation in, 234, 274–275, 276
  framing, 274, 277–279
  genres in, 234, 235, 277
  graphic analysis in, 248–251
  idea generation for, 256–260

795

Analytical writing (cont.)
  interpretation in, 234, 235, 256, 257–261, 264–277, 279–281, 293
  introduction in, 278
  issue analyses as, 240–247
  organization of, 248, 255, 279, 281
  outlines for, 279
  peer review of, 280
  project ideas for, 292–296
  purpose of, 234, 271, 280–281
  questioning for, 233, 240, 248, 252, 254, 256, 257–258, 278, 281
  readers of, 234, 271, 281
  reasons and evidence in, 274–275, 277
  refining question for, 261–262
  reflection in, 240, 244, 248, 252, 254, 255, 256, 276
  review and revision of, 279–281
  rhetorical analyses in, 248–251, 271, 293–294
  seeking fuller understanding of topic in, 262–263
  Smith, Kelsey, "Art Theft on the Rise with Social Media" (student essay), 282–292
  sources for, 234, 237, 240, 241, 256, 259–260, 271, 276, 280–281, 283–284, 285–286
  supporting points in, 244, 275, 277
  text analysis in, 269–270, 271, 272, 276, 278, 280, 294
  thesis statement in, 274, 278, 544
  topic for, 256–260, 262–263, 292–296
  trend analysis in, 257, 279, 292–293
Anecdotes
  in introduction, 169, 391
  in oral presentations, 643
  in problem-solving writing, 391
Annotated bibliographies, 522–524
  creating shared, 102
Annotation, in active reading, 51, 58–59, 61
Anthologies, works in, in MLA style, 671, 675–677, 699
APA style, 691–711
  citations and attributions, 215, 534–535, 588–589, 596, 597, 692, 693–696
  references list, 228, 604–605, 692, 696–711
    books, 692, 697–710
    field sources, 692, 705–706

  journals, magazines, newspapers, 692, 702–707, 710
  media sources, 692, 706–707
  other digital sources, 692, 707–710
  other sources, 692, 711
  reference works, 692, 705
  title pages, 223
Apostrophes, 780–782
Appeals
  argumentative writing using, 440, 446–449, 451, 452
  to authority, 447, 451
  to character (*ethos*), 271, 448
  choosing appropriate, 449
  to emotion (*pathos*), 271, 447, 451, 643
  to logic (*logos*), 271, 448–449, 451, 643
  rhetorical analysis of, 271
Aral, Sinan, 86
"Are We Rich?" (Jefferson), 152–158, 167
Argumentative writing, 404–466
  advertisements as, 413–418, 465
  Alcazar, Jeremy "Reforming, Not Defunding, the Police" (student essay), 455–462
  alternative/opposing claims addressed in, 406, 442–443, 449–451, 453
  appeals in, 440, 446–449, 451, 452
  building argument for, 435–445
  call to action in, 407, 413, 417, 429
  claims in, 406, 413, 437–443, 445–446, 449–451, 452
  collaboration on, 442
  conclusion in, 452
  context for, 405, 438, 454
  as conversation, 5–7
  conversations on topic of, 433
  counterarguments in, 407, 413, 442–443, 449–451, 453
  critical thinking in, 405, 412
  definition and description of, 404–406
  definition of claim in, 437
  design of, 416, 419, 427, 430, 451, 455
  drafting, 445–452
  essays as, 406–413, 431–462, 542
  exploring disagreements in, 432–434, 442–443
  framing, 451–452
  genres in, 406–430, 451
  idea generation for, 431–435, 438
  integrity of argument in, 443–445, 453
  introduction in, 452, 455
  logical fallacies in, 443–445

  open letters as, 426–429
  organization of, 451, 570
  peer review of, 454
  photographs and images in, 413–418, 419, 428, 440, 451
  point/counterpoint editorials as, 418–426
  project ideas for, 463–465
  purpose of, 405, 454
  questioning for, 434–435, 438, 452
  readers of, 405–406, 410, 429, 435, 446–449, 454
  reasonableness in, 405, 406, 450–451
  reasons and evidence in, 406, 421, 428, 437–441, 452
  review and revision of, 452–454
  role-playing in, 8
  sources for, 405, 406, 407, 421–422, 428, 434, 436, 454, 460–462
  supporting points in, 438–441
  thesis statement in, 445–446, 542, 544
  topic for, 431–435, 463–465
  tracking online discussions for, 434
Articles. *See also* Journal articles; Magazine articles; Newspaper articles; Online articles; Scholarly articles
  in APA style, 692, 702–704, 710
  checklist for writing, 630
  from databases, 678, 680
  drafting, designing, and review of, 628
  in MLA style, 678–682
  monthly/bimonthly, 681
  organization of, 627
  quotation in title of, 682
  sample/example, 628–629
  skipping pages, 681
  source selection for, 627
  in special issue, 682
  target publication analysis for, 625–627
  unsigned, 681, 703
  writing, 625–630
Articulation, in oral presentations, 648
Arts & Humanities Database, 488
Artstor, 488
"Art Theft on the Rise with Social Media" (Smith), 282–292, 691
Art works
  in APA style, 707
  in MLA style, 686
As if comparisons, 755–756
Assertions, evidence to support, 585. *See also* Claims

Assessing and evaluating sources, 84–97
Assumptions
　challenging, in revision, 659
　fallacies based on questionable, 444
　research question referring to shared, 474–475
Atlases, 498
Attributions
　APA style, 588–589
　common, 588–589, 656
　examples of, 602
　language in, 589, 655–656
　MLA style, 588–589
　plagiarism avoidance with, 534
　source identification with, 588–589, 602
　specific, 656
Attributive nouns, 781
Audience. *See also* Readers
　for analytical writing, 271
　for argumentative writing, 405–406, 409, 410, 429, 446–449, 454
　for assignment, 33, 34, 35, 619
　engaging, 566, 648–649
　for evaluative writing, 299, 321, 338
　for informative writing, 184, 222
　for multimedia presentations, 648–649
　for oral presentations, 641–645
　for problem-solving writing, 349, 352–353, 384, 394
　for reflective writing, 132, 180
　rhetorical analysis of, 271
　text analysis of, 269
　writing life inventory, 4
Audio clip
　in APA style, 707
　in MLA style, 685–686
Audio search sites, 492
Authority. *See also* Expert opinion
　appeals to, 447, 451
　argumentative writing aligned with, 430
　citing inappropriate, fallacy of, 444
　role-playing, 100
　sources aligning writer with, 585–586
　sources written by, 211
Authors
　in APA style, 693–695, 701, 704
　bias of, 85
　corporate, group, government, 670, 673, 694, 697
　with editors or translators, 674, 698
　identification of, 92–93

in MLA style, 400, 460–462, 669–672, 673–674, 677, 680, 689
　named in text, 669, 693
　not named in text, 669, 693
　one, 673, 697
　organizations as, 400
　quoted in another source, 671, 695
　role-playing, 100
　as search terms, 486
　three or more, 670, 673, 694
　two, 670, 673, 693–694
　two or more, 697
　two or more, with same last name, 670, 695
　two or more works by same, 400, 670, 674, 695, 698
　unknown, 670, 674, 694, 697
　website, 689

B

Baker, Peter C., 579–580
　"Reform of the Nerds, Starring Arthur Chu," 240–247, 248, 278
Base-rate fallacies, 444
"Basic Income after Automation? That's Not How Capitalism Works!" (Nieswandt), 418–423
Bartholomae, David, 28
Begging the question fallacy, 445
Bereiter, Carl, 28
Berlin, James, 28
Bias
　author's, 91
　editing to avoid, 663
　language free of, 732–733
　of sources, 85–86, 97
Bibliographies
　annotated, 102
　creation of, 102, 520–522
　searches of, 478, 488, 496–497
　working, listing sources in, 521–522
Bile, Simone, 574
Biographies, checking, 497
Bizzell, Patricia, 28
Blank on Blank (Videos), 252–253
Bloch, Ben, "Tax Robots and Universal Basic Income," 423–426
Block quotations
　citations and attributions for, 669
　punctuation for, 590–591, 593, 669
　strategic use of, 590–591

Blogs, 489
　analytical writing in, 235
　in APA style, 708
　argumentative writing in, 465
　assessing the relevance and credibility of, 94
　evaluation of, 94
　evaluative writing in, 299
　informative writing in, 190
　in MLA style, 688
　as reflective writing, 180
　searches of, 489
　text analysis of, 269
　topics from, 434
Bloom, Benjamin, 25
Bookmarks, saving in browser, 519
Boolean operators, 483–485
Brainstorming
　for analytical writing, 258
　for argumentative writing, 437
　for evaluative writing, 323, 326
　group, 99, 216
　for idea generation, 37, 99, 158–159, 164, 206, 216, 258, 323, 326, 468
　for informative writing, 206, 216
　for reflective writing, 158–159, 164
　research questions, 468
　supporting points and evidence, 216
Brochures. *See also* Pamphlets
　in APA style, 705
　genre and design of, 18, 21
　informative writing in, 181, 230–232
　in MLA style, 684
Bulleted lists, 614, 651, 782
Burke, Kenneth, 633

C

"Cancer Trends Progress Report" excerpts (National Cancer Institute), 311–320
Capitalization, 788–790, 792
Captions, 599–600, 614, 629
　in design, 617
Careless reasoning, fallacies based on, 444–445
Cartoons, in MLA style, 687
Causal analysis, 264, 265–266, 267, 279–280
Cause/effect
　analytical writing on, 258
　causal analysis, 227, 259–260, 272
　correlation *vs.*, 267, 269

Cause/effect (cont.)
  organization, 279, 548
  problem-solving writing on, 378, 380, 381
  reflective writing tracing, 162
  sentence starters for, 43
Character appeals (ethos), 271, 448
Charts
  active reading of, 60
  for analytical writing, 276
  in argumentative writing, 405, 419, 440, 451
  design of/with, 615, 627
  in evaluative writing, 315
  in informative writing, 182, 217–218
  in MLA style, 683
  in multimedia presentations, 644
  numerical information in, 598
  in problem-solving writing, 349, 375
Checklist
  for conducting interviews, 504
  for conducting observations, 507–508
  for conducting surveys, 512–513
  for creating multimedia presentations, 652
  for creating multimodal essays, 636–637
  for developing websites, 641
  for editing, 666
  for paraphrasing, 596
  for preparing and delivering oral presentations, 652
  for quoting, 594
  for reading laterally, 89
  for revision, 660
  for summarizing, 597
  for writing articles, 630
Cherry-picking, avoiding, 270, 276
Chronological order, 166, 219, 279, 548, 725–726, 727
Circular reasoning, 445
Cisneros, Sandra, 148
Citation indexes, 488
Citations
  in analytical writing, 291, 292
  APA style, 215, 534–535, 588–589, 596, 597, 692, 693–696
    corporate, group, government author, 694
    documents from websites, 696
    email, letters, personal communication, 695
    source quoted in another source, 695

sources named in text, 693
sources not named in text, 693
source without page numbers, 695
three or more authors, 694
two authors, 693–694
two or more authors with same last name, 695
two or more works by same author, 695
two or more works cited together, 694–695
unknown author, 694
websites, 696
checking for unattributed, 603
common, in multiple sources, 68
ethical use of, 529
in evaluative writing, 333–334, 341
in informative writing, 201, 224
in-text, 215, 588–589, 603, 604, 668, 669–672, 692, 693–696
MLA style, 534–535, 588–589, 590, 597, 603, 668, 669–672
  corporate, group, government author, 670
  entire source, 669
  literary work, 671
  sacred text, 671
  source quoted in another source, 671
  sources named in text, 669
  sources not named in text, 669
  source without page numbers, 671–672
  three or more authors, 670
  two authors, 670
  two or more authors with same last name, 670
  two or more works by same author, 670
  two or more works cited together, 671
  unknown author, 670
  work in edited collection or anthology, 671
of multiple sources, 671
in paraphrases, 595
parenthetical, 224, 529, 534, 591, 603, 604, 669–672
plagiarism avoidance with, 534–535
in problem-solving writing, 371
punctuation with, 593, 780
source identification with, 588–589
in summaries, 596–597

Citing inappropriate authorities fallacy, 444
Claims
  in argumentative writing, 406, 412, 437–443, 445–446, 449–451, 452–453
  conceding valid, 450
  defining of, 437
  ignoring competing, 450
  interpretive, 274, 279
  negative, 413
  opposing, identifying, and considering, 442–443, 449–451, 453
  problem-solving writing in response to, 363, 366
  reasons and evidence supporting, 437–441
  refuting widely held, 450
Clarity
  of analytical writing, 281
  of complex concepts, design for, 610
  of effective writing, 564–565
  of informative writing, 220
  of main point, in reflective writing, 169
  of peer review request/feedback, 115, 118
  of pronoun-antecedent references, 725, 762–765
  of sentences, 714–729
  of statements, sources used for, 586–587
  of survey questions, 511
  of thesis statement, 446
Classification
  library system of, 494
  proofreading by, 221
  scheme, 263
  of sources, 68–69
  of topic, in analytical writing, 263
Clauses
  antecedents as whole, 763
  main or independent, 714–715, 720, 772–773
  subordinate or dependent, 715–717, 718–719, 721, 773
Clichés, avoiding, 738
Clustering
  for analytical writing, 258
  for idea generation, 39–40, 69, 258, 385, 468
  in note taking, 69
  for organization, 551
  for problem-solving writing, 385
  research questions, 468

Collaboration
    on analytical writing, 258, 276
    on argumentative writing, 442
    to collect and work with information, 102
    to determine fairness of judgments, 334, 379
    on evaluative writing, 323, 334
    for field research, 514
    generating ideas in, 99–102
    in group projects, 104–108
    on informative writing, 209
    to make connections among sources, 102
    on opposing claim identification and consideration, 442
    on problem-solving writing, 379
    on reasons for interpretation, 275
    for refining arguments, 102–104
    on reflective writing, 163
    resources for, 116–118
    role-playing as, 100–101
    on search strategy/plan, 102
    technology for, 118
    to understand arguments, 62
    writing improved through, 99–104
Collective nouns, 747–748, 762
Columns
    analytical writing in, 235
    drafting and designing for magazine, 295–296
    opinion, 541–542
    page layout, 612, 614, 629
Colville, Gina, 5–6, 10, 11, 12, 14, 37, 54
Commas
    comma splices, 715, 720–721
    in dates, 776
    detours set off with, 773–775
    introductory elements set off with, 773
    with proper names, 774–775
    with quotations, 593
    in sentences, 715, 772–777
    separating main clauses, 715, 720, 772–773
    in series/serial, 775–776
    with *yes/no*, 777
Comments, on draft, making, 117
Common knowledge, 530–532
Compare/contrast
    in argumentative writing, 406–413
    comparative adjectives, 769
    comparative adverbs, 769
    in evaluative writing, 335, 339
    as if comparisons, 755–756
    in informative writing, 219
    in introduction, 576–577
    organization, 549
    in problem-solving writing, 391
    pronoun choice in, 760
    in reflective writing, 162, 163, 164
    sentence starters for, 43
    sentence structure for, 722–723
    of sources, 67–68
    sources used to, 584–585
    transitions to, 568–569
Complex sentences, 715–717
Composing process. *See* Writing process
Composing tools
    for multimedia presentations, 646–647
    for multimodal essays, 633–634
Comprehensiveness, evaluating, 91–92
Computer games
    in MLA style, 690
    text analysis of, 269
Computer software
    in APA style, 709
    in MLA style, 690
Concessions
    transitions signaling, 569
    to valid claims, 450
Conciseness
    editing for, 662
    of effective writing, 564–565
    of phrasing style, 735–736
Conclusion
    in analytical writing, 278, 290–291
    in argumentative writing, 452
    call to action in, 580
    challenging, 279
    closing with question in, 580
    closing with quotations in, 579
    drafting, 577–581
    drawing, in trend analysis, 268
    in evaluative writing, 336, 343
    framing topic in, 581
    in informative writing, 219, 220–221, 227
    link to introduction, 580–581
    offering additional analysis in, 578
    in problem-solving writing, 391
    in reflective writing, 168–169
    reinforcing main points in, 577–578
    restating thesis statement in, 577
    speculation about future in, 578–579
    storytelling in, 579–580
    strategy selection, 578–581
    transitions to introduce, 569
Conference proceedings
    in APA style, 699
    in MLA style, 677
Conflicts, in storytelling, 166
Conjunctions
    coordinating, 715, 720, 772–773
    as signposts in sentences, 724
    subordinating, 716, 718, 724
Connections, academic, personal, and professional, 30
Consensus, argument from, 444
Consistency
    in design, 607, 608, 610, 616, 634–635, 652, 663
    editing for, 663, 665
Context
    for analytical writing, 234, 235, 252, 264, 265, 269, 271, 272, 276, 278, 280, 294
    for argumentative writing, 405, 438, 454
    for assignment, 35, 619–620
    cultural, 13–15, 21, 28–29, 35, 132, 182, 271, 272, 296
    disciplinary, 13, 21, 28
    establishing, in introduction, 574
    for evaluative writing, 298, 334, 338
    genre shaped by, 21–22, 619–621
    historical, 28–29, 132, 182, 265, 269, 271, 272, 293, 296, 438
    for informative writing, 182, 222
    for multimodal essays, 633
    peer review consideration of, 118, 172, 222
    physical, 13, 116
    political, 28–29, 269, 272, 296
    for problem-solving writing, 349, 378, 394
    for reflective writing, 132, 172
    rhetorical analysis of, 271
    social, 13–14, 21, 28, 35, 132, 182, 271, 272
    for source information, 589–590
    technological, 28
    text analysis of, 269
    understanding, for effective writing, 562
    writing process shaped by, 28–29
    for writing situations, 13–15
Contractions, apostrophes in, 780–781

Conversation
  adopting roles through, 7–8
  exchanging information, ideas and arguments by, 5–6
  finding written, 8
  online and off, 3–4
  writing as, 2–3
Convincing. *See* Argumentative writing; Persuasive writing
Coordinating conjunctions, 715, 720, 772–773
Copy and paste, 518
Copyright, and plagiarism, 526, 530
Copyright Act of 1976, 530
Corporate authors
  in APA style, 694, 697
  in MLA style, 670, 673
Correlation *vs.* cause, 267, 269
Correspondence. *See also* Letters
  about topic, 46
  as field research, 513, 514
Costs/benefits
  argumentative writing on, 438
  evaluative writing on, 327
  organization, 549
  problem-solving writing on, 391
  reflective writing considering, 162
Council of Science Editors (CSE) documentation style, 604
Counterarguments
  in argumentative writing, 413, 442–443, 449–451, 453
  collaboration on, 103
Credibility
  of presenters, 642, 643, 645
  revising for, 654
  of sources, 87–89, 210
Criteria, for evaluation
  conclusions based on, 298
  defining of, 308, 314, 327–328, 332, 340
  evidence to meet, 329
  explanation of, 332
  identification of, 322
  judgments based on, 329–330
  organization relative to, 335
  review of, 336
Critical reading, 49–51, 61. *See also* Active reading, strategies for
Critical thinking
  in analytical writing, 234, 256
  in argumentative writing, 405, 406
  critical reading and, 49–51, 61
  definition of, 26
  in evaluative writing, 298
  in informative writing, 182
  in problem-solving writing, 349, 376
  in reflective writing, 132, 158
  skills, 50–51
  on source credibility, 81
  in writing process, 25–27
Criticism
  avoiding, in group brainstorming, 99
  openness to, 115
Crowley, Sharon, 27
CSE style, 604
Cultural context
  academic, 13–14
  for assignment, 35
  genre shaped by, 21
  for informative writing, 182
  text analysis of, 269
  writing process shaped by, 28–29
  for writing situation, 13–15

D

Dashes, 773, 785–786
Data analysis, 267–269
Databases
  articles from
    locating, 495
    in MLA style, 678, 680
  full-text, 488
  identifying relevant, 487–488
  media, 488
  news and information, 487
  professional or disciplinary, 488
  searches of, 47, 208, 209, 210, 259–260, 476, 478, 479, 487–489, 496
  search fields in, 488–489
  search plan for, 478
  subject, 487
  subscriptions to, 487
Date, assignment due, 34, 35, 620
Debate
  interpretive claims open to, 272, 279
  staging, in role-playing, 100
  thesis statement allowing for, 445–446
Deduction, 448–449
Definition
  of analytical writing, 233–234
  of argumentative writing, 404–406
  of claim, in argumentative writing, 437
  of concept, sources used for, 586
  of criteria for evaluation, 308, 314, 327–328, 332, 343
  of critical thinking, 26
  of evaluative writing, 297–298
  of informative writing, 181–182
  organization using, 548
  of paraphrases, 595
  of plagiarism, 526
  of problem, in introduction, 575
  in problem-solving writing, 348–350, 355, 376, 378, 380–381, 383, 384, 386–387, 392, 401
  of summary, 596
  of writing situation, 9
Department websites, in MLA style, 687
Dependent clauses, 715–717, 721, 773
Description
  details including, 163
  in informative writing, 219, 229
  organization using, 548
  in problem-solving writing, 355
  vivid, in oral presentations, 643
Design, 16–22, 606–617. *See also* Format
  of academic essays, 21, 611
  of advertisements, 416
  of analytical writing, 241, 277
  of argumentative writing, 416, 419, 427, 430, 451, 455
  of articles, 628, 629
  assignment requirements for, 34
  balance and symmetry in, 607
  color, shading, borders, and rules in, 340, 615, 621, 622, 636, 638, 652
  consistency in, 607, 608, 610, 616, 636, 652, 663
  effective use of elements of, 612–617
  emphasis in, 607
  of evaluative writing, 312, 321, 334–335, 339–340
  font, line spacing, and alignment in, 612–614, 629, 647–648, 672, 696
  genre and, 16–22, 611
  goal achievement with, 21–22
  of informative writing, 217–218, 222–229, 232
  moderation in, 608
  of multimedia presentations, 634–635
  of multimodal essays, 610, 617, 632
  of/with illustrations, 277, 609, 615, 617, 628, 629
  of open letters, 427
  page layout in, 612, 614, 629, 636, 647

placement in, 608, 612, 617
of point/counterpoint editorials, 419
principles of, 607–609
of problem-solving writing, 358, 375, 389–390, 394–395
for purpose, 21–22, 609–610, 615, 617
for readers, 610–611
of references lists, 696
of reflective writing, 132, 165, 168
repetition in, 608
revising for, 656–657
simplicity of, 608
of surveys, 382
of target publication, 627
to understand point, 609–610
of websites, 638, 640
of works cited lists, 672
in writing process, 25
as writing tool, 17
Devil's advocate role, 100, 101, 442, 659
Dewey, John, 377
Dialogue, in reflective writing, 167, 169–170, 182
Dictionaries/dictionary entries
in APA style, 705
in MLA style, 683
searches of, 478, 491
Digital documents
highlighting main point, reasons, and evidence in, 657–658
saving multiple drafts of, 657
Digital illustrations
active reading of, 60
in APA style, 695–696
integration of, 60, 598
Digital materials, keeping track of, 516–517
Digital notes, tagging and labeling in, 68–69
Digital object identifiers (DOIs), 673, 678, 697, 701, 702, 704, 705
Digital search tools, 478. *See also* Online searches
Digital sources
in APA style, 691–711
availability of, 632–633
citations for, 341
evaluation of, 93–95
file size of, 632
imported or linked, 632–633
labeling of, 550

locating, 480–493 (*See also* Online searches)
in MLA style, 668–690
for multimodal essays, 632–633
software constraints with, 632
Directories, 491
Disagreements
agree/disagree responses, 73
exploring, in argumentative writing, 432–434, 442–443
in sources, 48, 58, 67
Disciplinary context, 13, 14, 21, 28, 468–469
Discussion forums
assessing the relevance and credibility of, 94
Dissertations
in APA style, 700
in MLA style, 678
Distraction, fallacies based on, 443
Division, in analytical writing, 262–263
Documentation
APA style (*See* APA style)
Chicago style, 604
choosing system for, 603–604
common knowledge exceptions, 530
CSE style, 604
in-text references, 604–605 (*See also* Attributions; Citations)
MLA style (*See* MLA style)
process of, 603–605
publication information, 604–605 (*See also* References; Works Cited)
revising to improve, 655–656
DOIs. *See* Digital object identifiers (DOIs)
Drafting, 560–581
alternatives, 543
analytical writing, 274–279
argumentative writing, 445–452
argument clarification in, 569–570
articles, 628
clear and concise, 564–565
conclusion, 577–581
details to capture reader's attention in, 566–567
effective documents, 562–569
engaging readers, 566
evaluative writing, 331–336
feedback, 115
headings and subheadings, 561, 568
informative writing, 213–219

integration of source information in, 563–564
introduction, 571–577
outline or map for, 561
paragraph focused on central idea in, 562–563
paragraph organization in, 563
problem-solving writing, 386–391
reflective writing, 165–169
saving multiple drafts, 657
survey questions, 509–511
thesis statement, 541–542
topic sentences, 561, 562
transitions within and between paragraphs, 567–569
in writing process, 25, 27, 28

E

E-books, 673, 697
Echo chamber, 86
Edited collections, works in
in APA style, 700
in MLA style, 671, 677
Editing, 664–666
for accuracy, 662
of analytical writing, 280
of articles, 628
checklist for, 666
for consistency, 663, 665
for economy, 662
feedback/proofreading after, 666
making/highlighting document for, 664
purpose of, 662
reading carefully before, 664
searches for, 664–665
for spelling, grammar, and punctuation, 663, 665
strategies for, 664–665
for style, 663, 665
in writing process, 24, 26
Editorials
analytical writing in, 235
in APA style, 703
argumentative writing in, 418–426
in MLA style, 682
point/counterpoint, 418–426
problem-solving writing in, 363, 364
Editors
in APA style, 699
in MLA style, 674
Effect, cause and. *See* Cause/effect

Effectiveness
  drafting for, 562–569
  of evaluative writing, 327
  of sources, 582–605
  of words, in phrasing style, 735–736
Either/or arguments, 445
Elbow, Peter, 28
Electronic mailing list, message posted to
  in APA style, 708
  in MLA style, 688
Ellipses marks, 592, 594, 601, 787
Email
  in APA style, 695, 708
  collaboration and peer review using, 116–117
  conversations in, 3
  field research via, 502, 511, 512–513
  interviews via, 502
  in MLA style, 688
  problem-solving writing in, 350
  survey distribution via, 511, 512
  use, 518
Email lists
  assessing the relevance and credibility of, 94
Emig, Janet, 28
Emotional appeals *(pathos)*, 271, 447, 451, 643
Emphasis
  dashes for, 785–786
  in design, 607
  italics for, 790–791
  sentence structure conveying, 714–717, 727
Encyclopedias/encyclopedia entries
  in APA style, 705
  in MLA style, 683
  searches of, 478, 491, 496, 497, 498
  specialized, 498
ERIC, 487, 488
Essays. *See also* Student essays
  suggestions for, 292–294
Essays/writings
  academic, 4, 10, 16, 17, 21, 22, 526, 541–542, 611, 630
  analytical, 157, 256–294
  argumentative, 406–413, 431–462, 542
  evaluative, 299, 322–347
  informative, 181, 183–189, 205–230, 232
  multimodal, 630–637
  photo, 135–147, 179–180
  problem-solving, 350–354, 376–402

  reflective, 158–180
  text analysis of, 269–270
Ethics, research, 528–529
Ethos (character appeals), 271, 448
Evaluative writing, 297–347
  collaboration on, 323, 334, 338
  conclusion in, 341, 336
  conducting evaluation for, 327–330
  context for, 298, 334, 338
  conversations on topic of, 322–323
  criteria in, 308, 314, 321, 327–330, 331, 335, 336, 340
  critical thinking in, 298
  definition and description of, 297–298
  design of, 312, 321, 334–335, 339–340
  drafting, 331–336
  essays as, 299, 322–347
  evidence in, 298, 305, 313, 328–330, 333–334, 336
  fairness and reasonableness in, 334, 337
  framing, 335–336
  genres in, 299–321, 334–335, 344–347
  idea generation for, 322–327, 344–347
  judgments made in, 299, 322, 327, 329–330, 331–332, 333–334, 337
  media reviews as, 307–310, 324, 327–328, 346
  organization of, 335
  peer review of, 338
  presenting evaluation in, 332–334
  progress reports as, 311–320, 328, 346–347
  project ideas for, 344–347
  purpose of, 298, 331, 338
  readers of, 298, 302, 321, 338
  review and revision of, 336–338
  scholarly articles as, 299–303
  Shannon, Brooke, "Is *Wicked* All That Wicked?" (student essay), 339–344
  sources for, 298, 305, 309, 313, 329, 333–334, 336, 338, 341–342
  thesis statement in, 331–332, 544, 545
  topic for, 322–327, 328, 344–347
  visual images in, 315, 321
  web-based articles as, 304–306
Evaluator, writing role as, 122, 124, 126
Evidence
  in analytical writing, 275–276, 277
  in argumentative writing, 406, 421, 428, 439–441, 452
  brainstorming, 216
  collaborative feedback on, 103–104

  evaluation of, 90, 210
  in evaluative writing, 298, 305, 309, 313, 328–330, 333–334, 336
  highlighting, for revision and editing, 657–658, 664
  identification of, 328–329, 440
  in informative writing, 210, 215–217
  judgments supported by, 329–330, 333–334
  key-point summaries including, 76
  oral presentations of, 642, 643
  paragraph offering, 563
  in problem-solving writing, 364, 369, 372, 386, 388, 389, 390, 394, 402
  review and reconsideration of, 336
  rhetorical analysis of, 271
  searches driven by need for, 478
  sources used to provide, 585
  supporting main point, 62–63, 215–217, 545–546
  thesis statement supported by, 545–546
Exaggeration, avoiding, 733–734
Examples
  in analytical writing, 276
  in argumentative writing, 455
  in informative writing, 216
  as sentence fragments, 720
  sources to provide, 587
  transitions to elaborate or provide, 569
Exclamation points, 593, 777
Expert opinion. *See also* Authority
  appeals to authority with, 447
  argumentative writing with, 440
  evaluative writing supported by, 333, 342
  recurring voices in sources, 48
  search plan including, 478
Explanation
  in analytical writing, 274–276
  in argumentative writing, 437–441, 455
  in evaluative writing, 332, 335
  in informative writing, 229
  of interpretation, 274–276
  parentheses with, 786
  in problem-solving writing, 375, 376, 386–389
  process, as organizational pattern, 391, 548
  sentence starters for, 43
  of survey purpose, 512
Eye contact, in presentations, 648

F

Facebook posts
    in APA style, 709
    conversation in, 3, 4, 5
    "fake news" on, 86
    in MLA style, 688
    Search, 492
    topic discussion on, 47
    topics from, 434
Face-to-face interviews, 502
Fact-checking websites, 88
FactCheck.org, 88
Fair use provision, 530
"Fake news," 84, 86
Fallacies, logical, 271, 443–445
False analogies fallacy, 444
Family & Society Studies Worldwide, 488
"Fast Fashion? Not So Fast!" (Guerrero), 222–228, 691
Favorites, saving in web browser, 519–520
Feedback. *See also* Peer review
    on analytical writing, 280–281
    on argumentative writing, 453
    on editing, 666
    on evaluative writing, 337–338
    guidelines for, 115–116
    on informative writing, 221–222
    peer review, sample, 115
    on problem-solving writing, 393–394
    providing to writer, 116
    refining argument using, 103–104
    on reflective writing, 171–172
    for revision, 661
    skills for giving/receiving, 98
    student writers guided by, 54–58
Ferrer, Eileen, 573
Field research, 499–514
    appropriate use of, 499–500
    methods of, 500–514 (*See also* Interviews; Observations; Surveys)
    responsibility for, 102
    search tools and methods for, 478
Field sources
    in APA style, 692, 705–706
    evaluation of, 96
    in MLA style, 668, 684
Figures. *See also* Graphics; Illustrations
    active reading of, 52–53
    in analytical writing, 255, 277, 283
    design of/with, 628
    in informative writing, 218
    in problem-solving writing, 390
    source management with, 598–600
Figures of speech, 738
Files, backing up, 520
Films/movies
    in APA style, 706
    argumentative writing in, 430
    evaluative writing on, 307–310, 323, 327–328, 346
    in MLA style, 684–685
    reflective writing in, 157, 177–178
Filter bubble, 86
First-person point of view, 167
Flower, Linda, 28
Fonts, in design, 612–613, 629, 647, 650
Footers, 612, 614, 616
Foreign words, in italics, 790
Foreword, author of
    in APA style, 699
    in MLA style, 677
Formal outlines, 556–558, 561
Format. *See also* Design
    assignment requirements for, 34
    consistency of, 663
    of progress reports, 312
    of references, 696
    of surveys, 512
    of works cited, 672
"4 Ways 'Internet of Things' Toys Endanger Children" (Maras), 304–306
Franklin, Benjamin, 27
Freewriting
    for analytical writing, 258
    for argumentative writing, 437
    for idea generation, 37–38, 163, 206, 258, 386, 437, 468, 558–559
    for informative writing, 206
    for problem-solving writing, 386
    for reflective writing, 163
    research questions, 468
    zero draft as, 558–559

G

Galchen, Rivka, 562–563
"An Unlikely Ballerina: The Rise of Misty Copeland," 192–199, 215
Garcia, Henry, 37–42
Geisler, Cheryl, 472
Gender-neutral language, 732–733
Generalizations, sweeping, 444
Genre, 16–22, 618–652
    active reading of, 60
    analysis of, 21
    analytical writing, 234, 235, 277
    argumentative writing, 406–430, 451
    assignment requirements for, 34, 35, 619–620
    choosing appropriate, 619–621
    context shaping, 21, 619–620, 621
    design and, 16–22, 611
    documentation specific to, 604
    evaluating, 92–93
    evaluative writing, 299–321, 334–335, 344–347
    as general categories of documents, 16–17
    informative writing, 181, 183–189, 217–218, 229–232
    problem-solving writing, 350–374, 375, 389, 402–403
    purpose met through, 21–22, 619, 620
    reflective writing, 132–156, 157
    revising for, 656–657
    role of writer reflected in, 619, 620
    of sources, 60, 92–93
    suggestion for, 294–296
    text analysis of, 269
    thesis statement reflecting, 541–542
    writer's goals achieved through, 21–22, 619, 620
    writing guidelines for specific, 625–652 (*See also specific genres*)
    writing resources shaping, 620–621
Gladstone, Brooke, "The Goldilocks Number," 248–251, 272
"The Goldilocks Number" (Gladstone), 249–251, 272
Government authors
    in APA style, 694, 705
    in MLA style, 672, 683
Government search sites, 491
Grammar, 742–770
    adjectives and adverbs, 766–770
    editing for, 663, 665
    pronouns, 757–765
    verbs, 743–757
Grandin, Temple, 252, 254
"Grant Proposal for Second Harvest Food Bank of Central Florida" (Krepcho), 354–362
Graphic narratives, in MLA style, 678

Graphics. *See also* Figures; Illustrations
   clustering as (*See* Clustering)
   graphic analysis, 248–251
   infographics as, 190–192
   mapping as (*See* Mapping)
   on websites, avoiding overuse of, 638
Graphs
   active reading of, 60
   for analytical writing, 276
   in argumentative writing, 440, 451
   design of/with, 615, 628
   in evaluative writing, 315
   in informative writing, 217–218
   numerical information in, 598
   in problem-solving writing, 349
Gregory, Sean, 574
Grouping notes or sources, 69, 551
Group/group projects
   collaboration in, 104–108
   creating plan, 108
   ground rules, 107–108
   potential problems and developing solutions, 106–107
   purpose of, 105
Guariglia, Caitlin, 158, 161, 164, 170, 171, 173, 567, 575, 587
   "Mi Famiglia," 173–177, 667
Guerrero, Gabriella, 205, 207, 211, 212, 215, 219, 221, 222, 223, 529, 553, 577–578
   "Fast Fashion? Not So Fast!," 222–228, 691
Guidelines
   peer-review, sample, 117
"Guiding the Budding Writer" (Johnston), 54–58, 68

H

Handbooks
   in APA style, 705
   in MLA style, 683
   searches of, 478, 498
Harris, Jonathan, "The Magic Bean Shop and the Fries That Bind Us," 190–192
Harris, Joseph, 28
Hasty generalizations, 444
Hayes, John R., 28
Headers, 612, 614, 616, 617
Headings and subheadings
   active reading of, 52
   in argumentative writing, 419

design of, 610, 612, 614, 628, 640
drafting, 561, 568
in evaluative writing, 321, 335, 340
in problem-solving writing, 262, 356, 394
scanning, 660
as transitions, 568
on websites, 640
Highlighting, 58–59, 657–658, 664
Historical event, assessing the effects of, 293
Hyphens, 783–784

I

Ideas
   for analytical writing, 256–260, 292–296
   for argumentative writing, 431–435, 438, 463–465
   attribution of, to avoid plagiarism, 534
   brainstorming, 37, 99, 158–159, 164, 206, 216, 258, 323, 437, 468
   building on, 99
   central, paragraphs focusing on, 562–563
   challenging, 61
   clustering, 39–40, 69, 258, 385, 468, 551
   collaboration to generate, 99–102
   contrasting, sources used for, 584–585
   design to locate, 610
   for evaluative writing, 322–327, 344–347
   freewriting, 37–38, 164, 206, 258, 385, 437, 468, 558–559
   generation of, 37–43, 99–102, 158–160, 205–207, 256–260, 322–327, 377, 383, 385, 431–435
   identifying, for thesis statement, 542–543
   for informative writing, 205–207, 229–232
   key, in sources, 51, 58, 60, 61, 63, 76–77
   looping, 37, 38–39
   mapping of, 40, 42
   for problem-solving writing, 376–379, 386, 401–403
   for reflective writing, 158–160, 177–179
   related, keeping together, 570, 725–727
   revising to improve, 653
   sentence starters for, 40, 43
   sentence structure emphasizing, 714–717

sources of, distinguishing, 601–602
   writing sharing, 5–7
IEEE Xplore, 488
If statements, 755–756
Illustrations. *See also* Graphics
   active reading of, 60
   for analytical writing, 276
   in APA style, 707
   in articles, 627, 629
   captions of, 599–600, 612, 614, 617, 629
   charts and graphs as (*See* Charts; Graphs)
   design of/with, 277, 609, 616, 617, 629
   digital, 60, 598, 686
   emotional impacts of, 60, 587, 609
   figures as (*See* Figures)
   in MLA style, 678, 686
   in multimedia presentations, 651
   placement of, 616
   of process, sources used for, 586–587
   source management with, 598–600
   tables as (*See* Tables)
   titles of, 617
Illustrators, in MLA style, 678
Image search sites, 492
Imperative mood, 755
Indefinite pronouns, 746–747, 761
Independent clauses, 714, 720, 772–773
Indexes
   citation, 488
   government documents, 497
   of materials in books, 497
   pamphlet, 497
   periodical, 497
   searches of, 478, 488, 497
Indicative mood, 755
Induction, 449
Infographics, 190–192
Informal outlines, 554–555, 561
Information
   bubble, popping, 86–87
   collaboration to collect and work with, 102
   contact, for field research, 504, 508
   design to locate, 610
   identifying, for thesis statement, 542–543
   informative writing, 181–232, 544, 545
   integration of, 563–564, 588–600, 655–656
   inventory of activities locating, 4
   key, in sources, 51, 58, 60, 61, 63, 76–77

numerical (*See* Numerical information; Statistics)
recording new, 61
on topic, gathering, 41, 46, 163, 208–213
on trends, gathering, 257
verification of, 80–81
writing sharing, 5–7
Informative writing, 181–232, 545
articles as, 181, 183–189, 204, 231–232
in brochures, 181, 230–232
citations in, 201, 215, 225
clarity of, 220
collaboration on, 209
compare/contrast in, 219
conclusion in, 219, 220–221, 227
context for, 182, 222
conversations on topic for, 207
critical thinking in, 182
definition and description of, 181–182
description in, 219, 229
design of, 217–218, 232
drafting, 213–219
essays, 181, 183–189, 205–230, 232
evaluation of sources for, 210, 211–212
evidence in, 210, 215–217
explanation in, 229
focusing discussion in, 220
framing, 218–219, 220–221, 225
Gabriella Guerrero "Fast Fashion? Not So Fast!" (student essay), 222–228
genres in, 181, 183–189, 217–218, 229–232
idea generation for, 204–207
infographics as, 190–192
information gathering for, 208–213
instructor feedback on, 221
interests reflected in, 206
interviews for, 182, 194, 208, 209, 213
introduction in, 218–219, 220–221
library information for, 207, 208, 209, 210
main points in, 213, 214, 220
newsletter articles as, 181, 200–203
objectivity in, 213
observation for, 194, 208
organization of, 219
peer review of, 222
profiles as, 192–199, 230
project ideas for, 229–232
purpose of, 182, 222
questioning for, 213, 214

readers of, 182, 184, 222
review and revision of, 219–222
search plan for, 209, 213
sequence of events chronicled in, 229–230
sources for, 182, 189, 194, 200, 208–213, 220, 222, 224, 228
student essay, 222–228
supporting points in, 213–217
thesis statement in, 213, 214, 223, 544
topic for, 205–213, 229–232
websites as, 181, 183, 190, 231
Instagram post
in APA style, 709
in MLA style, 690
Intentional plagiarism, 527
Interlibrary loan, 494–495
Interpreter, writing role as, 121–122, 124, 126
Interviews
analysis of results, 505
for analytical writing, 241, 276
in APA style, 705
for argumentative writing, 421, 428, 440
candidate identification, 501
checklists for conducting, 504
collaboration on, 514
conducting, 500–505
evaluation of data from, 96
for evaluative writing, 305, 313
face-to-face, 502
for informative writing, 182, 194, 207, 209, 213
method selection, 502
in MLA style, 682, 684
as multimodal essay sources, 627, 631
notes and recordings from, 503–504
planning of, 501–503
for problem-solving writing, 352, 372
published
in APA style, 705
in MLA style, 682
questions in, 501–504
for reflective writing, 157, 163, 178
search plan including, 478
telephone, 502
on topic, 46
written, 502
Introduction
in analytical writing, 278
in argumentative writing, 452, 455

asking question in, 575
author of
in APA style, 699
in MLA style, 677
compare/contrast in, 576–577
conclusion linked to, 580–581
defining problem in, 575
drafting, 571–577
establishing context in, 574
framing, 572–573
historical accounts in, 576
in informative writing, 218–219, 220–221
in interviews, 504
leading with quotation in, 576
map or preview provided in, 577
in observations, 507
of point, sources for, 583–584
in problem-solving writing, 391, 394–395
quotations in, 364, 391, 396, 576
in reflective writing, 168–169, 179–180
selecting introductory strategy, 573–577
stating thesis in, 574
stating topic in, 573
storytelling in, 575–576
strategy selection, 573–577
surprising statements in, 169, 575
Introductory phrases
avoiding unnecessary, 565, 662
with commas, 773
Irrelevant history fallacy, 443
"Is *Wicked* All That Wicked?" (Shannon), 339–344, 667
Italics
for emphasis, 790–791
of foreign words, 790

J

Jackson, Quinn, 54, 64, 88, 103, 541, 542, 639, 649
Jargon, 731
Jefferson, Margo, 580
"Are We Rich?," 152–156, 167
Johnston, Peter, "Guiding the Budding Writer," 54–58, 68
Jong, Anneke, 576, 580
"Leveling the Playing Field: How to Get More Women in Tech," 350–354

Journal articles. *See also* Periodicals; Scholarly articles
　analytical writing in, 235
　in APA style, 692, 702–703
　genre and design of, 20
　informative writing in, 190, 231–232
　in MLA style, 668, 678–681
　skimming, 52, 54
　text analysis of, 269
JSTOR, 488
Jumping on bandwagon fallacy, 444

K

Kairos, 271
Kanoya, Justin, 578–579
　"Thoughts on *Crazy Rich Asians:* How Representation Impacts Self Worth," 307–310
Kaufer, David, 472
Kaufman, Scott Barry, 574
Keywords
　as search terms, 481, 482, 486
Kimble, Sophie, 376, 382, 383, 385, 390, 391, 393, 394, 395, 397, 398, 399, 556–557, 558
　"Sharks for Profit," 394–400, 667
King, Patricia, 25
Kitchener, Karen, 25
Knowledge
　conducting inventory, 532–533
Krepcho, Dave, "Grant Proposal for Second Harvest Food Bank of Central Florida," 354–362

L

Lateral reading, 87–89
Lateral thinking, 87
Layouts, symmetrical and asymmetrical, 607
Lectures
　in APA style, 706
　in MLA style, 684
Letters
　in APA style, 695, 706
　argumentative writing in, 426–429
　field research via, 502, 513
　interviews via, 502
　in MLA style, 684
　open, 426–429
　problem-solving writing in, 363
　unpublished, 684, 706
Letters to the editor
　in APA style, 703
　in MLA style, 682
　problem-solving writing in, 363
"Leveling the Playing Field: How to Get More Women in Tech" (Jong), 350–354
Lewis, Carly, 579
　"The Writing on the Virtual Bathroom Wall," 235–240
Librarian, consulting, 497
Library stacks, 494
Limiting adverbs, 770
Limiting modifiers, 726–727
Line spacing, 613
Literacy narratives, 148–152, 178–179
Literature
　analytical writing on, 275, 295–296
　in MLA style, 671
　reflective writing on, 177–178
　reviews, 80–83, 347
Live performance, in MLA style, 687
"Living Composition" (Sommers), 64–65, 71–75, 76, 77, 79
Logical appeals *(logos),* 271, 448–449, 451, 643
Logical fallacies, 271, 443–445
Logos (logical appeals), 271, 448–449, 451, 643
Looping, 37, 38–39

M

Macrorie, Ken, 28
Magazine articles. *See also* Periodicals
　analytical writing in, 235–240, 295–296
　in APA style, 692, 702
　argumentative writing in, 407–413
　design of, 614
　evaluative writing in online, 304–306
　informative writing in, 181, 183–189, 231–232
　in MLA style, 668, 679
　purpose of, 10
　text analysis of, 269
"The Magic Bean Shop and the Fries That Bind Us" (Harris), 190–192
Maheshwari, Sapna, "Why Elite Female Athletes Are Turning Away from Major Sponsors," 363–369
Main clauses, 714–715, 720, 772–773
Main points. *See also* Claims; Thesis statement
　active reading identifying, 62
　design to understand, 609–610
　highlighting, for revision and editing, 657–658, 664
　in informative writing, 213, 214, 220
　in main clauses, 714
　in reflective writing, 164, 165, 169
　reinforcing, in conclusion, 577–578
　stating, in introduction, 574
　summaries of, 76
Maisonet, Illyanna, "Why Aren't There More Puerto Rican Restaurants . . . in California," 200–203
Mapping
　drafting from, 561
　for idea generation, 40, 42
　in note taking, 69
　for organization, 551, 553, 559, 660
　research questions, 468
　for revision, 659
Maras, Marie-Helen, "4 Ways 'Internet of Things' Toys Endanger Children," 304–306
Marginal glosses, 614
McGrew, Sarah, 88
McQuide, MacKenzi, 559
Media reviews, 307–310, 323, 326, 346
Media sites, 492–493
Media sources
　in APA style, 692, 706–707
　in MLA style, 668, 684–687
Mediations, reflective writing, 133–135
Memoirs, 133, 152–155, 152–158, 179
Men Can Stop Rape, "Where Do You Stand?" campaign, 413–418
Metaphors, mixed, 740
"Mi Famiglia" (Guariglia), 173–176, 667
Misrepresentation, fallacies based on, 444
Mixed metaphors, 740
MLA style, 667–690
　argumentative writing in, 455, 460–462
　citations and attributions, 534–535, 588–589, 590, 597, 603, 668, 669–672
　description of, 603, 667
　design in, 672
　evaluative writing in, 344
　MLA Handbook on, 667
　problem-solving writing in, 395, 400
　student essays in, 667

Works Cited, list of, 344, 400, 459, 604–605, 668, 672–690
   books, 668, 673–678
   field sources, 668, 684
   journals, magazines, newspapers, 668, 678–682
   media sources, 668, 684–687
   other digital sources, 668, 687–690
   reference works, 668, 683–684
Works Consulted, list of, 672
Mobile app
   in APA style, 709
   in MLA style, 690
Modern Language Association style. *See* MLA style
Modifiers
   adjectives as, 766–767
   adverbs as, 767–768
   avoiding unnecessary, 565, 662
   dangling, avoiding, 728–729
   indefinite pronouns as, 747
   limiting, 726–727
   misplaced, 726–727
   verbals as, 719
Mollison, James, 135–148
   "Where Children Sleep," 145–147, 167
Mood
   setting, 587
   verb tense and, 748–757
      imperative, 755
      indicative, 755
      subjunctive, 755–757
Multimedia presentations
   accessibility of, 652
   audience for, 648–649
   checklist for creating, 654
   composing tools for, 646–647
   creation of, 645–648
   design of, 647–648
   informative writing in, 181
   multimodal essays as, 633–634
   oral presentations and, 645–648
   organization of, 646
   planning of, 642–645
   reflective writing in, 157
   sample/example, 650–651
Multimodal essays
   academic essay experience applied to, 630
   argument development and organization in, 630
   checklist for creating, 636–637
   composing tools for, 633–634
   context for, 633
   creation of, 630–637
   design of, 617, 632, 635–636
   engaging readers in, 631–632
   imported or linked sources in, 632–633
   navigation tools for, 617
   organization of, 630
   sample/example, 636
   source selection for, 631–633
Multiple strategies, search with, 487
Multiple works by author
   APA style of, 698
   MLA style of, 400, 670, 674
Multivolume works
   in APA style, 698
   in MLA style, 675
Murray, Donald, 28
Musical scores, in MLA style, 686

N

Narratives
   analytical writing drawing on, 244
   literacy, 148–152, 178–179
National Cancer Institute, "Cancer Trends Progress Report" excerpts, 311–320
Navigation tools, 617
Neither/nor, 745, 747
Neuwirth, Christine, 472
News
   consuming, 87
   creating analysis, 295
   distributed via social media, 86
Newsgroup, message posted to
   in APA style, 708
   in MLA style, 688
Newsletter articles
   informative writing in, 181, 200–203
   problem-solving writing in, 349, 373
Newspaper articles. *See also* Periodicals
   analytical writing in, 235–240
   in APA style, 692, 702–703
   informative writing in, 181, 190, 231–232
   in MLA style, 668, 679, 681
   purpose of, 10
   text analysis of, 269
   thesis statement in, 541–542
News reports
   analytical writing on, 295
News search sites, 491

New York Public Library Digital Collections, 487, 488
Nickerson, Angela, "An Open Letter to Lands' End," 426–429
Nieswandt, Katharina, "Basic Income after Automation? That's Not How Capitalism Works!," 418–423
Non sequiturs, 445
Notes, saving, 519
Note taking
   in active reading, 58
   classifying sources with, 68–69
   direct quotations, 64
   in group brainstorming, 99
   grouping in, 69, 551
   improving understanding with, 67–70
   in interviews, 503–504
   labeling in, 68–69, 550
   listing in, 69
   on observations, 506, 508
   paraphrases in, 65–66
   plagiarism avoided through careful, 63, 533
   on planning and organization, 69
   at public events, 513, 514
   quotations in, 63, 64
   on reactions and impressions, 67
   reasons for, 63–64
   for reflective writing, 160, 161
   review of, to develop thesis statement, 540
   for source comparison, 67–68
   on sources, 63, 102, 210
   speaker's notes, for oral presentations, 643–644
   summaries in, 66–67
   tagging in, 68
   tools for, 63
   visual elements in, 69
Nouns
   adjectives to modify, 766–767
   as antecedents, 725, 761–765
   attributive, 781
   collective, 747–748, 762
   noun complements *vs.*, 746
   possessives of, 781
   pronouns in place of (*See* Pronouns)
   singular that look plural, 748
   as subject of sentence (*See* Subject [of sentence])
Novel, analyzing, 295–296
Numbered lists, 614

Number (singular/plural)
alternative subject nearest to verb determining, 745
collective nouns, 747–748, 762
compound subject as plural, 744
indefinite pronouns, 746–747, 761
noun complements confusing, 746
pronoun-antecedent agreement, 761–762
singular nouns that look plural, 748
verb placement before subject, 745–746
verb-subject agreement, 743–748
words between subject and verb confusing, 744
Numerical information. *See also* Statistics
accuracy of, 662
for analytical writing, 276
in argumentative writing, 440
call numbers as, searches by, 486
consistent use of, 663
periods as decimal points in, 777
sources for, 598

O

Objectivity
fairness *vs.*, 334
in informative writing, 213
Object pronouns, 757–761
in comparisons, 760
paired with name or another pronoun, 758
whom/whomever, 759
Observations
analysis of results, 508
for analytical writing, 234, 241, 243, 276
for argumentative writing, 428, 440
checklist for conducting, 507–508
collaboration on, 514
conducting, 505–509
evaluation of data from, 96
in evaluative writing, 305, 313, 329
frequency and duration of, 505–506
for informative writing, 194, 208
notes and recordings of, 505–506, 507–508
permission for, 506–507
planning of, 505–507
for problem-solving writing, 372
for reflective writing, 132, 160, 161, 163, 169, 178

search plan including, 478
topic exploration through, 46
Observer, writing role as, 121, 123, 124, 125
Online articles
in APA style, 702–703, 710
evaluative writing in, 304–306
in MLA style, 400, 679, 680–682
problem-solving writing in, 350–353
Online discussion forum, message posted to
in APA style, 708
in MLA style, 688
Online file
in APA style, 709
in MLA style, 690
Online library catalog, 46, 207, 209, 217, 476, 478, 485–487
Online searches
of audio search sites, 492
of blogs, 489
Boolean operators in, 483–485
of databases, 47, 207, 217, 259–260, 476, 478, 479, 487–489, 496
exact phrases in, 482–483
of government search sites and directories, 491
of image search sites and directories, 492
locating digital sources with, 480–493
of media sites, 492–493
of news search sites, 491
of online discussions, 47
of online library catalogs, 47, 207, 209, 217, 476, 478, 485–487
of reference sites, 491
search limits for, 484–485
search plan for, 481–485
search terms generated for, 481, 482
of social media, 47, 492
strategies for, 482–485
of video search sites, 493
of web, 47, 208, 325, 477, 489–492
wildcards in, 483
Online surveys, 511
Only Daughter (Cisneros), 148
Open letters, argumentative writing in, 426–429
"An Open Letter to Lands' End" (Nickerson), 426–429
Opinion columns, 541–542

Oral presentations
checklist for preparing and delivering, 654
engaging with audience in, 648–649
language in, 643
multimedia presentations and, 641–642
narrowing scope of, 654
outlines for, 654
speaker's notes for, 643–644
Organizing your ideas, 547–559
of analytical writing, 255, 279, 280–281
argument arrangement for, 549–553
of argumentative writing, 451, 570
assessment of, 280–281
as author, in MLA style, 400
capitalization of names of, 789–790
cause/effect, 279, 548
choosing pattern for, 547–549
chronological, 166, 219, 279, 548, 725–726, 727
clustering for, 551
compare/contrast, 549
costs/benefits, 549
definition, 548
description, 548
design to clarify, 610, 615
of evaluative writing, 335
grouping for, 551
of informative writing, 219
labeling for, 550
mapping for, 551, 553, 659
of multimedia presentations, 646
of multimodal essays, 630
multiple patterns in one document, 548
multiple perspectives, 548
note taking on, 69
of oral presentations, 643
outlines for, 103–104, 219, 279, 335, 554–558, 561, 654, 659
in paragraphs, 563, 656
for peer review, 117
problem/solution, 549
of problem-solving writing, 391, 553
process explanation, 391, 548
pro/con, 548
of reflective writing, 168
related ideas kept together in, 570
revising to improve, 656
spatial, 168
strengths/weaknesses, 549
in writing process, 25

writing situation informing, 549
zero draft aiding, 558–559
Outlines
for analytical writing, 279
collaborative feedback on, 103–104
creation of, 554–558
drafting from, 561
for evaluative writing, 335
formal, 554–558, 561
informal, 554–555, 559, 561
for informative writing, 219
for oral presentations, 654
for revision, 660
sentence, 558
thumbnail, 554–555
topical, 556
zero draft aiding, 559

P

Page layout, 612, 614, 629, 636, 647
Page numbers, in design, 614
Pamphlets. *See also* Brochures
in APA style, 705
informative writing in, 181
in MLA style, 684
Paraphrases
accuracy and fairness of, 595, 601
to align writer with authority, 586–587
for analytical writing, 276
appeals to authority with, 447
in argumentative writing, 421, 440
checklist for, 596
context for, 589–590
to contrast ideas, 584–585
for definition, illustration, or clarification, 586–587
definition of, 595
effective and appropriate use of, 595–596
integration of, 595
to introduce a point, 583–584
note taking including, 63, 65
in problem-solving writing, 395
Parentheses, 773, 786–787
Park, Alice, 574
Partanen, Anu
"What Americans Keep Ignoring about Finland's School Success," 407–413
Particles, 729

Passive voice, 566, 736
Pathos (emotional appeals), 271, 447, 451, 643
Peer review
of analytical writing, 280
of argumentative writing, 454
of articles, 628
conducting effective, 110–116
context considered in, 110, 172, 222
for editing, 666
to enhance writing process, 117
of evaluative writing, 338
of field research, 514
guidelines for, 115–116
of informative writing, 222
instructors, classmates, friends, and family in, 118
of multimedia presentations, 651
needs as writer considered in, 115–116
plagiarism and, 527
of problem-solving writing, 394
of reflective writing, 172
resources for, 116–118
for revision, 115, 116, 661
role as reviewer, 116–117
technology for, 110–111, 116–117
using, to improve document, 117, 172, 222
writing improved through, 116–118
Periodicals. *See also* Journal articles; Magazine articles; Newspaper articles
in APA style, 692, 702–704, 710
indexes of, 497
microform of, 495
in MLA style, 679, 680–682
searches of, 46, 208, 209, 210, 494–495
Perl, Sondra, 28
Permission
for observations, 506–507
to record interviews, 503
sample request form, 507, 531
to use sources, 530–532, 598
Personal connections, considering, 30
Persuasive writing, 404–466
advertisements as, 413–418, 465
Alcazar, Jeremy, "Reforming, Not Defunding, the Police" (student essay), 455–462
alternative/opposing claims addressed in, 442–443, 449–451, 453
appeals in, 440, 446–449, 451, 452

building argument for, 435–445
call to action in, 417, 407, 413, 429
claims in, 406, 413, 437–443, 445–446, 449–451, 452–453
collaboration on, 442
conclusion in, 452
context for, 405, 438, 454
conversations on topic of, 433
counterarguments in, 413, 442–443, 449–451, 453
critical thinking in, 405, 406
definition and description of, 404–406
definition of claim in, 437
design of, 416, 419, 427, 430, 451, 455, 610
drafting, 445–452
essays as, 407–413, 431–462
exploring disagreements in, 432–434, 442–443
framing, 451–452
genres in, 406–430, 451
idea generation for, 431–435, 438
integrity of argument in, 443–445
introduction in, 452, 455
logical fallacies in, 443–445
open letters as, 426–429
organization of, 451–452
peer review of, 454
photographs and images in, 413–418, 419, 428, 440, 451
point/counterpoint editorials as, 418–426
project ideas for, 463–465
purpose of, 405, 454
questioning for, 434–435, 438, 452
readers of, 405–406, 408, 412, 429, 435, 446–449, 454, 610
reasonableness in, 406, 450–451
reasons and evidence in, 405, 406, 421, 428, 437–441, 452
review and revision of, 452–454
sources for, 405, 406, 407, 421–422, 428, 434, 436, 454, 460–462
supporting points in, 438–441
thesis statement in, 445–446, 545
topic for, 431–435, 463–465
tracking online discussions for, 434
Peterson, Savannah, "Advice for Generation Z from a Savvy Millennial," 369–374
Photo essays, reflective writing, 135–148

Photographs
  in APA style, 707
  in design, 615
  in MLA style, 686
Photos, taking, 519
Phrasal verbs, 729
Phrasing style
  active voice for, 736–737
  affirmative statements in, 741
  alternatives to forms of *to be* in, 737
  concise and effective words in, 735–736
  endings of *-tion, -ing, -ly,* avoiding, 740–741
  figures of speech in, 738
  relationships among words in, 738–740
  vivid and specific, 735
Plagiarism, 525–537
  accuracy to avoid, 601
  actions to avoid, 532–535, 601–603
  attribution of ideas to avoid, 535
  avoiding, 532–535, 537, 601–603
  careful note taking to avoid, 64, 533
  checking for unattributed sources to avoid, 603
  citations and source identification to avoid, 534–535
  common knowledge exceptions, 530
  conducting knowledge inventory to avoid, 532–533
  definition of, 526
  distinguishing source of ideas to avoid, 601–603
  in group projects, 527
  intentional, 527
  myths *vs.* facts, 536
  permission to use source and, 530–532
  reasons for, understanding, 535
  research ethics and, 528–529
  response to accusations of, 535–537
  self-, 528
  software to detect, 536
  unintentional, 526–527, 601
Planning
  interviews, 501–503
  multimedia presentations, 642–645
  note taking on, 69
  observations, 505–507
  searches, 208, 209, 477–478, 482–485, 494
  surveys, 509–511
  websites, 637–638
  in writing process, 24, 26, 27

Plural. *See* Number (singular/plural)
Podcasts
  in APA style, 707
  assessing the relevance and credibility of, 94
  in MLA style, 685–686, 690
Poetry
  analyzing, 295–296
  punctuation with, 778, 788
  reflective writing on, 177–178
  text analysis of, 269, 295–296
Point/counterpoint editorials, 418–426
Point of view
  first-person, 167
  in reflective writing, 133, 166, 167–168
  in storytelling, 166
  third-person, 167
PolitiFact, 88
Polk, Thomas, "A Review of the MLA Handbook, Eighth Edition," 299–303
Porter, James, 28
Position statements, 540–541, 543. *See also* Thesis statement
Possessives, apostrophes in, 781–782
Post hoc fallacies, 444–445
PowerPoint, 19, 60, 621, 633, 634, 646–647
Prepositions
  dangling, avoiding, 729
  sentence fragments with, 719
Presentations, 641–652
  analytical writing in, 235
  of evaluation, 332–334
  multimedia, 157, 181, 633–634, 641–652
  oral, 641–651
Prewriting activities
  brainstorming (*See* Brainstorming)
  clustering (*See* Clustering)
  freewriting (*See* Freewriting)
  looping, 38–39
  mapping (*See* Mapping)
  sentence starters, 40, 43
Print materials, keeping track of, 515–516
Print resources, locating and using, 493–498
Privacy policies, 491
Problem/solution
  defining, in introduction, 575
  organization, 549
Problem solver, writing role as, 122–123, 124, 126–127

Problem-solving writing, 348–403
  advice writing as, 369–374
  agent/goals/actions/results in, 381
  alternative perspectives/solutions addressed in, 349, 389, 393
  arguments in, 355, 363, 386, 389, 402
  articles as, 349, 350–354
  assessing practicality of solution in, 380, 384, 386
  clustering ideas for, 385
  collaboration on, 379
  conclusion in, 391
  considering potential solutions in, 381, 383, 383–384, 385
  context for, 349, 372, 374, 378, 393
  critical thinking in, 349, 376
  definition and description of, 348–350
  definition of problem in, 348–350, 355, 376, 378, 380–381, 383, 384, 386–387, 392, 401
  design of, 358, 375, 389–390, 402, 403
  developing a solution in, 380–386, 397, 401
  discussion in, 349
  drafting, 386–391
  essays as, 350–354, 376–402
  evaluations in, 299, 346, 402
  evidence in, 364, 369, 372, 386, 388, 389, 390, 394, 402
  explanation in, 349, 375, 379, 391
  exploring difficulties for ideas for, 377
  fairness and reasonableness in, 349, 386, 387, 392
  feasibility of solution in, 380, 384, 392
  framing, 391
  genres in, 350–374, 375, 389, 402–403
  goals and barriers in, 381
  idea generation for, 376–379, 386
  introduction in, 391, 395
  judgments on, 373–374, 379
  Kimble, Sophie, "Sharks for Profit" (student essay), 394–400
  objections to, 386, 393
  opinion pieces as, 363–369
  organization of, 391, 553
  peer review of, 394
  project ideas for, 401–403
  proposals in, 349, 354–362, 387–388, 401, 402–403
  purpose of, 349, 354, 369, 386, 394
  questioning for, 350, 378, 383

INDEX   **811**

readers of, 349, 352–353, 362, 371, 374, 375, 385–386, 392–394
review and revision of, 391–394
severity and duration in, 381, 385
solution explained in, 388–389, 392
sources for, 349, 350, 353, 389, 394, 395, 396, 400, 401
supporting points in, 388–389, 390
surveys for, 372, 379, 382, 401, 402
thesis statement in, 388, 391, 545
topic for, 376–379, 401–403
visual images in, 349, 375, 389–390
Process explanations organization, 548
Pro/con organization, 548
Professional connections, looking for, 30
Profiles, as informative writing, 192–199, 230
Progress reports, evaluative writing in, 311–320, 328, 346
Pronouns
adjectives to modify, 766–767
antecedents
agreement with, 761–762
clarity of reference to, 725, 762–765
as clauses or sentences, 763
it without, 765
referring to more than one thing, 764
same pronoun referring to two, 763–764
they, for specific, 765
in comparisons, 760
for gender-neutral language, 732–733
grammatical use of, 757–765
indefinite, 746–747, 761
it, used sparingly, 765
object, 757–761
possessive, 782
reflexive, 759
relative, 716, 718
subject, 757–761
they, for specified antecedent, 765
who/whom, 716, 759
you, in formal writing, 764–765
Proofreading, 221, 666
Proper names
capitalization of, 788, 789–790
commas with, 774–775
Proposals
evaluation of, 345–346
in problem-solving writing, 349, 354–362, 387–388, 401, 402–403
role-playing review of, 101

Publication Manual of the American Psychological Association, 691
Published conference proceedings
in APA style, 699
in MLA style, 677
Published interviews
in APA style, 703
in MLA style, 682
Publisher
in APA style, 701
evaluation of, 91
in MLA style, 675
Pull quotes, 52, 451, 614
Punctuation, 772–788
apostrophes, 780–782
brackets, 592, 594, 601, 787
colons, 591, 594, 782–783
commas, 593, 715, 719–721, 772–777
dashes, 773, 785–786
editing for, 663, 665
ellipses marks, 591–592, 594, 601, 787
exclamation points, 593, 777
hyphens, 783–784
parentheses, 773, 786–787
periods, 777
question marks, 593
quotation marks, 590–591, 593, 601, 602, 672
for quotations, 591–592, 593–594, 669, 776, 778, 780, 783, 787–788
semicolons, 594, 715, 721, 783
slashes, 788

Q

Quackenbos, John, 27
Questionable analogies fallacy, 444
Questionable assumptions fallacy, 444
Question marks, 594, 777–778
Quotation marks, 590–591, 594, 601, 602, 672, 778–780
Quotations
accuracy of, 601, 655, 662
to align writer with authority, 585–586
for analytical writing, 276
appeals to authority with, 447
in argumentative writing, 421, 430, 440, 451, 452
block, 591, 593, 669
checklist for, 594
complete, 590–591
in conclusion, 579

context for, 589–590
to contrast ideas, 584–585
for definition, illustration, or clarification, 586–587
emotion and mood conveyed in, 587
in evaluative writing, 341, 342
in informative writing, 185, 204, 216, 224, 226
to introduce a point, 583–584
in introduction, 364, 391, 396, 576
key-point summaries including, 76
leading with, in introduction, 576
modifications to, 591–593, 594, 601, 787
note taking including, 64
orphan, 590
partial, 341, 590–591, 602
in problem-solving writing, 364, 391, 396
pull, 52, 451, 614
punctuation for, 592, 593–594, 669, 776, 778, 780, 783, 787–788
strategic use of, 590–594
in titles, 682

R

Radio
in APA style, 706–707
in MLA style, 685
Radio program
in APA style, 706–707
in MLA style, 685
Readers. *See also* Audience
of analytical writing, 234, 236, 246, 248, 271, 280–281
appeals to (*See* Appeals)
of argumentative writing, 405–406, 408, 412, 429, 435, 446–449, 454, 610
for assignment, 33, 34, 35, 619
building on personal experiences of, 570
design for, 610–611
drafting argument for, 580
engaging, 566, 631
of evaluative writing, 298, 301, 321, 338
of informative writing, 182, 184, 222
map for, 570
of multimodal essays, 631–632
participation of, in online comments, 306, 321
of problem-solving writing, 349, 352–353, 362, 371, 374, 375, 385–386, 392–394

Readers (cont.)
  purposes, needs, interests, knowledge, and background of, 10–11, 323–324, 384, 405, 408, 412, 429, 435
  putting self in place of, 659
  of reflective writing, 132, 172, 180
  rhetorical analysis of, 271
  sentence structure signposts for, 724–728
  of target publication, 626
  writing situation considering, 11–12, 33
Reading
  about topic, 46–47
  active, 51–63
  aloud, 664
  with attitude, 50
  carefully before editing, 664
  close, 32, 277
  critically, 49–51, 61 (See also Active reading, strategies for)
  critical thinking while, 50–51, 61
  like a writer, 65–83
  literacy narratives on, 148–152, 178–179
  to make connections, 79–83
  questioning in, 50, 51
  rereading later, 51
  to respond, 77–79
  in reverse order, 664
  scanning, 659–660
  skimming, 51–54
  to understand, 70–71, 76–77
  writing informed by, 5–6, 49–83
  writing situation considered in, 50
Reasoning
  circular, 445
  deductive, 448–449
  fallacies based on careless, 444–445
  inductive, 449
  logical appeals referring to, 271, 448–449, 451, 643
Reasons
  to accept thesis statement, 544–545
  in analytical writing, 274–276, 277
  in argumentative writing, 437–441, 452
  collaborative feedback on, 103–104, 275
  generating ideas about, 438
  highlighting, for revision and editing, 657–658, 664
  for interpretation, 272–274
  key-point summaries including, 76
  for note taking, 63–64
  oral presentations drawing on, 643

  for plagiarism, 535
  supporting main point, 62–63, 215, 438–441, 545–546
  working together to generate, 275
Recordings. See also Videos
  in APA style, 707
  of interviews, 503
  makings, 519
  in MLA style, 685–686
  of observations, 505–506, 507–508
  of public events, 513
Red herring fallacy, 443
Redundancy, 739
References
  books in, 692, 697–701
  categories of entries, 668
  design of, 696
  field sources in, 692, 705–706
  for informative writing, 228
  journals, magazines, newspapers in, 692, 702–704, 710
  media sources in, 692, 706–707
  omissions from, 696
  other digital sources in, 692, 707–710
  other sources in, 692, 711
  publication information in, 604–605
  reference works in, 692, 705
  sites, 491
Reference works
  in APA style, 692, 705
  in MLA style, 668, 683–684
  searches of, 491, 495–498
Reflection
  in analytical writing, 256–260, 275
  in argumentative writing, 405, 406
  critical thinking and, 27, 61
  in evaluative writing, 298
  in informative writing, 182
  in problem-solving writing, 349, 369, 370, 374
  reflective responses, 73
  reflective writing, 119–130, 244, 248, 252, 254, 545
  on surroundings, 256–257
  on topic, 160–161
Reflective writing, 131–180
  analytical writing drawing on, 240, 244, 248, 252, 254, 255, 256, 276
  blog posts as, 180
  compare/contrast in, 162, 163, 164
  conclusion in, 168–169
  context for, 132, 172

  conversations on topic for, 163
  critical thinking in, 132, 158
  design of, 132, 168
  details in, 163, 167, 169, 170
  dialogue in, 169, 170, 171
  drafting, 165–169
  essays as, 158–160
  examination of topic for, 162–163
  framing, 168–169
  genres in, 132–156, 157, 168
  Guariglia, Caitlin, "Mi Famiglia" (student essay), 173–177
  idea generation for, 158–160, 177–179
  instructor feedback on, 171
  introduction in, 168–169, 179–180
  literacy narratives as, 148–152, 178–179
  main points in, 164, 165, 169
  meditations, 133–135
  memoirs as, 152–155, 158, 179
  note taking for, 160, 161
  observation for, 132, 159–160, 161, 163, 169, 178
  organization of, 168, 171
  personal experiences in, 136, 152, 158–160, 162–163, 167–168, 177
  photo essays as, 135–148, 179–180
  point of view in, 133, 166, 167–168
  project ideas for, 177–180
  purpose of, 131, 132
  questioning for, 159
  readers of, 132, 172, 180
  review and revision of, 169–170
  significance of, 164
  sources for, 132
  storytelling in, 166, 169
  thesis statement in, 165, 169, 545
  topic for, 158–161, 177–180
Reflexive pronouns, 759
"Reform of the Nerds, Starring Arthur Chu" (Baker), 240–247, 248, 278
Relative pronouns, 716, 718
Relevance
  of databases, 487–488
  of sources, 89–90, 210, 477, 487–488
  of topic, 378
Remembering
  in analytical writing, 256, 272
  in argumentative writing, 405
  critical thinking and, 27
  in evaluative writing, 298
  in informative writing, 182
  in problem-solving writing, 349

INDEX

in reflective writing, 158, 179
Reporter, writing role as, 121, 124, 125–126
Reports. *See also* News reports
  analytical writing in, 157
  evaluative writing in, 299, 311–320, 328, 345–346
Research. *See also* Searches
  ethics in, 528–529
  field, 102, 479, 499–514 (*See also* Field sources)
  informative writing on, 182
  methods of, 477–478
  progress reports presenting, 313
  research questions for, 467–472, 482
  responsibility for, 102
  scholarly articles presenting, 299–303
  in writing process, 26
Review. *See also* Peer review
  of analytical writing, 279–281
  in APA style, 703
  of argumentative writing, 452–454
  of articles, 628
  of criteria for evaluation, 336
  evaluative writing in, 307–310, 323–324, 327–328, 336–337, 344–347
  of informative writing, 219–222
  literature, 80–83, 347
  media, 307–310, 323, 326, 346
  in MLA style, 682
  of notes, to develop thesis statement, 540
  of problem-solving writing, 391–394
  of proposals, 101
  of reflective writing, 169–172
  of sources, 47–48, 80–83, 220
  in writing process, 24, 28, 117
"A Review of the MLA Handbook, Eighth Edition" (Polk), 299–303
Revision, 653–666
  of analytical writing, 279–281
  argument and ideas considered in, 654–655
  of argumentative writing, 452–454
  of articles, 628
  challenging assumptions in, 659
  checklist for, 661
  of evaluative writing, 336–338
  feedback for, 661
  focus of, 653–657
  for genre and design, 656–657
  highlighting main point, reasons, and evidence in, 657–658

of informative writing, 220–222
peer review incorporation in, 115, 116, 661
of problem-solving writing, 391–394
purpose of, 653
of reflective writing, 169–170
saving multiple drafts of, 657
scanning, outlining, and mapping document for, 659–660
for source use and integration improvement, 655–656
strategies for, 657–661
for structure and organization, 656
in writing process, 24, 26, 27, 28
writing situation shaping, 654
Rhetorical analyses, 248–251, 271, 292–293
Rhetorical situations, 9. *See also* Writing situation
Role of writer
  advocate, 8, 405–406
  assignment requirements, 619
  evaluator, 8, 297–298, 322
  genre reflecting, 619, 620
  interpreter, 8, 234
  observer, 8, 167, 172, 470
  oral presentations considering, 643
  problem solver, 8, 349–350, 470
  reporter, 8, 181–182, 205, 470
  revising to reflect, 664
  searches driven by, 470
Roy, Deb, 86
Run-on sentences, 715, 720–721
Russell, David R., 27
Ruta, Izzy, 635

S

Sacred texts
  in APA style, 700
  in MLA style, 671, 678
Scardamilia, Marlene, 28
Scholarly articles. *See also* Journal articles
  evaluative writing in, 299–303
  genre and design of, 20
  problem-solving writing in, 349
Scibona, Salvatore, 575
Screenplay, in MLA style, 677
Searches
  collaborative strategy for, 102, 209
  editing using, 664–665
  gaps in conversation driving, 472

informative writing search plan, 208, 209
locating sources with, 102, 436, 480–498
methods to focus, 467–472
online (*See* Online searches)
preliminary, conducting, 476
print resources, 473, 493–498
purpose and role driving, 470–472
questions about issue driving, 473–475
relevant sources identified for, 477–478
research methods shaping, 477–479
research question to narrow, 467–472
search limits for, 484–485
search plan for, 208, 209, 477–478, 482–485, 494
search terms generated for, 481, 482, 486, 494
search tools for, 477–478
for topic, 47, 208, 325, 486
Self-plagiarism, 528
Sentence mechanics
  abbreviations, 4, 777, 791
  acronyms, 786, 792
  capitalization, 788–790, 792
  italics, 612, 672, 779, 790–791
Sentences
  antecedents as whole, 763
  breaking into separate, 721, 728
  complete, 717–720
  complex, 715–717
  compound, 714–715, 783
  compound-complex, 717
  dangling words/phrases avoided in, 728–729
  detours in, 773–775, 784–786
  editing style of, 663
  flow of, moving forward, 727–728
  main clauses of, 714–715, 720
  parallel structure in, 722–724
  periods ending, 777
  reader signposts in, 724–728
  related ideas together in, 725–727
  run-on, 715, 720–721
  scanning first, 660
  sentence fragments, 717–720
  structure of, choosing right, 714–717
  subordinate clauses of, 715–717, 718–719, 721, 773
  topic, 215, 561, 562
  transitional, 568
  transitions in, 721, 724–725, 774
  writing clear, logical, 714–729

Series
  books in
    in APA style, 698
    in MLA style, 675
  commas/serial commas in, 775–776
  connecting to rest of sentence, 723–724
  flow of, in sentences, 727
  parallel sentence structure for, 722
  semicolons in, 783
Shannon, Brooke, 322, 325, 326, 330, 333, 337, 339, 563
  "Is *Wicked* All That Wicked?" 339–344, 667
"Sharks for Profit" (Kimble), 394–400, 667
Short story, analyzing, 295–296
Sidebars, in design, 614
Singular. *See* Number (singular/plural)
Situation/effects, in problem-solving writing, 380, 383, 385, 395
Slashes, 788
Slippery slope arguments, 445
Smith, Kelsey, 256, 260, 264, 273, 277, 278, 281, 282, 293, 554, 578
  "Art Theft on the Rise with Social Media," 282–292, 691
Snopes.com, 88
Social media
  assessing the relevance and credibility of, 94
  news distributed via, 86–87
  sites, 492
Social Science Abstracts, 488
Sommers, Nancy, "Living Composition," 64–65, 71–75, 76, 77, 79
Sound recording
  in APA style, 707
  in MLA style, 685–686
Sounds, words with similar, 738–739
Sources
  to align writer with authority, 585–586
  for amplifying or qualifying a point, 587–588
  for analytical writing, 234, 237, 240, 241, 259–260, 264, 268, 269, 270, 271, 272, 280–281, 285–286
  for argumentative writing, 405, 406, 407, 421–422, 428, 434, 436, 454, 460–462
  for articles, 627
  assessment and credibility of, 85–89, 210, 368
  assessment of, 85–87
  for assignment, 33, 35
  audience for, 92–93
  authority of, 210
  author of, 91, 400
  bias of, 85, 86
  bibliographies of (*See* Bibliographies)
  building on, in writing situation, 12–13, 33
  central concepts in, 47 (*See also* Main point)
  citations of (*See* Citations)
  classification of, 68–69
  collaboration to collect and work with, 75, 102
  collection of, 210
  comparison of, 67–69
  connection to topic, 87
  consistent treatment of, 663
  context for, 589–590
  to contrast ideas, 584–585
  for definition, illustration, or clarification, 586–587
  digital (*See* Digital sources)
  disagreement in, 48, 58, 61, 67
  documentation of (*See* Documentation)
  downloading, 517
  effective use of, 582–605
  emotions/mood conveyed using, 585, 587
  entire, references to, 596, 669
  evaluation and credibility of, 87–89, 102, 210, 211–212, 299
  for evaluative writing, 298, 309, 313, 329, 333–334, 336, 338, 341–342
  evidence from (*See* Evidence)
  examples from, 587
  expert (*See* Expert opinion)
  field, 96, 102, 668, 684, 692, 705–706 (*See also* Interviews; Observations; Surveys)
  genre of, 60, 92–93
  grouping, 69, 551
  identifying in document, 534–535, 588–589
  identifying relevant types of, 477
  information gathering from, 46–48, 208–213
  for informative writing, 182, 189, 194, 200, 208–212, 220, 222, 224, 228
  integration of information from, 563–564, 588–600, 656–657
  to introduce a point, 583–584
  key information, ideas, and arguments in, 51, 58, 60, 61, 70, 76–77
  labeling of, 68, 550
  learning from, 93
  listing in working bibliography, 521–522
  literature reviews of, 80–83, 347
  locating, 102, 436, 480–498 (*See also* Searches)
  main point of, 62, 76
  making connections between, 79–83
  managing, 515–524
  marking and annotation of, 51, 58–59, 61
  media, 668, 684–687, 692, 706–707 (*See also specific types*)
  for multimedia presentations, 645–646
  for multimodal essays, 631–633
  note taking on, 63, 102, 210
  paraphrases of (*See* Paraphrases)
  paying attention to, 59–61
  permission to use, 530–532, 598
  plagiarism by lack of acknowledging (*See* Plagiarism)
  for problem-solving writing, 349, 350, 353, 389, 394, 395, 396, 400, 401
  to provide evidence, 585
  publisher of, 91, 675, 701
  purpose accomplished by using, 583–588
  purpose of, 92
  questioning, 50
  quotations from (*See* Quotations)
  quoted in another source, 671, 695
  reactions to, 51, 63, 68
  reading of, 5–6, 49–83
  recurring voices in, 48
  for reflective writing, 132
  relevance of, 89–90, 210, 477–478, 487–488
  responses to, 69, 77–79, 86
  responsibility for locating, 102
  review of, 47–48, 80–83, 220
  revising for best use, integration, and documentation of, 655–656, 664–665
  rhetorical analysis of, 271
  searches for (*See* Searches)
  to set mood, 587
  similarities/differences in, 61
  skimming, 51–54
  summaries of, 66–67, 76–77, 596–597
  text analysis of, 269
  themes in, 48

timeliness of, 91, 210
visual links within, 51
without page numbers, 671–672, 695
writer's argument in, 62–63
written conversation based on, 5–6, 9
Speaker's notes, 643–644. *See also* Oral presentations
Speeches
  oral presentations, 643
  problem-solving writing in, 369
Spelling, 665, 666
Stacking the deck fallacy, 444
Statistics
  in analytical writing, 252, 267, 268, 269, 278
  in argumentative writing, 421, 440
  base-rate fallacies with, 444
  data analysis of, 268–269
  in evaluative writing, 305
  in informative writing, 213
  in introduction, 391
  in problem-solving writing, 391
Straw-man attacks, 444
Student essay, 222–228
Student essays
  Alcazar, Jeremy, "Reforming, Not Defunding, the Police," 455–462, 667
  APA style documentation, 691
  Guerrero, Gabriella, "Fast Fashion? Not So Fast!," 222–228, 691
  Guariglia, Caitlin, "Mi Famiglia," 173–177, 667
  Kimble, Sophie "Sharks for Profit," 394–400, 667
  MLA style documentation, 667
  Shannon, Brooke, "Is *Wicked* All That Wicked?," 339–344
  Smith, Kelsey, "Art Theft on the Rise with Social Media," 282–292
Style, 713–741
  editing for, 663, 665
  language usage, 730–734
  phrasing, 735–741
  sentence composition, 714–729
Subject (of sentence)
  alternative, nearest to verb determining number, 745
  collective nouns as, 747–748, 762
  compound, as plural, 744
  indefinite pronouns as, 746–747, 761
  in main clauses, 714
  noun complements confused with, 746

  number (singular/plural) matching verb, 743–748
  reflexive pronouns referral to, 759
  subject complements, 760–761
  subject pronouns, 757–761
    in comparisons, 760
    paired with name or another pronoun, 758
    for subject complements, 760–761
    who/whoever, 759
  in subordinate clauses, 715
  verb placement before, 745–746
  words between verb and, 744
Subjunctive mood, 755–757
Subordinate clauses, 715–717, 718–719, 721, 773
Subordinating conjunctions, 716, 718, 724
Summaries, in note taking, 66–67
Superlatives, 769
Surveys
  for analytical writing, 234, 241, 255, 264, 267–268
  anonymity of, 512
  for argumentative writing, 407, 440
  checklist for conducting, 512–513
  conducting, 509–513
  data analysis of, 96, 267–268, 513–514
  development and design of, 382
  distribution of, 511
  for evaluative writing, 305, 313
  for informative writing, 208
  online, 511
  paper-based, 511
  planning of, 509–511
  for problem-solving writing, 372, 379, 382, 401, 402
  questions in, 509–511
  respondent identification, 509
  telephone, 511
  unpublished data, in APA style, 706
Sweeping generalizations, 444

T

Table of contents, 617
Tables
  active reading of, 60
  for analytical writing, 276, 277
  in argumentative writing, 405, 419, 440, 451
  design of/with, 615, 627
  in informative writing, 182, 217

  in multimedia presentations, 645
  in multimodal essays, 631
  numerical information in, 598
  in problem-solving writing, 349
"Tax Robots and Universal Basic Income" (Bloch), 423–426
Technical language, 731
Television program
  in APA style, 706–707
  in MLA style, 685
Tense, verb. *See under* Verbs
That/which, 774
There is/there are sentences, 745–746
Thesis
  in APA style, 700
  in MLA style, 678
Thesis statement, 539–546. *See also* Main points
  in analytical writing, 274, 278, 544
  in argumentative writing, 445–446, 542, 544
  choosing reasons to accept, 544–545
  clear, 446
  collaboration to refine, 102–103
  debatable, 445–446
  developing position for, 539–541
  drafting of, 541–544
  in evaluative writing, 331–332, 545
  evidence supporting, 545–546
  focusing or narrowing, 543–544
  in formal outlines, 558–559, 561
  genre and, 541–542
  information, ideas, and arguments in, 542–543
  in informative writing, 213, 214, 223, 544
  interpretive claims in, 274
  in introduction, 574
  judgments expressed in, 331–332
  main point expressed in, 62, 102–103, 165, 169, 214
  oral presentations drawing on, 642
  placement of, 332
  plausible, 446
  position statements underlying, 540–541, 543
  in problem-solving writing, 388, 391, 545
  in reflective writing, 165, 169, 545
  restating, in conclusion, 577
  revision of, 653–654
  support for, 545–546

Third-person point of view, 167
"Thoughts on *Crazy Rich Asians:* How Representation Impacts Self Worth" (Kanoya), 307–310
Thumbnail outlines, 554–555
TikTok, 493
"Time 2021 Athlete of the Year: Simone Biles" (Park and Gregory), 183–189, 190
Timeline, creating project, 30
Time management, 31
Title
   active reading of, 52–53
   in APA style, 223
   in argumentative writing, 455
   of articles, 629, 678, 682
   capitalization of, 788–789
   design of, 629, 672
   in evaluative writing, 321, 339
   of illustrations, 617 (*See also* Captions)
   italics for, 779, 790
   in MLA style, 395
   of multimedia presentations, 650
   in problem-solving writing, 394
   quotation marks around, 779
   quotations in, 682
   as search term, 486, 495
   within title, 675
   of websites, 689
Tone, design for setting, 609
Topic
   for analytical writing, 256–260, 262–263, 292–296
   appropriateness of, 327
   for argumentative writing, 431–435, 463–465
   asking questions on, 44–45, 159, 208, 209, 264, 378, 434–435, 473–474
   of assignment, 32, 34, 35
   categories for, 258
   cause/effect analysis of, 258
   classification for examination of, 263
   developing interest in, 36–45
   discussing with others, 46, 47, 150, 207, 258, 322–323, 433
   division for examination of, 262–263
   elements of, 258
   for evaluative writing, 322–327, 328, 344–347
   examination of, 162–163, 262–263
   exploring difficulties for, 162, 377
   finding interesting, 44

   framing, in conclusion, 581
   fuller understanding of, 262–263
   generating ideas for, 37–43, 99–102, 158–160, 205–208, 256–260, 322–327, 377–379, 431–435
   history or origins of, 258
   importance of, 326
   information gathering on, 46–48, 208–213
   for informative writing, 205–213, 229–232
   listening in on conversation about, 45–48, 158–160, 205–207, 253–260, 322–327, 376–379, 431–435
   meaning of, 259
   narrowing focus of, 326–327, 378
   observation of, firsthand, 48
   position statements on, 540–541, 543
   prevailing opinions on, 326–327
   print resources classified by, 494
   for problem-solving writing, 376–379
   reading about, 46–47
   reflection on, 160–161
   for reflective writing, 158–161, 177–180
   relationships with, 258, 263, 269
   relevance of, 378
   searches for, 47, 208, 324–327, 486
   source connections to, 87
   stating, in introduction, 573
   timeliness of, 477
Topical outlines, 556
Topic sentences
   drafting, 561, 562
   paragraph focus in, 562
   supporting points in, 215
Transcripts of interviews, 503, 631
Transitions
   common, 568–569
   drafting, within and between paragraphs, 567–569
   editing of, 663
   in oral presentations, 644, 645, 648
   in sentences, 721, 724–725, 774
Translation tools, 528
Translators
   in APA style, 698
   in MLA style, 674
Trend analysis, 257, 279, 292–293
Twitter post (tweet)
   in APA style, 709
   in MLA style, 690

Typeface, in design, 612. *See also* Fonts, in design

U

Unintentional plagiarism, 526–527, 535, 601
Unknown authors
   in APA style, 697
   in MLA style, 670, 674
"An Unlikely Ballerina: The Rise of Misty Copeland" (Galchen), 192–199, 215
Unpublished letters
   in APA style, 706
   in MLA style, 684
Unsigned articles
   in APA style, 703
   in MLA style, 681

V

Verbals, 719
Verbs
   for active *vs.* passive voice, 566, 736–737
   adverbs to modify, 767–768
   affirmative *vs.* negated, 741
   to be
      alternatives to, 737
      as linking verb, 766
      matching to subject, 743
      noun complements with, 746
      placement before subject, 746
      subject complements with, 760–761
      tense and mood, 751, 756
   collective nouns with, 747–748
   grammatical use of, 743–757
   helping, 750–751
   indefinite pronouns with, 746–747
   infinitives of, 719
   -ing form of, 719, 740, 750
   irregular, 751–755
   linking, 766
   in main clauses, 714
   number (singular/plural) matching subject, 743–748
   parallel structure of, 722–724
   past participles of, 750, 751–755
   phrasal, 729
   placement before subject, 745–746
   present participles of, 750
   regular, 749–751

in subordinate clauses, 715
tense and mood, 748–757
  imperative, 755
  indicative, 755
  with irregular verbs, 751–755
  perfect, 750, 751–755
  progressive, 750
  with regular verbs, 749–751
  simple, 749, 751–755
  subjunctive, 755–757
words between subject and, 744
Video games
  in APA style, 709
  in MLA style, 690
Videos
  active reading considering, 53, 60
  in APA style, 706
  in argumentative writing, 440
  assessing the relevance and credibility of, 94
  Blank on Blank, 252–253
  in MLA style, 684–685
  in multimedia presentations, 645, 648
  in multimodal essays, 630, 631–632, 634
  news reports in, 189
  reflective, 157
  searches for, 488, 493
  source management with, 598–600
  text analysis of, 269
  on websites, 637
Visual search tools, 492
Vivid language, 643, 735
Vosoughi, Soroush, 86

W

Warrants, 438–439
Web search engines, 489–490
Websites
  in APA style, 696, 710
  assessing the relevance and credibility of, 94, 95
  checklist for developing, 641
  content creation for, 637
  creation of, 637–641
  design of, 19, 22, 617, 638, 640
  documents from, in APA style, 696, 710
  entire, references to, 687, 696
  evaluation of, 94, 211–212
  genre in, 19, 22
  informative writing in, 181, 184, 190, 231
  links to, 631–632, 638, 639

in MLA style, 687–690
multimodal essays on, 635
navigation tools, 612, 617, 640
planning of, 637–638
problem-solving writing on, 350
sample/example, 639–640
skimming, 54
tools for, 639
uploading online, 639
Web tools, using, 520
"What Americans Keep Ignoring about Finland's School Success" (Partanen), 407–413
"Where Children Sleep" (Mollison), 135–148, 167
"Where Do You Stand?" (Men Can Stop Rape), 413–418
White space, 614
Who/whom, 716, 759
"Why Aren't There More Puerto Rican Restaurants . . . in California?" (Maisonet), 200–203
"Why Elite Female Athletes Are Turning Away from Major Sponsors" (Maheshwari), 363–369
Wikis
  in APA style, 705
  evaluation of, 94
  in MLA style, 683
Wineburg, Sam, 88
Words
  capitalization of, 788–790, 792
  compound, 783–784
  concise and effective, in phrasing style, 735–736
  contractions of, 780–781
  dangling, avoiding, 728–729
  familiar and simple, 734
  foreign, in italics, 790
  keywords, 481, 482, 486
  new terms, 779
  paying attention to relationship among, 738–740
  question, 44, 159, 379, 473
  in quotation marks, 779
  with similar sounds, 738–739
  between subject and verb, 744
  syllables of, 785
  used as words, 779
Works Cited. *See also* Citations
  in argumentative writing, 460
  books in, 668, 673–678

categories of entries, 668
design of, 672
in evaluative writing, 344
field sources in, 684
journals, magazines, newspapers in, 668, 678–682
media sources in, 668, 684–687
other digital sources in, 668, 687–690
preparation of, 672–690
in problem-solving writing, 400
publication information in, 604–605
reference works in, 668, 683–684
Works Consulted, 672
Writers, reason for plagiarism, 535
Writer's argument, understanding, 62–63
Writer's notebook
  project timeline, 31
  steps of creating, 31
Writing lives, inventory your, 4
"The Writing on the Virtual Bathroom Wall" (Lewis), 235–240
Writing process, 22–29
  comparison to other complex activities, 22–23
  critical thinking in, 25–27
  genre and design in, 24
  peer review to enhance, 117
  project-to-project variation in, 24
  recursion in, 25
  study of, 27–29
  time and effort in, 23–24
Writing project, preparing, 29–30
  academic connections, 30
  taking ownership, 29–30
Writing role, 120–130. *See also* Writing role selection
  as advocate, 123, 124, 127
  as evaluator, 122, 124, 126
  as interpreter, 121–122, 124, 126
  as observer, 121, 124, 125, 132
  as problem solver, 122–123, 124, 126–127
  purpose in choosing, 125
  as reporter, 121, 124, 125–126
Writing role selection
  adopting more than one role, 129
  choice of sources, 128
  context of document, 127
  critical thinking and, 128–129
  purpose, 125, 132
  readers and, 125–127, 132

Writing situation, 9–16
  analysis of, 15, 248–251, 269, 271, 272, 292–293
  assessment of, for assignment, 33–35
  building on work of others in, 12–13, 33
  context for, 13–15, 35
  definition of, 9
  genre and design reflecting, 21
  language style matching, 730–731
  organization reflecting, 549
  position statements informed by, 540–541
  purpose in, 9–11, 33
  readers considered in, 11–12, 33
  reading critically and consideration of, 50
  revision considering, 653–654, 665
  as rhetorical situations, 9
  scholarly inquiry on, 15–16
  text analysis of, 269

Writing style. *See* Style

Y

Young, Richard E., 27
YouTube, 253

Z

Zero draft, 558–559